MANTEGNA & BELLINI

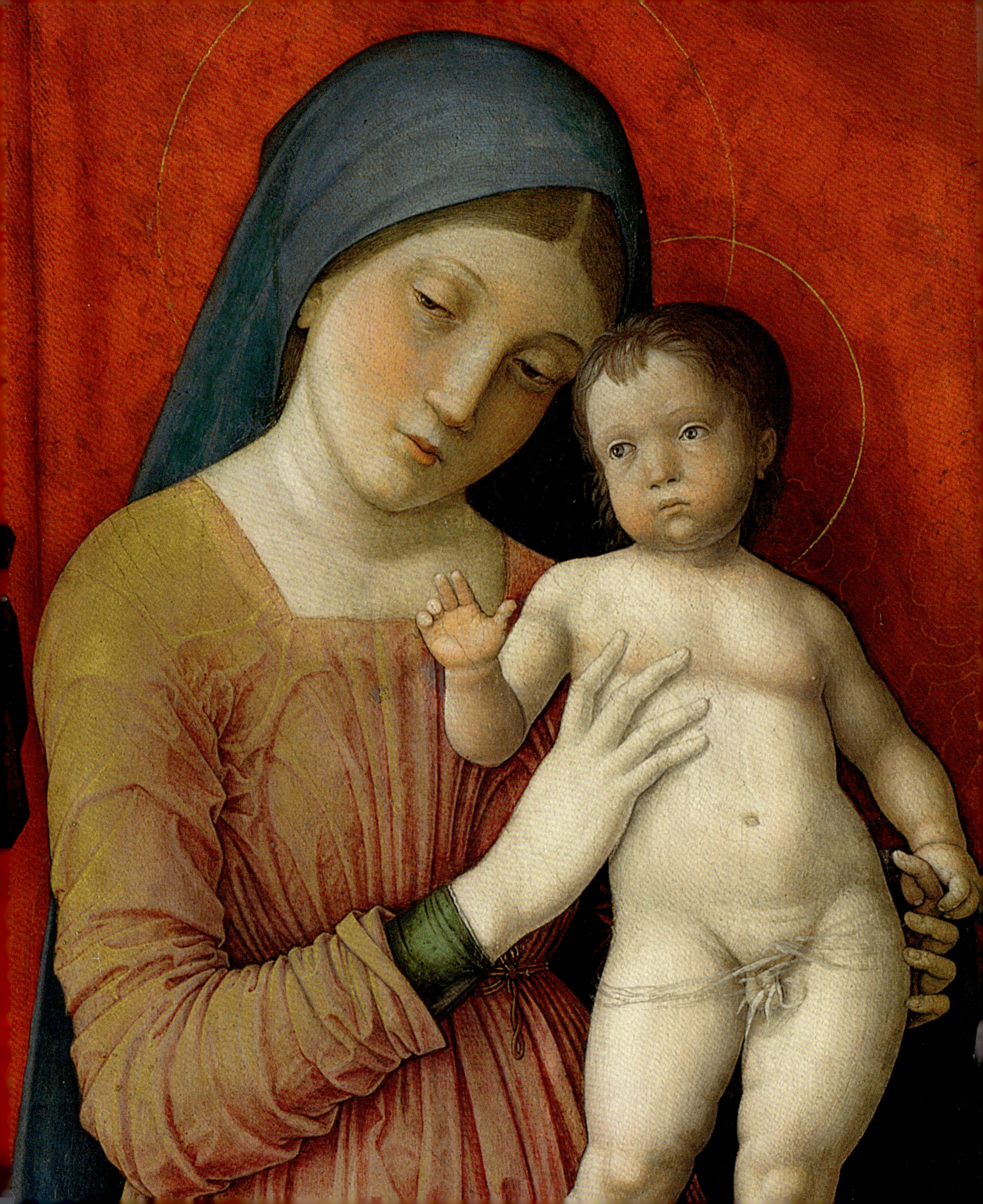

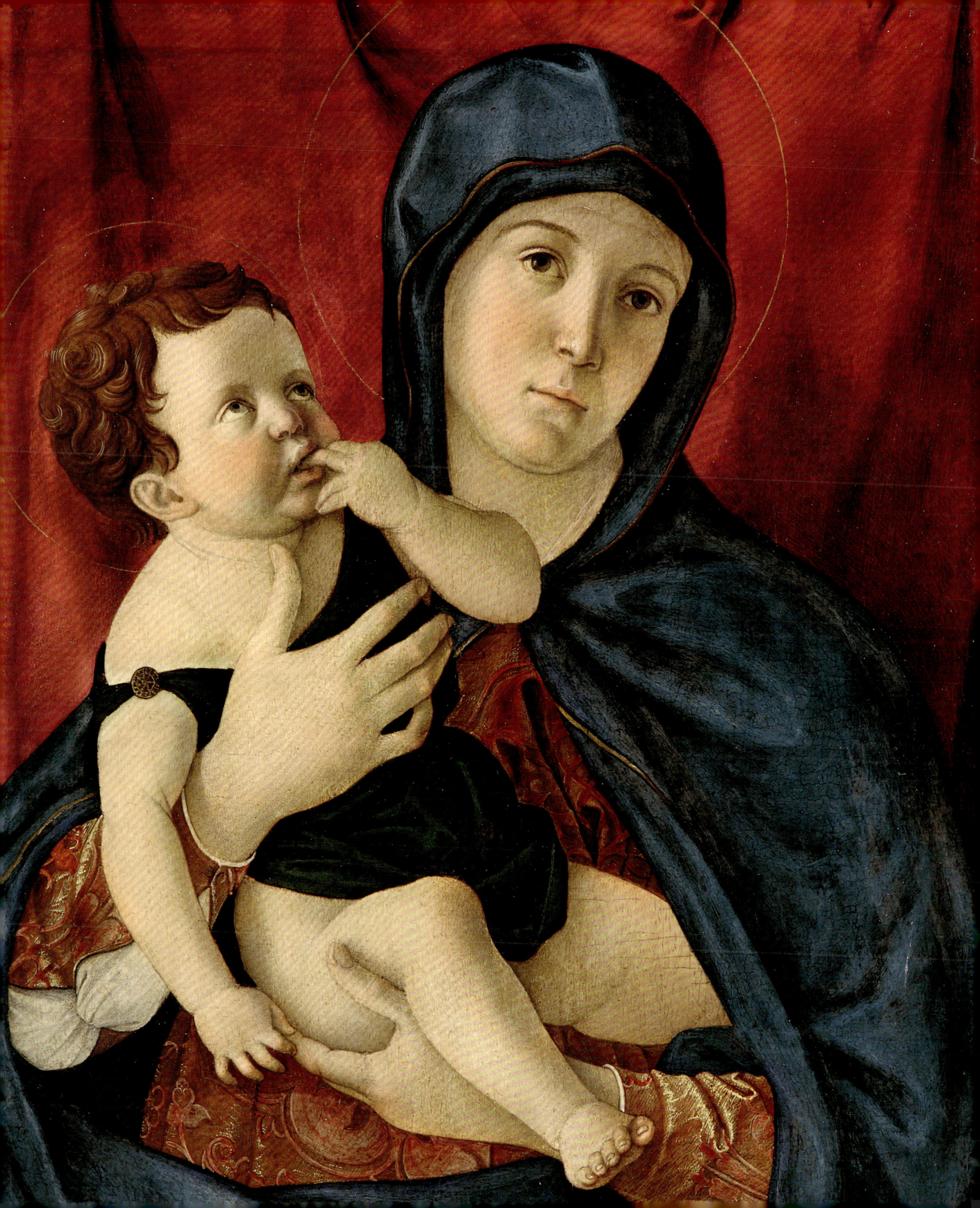

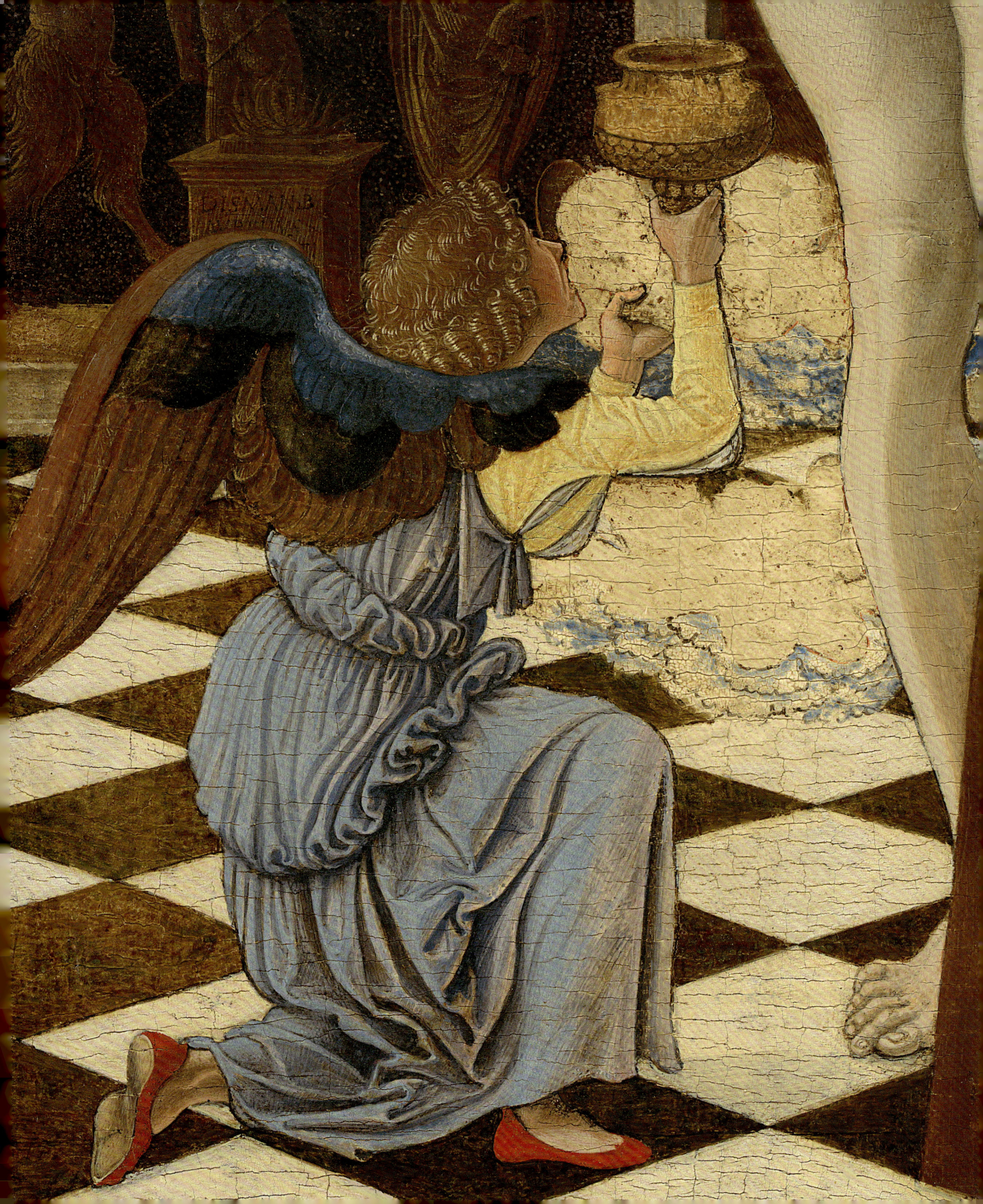

MANTEGNA & BELLINI

Caroline Campbell, Dagmar Korbacher,
Neville Rowley and Sarah Vowles

WITH CONTRIBUTIONS BY

Andrea De Marchi, Jill Dunkerton, Babette Hartwieg
and Katharina Weick-Joch

Published by
NATIONAL GALLERY COMPANY, LONDON
in association with
STAATLICHE MUSEEN ZU BERLIN

DISTRIBUTED BY YALE UNIVERSITY PRESS

Published to accompany the exhibition

MANTEGNA & BELLINI

The National Gallery, London
1 October 2018 to 27 January 2019

MANTEGNA und BELLINI
Meister der Renaissance

Gemäldegalerie, Staatliche Museen zu Berlin
1 March to 30 June 2019

Exhibition generously supported by

The Julia and Hans Rausing Trust
The Thompson Family Charitable Trust
The Robert Lehman Foundation

With additional support from

Graham and Amanda Hutton
Elizabeth and Daniel Peltz OBE
The Tavolozza Foundation – Katrin Bellinger
The Vaseppi Trust
Andrew Bentley and Fiona Garland
And other donors

Exhibition sponsored by

Italian National Tourist Board

This exhibition has been made possible by the provision of insurance through the Government Indemnity Scheme. The National Gallery would like to thank HM Government for providing Government Indemnity and the Department for Digital, Culture, Media and Sport and Arts Council England for arranging the indemnity.

First published in 2018 by
National Gallery Company Limited
St Vincent House
30 Orange Street
London WC2H 7HH
www.nationalgallery.co.uk

HB 978 1 85709 634 7 / 1046329
PB 978 1 85709 635 4 / 1046330

British Library Cataloguing-in-Publication Data
A catalogue record is available from the British Library
Library of Congress Control Number: 2018943342

Publisher Jan Green
Project Editor Claire Young with Elin Sandell
Editor Kate Bell
Picture Researcher Félix Zorzo
Production Jane Hyne and Amanda Mackie
Designer Philip Lewis

Translation of texts from Italian to English (Andrea De Marchi) and from French to English (Neville Rowley) by Frank Dabell

Translation of texts from German to English (Dagmar Korbacher and Katharina Weick-Joch) by Melissa M. Thorson

Origination by DL Imaging, London
Printed in Italy by Conti Tipocolor

FRONT COVER Giovanni Bellini, detail from *The Virgin and Child with Saints Catherine and Mary Magdalene* (fig. 187)

BACK COVER Andrea Mantegna, detail from *The Crucifixion* (fig. 101)

PAGE 2 Andrea Mantegna, detail from *The Virgin and Child with the Magdalen and Saint John the Baptist* (fig. 173)

PAGE 3 Giovanni Bellini, detail from *The Virgin and Child* (fig. 179)

PAGE 4 Giovanni Bellini, detail from *The Blood of the Redeemer* (fig. 192)

PAGE 8 Andrea Mantegna, detail from *Saint Sebastian* (fig. 193)

PAGES 86–7 Giovanni Bellini, detail from *The Dead Christ supported by Four Angels* (fig. 156)

PAGE 256 Andrea Mantegna, detail from *The Presentation of Christ in the Temple* (fig. 128)

PAGE 257 Giovanni Bellini, detail from *The Presentation of Christ in the Temple* (fig. 132)

PAGE 304 Andrea Mantegna, detail from *The Agony in the Garden* (fig. 125)

CONTENTS

DIRECTORS' PREFACE

THIS IS THE FIRST EXHIBITION EVER DEVOTED to Andrea Mantegna and Giovanni Bellini, both of them artists of enormous importance for the Italian Renaissance and for the tradition of European painting. They each represent something new in art: Mantegna revived the world of classical antiquity with a ferocious precision and a preternatural clarity. His contemporary Giovanni Santi, the father of Raphael, recognised in him the unequalled and resplendent successor of the ancients. Bellini was the poetic interpreter of landscape, colour and light, whose painting was, according to Marco Boschini, the Venetian painter and writer who looked back at his achievement a century and a half later, like 'a new springtime for the whole world'.

Mantegna was born near Padua in about 1431 and Bellini a few years later in Venice. When the former married Giovanni's sister, Nicolosia, in 1453, they became brothers-in-law at a time when family relationships were central to artists' success. To be family meant strengthening the studio against rivals, extending patronage networks, and benefiting from the practices and secrets of the workshop. Mantegna remained in Padua and was later to pursue his career in Mantua as court painter to the ruling Gonzaga family, whereas Bellini spent his entire career in Venice, painting for churches, private patrons and for the Venetian Republic.

This exhibition is a special collaboration between our two institutions, the National Gallery in London and the Staatliche Museen zu Berlin. Paintings and drawings from both our institutions form the core of the exhibition and our curators, Caroline Campbell, Dagmar Korbacher and Neville Rowley, have worked closely together to conceive and develop the project. A third partner in the venture is the British Museum, which has supported the exhibition both with loans and the integration in the curatorial team of Sarah Vowles. Our debt of gratitude to the curators of the exhibition and to the Director of the British Museum, Hartwig Fischer, is enormous.

We also wish to express our thanks to the other catalogue authors, Andrea De Marchi, Babette Hartwieg, Katharina Weick-Joch and Jill Dunkerton. The last named of these undertook over a four-year period the painstaking and impressive restoration of Giovanni Bellini's *Assassination of Saint Peter Martyr* in the National Gallery's collection, a painting that had previously been thought to be compromised beyond saving. Alexander Röstel compiled the provenance and references for the List of Works. The catalogue has been designed by Philip Lewis, edited by Kate Bell and project-managed by Claire Young.

We wish to acknowledge the generosity of lenders from several different countries, both institutional and private individuals. Her Majesty Queen Elizabeth II has been most gracious in lending three of the canvases of the *Triumphs of Caesar.* We feel the obligation to highlight the extraordinary beneficence of the National Gallery of Art in Washington (and to thank Earl A. Powell III and David Alan Brown), which has agreed to lend *The Feast of the Gods* to both venues, the museums of Venice (Musei Civici, the Accademia and the Fondazione Querini Stampalia), the Statens Museum for Kunst in Copenhagen, and the Louvre (especially Jean-Luc Martinez, Sébastien Allard and Xavier Salmon). We are grateful to the owner of Mantegna's *Descent of Christ into Limbo* for letting it be seen in both exhibitions in London and Berlin.

At the National Gallery we are grateful to the following sponsors and supporters who have made the exhibition possible: The Julia and Hans Rausing Trust, The Thompson Family Charitable Trust, The Robert Lehman Foundation, Graham and Amanda Hutton, Elizabeth and Daniel Peltz OBE, The Tavolozza Foundation – Katrin Bellinger, The Vaseppi Trust, Andrew Bentley and Fiona Garland and other individual donors and trusts. We are also grateful to Italian National Tourist Board for their sponsorship of the exhibition.

In Berlin we are extremely grateful for the exceptional support of the Kaiser Friedrich Museumsverein, without which the exhibition and its publication would not have been possible. Further thanks are owed to the Istituto Italiano di Cultura – Berlino for their important cooperation with us.

Gabriele Finaldi
Director, The National Gallery, London

Michael Eissenhauer
Director General, Staatliche Museen zu Berlin
Director, Gemäldegalerie and Skulpturensammlung

CURATORS' INTRODUCTION

Caroline Campbell, Dagmar Korbacher, Neville Rowley and Sarah Vowles

IN 1453 A BRILLIANT YOUNG ARTIST FROM PADUA, Andrea Mantegna, married into the Bellini family, which would become the greatest dynasty of painters from the nearby city of Venice. The talents of Mantegna and his brother-in-law, Giovanni Bellini, shaped the course of the art of the Renaissance.

In many respects, it is hard to think of artists more different than Mantegna and Bellini. Mantegna's talent lay in his powers of invention, his mastery of storytelling and his ability to bring the long-dead world of classical antiquity to life. Bellini was no less innovative. He used his interests in light, colour and landscape to create a new kind of art – one that still dazzles by its beauty and demands an emotional response from the viewer.

Our exhibition traces Mantegna and Bellini's artistic dialogue and interaction, which waxed and waned at different periods during their lives. For a brief while, they worked in close artistic dialogue. But in 1460, Mantegna left Padua to become court painter to the powerful Gonzaga family of Mantua. Bellini remained in Venice. Although Mantegna and Bellini's art developed in exciting and different ways, they were shaped by their time together and their knowledge of each other's skills and achievements. This is the first exhibition to focus on the creative exchange that left an indelible impression on their lives and their art.

Mounting an exhibition of this sort is reminiscent of the activity of a Renaissance artist's workshop. As curators, we have worked together on this project for three years. Its genesis came in our joint realisation that the collections of London and Berlin, rich in paintings and drawings by Mantegna and Bellini, provided a uniquely appropriate core from which to create this exhibition. It has been a very fruitful and collegial collaboration. Without this, we could have constructed neither the exhibition nor the scholarly research that underpins it.

We are extremely grateful to the many people without whose support this exhibition and catalogue could not have come to life. Firstly, the exhibition could not have happened without the enthusiastic advocacy of our directors, Michael Eissenhauer, Gabriele Finaldi and Hartwig Fischer. Within our institutions, we would like particularly to thank our senior conservation colleagues Jill Dunkerton and Babette Hartwieg, with whom we have examined many of the paintings in our collections, and who have contributed a jointly authored essay to the catalogue. Jill Dunkerton has also undertaken the challenging and lengthy restoration of Giovanni Bellini's *Assassination of Saint Peter Martyr*, together with Britta New who treated the fragile panel, while at the same time Cinzia Pasquali and her team have worked tirelessly to ensure that *The Drunkenness of Noah* could be shown for the first time following a cleaning that transforms our understanding of Bellini's late works. At the National Gallery, Marika Spring and her team in the scientific department and Rachel Billinge have contributed their invaluable expertise in undertaking technical examination of Renaissance paintings, in particular to the *National Gallery Technical Bulletin* dedicated to Giovanni Bellini that is published in tandem with the exhibition. Scientific analyses for the paintings of the Gemäldegalerie were undertaken by Ina Reiche and her team at the Rathgen-Forschungslabor of the Staatliche Museen zu Berlin, while Maria Reimelt and Maria Zielke undertook major conservation treatments on the paintings from Berlin in this exhibition. We thank Georg Josef Dietz, Luise Maul and Hanka Gerhold for preparing the exhibits from the Kupferstichkabinett. At the British Museum, we would like to thank Hugo Chapman for his generous understanding and support. Jane Knowles, Head of Exhibitions at the National Gallery, and Samantha Cox, Exhibitions Manager, have worked tirelessly on the management of the exhibition. We are indebted also to Katharina Weick-Joch at the Gemäldegalerie and Alexander Röstel, Simon Sainsbury Curatorial Fellow at the National Gallery, who have worked with us on multiple aspects of the exhibition and the publication. Claire Young, Philip Lewis, Kate Bell, Jan Green, Félix Zorzo, Elin Sandell, Jane Hyne and Amanda Mackie have been indefatigable in producing a beautiful book that is the long-term legacy of the exhibition, while Karen Angne and Lutz Stirl, with translators Birgit Lamerz-Beckschäfer, Bernadette Ott and Achim Wurm, have taken care of its German version. And lastly, we would like to thank our families, without whose support none of our work would have been possible.

We would like to thank the following supportive colleagues without whom the exhibition could not have been realised, in particular our generous lenders, including those who wish to remain anonymous:

Marion Ackermann, Giovanni Agosti, Sébastien Allard, Denise Allen, Dita Amory, Susanne Anger, Anne Auber, Jean-Pierre Babelon, Martina Bagnoli, Sophie Ballinger, Davide Banzato, Andrea Bayer, Alex Bell, Peter Bell, Sylvain Bellenger, Gabriella Belli, Andrea Bellieni, Ines Bellin, Roberto Bellucci, Annamaria Bernucci, Brigit Blass-Simmen, Bruno Blasselle, Heidi Blöcher, Jean-Baptiste Bodiguel, Thomas Bohl, Suzanne Boorsch, Olivier Bosc, Tiziana Bottecchia, Anna Bottinelli, Stephanie Brodel, Xanthe Brooke, Beverly Brown, David Alan Brown, Emmanuelle Brugerolles, Stephanie Buck, Babette Buller, Massimo Busetto, Francesco Caglioti, Giacomo A. Calogero, Marina Calow, Lorne Campbell, Laura Cavazzini, Matteo Ceriana, Julien Chapuis, Keith Christiansen, Giancarla Cilmi, Roberto Contini, Donal Cooper, Dominique Cordellier, Marino Cortese, Alberto Craievich, Pierre Curie, Frank Dabell, Roberta D'Adda, Emanuela Daffra, Anne Dary, Glyn Davies, Wolfgang Davis, Ana Debenedetti, John Delaney, Francesca Del Torre Scheuch, Vincent Delieuvin, Alessandro Della Latta, Philipp Demandt, Stéphanie Deprouw-Augustin, Jocelyne Deschaux, C.D. Dickerson, Luigi Maria Di Corato, Andrea Di Lorenzo, Helen Dowding, Bastian Eclercy, Kate Edmondson, Robert M. Edsel, Maren Eichhorn, David Ekserdjian, Caroline Elam, Sabine Engel, Alexandra Enzensberger, Stéphane Épin, Christine Exler, Gabriele Fabbrici, Marzia Faietti, Miguel Falomir, Markus Farr, Katharina Fendius, Julie Firth, Fritz Fischer, Jennifer Fletcher, Susan Foister, Fondazione Giorgio Cini, Ramona Föllmer, Fabian Fröhlich, Francesca Gabrieli, Aldo Galli, Jenny Gaschke, Davide Gasparotto, Elisabetta Gastaldi, Yvonne Geister, Laura Gnaccolini, Ketty Gottardo, Barbara Gottschalk, Simone Guerriero, Sabine Haag, Gill Hart, Bettina Held, Miguel Helfrich, Andreas Henning, Catalina Heroven, Paul Hills, Gretchen Hirschauer, Anne Hodge, Sabine Hoffmann, Paul Hofmann, Michaela Humborg, Peter Humfrey, Nicola Kalinsky, Guillaume Kazérouni, Stephan Kemperdick, Leah Kharibian, Stephan Koja, Philippa Kramer, Mechtild Kronenberg, Michel Laclotte, Lisa Lang, Amélie Laurent, Tom Laver, Marigusta Lazzari, Eric M. Lee, Amanda Lillie, Antonella Longo-Turri, Maria López-Fanjul, Bertram Lorenz, Mauro Lucco, Alison Luchs, Emanuele Lugli, Andreas von Majewski, Ilenia Malavasi, Lara Marchese, Elena Marchetti, Giorgio Marini, Paola Marini, Jane Martineau, Jean-Luc Martinez, Daniel W. Maze, Antonio Mazzotta, Luciano Migliaccio, Julie Molloy, Fabrizio Moretti, Anna Mosig, Peta Motture, Andrea Müller, Nicola Müller, Sophie Nawrocki, Michele Nicolaci, Christina Nielsen, Alison Nogeira, Elke Obertaler, Daniela Parenti, Milly Passigli, Maria Cristina Passoni, Adriano Pedrosa, Sandra Penketh, Nicholas Penny, Belinda Phillpot, Lucia Pini, Orietta Piolanti, Timothy Potts, Earl A. Powell III, Hannah Prinz, Massimo Pulini, Cristina Quattrini, Sean Rainbird, Richard Rand, Guido Rebecchini, Anika Reineke, Eleanor Richards, Yohan Rimaud, Maria Cristina Rodeschini, Christiana Romalli, Bernd Rottenburg, Julie Rowlins, Susannah Rutherglen, Xavier Salmon, Sarah Salomon, Xavier F. Salomon, Lois Salter, Paolo Sanvito, Marta Savaris, Don Stefano Savoia, Marco Scansani, Volker Schaible, Peter Scheel, Thomas Schelper, Andrea Schindlmeyer, Konrad Schlegel, Christoph Schmidt, Eike D. Schmidt, Andreas Schumacher, Sabine Schwerdtfeger, Karen Serres, Nathaniel Silver, Rachel Sloan, Carolin Stanneck, Ute Stehr, Maria Stein, Sandra Stelzig, Sven Stienen, Maria Stölzer, Luke Syson, Francesca Tasso, Dominique Thiébaut, Dodge Thompson, Veronika Tocha, Marcello Toffanello, Ceren Topcu, Louisa Torres, Letizia Treves, Babet Trevisan, Giovanni Valagussa, Ernst Vegelin van Claerbergen, Federica Veratelli, Giovanni C.F. Villa, Mattia Vinco, Antje Voigt, Jörg Völlnagel, George Wachter, Christine Waidenschlager, Rainer Wendler, Robert Wenley, Stefan Weppelmann, Catherine Whistler, Tanja Wieczorek, Matthias Wivel, Sigrid Wollmeiner, Annalisa Zanni, Giulio Zavatta, Kurt Zeidler, Maria Zielke, Marta Zoppetti, Michela Zurla.

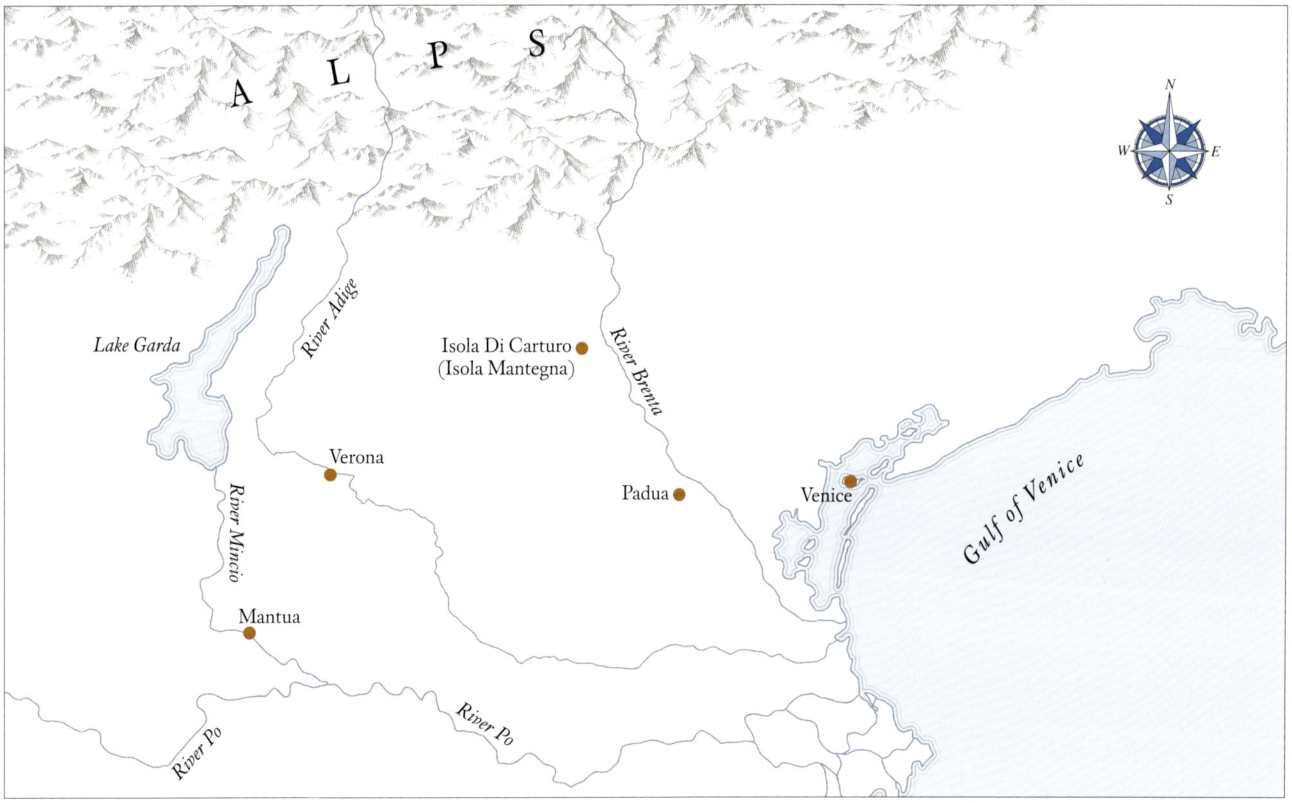

ALPS
N
W
E
S
Lake Garda
River Adige
Isola Di Carturo
(Isola Mantegna)
River Brenta
Verona
Padua
Venice
Gulf of Venice
River Mincio
Mantua
River Po
River Po

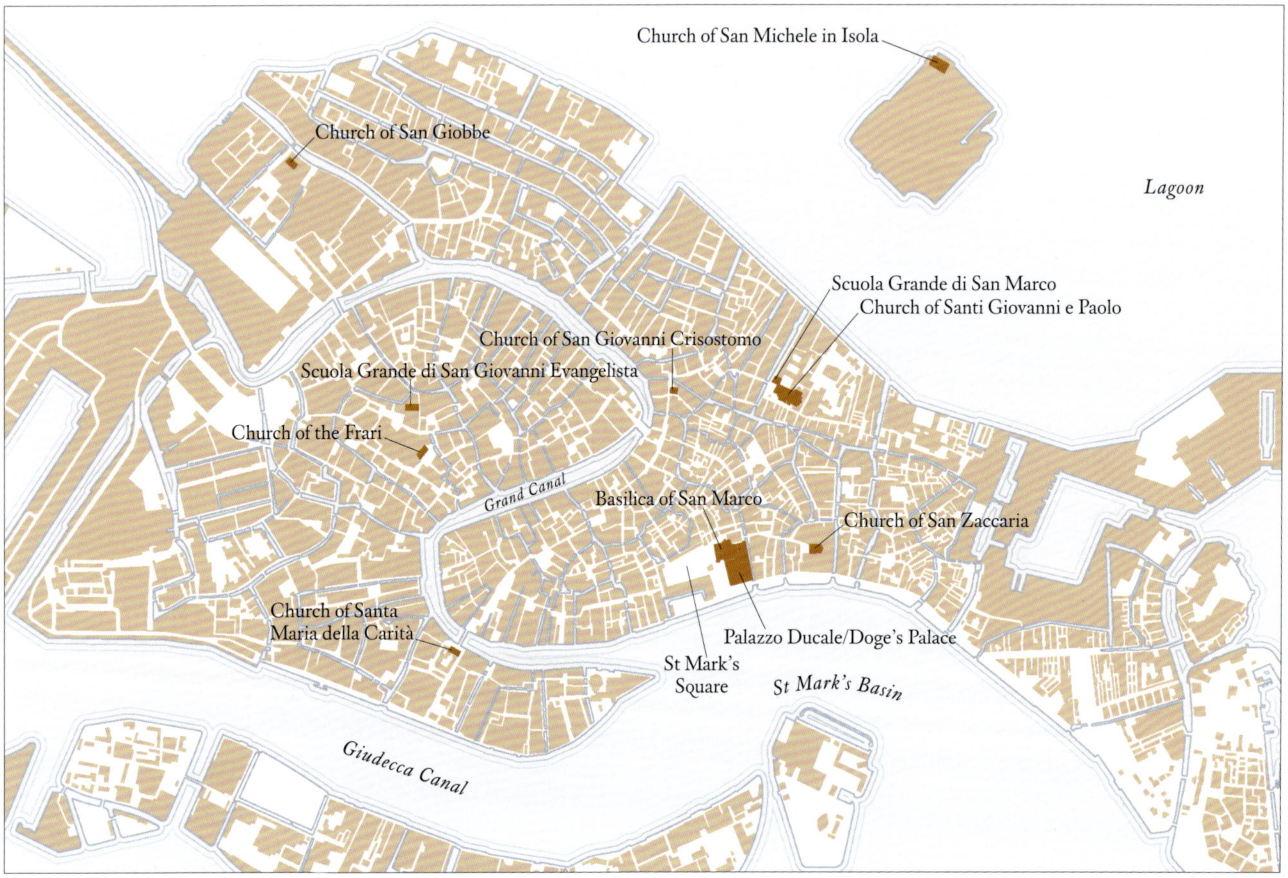

Church of San Michele in Isola
Church of San Giobbe
Lagoon
Scuola Grande di San Marco
Church of Santi Giovanni e Paolo
Church of San Giovanni Crisostomo
Scuola Grande di San Giovanni Evangelista
Church of the Frari
Grand Canal
Basilica of San Marco
Church of San Zaccaria
Church of Santa
Maria della Carità
Palazzo Ducale/Doge's Palace
St Mark's
Square
St Mark's Basin
Giudecca Canal

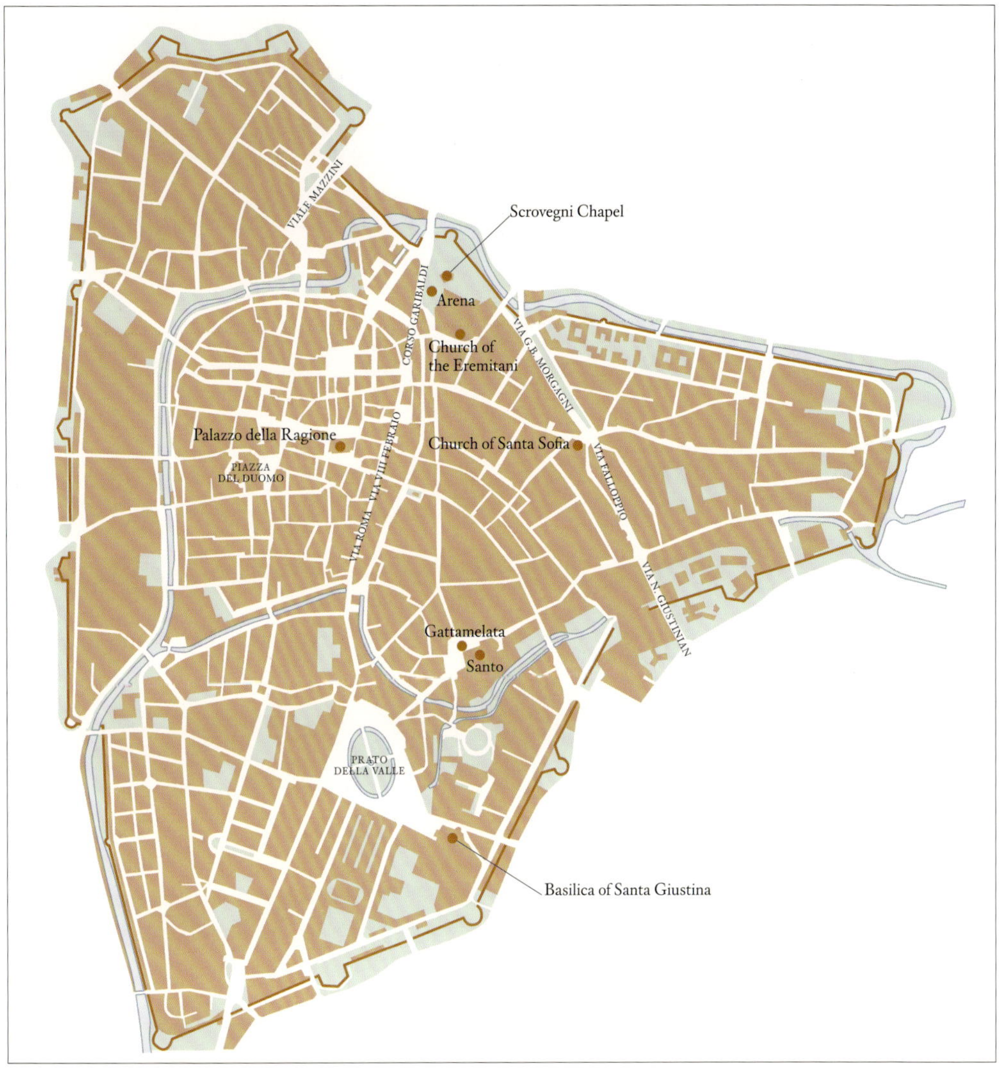

PADUA

Family of Giovanni Bellini

Zanine [1] = Nicolo Bellini = [2] Franceschina
deceased c.1460

'Rinversi' = Gera

Elena = Paolo dai Remi (deceased by 1443)

Giovanni

Jacopo = Anna Rinversi (about 1400–about 1470)

Francesco da Pesaro

? = Giorgio Bocheta (deceased by 1489)

Katarucie

Leonardo (miniaturist)

Andrea Mantegna = Nicolosia
(about 1431–1506) c.1429–1475/80

Nicolò
c.1430–after 1512

Cattarina Barasina [1] = Gentile = [2] Maria di Antonio Trevisano
deceased c.1469 c.1431–1507 ('Gaban')
testament 1503;
no known issue

? [1] = GIOVANNI = [2] Ginevra
(about 1435–1516)

Gabriele = Lucrezia

Francesco (priest)

Giovanni (illegitimate)

Giovanni Andrea (illegitimate) born c.1480

Federico

Girolamo

Ludovico

Francesco

Taddea

Laura

Bernardino? deceased 1493

Alvise deceased 1499

Elena = Matteo Mondo married 1481

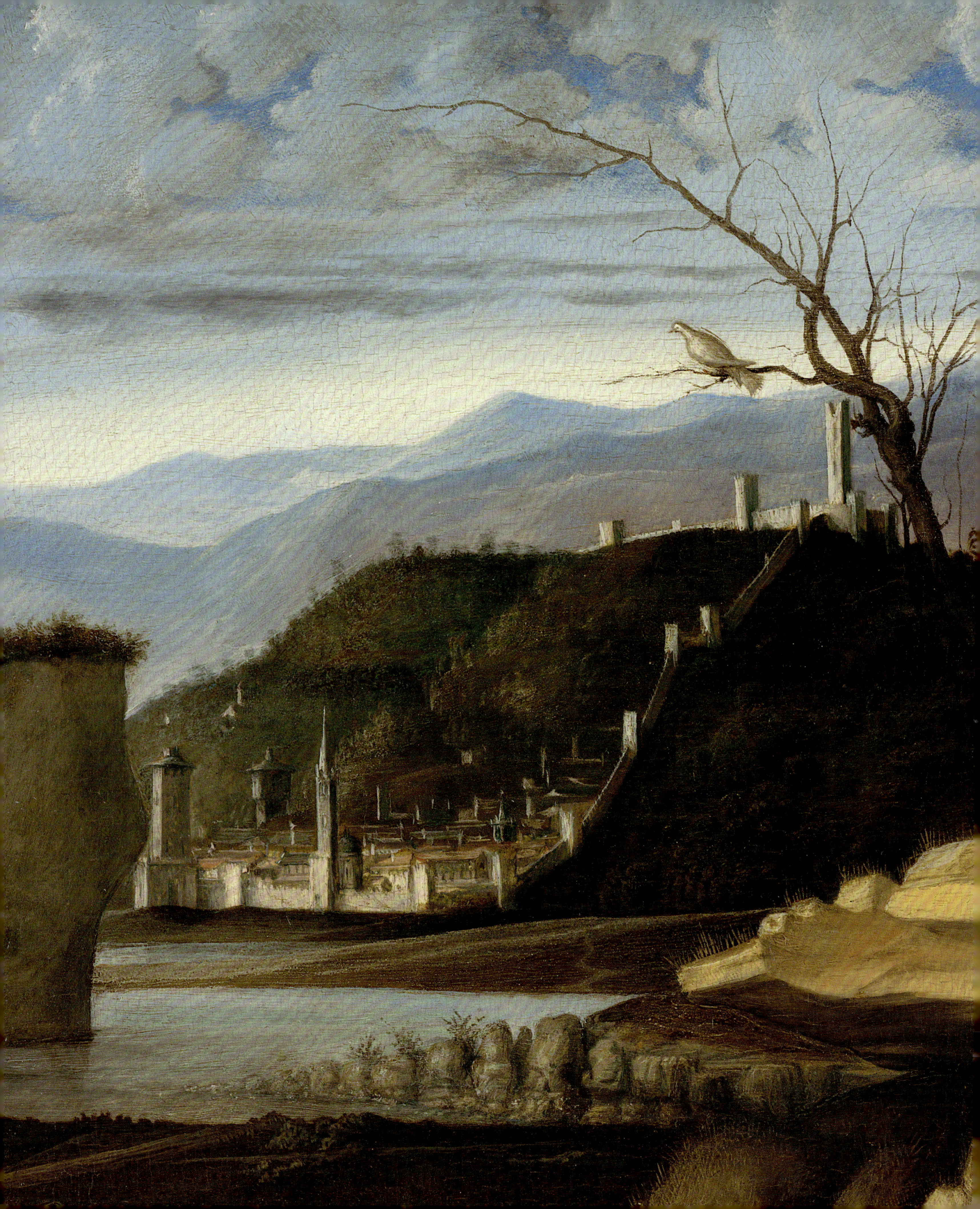

I

A Tale of Two Artists and Two Cities: Mantegna, Bellini; Padua, Venice

CAROLINE CAMPBELL

FROM THE PERSPECTIVE OF THE TWENTY-FIRST century, when personal celebrity is all-important, and we are accustomed to famous artists and architects, it is hard to conceive of the centrality of family relations to artistic production in the Renaissance. Andrea Mantegna and Giovanni Bellini were both acclaimed artists of their day and, in a way that seems superficially familiar today, individually adulated and engaged in artistic competition. They were also, however, brothers-in-law, linked through Mantegna's marriage to Bellini's half-sister, Nicolosia. This is a tale of two artists, their families and their cities; an interlinked story of art, family, rivalry, marriage, pragmatism and personality.

PROLOGUE: 1501 – MANTEGNA AND BELLINI

In 1501 Mantegna's patron, Isabella d'Este, the young, incessantly demanding Marchioness of Mantua, was eager to acquire a work by his brother-in-law, the Venetian artist Giovanni Bellini. By this time Bellini was generally agreed to be – as Albrecht Dürer was to write five years later, on his second visit to Italy – the 'best' of all Venetian painters.[1] Isabella wished Bellini to produce an *istoria*, a narrative painting based on a learned source, and for this to be hung beside the work of the Mantuan court artist, Mantegna, in her rooms in the city's Ducal Palace. This was a genre in which Mantegna excelled: as his *Triumphs of Caesar* (figs 235, 236, 237) demonstrate. It was not one, however, in which Bellini was accustomed to working. Landscapes, devotional paintings, altarpieces, portraits: these were all part and parcel of Giovanni Bellini's usual production. But an *istoria* was different. By 1501 Bellini was the most admired painter in Venice. He was a state official, prosperous and well connected. Why should he accede to the request? This was Mantegna's territory, and Bellini – despite his fame – seems to have felt distinctly uncomfortable about a direct comparison with his brother-in-law's work.

As Isabella's correspondent, the Venetian art collector Michele Vianello, wrote in June 1501:

> But of that narrative your ladyship gave [Bellini], he cannot say how unwillingly he would do it because he knows your ladyship's discernment and also that [the picture] would be compared with those works by messer Andrea [Mantegna], and thus he wishes to do as he knows [best] and he says that in this narrative he cannot do something that will come out well or in which there will be something good...[2]

Finally, after years of negotiation over this picture, Isabella admitted defeat. Bellini ultimately produced a *Nativity*, which hung in the Marchioness's bedchamber and is unfortunately lost. The instrument-maker (and another of Isabella's Venetian agents) Lorenzo da Pavia's description of this painting during its production in the summer of 1504 praises this 'beautiful thing', for, as he goes on: 'In this work he [Bellini] has really pushed himself, partly out of a sense of honour, and especially out of respect for master Andrea Mantegna.'[3]

This anecdote bears witness to the close ties that linked Mantegna and Bellini throughout their lives, even though for much of it they inhabited very different worlds. Mantegna spent most of his life as a court painter, active in the small but refined ambiance of Mantua, south-west of Verona, wholly reliant on the largesse and patronage of the ruling Gonzaga family. In contrast, Bellini, a Venetian citizen recognised by

GIOVANNI BELLINI, detail from *Saint Jerome reading in Landscape* (FIG. 117)

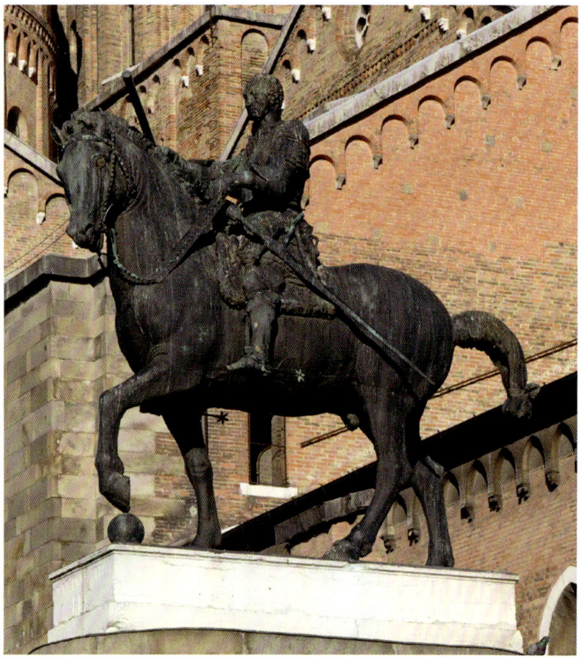

FIG. I
DONATELLO
Equestrian statue of Erasmo da Narni, known as Gattamelata (1370–1443), 1447–53
Bronze, 340 × 390 cm
Piazza del Santo, Padua

his peers as the Republic's greatest painter, had more autonomy and the ability to resist at least some of the blandishments of a Marchioness. Their admiration and respect, however, was mutual. Inspired by each other's example, they both experimented and worked in ways they were not entirely comfortable with in order to hone the essence of their artistic identities. While Mantegna exemplified the intellectual artist, Bellini was the archetypal landscape painter, the first to use nature comprehensively to convey emotion. For these reasons, the course of Italian Renaissance painting and the careers of Titian, Correggio and Veronese – to name but a few – are inconceivable without their example.

PADUA: A CENTRE OF INNOVATION AND EXCHANGE

Although Mantegna spent most of his life in Mantua, his upbringing and early career in Padua set the pattern for his artistic production. The university town of Padua, 24 miles from the 'Most Serene Republic (La Serenissima)' of Venice (in the fifteenth century it was possible to travel between the two by boat in an evening),[4] has long been overshadowed by its more glamorous neighbour. But in the fifteenth and sixteenth centuries Padua, although a subject of the Venetian Empire from 1405, was the centre of a vibrant intellectual, artistic and religious life without which the history of Europe – let alone that of Venice herself – would have been very different.

Padua, unlike Venice, claimed its descent from a hero of classical antiquity, following assertions made by the great Roman authors Livy and Virgil. According to these sources, Padua was founded by the Trojan Prince Antenor in the year 1180 BCE. In the late twelfth century, when a stone sarcophagus was exhumed in the city, the remains found within were declared to be those of Antenor. An inscription by the early humanist scholar Lovato de' Lovati, placed near the tomb in 1294, refers to the 'noble Antenor' who 'founded Padua'.[5] This creation myth, as potent in different ways as Venice's supposed foundation by Saint Mark, was believed even in Mantegna and Bellini's day. It gave Padua a longer history and pedigree than its nearby rival. Padua's Roman remains were celebrated throughout the Middle Ages, the most notable being the Roman amphitheatre or Arena, which was partially cleared to make way for the palace (now destroyed) and chapel built by Enrico Scrovegni in the early fourteenth century.

By the early thirteenth century Padua was one of the most confident and important cities of North-Eastern Italy, and still one that believed (as the name of its late medieval communal hall, the Palazzo della Ragione suggests) that reason was the root of civic government. To this period can be dated the city's greatest institutions, its university (the second oldest in Italy), and the pilgrimage church housing the shrine of the Franciscan friar Saint Anthony of Padua (who died outside the city in 1231), commonly known as the Santo. Although Padua ceased to be self-governing in the early fourteenth century, when it fell under the control of the Scaliger family, its identity remained strong, based on three foundations: the city's ancient heritage, its university and the Santo.

Padua was a city where a tradition of innovative intellectual and cultural life was paramount. Together

FIG. 2
DONATELLO
Crucifix and high altar of the Santo, 1446–50
Basilica of Sant'Antonio, Padua

with Florence, it was one of the most creative and interdisciplinary milieux in fifteenth-century Europe. Students flocked to its university, renowned for its scholarship in law, the classics and medicine, and from 1443, Venetians were forbidden to study anywhere else.[6] Such was its draw that talented individuals from other spheres also gravitated to Padua, most famously the Florentine painter Giotto, who frescoed the Scrovegni Chapel between 1303 and 1305, and his Tuscan compatriot, the poet and humanist Francesco Petrarch, who died in Arquà near Padua (1368–74).

In the fifteenth century the intellectual tradition of Padua was continued by the renowned humanists Guarino da Verona and Vittorino da Feltre, who studied and, in the case of the latter, taught in the city. Scholars and collectors made extended stays: for instance, Ciriaco d'Ancona (1392–1452), the pioneering collector of antiquities, spent a year in Padua in the early 1440s.[7] Among Ciriaco's friends was Pietro Donato (Dona), the Venetian who was the city's bishop from 1428 to 1447, and who established the first scribal school attached to the cathedral. Paduan manuscripts, from Donato's scriptorium and other centres, were celebrated for their unity of classical form and content – the ideal of humanist studies.[8]

A similar goal motivated the Florentine artist Donatello, who spent a decade working for the friars of the Santo and producing the first free-standing equestrian monument since antiquity (fig. 1), and the artist Francesco Squarcione, who established an 'Academy of Design'. Paduan artists, often inspired or trained by them, had pronounced intellectual interests, particularly in classical antiquity (about 100 BCE to 450 CE). The *istorie* drawn on parchment by Bernardo Parentino, the sketchbook of Marco Zoppo, or – far later in the century – the small bronzes of sculptor Andrea Riccio, reveal how easily artists could invent successful compositions in the ancient manner (*all'antica*). Paduan humanism, and humanist art, were strongly connected to studies of coins (numismatics), ancient inscriptions (epigraphy) and manuscripts, all subjects that attracted intense interest in Italy in the fifteenth century.

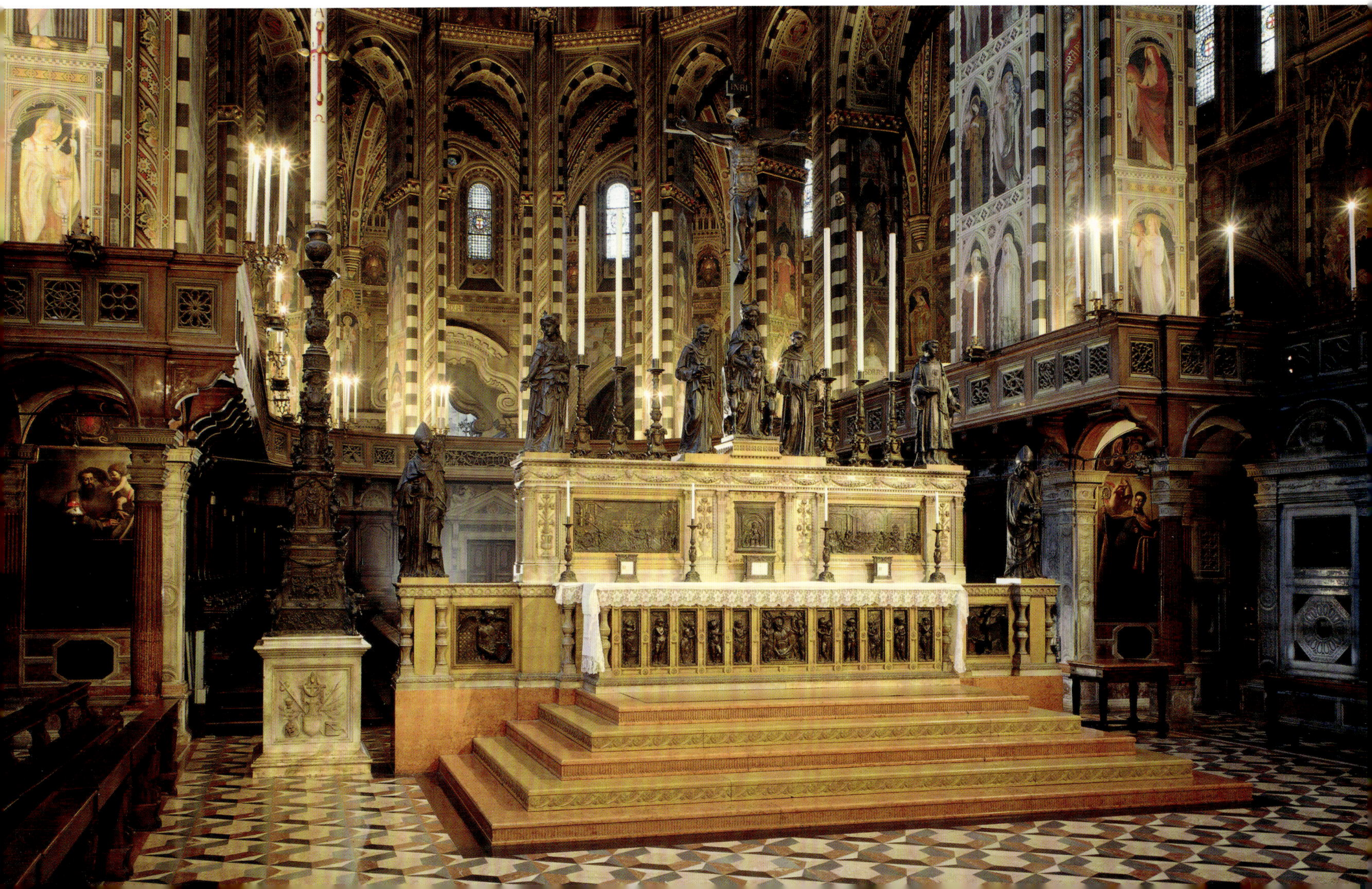

FIG. 3
ANDREA MANTEGNA
Ceiling oculus from the Camera Picta, 1465–74
Fresco, Ducal Palace, Mantua

ANDREA MANTEGNA

The son of a carpenter, Andrea Mantegna[9] was a self-made man. His rise to fame, as recounted by the sixteenth-century Tuscan artist and writer on art, Giorgio Vasari (among others), saw him carried by extraordinary talent far beyond the social and cultural sphere of his birth.[10] He ended his days in Mantua as court painter to the Gonzaga dukes, and was buried in an elaborate funerary chapel, in the church of Sant'Andrea. It was apparently designed by Mantegna himself, and incorporated paintings by the artist (including figs 243, 244) and his two sons, as well as a bronze portrait (fig. 242) based on ancient Roman precedents, accompanied by an inscription that he must at least have approved, if not invented, praising him as the 'new Apelles'.

Mantegna's admiration for himself was shared by all fifteenth- and sixteenth-century commentators on art. Even as a teenager, in the 1440s, a realistic portrait of a nun (now lost) was singled out for its lifelike qualities by the Venetian humanist (and friend of Giovanni's father, Jacopo) Ulisse degli Aleotti (1412–1468).[11] Giovanni Santi, Raphael's father, and author of an elogium of fifteenth-century painters, ranked Mantegna as the finest artist of his day. Santi was a great admirer of what he called Mantegna's 'marvellous painting and exalted art', praising him for his skills in drawing, compositional invention, perspective, grace, fine colouring and three-dimensionality.[12] But perhaps the most interesting contemporary perspective on Mantegna as an artist comes from the Hungarian humanist poet Janus Pannonius, who compared Mantegna not to any painter, but to the Roman historian Livy, who was beloved of fifteenth-century scholars for his moralistic histories and invention of *istoria*.[13]

Mantegna was born in the small community of Isola di Carturo, a few miles north of Padua. He was a precocious talent, and in 1442, when he can have been no more than 11, he was taken on as a pupil by Francesco Squarcione (see figs 79, 80), a painter of limited ability who adopted the most gifted of his students (including, successively, Mantegna and Marco Zoppo) so that he could benefit financially from their work. Yet Squarcione's *Studium* formed the basis of Mantegna's artistic identity and success.[14] In 1448, after alleging that he had been shamelessly exploited, Mantegna was able to annul his adoption.[15] The subsequent 12 years of independent activity in Padua shaped the course of his artistic development.

In Padua, in the late 1440s and early 1450s, Mantegna established himself as the most exciting artist of his generation. Here he associated regularly with talented artists and intellectuals including Zoppo, his own erstwhile friend and partner Niccolò Pizzolo (d. 1453),[16] Ulisse degli Aliotti, the epigrapher and doctor of medicine Giovanni Marcanova (d. 1467) and the calligrapher, writer and artist Felice Feliciano (1433–1479). With Pizzolo (as well as two other younger artists, Giovanni d'Alemagna and Antonio Vivarini), he was commissioned to paint half of the notary Antonio Ovetari's funerary chapel in the Church of the Eremitani (figs 248, 249, 250, 251) by his widow Imperatrice Forzatè. Although the destruction of the chapel by Allied bombardment in 1944 has hampered our full understanding of this cycle, Mantegna's contributions are remarkable for their dramatic foreshortening and convincing archaeological reconstructions of classical settings and spaces.

It was through Pizzolo, who had been Donatello's assistant, that Mantegna formed a connection with the workshop of the great Florentine sculptor, who came to Padua in 1443 to make a life-size bronze Crucifix for the Santo, and who was to stay for a decade, engaged on a monumental bronze high altar for the church (fig. 2), unfortunately dismembered in 1579, although the individual figures and reliefs survive. Donatello's work – which had an impact on every artist in mid-century

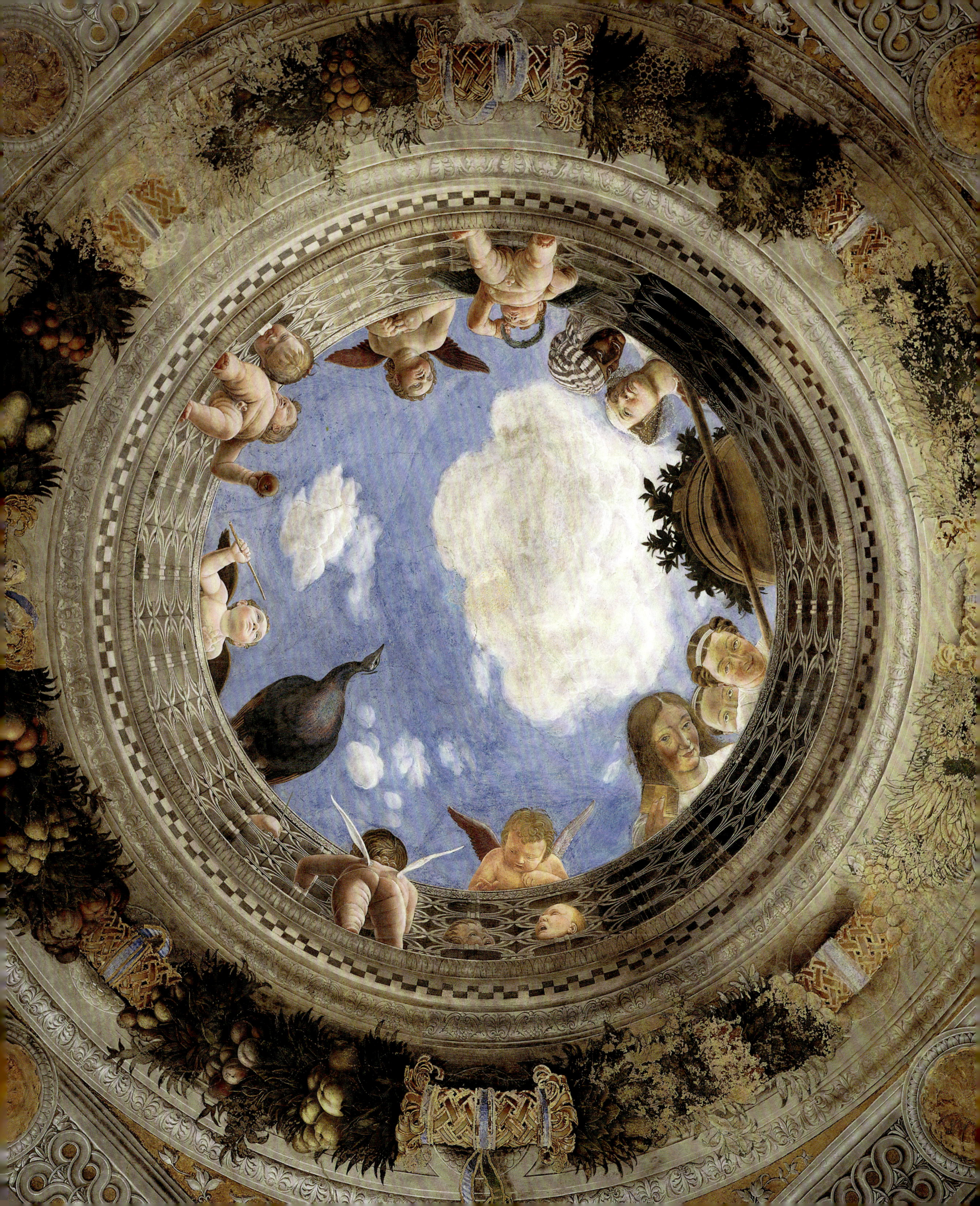

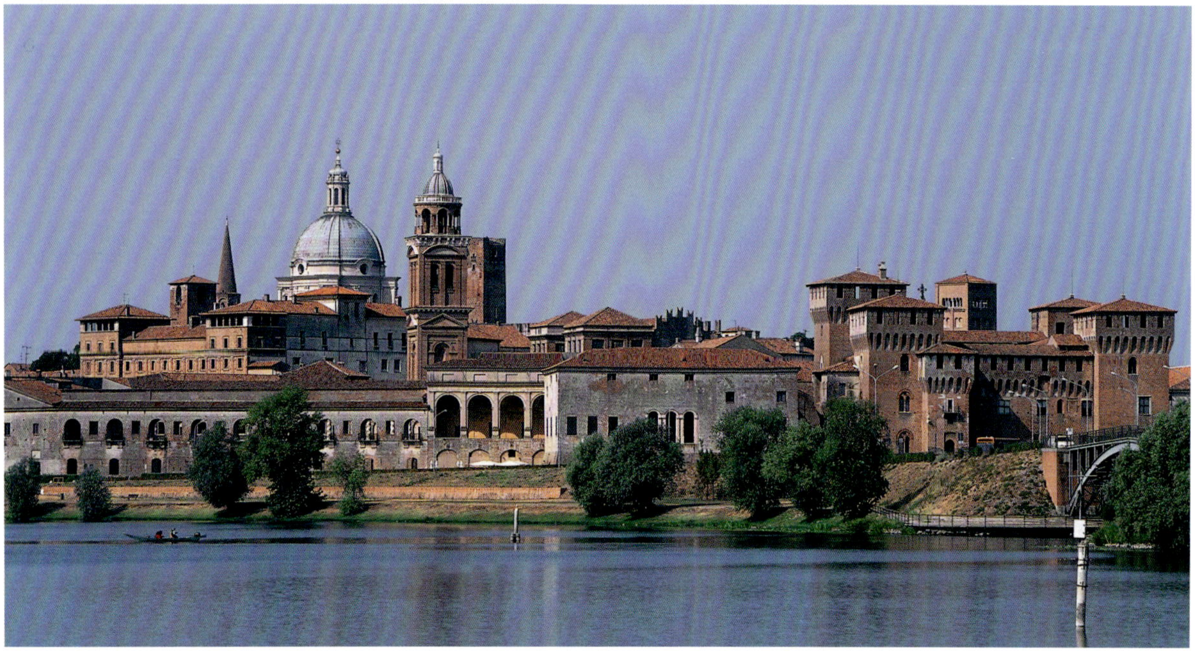

FIG. 4
View of Mantua

Padua – showed Mantegna how to fit his beautifully constructed figures into a naturalistic setting, and to think about perspective – the most radical element of the Ovetari frescoes. The most 'Donatellian' of Mantegna's works in Padua was the altarpiece commissioned by the reformed Benedictine Abbot Gregorio Correr for his abbey church, San Zeno in Verona (1456–9; fig. 252). All of it (apart from the predella, including fig. 101) remains *in situ* in the church, in the classicised frame which Mantegna must have designed.[17]

Mantegna's work for San Zeno prevented him taking up immediately the generous offer of employment he had received in 1456 from Ludovico III Gonzaga, Marquess of Mantua. Finally, in 1460, Mantegna moved his wife and family permanently to the small, marshy city of Mantua (fig. 4). Here he was to spend almost 50 years, working as court painter to the Gonzagas. His salary and prerequisites (if paid) were generous: over his lifetime in the city they included several gifts of land, as well as money.

Much of Mantegna's work in Mantua has disappeared; we know nothing for instance, save four paintings (including figs 213, 214), about his decoration of the new chapel in the Ducal Palace. Yet in the Camera Picta (Camera degli Sposi) we still have one of the most famous of all Renaissance fresco cycles (figs 3, 203). This smallish room, a picture gallery of Ludovico, his consort Barbara of Brandenburg, their families and their court, is notable for its naturalism, and for its audacious spatial effects. It anticipates the Baroque in its complete integration of pictorial and architectural spaces. Mantegna's relative isolation in Mantua gave him the incentive to spread knowledge of his work outside the court through the then extremely innovative technique of printmaking. He was among the very first Italian artists involved in engraving, and his zealous protection of his intellectual copyright is one of the most striking examples of his spiky and argumentative personality.[18]

Building on his Paduan formation, Mantegna developed a deep understanding of ancient Roman art and archaeology. His house, the Casa del Mantegna, with its square ground plan and round courtyard, is uniquely classical for an artist's dwelling of the fifteenth century. Mantegna's understanding of antiquity was drawn from the towns and countryside around him. His two years in Rome (1488–90), where he was summoned by Pope Innocent VIII to fresco the Belvedere Chapel in the Vatican (destroyed by fire in 1780), seem to have deepened rather than changed his attitude to the ancient world. On his return to Mantua he embarked on his most influential series of works, nine large paintings of Julius Caesar's Gallic Triumphs (figs 235, 236, 237), an evocative recreation of the world of classical antiquity.[19]

The last years of Mantegna's life were marked by never-ceasing inventiveness, and work for a greater range of patrons than simply the Gonzaga family. He found Isabella d'Este, the new Marchioness, exacting and difficult, but whether in his work for her or for others, he always sought new pictorial solutions. The *Dead Christ* (fig. 199) is unparalleled in its illusionism among any work of fifteenth-century Italian art. He experimented afresh with formats including paintings for secular settings which mimic bronze or stone (figs 238, 240, 241, 245), as well as the half-length narrative (such as *The Adoration of the Magi*, fig. 136) – while continuing to produce major altarpieces, including *The Virgin and Child with the Magdalen and Saint John the Baptist* in the National Gallery (fig. 173). The inscription on the *Saint Sebastian* (now in Ca' d'Oro) recorded in his studio at his death can perhaps stand as his true epitaph: 'Nothing stands firm but the divine; all else is smoke.'

VENICE

Padua was important, but it was not Venice. During the fifteenth century Venice was the pre-eminent city in Europe, the continent's business and luxury goods capital, and her most significant port, controlling Christian commercial activity in the Mediterranean basin. A Milanese pilgrim, Canon Pietro Casola, recorded his excitement on arriving in Venice in 1494:

> And I declare that it is impossible to tell or write fully of the beauty, the magnificence or the wealth of the city of Venice.... Indeed it seems as if all the world flocks there, and that human beings have concentrated there all their force for trading.[20]

All this was to change with the opening of the Atlantic sea routes to Asia, Africa and the New World, but in the 1400s there was no other city in Europe where so many of the best and most valued items from around the world could be purchased: exotic spices including pepper, Chinese porcelain, Ottoman carpets and textiles, Syrian metalwork and lapis lazuli from Afghanistan. One benefit for artists was the ready availability of the best and most intensely coloured pigments. Venice's export and import trade was guaranteed by the galleys built in her great shipyard, the Arsenal, which accompanied every convoy across the sea, and the Venetian officials and ambassadors who resided in every port of note.

But fifteenth-century Venice was not simply the leading trade centre in Europe, it was also the Christian superpower of its day in the Eastern Mediterranean. Following the Venetian-led sack of Constantinople (Istanbul), during the Fourth Crusade of 1204, the Byzantine Empire had begun to collapse as a coherent political and territorial state. Venice presented herself as the only plausible Christian alternative to Byzantium, and the only possible opponent to the Ottoman Turks, who were making great territorial advances in the Levant and South-Eastern Europe. By the fifteenth century Venice's empire included much of the Slovenian, Croatian and Dalmatian coast, parts of the Peloponnese and sundry islands in the Adriatic and Aegean seas, as well as the Mediterranean. European travellers to Venice often commented on the extraordinary mix of peoples to be found there. Typical of such fifteenth- and sixteenth-century accounts is that of Sir Lewes Lewkenor, the first English translator of Cardinal Gasparo Contarini's *The Commonwealth and Government of Venice*, who singles out the 'wonderful concourse of strange and forraine people ... of the farthest and remotest nations' to be found in this 'glorious' city.[21] In the fifteenth century, Venice was home to substantial communities of Sephardic and Ashkenazi Jews, Albanians and Greeks – not to mention Germans, Spaniards and the citizens of other Italian states, such as Genoa, Florence and Milan. On Cyprus, Venice's most important colony (formally incorporated into the state in 1489), Cypriots, Greeks, Jews and Turks co-existed, if not always peacefully.

Venice was defined by her relationship with the Mediterranean and divinely appointed position (or so it was believed) to be neither the new Rome or the new Byzantium, but the 'new' Jerusalem, a heavenly city rising supernaturally from the waves. Unlike practically every other city in the area, Venice did not claim to have been founded by the ancient Greeks or Romans. The city's birth was even more illustrious: she asserted no less than the evangelist Saint Mark – who was believed to have brought Christianity to North-East Italy – as her patron. According to a thirteenth-century rewriting of the life of Saint Mark, it was while crossing the Venetian lagoon, following his mission to Aquileia, that the saint had received the angelic message 'Peace be with you, Mark, my evangelist' ('*Pax tibi Marce Evangelista meus*'), and understood that his body would find its resting place in Venice.[22] Such retrospective myth-making made sense of the theft perpetrated by two Venetian merchants in 827, when they appropriated Mark's relics from Alexandria and 'returned' them to Venice. These were placed in the church of San Marco, founded on that occasion, which dominated Venetian life henceforth, both figuratively and physically. In the early thirteenth century the Basilica, built in the Byzantine style and adorned with narrative mosaics (only completed many centuries later, worked on by artists including Jacopo Bellini and Titian), was further adorned with some of the best *spolia*, or loot, brought back from Constantinople by the victorious Crusaders of 1204. These were incorporated throughout the city, making good Venice's claim to be Byzantium's temporal and spiritual heir. By the fifteenth century the Basilica had already assumed its distinctive Venetian combination of Western and Eastern forms, with Gothic cusps and crockets, and Mediterranean onion domes.

Venice was also, for many statesmen and philosophers, 'the' model of how a state should be governed, admired throughout Europe for its combination of monarchy, oligarchy and a limited 'democratic' franchise. As Cardinal Johannes (Basilios) Bessarion wrote in 1468, in the act of giving his library to the procurators of San Marco in Venice: 'men of prudence ... hold the keys of empire ... Forgetful of their own private advantage, they set the good of the whole body politic, with common purpose and with the highest integrity.'[23] Roger Ascham, one-time tutor to the English Queen Elizabeth I, praised Venice as 'the seat of just laws, wise rulers and free citizens', while warning his students against visiting the rest of Italy, declaring it full of the 'inchantme[n]tes of Circes [*sic*]'.[24]

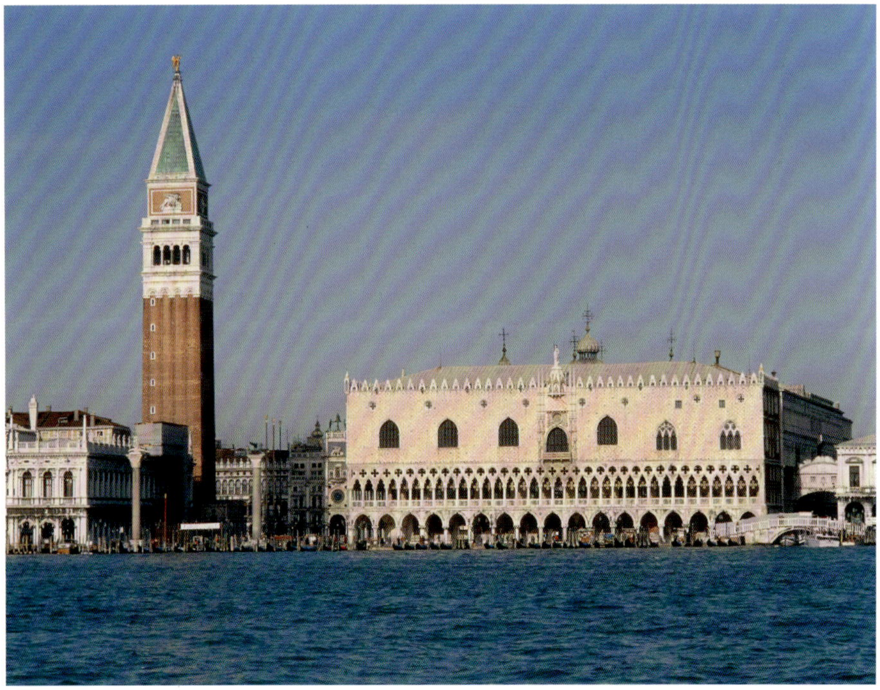

FIG. 5
View of the Doge's Palace and the Campanile, Venice

Venice was ruled by an elected prince, the Doge, who was chosen by representatives of the Greater Council (Maggior Consiglio). Membership of this council was restricted to the small number of noble families whose names were registered in the Golden Book (*Libro d'Oro*), access to which was confined to male descendants of those who were part of the Greater Council in 1297. From this small group of families were drawn the elected members of the Senate, as well as the Procurators of Saint Mark and other important officials who acted as the Doge's representatives and were the heads of various government offices. Much of the actual business of day-to-day government was undertaken by a further group: the Venetian citizens (*cittadini originari*).

To be a Venetian citizen, and to be born into such a family, as were Giovanni Bellini and his brother Gentile, was a considerable advantage in life. In Venetian society, they were next in rank to nobles. *Cittadini originari* enjoyed special dispensations, such as the right to hold certain posts in the civil service, the ability to trade freely and the eligibility to sit on the board of the *Scuole Grandi*, or large confraternities (a privilege reserved exclusively for citizens). We know that by the fifteenth century nobles and citizens mixed regularly and intermarried. It could also be hard to tell them apart, as both castes wore the same long black robes and cap.[25] In addition they met at small intellectual gatherings. Ulisse degli Aleotti, who wrote a eulogy of Jacopo Bellini and his achievements, and who also knew the Bellini brothers and Mantegna, was at the centre of one of these informal circles.[26]

The role of the confraternities (*scuole*) in providing the glue that bound civic life together, should not be underestimated. Confraternities existed in every late medieval city across Europe. They grew out of the flagellant movements of the early thirteenth century, when men banded together in civic spaces to celebrate their commitment to a life of devotion to Christ. They buried the dead, provided dowries for young virtuous women and supported the families of their former members. In Venice, their role was stronger than anywhere else in Europe, a feature that was remarked on by every visitor to the city. Not only did the confraternities process through the city, in company with the holy relics that were their most prized possessions, but they also commissioned art and architecture of the highest possible standard to decorate their meeting houses. The greatest artists worked across the social scale, from the Patriarch of Venice at San Pietro di Castello, to the Doge in the Doge's Palace (fig. 5), the Procurators of the Basilica of San Marco and the patricians and citizens in their *scuole*.

GIOVANNI BELLINI

If Mantegna, with his abiding passion for antiquity and intellectual inquiry, can be seen as the quintessential Paduan artist of the fifteenth century, Giovanni Bellini[27] was the archetypal Venetian. For an artist of his day he was born with a silver spoon in his mouth,[28] even if he was (as is sometimes assumed) illegitimate. He came from a family who had, for at least one generation, been *cittadini originari*, with all the social advantages that this brought. He was fortunate not just to have a genuinely loving brother, Gentile, and other family members active in influential civic, artistic and social circles in Venice, but also to be legally recognised as the son of the painter Jacopo Bellini.[29] One of the greatest artistic inventors of his generation, Jacopo combined skill with business sense and general astuteness to an unusual degree. As paterfamilias it was his duty to settle his children well in life, but he also saw their talents and the family's interests as interlinked. He was well connected, in Venice and further afield – in his youth, it is very likely that Jacopo travelled with his master Gentile da Fabriano to Florence – and as a mature artist he worked for and had good relations with the cities and princely courts of North-Eastern Italy, particularly the Este family of Ferrara. In Venice, Jacopo worked for the state, and was an active member of his *Scuola Grande*, San Giovanni Evangelista, which he served in the capacity of dean, as well as painting scenes from the New Testament (including fig. 6) together with his son Giovanni for the *Sala* (meeting room) of the Scuola.[30] His last recorded commission was for the Scuola di San Marco, the confraternity that his artist sons, as well as his grandson Alvise (Giovanni's son) would join.

It was through the agency of Jacopo that Giovanni Bellini and Andrea Mantegna must have met, and his legacy is crucial to understanding not only their careers but also their artistic output. Very few of Jacopo's paintings now survive but his two Drawing Books in the British Museum (figs 7, 92, 215) and the Louvre (figs 89, 90), offer an immediate insight into what they looked like. The books constitute an astonishing compendium of visual and intellectual ideas, with a particular interest in spectacular architectural and landscape settings (fig. 7). These preoccupations, as well as many motifs from them, found their way into the art of Mantegna and Giovanni Bellini.

Giovanni's career, like that of his brother Gentile,[31] fitted into a typical Venetian pattern, which depended on family. Well into the eighteenth century, Venetian artists tended to work in dynasties. It was for this reason that Canaletto preferred to take his sister's son Bernardo Bellotto into his business rather than train a stranger. And, sometimes, a gifted woman, such as Marietta Tintoretto, was allowed to practise as a painter. But more often daughters or sisters of artists, as was the case with Giovanni and Gentile Bellini's sister Nicolosia, were married to promising talents who could supplement the family fortunes, and who would not, now that they were family, be as demanding of payment. Family provided a means of preventing other artists from gaining prestigious commissions. In 1479, when Gentile Bellini was sent to Constantinople by the Venetian state, Giovanni and his assistants took on his brother's work in the Sala del Maggior Consiglio in the Doge's Palace.[32]

Mutual ties of affection as well as economic advantage bound Gentile and Giovanni together. Following his death in 1507, Gentile bequeathed the remaining book of drawings by their father, Jacopo, to his 'most dear' brother, provided that he completed the vast canvas of *Saint Mark preaching in Alexandria* (fig. 8) for the Scuola Grande di San Marco.[33] In fact, Giovanni agreed

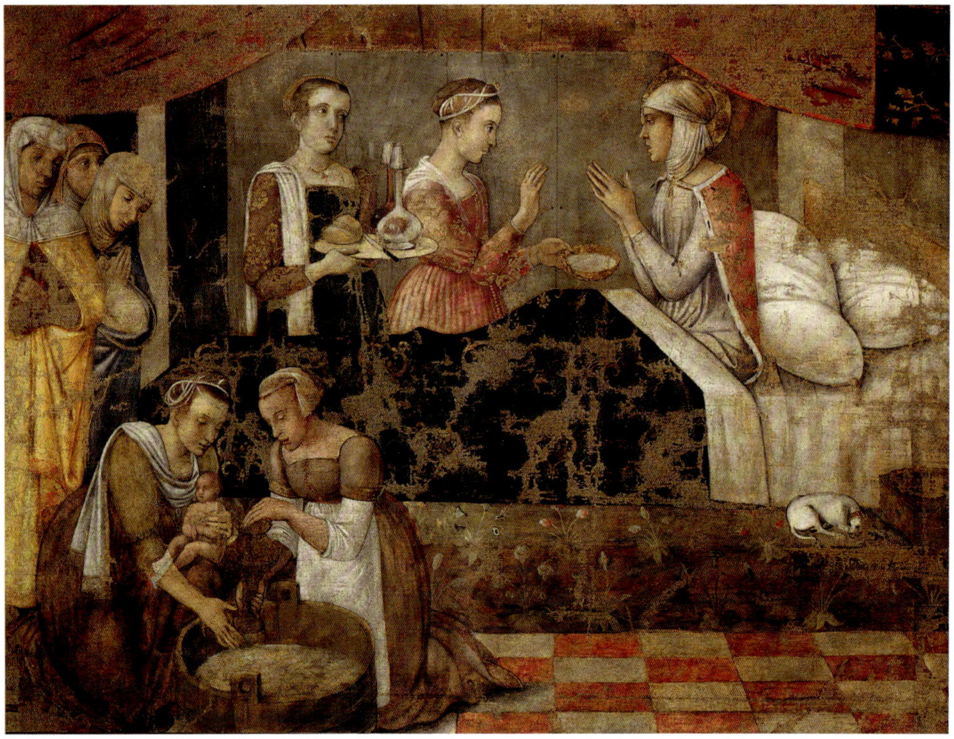

FIG. 6
Attributed to
GIOVANNI BELLINI
The Birth of the Virgin, about 1453
Egg tempera on canvas, 112 × 152 cm
Galleria Sabauda, Turin (158)

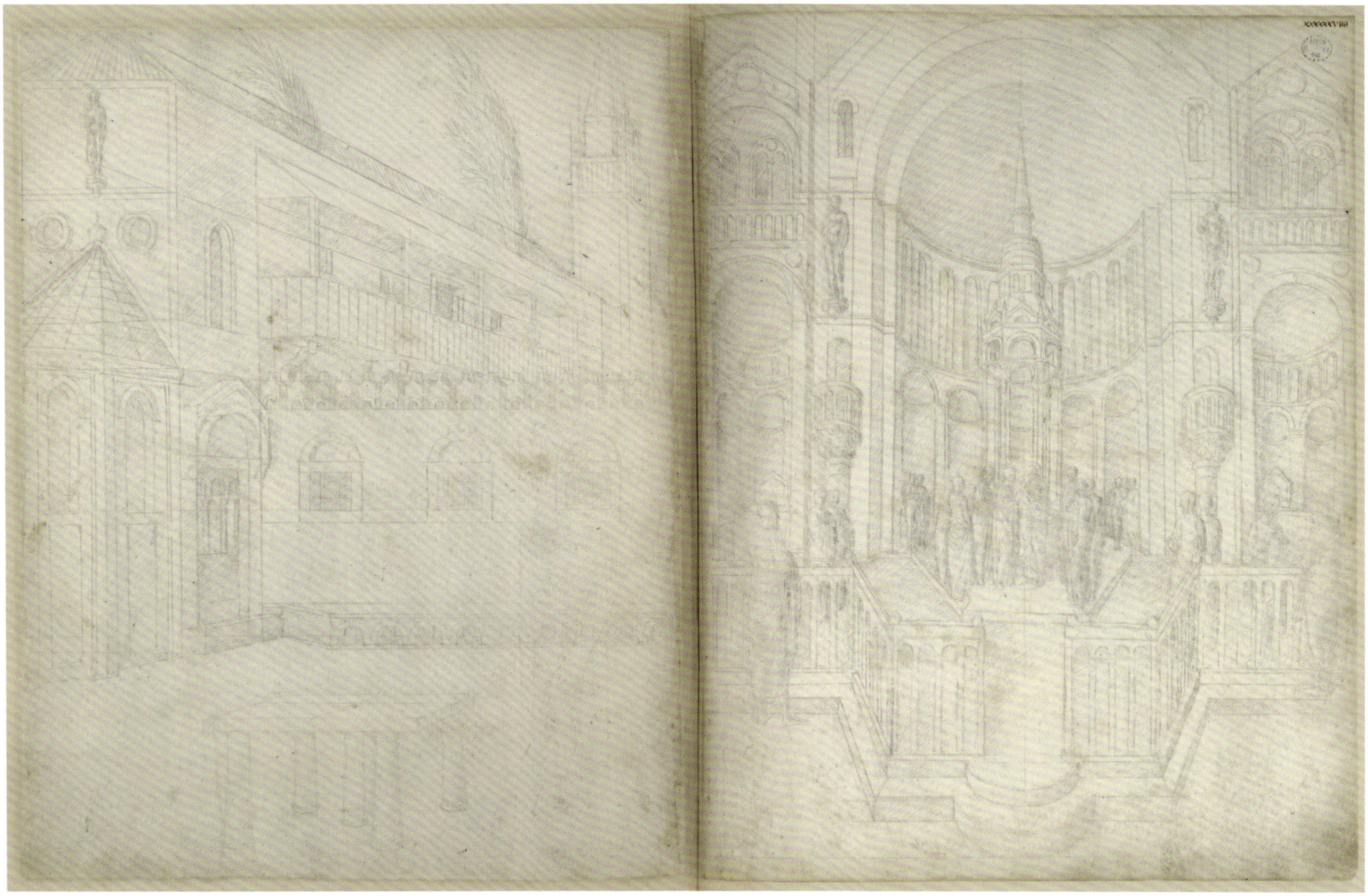

FIG. 7
JACOPO BELLINI
The Presentation of Christ in the Temple, from *The London Drawing Book of Jacopo Bellini*, 1440–70
Leadpoint and stylus on paper, each 41.6 × 33.6 cm
The British Museum, London (1855,0811.67v and 1855,0811.68r)

to bring the whole cycle of paintings to completion. Giovanni revered his brother and was happy to follow where he trod. Although he served, like Gentile, on the Board of Management of the Scuola, he was content not to hold the prestigious but demanding positions this could bring.[34]

Giovanni's life was grounded in Venice.[35] He seems rarely to have left the *sestiere* of Castello, and spent the majority of his adult life in the adjacent parishes of San Lio and Santa Marina.[36] It is likely that he also met his wife, Ginevra, in the latter parish, where he lived from at least 1459.[37] We can be certain, however, that he knew Padua. In the late 1450s, Jacopo Bellini was commissioned to paint an altarpiece for the Paduan *condottiere* Gattamelata's funerary chapel in the Santo. Jacopo, Gentile and Giovanni's hands all signed the altarpiece, but it is difficult to discern their individual hands in the parts of the altarpiece that survive (figs 85, 86, 87).[38] Although these could have been painted in Venice, and shipped to Padua, the artistic sources for these and other contemporary works virtually confirm Giovanni's presence there. Many of his first independent works show his interest in sculptural form, and in particular in Donatello's Paduan reliefs and bronzes. *The Dead Christ supported by Four Angels* (fig. 156) is closely related to a relief by Donatello or a follower (fig. 149); while the musculature and melancholy of his *Dead Christ supported by the Virgin and Saint John* of about 1460–70 (fig. 11) is indebted to Donatello's much admired and much copied *Pietà* from the *Santo Altarpiece* (fig. 2).

From 1479, when Giovanni began to receive a regular income from the Venetian state (which included a tax-free brokerage in the Fondaco dei Tedeschi) there was even less reason for him to seek work outside Venice (as Jennifer Fletcher has pointed out, this was paid far more regularly than the salary of his brother-in-law in Mantua).[39] In any case, Giovanni was evidently able, throughout his career, to be adequately remunerated by Venetian patrons, who included – apart from the

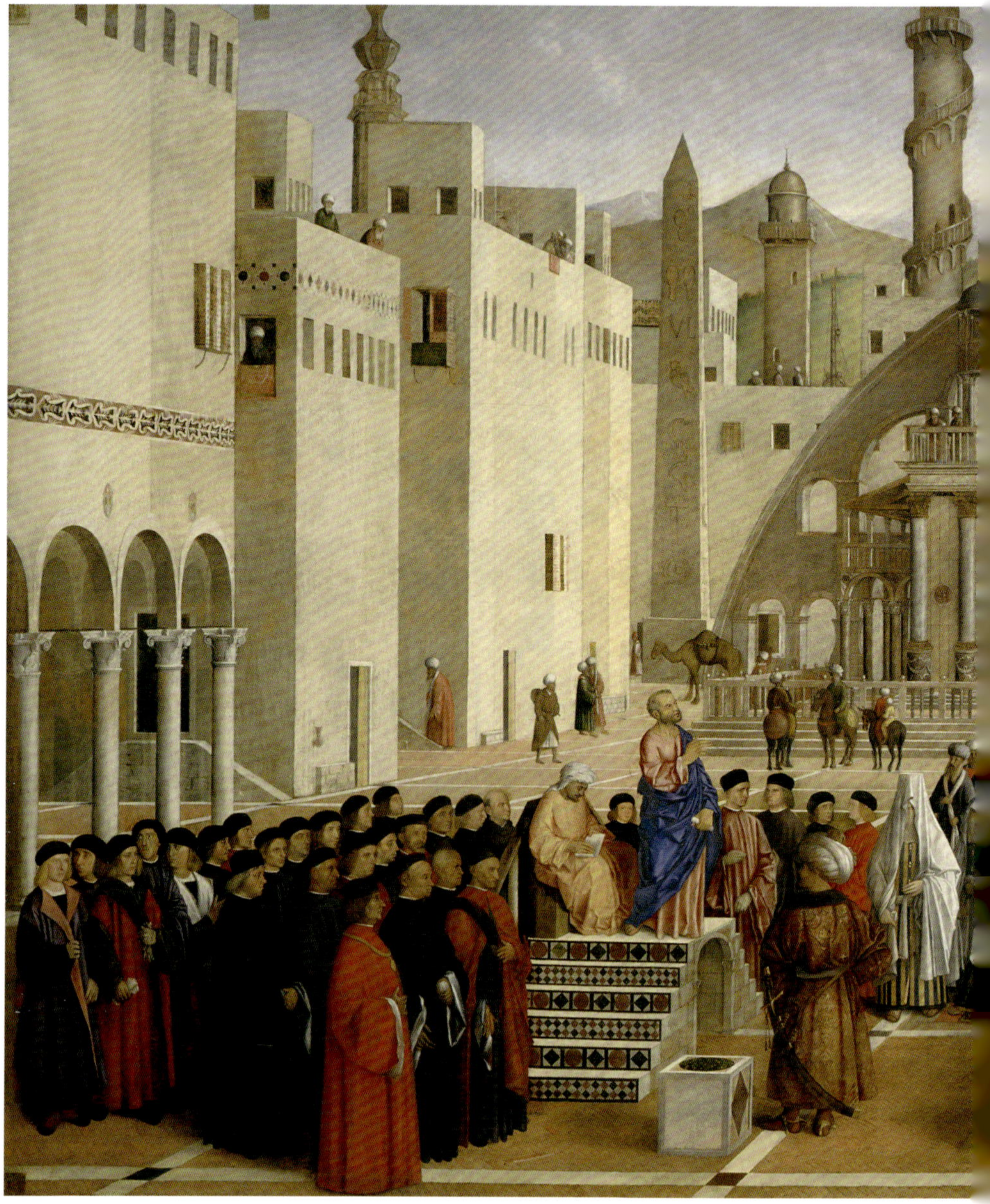

FIG. 8
GENTILE and GIOVANNI BELLINI
Saint Mark preaching in Alexandria, 1504–7
Oil on canvas, 347 × 770 cm
Pinacoteca di Brera, Milan (160)

government and the *scuole* – individual parishes and churches, religious foundations including the Dominican monastery at Santi Giovanni e Paolo, cultured fellow citizens such as Zuan Michiel (the patron of the *Saint Francis* now at the Frick, fig. 219),[40] his father and brother-in-law's friend Jacopo Antonio Marcello, and representatives of various generations of the Bembo and Corner (Cornaro) families. It was very different for the Bellini family's principal rivals in Venice, the Vivarini, who were obliged to work extensively for clients on the mainland and on the Adriatic coasts.

The core of Giovanni's activity as a painter was his work for the state (most of which was lost in a fire at the Ducal Palace in 1577) and the production of small-scale devotional works, often placed in landscape settings which evoke the land-, water- and skyscapes of Venice and the Terraferma. There has long been debate concerning Giovanni's residence on the mainland; but it seems probable that by the early sixteenth century he had such a second home, and in June 1501 he is said to be out of the city 'alla villa'.[41] Such uncertainty surrounds much of Giovanni Bellini's career, which is not as straightforward to reconstruct as that of Mantegna.

MEETING

The Bellini family may have become aware of the talented Padua painter through Jacopo's friend Ulisse degli Aleotti, or it may have been Mantegna's work in the Ovetari Chapel that brought him to Jacopo Bellini's attention. Certainly, by the late 1440s Mantegna was the most promising young artist in North-Eastern Italy, and Jacopo Bellini, hoping to marry his daughter to someone of use to his business, would have viewed him as an attractive prospect. Sadly, we will never know what Nicolosia Bellini's views were on the matter. Externally, it appeared to be a successful match. The marriage, which took place in 1453, produced several surviving children,[42] lasted until Nicolosia's death[43] and her widower did not remarry. But Mantegna put a spanner in the works by accepting the post of court painter in Mantua and removing his wife and family to the Gonzaga court. Nevertheless, the impact of the match would prove strong, and long lasting, above all in the enduring influence that Andrea Mantegna and Giovanni Bellini had on each other's art.

Both artists, on occasion, changed the way that they worked in response to each other. Many paintings by Bellini from the middle of the 1450s to the early 1460s, including *Saint Jerome* (fig. 114) – are so evidently in the

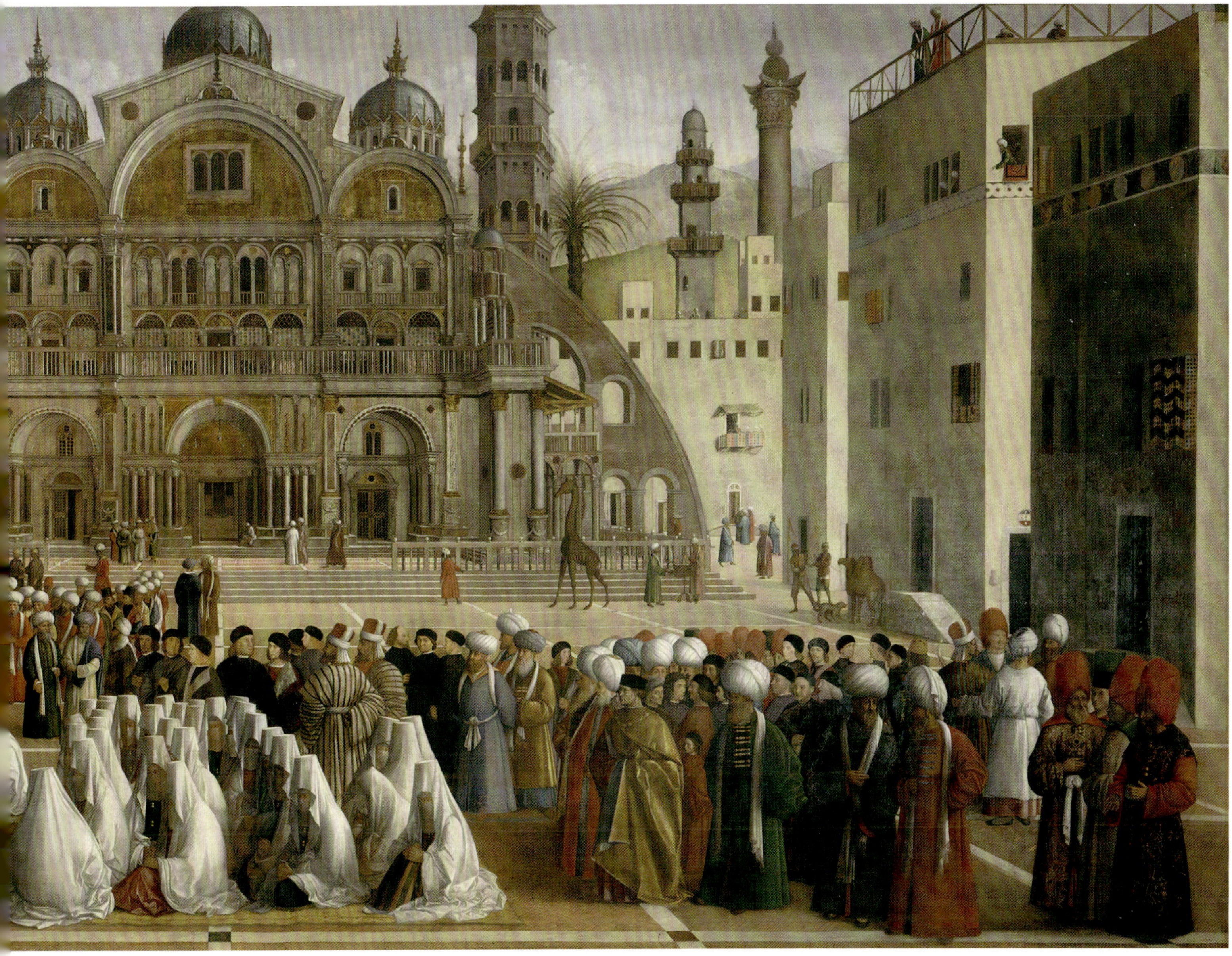

manner of Mantegna that it is hard to conceive of them not being painted in close proximity and in deliberate response to his brother-in-law's work. Bellini's earliest autograph paintings, moreover, where we can see his separation from his father, are very evidently in Mantegna's mode. Sometimes they copy motifs – as in the Birmingham *Saint Jerome* or the *Lehman Madonna* (fig. 175). On other occasions, such as the *Davis Madonna* (fig. 111) or in the figures in the National Gallery's *Agony in the Garden* (fig. 126), they replicate Mantegna's insistence on outlines and strong form. For Bellini, the creative stimulus of Mantegna is apparent throughout his career. It is there for Mantegna too, but in less immediately obvious ways. Landscape, for example, is present as an element in Mantegna's work from the beginning of his career. The combination, however, of landscape and light – as rare as it is spectacularly beautiful – is in response to Bellini. So Michele Vianello's anecdote, cited at the opening of this essay, about Bellini's reluctance to place himself in competition with his brother-in-law was much more than a matter of merely professional rivalry. The special effort that Bellini made 'partly out of a sense of honour, and especially out of respect for master Andrea Mantegna' was also born of a family connection from which – in the many complex ways outlined above – both their careers drew such strength and brilliance.

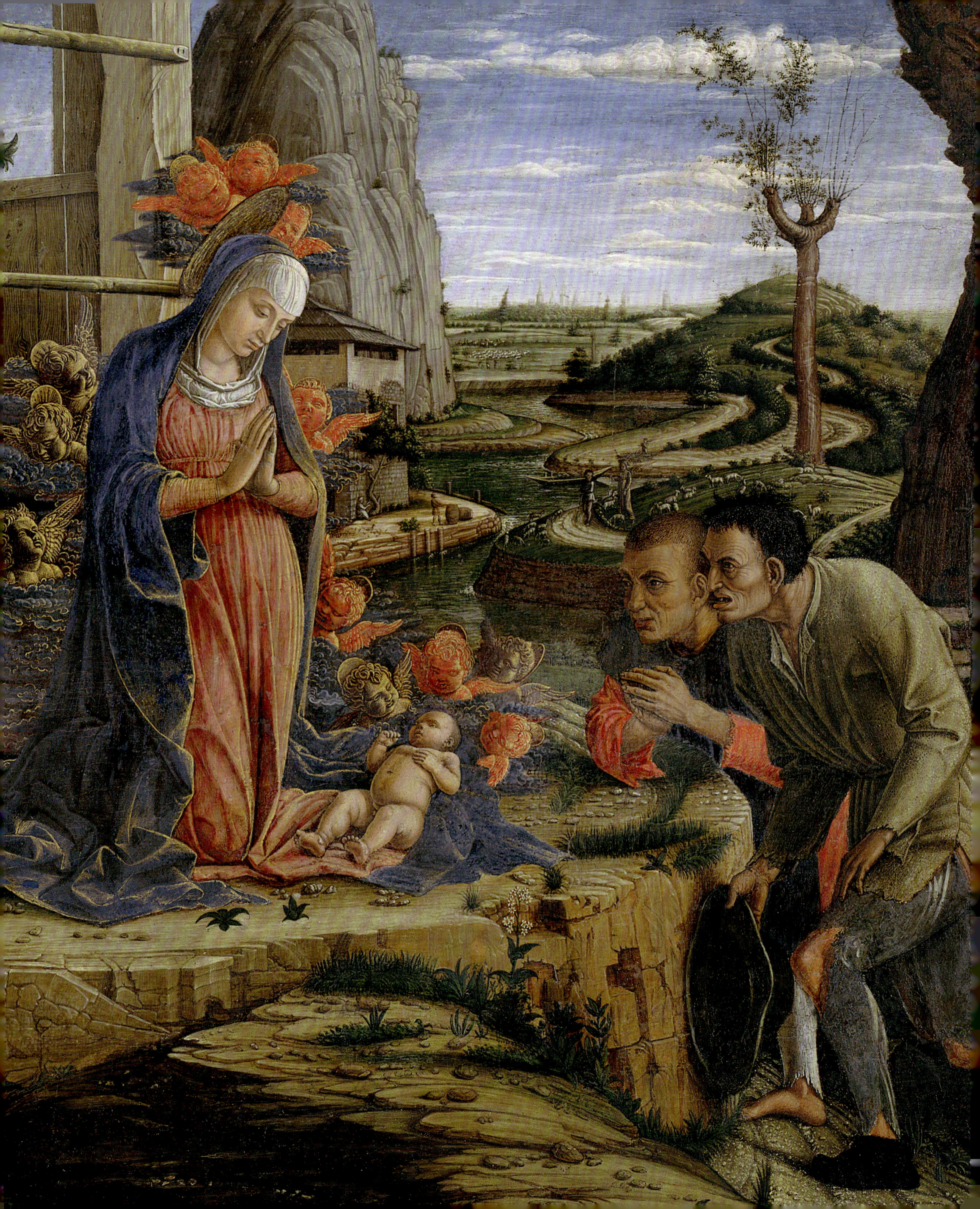

II

Mantegna / Bellini: Invention versus Poetry

ANDREA DE MARCHI

THE PARADOX IN THE ART OF GIOVANNI BELLINI is that while he was one of the greatest painters of all time, whose style evolved over six decades, yet over the same period he often repeated certain motifs with slight variations, and combinations of figures, entrusting them to his workshop assistants to paint in works bearing his signature.[1] Both a peerless poet and a skilled manager! It can be entertaining to trace the same tree, the same rock, or a similar gesture in different compositions.[2] The master's touch lies in the quality of his technique, which blends these elements into a carefully defined whole. Bearing this in mind, it is hardly surprising that in his relationship with Andrea Mantegna (who became his brother-in-law in 1453 when Andrea married his half-sister Nicolosia Bellini) Giovanni had no misgivings about lifting entire compositions or individual motifs from him – sometimes after many years had passed, such as a soldier's shield in the Berlin *Resurrection of Christ* (about 1478–9; fig. 218), taken from the scene of *Saint James before Herod Agrippa* in the Ovetari Chapel (1451; fig. 249)[3].

The most blatant example of such borrowing is *The Presentation of Christ in the Temple*. In the present exhibition it will be possible to see – for the first time, side by side, in Venice,[4] then in London and Berlin – Mantegna's version, from Berlin (fig. 128), perhaps painted on the occasion of his marriage, in 1453, and Bellini's later iteration of it in the Fondazione Querini Stampalia (fig. 132). Notwithstanding the directness of the derivation, what is striking is how Bellini makes the work his own in a radical way; and not only through the addition of two onlookers flanking the central figures. In Mantegna's painting, the powerfully modelled bodies of the Virgin and Simeon are pushed up against the lower edge of a marble frame that surrounds them on all sides. This frame defines the conceptual threshold between their virtual reality and that of the beholder: the scene becomes theatrical. Bellini, on the other hand, abolishes this inner frame and extends the parapet laterally, indefinitely; the figures no longer have haloes and are not set within a quadrangular frame, they inhabit a potentially limitless space and breathe naturally. This is a snapshot, not something set within a stage. To use cinematic terms, we might say this marks a shift from a medium close-shot to a panoramic view.

The fact that the setting of the *Pietà* in the Museo Poldi Pezzoli (fig. 148), one of Bellini's first works after the *Saint Jerome* in Birmingham (fig. 114), is taken from that of *The Adoration of the Shepherds* by Mantegna in the Metropolitan Museum of Art (fig. 221)[5] in no way lessens its originality. The two rocky wings that frame the winding stream are reduced to their essence, stripped of Mantegna's myriad, minutely described details. On the other hand, the cliffs are bathed in a uniform play of light and shadow, imitating the diffusion of the first rosy touches of dawn, thus creating an elegiac and subtly melancholy backdrop for the almost dazzling display of the pearl-grey flesh tones of the Dead Christ in the foreground. During the 1450s, both masters were taking up the challenge of the Netherlandish treatment of nature and atmosphere (found in the work of contemporary Netherlandish painters such as Jan van Eyck and Dirk Bouts), but in diametrically opposite ways. Mantegna sculpts and engraves with his paintbrush, giving spectacular emphasis to the slightest fold of drapery, to every nook and cranny. Bellini instead caresses with his brush, lending vital life to flesh, shrouding and dissolving his figures and objects as they blend with light (but never that of the

ANDREA MANTEGNA, detail from *The Adoration of the Shepherds* (FIG. 221)

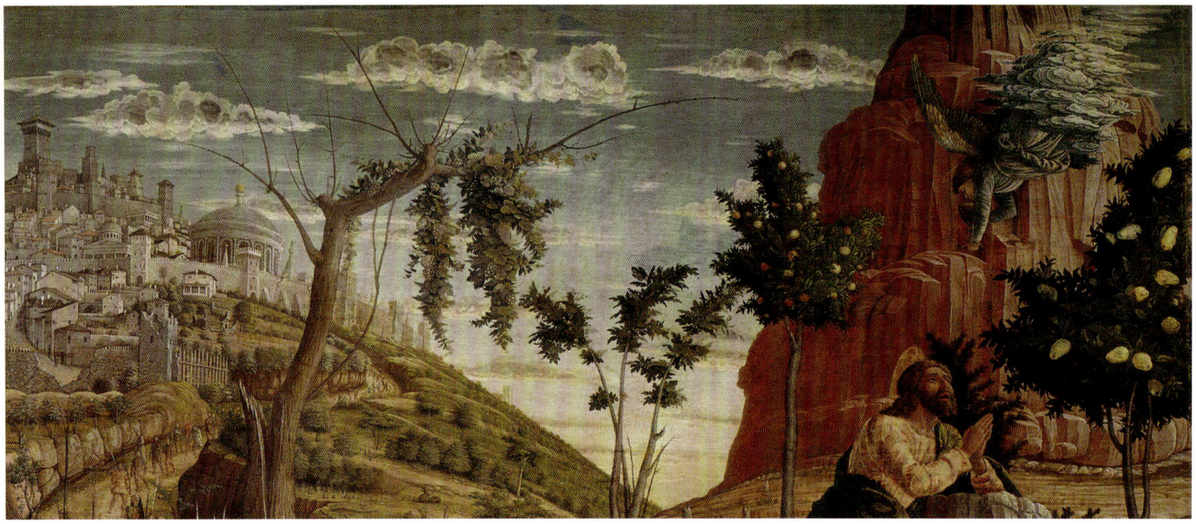

FIG. 9
ANDREA MANTEGNA, detail from *The Agony in the Garden* (FIG. 124)

noonday sun), always changing and softened, with a wealth of reflections.

For Mantegna, *inventio* (invention) was everything, the result of a carefully devised and complex intellectual reflection; for Bellini, on the other hand, the magic of painting lay in certain accidental details and the atmospheric quality of a given composition. As for the expression of sentiment, or emotion, a preoccupation for both of them, Mantegna chose to do this through gesture and expression, while Bellini used the harmonious inter-relationship of figures in a specific situation to convey meaning. This sense of harmony was reached through the play of light on different surfaces – in a word, by 'tone', an expression used by Pliny the Elder in his *Natural History* (XXXV, 29) to indicate the blending of colours ('*commissuras vero colorum*') from whose modulation ('*transitus*') harmony ('*harmogé*') was produced. Harmony creates 'tonal' painting, a glorious tradition considered to have originated in Venice, and in particular with Giovanni Bellini.

The laboured negotiations of 1501–5 that pitted Bellini against Isabella d'Este, the Marchioness of Mantua – who demanded an *istoria* from him, while the artist stated that he would much rather paint a devotional picture, a Nativity ('*Presepe*'), and not to be burdened with excessively precise or limiting iconographic dictates[6] – reveals Giovanni Bellini's scant regard for the genre of history painting. In part, this was because of his fear of undermining his reputation when his paintings were compared with the learned, complex works of his brother-in-law.[7] In Venice the role of official painter to the Doge – and the 'state' painter of *istorie* – was held not by Giovanni but by his brother Gentile, who continued in their father Jacopo's footsteps, and was the preferred painter of the *Scuole,* or confraternities, when it came to grand narrative canvases. Gentile – who had been commissioned to paint subjects from Venice's history for the Sala del Maggior Consiglio in the Doge's Palace in 1474 – only relinquished this post to Giovanni in 1479 because he was ordered by the Venetian state to journey to the court of Mehmet II in Constantinople.

For decades Giovanni Bellini had known that his own privileged realm was that of devotional painting. These paintings were intended to be experienced intimately, at close range, his figures bathed in light that evoked the atmosphere of a specific time of day. Thus it was that he sought in vain to make Isabella understand, through her agents and even Pietro Bembo, that it would be better to leave him free to follow his own whims, to do what was congenial to him ('*vole fare quanto saperà*').

In his altarpieces, too, and in large-scale works, Bellini's greatest compositional inventions are always concerned with the relationship between his figures and nature, between architecture and landscape. He created audacious compositional solutions in this field, such as his altarpiece still *in situ* in the chapel of Giorgio Diletti in San Giovanni Crisostomo (1513) where the mosaic inner arch encloses an Alpine landscape, with Saint Jerome silhouetted against the view. The idea of sculptural and architectural enclosures opening onto open-air spaces is a leitmotif running through his entire oeuvre, beginning with *The Blood of the Redeemer* in the National

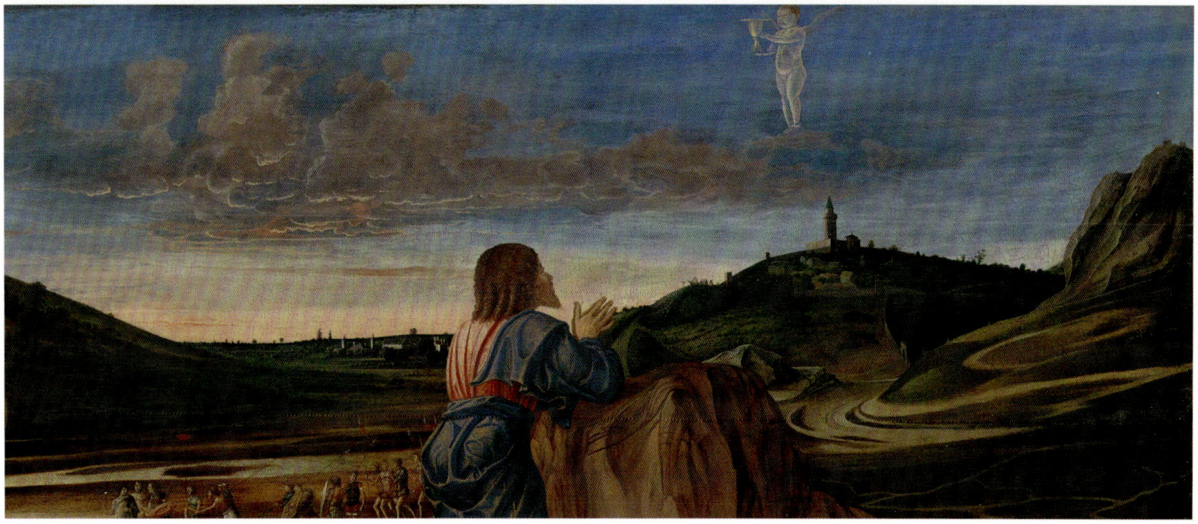

FIG. 10
GIOVANNI BELLINI,
detail from *The Agony in the Garden* (FIG. 126)

Gallery (fig. 192). The back of the throne in the *Coronation of the Virgin* in Pesaro (fig. 255), pierced so that the marble acts as a frame to the background view of the castle of Gradara, is a wonderful invention, but it does not fit into the canonical category of *inventio* appropriate to history painting. Nor, ultimately, does the unitary solution of the Frick *Saint Francis* (fig. 219), which strays from the ordinary attributes of the scene of the Stigmatisation, giving the leading role not to the wounds of the saint, or to Francis's vision of Christ as a seraph (as was normal in such scenes), but to the beauty of nature and its variable weather. The painting thus presents an 'unusual iconography', or better, a 'lack of iconography'.[8] It would be pleasant to think that it was Bellini himself, in those years, who was the first artist to paint a vaulted canopy with no walls over the enthroned Virgin providing a view of limitless sky and landscape, for the altar of Saint Catherine of Siena in Santi Giovanni e Paolo (the panel was destroyed by fire in 1867, and is now only known through prints).

Bellini's inclination to immerse his figures in a particular atmosphere, and ultimately to make that atmosphere the protagonist of his paintings, was not simply a response to the challenge posed by mimetic Netherlandish painting, which was known and loved in Venice from the middle years of the fifteenth century onwards. Rather, it arose as a reaction to the obsession with history painting, with rigorously organised settings, and with gesture and the rendering of expression which pervade every aspect of Mantegna's work. The early years of the relationship of the two artists, around 1460, were decisive in this respect. A comparison between the three versions of *The Agony in the Garden* – Mantegna's in the National Gallery, London (about 1453–4; fig. 125) and Musée des Beaux-Arts, Tours, from the predella of the *San Zeno Altarpiece* (1459; figs 9, 124); Bellini's, in the National Gallery, London (about 1460; figs 10, 126) – is illuminating for our understanding of the interaction between the two painters, which in that period was reciprocal.

Bellini's painting lacks the *di sotto in su* (foreshortened from below) arrangement that lends greater monumentality to Mantegna's two *Agonies*; the setting essentially repeats that of a drawing of *Saint Jerome in the Wilderness* in Jacopo Bellini's Drawing Book in Paris.[9] It disperses the figures, but concentrates a sudden band of light (incongruous, given the hour, as the sun has not yet risen) on the figure of Christ, whose partially shadowed head stands out against the dawning sky.

Mantegna, whose first version of the Agony set the story in a bare, rocky valley resembling the harsh scenery of the Ovetari frescoes, implements a substantial change in the Verona predella, reacting to the more expansive atmosphere of Bellini's paintings. Now he peoples his landscape with myriad details, teeming with life, and accentuates the effect of dawn on the brightened, backlit clouds and the dry tree with its clinging vine, loaded with symbolism. All nature awakens to new life, heralding the future Resurrection of Christ. Mantegna here is seeking a fresh challenge: his aim is to make nature a living witness to the unfolding drama, and to the tense expectation at its heart – the presentiment that Christ will be taken by soldiers to his passion and death.

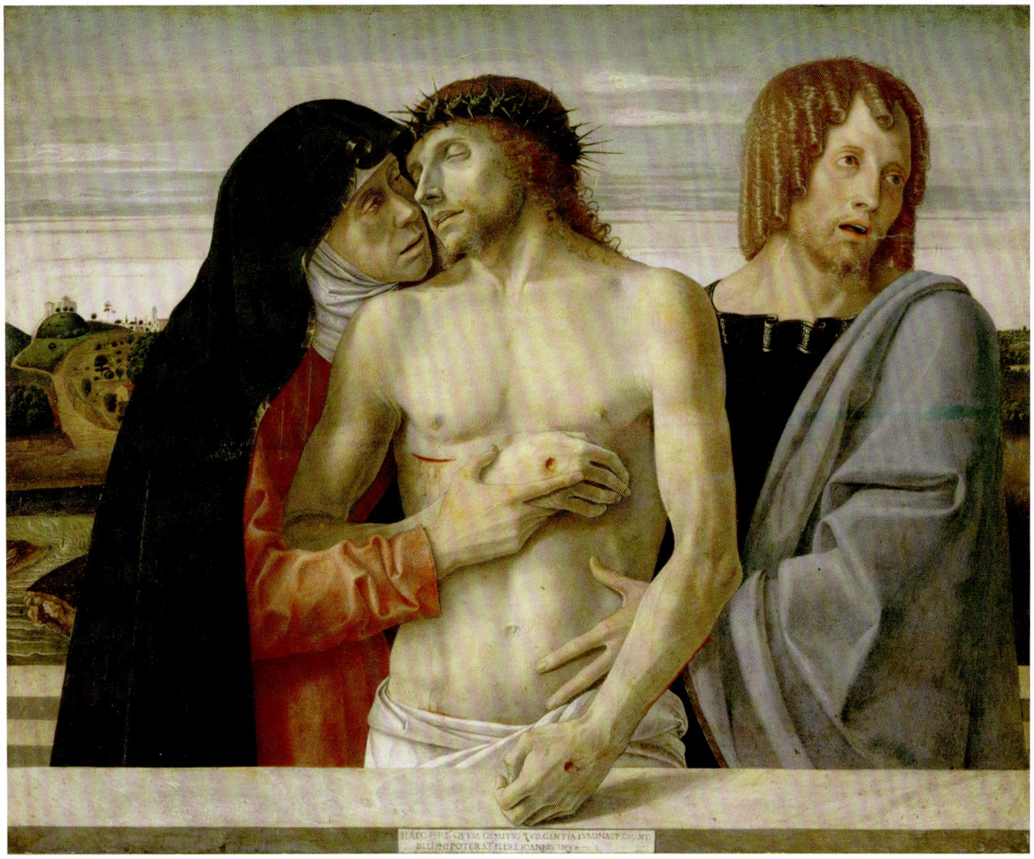

FIG. 11
GIOVANNI BELLINI
The Dead Christ supported by the Virgin and Saint John, about 1465–7
Egg tempera on panel, 86 × 107 cm
Pinacoteca di Brera, Milan (228)

By contrast, Bellini reduces, simplifies and empties out the composition, yet seeks to capture specific atmospheric conditions: the broad landscape lies partly in shadow, partly struck by sudden flashes of light; clouds are illuminated from below by a golden glow. Even the angel is a luminous revelation, a little ghost who materialises at the first light of dawn. The human figures are small, with the modern-seeming effect of being wholly enveloped in their environment. As Davide Gasparotto has written, 'the overall result is the first fully accomplished atmospheric landscape in Italian art'.[10]

But what were the exact phases of the dialogue between Bellini and Mantegna? In a celebrated passage of his *Viatico per cinque secoli di pittura veneziana*, Roberto Longhi wrote that Giovanni Bellini had been 'first Byzantine and Gothic, then Mantegnesque and Paduan'.[11] Such a statement might have seemed exaggerated, but it certainly aided the assertion of Bellini's seniority over Mantegna, both artistically and biographically, made by Longhi when he argued that the latter's *Saint Luke Polyptych* of 1453–4 (fig. 129) showed the influence of the Venetian master's tenderness of sentiment; Bellini's birthdate was at this time believed to be about 1425.[12] Yet there was truth in this statement, as Bellini succeeded in being skilfully '*antico-moderno*'. He was 'Byzantine' not only because he often used the Greek acronyms for the Mother of God in his paintings, but also because his emotional reworking of subjects such as the Virgin embracing the Christ Child and the Pietà, reinvigorated a venerable Byzantine tradition, creating modern icons with his intimate devotional images.[13] And he was 'Gothic' because he was profoundly marked by his apprenticeship with his father, Jacopo, a pupil of Gentile da Fabriano who – notwithstanding his infatuation with dizzying para-perspective projection, especially in the late drawings in his two Drawing Books – introduced a manner of painting with gentle interwoven short brushstrokes that was fundamental for Giovanni.

As Luciano Bellosi pointed out, the early dating of the *Pietà* in the Museo Poldi Pezzoli (fig. 148), well before the one in the Brera (fig. 11), for example, or the polyptych in Santi Giovanni e Paolo (fig. 253), which must date from around 1467, is manifest in the painterly texture, especially in the body of Christ, described in liquid, vibrant little strokes. This is even more evident in the illuminated folios of the *Passion of Saint Maurice* commissioned in 1453 (figs 94, 95).[14]

Giovanni is not mentioned in the will of Jacopo's widow, Anna Rinversi, in 1471, because he was born out of wedlock, probably after 1435, or even later.[15] Public success was slow to come.[16] Bellini's first significant commission was the polyptychs for the church of the secular Lateran canons of Santa Maria della Carità (figs 84, 120) between 1462 and 1464. By contrast, for Mantegna, success came early, in 1448, aged 17, when he signed his name on the polyptych commissioned for Santa Sofia in Padua.[17]

Secure chronological markers for the first phase of Bellini's life are scarce, leading scholars to propose some wildly discordant opinions, some of which are paradoxical, if one bears in mind the huge stylistic evolution that marks his early works, much stronger in fact than that between the *Madonna degli Alberetti* of 1487 in the Accademia, Venice, and Bellini's death in 1516. Nonetheless there are many almost certain dates, such as that of the *Saint Giustina* in the Museo Bagatti Valsecchi in Milan (fig. 22), sent to Milan in 1475, which is very close in date to the *Pesaro Altarpiece*. Other dates are still conjectural, such as those of the Museo Correr *Transfiguration of Christ* (fig. 105), which must have been painted just after the institution of the eponymous feast by Pope Calixtus III in 1457, and of *The Blood of the Redeemer* in London (fig. 192), which is likely to have been made as a result of the promotion of the cult of the relic of the Holy Blood by Pope Pius II during the Church Council held in Mantua in 1459.[18] There are two key points of reference: the miniatures made for the *Passion of Saint Maurice* of 1453 (figs 94, 95), mentioned above, and those for Strabo's *Geography* in 1459 (fig. 97), both codices commissioned by the learned Venetian patrician Jacopo Antonio Marcello as diplomatic gifts respectively for Jean Cossa, councillor of King René of Anjou, and for the Provençal monarch himself. Bellini's authorship of the second series of miniatures is now generally accepted, and indeed it is possible that this was the '*operetta*' (small work) for Marcello that Mantegna was supposed to execute, and which he cites in March 1459 to justify the delay in his entering the service of Ludovico III Gonzaga,[19] while the attribution of the first miniatures to Giovanni are more controversial, showing him at the start of his career, and still closely tied to his father, Jacopo.

What is there in the scene of the assembly of the Knights of the Crescent (fig. 95) that could be called Mantegnesque? Nothing! The architecture could have been designed by Jacopo Bellini.[20] The softly rendered faces and robes of the knights, the beams, the ashlar blocks, plastered walls and fabric on the benches are all brushed by glancing light, midway between Gentile da Fabriano and the *ars nova* of the Flemings. The portrait of the patron himself, Jacopo Antonio Marcello, exudes intrepidness, yet the figure's volume is weak, whereas Mantegna, to whom Millard Meiss ascribed the work,[21] would have emphasised its sculptural form; the surfaces, touched with only the tip of the brush, have an intimate quivering that reveals Giovanni Bellini's talent. Only the folio with Saint Maurice (fig. 94), in its whimsical imitation of *all'antica* armour, wears a light Mantegnesque patina, but here too, the gentleness of the adolescent face, submerged in light shadow, is redolent of Bellini's style. We see a copious use of shell gold, much favoured by Jacopo Bellini, which would subsequently be adopted by both Mantegna and Bellini, in different ways, to convey either effects of intense shininess or of suffused luminosity. In Mantegna's *Adoration of the Shepherds* in the Metropolitan Museum of Art (fig. 221), cherubim and seraphim sparkle with bronzed reflection, as do the ridges of the folds of drapery worn by the Virgin as she adores the Child. In Bellini's Poldi Pezzoli *Pietà* (fig. 148), Christ's halo is indicated by the short strokes

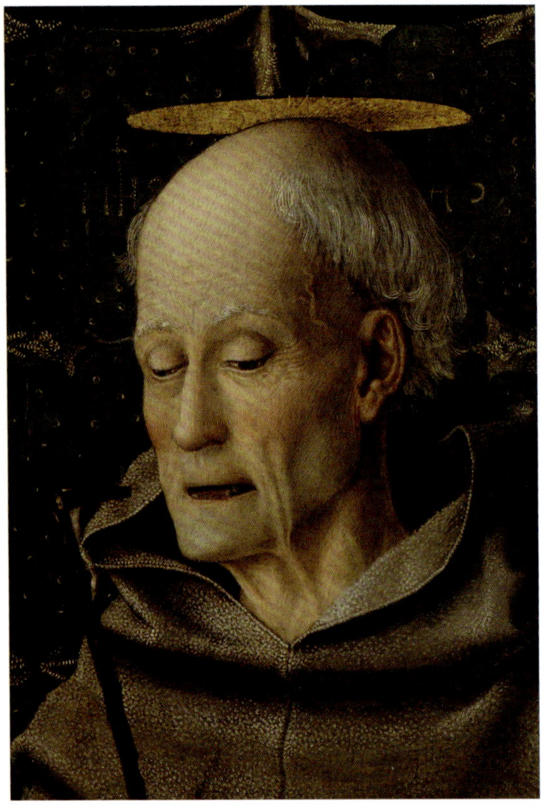

FIG. 12
Attributed to GIOVANNI BELLINI
Saint Bernardino of Siena,
about 1450–5
Egg tempera on panel, 30 × 21 cm
Private collection, New York

of almost impalpable gilding which is also used on the edge of the tomb.

Some 25 years ago, I suggested that a *Saint Bernardino of Siena* (fig. 12) in a private collection, at that time on long-term to the Metropolitan Museum of Art, might be an early work by Giovanni Bellini.[22] This attribution has not been the subject of serious discussion, though Keith Christiansen has cited it as a possible alternative attribution, that 'has the virtue of underscoring the fundamental novelty of this extraordinary portrait and cult image, and the way its descriptive naturalism is directed towards an enhanced emotional intensity'.[23] Notwithstanding the fact that this superb painting holds a stellar position on the cover of Colin Eisler's 1989 monograph on Jacopo Bellini, the attribution is anything but secure. Composed only of the saint's face, shown in absorbed contemplation of a humble little cross of bare twigs, the picture shuns the traditional portrait in profile always used in the Veneto after the great preacher's canonisation in 1450.[24] When did Jacopo ever succeed in generating such an almost pitiless physical truth, as in this toothless old man with withered skin, and at the same time ennoble it with an interior moral fervour? When did he ever brighten dimness with warm, reflected light, with a truly atmospheric effect, as we see here between the ear, the beardless cheekbone and the temple, with its pulsing little vein? When did he ever modulate his Gentile-inspired stippling to achieve the effect – not of sumptuous *sfumato*, but of the thickness of a crumpled habit effected by graduations of light? The answer is clear, at least for me: we are witnessing the feverish mind and sensitive brush of Jacopo's son Giovanni, still moving in his father's shadow but clearly presaging what he will become.

Among Bellini's most Mantegnesque works is *The Transfiguration of Christ* (fig. 105), but it should be noted that the closest parallels for the crinkled drapery of the three Apostles are the two scenes of *The Calling of Saint James and John* and *Saint James talks to the demons* in the lunette of the Saint James cycle in the Ovetari Chapel, painted by Mantegna between 1449 and 1450, whereas by the mid-1450s, in *The Martyrdom of Saint Christopher*, Mantegna had tempered the Donatellian intensity of those early works. Bellini's *Transfiguration* has been cut down; originally it had an arched top in which a vortex of clouds and a corolla of cherubs must have surrounded a source of divine light, a *dextera Dei* (hand of God) or, less likely, a bust of God the Father, never explicitly depicted in representations of this subject – the sense of a vast, infinite sky and distant darkness must have surmounted the foreshortened figures in the foreground seen *di sotto in su*, isolated from one another.

Slowly and by degrees Bellini assimilated the progressive aspects of his brother-in-law's art. One crucial point of contact occurred when Mantegna was in his Paduan workshop painting the great altarpiece for San Zeno in Verona (fig. 252), between 1457 and 1459, while the Bellini family was also working for Padua (the *Gattamelata Altarpiece* for the Santo). It was then that Giovanni began to take the measure not only of Mantegna's elaborate modelling of figures, but also of the compositional framework that creates such a supreme

FIG. 13
ANDREA MANTEGNA,
detail from *The Crucifixion*
(FIG. 101)

FIG. 14
GIOVANNI BELLINI
The Crucifixion, about 1457–9
Egg tempera on panel,
54 × 30 cm
Museo Correr, Venice
(Cl. I n. 0028)

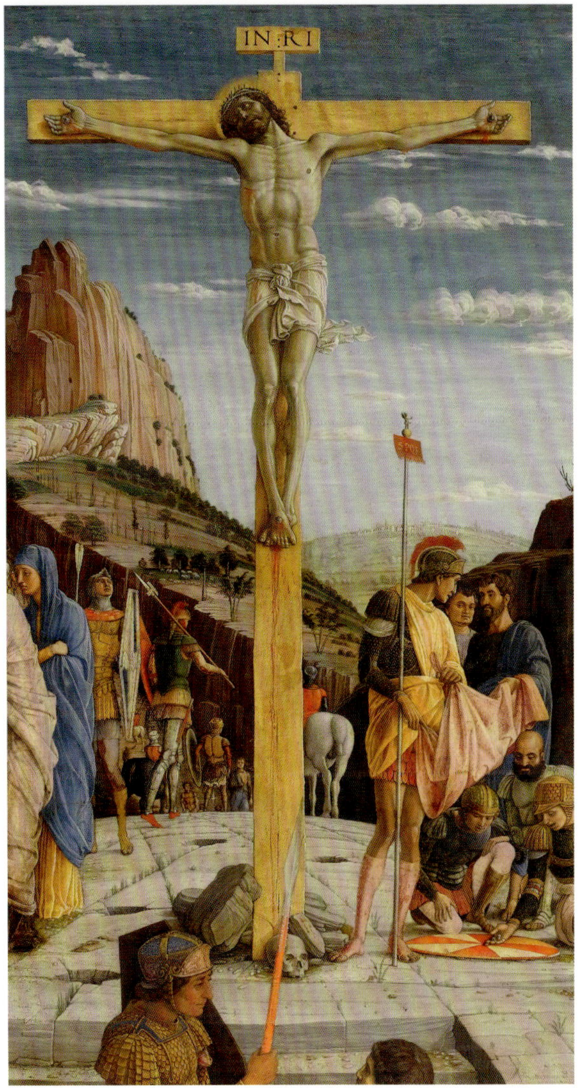

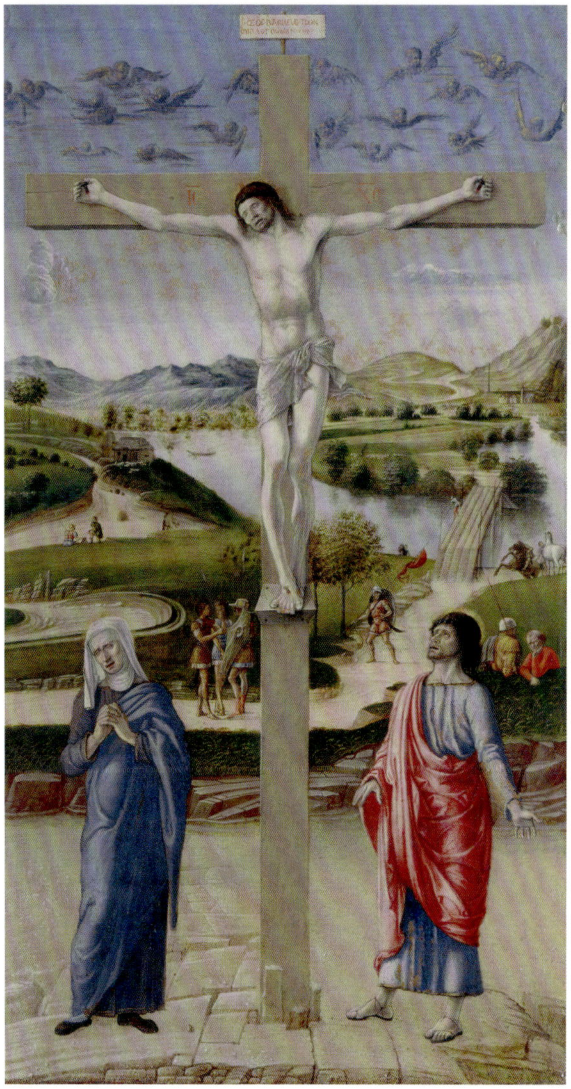

bond between each gesture and each foreshortened figure in the works painted before he moved to Mantua to serve Ludovico III Gonzaga in 1460.

The *Crucifixion* in the Museo Correr (fig. 14) is the result of Bellini's taking on what Mantegna was doing in the *Crucifixion* in the Verona predella (fig. 13), perhaps the last part of the altarpiece to be painted during the first half of 1459. One can make a close stylistic comparison of the Correr *Crucifixion* with the Strabo miniatures made for Jacopo Marcello, from the same year:[25] the delicate brushwork that gives a melancholy cast to some of the faces in the Strabo is the same as that of the sorrowful Saint John in the Correr panel. But what an abyss lies between the *Crucifixions* of Bellini and Mantegna! From the great theatre of Mantegna's Calvary, Bellini has extracted the body of Christ, no longer silhouetted against the sky, but set within an expansive landscape of hills and water, its vanishing point deliberately high, unfurling a bird's-eye view of the landscape, over which the beholder's gaze flows and wanders. In the Verona predella, on the other hand, one's gaze is invited to measure the distances, to distinguish and arrange the actors in this drama, to recognise the arcane grandeur of a Jerusalem on its great hillside entrenchment, to be aware of the gravity of the event. In Bellini the drama becomes internal, concentrating on the solitude of Christ and the two mourners. The foreground is derived from the great fissured rock in Mantegna's scene, but Mantegna's concept depended on his *sotto in su* perspective, rejected by Bellini. The shift to the background mediated by splintered rocks (fig. 17), a partial repeat of the rocks in the foreground of *The Transfiguration of Christ* (fig. 16), is in turn derived from Mantegna's *Descent of Christ into Limbo* (fig. 15).[26]

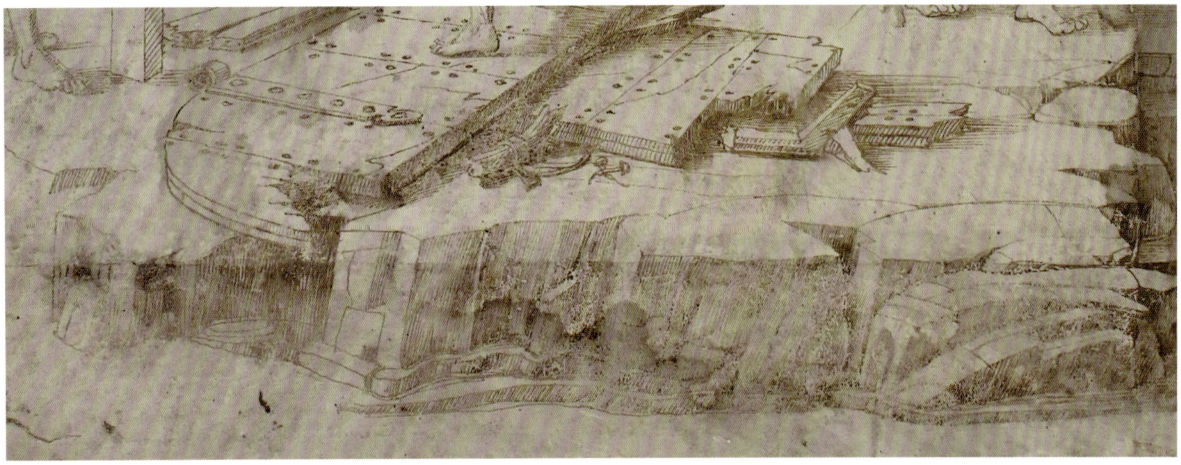

FIG. 15
ANDREA MANTEGNA,
detail from *The Descent of Christ into Limbo* (FIG. 143)

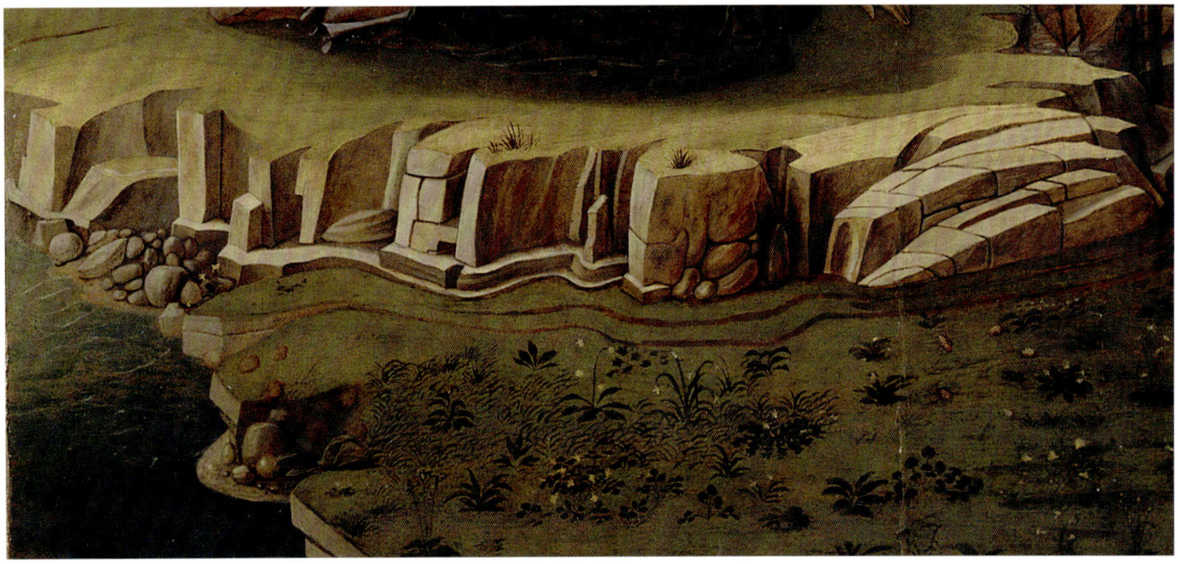

FIG. 16
GIOVANNI BELLINI,
detail from *The Transfiguration of Christ* (FIG. 105)

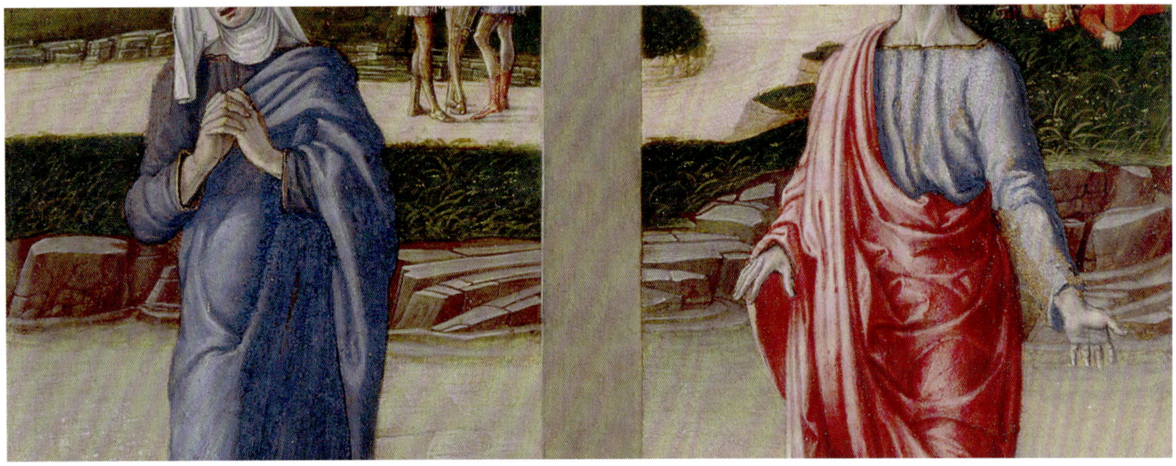

FIG. 17
GIOVANNI BELLINI,
detail from *The Crucifixion* (FIG. 14)

FIG. 18
GIOVANNI BELLINI,
detail from *Three Stories of Drusiana and Saint John the Evangelist* (FIG. 103)

FIG. 19
ANDREA MANTEGNA,
detail from *The Death of the Virgin* (FIG. 214)

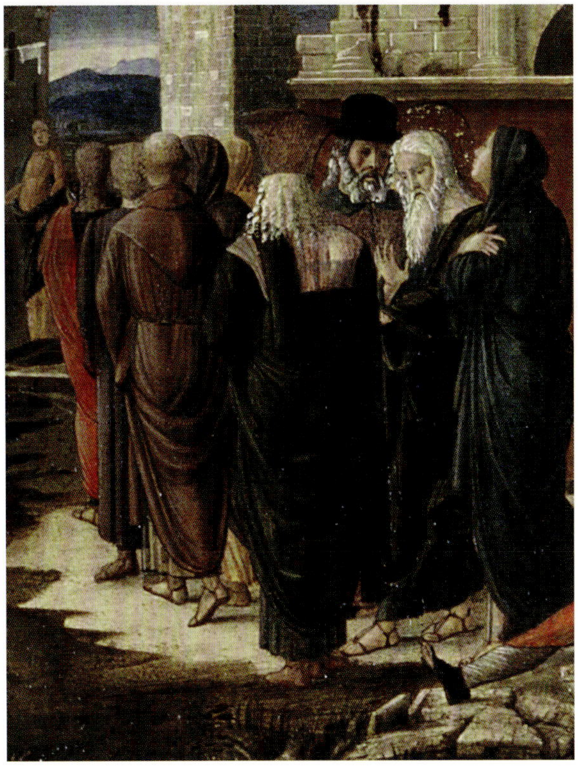

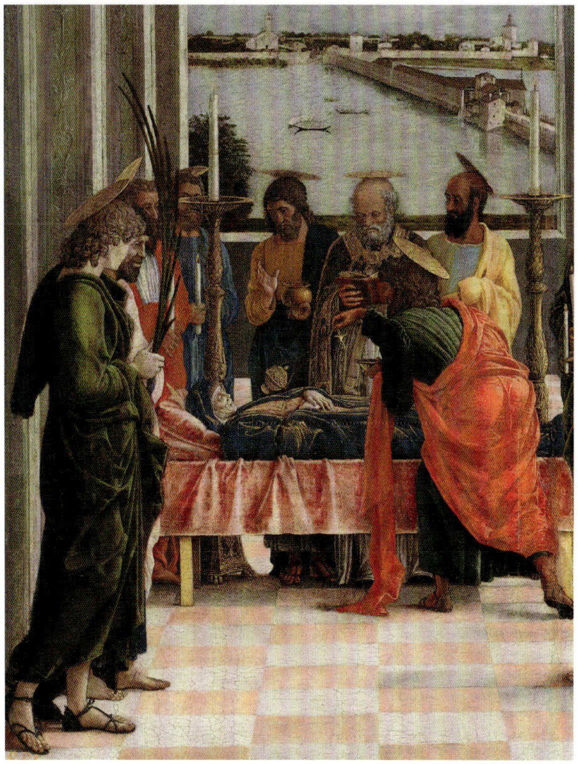

The anatomy of Christ's body does not stand out in sharp relief, as in Mantegna's scene and in the bronze *Crucifix* by Donatello in the Santo (though it would later, starting with the figure of the Dead Christ and angels in the polyptych for Santi Giovanni e Paolo). The design of the bowed legs of Christ in the two Crucifixions is almost identical, but we only need one detail to perceive the distance between them: in Bellini's work a shaft of light filters under Christ's right leg and strikes his other calf. Light quivers on the tranquil surface of the river, which reflects bushy trees, and suggests those qualities of dissolved atmosphere antithetical to the spectacular, micrographic clarity of Mantegna. Bellini's Christ's suffering is less heroic, his face is not sculpted by the shadow, it does not jerk backwards to reveal a view from below, instead it bears the signs of the physical ugliness of pain. Bellini counters the startling novelty of Mantegna's *mise en scène* with quiet tributes to a very ancient iconographical tradition: in the footrest on the cross, omitted by his brother-in-law; in the wooden wedges holding the Cross in the ground, in the Byzantine tradition; and in the flight of weeping cherubim, a poetic reworking of the crying angels of Giotto's *Lamentation* in the Scrovegni Chapel. They almost look like a flock of birds, were it not for the presence of tiny shell gold highlights.

The increased awareness of perspective thus reached a climax in Bellini's predella with *Three Stories of Drusiana and Saint John the Evangelist* owned by the Wittelsbacher Ausgleichsfonds in Munich (fig. 103), and in the Louvre *Crucifixion* (fig. 102), which comes from the same altarpiece painted for the chapel on the right side (*a cornu epistolae*) of the altar in Santa Maria della Carità.[27] The predella has been wrongly dated to after 1468, a misunderstanding, since the '*mansioneria*' instituted in that year by the patron, Domenico Marin, is for endowing the altar, that is, providing it with an income for officiating it – something generally done after a chapel is erected and decorated. On the other hand, a dating to about 1453–5, as Bellosi proposed, is not viable. The three episodes unfold with a cinematic intensity from right to left (because the high altar of the church was on that side), but also with an unprecedented *gravitas*. Gestures are contained. The procession on the left turns towards the far distance, and the foreshortened figures, some of their faces shown in lost profile, recall the figures flanking the Virgin's bier in the *Death of the Virgin* now in the Prado painted by Mantegna for the chapel of the Castello di San Giorgio in his first years in Mantua (figs 18, 19). Drusiana moves forward, her hands clasped around her shoulders, isolated and gazing heavenwards, in a state of grace.

We are a long way from the tormented forms we find in the *Transfiguration* or the *Agony in the Garden* in London! Instead, this was the moment of the *Pietà* (or *Dead Christ supported by Two Angels*) of about 1460 at the Museo Correr in Venice, a composed and almost Neo-Attic image, in which the painter takes pains to depict Jerusalem as a vision mingling Roman monuments and medieval walls. Above all, it was the moment of the four polyptychs erected along the *barco* (rood-screen) of the Church of the Carità; their altars had been erected between 1462 and 1464, as is well documented.[28] Even though – unlike the predella panels of *Drusiana and Saint John the Evangelist* – their execution is not completely autograph, these triptychs reflect the spirit of Giovanni Bellini. In the same years, Gentile Bellini was painting the organ shutters for the Basilica of San Marco, and in comparison, his figures resemble manikins set against absurd geological forms. Scholars persist in associating them with the style of his father, Jacopo Bellini,[29] but they are totally emancipated from it, looking towards a different sense of monumentality and atmosphere. If ever the payments are found, we could bet that the whole project was entrusted to Giovanni, who for the first time subcontracted some of the work, which from this point onwards was to mark much of his output, especially paintings of the Virgin and Child and other devotional subjects. I believe that the young Alvise Vivarini and Lazzaro Bastiani collaborated on the Carità triptychs, even if their subordinate role, subject to the strict direction, design and finishing touches of Giovanni Bellini – as Giotto had done and as Raphael would in Rome – is not immediately recognisable.[30] These stand as key works in the evolution of the Venetian Renaissance altarpiece, because they adapt the innovative structure of the *pala quadra lunettata* – the quadrangular altarpiece topped by a lunette derived from Donatello's altar in the Santo – to the rhythmical cadence of the triptych.[31] The loss of the pilasters and frames impairs our perception of these altarpieces. Unique to these triptychs is the idea of hollowing out each panel, as though they were recesses, echoed in the half-shell above. They stand as a tribute to the tradition of medieval architecture in San Marco, recessed with half-shell canopies that look back to its early Christian and Byzantine origins.

It was when his brother-in-law had moved permanently to Mantua that Bellini engaged with aspects of his art with renewed intensity. Otherwise it is impossible to explain this period, during which he painted the Santi Giovanni e Paolo polyptych (fig. 253) which marks a stylistic advance, with a tauter, more restless figurative style, imbued with vivid, powerful light. The predella, with the miracles of Saint Vincent Ferrer, is constructed in discrete units, apparently fragments of scenes, with contradictory vanishing points and horizons. By contrast, in the *Stories of Drusiana and Saint John the Evangelist* (fig. 103), the urban setting is extraordinarily complex, well-coordinated and perspectivally foreshortened; Drusiana, in the centre, is shown in daring frontal foreshortening. The scenery changes, as it would in the various acts of a play, but the sky unites the second and third scenes. The scenes are separated by painted pilasters, and the idea of an apparent continuity that masks the breaks in time has emerged after the experiments in spatial unity in the great triptychs: Jacopo Bellini's, painted for the Gattamelata Chapel in the Santo, in which the cover of the sarcophagus can just be glimpsed in the side panel of *Saint Anthony Abbot and Saint Bernardino of Siena*, now in the National Gallery of Art in Washington; and Mantegna's in San Zeno in Verona (fig. 252), in which the continuous architectural loggia imposes a unity on the composition.

Never again did Mantegna study sources of natural light as he did in the triptych for San Zeno, nor attempt

FIG. 20
GIOVANNI BELLINI
San Giobbe Altarpiece, 1480s (reconstruction)
Oil on panel, 471 × 258 cm
Gallerie dell'Accademia, Venice (38)

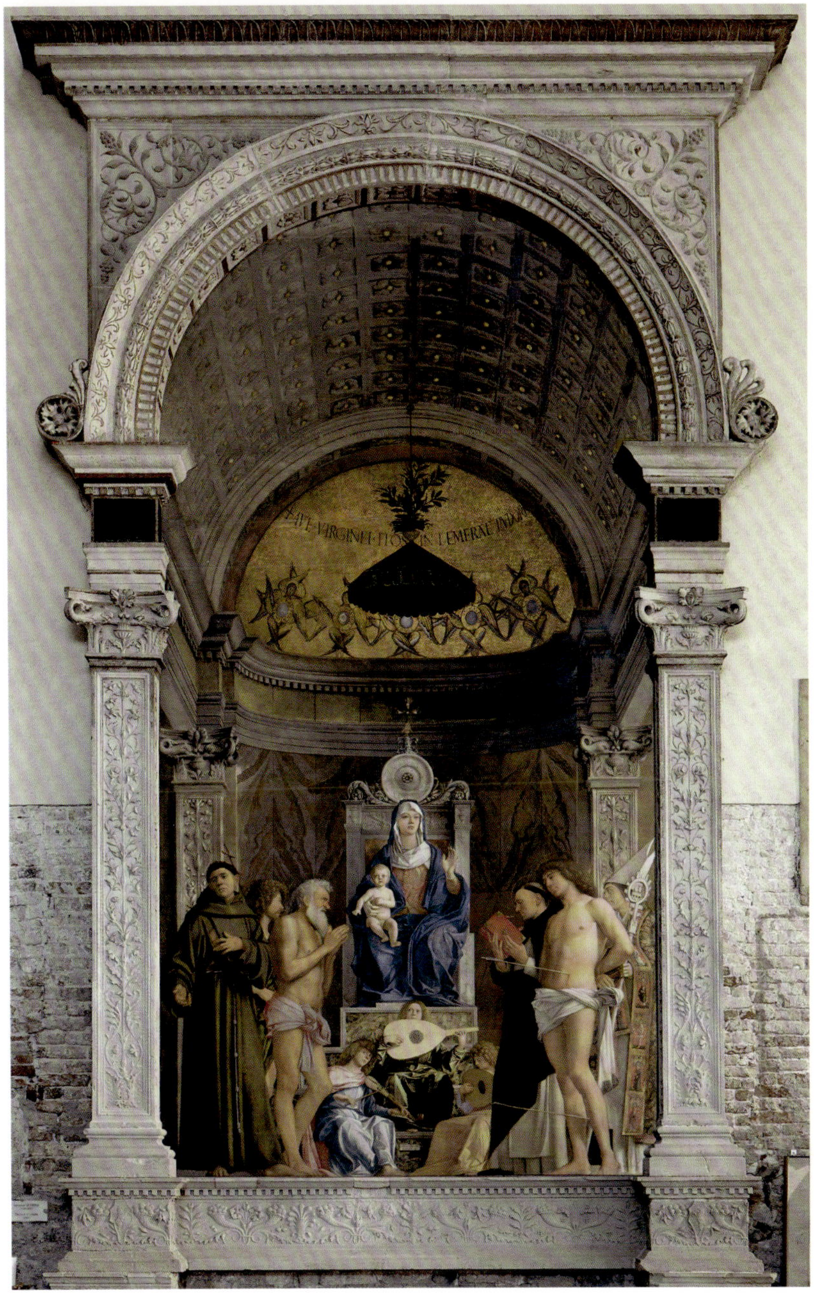

such a tender sense of pathos. This was the result of the influence of a radically different artist, his Venetian brother-in-law. At the same time the *San Zeno Altarpiece* (fig. 252) made a profound impression on Giovanni Bellini, who constantly measured himself against it in the concept of altarpiece design, and in how he established the illusion of its painted architecture with respect to the real frame. That the *San Giobbe Altarpiece* (fig. 20), painted over 20 years later, is in some sense a descendant of the one in Verona, is underlined by the use of a marble disk at the top of the throne that in Mantegna's work enhances the Virgin's halo and in Bellini's directly stands in for it. However, in the overall planning of the work, Bellini once again set himself apart. Mantegna's pavilion of ten marble piers is set off by fictive garlands which, seeming to entwine and separate the four columns of the wooden frame, emphasise the mental threshold between reality and artifice. The architecture painted by Giovanni Bellini, instead, forms an organic continuation of the stone frame, reproducing the same capitals and relief carving on the pilasters, and diminishing their size perspectivally, so as to suggest the gulf between the ecclesiastical space and that of the *sacra conversazione*. Naturalism triumphs over artifice.

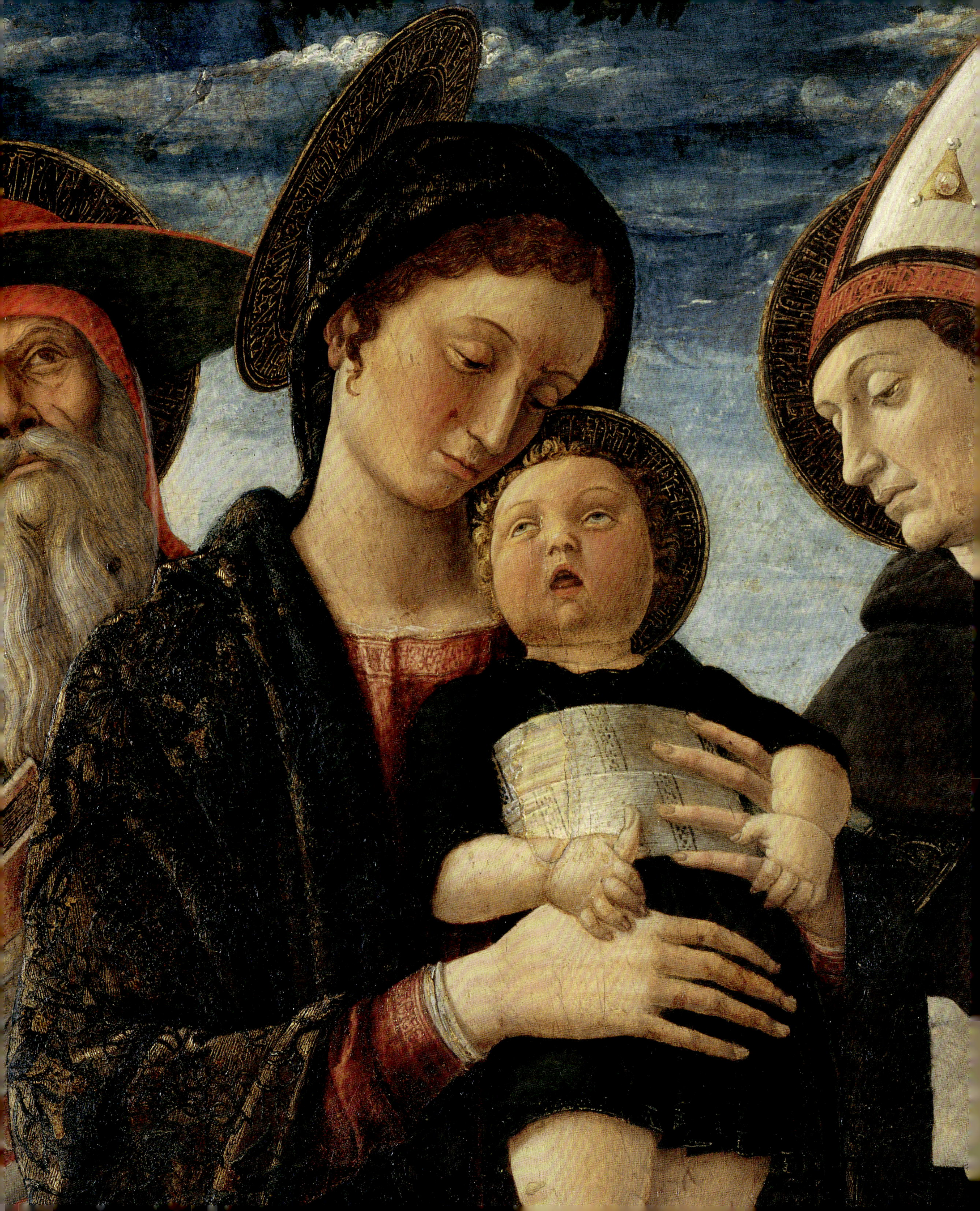

III 'Bellini stands higher … than Mantegna'

NEVILLE ROWLEY

PARIS/ROME 2008: TWO COMPETING EXHIBITIONS

THE AUTUMN OF 2008 WILL BE REMEMBERED AS a great moment for the joint commemoration of Andrea Mantegna and Giovanni Bellini. Mantegna, who had already been celebrated two years earlier in Italy by ten or so related exhibitions marking the fifth centenary of his death – in Padua, Verona and Mantua – was the object of a spectacular retrospective at the Musée du Louvre, boasting almost 200 works. These ranged from the reassembled predella of the *San Zeno Altarpiece* (fig. 252) to one of the nine *Triumphs of Caesar* from the Royal Collection, which had never left England since the seventeenth century (fig. 236). As for Bellini, he was the hero of another exhibition, at the Scuderie del Quirinale in Rome. This may have comprised a smaller number of works (62), but nearly all were by the master himself and often of essential historical interest, such as the *Pesaro Altarpiece*, a work that offered a theatrical opening to the exhibition, crowned as it was by the *Lamentation* from the Vatican Picture Gallery that was originally part of the altarpiece (fig. 255).

However extraordinary they might have seemed to their visitors, these exhibitions did not succeed in reuniting all the objects sought by their curators. In her introductory essay to the Paris show, the Louvre curator Dominique Thiébaut made a point of regretting the absence of the *Presentation of Christ in the Temple* from the Gemäldegalerie in Berlin (fig. 128), which 'so cruelly made itself felt in evoking the proximity of Mantegna and Giovanni Bellini'.[1] The author implicitly evoked a slightly modified replica of Mantegna's painting in the Fondazione Querini Stampalia in Venice (fig. 132), painted by Giovanni Bellini and providing the poster image for the exhibition in Rome.[2] On their side, the organisers of the Italian event must have regretted the absence of a key picture in the reconstruction of Bellini's youthful phase, to which they nonetheless made significant contributions, namely the predella with the *Three Stories of Drusiana and Saint John the Evangelist* owned by the Wittelsbacher Ausgleichsfonds in Munich (fig. 103). Not that the owners had prohibited the work from being shipped, as had been the case with the *Presentation* in Berlin; in fact the predella had been lent at the same time, not to Rome for Bellini, but to Paris for Mantegna.[3] The events of autumn 2008 were thus not only contemporaneous, but also competing against one another.

This competition between Paris and Rome was not limited to the realm of loans; the historical interpretation of the relationship between Mantegna and Bellini was also radically different, and therefore in potential conflict. These divergences became real through the question regarding one historical fact – the date of birth of Giovanni Bellini – which differed by no less than a decade in the respective exhibitions. In Paris, Bellini, born around 1430, was the equal in age of Mantegna (who was born at the end of that year, or more likely in 1431), his contemporary, if not his senior, and certainly influenced by him, but also capable of transmitting his unique understanding of light and colour to Mantegna.[4] In Rome, on the contrary, Bellini was born about ten years after Mantegna, whom he began to imitate only when the latter had moved from Padua, in 1460, to settle at the Mantuan court. One example of what this implied involved the predella with *Drusiana and Saint John*, which in Rome was dated to between 1468 and 1471, based on the date of the consecration of the chapel in the Church

ANDREA MANTEGNA, detail from *The Virgin and Child with Saints Jerome and Louis of Toulouse* (FIG. 108)

of the Carità, from which the work appears to have come – a dating that should have established that customarily given to the *Crucifixion* in the Louvre (fig. 102), which was connected for the first time with the same altarpiece.[5] In Paris, such a dating was considered 'extraordinarily late', as the work was considered as an echo not so much of Mantegna as of Donatello, and therefore datable to 1453–5.[6]

Points of disagreement are not uncommon, yet with respect to a field as studied as Italian painting of the fifteenth century, they rarely stretch beyond 15 years or so – and especially when this concerns the art of one of the most famous artists and is discussed by recognised art historians, Luciano Bellosi in Paris and Mauro Lucco in Rome. The bout might have ended with the combatants merely pulling their punches were it not for the fact that in the catalogue of the Louvre exhibition one of the two curators, Giovanni Agosti, had explicitly chastised the

> revisionisms of our time, all set on post-dating Giovanni's date of birth, even going as far as the mid-1440s, and thus ruling out any possibility of reciprocal relations [with Mantegna]. Such a chronology has endless consequences for the interpretation of the entire Quattrocento, one of which can stand for all the rest: it would invalidate the possibility that Bellini's shift towards modernity was a result of his contact with Piero della Francesca in the mid-1470s – that is, the keystone of all of Roberto Longhi's scholarly activity. And who knows, perhaps this desire to demolish was the spur for revisions of this kind.[7]

According to Agosti, a rejection of Longhi's writings thus formed the basis of the position adopted by the Rome exhibition, though in its catalogue Lucco forestalled this criticism and defended himself against the charge of being anti-Longhian.[8] In order to understand what was at stake in the 2008 debate, we should therefore go back almost a century earlier and study the series of publications on this topic by Longhi, the putative target of the Roman catalogue and one of the authorities for the Paris volume. It will then be possible to assess each side's position and, perhaps, decide which camp lies closer to historical truth.

ROBERTO LONGHI: FOR BELLINI / AGAINST MANTEGNA

In 1914, Roberto Longhi was a 24-year-old art historian, teaching in two Roman secondary schools. In the journal directed by one of his former professors, *L'Arte*, he published a long article entitled 'Piero dei Franceschi e lo sviluppo della pittura veneziana' (Piero della Francesca and the Development of Venetian Painting).[9] Its thesis was simple: Piero della Francesca (whose name Longhi preferred to write with historical correctness, not without a certain pedantry) is considered as the first painter to have succeeded in uniting flat colour and forms in depth in a unique combination at once inspired by the Gothic love of colour and the Florentine discoveries in the representation of space. This combination would have served in founding a new pictorial tradition initiated by Antonello da Messina and continued, in Venice, by Giovanni Bellini, Giorgione and the young Titian. Whereas the painting of Florence and that of Venice had been thought of as opposites since the mid-sixteenth century by Giorgio Vasari, who praised Florentine drawing in order to criticise Venetian colour, Longhi set out to unite the two traditions in a peculiar genealogy: what Florence had invented as regards perspective must have been filtered through the (supposedly) Umbrian painter, Piero della Francesca, in order to be able to be interpreted by the artists of the Serenissima, notably Giovanni Bellini.

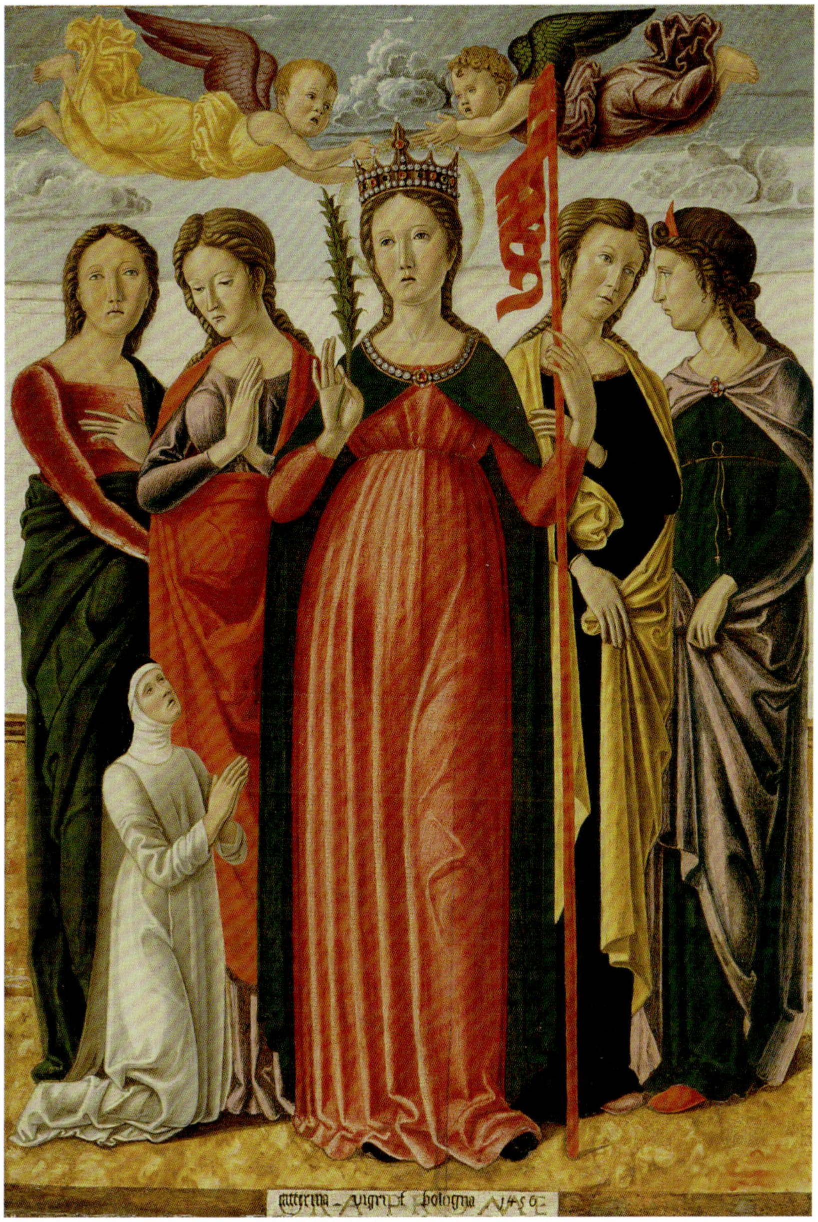

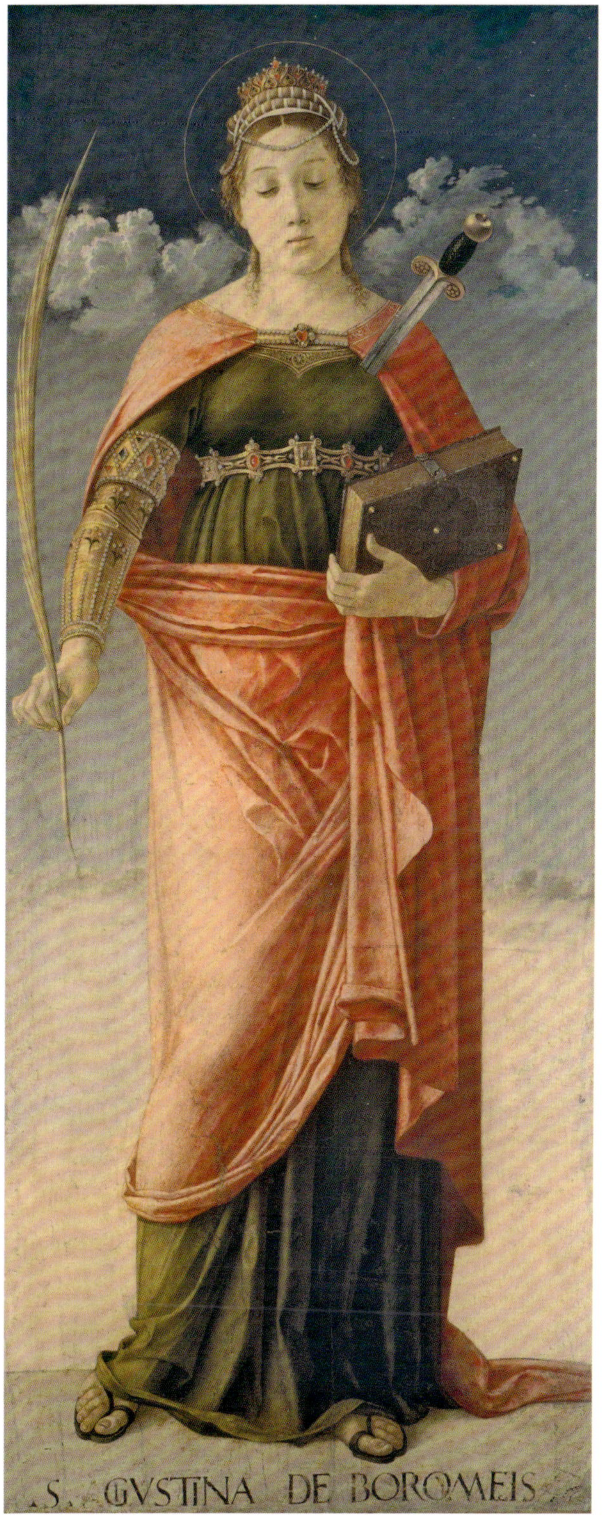

FIG. 21
VENETIAN PAINTER
Saint Ursula and her Companions, 1456 (?)
Egg tempera on panel, 64 × 45 cm
Gallerie dell'Accademia, Venice (188)

FIG. 22
GIOVANNI BELLINI
Saint Giustina, about 1474–5
Oil (?) on panel, 129 × 55 cm
Museo Bagatti Valsecchi, Milan (986)

FIG. 23
GIOVANNI BELLINI
Saint Christopher, detail from the *Saint Vincent Ferrer Altarpiece*, about 1467
Egg tempera (?) on panel, 167 × 67 cm (panel)
Church of Santi Giovanni e Paolo (San Zanipolo), Venice

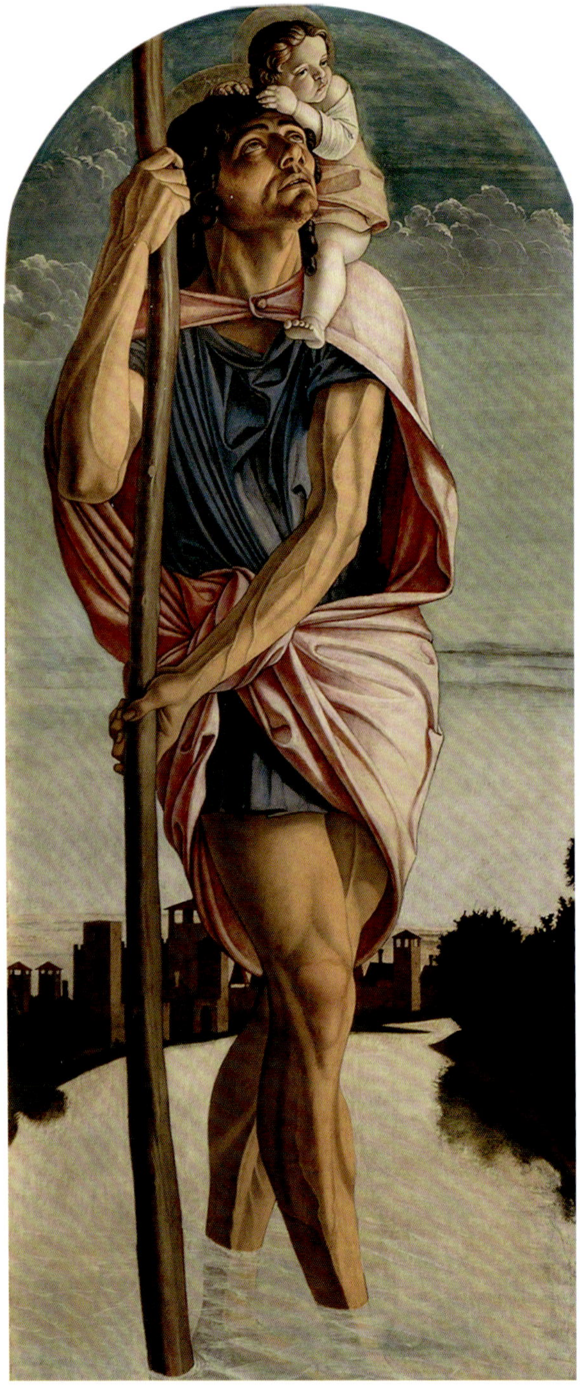

Longhi in this way sought to justify the evident transformation that occurred in the art of Giovanni Bellini during the 1470s, a transformation which the Lithuanian-American art historian Bernard Berenson had at the turn of the century referred to as a 'change of visualisation': 'hitherto an adept of the plastic vision, [Bellini] began all at once to visualise in still another mode, which, to differentiate it from the linear and the plastic, I may call the commencement of the pictorial mode.'[10] In 1913, Berenson had added a *Saint Giustina* in the Museo Bagatti Valsecchi in Milan (fig. 22) to Giovanni Bellini's oeuvre from these years of the 'shift towards modernity' (Agosti); the picture was until then considered to be by Alvise Vivarini.[11] In his essay of 1914, Longhi used this attribution as a basis for recognising the artist's hand in another work traditionally attributed to Alvise, the *Saint Vincent Ferrer Altarpiece* in the Venetian church of Santi Giovanni e Paolo (figs 23, 253).[12] But Bellini was no longer the 'unconscious revolutionary' described by Berenson:[13] the modulation towards colour and light was now explained by the influence of Piero della Francesca. Initially ignored, notably by Berenson (who was Longhi's model, and about to become his nemesis), the attribution was subsequently accepted by most scholars; and likewise, the hypothetical influence of Piero della Francesca on Giovanni Bellini would soon become a certainty for numerous art historians, both in Italy and beyond.[14]

This new reading of how Italian Renaissance painting evolved nonetheless created collateral damage. For biographical as well as formal reasons, the art of Giovanni Bellini had long been regarded as inherited from the works of Jacopo Bellini and Andrea Mantegna, the painter's father and brother-in-law. Had Jacopo, together with his sons Gentile and Giovanni, not signed the altarpiece of the Gattamelata Chapel in the Basilica of the Santo in Padua?[15] As for the many works by

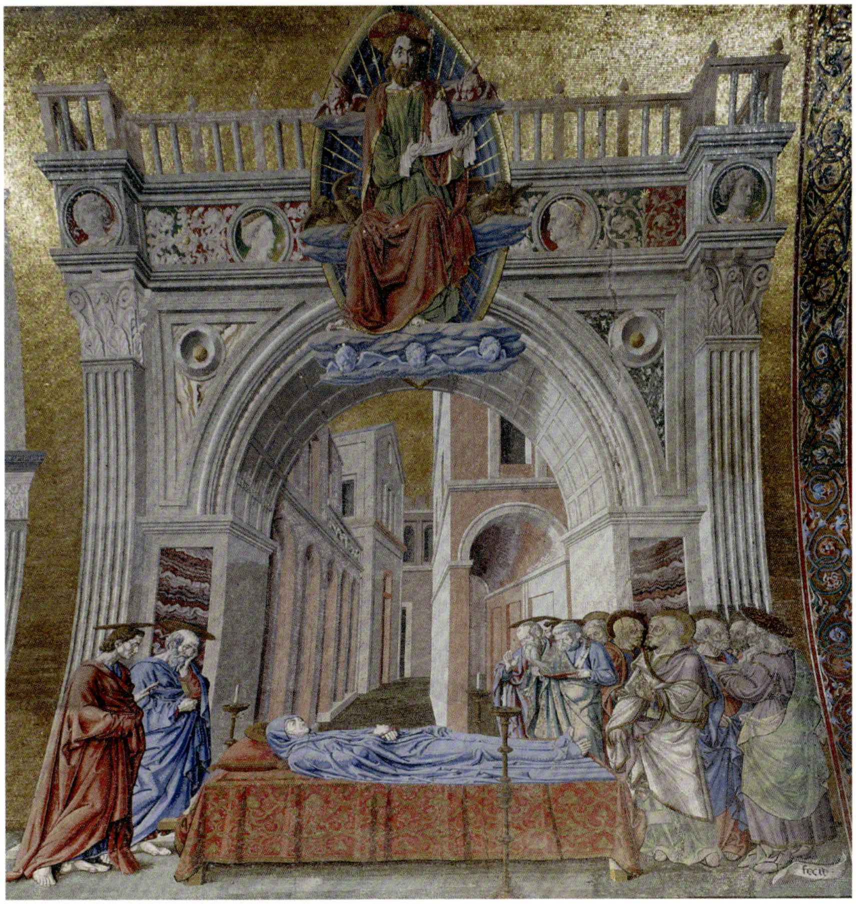

FIG. 24
The Death of the Virgin, 1450s
Mosaic, Mascoli Chapel
Basilica of San Marco, Venice

Giovanni Bellini which had been ascribed to Mantegna over the course of the centuries – for instance *The Transfiguration of Christ* in the Museo Correr (fig. 105), or *The Agony in the Garden* in the National Gallery (fig. 126) – were they not perfect demonstrations of how much the style of the two painters had once been very similar, in a style that properly belonged to Mantegna, since, unlike Bellini, he would remain faithful to it throughout his life? For Longhi, these arguments were worthless. Jacopo Bellini is scarcely mentioned in the article, while the influence of Mantegna on the young Bellini is certainly not denied, but his historical importance strongly minimised. It is only when Bellini encountered the art of Piero that he succeeded in 'reforming' what Longhi called *mantegnismo*, and clearing the way for the truly Venetian tradition, that of the painting of light and tone. Thus, Bellini would only have become Bellini when he had begun to distance himself from his invasive brother-in-law.

During the decades that followed, Roberto Longhi engaged himself in defending his analysis of 1914, while taking an ever more disparaging view of the role played by Mantegna. In 1926, a monograph on the latter written by Giuseppe Fiocco offered him a pretext for a review that was polemical, to say the least.[16] Fiocco saw the art of Mantegna as an extension of the artistic discoveries made in Florence in the early fifteenth century, brought to the Veneto by a substantial number of artists ranging from the sculptors Niccolò and Pietro Lamberti (and not so much Donatello) to the painters Paolo Uccello, Andrea del Castagno and Filippo Lippi. For Longhi, this direct influence of Florence on Padua competed with the crucial link he had established between Piero della Francesca and Giovanni Bellini. In his review, written as an open letter, he took pains to invalidate Fiocco's thesis while presenting in detail some new attributions to bolster his case. Fiocco, who recognised Mantegna's hand in the mosaic of *The Death of the Virgin* in the Mascoli Chapel at San Marco (fig. 24), especially in the passage representing Christ holding the Virgin's soul in his arms, was turned down flat by Longhi, who for his part mentioned a work (at that time unknown) of the same subject, which he gave to Mantegna (fig. 213).[17] The conclusion was a matter of course: the finest connoisseur is implicitly the one who has looked at the works in the best way, and thus the one who will provide the best historical interpretation.[18] For Longhi, Mantegna and the artists of Padua had so insistently copied Donatello without understanding his spirit that they became 'anti-classical':

> Before the truly Hadrianic Donatello of the Santo altar [in Padua], or to the Masaccio of the Brancacci Chapel [in Florence], the frescoes in the Eremitani Chapel [in Padua] seem to have been painted by a team of barbarians preparing ferociously for their Latin diploma.[19]

The art of Venice was thus said to have been born under the aegis of Piero della Francesca, about whom Longhi published a monograph in 1927 that met with considerable success.[20] Giuseppe Fiocco did his best to respond to these attacks, reproaching this competing interpretation for being 'anti-national', but in vain – of course the adjective does veer dangerously close to the rhetoric used by the Fascist regime, which Longhi did not fail to point out.[21]

After the Second World War, Longhi pushed his interpretation further. From having been a pre-war adversary, Fiocco became an objective ally when he suggested in a 1949 lecture that Giovanni Bellini's birth date should be set around 1425, that is, far earlier than had been hitherto proposed and six years before the birth of Mantegna. The 'Mantegnesque phase' of Bellini, in which everyone had believed for decades, subject to the erroneous attributions encompassing the two painters, was only an illusion: the sculptural style long associated with Mantegna could now pass as an invention by Bellini himself, which meant that: 'to-day, for all of us, Giovanni Bellini stands higher as an example of independence of spirit than Mantegna and, *a fortiori*, than every other Venetian or Paduan contemporary.'[22]

This judgement leads to a chronology of Bellini's work that starts at the beginning of the 1450s, including paintings such as *Saint Ursula and her Companions* in the Accademia (fig. 21), and it always rules out Mantegna's oft-formulated precedence: the two versions of *The Agony in the Garden* in the National Gallery (figs 125, 126) would both date from the mid-1450s, while ten years later it would be equally impossible to decide which of the two depictions of *The Presentation of Christ in the Temple* (Mantegna's in Berlin and Bellini's in Venice, figs 128, 132) was painted first. One work sums up this creative simultaneity by itself, *The Virgin and Child with Saints Jerome and Louis of Toulouse* in the Musée Jacquemart-André in Paris (fig. 108): long attributed to Mantegna, its light-filled quality made it possible, for Longhi, to attribute it to Giovanni Bellini.

FOR OR AGAINST LONGHI: TWO FACTIONS

Nearly half a century after the death of Roberto Longhi, we may wonder why the exhibitions of 2008 were so bitter in their reaction to his legacy. At first sight, it seems hard not to agree with the view upheld in Rome, given the seemingly excessive stances taken by Longhi. A good number of attributions to Bellini have been forgotten, such as the *Saint Ursula* in the Accademia (fig. 21). Others have endured, but it is their dating that poses a question. Historical data enabled the exhibition in Rome to date the predella with *Drusiana and Saint John the Evangelist* (fig. 103) to between 1468 and 1471, as we saw, rather than to the 1450s. Likewise, Bellini's *Presentation of Christ in the Temple* in the Fondazione Querini Stampalia (fig. 132) is now commonly dated over 15 years later than the version by Mantegna in Berlin (fig. 128), though Longhi said they were contemporaneous. The similarity of the rock motif in the foreground of the *Transfiguration* by Bellini in the Museo Correr (fig. 16) and Mantegna's drawing of *The Descent of Christ into Limbo* in the École des Beaux-Arts in Paris (fig. 15) provides another argument for the Roman catalogue to place these two works in the second half of the 1460s: a letter of 28 June 1468 from Mantegna to the Marquess of Mantua Ludovico III Gonzaga asserts that the painter had begun to work on the picture with 'the story of limbo'.[23] How could Bellini have prophesied – alone – this eminently Mantegnesque motif?

As for the putative relationship between Piero della Francesca and Giovanni Bellini, it is all very well for the Roman catalogue to underline that this theory is not founded on a single direct borrowing, unlike the numerous literal reiterations made by the Venetian painter from the work of his father Jacopo or his brother-in-law Mantegna: how can it therefore be relevant?[24] More generally, is it not somewhat problematic to consider Longhi's article of 1914 as a keystone of current history of art – an inspired text, to be sure, but more than a little cursory in method, and written so long ago by a young man of 24?[25]

Yet making the Paris exhibition of 2008 a simple re-affirmation of Longhi's positions would be equally hasty. Had not one of its organisers, Giovanni Agosti, a fierce opponent of the Rome exhibition, ascribed to Mantegna the *Virgin and Child* in the Musée Jacquemart-André (fig. 108), which Longhi had almost judged to be worthy of Bellini's hand?[26] As for the scholar responsible for the section dedicated to Mantegna and Bellini, Luciano Bellosi, he may well have been Roberto Longhi's student in the 1960s, but his own reputation was founded on his gifts as connoisseur and his qualities as historian, reaching certain conclusions that did not always confirm his teacher's points of view.[27] In the 2008 catalogue, Bellosi hardly refrained from applauding the Longhian attributions he approved of, such as the *Saint Vincent Ferrer Altarpiece* (fig. 253) and the predella with *Drusiana and Saint John* (fig. 103), while making no mention of the less relevant ones, such as the *Saint Ursula* in the Accademia (fig. 21). All the same, other 'erroneous' attributions seemed to contain an element of truth. If the Jacquemart-André *Virgin and Child* (fig. 108) had been given to Bellini when it was in fact by Mantegna, did this not show that the latter had learned from his brother-in-law, and not vice-versa?[28] Bellini, therefore, was not a precursor of Mantegna, as Longhi wanted him to be, but a painter who had been able to understand his style and, in his turn, lend him his own inventions.

In support of his proposals, Bellosi asserted the attribution to the young Giovanni Bellini of several illuminated sheets belonging to two manuscripts commissioned by Jacopo Antonio Marcello and now housed in the Bibliothèque de l'Arsenal in Paris and in the Médiathèque Pierre-Amalric in Albi (figs 94, 95, 97).[29] The secure date of these works – 1453 and 1459 respectively – allowed for Giovanni's artistic beginnings to be assigned no longer to the same dates as those of Mantegna (whose activity as painter had begun at the end of the 1440s), but precisely when the latter became a member of the Bellini family through his marriage to Nicolosia in 1453. One could thus explain the dating of the *Drusiana and Saint John* predella (fig. 103) to about 1453–5, while the resemblance of the rocks in Bellini's *Transfiguration* (fig. 105) and those in the *Descent of Christ into Limbo* by Mantegna (fig. 143), also highlighted in the catalogue, was not interpreted as sufficient evidence for a late dating.[30]

The way in which the young Bellini now appeared to show immediate sensitivity to Mantegna's innovations seemed to herald the rest of his career. He was to react promptly to the presence of Antonello da Messina in Venice, in the mid-1470s, and the same would apply towards the end of his life, when he showed no hesitation in adapting his style as he absorbed the discoveries made by Giorgione. There was thus a certain logic in interpreting his debut as painter in this way, rather than dating Bellini's most 'Mantegnesque' works after Mantegna's departure for Mantua in 1460, as the Roman exhibition saw it. If Bellini had always been inspired by other painters to advance his own art, it became logical to interpret this 'change of visualisation' in favour of a more luminous and space-filled painting, which emerged in the 1470s, as the result of an artistic encounter. To Antonello da Messina one could now add Piero della Francesca, whose *Montefeltro Altarpiece*, painted for the church of San Bernardino in Urbino and now in the Brera (fig. 25), appears very close to Bellini's creations of this period, starting with the *Coronation of the Virgin* in the Musei Civici in Pesaro (fig. 255). To these formal antecedents one can add the geographical proximity of Urbino and Pesaro, as well as Franciscan commissions. A century after its declaration, Longhi's thesis does not seem totally devoid of foundation.[31]

FIG. 25
PIERO DELLA FRANCESCA
Montefeltro Altarpiece, about 1465
Oil on panel, 251 × 172 cm
Pinacoteca di Brera, Milan (180)

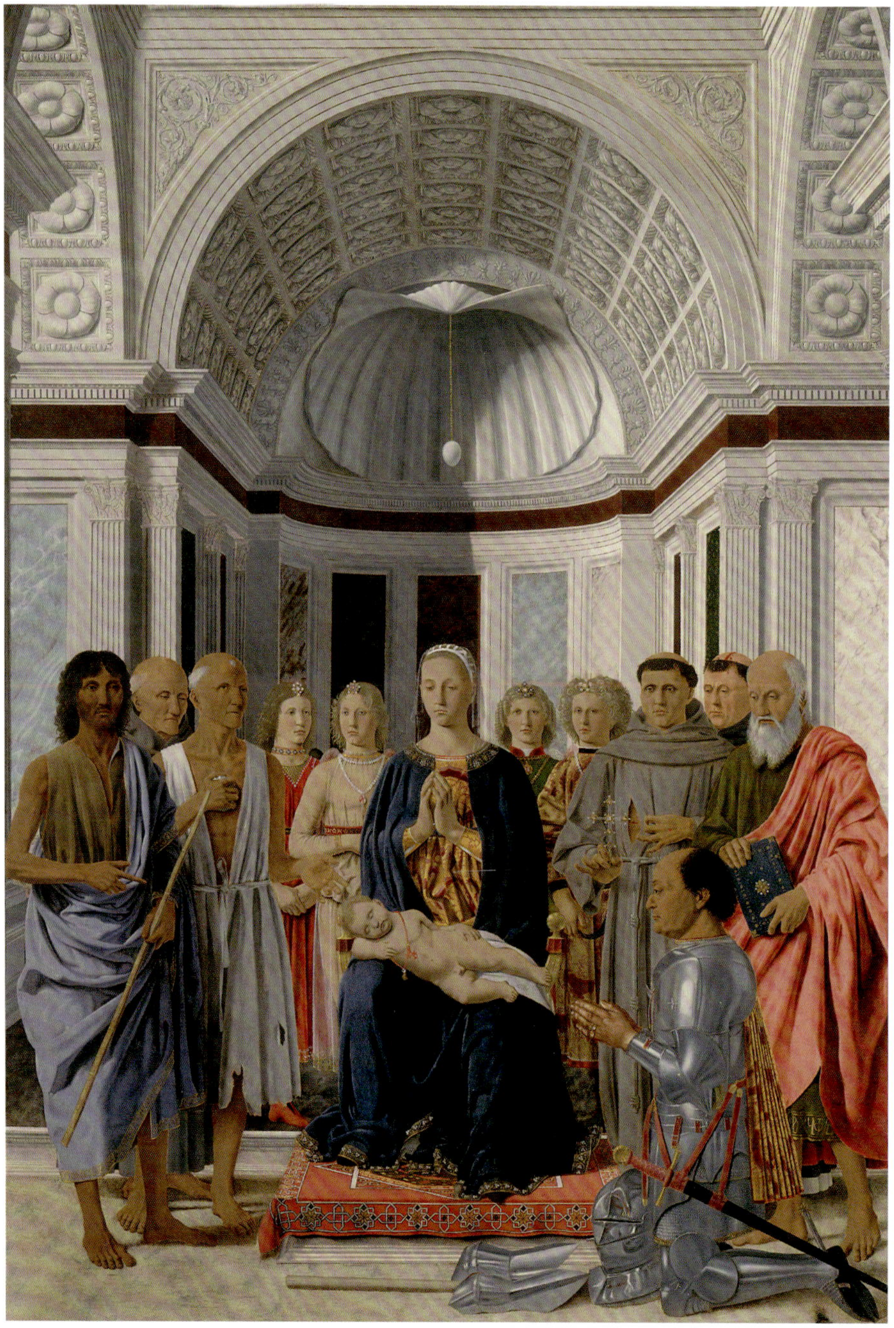

ACCEPTING THE LIMITS OF CURRENT KNOWLEDGE

The pitched battle of autumn 2008 could have produced a winner, but none was declared, with the exhibition reviews leaning either towards one thesis or the other – that is, when they did take a side.[32] The last decade has not been lacking in archival discoveries, yet these have not resolved the issue. The will of an aunt of Giovanni Bellini has been interpreted as proof of his birth around 1440 – which is actually no more than supposition – while it has also been suggested that Giovanni was not the illegitimate son of Jacopo, but his half-brother, born in about 1425 – hardly an easy argument to accept in the light of historical sources, even for the partisans of Longhi, who had after all used this date of birth to assert the painter's seniority over Mantegna.[33] As for the latest proposal from the Longhi camp, put forward by Antonio Mazzotta, Bellini is given the authorship of the *Saint Ursula* (fig. 21), as once proposed by Longhi – an opinion as hard to accept as it is to find a satisfactory alternative.[34] Following one side or the other seems to be a matter of faith, such is the struggle required for scholarly consensus to be given to putatively fundamental attributions, and given the only relative certainty of dates cited as supporting evidence.[35]

Better than any other work, Giovanni Bellini's monumental *Lamentation* in the Doge's Palace in Venice (fig. 26) illustrates the discordance of the two positions. Several eighteenth-century sources indicate that the painting bore the date 1472 alongside the surviving inscription with the painter's signature. For Lucco and the Roman camp, this date was evidence for Bellini's late chronology; for Bellosi and 'the Parisians', the style of the work was totally incompatible with the more light-filled creations of the 1470s, starting with the *Coronation of the*

FIG. 26
GIOVANNI BELLINI
The Lamentation over the Dead Christ, with Saints Mark and Nicholas of Bari,
about 1457–9
Oil (?) on canvas,
116 × 319 cm
Ducal Palace, Venice (433)

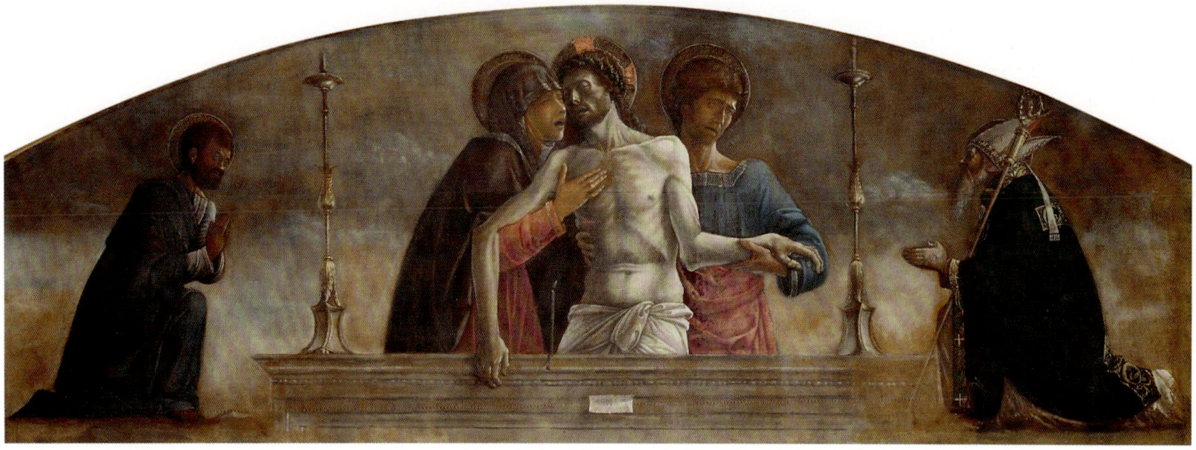

Virgin in Pesaro (fig. 255).[36] In this instance, Longhi's authority is of no use, since by turns the art historian upheld both an early dating and a late one.[37] Two reconstructions of Giovanni Bellini's youthful phase face one another here, both possible if we take into account what we know historically – and both defended by two of the principal Mantegna and Bellini specialists of recent decades, Giovanni Agosti and Mauro Lucco.

Rather than choosing between the two sides, a number of scholars now stand behind an interpretation midway between the positions put forward in 2008. Giovanni Bellini's birth would be around 1435, making him neither an alter ego of Mantegna nor a *retardataire* follower, but rather a painter slightly younger than his brilliant brother-in-law, who was clearly his initial model.[38] Bellini's Mantegnesque phase would thus not be limited to the 1450s, when Mantegna was working in Padua, but would also stretch a good way into the 1460s.[39] As for the influence exerted by the works of Piero della Francesca during the 1470s, this must remain in the realm of the possible. Frustrating though it may be, this absence of certainty forces us to accept the limits of current knowledge – limits only highlighted by the polemics of the last century. Rather than resolving these problems, the catalogue of the present exhibition seeks to cast light on them. If comparing numerous works by Mantegna and Bellini might enable scholars to fine-tune the historical relationship between the two painters, one of its aims would be achieved.

But let us return to the young Longhi one last time. In 1910, four years before the publication of his much-discussed article, Roberto Longhi visited the Venice Biennale, where he discovered the French painters of the nineteenth century, and especially Renoir and the Impressionists.[40] It was at this moment that a taste for colour rather than drawing took shape within him, a penchant for handling rather than finish, for partial rather than overall light, and for painting without subject rather than history painting. In one sense, Longhi had already begun to prefer Bellini over Mantegna even before he took a close interest in the oeuvre of the two painters. A supporter of art history founded on art criticism, Longhi always sought to transform his personal tastes into an artistic hierarchy. For example, he was one of the first to establish Piero della Francesca and Caravaggio as artists of prime importance. This parable-like approach continued in the case of Mantegna and Bellini: for the second one to wax, the first had to wane. Whether one admires Longhi's genius or finds his value judgements exasperating, this new interest in Bellini at the expense of Mantegna is only a symptom of a more global change of perception: at the beginning of the twentieth century, the period was no longer attuned to Mantegna's line, finding more favour in Bellini's brushstrokes.[41] A century after this 'change of visualisation', this exhibition provides the occasion, for once, to set the same level for such complementary and exceptional geniuses as Mantegna and Bellini.

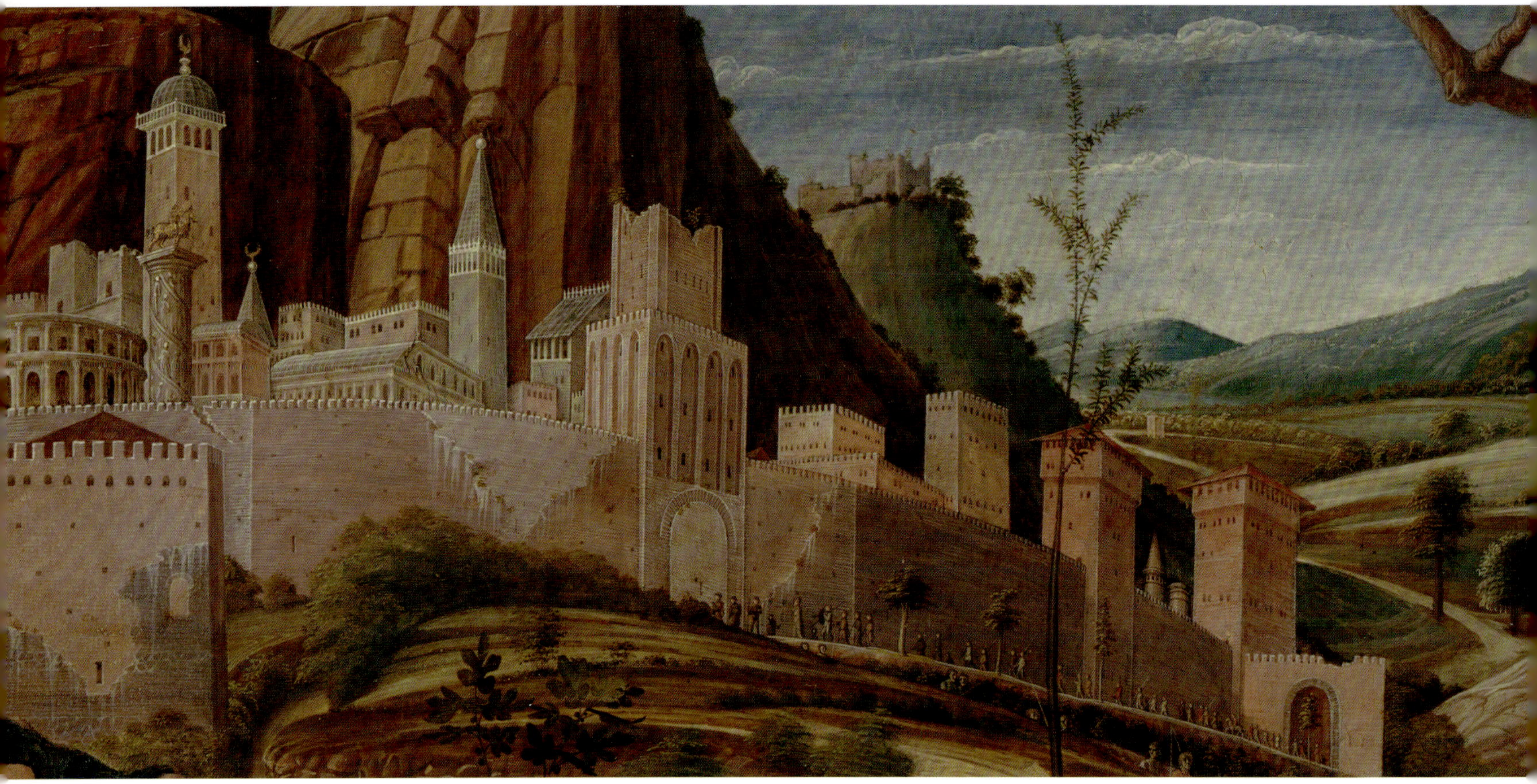

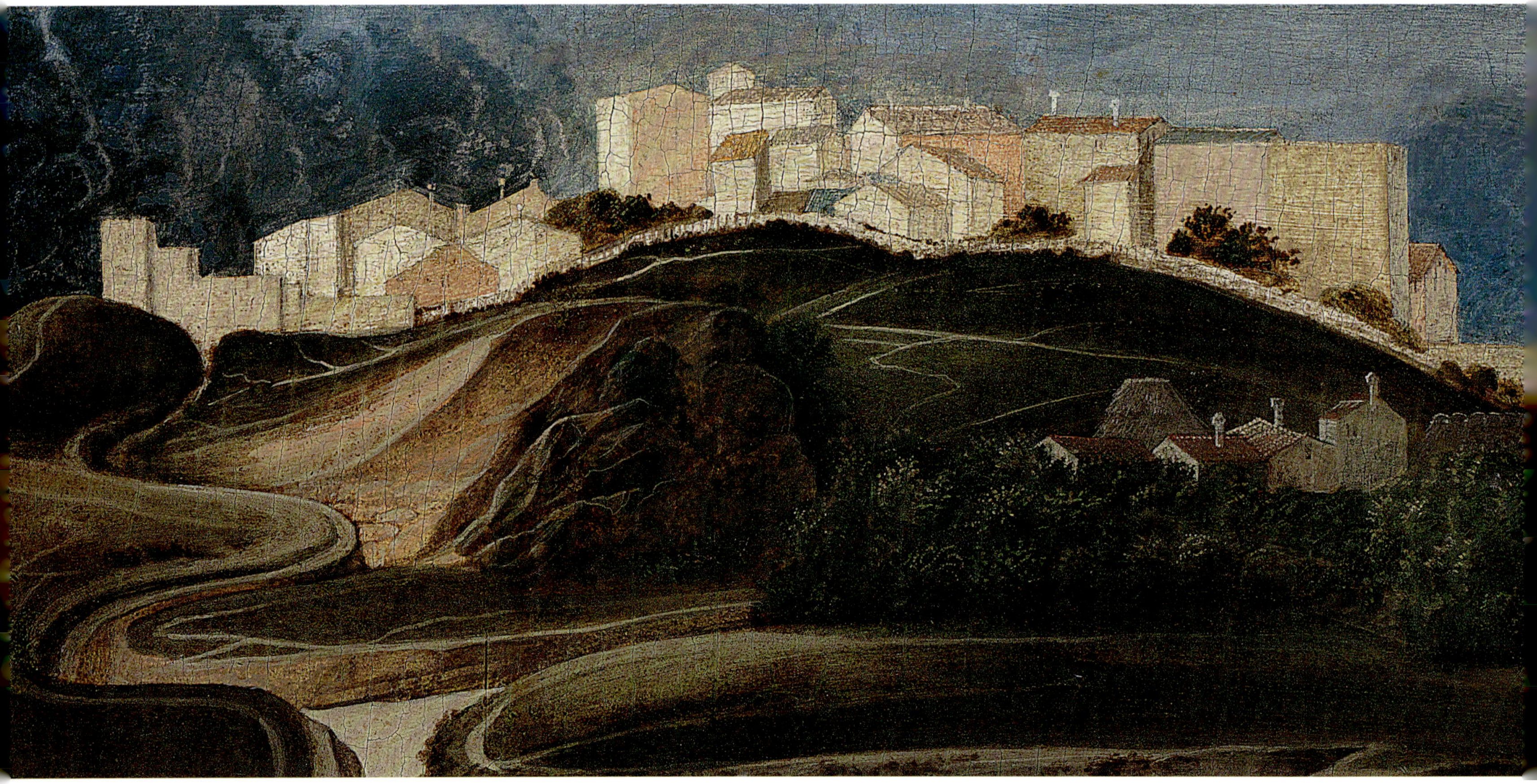

IV

Mantegna and Bellini: Contrasting Approaches to Technique

JILL DUNKERTON AND BABETTE HARTWIEG

IT MIGHT BE EXPECTED THAT AS BROTHERS-IN-LAW Andrea Mantegna and Giovanni Bellini would employ similar painting techniques, thereby reinforcing their apparently close connection. In fact, beyond the use of pigments and materials and basic practical traditions common to all painters in Northern Italy at the time, their techniques are notably different and distinctive and were to become ever more divergent over the course of their long careers.

As a standard part of their training in the workshops of Venice and Padua, both artists were instructed on how to paint on panels. These were prepared in the usual way with gesso in preparation for gilding and painting. Early in their careers they were still expected to paint altar-pieces with figures set against backgrounds of burnished gold leaf, Mantegna in the *Saint Luke Polyptych* of 1453–4 (fig. 129),[1] and Giovanni Bellini some ten years later with the set of triptychs painted for the Church of the Carità in Venice (for example, fig. 84).[2] Both also gained early experience in painting on canvas, a support that was more widely used than is commonly supposed, especially in Northern Italy.[3] Two of Mantegna's earliest surviving paintings, the *Saint Mark* (fig. 77) dating from around 1448 and the *Saint Euphemia* (Museo Nazionale di Capodimonte, Naples) of 1454 were painted on canvas, while Giovanni may have collaborated with his father, Jacopo, on a cycle of canvases showing Scenes from the Life of Christ and the Virgin for the Scuola Grande di San Giovanni Evangelista (including fig. 6).[4] In Venice it was becoming common for such narrative cycles to be painted on canvas instead of directly on the walls of a church or meeting room, most probably because of the effects of the damp Venetian climate on murals. On the mainland, however, fresco painting was widely employed, and it was in this medium that Mantegna first made his name with his contribution to the decoration of the Ovetari Chapel (fig. 250), commissioned in 1448 and completed in 1457. Subsequent wall painting projects were to include his celebrated Camera Picta (figs 3, 203), painted from 1465–74 in the Ducal Palace at Mantua, and a chapel in the Vatican frescoed during his stay in Rome from 1488–90 (now lost). The high-key palette of fresco continued to influence Mantegna's technical preferences when painting on panel and canvas.

Even at the point when Mantegna and Bellini appear closest in their artistic and technical interests, the two versions of *The Agony in the Garden* in the National Gallery, their differences in approach are striking, and especially in their depiction of landscape (figs 125, 126).[5] Both versions were painted in egg tempera on panel. Mantegna used the precision of the medium to depict each element with an almost equal degree of attention. With a fine pointed brush he defined in lead white every detail of the buildings as the dawn light rakes across them (fig. 29) and described with meticulous attention the condition of the city walls. The equestrian monument and the golden crescents surmounting the towers and spires were picked out in gold leaf, here applied using a mordant. While the townscape on the left of Bellini's composition has clearly been damaged in a past cleaning, it must always have been painted more broadly. The absence of detail confirms Bellini's observation that the brilliant early morning sun has bleached out much of the information about the structure of the distant buildings. In the painting of the group of rustic buildings below, still in the shade, the effects of light on the roofs and haystack are suggested with a few quick flicks of the brush. There is no gold leaf – the crescent

ANDREA MANTEGNA, detail from *The Agony in the Garden* (FIG. 125)

GIOVANNI BELLINI, detail from *The Agony in the Garden* (FIG. 126)

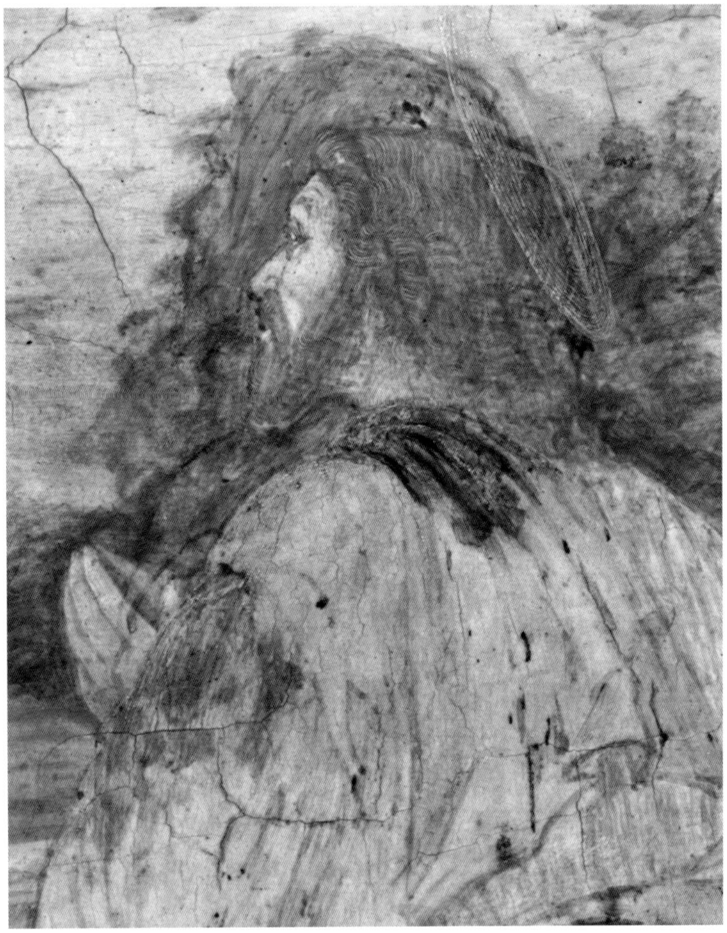

FIG. 27
ANDREA MANTEGNA, *The Agony in the Garden* (FIG. 125)
Detail of infrared reflectogram

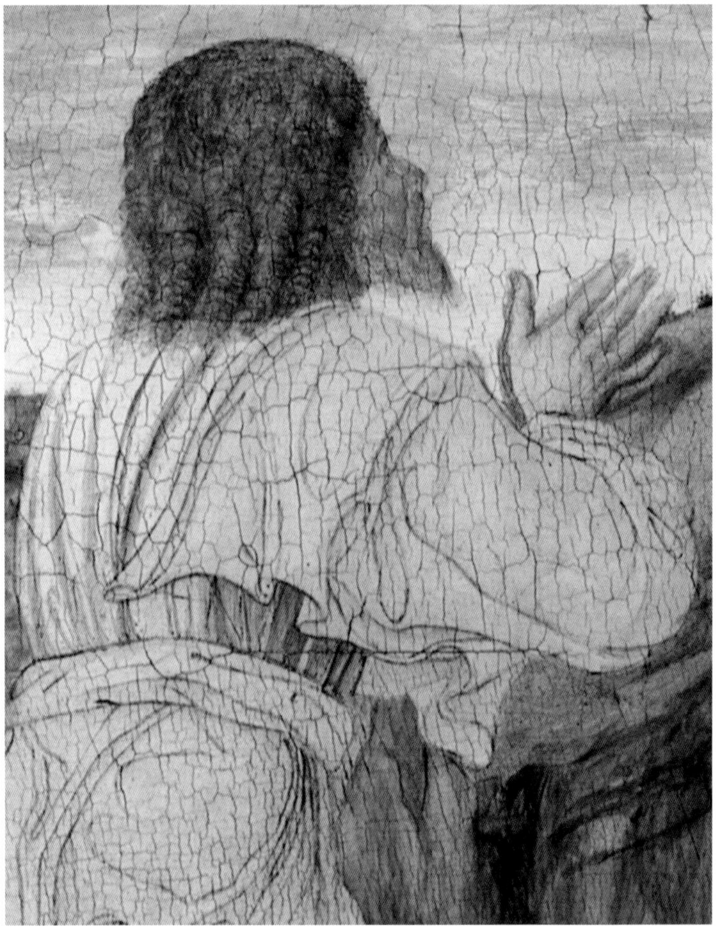

FIG. 28
GIOVANNI BELLINI, *The Agony in the Garden* (FIG. 126)
Detail of infrared reflectogram

that crowns the stubby tower in his view of Jerusalem consists of no more than a stroke of azurite-containing paint, its greenish blue colour contrasting with the cooler lapis and white of the sky (fig. 30).

Even though periods of direct contact and discussion about painting technique between the brothers-in-law may have been rare, details of the execution of the figures in these two compositions suggest that at this point there may have been a moment of connection. Examination by infrared reflectography confirms that they both made careful underdrawings before beginning to paint, drawing outlines on their gessoed panels with a liquid black medium and a fine brush. Mantegna, as always, had planned his design with particular care. Most of the landscape elements, even including the clouds, were established in the underdrawing, as well as the figures. If necessary, however, he was prepared to make adjustments. Christ's head and shoulders were first drawn higher and to the left, before being redrawn in their painted position, with his profile now set against the trees and rocky outcrop (fig. 27).[6] Bellini also set out the general topography of his landscape in the underdrawing but concentrated his efforts on the principal figures. They are drawn with a precise linear technique (fig.28),[7] which, with its schematic construction of the drapery folds, is unlike the underdrawing to be seen in his subsequent production.

Bellini's ambitious foreshortening of the sleeping disciple on the right may well have been inspired by Mantegna's figures from both the National Gallery panel and the predella of the *San Zeno Altarpiece* (fig. 252). When viewed under magnification, the depiction of the heads in each painting, with their triangular noses and open mouths showing glimpses of teeth, appear strikingly similar, but with Bellini's version painted, as always, in a more generalised, less sharply graphic way (figs 31, 32).

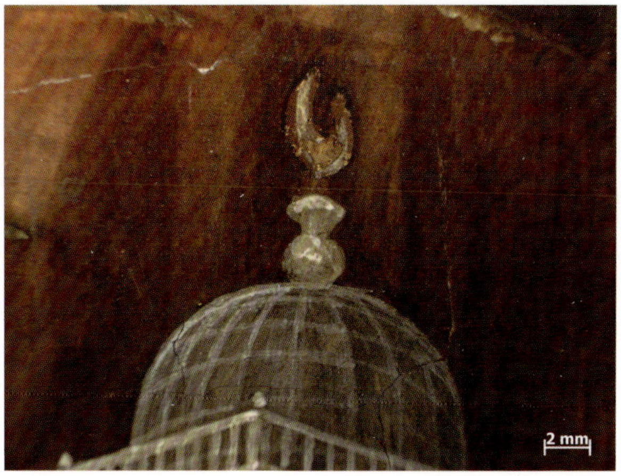

FIG. 29
ANDREA MANTEGNA, *The Agony in the Garden* (FIG. 125)
Photomicrograph of tower

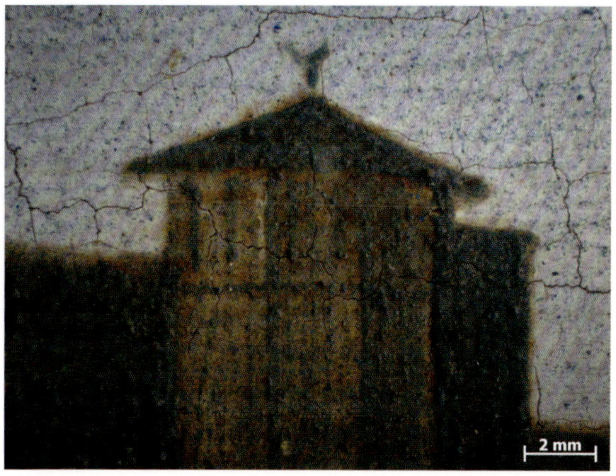

FIG. 30
GIOVANNI BELLINI, *The Agony in the Garden* (FIG. 126)
Photomicrograph of turret

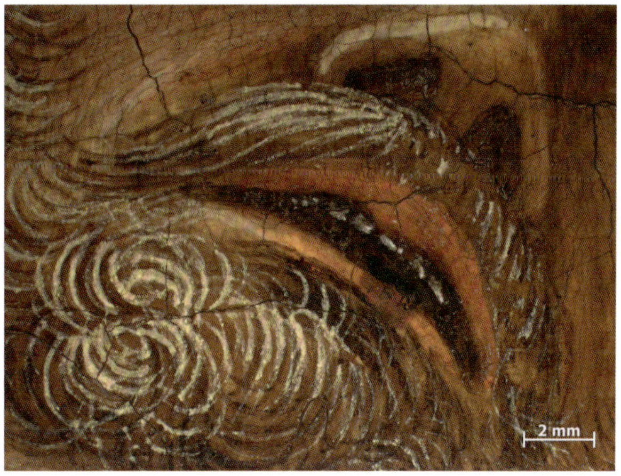

FIG. 31
ANDREA MANTEGNA, *The Agony in the Garden* (FIG. 125)
Photomicrograph of the mouth of a sleeping Apostle (Saint James?)

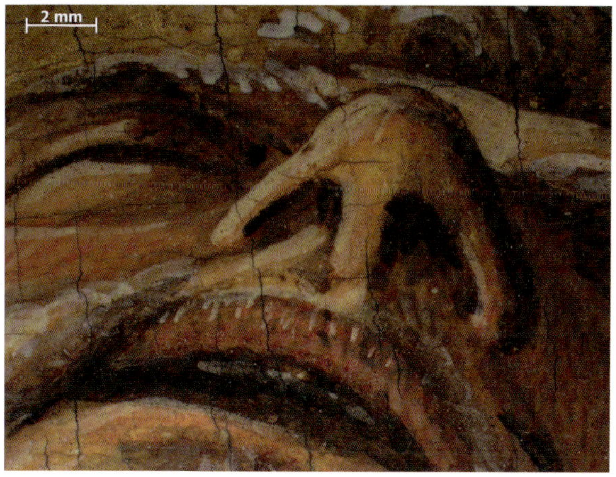

FIG. 32
GIOVANNI BELLINI, *The Agony in the Garden* (FIG. 126)
Photomicrograph of the mouth of Saint Peter

In both panels the fine hatched brushstrokes typical of modelling in egg tempera are clearly visible. A particular technique that works best with the egg medium is that of spattering to suggest the flecks of coloured stones and marble or small pebbles in the foregrounds of outdoor scenes. This was probably done by flicking the end of a stiff brush loaded with paint, resulting in small dots of colour, easily recognised under magnification by the craters formed by the collapse of air bubbles in the aerated egg-based paint (fig. 33). Mantegna can be described as a master of the technique (which must have involved the careful masking of the painted figures) and was to use it throughout his career. Bellini tried it out in the foreground of his *Agony in the Garden* (fig. 34), perhaps at the suggestion of his brother-in-law, but seems not to have used it again. The tiny pebbles in the background of *The Blood of the Redeemer* (fig. 192), also a tempera painting, were all dotted individually with the point of a brush.[8]

As well as the mordant gilding of the architectural details on Mantegna's panel, further gold decoration was applied in the form of powdered gold paint, also known as shell gold. The technique had been more widely used in manuscript painting but was only just coming into common use on panel paintings. Instead of painting the lines of a halo or pattern with an adhesive mordant, waiting for it to become almost dry and then laying the loose gold leaf over it, it was possible to work with the gold as if it were paint. Shell gold was applied in this way for the light that falls on the robes of the figure of Christ (fig. 35) – an effect now compromised by the darkened and damaged condition of the blue paint – and for the haloes of Christ and his sleeping disciples. Bellini took up the technique to beautiful effect for his figure of

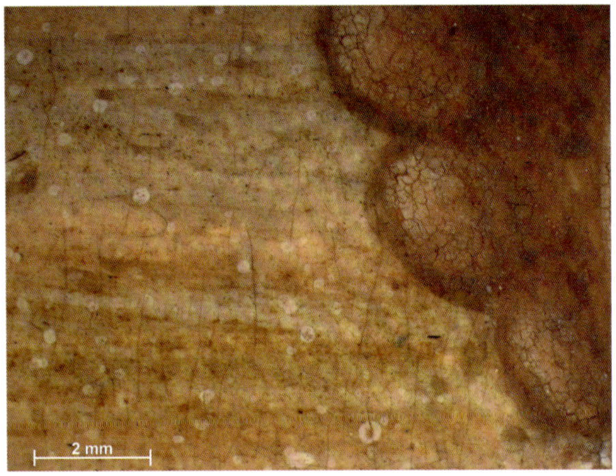

FIG. 33
ANDREA MANTEGNA, *The Agony in the Garden* (FIG. 125)
Photomicrograph showing spattered paint

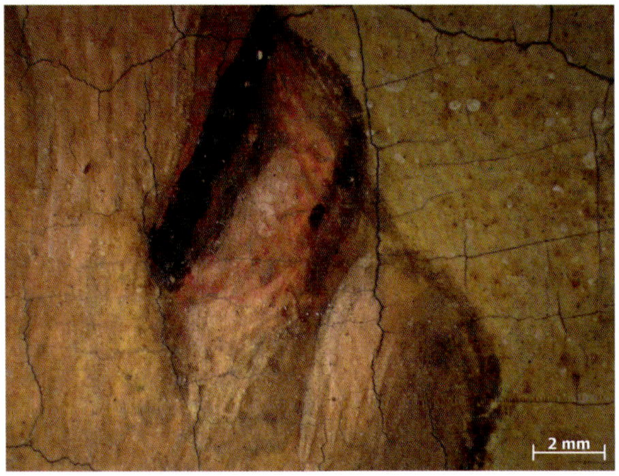

FIG. 34
GIOVANNI BELLINI, *The Agony in the Garden* (FIG. 126)
Photomicrograph of the mouth of Saint John

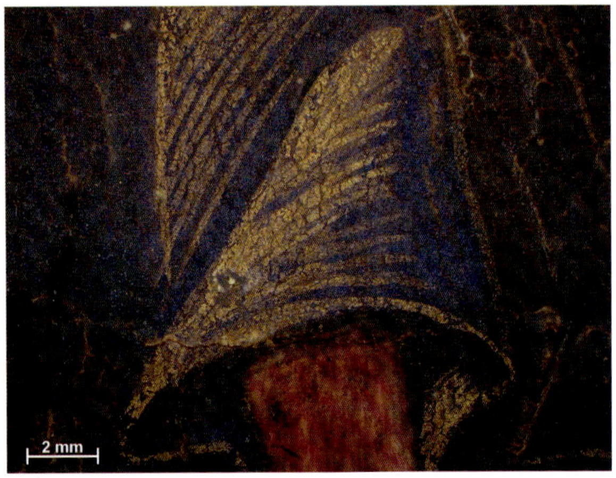

FIG. 35
ANDREA MANTEGNA, *The Agony in the Garden* (FIG. 125)
Photomicrograph of shell gold on Christ's robe

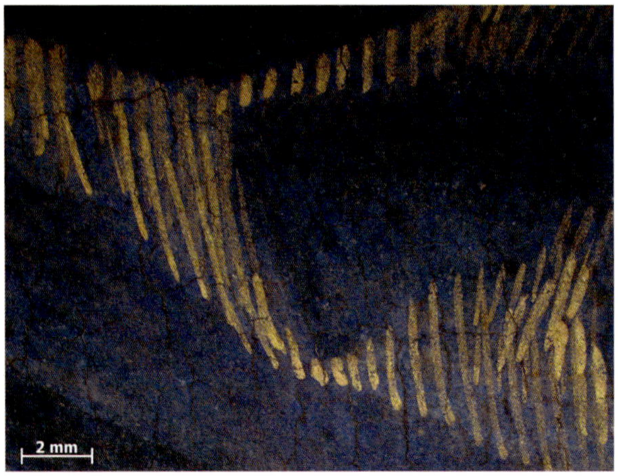

FIG. 36
GIOVANNI BELLINI, *The Agony in the Garden* (FIG. 126)
Photomicrograph of shell gold on Christ's robe

Christ (fig. 36) and more discreetly in the haloes of his disciples.

While Bellini's version of *The Agony in the Garden* was almost certainly painted within a few years of Mantegna's models, the same cannot be said of his second direct response to a painting by his brother-in-law, his version of the composition showing *The Presentation of Christ in the Temple* (fig. 132). It is generally agreed that Mantegna's canvas (fig. 128) was painted in the 1450s, either to celebrate his marriage to Nicolosia in 1453, or more probably to commemorate the birth of their son the following year. The painting has long been of interest to historians of painting technique as it is a rare example of an early canvas painting that has escaped structural alteration. Therefore it is still possible to see how the linen canvas was originally stretched with tacks that were hammered into the front face of the fixed wooden strainer (fig. 37). Smaller canvases were often stretched in this way in the fifteenth and early sixteenth centuries. In this instance the original strainer has survived, complete with the thin boards of spruce-wood set into it to support the canvas (fig. 38).[9] A wooden frame would then have been attached to the front face of the strainer, covering the tacking margin. A ridge of gesso covered with original paint can be seen around the perimeter of the painted image, which confirms that the frame mouldings were prepared with gesso and painted at the same time as the picture.

Examination of the painting by infrared reflectography and X-radiography (figs 39, 40, 41) has shown that the composition developed in a surprisingly ad hoc fashion, at least by Mantegna's normal highly organised standards. This may be connected with the likelihood that this was a private project, painted for family reasons.

FIG. 37
ANDREA MANTEGNA
The Presentation of Christ in the Temple (FIG. 128) showing the tacking margins

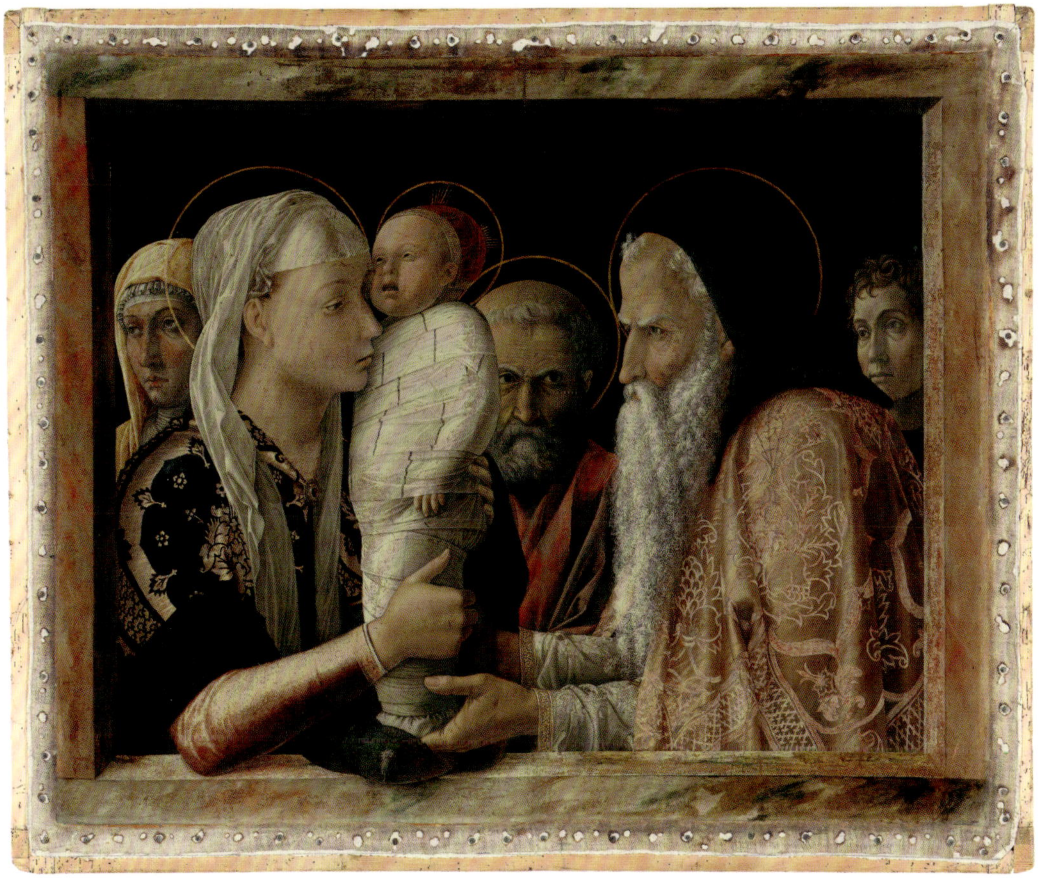

FIG. 38
ANDREA MANTEGNA, reverse of *The Presentation of Christ in the Temple* (FIG. 128) with original strainer and backing boards

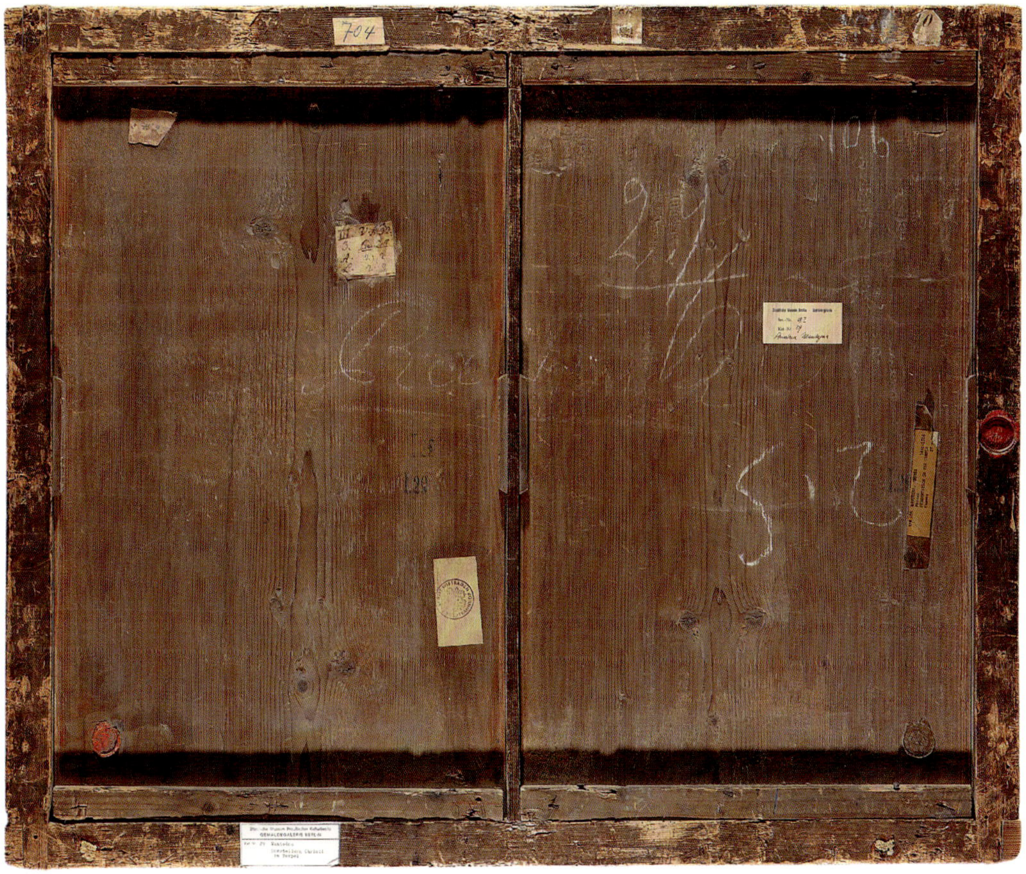

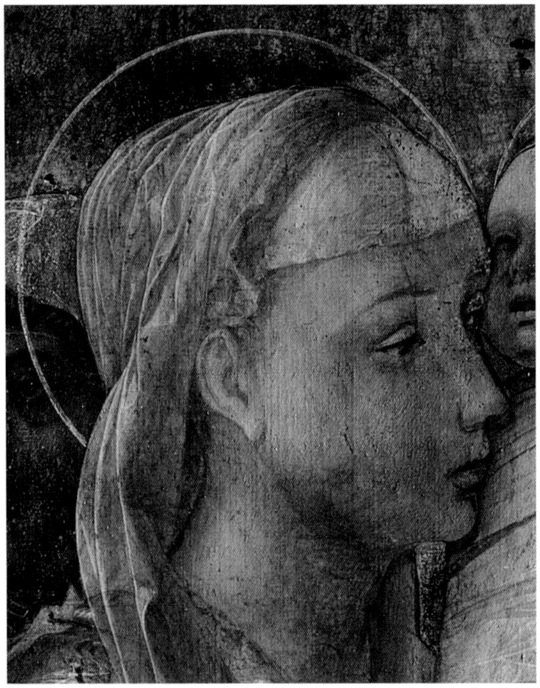

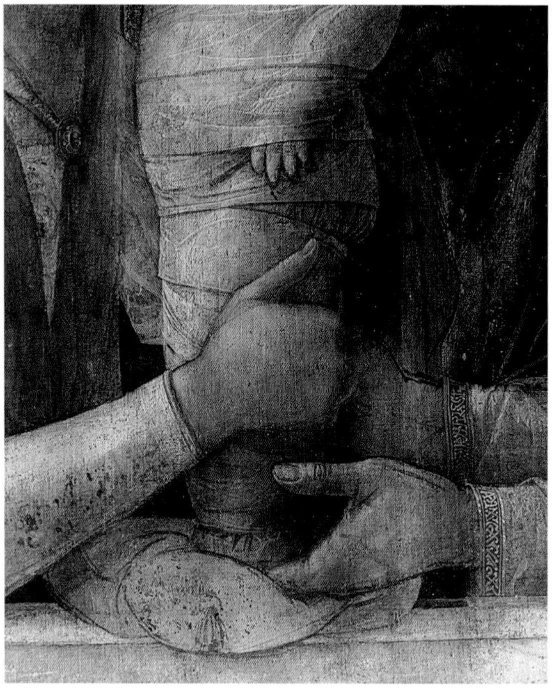

FIGS 39, 40
ANDREA MANTEGNA,
The Presentation of Christ in the Temple (FIG. 128)
Details of infrared reflectogram

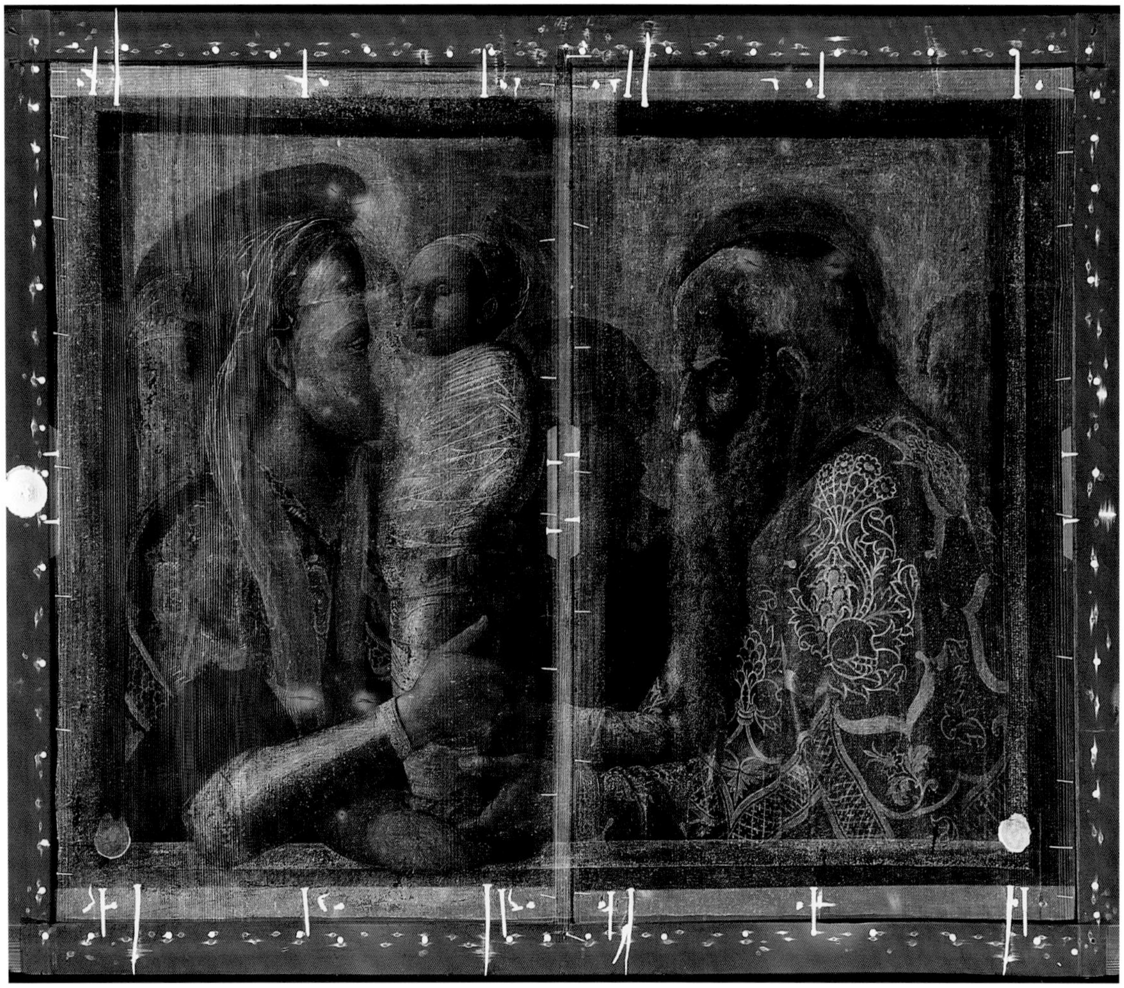

FIG. 41
ANDREA MANTEGNA,
The Presentation of Christ in the Temple (FIG. 128)
X-radiograph

The underdrawing that can be detected is characteristic in that it mainly consists of outlines, drawn with a brush and a liquid black paint or ink, but the lines are unusually broad and free. The sense of improvisation is confirmed by the Virgin's profile, for example, which seems to have first been sketched much further to the left and higher up. Mantegna then began to block in the background with a light-coloured underpaint. This appears to be a greyish colour, containing sufficient lead white to register clearly in the X-radiograph (fig. 41). The X-ray image confirms that an area was reserved for the Virgin's head, complete with halo, well to the left of her present position. The only other heads to be reserved were those of the Christ Child and Simeon, which seems to have been a little higher. The heads of Joseph, and, more importantly, those taken to represent Mantegna and Nicolosia, appear to have been afterthoughts, and indeed the head of the latter could only be fitted in by adjusting the Virgin's position. The infrared image confirms that the Virgin's profile was redrawn in its present position. Another significant change was to Simeon, originally painted wearing a kippah and with a high stiff collar, all now covered by a dark blueish shawl.[10]

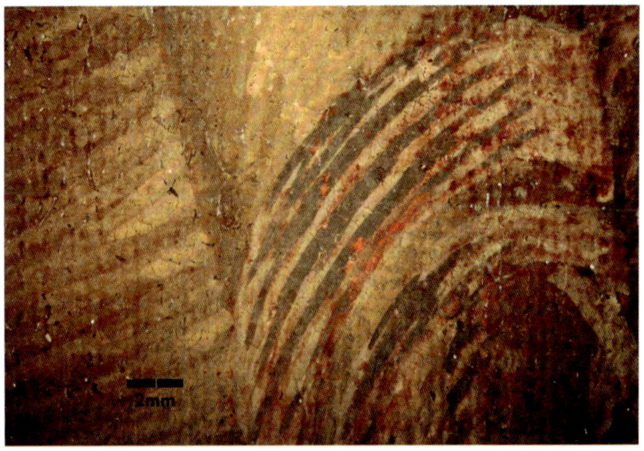

FIG. 42
ANDREA MANTEGNA,
The Presentation of Christ in the Temple (FIG. 128)
Photomicrograph of darkened vermilion on Simeon's robe

This shawl was almost certainly originally brighter in colour as indeed were almost all the draperies in this much-altered painting. The malachite of the green lining to the Virgin's cloak has darkened as has the pattern on her cloth of gold, which must once have been a rich azurite blue. The red pigments have fared even worse: the translucent red lakes have faded, reducing the colour of her sleeve to a pale pink, and the bright red vermilion pigment has developed surface blackening so that Joseph's robes are now a patchy combination of red and purplish grey. The red pattern on Simeon's robe has been affected by both fading and abrasion of the red lakes (in places applied over a white underlayer to enhance their translucency) and by blackening of the vermilion highlights (fig. 42). Originally it must have been as splendid as the very similar textile worn by the figure of Saint Gregory in the right panel of the *San Zeno Altarpiece* (fig. 252). The background, which now appears to be black, was originally a rich deep blue, containing mainly azurite. It is also obscured by a later overpaint and so the gold haloes are all false.[11] The appearance of this once brilliant painting is further muted by layers of discoloured varnish and dirt.

The dull greyish surface is one reason why the Berlin *Presentation* has always been assumed to be an example of a canvas painted using a medium of glue size rather than egg tempera.[12] Mantegna did indeed use this technique, but recent research has shown that several of the paintings previously described as being in this medium were actually painted using the egg medium.[13] This is also the case with the *Presentation* where egg has been identified.[14]

Furthermore, it may be significant that the relatively small group of canvas paintings to have been established (mostly through analysis) as having been painted in glue size are all generally dated to the later part of his career. In this exhibition they include the two so-called 'monochromes' in the National Gallery (figs 240, 241),

FIG. 43
ANDREA MANTEGNA,
Samson and Delilah
(FIG. 238)
Photomicrograph of grapes

FIG. 44
ANDREA MANTEGNA,
detail from *Samson and Delilah*
(FIG. 238)

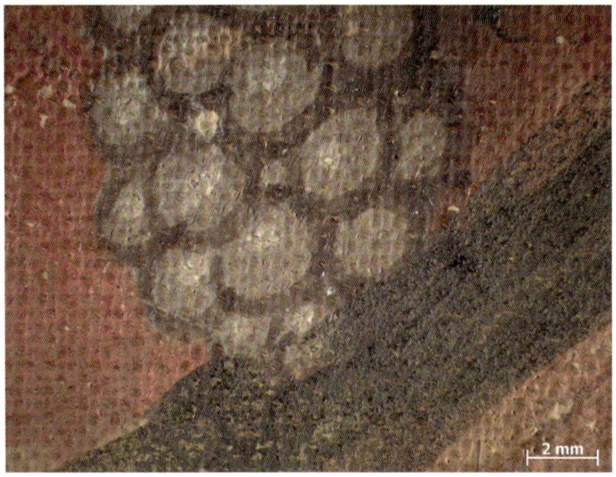

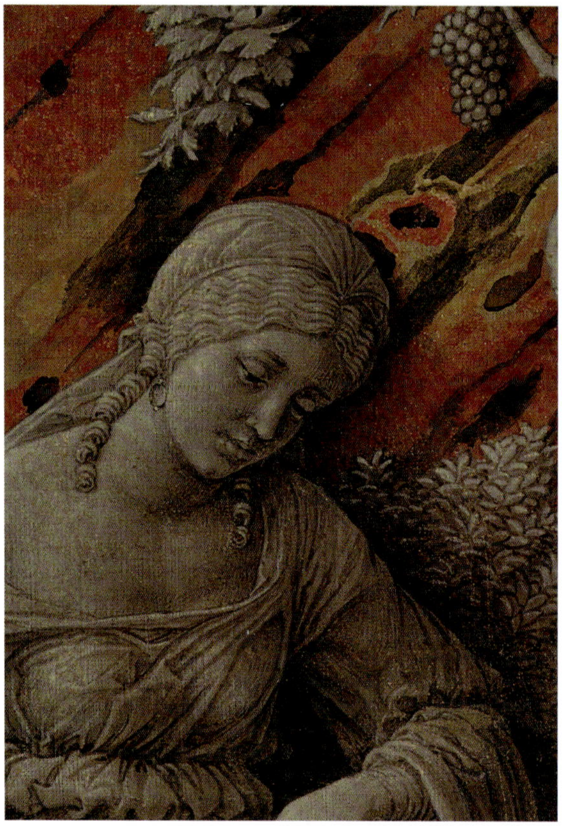

The Adoration of the Magi (fig. 136) and probably the small canvas painting of *The Virgin and Child* in Berlin (fig. 188) – sometimes dated early but its technique might suggest otherwise. It seems likely, therefore, that in common with the *Presentation*, further early canvases such as the *Saint Mark* in Frankfurt (fig. 77) are conventional tempera paintings and not painted in other media as has previously been stated.[15]

Mantegna's glue-size paintings have a distinctive surface appearance, particularly when viewed under magnification (fig. 43). For the smaller ones such as *Samson and Delilah* (fig. 238) he chose linen with an exceptionally fine weave (sometimes stated in the past to have been silk), which he may have rendered even smoother by burnishing.[16] The technique of painting in glue size is simple and direct. The nature of the glue medium means that when the paint has dried the pigments appear clear and bright (close to their appearance when seen as a dry powder) and the surface is matt. Unlike egg tempera, in which the paint begins to harden the moment that the water content has evaporated, glue-based paints remain resoluble. Therefore any superimposed brushstrokes have to be made with the lightest of touches.[17] Mantegna's glue-size technique, as exemplified by *Samson and Delilah* (fig. 44), has much in common with his coloured drawings on paper, for instance the *Virtus Combusta* (fig. 229).

If Mantegna only began to work in the medium relatively late in his career, it is possible that he was inspired by the example of his Venetian relations. Techniques of painting on canvas using a glue medium were common in Northern Europe. The most significant surviving example of such a work from the fifteenth century is the polyptych of which *The Entombment* in the National Gallery is part. This was painted in Louvain by Dirk Bouts in the 1450s and probably sent immediately to Venice.[18] In 1465 Gentile Bellini adopted the technique for the canvas banner showing *The Blessed Lorenzo Giustiniani*, now in the Accademia, Venice.[19] Mantegna may well have seen the Bouts altarpiece on visits to Venice, but it was Giovanni who was to learn the most from its example. Many of the elements that make his landscape in *The Agony in the Garden* so different from Mantegna's equivalent landscapes can be attributed to the careful study of this canvas polyptych.

The import of paintings from across the Alps to Venice and the immediate mainland, and also the increasing presence of Northern artists and craftsmen

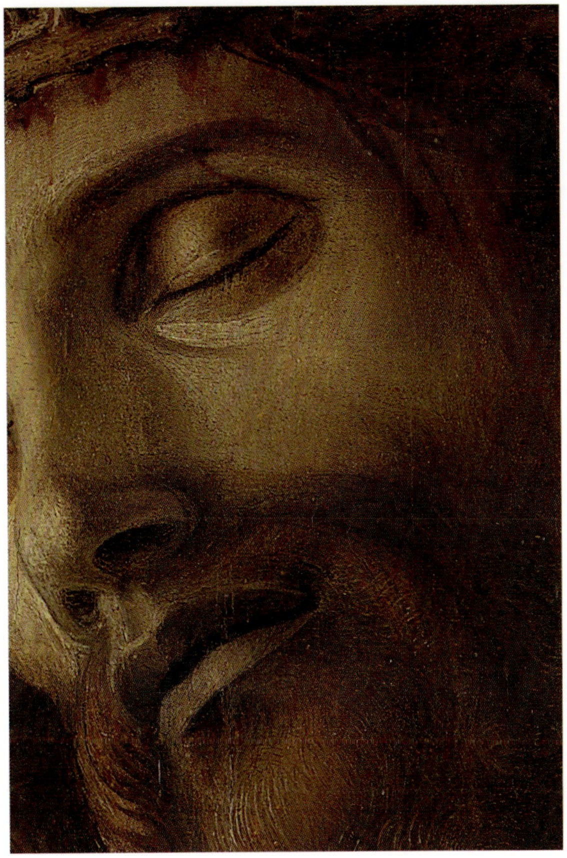

FIG. 45
GIOVANNI BELLINI, detail from *The Dead Christ supported by Two Angels* (FIG. 151)

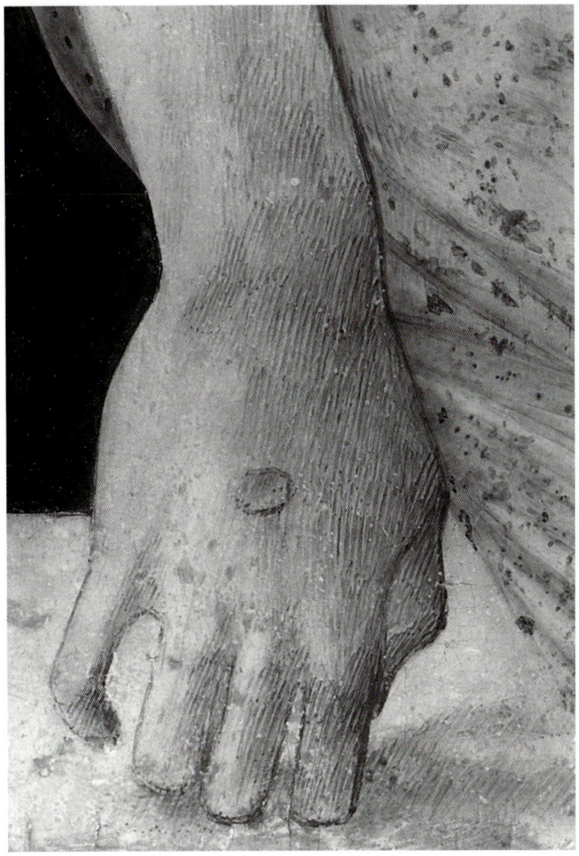

FIG. 46
GIOVANNI BELLINI, *The Dead Christ supported by Two Angels* (FIG. 151)
Detail of infrared reflectogram showing Christ's right hand

in the region, had a radical effect on Giovanni's panel painting technique. He was among the first Italian painters to abandon the tradition of painting in egg tempera for the advantages of working in oil. Drying oils were not unfamiliar materials in the workshops of earlier painters but the idea of using them as the medium for panel painting does seem to have been triggered by the astonishing effects that were to be seen in works arriving in Italy from the great Netherlandish painters of the early and mid-fifteenth century.

Difficulties in dating Bellini's earlier production mean that it is impossible to determine exactly when he began work in oil, but analysis of the medium of the National Gallery *Dead Christ supported by Two Angels* (fig. 151), usually dated to about 1465–70, confirms that it is painted in oil. This was before the arrival in Venice of Antonello da Messina, who is traditionally credited with introducing oil painting to that city. The *Dead Christ* is a much damaged painting, considerably altered by time, but it is evident that Bellini had already discovered the potential of the oil medium for rapid and direct execution of passages of painting. The boldness and economy of the painting of Christ's proper left eye (the other consists entirely of restoration) is remarkable (fig. 45). The broad handling of the highlight beneath it contrasts with the delicate touches used to pick out the hairs of his beard. Unfortunately this direct technique may have contributed to the drying defects which have affected the surface of the painting, causing wrinkling and wide drying cracks even in light colours and not just the areas of black where poor drying is more common. The latter problem may be connected with his choice of walnut oil (which tends not to dry as well as linseed) but he perhaps also had difficulty in determining the correct proportion of oil to pigment. This might be put down to inexperience but similar drying defects appear in many later works as well.[20]

Underlying the confident painting of *The Dead Christ supported by Two Angels* is a highly worked up underdrawing (fig. 46) of the type found consistently on most of Bellini's panel paintings,[21] the exceptions being mainly

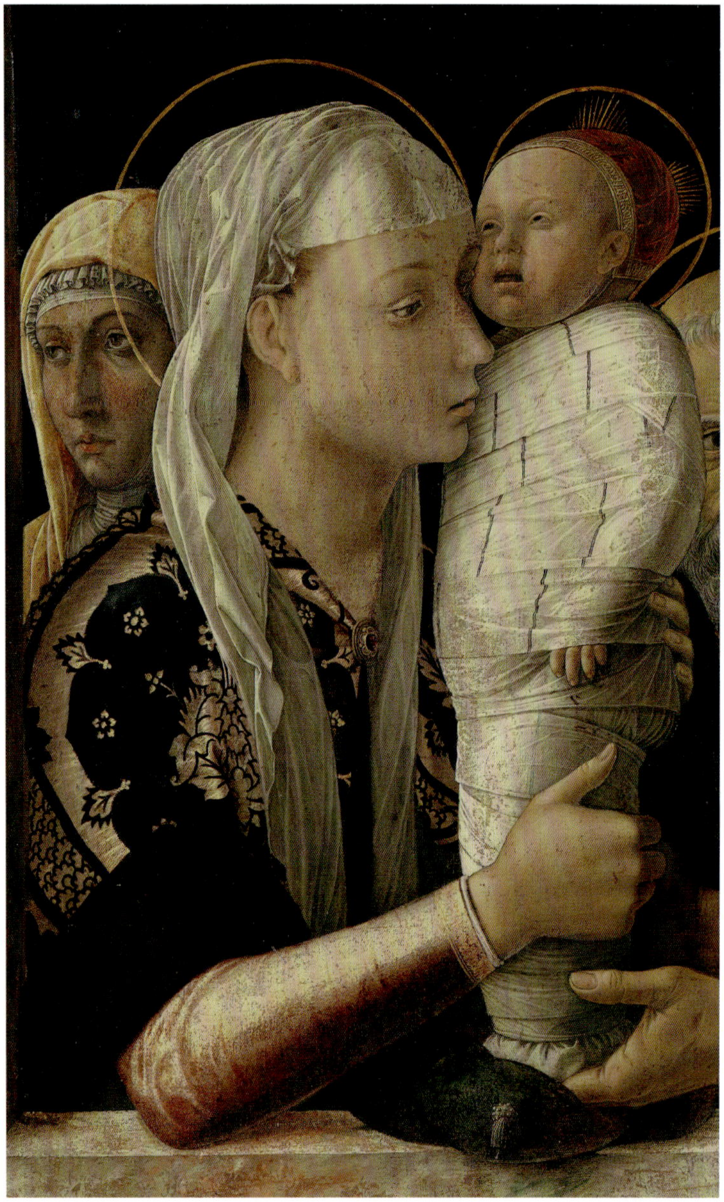

FIG. 47
ANDREA MANTEGNA, detail from *The Presentation of Christ in the Temple* (FIG. 128)

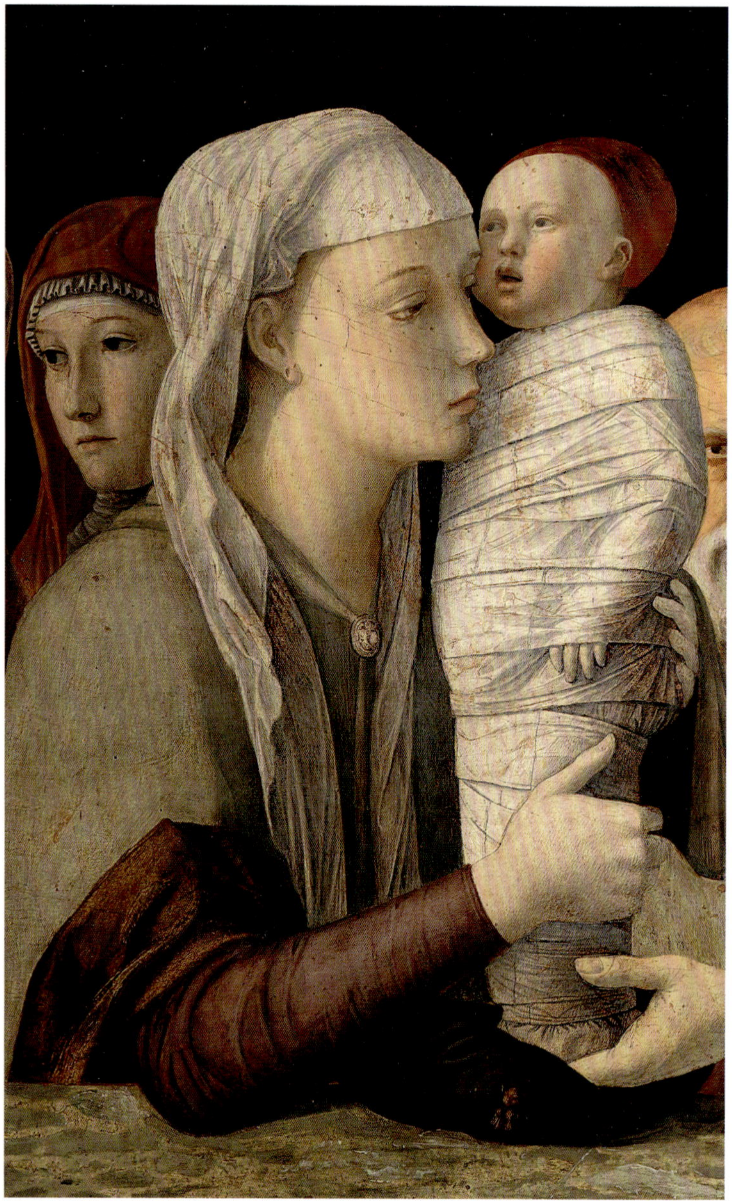

FIG. 48
GIOVANNI BELLINI, detail from *The Presentation of Christ in the Temple* (FIG. 132)

the earliest and latest works and those produced by his ever-growing workshop where replicas and variations on his designs were usually generated by means of tracings and pounced cartoons.[22] When creating a new composition Bellini drew on the gesso with a liquid black paint or ink and a fine brush, modelling his figures and draperies with fine hatched strokes and paying particular attention to the fall of light across the forms. Such underdrawings might be thought to be connected with his adoption of oil paint but they also occur in some of his tempera paintings, most strikingly the *Dead Christ* in the Brera (fig. 199).[23] Mantegna, however, only included the occasional passage of shading in his underdrawings. Such is the extent of the underdrawing discovered in some of Bellini's works that some scholars have taken *The Lamentation over the Dead Christ* (fig. 161) to be an underdrawing that was never painted. However, the subtle tonal differentiation between the drawing of figures in the foreground and those towards the rear of the group and other technical features indicate that the work is a finished form of grisaille.[24]

By the time Bellini came to paint his version of *The Presentation of Christ in the Temple* (fig. 48) these detailed underdrawings were an established part of his

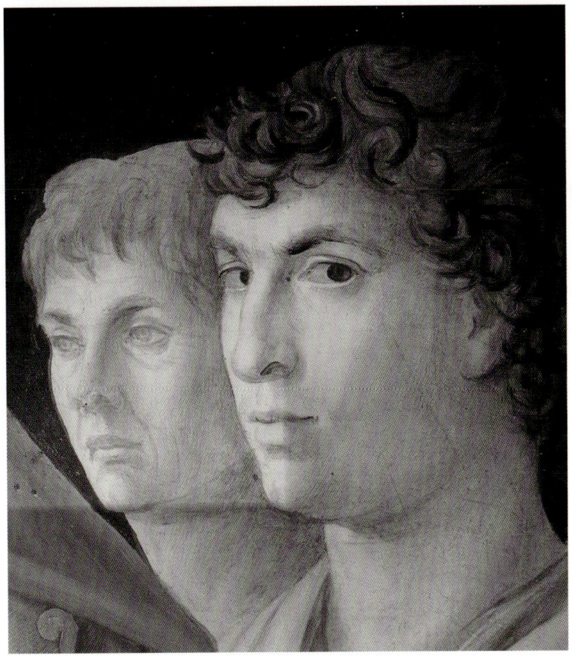

FIG. 49
GIOVANNI BELLINI, *The Presentation of Christ in the Temple* (FIG. 132)
Detail of infrared reflectogram

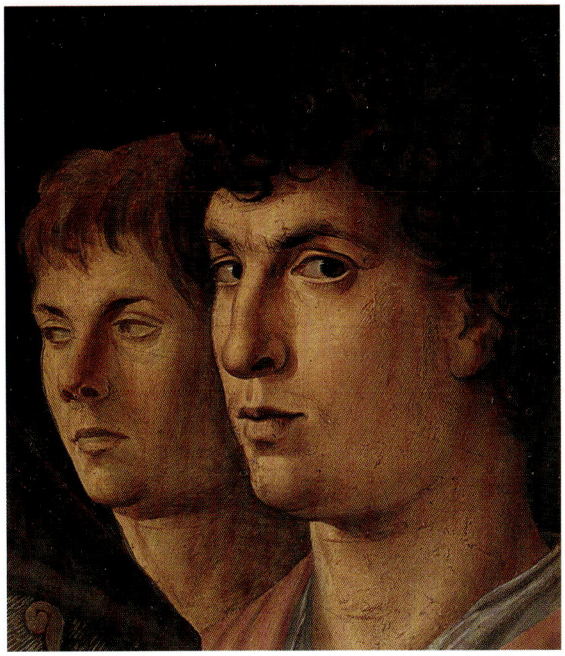

FIG. 50
GIOVANNI BELLINI, detail from *The Presentation of Christ in the Temple* (FIG. 132)

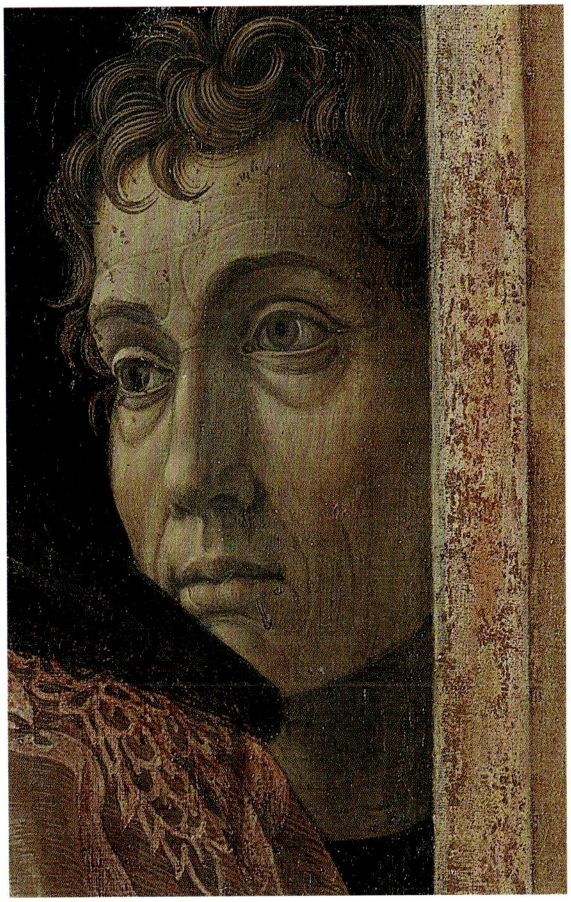

FIG. 51
ANDREA MANTEGNA, detail from *The Presentation of Christ in the Temple* (FIG. 128)

technique and he was a confident user of the oil medium. The occasion that called for the making of this painting must therefore have been at least 20 years after the production of Mantegna's original design. Bellini's transcription (for it is not a copy) was painted on panel, not canvas. It was considerably wider, necessitating the addition of two figures, and the fictive frame abandoned in favour of the parapet employed to set back his Madonnas and half-length devotional figures. The discovery of so many alterations to Mantegna's canvas means that Bellini's version cannot be derived from a shared cartoon. Instead he must have had access to a tracing, either sent by Mantegna or that he made himself, depending on the whereabouts of the canvas. By overlaying a tracing made from the Berlin painting over the Venice panel it has been possible to confirm that this was the process.[25] The figures of the Virgin and Child align perfectly (figs 47, 48), while the woman taken to represent Nicolosia also fits if the tracing is shifted slightly – Bellini's tracing must have slipped a little during the transfer process. The 'Mantegna' head (fig. 51) can only be made to fit for some of the features by a slight rotation of the tracing but it is clear that Bellini has converted the first traced outlines into the head of someone else. The original nose visible in the underdrawing (fig. 49) matches that in Mantegna's version, but was changed at the painting stage to a broader, more upturned nose, and the features softened into those of a younger man (fig. 50). Curiously the detailed shaded underdrawing seems still to follow the Mantegna model, including the nose, the deep cheek creases and the direction of the gaze. The figure on the far right was also underdrawn with hatched shading. There is nothing to indicate that this head is extensively overpainted as has recently been suggested[26] and even the heavy black appearance of his curly hair in infrared is likely to be the result of the use of a great deal of black pigment in the paint rather than a later restorer's intervention.

The difference in the handling of the paint between Mantegna's and Bellini's versions is striking, especially in the male heads. The fluidity of Bellini's oil technique and the soft, suggestive depiction of their features seem almost to be a critical commentary on the meticulous and uniformly crisp tempera of his brother-in-law (figs 52, 53). Only in the painting of the Virgin and Child does Bellini try to imitate more closely his model. They too appear to have been painted in oil but damage to the paint surface and an increase in transparency means that some of the shaded underdrawing is now showing through, giving the impression of the hatched brushwork of tempera. Bellini's chosen palette for the *Presentation* is also very different, replacing the once brilliant local colours of Mantegna's version with a more muted range of red, browns and purples. The expensive lapis that appears in so many of his altarpieces and luxury Madonnas for rich patrons is absent. This may also be connected with the peculiar circumstances of this commission, which have yet to be fully explained.

That Bellini was not too proud to make paintings based on designs by his brother-in-law is confirmed by the painted version of *The Descent of Christ into Limbo* (fig. 145). Recent examination has shown that this was painted over a detailed copy drawn on vellum[27] of Mantegna's highly detailed study of the subject usually dated to 1468 (fig. 143). The character of the drawing visible through the thin paint film – probably in iron gall ink since it disappears when imaged in infrared – is unlike Bellini's own drawing or underdrawing style. The outlines are precise and the hatched shading is regular and evenly spaced, with something of the character of an engraving. It seems therefore, that a careful copy was made of Mantegna's drawing, perhaps by a member of his workshop, and was sent to Venice as a basis for Bellini to make his painting. This he did, employing his now standard oil technique, creating his own rock formations in the upper part where Mantegna's design terminated. The fact that these resemble rock structures in paintings usually dated to the late 1470s or even early 1480s suggests that again Bellini's painted version was made long after Mantegna's original invention.

In the 1470s Mantegna's appointment as painter to the Gonzaga court had taken him back to his early experience as a fresco painter but also led to a new emphasis on the need for portability in his production. The technique he used for the murals in the celebrated Camera Picta appears to be essentially *buon fresco* but with extensive additions carried out *a secco*. The ordering in 1471 by Ludovico III Gonzaga of a large amount of walnut oil 'for the work on that room of ours' might suggest that some secco work was carried out in oil, which would not be unusual in Northern Italy, but there are also other purposes to which the oil might have been put, not necessarily directly linked with Mantegna's painted parts of the decoration. Certainly Mantegna seems to have had little interest in following the example of his brother-in-law in abandoning his favoured egg tempera for oil when working on panel.[28] In the later part of his career he was still able to produce tempera

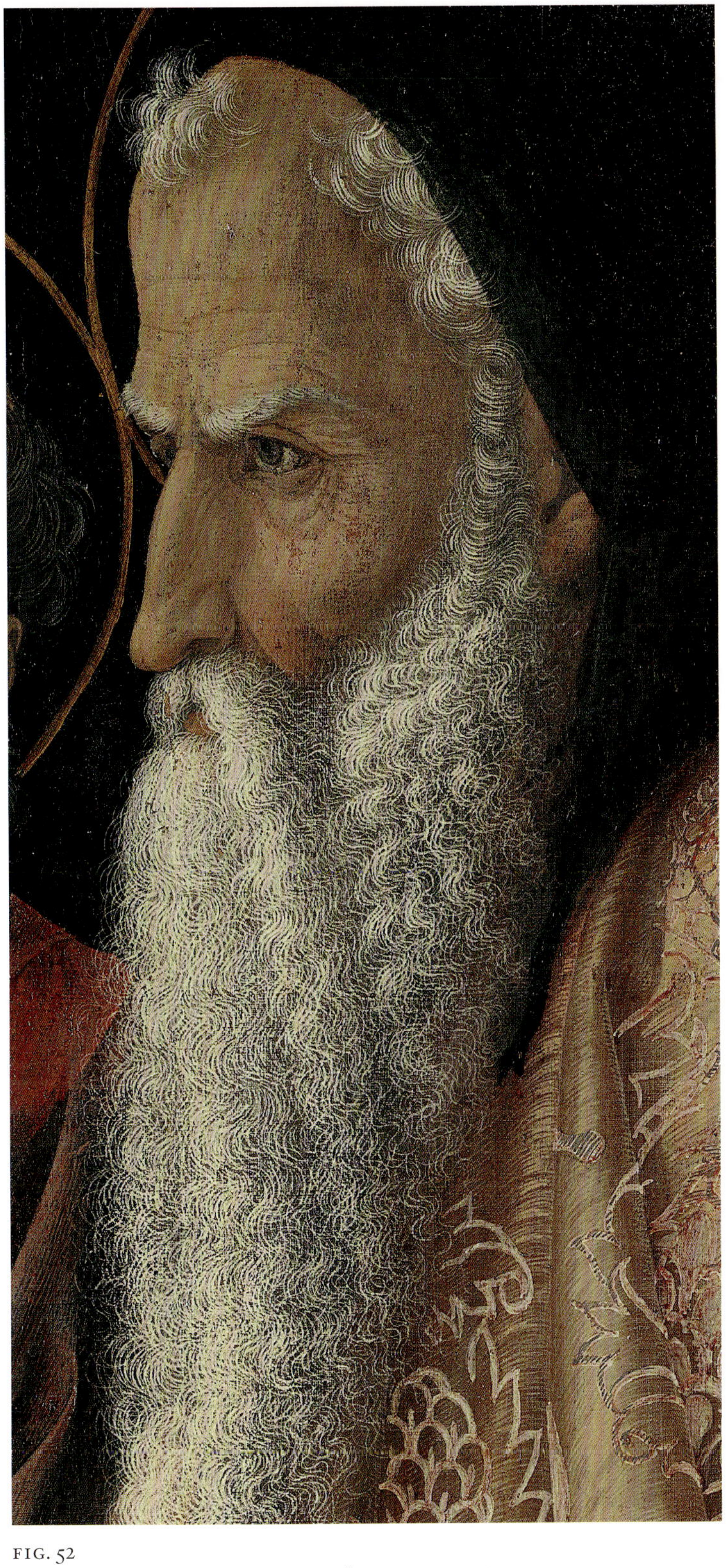

FIG. 52
ANDREA MANTEGNA, detail from *The Presentation of Christ in the Temple* (FIG. 128)

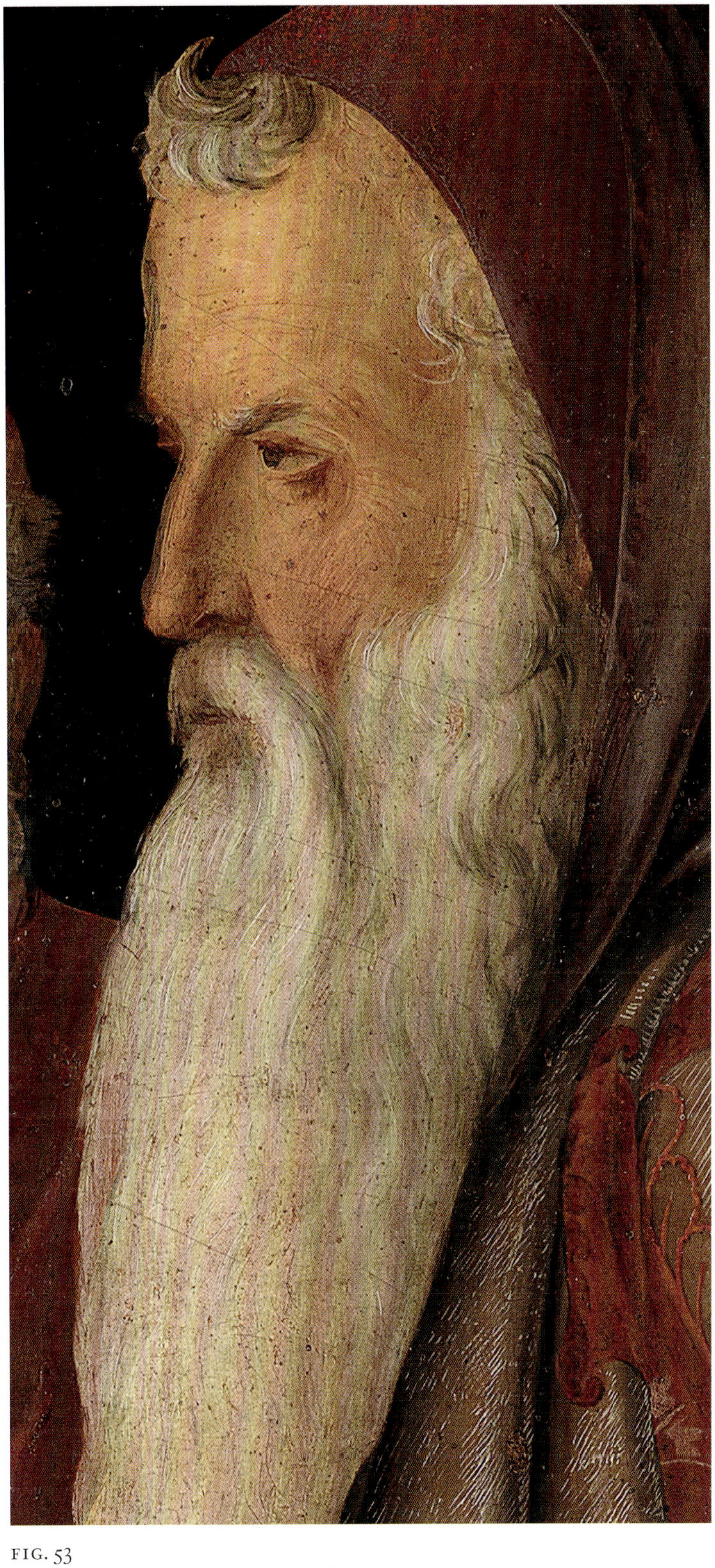

FIG. 53
GIOVANNI BELLINI, detail from *The Presentation of Christ in the Temple* (FIG. 132)

FIG. 54
ANDREA MANTEGNA,
detail from *The Introduction of the Cult of Cybele at Rome*
(FIG. 245)

paintings of a level of detail and technical refinement that matched those of the 1450s and 1460s, displaying an undiminished virtuosity in the execution of the exceptionally well-preserved Copenhagen *Dead Christ supported by Two Angels* (fig. 150),[29] or the rendering of the watered silk of the Virgin's mantle in the Dresden *Holy Family* (fig. 190), with highlights of powdered silver over the deep blue. This has survived in remarkably untarnished condition.[30]

The Virgin's red dress in the small altarpiece in the National Gallery of *The Virgin and Child with the Magdalen and Saint John the Baptist* (fig. 173) is decorated in a similar way, but this time using gold over the pink – the original effect is likely to be diminished by fading of the red lake. This painting is on a canvas support, consisting of a twill-weave linen of the type noted on many of Mantegna's paintings. The advantage of canvas was its lightness and portability; as Mantegna himself observed, 'it can be wrapped round a rod' for transport.[31] In his role as painter to the Mantuan court, he was increasingly expected to produce works, including altarpieces, that were to be sent out of the city for political reasons.[32] Even within the Ducal Palace, however, canvas was a logical choice for decorative paintings that functioned in a similar way to tapestries such as the *Triumphs of Caesar*, now so damaged and altered perhaps in part because of the way in which they were moved around. Their poor condition has led to the belief that they were painted in glue size, but analysis of samples has shown that they are in fact egg tempera paintings.[33]

Not only did canvas displace panel for Mantegna's altarpieces but it was also chosen for the paintings destined for Isabella d'Este's *studiolo*, a type of room that would previously have been decorated with panel paintings. The lightweight support was also an advantage for Isabella's ambition to obtain works by other celebrated painters. Mantegna's canvases from the *studiolo* now in the Louvre, the *Parnassus* (fig. 57) and *Minerva expelling the Vices from the Garden of Virtue* (fig. 225) are essentially egg tempera paintings but we know that they were varnished, because of the efforts of the instrument-maker Lorenzo da Pavia to obtain the best varnish from Venice for Mantegna, first for the *Parnassus* in 1497 and subsequently for the *Minerva* in 1502.[34] Earlier references in documents to varnishing by Mantegna indicate that this was his practice for most paintings and that, however altered their current appearance, they were all once brilliantly coloured with a rich saturated surface.

The exceptions were those canvases painted with glue size. In these instances Mantegna evidently sought a matt, unreflective finish closer to that of fresco. This surface was particularly appropriate for the imitations of sculpted reliefs that he produced later in his career.

For *The Introduction of the Cult of Cybele at Rome* (fig. 245) the base colour was a warm mid-grey, applied with broad brushstrokes over a layer of gesso that was sufficiently substantial to fill in much of the texture of the canvas weave.[35] The colours for the marbling were brushed on fluidly, often leaving patches of the base colour exposed, but the sculpted figures and architecture were all painted with fine outlines and hatched strokes made with the point of the brush and working entirely with black and white paints as if it were an enormous drawing on paper (fig. 54). The impression of a warmer, brownish colour on some figures, notably the supplicant Claudia Quinta, is actually where the colour of the canvas has become exposed as a result of damage to the fragile paint surface. The canvas was one of a set of four, commissioned in 1505 by Francesco Cornaro for his Venice palace, where it was to be set into a room in imitation of a sculpted frieze. It was evidently placed to the left of the slope of a chimney as the lower right corner was only made up to a rectangle at a much later date

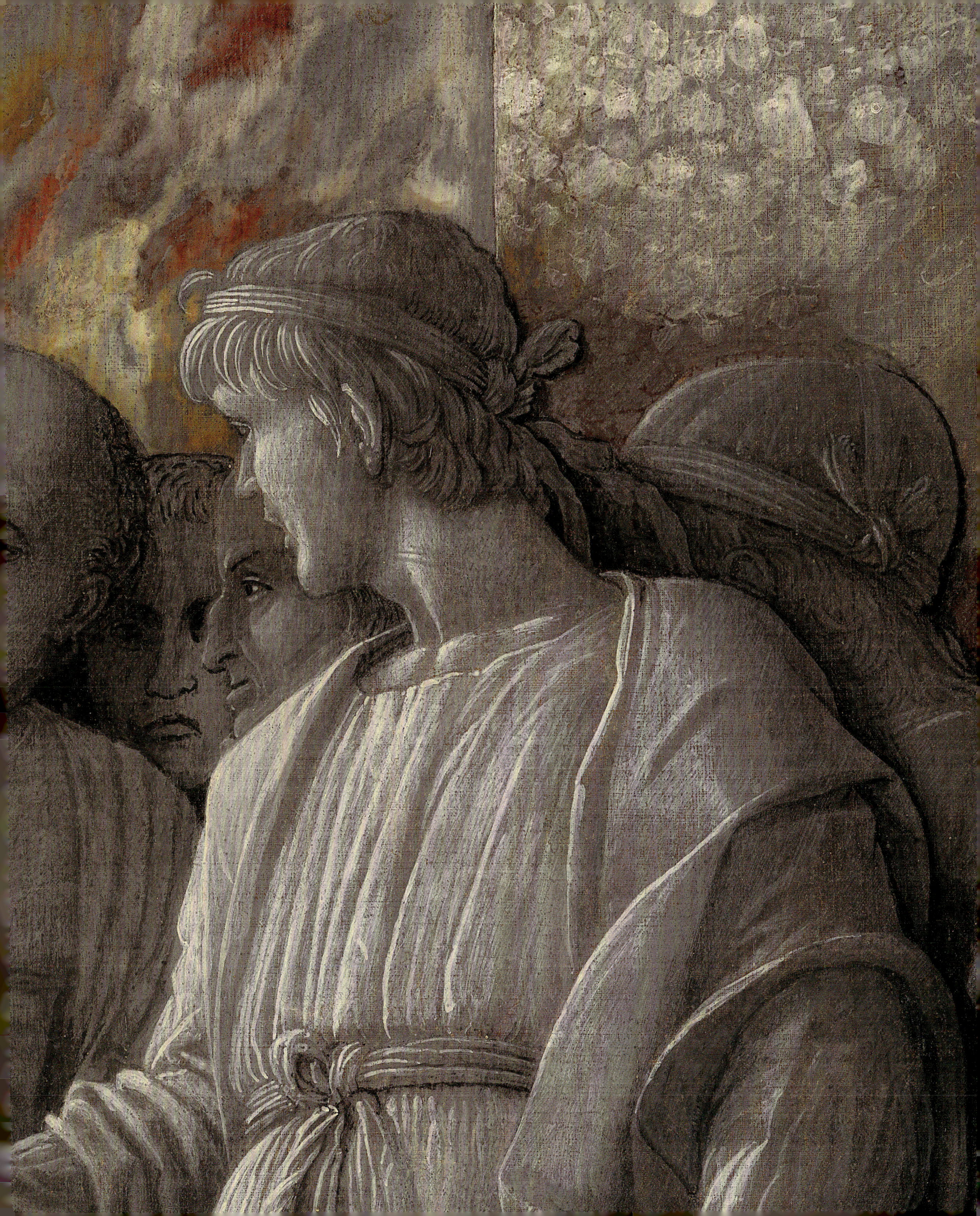

FIG. 55
GIOVANNI BELLINI,
detail from *The Continence of Publius Cornelius Scipio*
(FIG. 246)

using a piece of canvas that appears to have been cut from another part of the room decoration.

On Mantegna's death in September 1506 a canvas from the series showing 'Publius Cornelius' was, according to his son, Ludovico, still in his Mantua studio. This was probably the completed National Gallery canvas that had not yet been dispatched to Venice, but it was also the subject of the canvas that was eventually painted by Giovanni Bellini (fig. 246). The weave of Bellini's canvas and the spacing of the tack holes are very similar to those of Mantegna's completed work. If all the canvases had been prepared in advance so that they fitted this specific site, then any unpainted ones may have been sent back to Venice for completion by Bellini. If so, he seems to have started over again with a new design and using his own technique. From 1479 onwards he had been engaged, with his workshop, in the production of paintings on canvas on a large scale for the decoration of Sala del Gran Consiglio in the Ducal Palace. These were destroyed in the fire of 1577, but some idea of his likely technique can be gained from surviving canvas paintings such as the *Votive Picture of Doge Agostino Barbarigo* painted in 1488 (San Pietro Martire, Murano). This was much the same as for his panels, with a gesso ground and using an oil medium, but the rougher and more absorbent surface of the canvas allowed him to work with thicker, more opaque paints, often covering the surface with a single layer of paint.[36]

In bringing this experience to his completion of the Cornaro palace canvases, Bellini completely disregarded the matt surfaces and precise application of his late brother-in-law. Instead he painted his relief in oil, the contours and internal modelling of the figures softened by the blending of the white and grey paints into one another while still wet (fig. 55). Details were also mostly worked wet-in-wet so that they are suggested but remain indistinct. Black paint was used very sparingly, for example the broad final touches to the mouth of the bearded figure wearing a curious domed helmet, and to the background around him. More often relief was achieved by bold highlights of lead white, the stiff paint forming a slight impasto.

By the time of Mantegna's death, therefore, Bellini's technique had evolved in new directions, suited to his very different artistic personality and interests. With his adaptability and openness to new sources, he continued to change as a painter.[37] Despite his great age, in his last works such as *The Feast of the Gods* (fig. 226) and *The Drunkenness of Noah* (fig. 247) he showed how he could both inspire and absorb the innovations of a new generation of painters, a generation that could not have existed without his example.

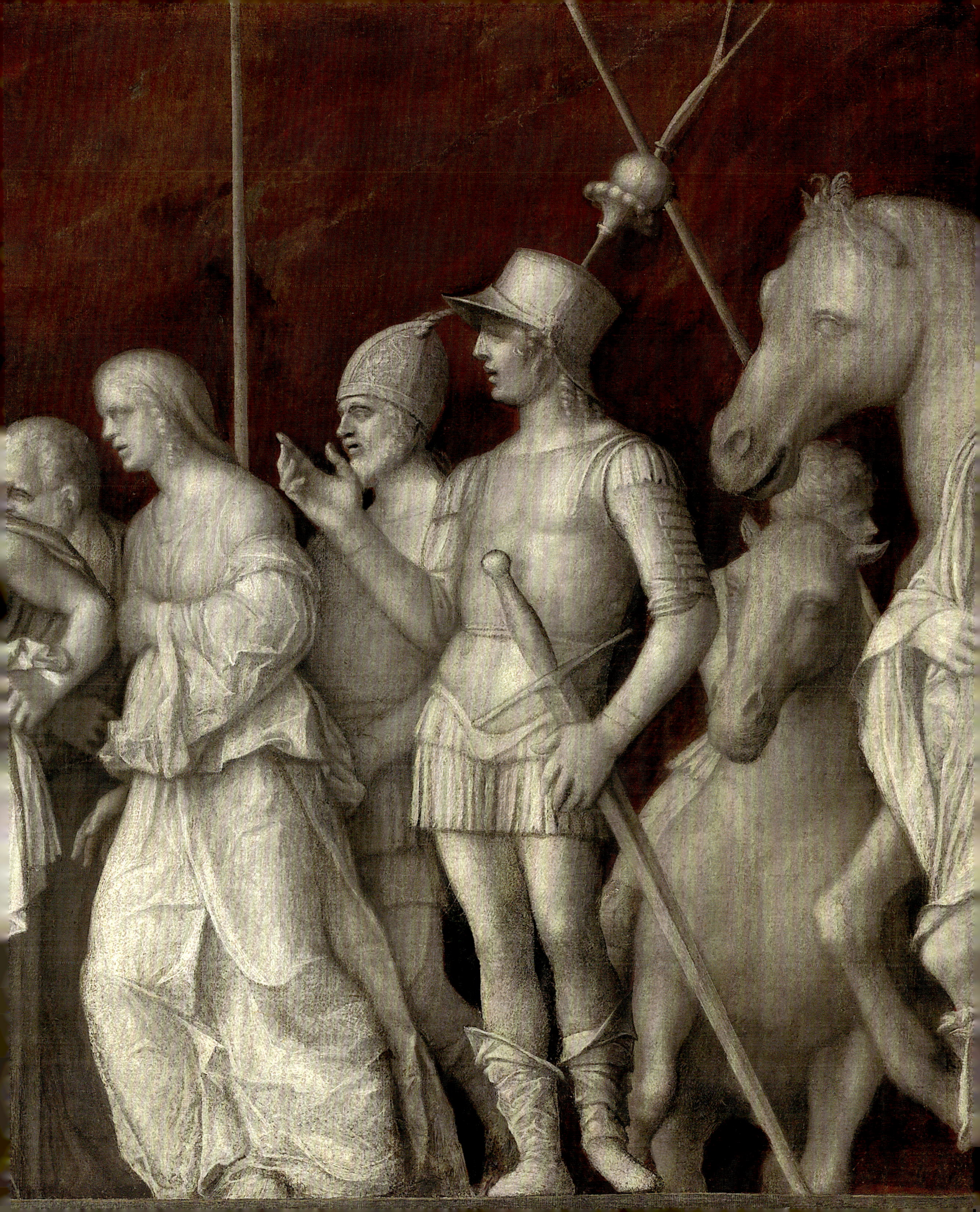

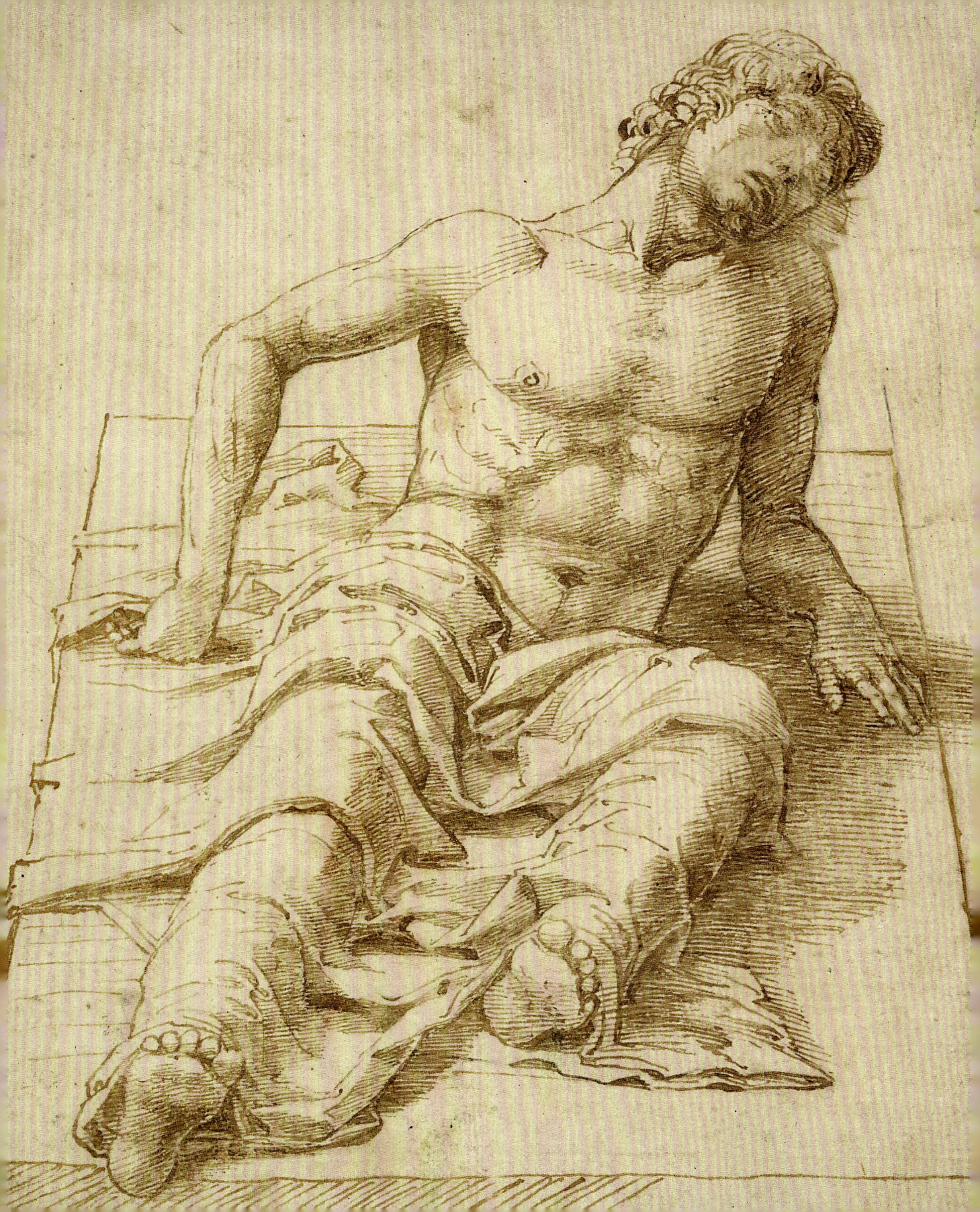

V

Drawing Conclusions: The Graphic Work of Mantegna and Bellini

SARAH VOWLES AND DAGMAR KORBACHER

IN 1502, THE ASTROLOGER CAMILLO LUNARDI listed the greatest artists of the day in *The Mirror of Stones* (*Speculum lapidum*). Giovanni Bellini was praised for his abilities with the brush, but Lunardi's greatest admiration was reserved for Andrea Mantegna, 'who not only surpassed all with the brush, but also with the pen and charcoal in the wink of an eye draws true images... so that they almost seem to move'.[1] Fifty years later, Giorgio Vasari commended Mantegna for his ingenious invention, a quality that for Vasari was expressed through the drawn line, whereas Bellini was noted for his 'beautiful colouring'.[2] These accounts have shaped most subsequent discussion of Mantegna and Bellini as exemplars of different painterly traditions, claiming that Mantegna was indivisibly wedded to graphic expression, while Bellini was a painter of colour and atmosphere, for whom drawing held little appeal. This is, unsurprisingly, a great oversimplification. In the last century it has become clear that drawing was central to the artistic processes of both artists.

Like all their contemporaries, Mantegna and Bellini began their artistic training by learning to draw – Mantegna in the Paduan 'academy' of Francesco Squarcione, Giovanni Bellini from his father Jacopo.[3] Drawing was, first and foremost, a medium of study which could take different forms dependent on its function. Its most ephemeral form was the sketch, drawn roughly and quickly to fix an idea. Most have been lost, as they had little appeal for early collectors, but a group of tiny figures by Mantegna survives in the upper corner of a drawing from his workshop (fig. 197), while Bellini sometimes made initial sketches on the back of his panels (see fig. 104 and back of fig. 103).[4] Such ideas would be developed further in a dedicated study, perhaps exploring several possibilities for a single figure, for example Bellini's studies of *Saint Louis of Toulouse* (figs 118, 119) or Mantegna's *Three studies for Saint John the Baptist* (fig. 122). Simultaneously, the artist would study the overall design of a composition, as in Mantegna's *Saint James led to martyrdom* (fig. 83), which is already very close to the final arrangement of the painted scene in the Ovetari Chapel, Padua (fig. 251).

Preparatory drawings would then give way to working drawings, such as the cartoon: a life-size copy of a figure or a whole composition that would be used for transfer onto the canvas, panel or plastered wall. In order to transfer the image, artists would prick holes around the contours and press through powdered chalk (*spolvero*), or even incise the outlines with a knife or stylus. Although few cartoons survive, examinations with infrared technology have revealed that Bellini occasionally used cartoons to prepare and replicate his paintings, while Mantegna's workshop also used the practice: the *Dancing muse* (fig. 56), related to the *Parnassus* (fig. 57), is a rare testament to such use.[5]

Less common in Renaissance practice are highly finished drawings of the type produced by Mantegna. These meticulously detailed works, which seem to have been made as an end in themselves (figs 106, 107), sometimes show traces of underdrawing in chalk or metalpoint subsequently overdrawn in ink.[6] It appears that Mantegna intended the drawings to be seen beyond the workshop, perhaps as independent works, as designs to discuss with a patron or models for professional engravers.[7] However, the most complex question posed by Mantegna's and Bellini's graphic works is not their function, but their attribution.

ANDREA MANTEGNA, detail from *A man lying on a stone slab* (FIG. 198)

FIG. 56
Studio of ANDREA MANTEGNA
Dancing muse, about 1497
Pen and black ink, blue-grey wash, white heightening, over black chalk on brown prepared paper, traces of spolvero transfer, 45.6 × 31.2 cm
Kupferstichkabinett, Staatliche Museen zu Berlin (KdZ 5058)

FIG. 57
ANDREA MANTEGNA
Parnassus, 1496–7
Egg tempera on canvas, 161 × 192 cm
Musée du Louvre, Paris (370)

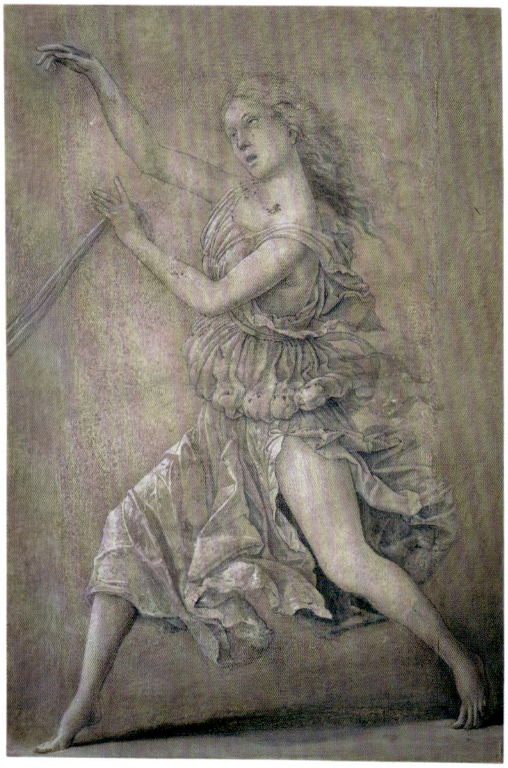

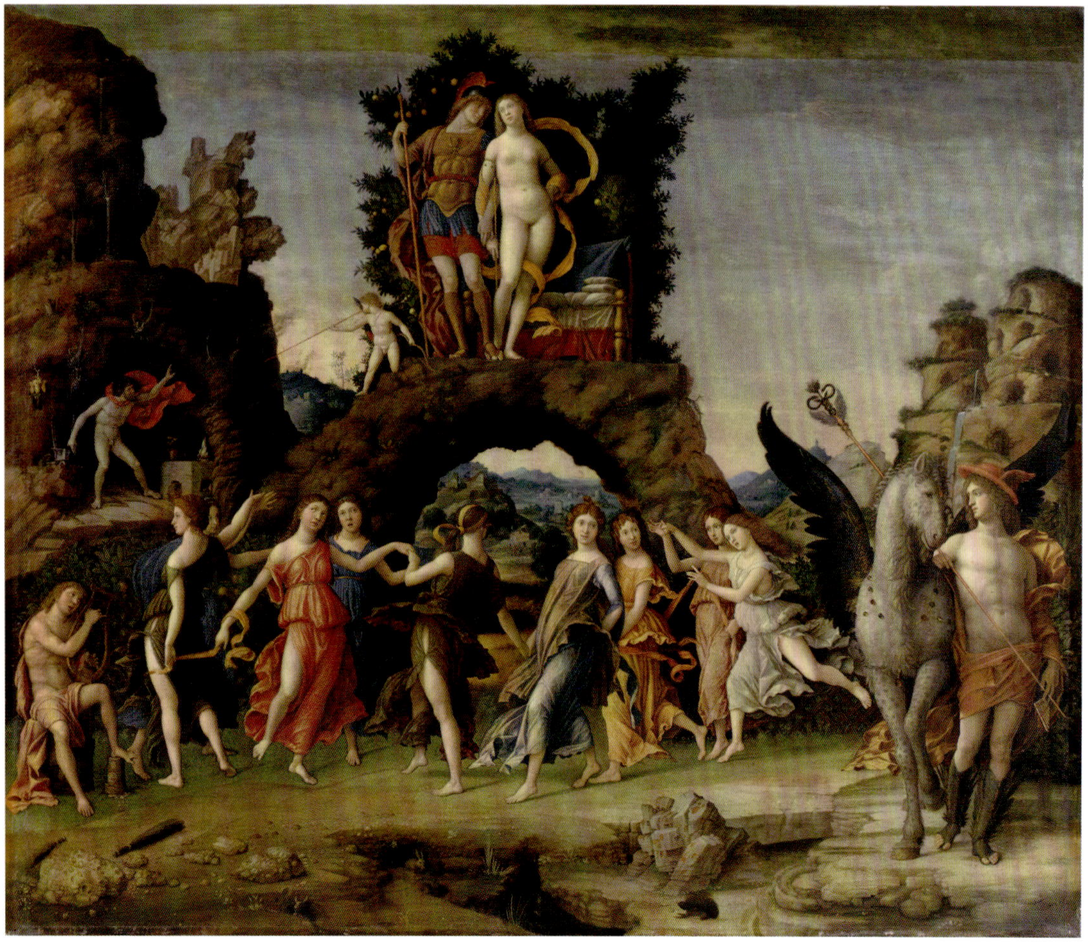

FIG. 58
ANDREA MANTEGNA
Judith and Abra, 1491
Pen and brush and brown ink,
black chalk (?) on paper, 39 × 25.9 cm
Gabinetto dei Disegni e delle Stampe,
Galleria degli Uffizi, Florence (404 E)

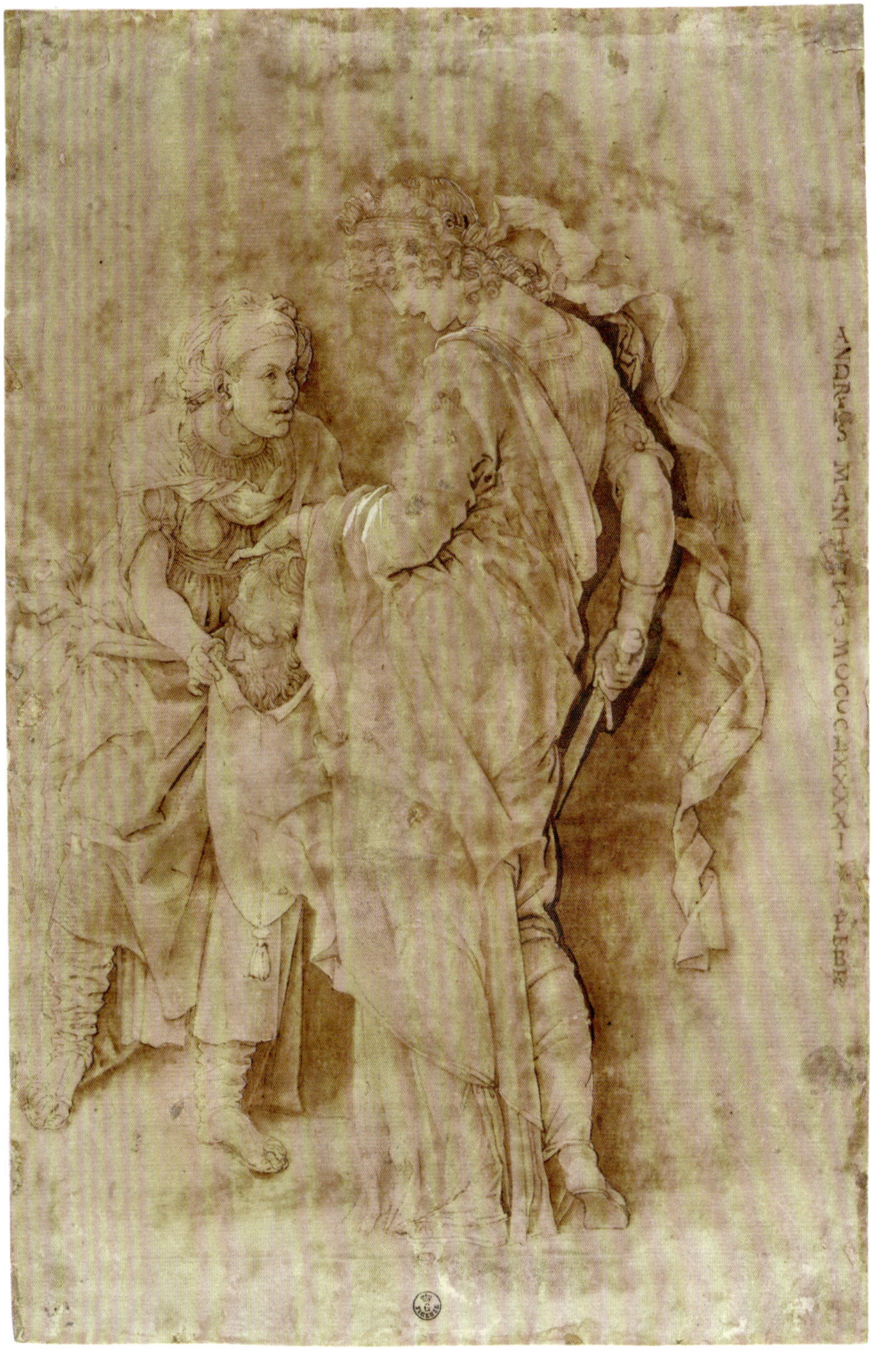

A QUESTION OF ATTRIBUTION

Every attempt to establish the attribution of drawings by the two artists is frustrated by the lack of documentary evidence. *Judith and Abra* (1491, fig. 58) is Mantegna's only signed and dated drawing, although *Saint James led to martyrdom* (figs 59, 83) is also universally accepted, because it is clearly a preparatory work for one of the Ovetari frescoes (1450–4). These works form the certain parameters of Mantegna's career as a draughtsman, but much of what lies between them is attributed on the basis of stylistic or thematic likelihood.[8] The challenges are even more extreme for Bellini. None of his drawings is dated or inscribed, and only four can be linked to compositions associated with the artist: the *Man in a turban* (fig. 160), connected to the grisaille *Lamentation* from the Uffizi (fig. 161); and three studies of *Saint Sebastian* (fig. 71) and *Saint Louis of Toulouse* (figs 72, 118, 119), which are apparently related to the triptychs painted by Giovanni Bellini's studio for the Church of the Carità (figs 84, 120) in the early 1460s. These drawings are so different in style that they do not easily form a core against which to judge other works. The rest of Bellini's drawings are attributed on the basis of assumptions about his style. Despite two serious attempts to catalogue his drawings – by Fritz Heinemann in 1962 and George Goldner in 2004 – Bellini remains an elusive draughtsman. The works catalogued under his name are so varied in media and quality that they simply cannot all be by him.[9] Our aim in this essay is to explain our attributions for the drawings in this exhibition. Such firm opinions are held on the matter that we do not expect to convert those with other views but we hope, with the use of details from various drawings, to justify our own interpretations.

FIG. 59
ANDREA MANTEGNA,
detail from *Saint James led to martyrdom* (FIG. 83)

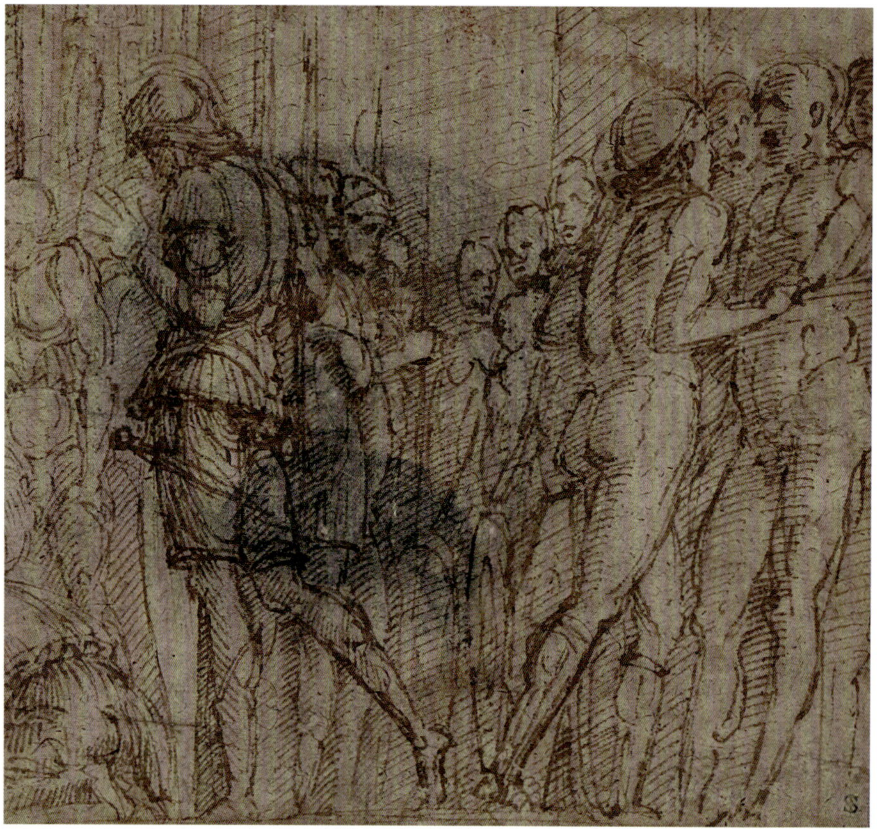

MANTEGNA'S DRAWINGS

By the time Mantegna embarked on his independent career in the late 1440s, he was a profoundly confident draughtsman. *Saint James led to martyrdom* (fig. 83) includes figures at rest and in movement, seen at different angles and levels, probably inspired by Donatello's narrative reliefs (figs 2, 131, 147) in the nearby Santo. Mantegna had already adopted the parallel hatching which would become such a characteristic feature of his mature style (fig. 59). As his career progressed, his hatching would become tighter and his pen line more delicate, as can be traced by comparing the *Pietà* of 1460–5 (fig. 60) with *The Virgin and Child with an angel* from about 1485 (fig. 61).

The figures in *Saint James led to martyrdom* are slender and attenuated, their legs tapering to pointed ankles. This abbreviated approach to anatomy continued in Mantegna's work of the 1460s, such as the verso of *Christ at the column* (fig. 195), where Christ's tormentor has been drawn so swiftly that his foot is almost overlooked. Similar features are seen in the lightly sketched composition at the upper left of *Study for a soldier of the Resurrection and other figures* (fig. 197).[10] The stiff and heavy main figure is undoubtedly by a workshop hand, but the small figures at upper left are drawn with greater competence, their limbs abbreviated to points in the artist's haste. The composition is similar in reverse to Mantegna's *Saint James before Herod Agrippa* (fig. 249), another of the frescoes in the Ovetari Chapel.

By the early 1460s, Mantegna's figural drawings had become sturdier and less elongated. This may reflect his awareness of Jacopo Bellini, whose Drawing Books are populated by compact, rounded forms; and pen drawings from the 1460s pose the knottiest conundrum in the field of Mantegna-Bellini attributions.[11] Yet at the same period Mantegna adopted a graphic shorthand, which he continued to use in working drawings throughout his career. He plotted in facial features with a rough T-shape for the eyes and nose, and used rows of small circles to draw hair. These motifs appear in his pen-and-ink studies of saints for an altarpiece which is now lost but was probably commissioned shortly after he arrived in Mantua (figs 62, 123).[12]

Mantegna's drawings from the early 1460s also became increasingly emotional. *Christ at the column* (fig. 195) focuses on the anguish of Christ's twisted body, while the *Pietà* (figs 60, 153) concentrates attention on the grieving figures (presumably the three Marys) who support Christ's body. This intensity of feeling is equally evident in Mantegna's contemporary studies of the *Lamentation* (figs 73, 159), and it probably derived from his admiration for Donatello, particularly the *Dead Christ* (fig. 147) for the high altar of the Santo.

Certain technical challenges held an enduring appeal for Mantegna: the extreme foreshortening of the figures in his *Agony in the Garden* from the late 1450s (fig. 125) is repeated in his *Lamentations* of the 1460s and reappears in the mid-1470s with the *Dead Christ* (fig. 199). The *Man lying on a stone slab* (fig. 198), which must date from the same period even if it is not a direct study for the Brera picture, demonstrates how far his graphic style had developed.[13] It displays greater modulation of the pen line,

FIG. 60
ANDREA MANTEGNA,
detail from *Pietà* (FIG. 153)

FIG. 61
ANDREA MANTEGNA,
detail from *The Virgin and Child with an angel* (FIG. 107)

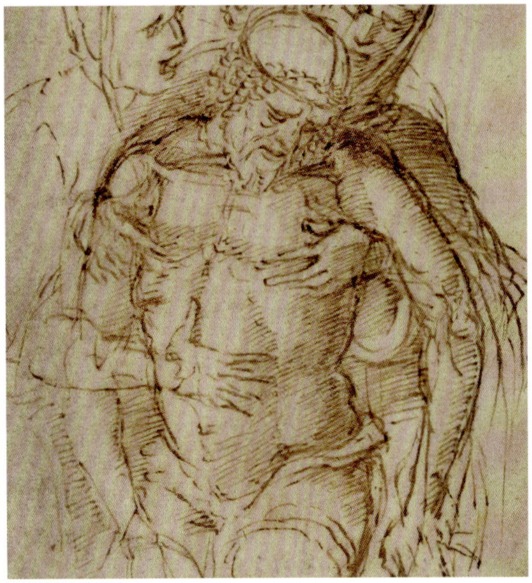

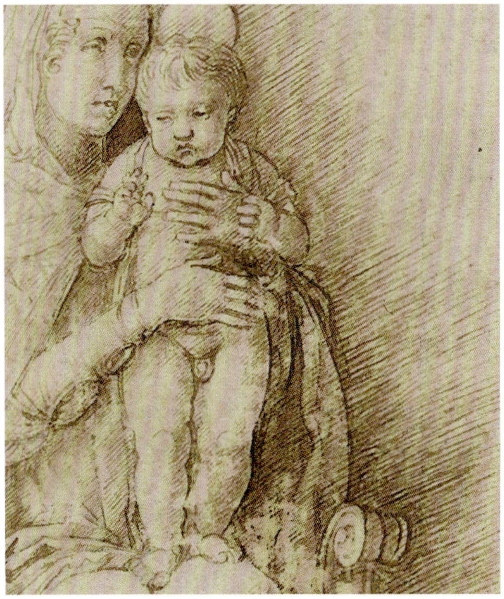

FIG. 62
ANDREA MANTEGNA
Three standing saints,
1460s
Pen and brown ink on paper toned with red chalk,
17.5 × 18.8 cm
The Morgan Library & Museum, New York, Thaw Collection (1985.100)

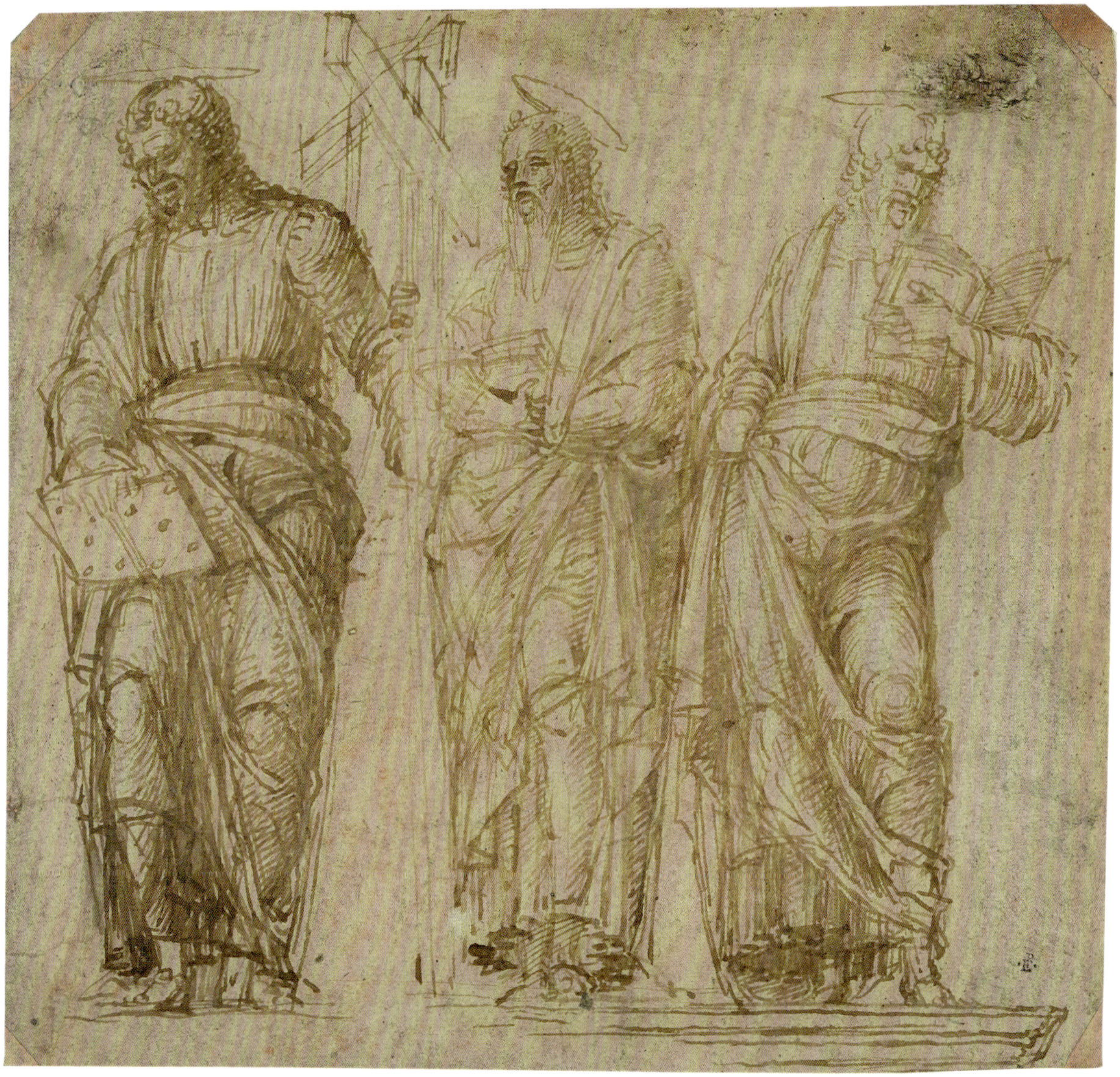

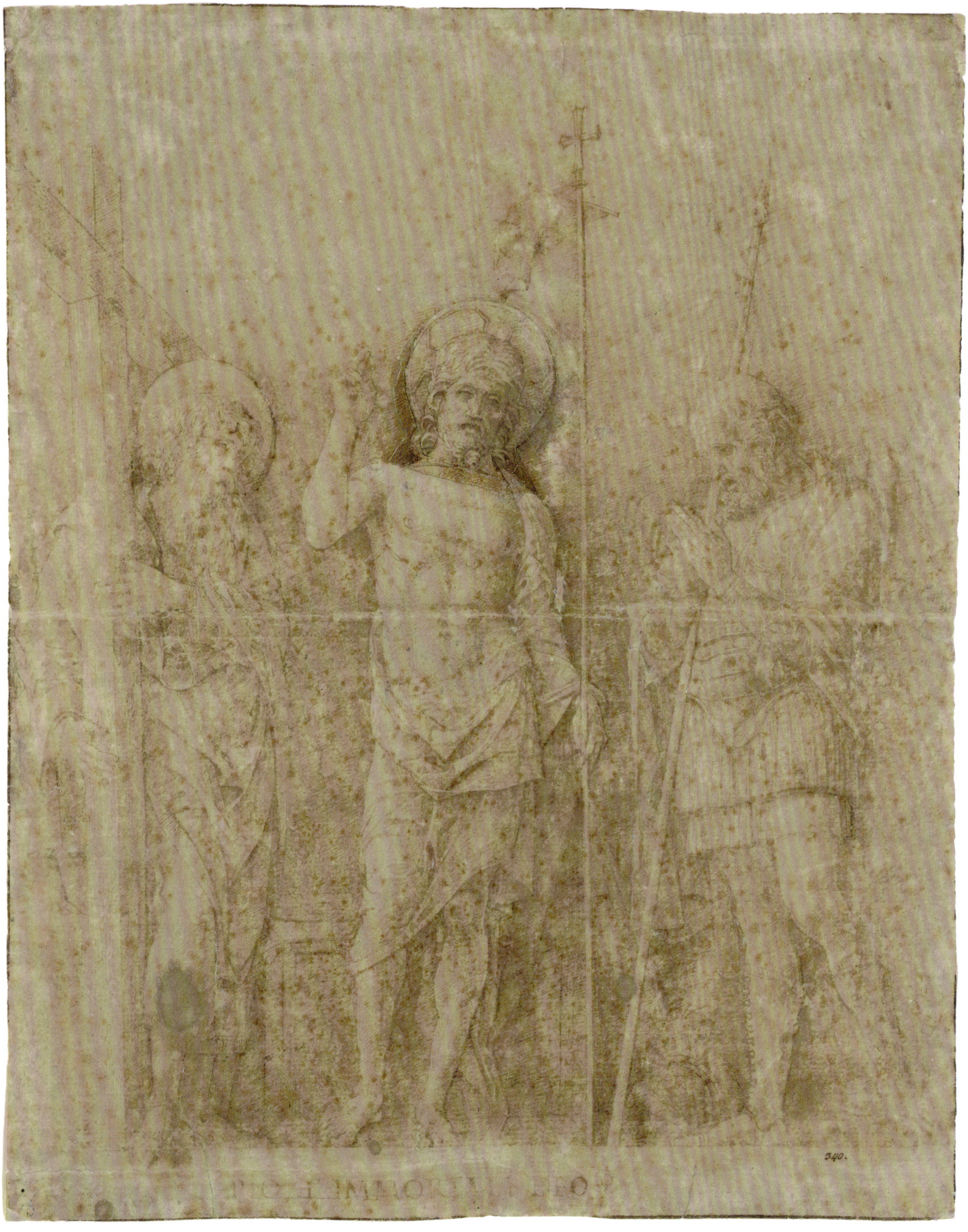

FIG. 63
ANDREA MANTEGNA
The Resurrected Christ with Saints Andrew and Longinus, 1470–5
Pen and brown ink, brown wash, on paper, 35 × 28.5 cm
Staatliche Graphische Sammlung, Munich (3065 z)

and a more sophisticated use of hatching, and is extremely close in style to the damaged *Resurrected Christ with Saints Andrew and Longinus* (fig. 63). This equally polished drawing seems to have been made for translation into print.[14] In both drawings, Mantegna reinterprets the horseshoe-shaped ribcages of his earliest works in a more classical idiom, using fine hatching and short, curving lines to delineate muscles beneath the skin. The bodies and draperies have an almost sculptural quality, which is also evident in prints associated with Mantegna, such as *The Entombment* of the mid-1470s.

Fine parallel hatching outlines the right-hand side of the *Man lying on a stone slab*, which indicates shadow and helps to define the contours. A similar technique recurs in several of Mantegna's late, highly finished drawings: *A bird catching a fly* (fig. 233) from around 1480; *The Virgin and Child with an angel* from some years later (figs 61, 107); and *The Calumny of Apelles* (fig. 230), which may date from as late as 1505. This technique perhaps originated in Mantegna's knowledge of drawings by Pisanello, his predecessor as court artist in Mantua.[15]

The recent discovery of a drawing of *A Roman triumph* (fig. 65) fits into this tradition of refined, delicately hatched drawings made by Mantegna in the 1480s and 1490s.[16] It is connected to Canvas II of *The Triumphs of Caesar* (fig. 235) and appears to be a first idea for the composition, as there are small but significant differences between the arrangement of figures in the final picture. The drawing's compromised condition means that its sophistication is less evident to the naked eye, but UV investigation has revealed fine hatching along the contours and a subtlety of description worthy of Mantegna (fig. 77). Of all the surviving drawings linked to the *Triumphs*, this has the best claim to be by Mantegna himself. It is instructive to compare it with the *Trumpeters* in the Louvre, connected to Canvas I and sometimes championed as autograph.[17] In comparison with the newly discovered *Triumph*, the Louvre sheet appears heavy and pedantic, with anatomical infelicities that seem unlikely for Mantegna at this date.

During the 1490s, Mantegna produced the most classical of his works: the magnificent painted *Triumphs* and the allegorical puzzles of *Virtus Combusta* (fig. 229) and the *Three deities* (fig. 231). These are the most painterly of Mantegna's drawings. Delicate shading with the point of a brush replaces the usual pen hatching, yet even here the red, blue and white washes are applied in thin, tightly spaced strokes, suggesting that Mantegna found it difficult entirely to sacrifice his notions of linear shading. In other ways, too, these drawings are faithful to his graphic aesthetic: note the abdominal musculature of ass-eared Folly, or the thick locks of hair, like those of the *Man lying on a stone slab* (fig. 198) and *The Resurrected Christ with Saints Andrew and Longinus* (fig. 63).

The vagaries of chance mean that far fewer working drawings survive from Mantegna's final years. A rare example is the *Three studies for Saint John the Baptist* (fig. 122). Originally attributed to Giovanni Bellini, the drawing is now generally accepted as Mantegna, although its date remains controversial. It was formerly considered an early work, connected to the *Reading saint* (fig. 123) and *Three standing saints* (fig. 62) of the 1460s, but several recent scholars have argued that it dates from the 1490s.[18] We are persuaded by this later dating, because the delicate pen line is far removed from Mantegna's broader, weightier line of the 1460s. However, this sheet also demonstrates how little Mantegna's graphic shorthand changed. Here, as in works of the 1460s, the eyes and nose are sketched in a T-shape and minimalist figures are conveyed with a few strokes of the pen. Arms and legs taper to points, while scrawled circles represent the hair of the seated figure on the right.

FIG. 64
ANDREA MANTEGNA,
A Roman triumph (FIG. 65)
Photograph taken in
ultraviolet light

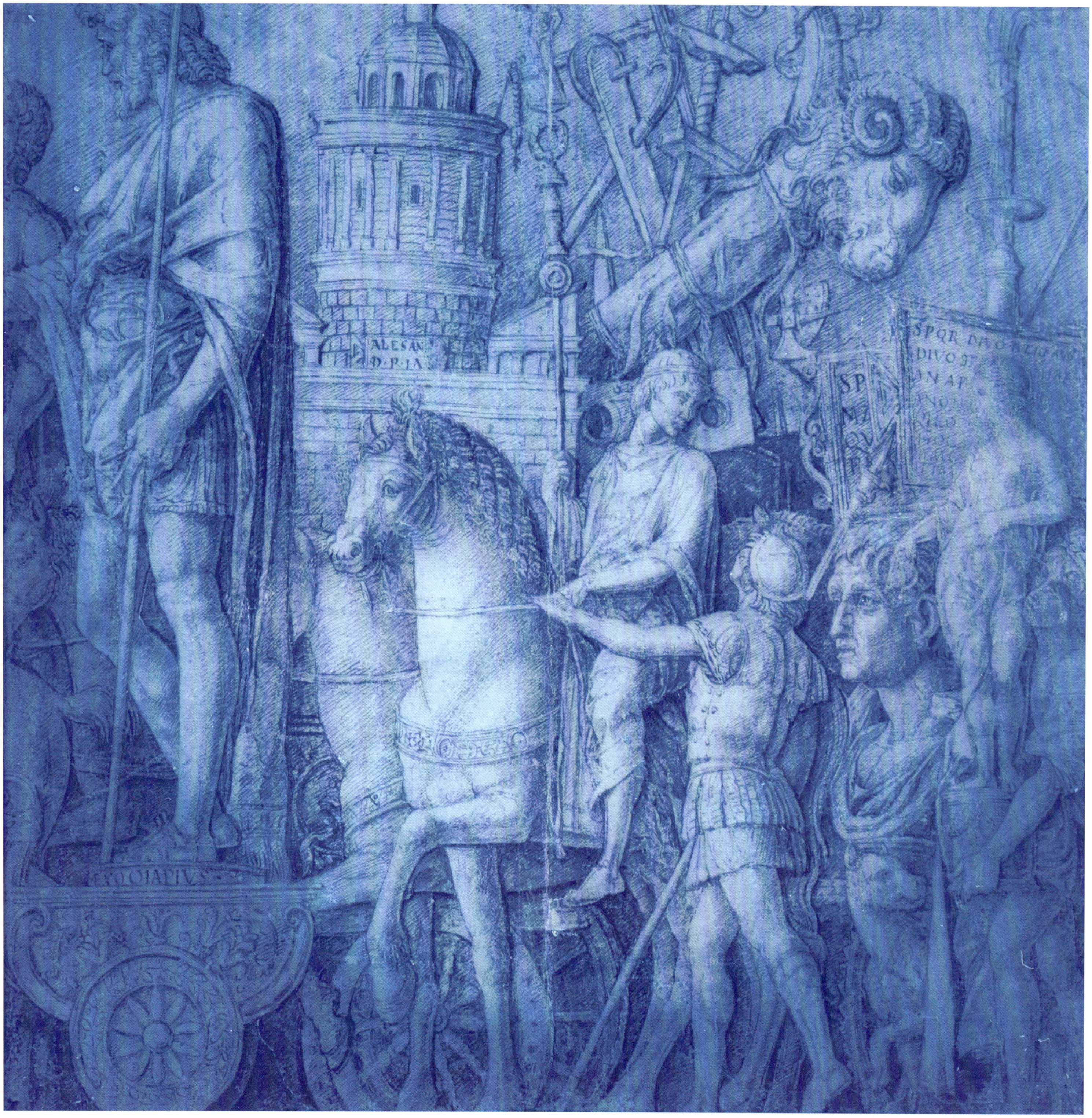

FIG. 65
ANDREA MANTEGNA
A Roman triumph, 1475–90
Pen and ink on brown paper,
26.6 × 26.6 cm
Private collection

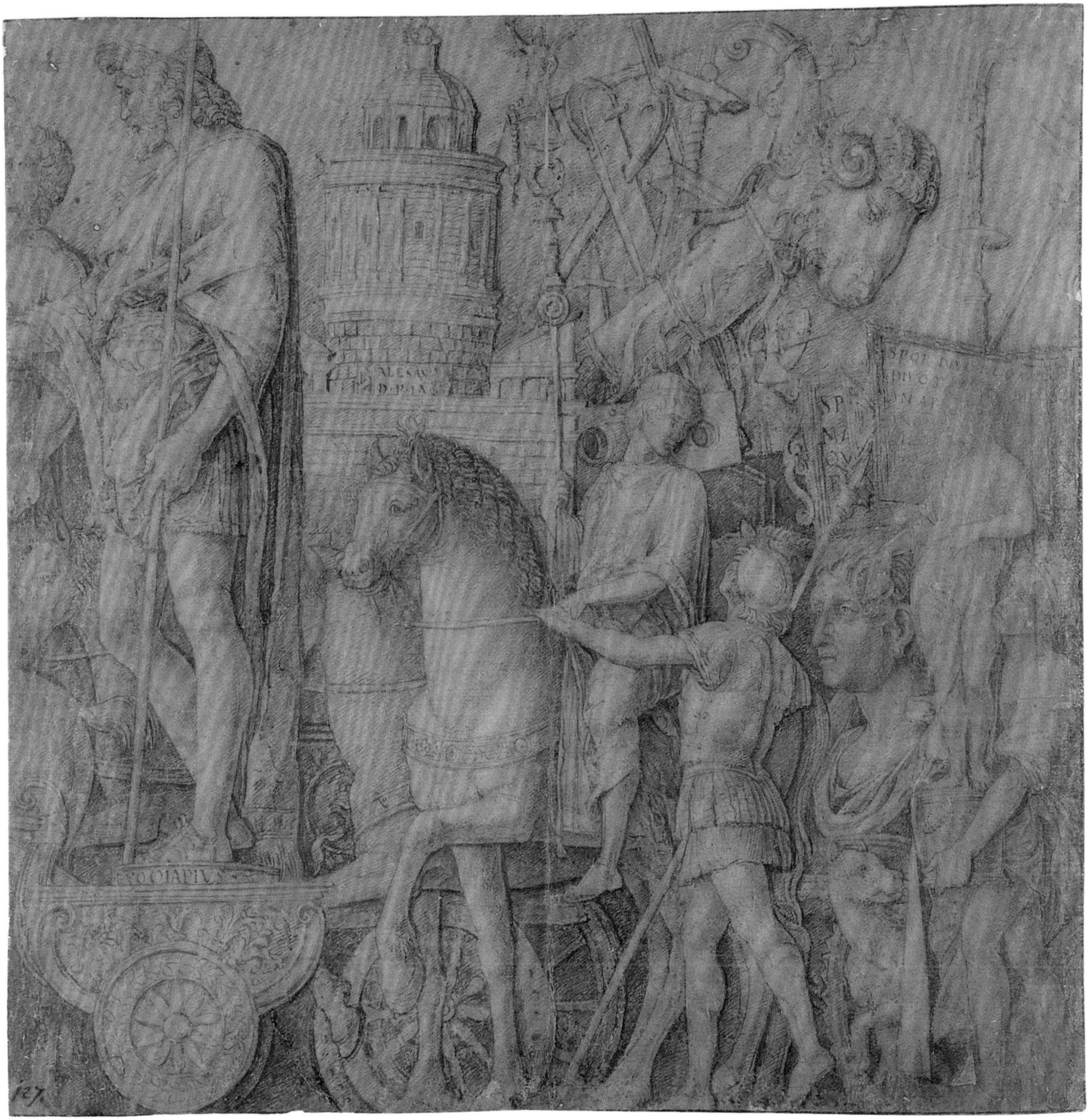

MANTEGNA AND THE ART OF PRINTMAKING

This exhibition focuses on subjects that inspired both Mantegna and Bellini, and so prints occupy a relatively minor place in the selection. Bellini himself appears to have had little interest in printmaking and so there is no cause for an extended discussion of the topic. Nevertheless, we felt it important to state our position with regard to the attribution of Mantegna's prints.

The question of Mantegna's activity as printmaker is even more controversial than the attribution of certain drawings. For some scholars he is one of the most innovative engravers of the Renaissance, while others see him as a supervisor, not a practitioner. A core group of seven engravings lies at the heart of this debate: *The Entombment* (fig. 66), *The battle of the sea gods* (engraved on two plates), *The Resurrected Christ between Saints Andrew and Longinus*, *A bacchanal with a wine vat*, *A bacchanal with Silenus* and *The Virgin and Child* (fig. 183). All demonstrate a level of sophistication that places them apart from other prints made by Mantegna's followers, and all but the *Virgin and Child* (probably engraved in the mid-1480s) should be dated to the 1470s. Five of the plates for these engravings still belonged to Mantegna's son Leonardo in 1510.[19]

Mantegna became fascinated by the potential of printmaking in the mid-1470s, but the engraving of lines into copper with a burin was a demanding task, usually undertaken by trained goldsmiths. Mantegna had no such training and, with his responsibilities for the Gonzaga court, would have had little time to study it. We are inclined to see Mantegna taking on a role like that which Raphael later assumed with Marcantonio Raimondi: as supplier of designs, supervisor of execution and controller of the resultant plates.[20] In April 1475, Mantegna drew up a contract with the goldsmith Gian Marco Cavalli, who promised, on pain of 100 ducats, 'that he will not show the designs and plates, nor allow

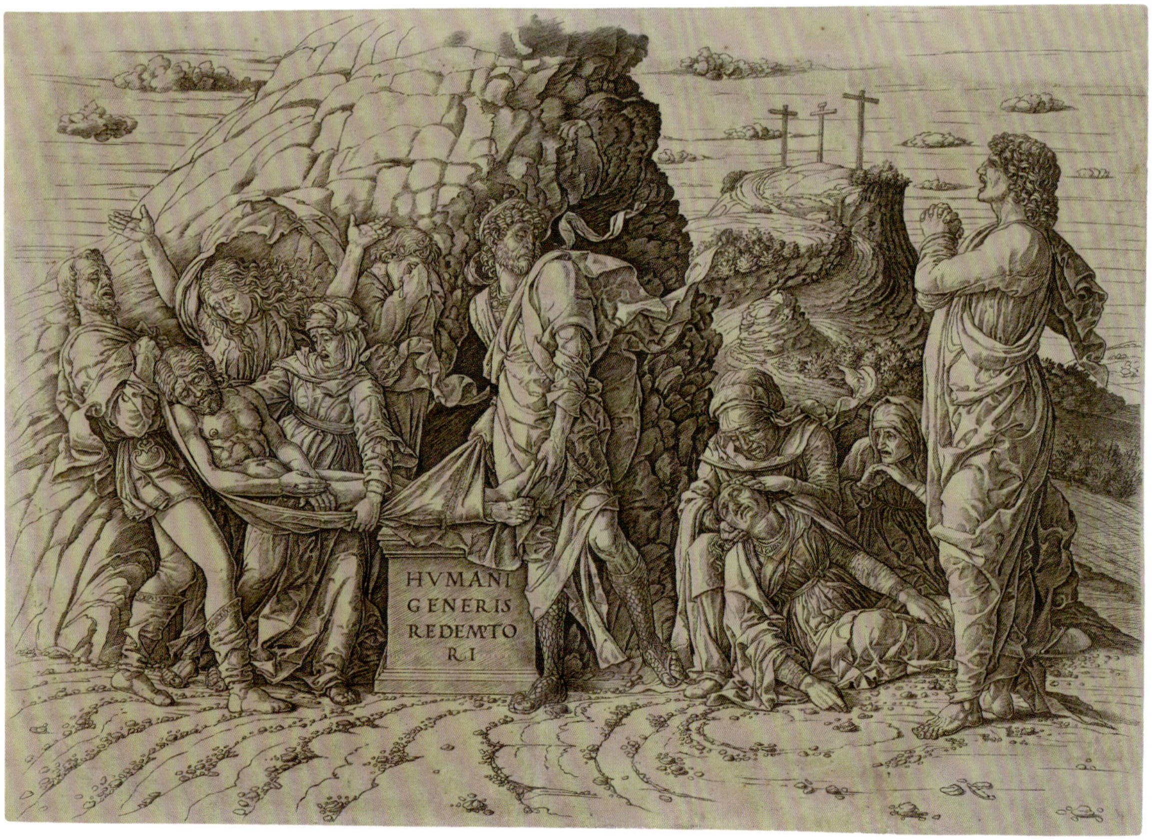

FIG. 66
Circle of ANDREA MANTEGNA
The Entombment, about 1480–5
Engraving, 30.4 × 44.4 cm
Kupferstichkabinett, Staatliche Museen zu Berlin (95-1893)

said designs to be copied by anyone without permission from Messer Andrea'.[21] Mantegna was determined to protect his monopoly, and when another printmaker, Simone da Reggio, began engraving plates for other Mantuan artists in 1475, Mantegna threatened him, had him waylaid by thugs and finally accused him of sodomy, forcing Simone to flee the city.[22] Evidently Mantegna was a difficult collaborator, but he and Cavalli were still working together in 1483, when Cavalli cast some vases in the antique style for Federico Gonzaga, after designs supplied by Mantegna.[23]

If Mantegna had learned to engrave plates, why was he only active in the 1470s and 1480s? It is most logical to see the seven core prints as the result of a productive artistic partnership between Mantegna and a skilled technical partner, probably Cavalli himself.

In contrast to Mantegna, printmaking held no imaginative appeal for Bellini, and Girolamo Mocetto's prints after Bellini were apparently undertaken at Mocetto's initiative.[24] Perhaps Bellini – whose genius lay in subtle variations of tone or colour – saw little potential in what was at this date a primarily linear medium. Giulio Campagnola's experiments with stipple engraving, which permitted the production of more atmospheric prints, ultimately arrived too late to be of interest to Bellini.

BELLINI'S DRAWINGS

No documentary evidence survives for Bellini's drawings, and few sheets can be linked with paintings. Even those drawings most commonly accepted as by Bellini, such as *The Nativity* (fig. 216), have been published with the qualifier 'attributed to'.[25] Moreover, the question of date often remains unresolvable. Yet it is clear that Bellini did draw and that drawing played a central role in his artistic process. Many of his pictures reveal extensive underdrawing in brush or chalk, sometimes with traces of *spolvero*, suggesting that he and his assistants used full-size cartoons to replicate his most popular compositions of the Virgin and Child.[26]

We need to start with the four drawings most commonly accepted as works by Bellini (although all at some point have also been attributed to Mantegna). *The Nativity* is a compositional study in pen and ink that juxtaposes the highly finished foreground figures of the Virgin and Child with the roughly drawn fence and the shepherds and their herds on the hills beyond. This drawing is frequently compared to *Saint Mark healing Ananias* in Berlin (figs 69, 217), which includes a similar range of mark-making, from roughed-in incidental details, like the shoes hanging from a rack at upper left, to carefully drawn main figures. These drawings are confidently executed, and this leads one to overlook compositional infelicities, such as the break between foreground and background in *The Nativity*, or the disproportionately tall saint in *Saint Mark healing Ananias*.

The figures in both drawings have individually delineated eyes, nose and mouth. There is no parallel to Mantegna's T-shaped shortcut. Noses tend to be straight, and that of the Virgin in *The Nativity* has been defined with an added line that gives it a broad, flat bridge. Eyes are heavily lidded and the outer eyebrows slope down. Secondary figures, such as the herdsmen arriving at the gate in *The Nativity*, have features blocked in with brief dabs of ink. These characteristics reappear in two drawings of the *Pietà* in the British Museum (figs 67, 162) and in Rennes (figs 68, 154), which are more vigorous in style and show the artist experimenting with the emotive theme of the Virgin cradling her dead son. In these drawings, too, the Virgin's eyes slope down at the outer edges, with heavy lids and arched brows. In all cases the heads and bodies are more rounded and more robust than those found in

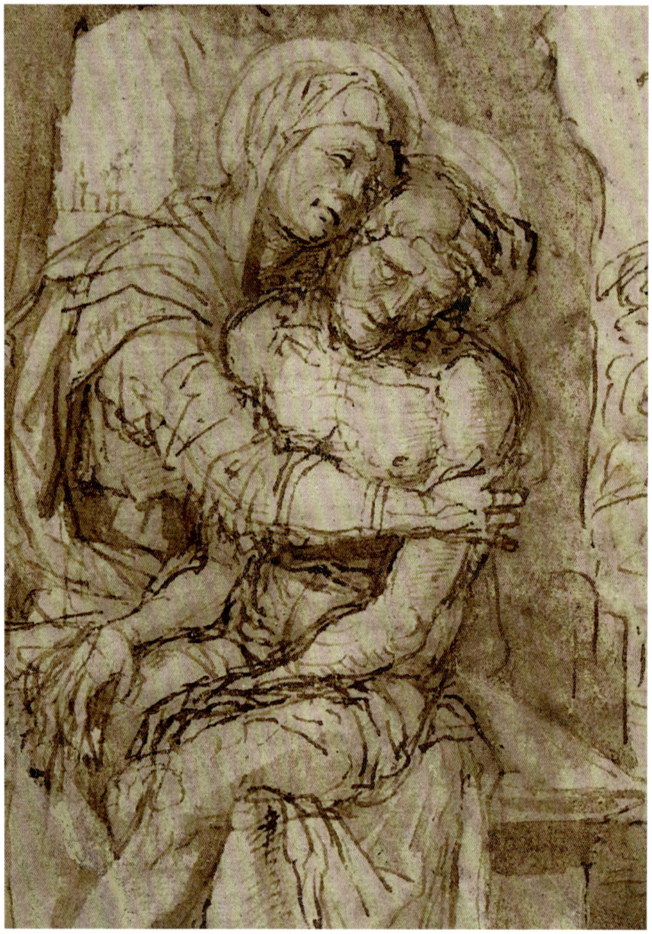

FIG. 67
GIOVANNI BELLINI, detail from *Pietà* (FIG. 162)

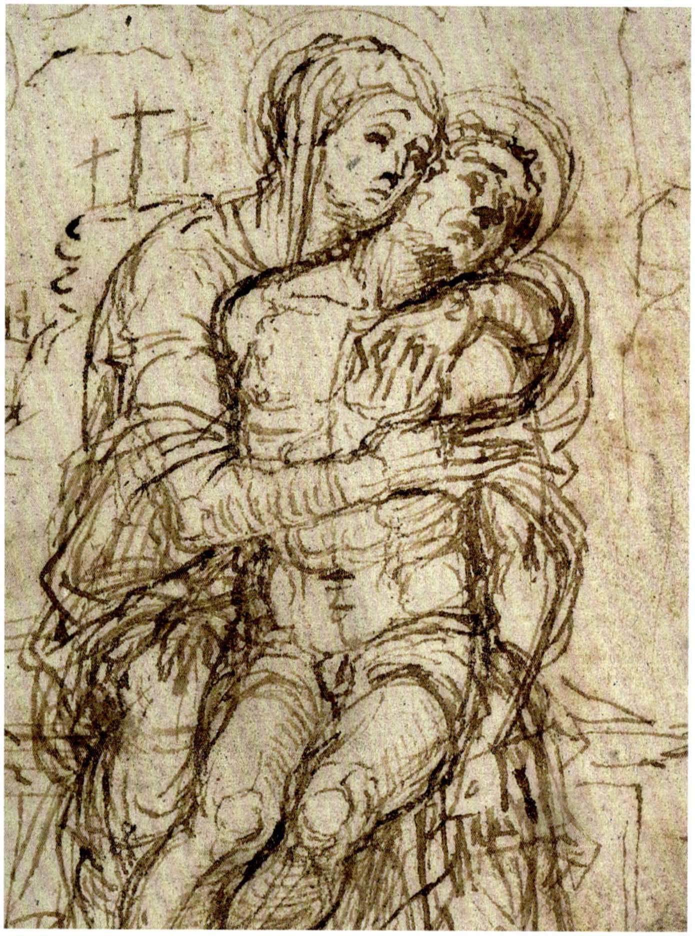

FIG. 68
GIOVANNI BELLINI, detail from *Pietà* (FIG. 154)

Mantegna's drawings. Mantegna's favoured technique of parallel hatching is used in *The Nativity* and *Saint Mark healing Ananias*, but it is less dominant than in Mantegna's work, and draperies are drawn more fluidly. This tendency is especially apparent in the vigorous quest for form in the two *Pietà* drawings.

We can cautiously suggest dates for these sheets. The *Saint Mark healing Ananias* (fig. 69) is related to a relief of the same subject, sculpted by Pietro and Tullio Lombardo for the exterior of the Scuola Grande di San Marco in 1485–9 (fig. 70).[27] Although the two compositions differ, there is a close enough correspondence to suppose they are related. As a member of this Scuola, twice holding office as its *degano* or dean, Bellini may well have been involved in planning the decorative scheme for its façade.[28] A date of around 1485 is likely for that drawing. *The Nativity*, with its less monumental figures, is generally supposed to be a little earlier than the *Saint Mark*, perhaps around 1480.[29] The two drawings of the *Pietà* seem to be earlier works (figs 67, 68).[30] Their emotional intensity jars with the serenity of Bellini's mature religious pictures, even the *Lamentation* for the *Pesaro Altarpiece* of the early 1470s (fig. 255). They are more comparable to the *Dead Christ supported by the Virgin and Saint John* of around 1460–70 (fig. 11), where the Virgin's expression displays similar anguish, and her right arm extends across Christ's chest in a similar manner.

These four drawings constitute a basis for reconstructing Giovanni Bellini's activity as a draughtsman. The earliest drawing that can be given with relative confidence to Bellini is the *Saint Sebastian* (figs 71, 194), which is connected not only to the triptych designed by the Bellini workshop for the Carità in 1462–4 (fig. 84), but also to Mantegna's first depiction of the saint (fig. 193). The saint's pose, his wiry legs and the curved lines of shadow on his shins recall Mantegna, and particularly his Saint Sebastian. Yet Bellini is already more interested

FIG. 69
Attributed to GIOVANNI BELLINI, detail from *Saint Mark healing Ananias* (FIG. 217)

FIG. 70
PIETRO AND TULLIO LOMBARDO
Saint Mark healing Ananias, about 1489
Marble, 130 × 76 cm
Scuola Grande di San Marco, Venice

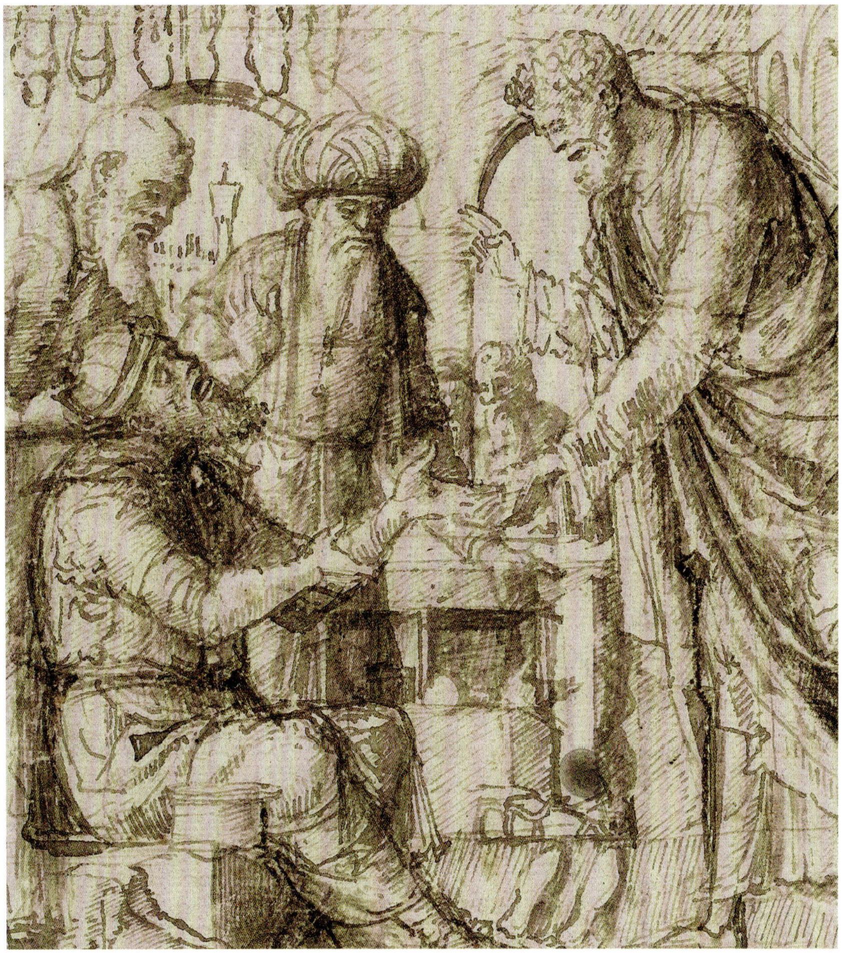

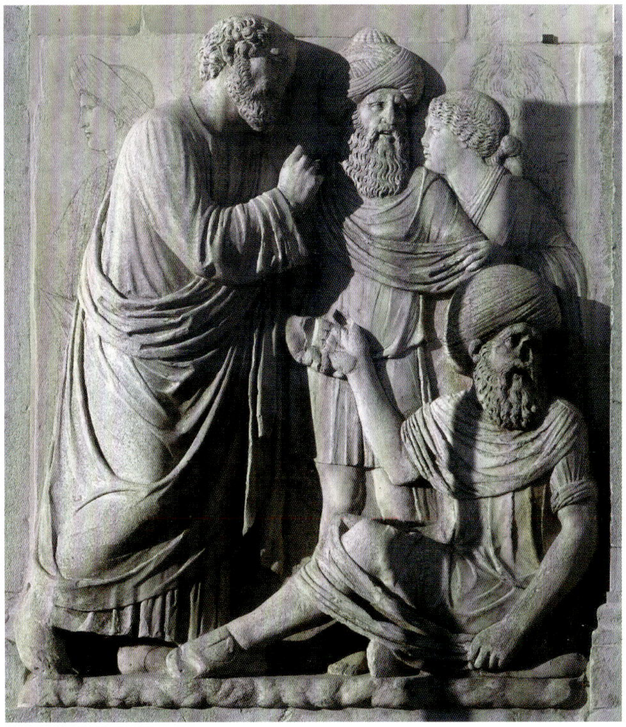

in light and tone than his brother-in-law. The facial features – such as Sebastian's eyes, composed of wells of ink, topped with arched brows – are reminiscent of those in Bellini's later drawings. Similar features appear in *The three crosses* (fig. 99), attributed by us to the young Bellini, which was probably drawn in response to Mantegna's *Crucifixion* from the predella of the *San Zeno Altarpiece* (fig. 101).

Two small, exploratory studies of *Saint Louis of Toulouse* (figs 72, 118, 119) can be connected to the depiction of that saint in another triptych (fig. 120) painted for the Carità. They are more confident than the *Saint Sebastian* and show Bellini's use of a stocky figure type inspired by his father Jacopo, and the blocking in of eyes, nose and mouth with blots of ink.[31]

A drawing of a different type is the *Head of an old man* (fig. 211), perhaps a study for the painting of Saint Anthony Abbot in the Carità *Saint Sebastian Triptych* (fig. 84).[32] Its hard, sculptural style seems to date it to the 1460s when Bellini was still very much inspired by Mantegna's works, yet it already displays his acute sensitivity to light. Using alternating strokes of pen and white heightening, he conveys the stronger fall of light from the left, illuminating the sitter's beard and hollowing out his sunken cheeks. A similar though more painterly approach characterises the *Head of a man in a turban* (fig. 160), which is connected to Bellini's large grisaille *Lamentation*, datable to around 1490 (fig. 161). Sometimes catalogued as a copy after the picture, the drawing of the turbaned man is worthy of reconsideration.[33] While it is looser in conception and less finished than the *Head of an old man*, its serene confidence and attention to the construction of form through light is worthy of Bellini himself.

Bellini's most puzzling drawings are three grisaille studies of standing men in classical costume (including fig. 239).[34] These are usually discussed in the context

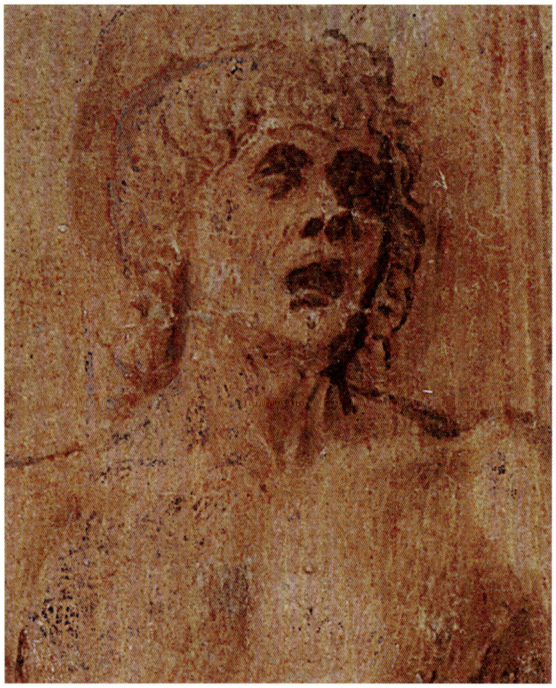

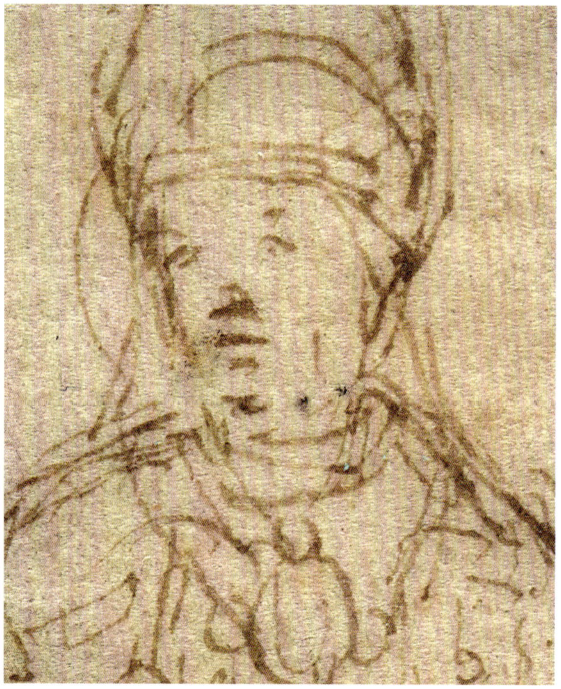

FIG. 71
GIOVANNI BELLINI,
detail from *Saint Sebastian*
(FIG. 194)

FIG. 72
GIOVANNI BELLINI,
detail from *Saint Louis of Toulouse holding a book*
(FIG. 118)

of *The Continence of Publius Cornelius Scipio* (fig. 246), commissioned by Francesco Cornaro from Mantegna and completed by Bellini after his brother-in-law's death. Goldner has identified all six figures in a *Christ and the Adulteress* (private collection), painted in Bellini's workshop.[35] However, it seems unlikely that this was their original destination, given the figures' Roman dress and the wreath of oak leaves (the Civic Crown) worn by the man on the left in fig. 239. They are sometimes linked to the two final – now lost – paintings for the Cornaro commission, as there are stylistic similarities between the figures and those in Bellini's *Scipio*, with the same soft, rounded faces and a sophisticated modulation of light and shade.

What was the function of these works? The drawings are carefully executed, with no compositional freedom or experiment. They must have been made after rather than in preparation for a painting, as each figure's outline is interrupted by its neighbours' shadows. The Paris drawing and its two companions are most convincingly interpreted as *ricordi* – probably by Bellini himself – after a lost painting, to be kept in the workshop for future reference.

The key to understanding Bellini's draughtsmanship may lie, as Giovanni C.F. Villa has suggested, in study of the underdrawing of his paintings.[36] In the 1548 *Dialogo di Pittura*, Paolo Pino advised painters not to follow Bellini's example in making elaborate underdrawing, as their hard work would simply be obliterated by colour.[37] Improved scientific equipment has recently allowed a better appreciation of the various techniques Bellini used, ranging 'from almost free-hand with a variety of strokes and broken lines, to an incisive mapping of a design, and to a carefully modelled, detailed technique'.[38] Further study of these underdrawings may help scholars to understand more about how Bellini's only grisaille, the Uffizi *Lamentation* (fig. 161), fits into his wider artistic practice.[39] *The Descent of Christ into Limbo* in Bristol (fig. 145) offers further evidence of Bellini's ability to build his painted works upon carefully drawn substructures.[40]

Bellini's activity as a draughtsman remains problematic, in the absence of documents and paintings that further elucidate the date and purpose of his drawings. This would be especially helpful for the 1460s, a period where the division of drawings between him and Mantegna remains uncertain.

FIG. 73
ANDREA MANTEGNA,
detail from *Two studies of the Lamentation* (recto) (FIG. 159)

FIG. 74
ANDREA MANTEGNA,
detail from *Three studies for the Dead Christ* (recto) (FIG. 163)

FIG. 75
ANDREA MANTEGNA,
detail from *The Deposition of Christ* (FIG. 158)

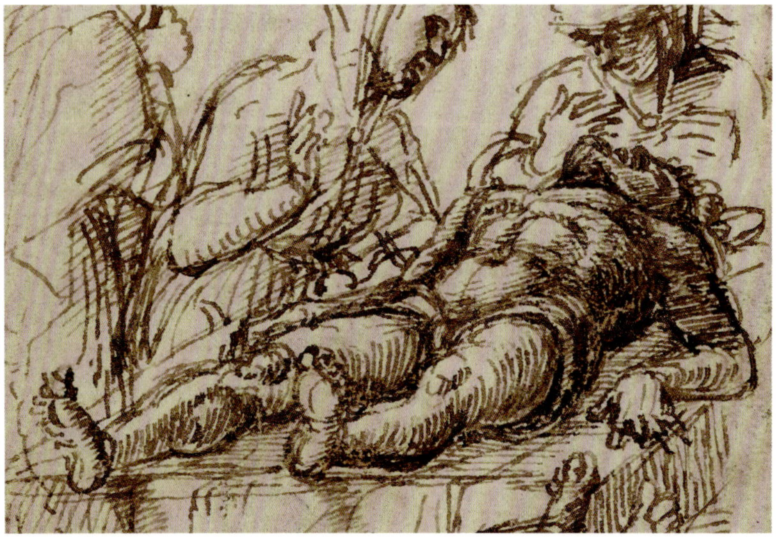

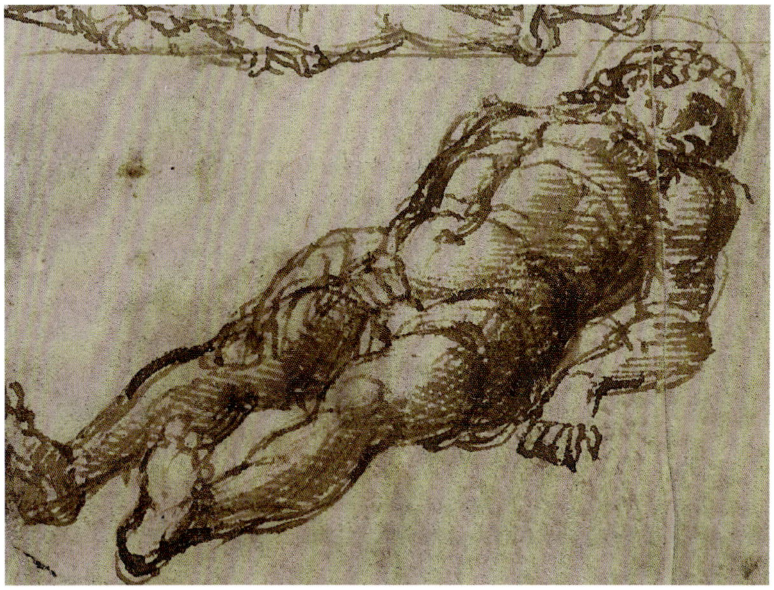

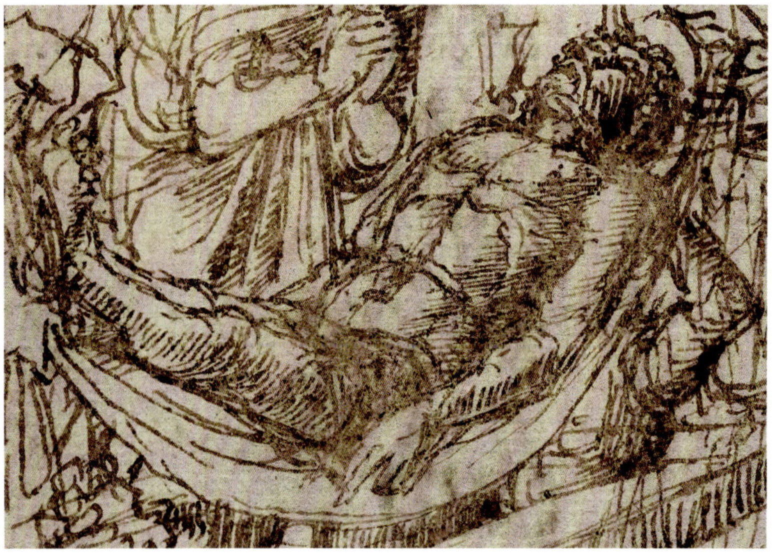

THE *LAMENTATIONS*

The 2013 discovery of Mantegna's *The Lamentation* (figs 73, 159) was greeted with reactions ranging from enthusiasm to scepticism. This drawing, now in a Milanese private collection, has been seen by very few scholars and its inclusion here, alongside related sheets from London (figs 74, 163) and Brescia (figs 75, 158), will facilitate further discussion.

The Milan drawing is extremely close to that in Brescia, both thematically and stylistically. Both exhibit the same vigorous hatching, with short, broad strokes defining the foreshortened figure of Christ, and in both cases the three mourning Marys are left unfinished, their heads receiving more attention than their bodies. Both sheets have the same inscription at the upper edge of the verso, which was only revealed on the Brescia drawing when it was lifted from its old mount during preparation for the 1992 Mantegna exhibition.[41] The bulging ribcage and pointed chin of the foreshortened Christ in the Milan drawing are awkward, but no more so than the rather flat, unarticulated torso of the Christ in Brescia. It seems highly likely that the two drawings are by Mantegna, made in Mantua in the early 1460s. Their technique and evocative pathos are close in spirit to the *Pietà* in the Accademia (figs 60, 153).

The British Museum *Three Studies for the Dead Christ* (fig. 74) has often been compared to the Brescia sheet, but the emergence of the Milan drawing underscores its differences. Although it deals with the same themes as the other drawings – the foreshortened body of the Dead Christ and the mourning holy women – the pen-work is different, drawn with an ink so fluid that in places it almost gives the impression of wash, while the outlines have a wiry nervousness recalling the Rennes *Pietà* (fig. 154). In 2004, Goldner attributed the British Museum drawing to Bellini, citing the different aesthetics of the Brescia and London sheets.[42] Despite this, and the British Museum drawing's similarities with Bellini's *Lamentation* in the Louvre (fig. 155), an attribution to Mantegna still seems most plausible. The subject matter of the London sheet is intimately linked to those of the Brescia and Milan drawings, while the obsessive studies of foreshortened figures link directly to a similar sketch on the recto of the Milan sheet. It is most convincing to see all three drawings as the product of the same hand. However, the British Museum and Louvre drawings – the former given to Mantegna and the latter to Bellini – demonstrate the challenges of distinguishing the work of the two artists around the year 1460, a time of extremely close reciprocal influence. This was the period when they produced their *Agonies in the Garden* (figs 125, 126) and it is very likely that they explored other themes in tandem.

STYLISTIC OUTLIERS

Mantegna and Bellini both drew most frequently in pen and ink, yet their names have also been attached, with varying degrees of plausibility, to drawings in other media. Chief among these are four highly finished black-chalk portrait drawings, whose attributions have oscillated between Mantegna, Bellini and their contemporary, Francesco Bonsignori.[43] Pisanello had popularised black chalk as a portrait medium in the early fifteenth century,[44] and it was used in Bellini's circle, as in the *Portrait of Gentile Bellini* (Kupferstichkabinett, Berlin), made in 1496 and traditionally regarded as a self portrait by Gentile (although sometimes attributed to Giovanni).[45]

The portrait of *Francesco II Gonzaga* from Dublin (fig. 204) is, in our view, the most likely to be by Mantegna. The format differs from the rest: rather than a stand-alone portrait, it is probably a fragment cut down from a larger composition, while the choice of an unusual full-face view may point to its intended function as part of a broader, more narrative scene, like the Camera Picta (fig. 203). We know that Mantegna made portrait drawings for that project, and that he was open to the idea of drawing portraits of the Gonzaga in the late 1470s.[46] Equally, the *Portrait of a man* at Christ Church Picture Gallery (fig. 76) is convincing as a work attributed to Bellini.[47] The handling of light is more delicate than that of the Dublin drawing and the sitter's refined aloofness is comparable to Bellini's painted portraits of around 1500, such as the portrait of *Doge Leonardo Loredan* (fig. 207).

The attribution of the two drawings in Besançon – neither of which we believe to be Mantegna or Bellini – is less certain. They are certainly of the period, as one of the sheets bears the basilisk watermark found in Northern Italy in the late fifteenth century, which is present on some drawings and prints by Mantegna.[48] Yet this is not enough to support an attribution to him. Until further research produces a more convincing attribution, we feel that the Besançon drawings should be regarded as the work of another talented North Italian artist, around 1500.[49]

THE PLACE OF DRAWING IN THE ART OF MANTEGNA AND BELLINI

The limitations of the evidence mean we must be careful in our conclusions. However, the extant sheets suggest that drawing was of fundamental importance to both artists, even if they came to use it in very different ways. Mantegna developed a strongly individualistic style, based on parallel hatching and contour lines, while Bellini adopted a more fluid technique, modelling with small strokes to soften his forms. Yet their understanding of draughtsmanship derived ultimately from the Paduan style leavened with their knowledge of Jacopo Bellini's drawings. Neither Mantegna nor Bellini ever abandoned these early lessons.

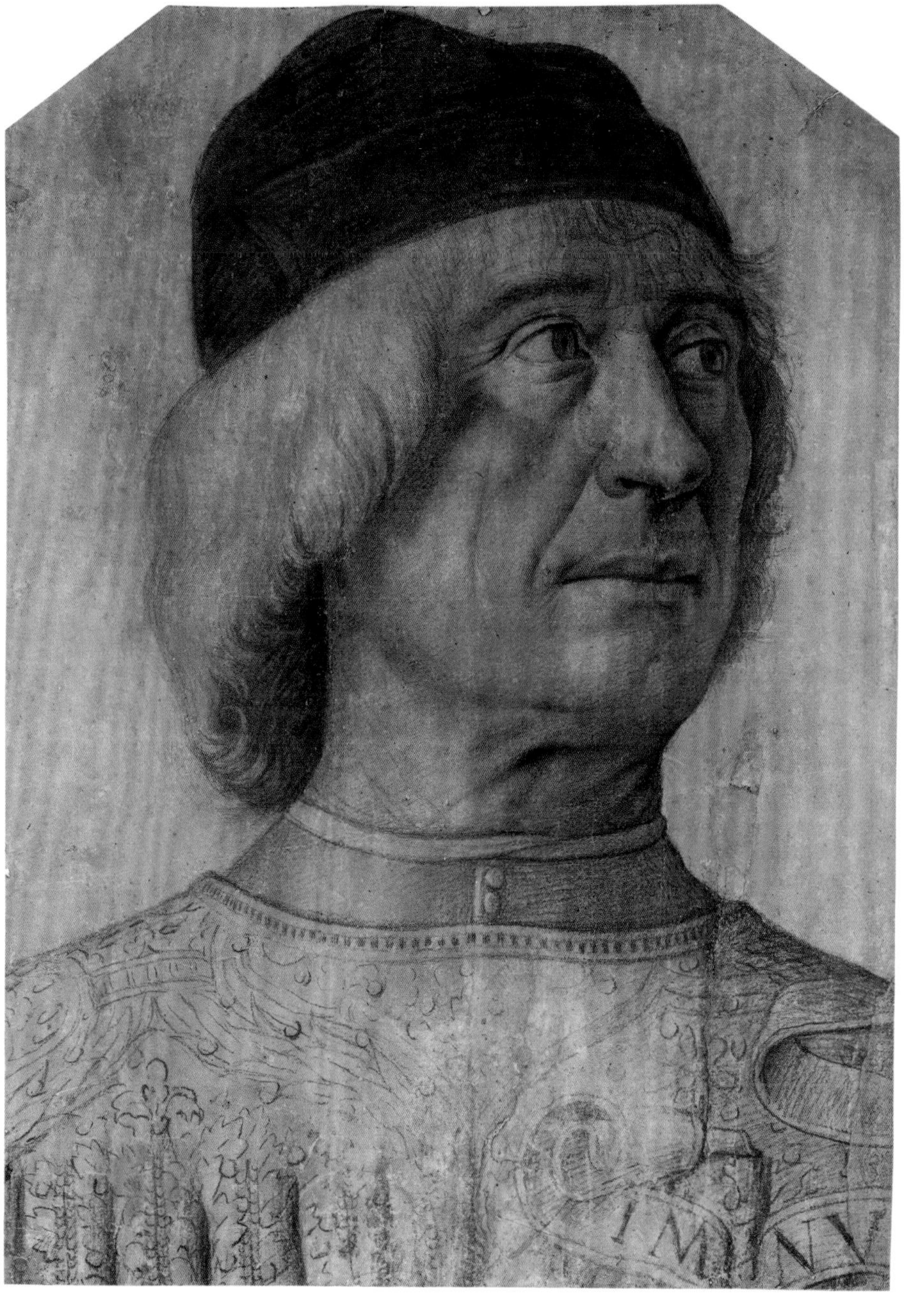

FIG. 76
Attributed to GIOVANNI BELLINI
Portrait of a man, about 1495
Black chalk, washed over, on paper, 39.1 × 28 cm
Christ Church Picture Gallery, Oxford (JBS 702)

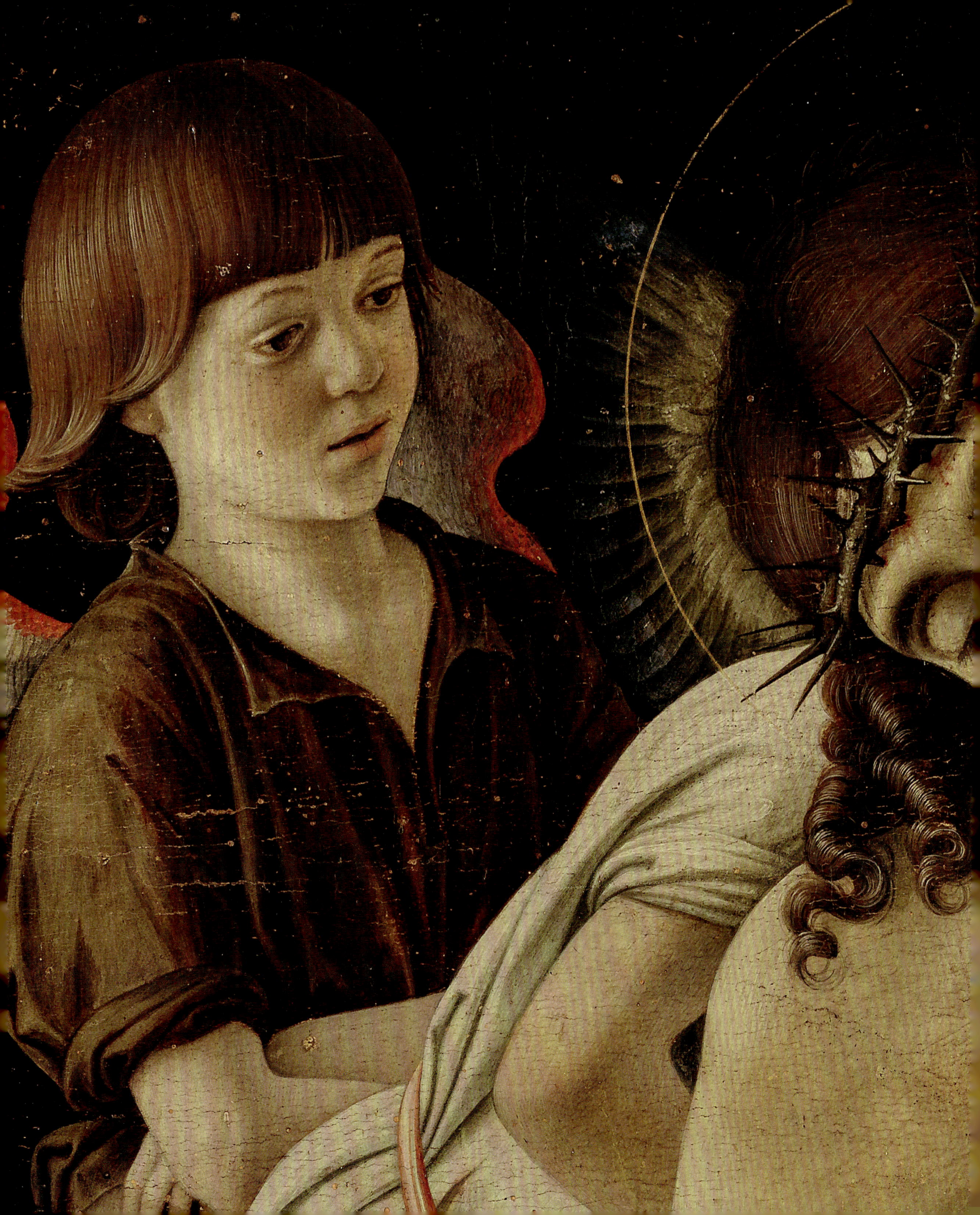

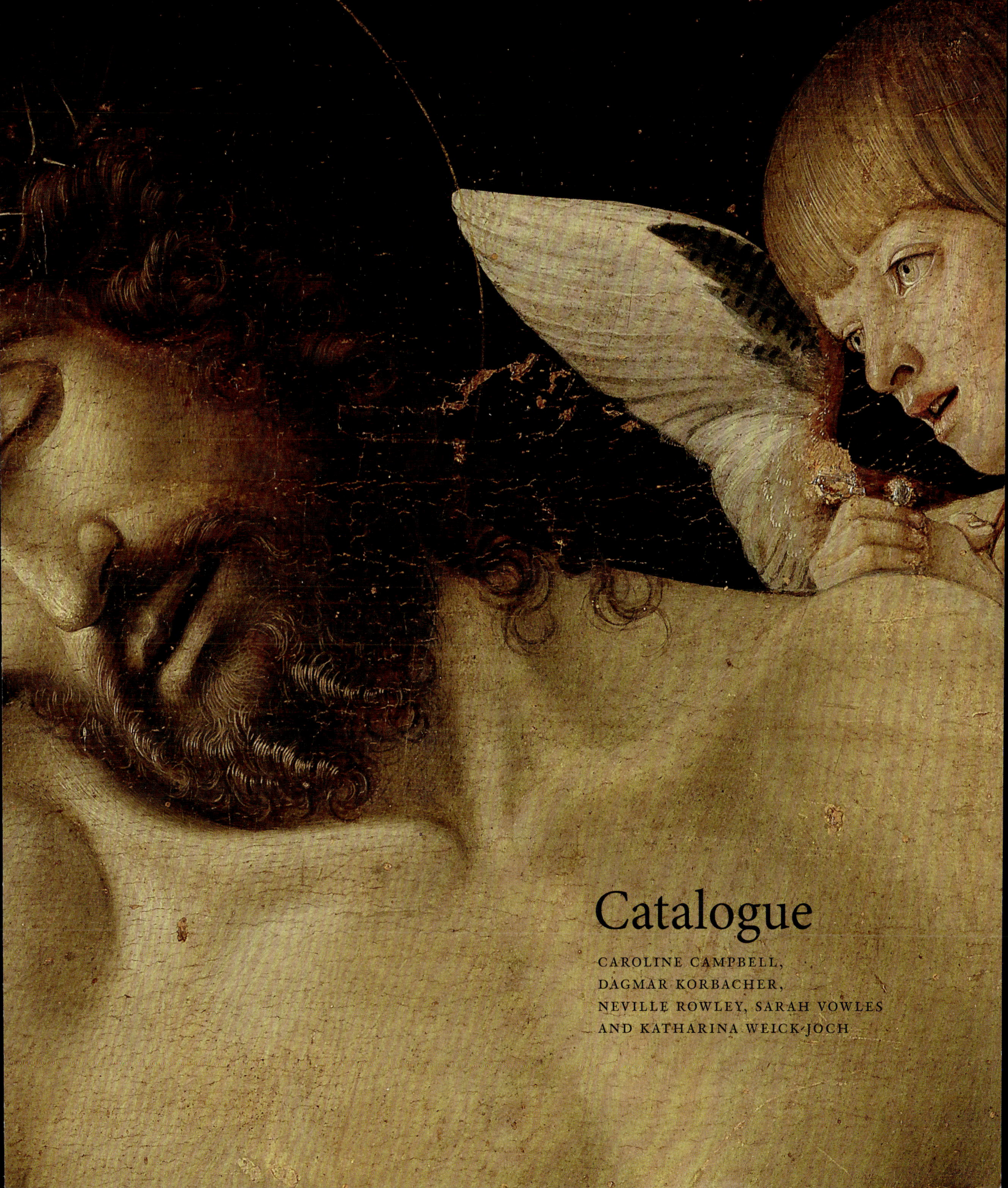

Catalogue

CAROLINE CAMPBELL,
DAGMAR KORBACHER,
NEVILLE ROWLEY, SARAH VOWLES
AND KATHARINA WEICK-JOCH

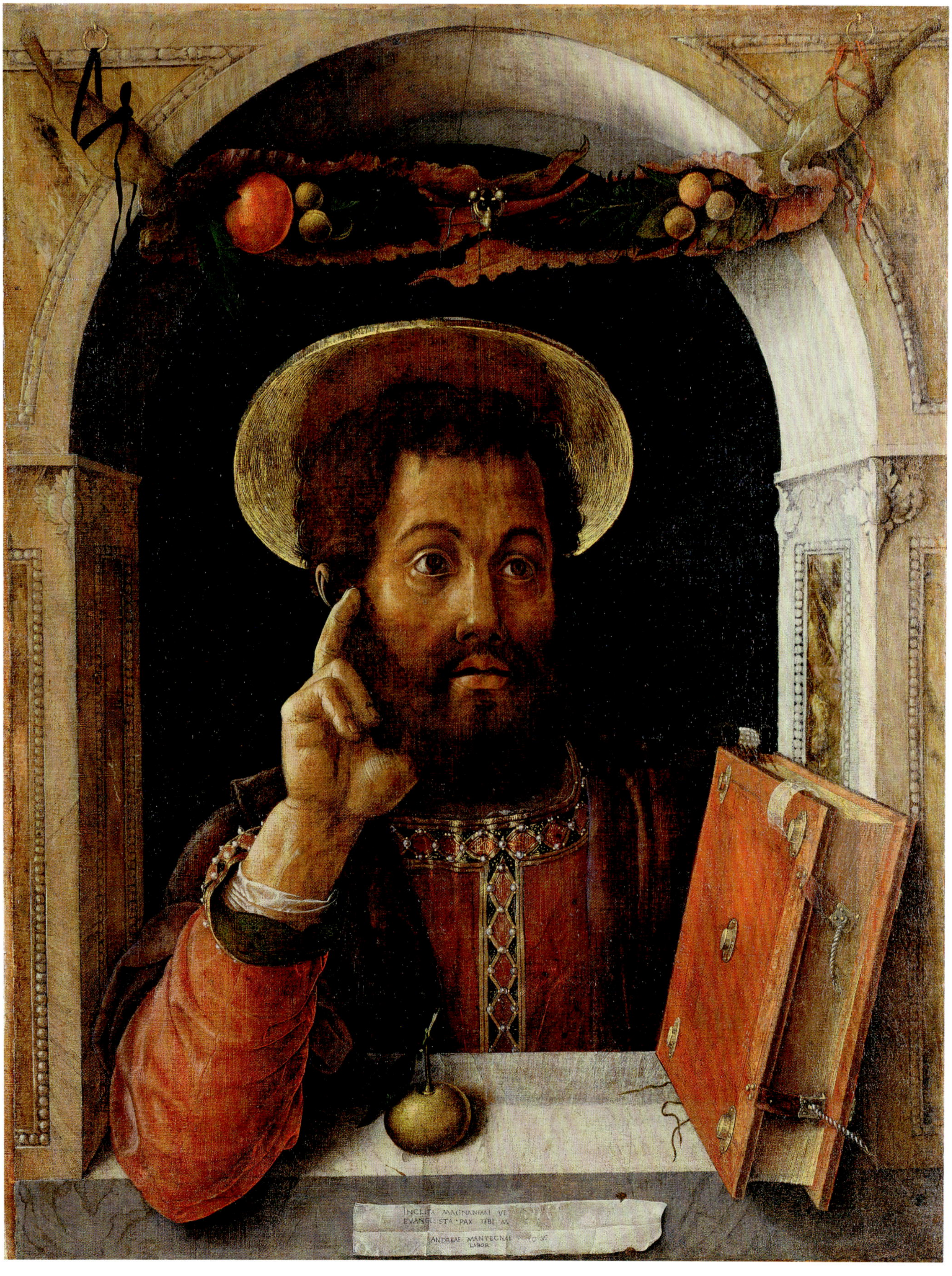
INCLITA MAGNANIMI
EVANGELISTA ·PAX TIBI
ANDREAE MANTEGNAE
LABOR

'Sculpting in paint': Mantegna's Training in Padua

NEVILLE ROWLEY

FIG. 77
ANDREA MANTEGNA
Saint Mark the Evangelist, about 1448
Egg tempera on canvas, 81.1 × 63.6 cm
Städel Museum, Frankfurt (1046)

The respective beginnings of Mantegna and Bellini are marked by a great difference in temperament. While the modest Giovanni took his time in emerging from the bosom of his father Jacopo, the proud Andrea proclaimed his merits in his very first works. There he stands in 1448, aged 17, already personally entrusted with painting the high altar of the Church of Santa Sofia in Padua. In the mid-sixteenth century, the painter, architect and art historian Giorgio Vasari admired the work, its signature declaring its author's age: 'it appears made by someone mature and well-practised, not by a youth.'[1] The *Santa Sofia Altarpiece* is unfortunately lost, but another painting executed by Mantegna in the same period, a *Saint Mark* housed in the Städelsches Kunstinstitut in Frankfurt (fig. 77), enables us to grasp the range of his precocious genius. Here too, Mantegna felt the need to sign his work, in calligraphic writing inspired by antiquity, applied to a piece of parchment that seems to have been glued onto the painting itself.[2] Even more than this virtuoso *trompe l'oeil*, it is the overall image that draws in our gaze. The niche surrounding the saint forms a fictive frame that allows the evangelist to emerge into the world of the beholder, thanks to his right elbow, nonchalantly resting on the ledge, and the book, as scarlet as his sleeve, depicted in striking foreshortening. In about 1448, no one had painted in this manner, either in Padua or Venice.

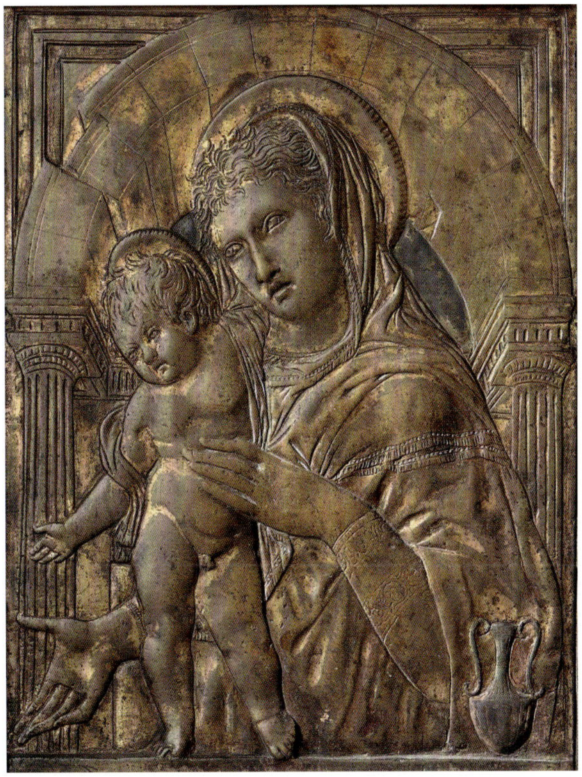

FIG. 78
After DONATELLO
Virgin and Child in a Niche, about 1440–50
Bronze and silver, 20.5 × 15.5 × 0.9 cm
Skulpturensammlung und Museum für Byzantinische Kunst, Staatliche Museen zu Berlin (3044)

The young Andrea's pictorial models were elsewhere. First of all, there was Flanders: during the 1430s, Jan van Eyck had invented a new way of painting, enabling artists to convey an unheard-of degree of detail and soon eliciting admiration throughout Europe. While Mantegna was not using oil here, like van Eyck, but tempera, he was aiming for Netherlandish pictorial illusion in the *trompe-l'oeil* piece of paper in the foreground, and in the open clasps of the closed book.[3] As for his interest in the depiction of space, that came from elsewhere – Florence. In about 1415, the goldsmith and sculptor Filippo Brunelleschi had set off a figurative revolution by inventing a system of realist representation in which lines parallel to the plane of a painting converge on a single point. This 'mathematical perspective' initially left painters indifferent, the first artist to take an interest in it being a great friend of Brunelleschi's, the sculptor Donatello. During the 1420s, the invention was taken up by Florentine painters, thanks to Masaccio, and soon it spread through the whole city, Tuscany and a good part of Italy. Several followers of Masaccio were summoned to the Veneto, ranging from Paolo Uccello to Andrea del Castagno and including Filippo Lippi, and the works they left there could not have failed to intrigue the young Mantegna.[4] At the end of 1443, another Florentine,

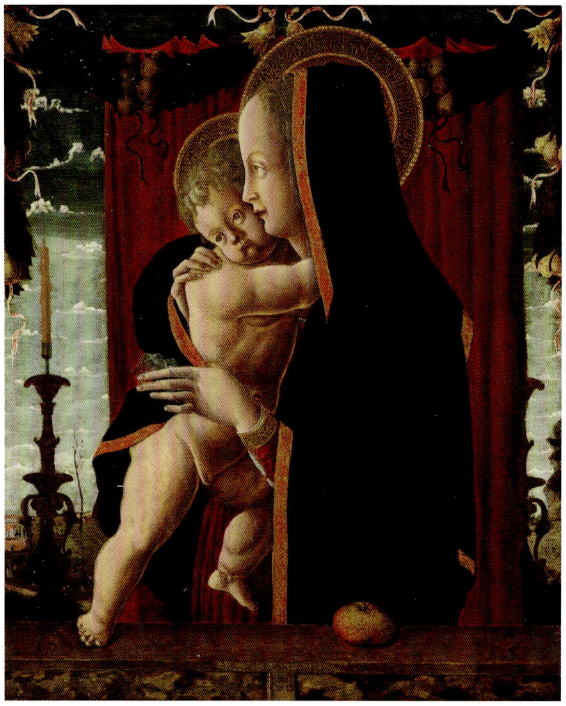

FIG. 79
FRANCESCO SQUARCIONE
The Virgin and Child, 1449–52
Egg tempera on poplar, 87 × 69.5 cm
Gemäldegalerie, Staatliche Museen zu Berlin (27A)

FIG. 80
FRANCESCO SQUARCIONE
De Lazara Polyptych, about 1452
Egg tempera on panel, 175 × 220 cm
Musei Civici Eremitani (Archaeological and Art Museum), Padua (399)

Donatello, settled in Padua. Mantegna was 12, the ideal age for learning this new art like a mother tongue.

When he arrived in Padua, Donatello was nearly 60 and hardly lacked laurels: he had sculpted some fundamental works for the greatest Florentine institutions and for the Medici, who had controlled the city since 1434; he had gone to Rome to serve the pope and had worked in a number of Italian cities including Siena and Naples. Yet his glory was limited. In Florence people spoke more about the bronze doors of the Cathedral Baptistry, cast by Lorenzo Ghiberti, than those made by Donatello for the Old Sacristy in the Church of San Lorenzo.[5] Above all, the city only had eyes for Brunelleschi, who had just built a monumental dome for the Cathedral using technical procedures forgotten since antiquity. Donatello did not want to stay in the shadows: in Padua, he was promised substantial funding for producing bronze sculpture on an unprecedented scale. Soon enough a decade-long project began, leading to the creation of a Crucifix and the high altar for the Franciscan Basilica of the Santo (fig. 2), as well as an equestrian monument on the adjacent piazza representing the *condottiere* Erasmo da Narni, nicknamed Gattamelata (fig. 1). No horse had been cast in bronze since antiquity, nor had anyone had the idea (or the means) of erecting an immense altarpiece in the same medium.[6] For Donatello, his sojourn in Padua was a dream opportunity to pit himself against the Ancients, and to contribute to their 'renaissance' while creating his own legend.

If the sojourns made by the Florentine painters in the Veneto had only a limited influence on local artists, none of the latter could remain indifferent to the innovative art imported by Donatello. For his work in the Santo, he recruited numerous collaborators, first and foremost sculptors and smelters, but also painters for certain decorations. What soon became evident was just how pictorial the art of Donatello is: apart from the monumental sculptures of the Virgin and Child surrounded by saints, he executed four notable narrative scenes in low relief, conceived as paintings – each created with virtuoso perspective and narration animated by a constant flow of figures with a wealth of expressions. Mantegna absorbed this narrative vein, and lost no time in reiterating it, in his own manner, in the frescoes for the Ovetari Chapel in the Church of the Eremitani in Padua, where he began to work as soon as he had completed the *Santa Sofia Altarpiece*, in 1448.[7] He was equally impressed by the figures surmounting the altar in the Santo: his *Saint Mark* has a face of bronze, while the niche from which he emerges seems almost transposed from a Donatellesque plaquette produced in the same moment (fig. 78).[8] Donatello may thus be considered the true master of Mantegna, of whom it was said as early as 1449 that he 'sculpted in paint, truly lifelike and real'.[9]

Before the arrival of Donatello, Mantegna nonetheless needed a painter to teach him the rudiments of his profession. Born in a small village not far from Padua, Isola di Carturo, Andrea came into the city in about 1441, aged 10 or so, to settle under the wings of a weaver turned painter, Francesco Squarcione.[10] Mantegna soon became his adoptive son, a common practice which enabled a master to avoid having to pay a young collaborator.[11] The value of this new paternal situation cannot be overestimated: the son of a carpenter who had tried in vain to set up shop in the city, Andrea was now the heir of a painter of swiftly increasing renown. When, only a few years later, he regarded himself a better artist than his adoptive father, Mantegna had no hesitation in regaining his freedom; and one more clearly understands why he insisted on signing his first works.[12]

If one compares the *Saint Mark* with the sole documented work by Squarcione that has come down to us, the *De Lazara Polyptych* (fig. 80), originally painted between 1449 and 1452 for the Carmelite church in Padua, Mantegna's artistic superiority is obvious. Squarcione unquestionably knew mathematical perspective, *all'antica* architectural vocabulary and Netherlandish realism, but he used them with far less mastery than his brilliant former pupil. As for the *Virgin and Child* now in the Gemäldegalerie in Berlin (fig. 79), the only other work certainly by the master's hand, we are no doubt looking at a later work, which cannot therefore be regarded as playing a decisive role in the development of Mantegna.[13] From a general point of view, the multi-coloured fruit garlands, refined architectural niches, gilded candelabra and antique putti found in the oeuvre of many of the artists who passed through Padua in the middle years of the century, including Giorgio Schiavone, Marco Zoppo, Cosimo Tura, Carlo Crivelli and Giovanni Boccati, all the aspects referred to as 'Squarcionesque' were in fact first assimilated by Mantegna himself: suffice it to cite the apple in the foreground of the *Saint Mark*, which recurs almost identically in the Berlin *Virgin*.[14] Squarcione's future fame, founded on his intimate rapport with humanists and his important collections of

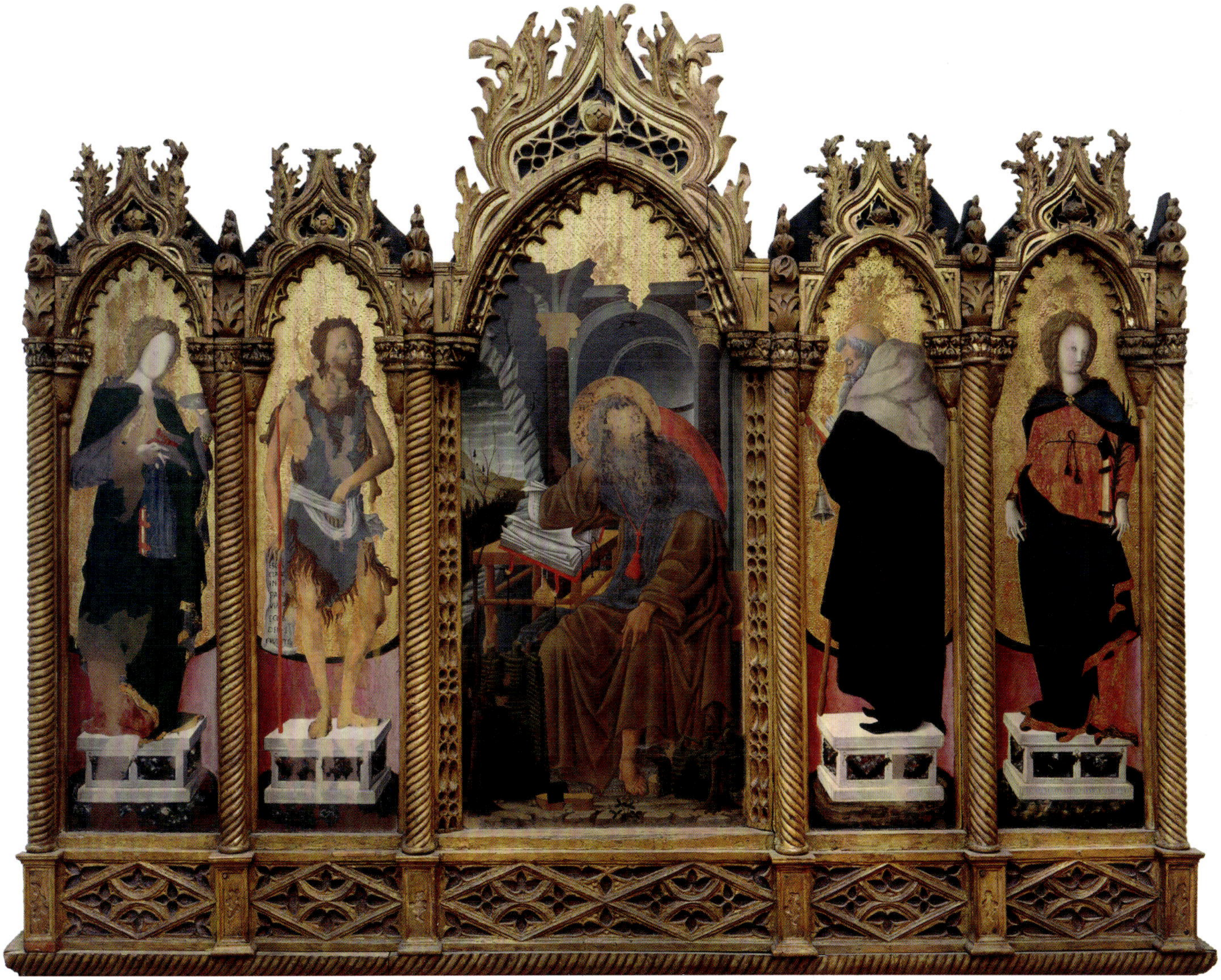

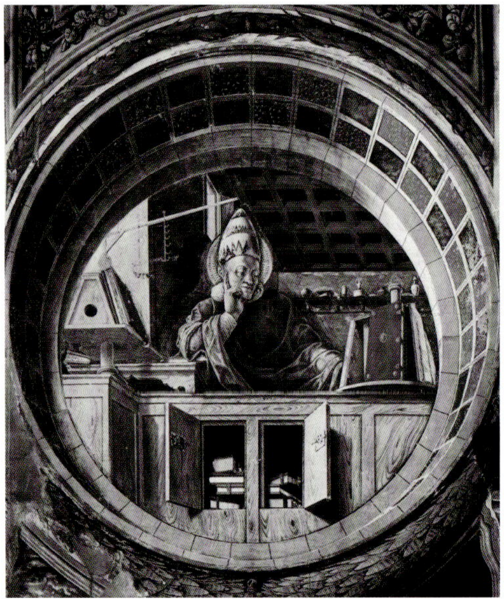

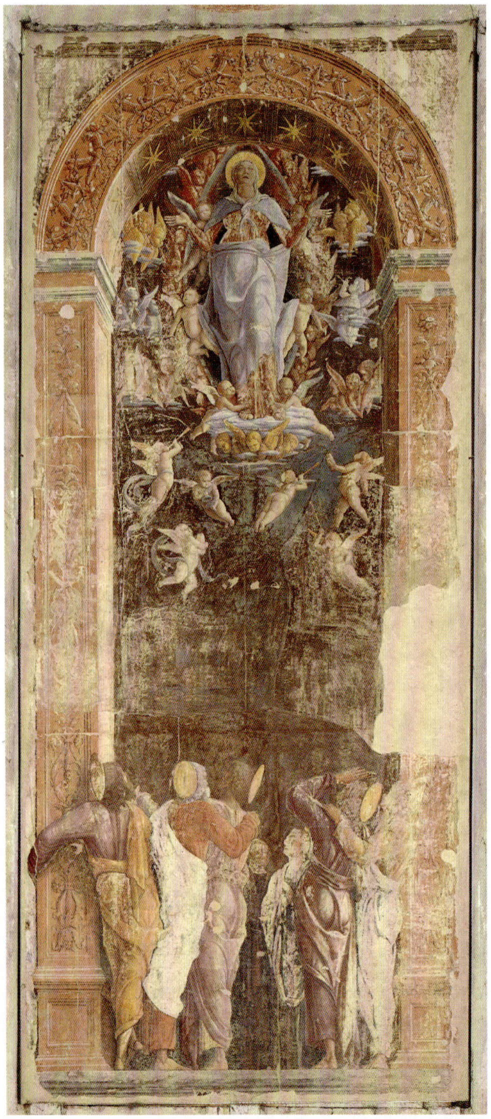

FIG. 81
NICCOLÒ PIZZOLO
Saint Gregory, about 1449
Fresco, Ovetari Chapel, Church of the Eremitani, Padua (destroyed), photograph taken before Allied bombing in 1944
Church of the Eremitani, Padua

FIG. 82
ANDREA MANTEGNA
The Assumption of the Virgin, about 1456
Fresco, Ovetari Chapel
Church of the Eremitani, Padua

drawings and ancient and modern reliefs, was certainly taking root when Mantegna was in his workshop. However, the works that have come down to us suggest that it was in fact Mantegna's painting, with its immediate novelty, that greatly contributed to the shaping of Squarcione's style as we know it today, as well as the reputation he was proud of vaunting throughout his life.[15]

Yet at the end of the 1440s, Mantegna was not the only artist from Padua who 'painted in the latest fashion'; Niccolò Pizzolo, ten years his senior, was that much closer to the innovations introduced by Donatello in the Santo as he had worked on the project in 1447.[16] The following year, Mantegna and Pizzolo were hired to paint frescoes in the chapel dedicated to the memory of Antonio Ovetari, in the Church of the Eremitani in Padua; and alongside these young local artists, the patron's widow, Imperatrice Forzatè, summoned two more experienced painters active in Venice, Giovanni d'Alemagna and Antonio Vivarini.[17] Giovanni died in 1450 and Antonio abandoned the project in the following year, so two new painters, Ansuino da Forlì and Bono da Ferrara, were brought in as reinforcements. By now the Ovetari Chapel had become a merciless competition ground between Pizzolo and Mantegna, who rivalled one another in ingeniousness, creating the most audacious foreshortening, such as those in the tondi of the chapel's pendentives by Pizzolo (fig. 81).[18] The latter's murder in 1453 allowed Mantegna to reign over the chapel's decoration alone, and thus to carry out the frescoes on the lower register (the most visible ones), not to mention the monumental *Assumption of the Virgin* behind the altar carved by Giovanni da Pisa (figs 82, 250). Having seen Mantegna's *Assumption*, Imperatrice Forzatè sued the young artist for having painted only eight Apostles around the Virgin, not twelve.[19] Mantegna won the case; for him, the spatial dynamics counted more than the sacred texts he was supposed to describe.

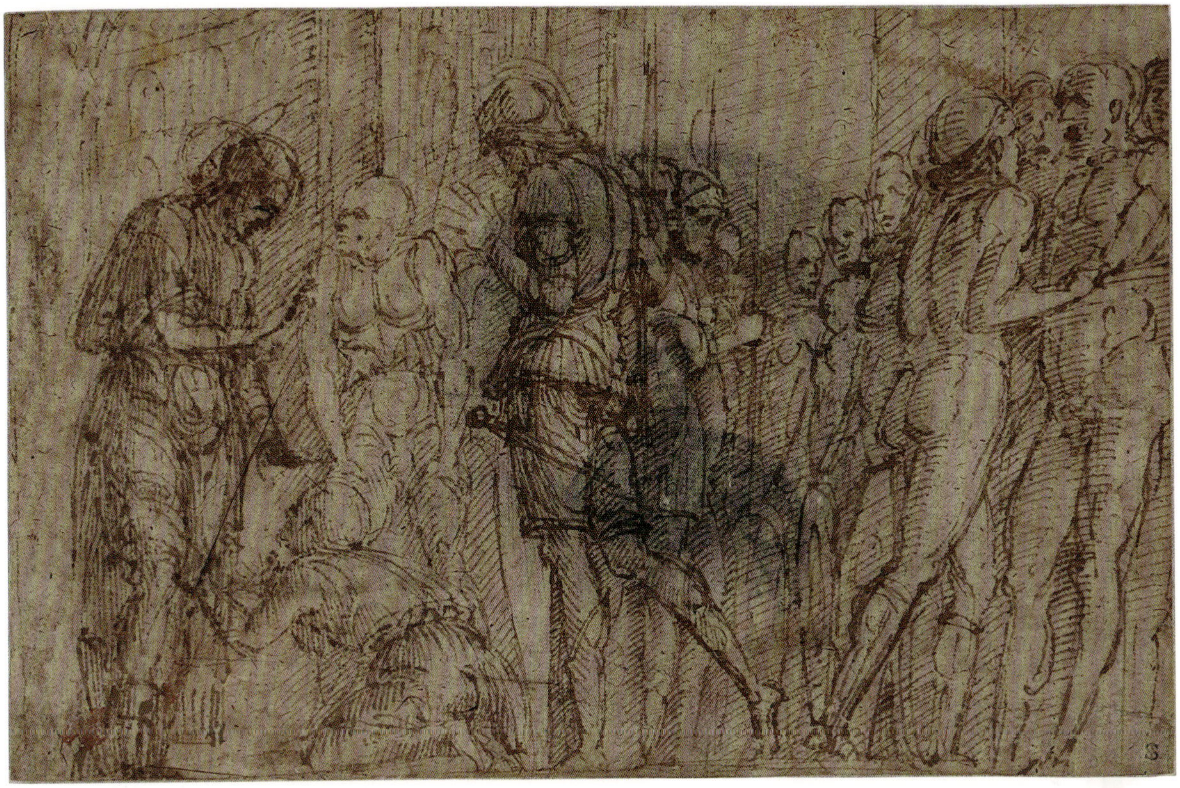

FIG. 83
ANDREA MANTEGNA
Saint James led to martyrdom, about 1453
Pen and brown ink on paper, 16.4 × 25.6 cm
The British Museum, London (1976,0616.1)

A preparatory drawing by Mantegna for one of the frescoes in the Ovetari Chapel, now in the British Museum, represents one of the scenes on the lower register with *Saint James led to Martyrdom* (fig. 83). The composition of the fresco (fig. 251) is already present: a crowd gathered to watch the last moments of a condemned man, barely held back, on the right, by a Roman soldier. In the drawing, this figure is represented nude the better to study his anatomy – a procedure that would become common to all art academies but which in Mantegna's day was only adopted by very few artists.[20] On the left, Saint James has just healed a crippled man, and the artist was initially unsure about the position of the saint's head, which was originally more inclined.[21] The greater extension of vertical space in the fresco allowed Mantegna to place a monumental *all'antica* triumphal arch on the left, balanced on the right by a flag on a long pole, topped by mysterious scales. The artist also accentuated the effect of perspective, as if the figures were in reality on a platform over the beholder's head – like Donatello's bronze saints in the Santo altar. Leaning against the triumphal arch, in the middle, is a pensive soldier holding a shield, the object of much admiration through the centuries, right up to Marcel Proust in *À la recherche du temps perdu*.[22] Sadly, this is not entirely possible to appreciate today: on 11 March 1944, the Ovetari Chapel was destroyed by Anglo-American bombardment. Mantegna's first masterpieces only survive in fragmentary form.[23]

At the beginning of 1454, Donatello returned to Florence after ten years in Padua. Through his contact with him, Mantegna had become a respected master, the author of significant commissions in the city and beyond; in 1449 he even painted a double portrait of the future Marquess of Ferrara, Leonello d'Este, and his treasurer.[24] In 1453, Andrea's marriage to Nicolosia Bellini[25] gave him access not only to the Drawing Books of his father-in-law Jacopo – albums of endlessly rich compositional inventions, but also to an ever larger client base.[26] As for Jacopo, he had already worked in Padua, but he would certainly not have looked down on his already celebrated son-in-law, who could strengthen his position there. No doubt Jacopo's sons Gentile and Giovanni, who were then apprentices, regarded Mantegna with envy and admiration. During these years, when the Ovetari project was being completed (the chapel was inaugurated in 1457), Giovanni often came to Padua, admiring the work of his brother-in-law, whom he always wished to outdo.[27]

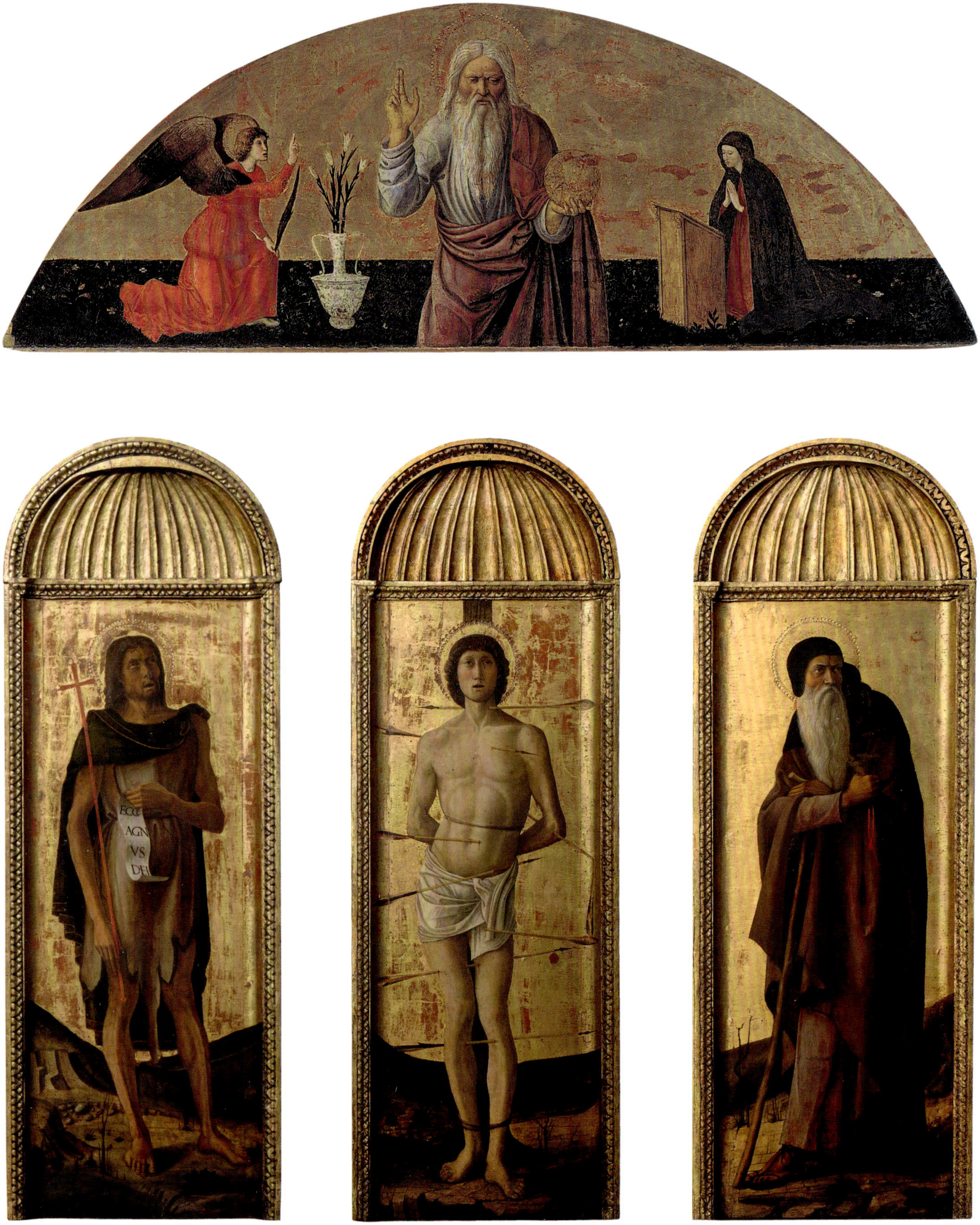

Jacopo Bellini and the Formation of Giovanni

SARAH VOWLES AND
DAGMAR KORBACHER

FIG. 84
Attributed to
GIOVANNI BELLINI
Saint Sebastian Triptych,
1462–4
Egg tempera on panel;
lunette above (studio of
GIOVANNI BELLINI)
God the Father blessing, with the Annunciation 59 × 170 cm;
left *Saint John the Baptist*
126 × 48.4;
centre *Saint Sebastian*
125.5 × 46.5 cm;
right *Saint Anthony Abbot*
126 × 46.5 cm
Galleria dell'Accademia,
Venice (621a)

Giovanni Bellini's path to success was smoothed by his family's artistic standing. This was true as late as 1479 when, with the departure of his brother Gentile for Constantinople, Giovanni inherited his role as official painter to the Serenissima. As a younger man, his social and artistic status had been bolstered by his father's reputation, and he had made his name working as part of the energetic, ubiquitous Bellini workshop. This family business had been established by Jacopo Bellini, along with his own half-brother Giovanni, during the 1430s, when demand for Jacopo's works was growing.[1] Over the next 20 years, Jacopo was kept busy with commissions in Padua and Verona as well as Venice, and even attracted the attention of foreign lords such as Leonello d'Este of Ferrara.[2] He worked as a sculptor as well as a painter, evidently feeling confident enough to submit (unsuccessful) proposals for an equestrian monument to Leonello in the early 1440s.[3] Jacopo trained his two sons to become his chief assistants in the studio and, between 1459 and 1465, two different commissions testify to the family's collaboration on major projects.

In either 1459 or 1460, Jacopo, Gentile and Giovanni jointly signed an altarpiece commissioned for the funerary chapel of the *condottiere* Erasmo da Narni, known as Gattamelata, in the Santo in Padua.[4] Only one of the main panels now survives: the *Saints Anthony Abbot and Bernardino of Siena* in the National Gallery of Art, Washington.[5] Three small paintings, however, are usually thought to have formed the predella of the altarpiece: *The Adoration of the Magi* in Ferrara (fig. 85), *The Crucifixion* in Venice (fig. 86) and *The Descent of Christ into Limbo* in Padua (fig. 87). All three derive to some extent from Jacopo's designs on the same theme in his Drawing Books, although they do not appear to be by his own hand.[6] It was suggested that they are works by the young Giovanni, although there is no documentary evidence of the division of labour among the studio. While it may not be possible conclusively to attribute the panels of the altarpiece to a particular hand, it is nevertheless clear that father and sons worked closely together, sublimating their personal styles into a single workshop aesthetic that defies individuation even today.

Shortly after completing the *Gattamelata Altarpiece* in 1460, the Bellini workshop was commissioned to paint the first of four memorial triptychs for Santa Maria della Carità, all now in the Accademia, Venice. Possibly executed under Giovanni's leadership rather than that of Jacopo, the triptychs were evidently conceived as a set, despite being commissioned by different patrons.[7]

The *Saint Sebastian Triptych* (fig. 84), was one of the first to be completed: commissioned by Zaccaria Vettori, it shows Sebastian flanked by saints John the Baptist and Anthony Abbot, with a lunette of God the Father and the Annunciation above. Once again, the figures appear to be based on the types of saints in Jacopo's Drawing Books.[8] They were probably painted by either Gentile or Giovanni, but attempts to assign particular figures to Giovanni have been inconclusive: the main level of the *Saint Sebastian* triptych has, however, been cautiously attributed to him.[9]

The triptych blends conservatism with innovation: while the saints are shown against traditional gold grounds, there is an effort to unify their fictive space. A low, shallow band of landscape seems to connect the panels, while the same light source falls on all three saints from the left. While it is tempting to read such spatial construction as the work of the young Giovanni, perhaps in response to Mantegna's achievement of the same principle in his *San Zeno Altarpiece*, it is clear that Jacopo had been making similar attempts at unity 20 years previously in a polyptych now partly in Berlin (fig. 88), discussed below. The desire to articulate and define the interior space of a picture was brought to life by Mantegna, but it may have been born with Jacopo.

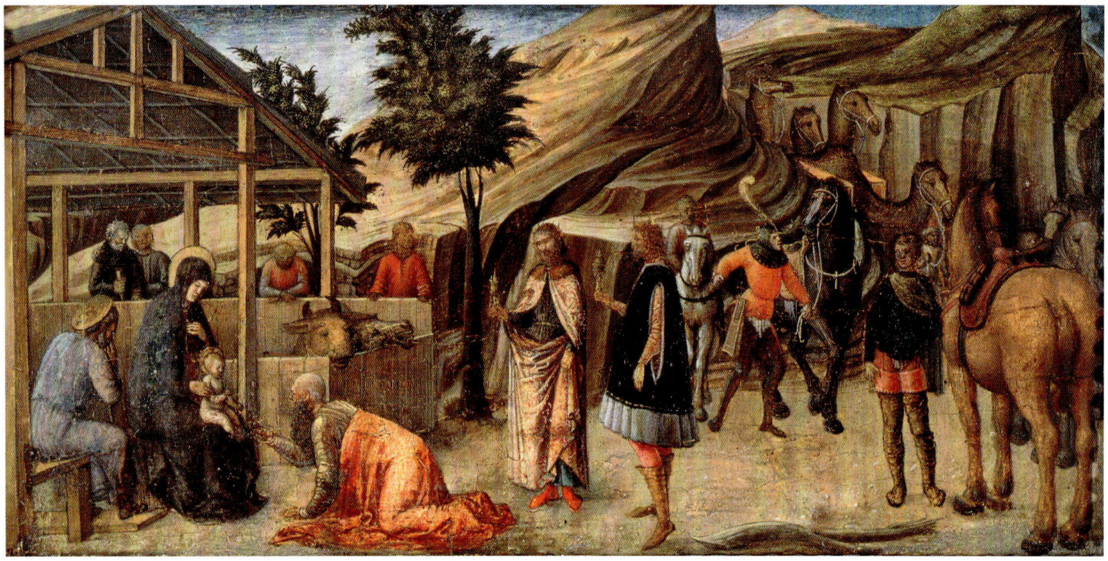

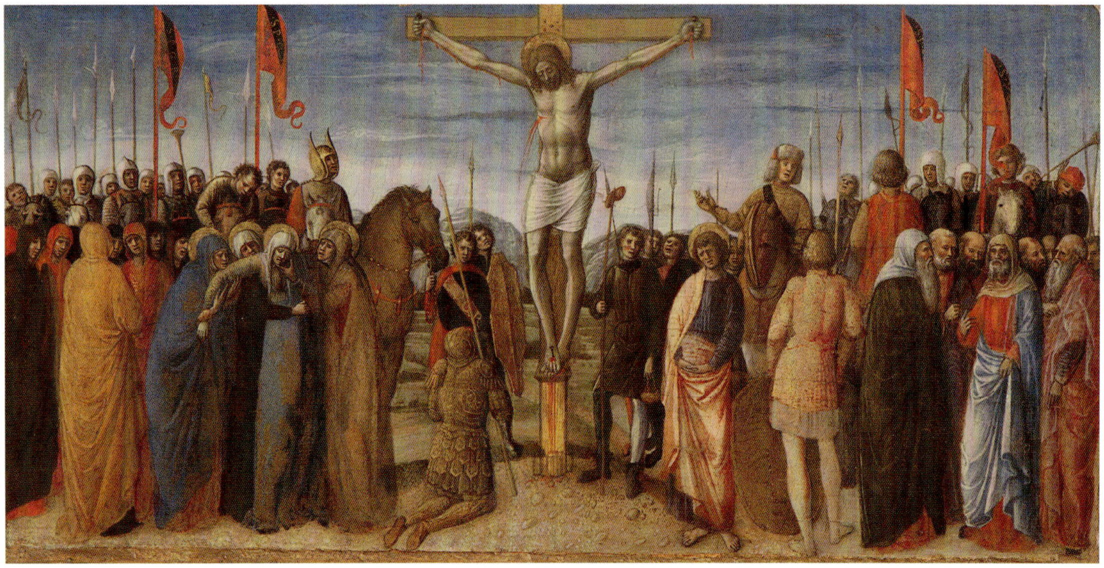

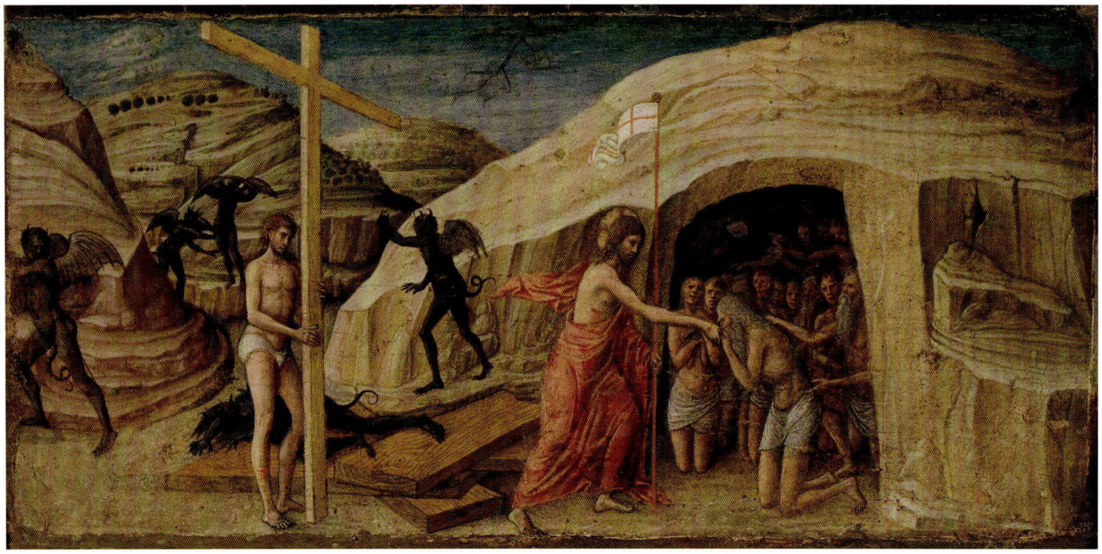

FIG. 85
JACOPO BELLINI, with possible contributions by GIOVANNI and GENTILE BELLINI
The Adoration of the Magi, about 1459–60
Egg tempera on panel, 29 × 57 cm
Pinacoteca Nazionale, Ferrara (327)

FIG. 86
JACOPO BELLINI, with possible contributions by GIOVANNI and GENTILE BELLINI
The Crucifixion, about 1459–60
Egg tempera on panel, 28.6 × 57 cm
Museo Correr, Venice (29)

FIG. 87
JACOPO BELLINI, with possible contributions by GIOVANNI and GENTILE BELLINI
The Descent of Christ into Limbo, about 1459–60
Egg tempera on panel, 28.5 × 58 cm
Musei Civici agli Eremitani, Museo d'Arte Medievale e Moderna, Padua (416)

JACOPO BELLINI, with possible contributions by GIOVANNI and GENTILE BELLINI, detail of *The Crucifixion* (FIG. 86)

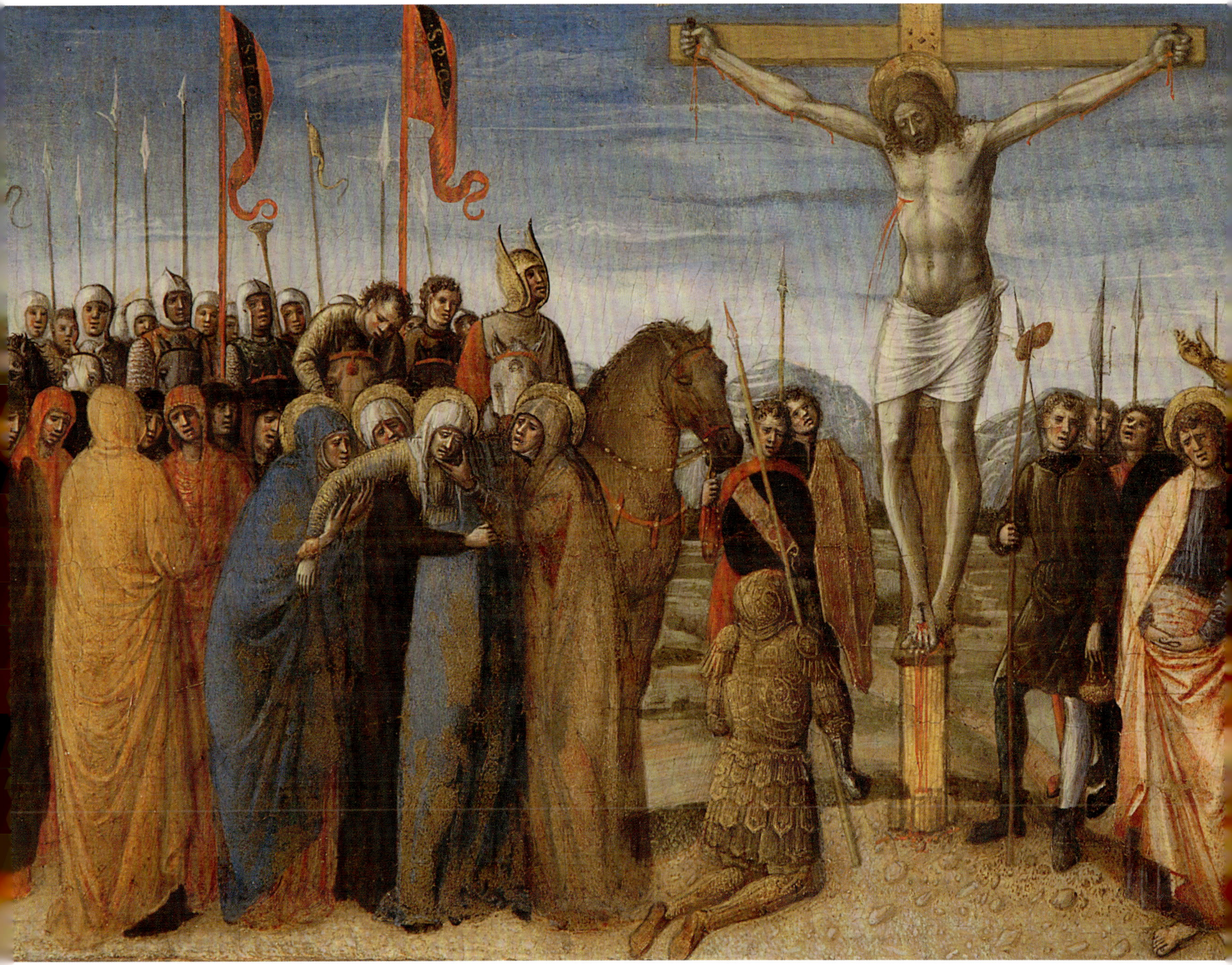

When the young Giovanni witnessed a will in 1459, he was already living away from home in the parish of San Lio, where he presumably had a workshop of his own while still employed in the family workshop in San Marco. His residence in another part of the city may have been part of a business strategy, intended to establish the Bellini family more widely and to help them compete with their chief rivals, the Vivarini.[10] If so, Jacopo evidently planned to add geographical reach to their business, alongside an increasingly broad selection of artworks.[11]

Jacopo's training

> Jacopo painted this with his slender genius as far as his artistry allowed. Gentile, this Venetian's teacher, [was] most renowned for his fame throughout the world. In that excellent Venetian man, his native city of Fabriano rejoices.[12]

With these words, Jacopo Bellini signed his fresco of the *Crucifixion* in Verona Cathedral in 1436.[13] Born in around 1400, he was then an established master in his own right but his affection for his teacher Gentile da Fabriano remained strong. He named his eldest son in his master's honour and painted a profile portrait of Gentile (now lost) which, by the early sixteenth century, was in the collection of the poet Pietro Bembo in Padua.[14] There is no firm documentation of when or where Jacopo began working with Gentile, although he is sometimes identified with the Jacopo, pupil of that master, who was arrested for assault in Florence in the early 1420s.[15] He clearly placed a high value on Gentile's teaching and may have accompanied his master not only to Tuscany but also to Rome.

Jacopo was born into a world where the International Gothic aesthetic of courtly elegance, elongated figures and intricate surface decoration still held sway. His early works, such as four panels from a polyptych now divided between Berlin and a private collection, preserve traces of this style. Dating from the mid-1430s, they represent Saint Peter and a male saint reading (fig. 88), Saint Jerome and an unidentified female saint, who seems to be the central figure and thus the key to the original destination of the panels.[16] All are elegantly clad in rather flat Gothic draperies, but their heads are framed by shell-shaped niches which appear to have Florentine origins, suggesting Jacopo's desire to blend Venetian tradition with Tuscan innovation.[17] The different viewpoints of the niches also indicate an attempt to unite the narrative world of the four panels with an overriding single-point perspective. In this, Jacopo's work may reflect not so much his awareness of Gentile da Fabriano's work, but that of the perspective enthusiast Paolo Uccello, who came to work on the mosaics of San Marco in 1425. He also drew inspiration from the powerfully emotive work of Donatello: the motif of the half-length *Dead Christ* with mourning saints or angels, which appears in a drawing by Jacopo in the London Drawing Book[18] as well as later paintings by Giovanni, was surely based on Donatello's bronze relief for the high altar of the Santo in Padua, executed in 1449 (fig. 2).[19]

Like his son Giovanni, Jacopo eagerly assimilated new styles and ideas. From 1430 he worked for patrons in Verona and Padua, where scholarly artistic circles may have ripened an interest in antiquity that he originally derived from Gentile da Fabriano. By the end of his life Jacopo, like his contemporary Francesco Squarcione, had built up his own collection of antiquities and may have been planning to catalogue them: the rows of empty circles on pages from his London Drawing Book may have been intended to record antique coins.[20] His work also became increasingly classical, with the Gothic saints of his early altarpieces metamorphosing into the more compact figures recorded in his later Drawing Books.[21]

FIG. 88
JACOPO BELLINI
Saint John the Evangelist (?) and Saint Peter, about 1430–5
Egg tempera and gold on poplar, 88 × 26.6 cm (left); 88.1 × 26.8 cm (right)
Gemäldegalerie, Staatliche Museen zu Berlin (1161)

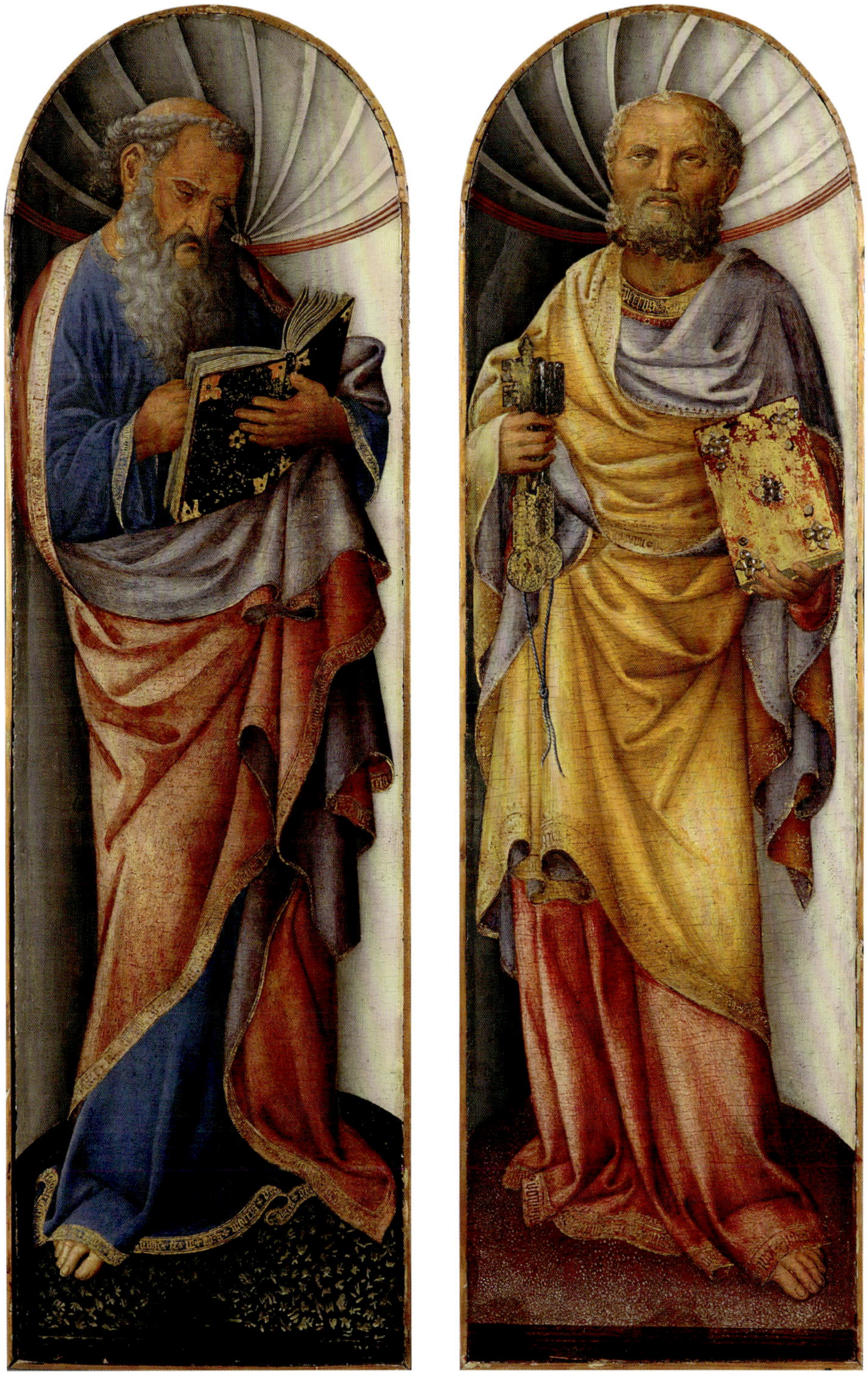

The Drawing Books

Two albums of Jacopo's drawings survive: one of 93 vellum pages in the Louvre in Paris and another of 99 paper pages in the British Museum in London. They underscore the importance of drawing in the Bellini workshop as a medium suitable for recording, exploring and preparing compositions. Differences between the supports and media of the two Books suggest they may have had distinct functions: the drawings on vellum in Paris tend to have been reinforced with pen and brown ink, while those on paper in London are in friable lead-point, which in some places is now barely legible.[22]

The Paris Book contains scenes in both upright and horizontal formats, including pages of a model-book type which assembled motifs for future use. Some were compositions that could be translated into fresco cycles, paintings or predellas, such as *Three dead kings* (fig. 89); others were ideas for decorations or fictive sculpture, such as the *Tomb of a prince* (fig. 90); and a handful were isolated motifs, like the page of lion studies (fig. 91), one of which was adapted by the young Giovanni Bellini in his early *Saint Jerome* (fig. 114).[23] Alongside products of the Bellini studio, the Book also contains pages from an

FIG. 89
JACOPO BELLINI
Three dead kings, from *The Paris Drawing Book of Jacopo Bellini*, about 1455–60
Pen and brown ink and metalpoint on vellum, 22 × 41 cm
Musée du Louvre, Paris (RF 425r)

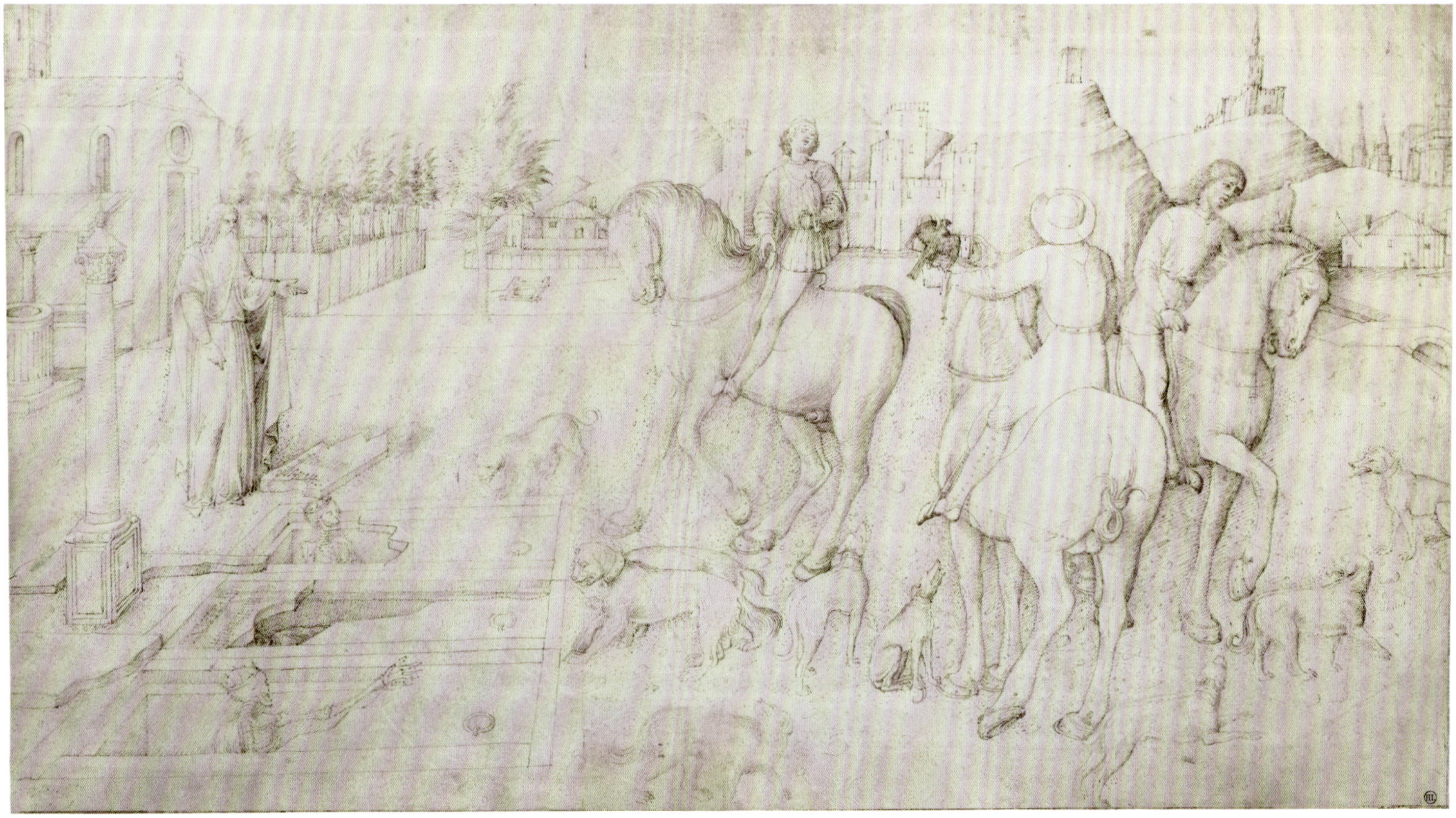

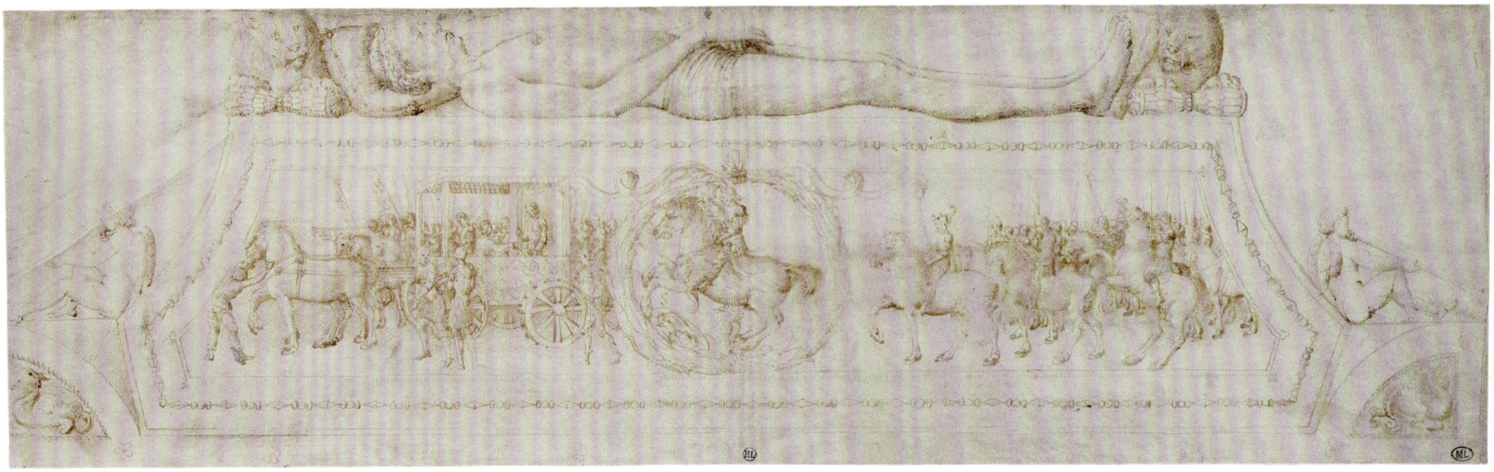

FIG. 90
JACOPO BELLINI
Tomb of a prince, from *The Paris Drawing Book of Jacopo Bellini*, about 1455–60
Pen and brown ink on parchment, 12 × 39.7 cm
Musée du Louvre, Paris
(RF 428r)

earlier fourteenth-century model-book, including an earlier study of lions.[24] The apparent function of this Book as a storehouse of studio repertoire may explain the choice of vellum for its support: expensive but durable, it was traditionally used for model-books that would be much handled.

Paper was slightly less expensive than vellum but also less robust. The same paper, watermarked with scales in a circle, is used throughout the London Book (fig. 92), indicating that the drawings were made over a relatively short period of time. Here only upright scenes are shown, although Jacopo returned at a later stage to expand many of the compositions onto the facing pages: the fact this was possible suggests the drawings were made in loose quires, before binding made it difficult to access the central gutter of the pages.[25]

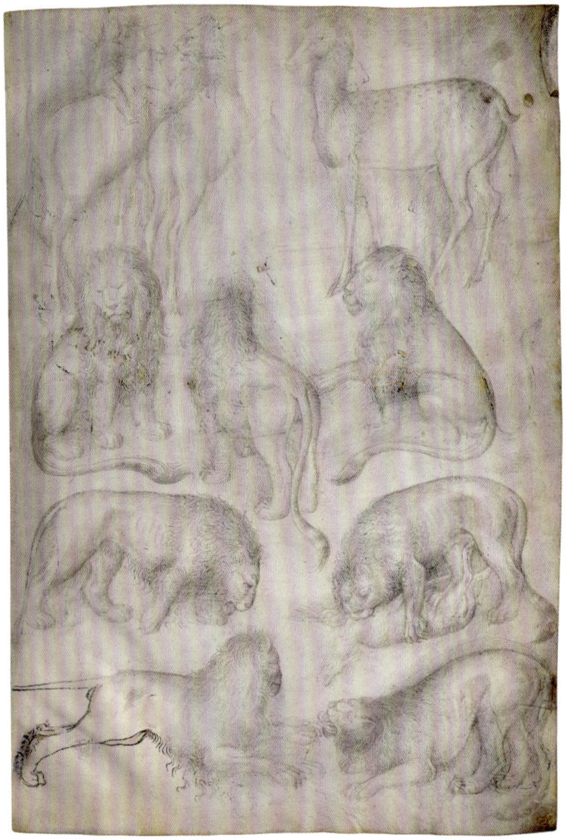

FIG. 91
JACOPO BELLINI
Studies of seven lions and three deer, from *The Paris Drawing Book of Jacopo Bellini*, about 1455–60
Silverpoint on a grey chalk ground, with pen and brown ink, on vellum, 38 × 26 cm
Musée du Louvre, Paris
(RF 1540-91 f. 72v)

The content of the London Book is also puzzling: it includes courtly and religious scenes, but no studies of the Virgin and Child, which would have been a useful resource for a studio who produced so many variants on the subject. Instead, this Book has been convincingly interpreted as a demonstration of Jacopo's *ingegno* or inventiveness, which could be used to impress potential clients with the intellectual capacity of the studio.[26] It is particularly notable for its extravagant architectural drawings which allowed Jacopo to demonstrate his skill in using perspective. This interest seems to have been encouraged among his followers, as can be seen in the drawing of *Two arcades, figures and view* (fig. 93), with its sharply receding colonnades. The Book was probably put together in the mid-1450s, as two studies of equestrian monuments indicate Jacopo's awareness of Donatello's *Gattamelata* in Padua (fig. 1), and the figural types are close to those of paintings produced in the workshop at this period (figs 85, 86, 87). While a wider range of dates has been argued for the Paris Book, it may well have been compiled at the same date as the London Book.

The two Drawing Books had a powerful impact on the young Giovanni, who found the seeds of many aspects of his later work in his father's drawings. Jacopo's

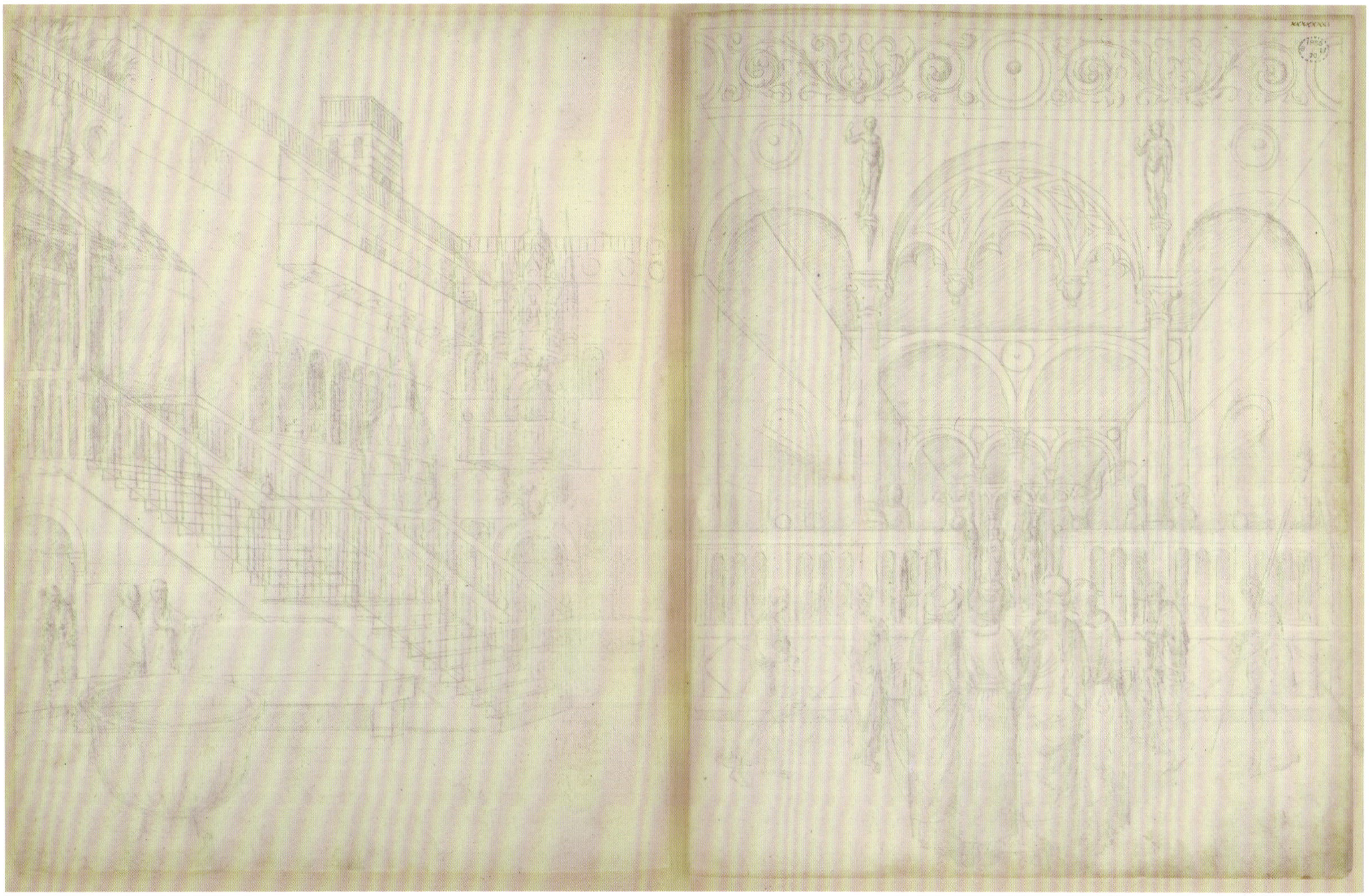

FIG. 92
JACOPO BELLINI
A courtyard of a palace with a staircase on the left and a basin in the foreground (left), *The Flagellation of Christ* (right), from *The London Drawing Book of Jacopo Bellini*, 1440–70
Leadpoint, some of the architecture drawn with the aid of a ruler and a compass, 41.5 × 33.6 cm each page.
The British Museum, London (1855,0811.69v and 1855,0811.70r)

FIG. 93
School of JACOPO BELLINI
Two arcades, figures and view, about 1470–80
Pen and brown ink on vellum, 14.2 × 14.1 cm
Kupferstichkabinett, Staatliche Museen zu Berlin (KdZ 418)

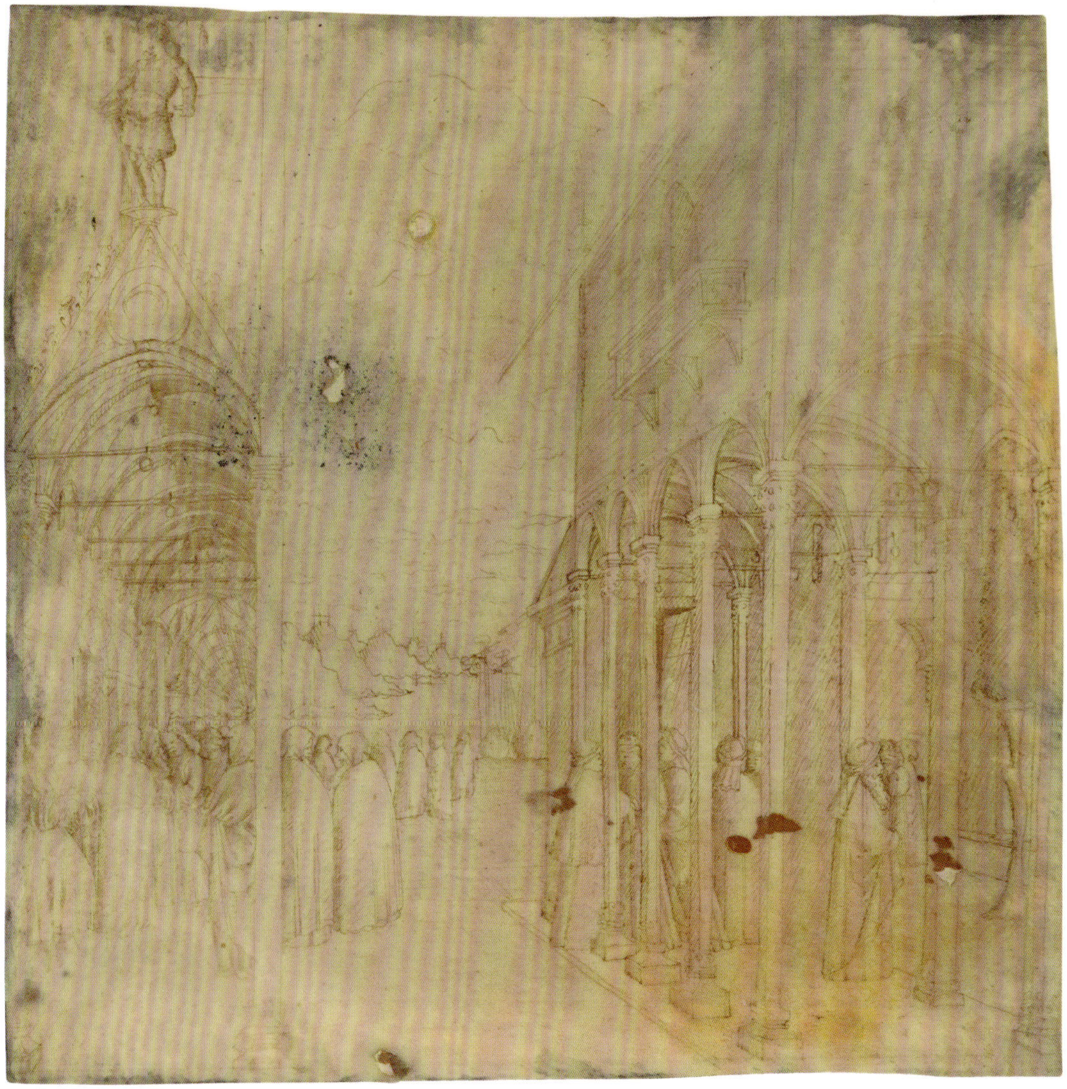

studies already strove to reduce narrative to its barest, most powerful elements and to evoke emotion through stressing the humanity of the Holy Family. His holy scenes were set within broader landscapes, which he often extended even further onto the facing pages and in which he added incidental details of rural or courtly life. Yet these landscapes preserve an enigmatic, half-sacred quality of their own and become part of the storytelling, as in the haunted wastelands of Jacopo's *Saint Jeromes*.[27] Rich in inspiration and meaning, the Books remained treasured objects in the studio even after Jacopo's death and Gentile and Giovanni probably strengthened and retouched drawings which had faded, as they were also prepared to do with their father's stand-alone drawings.[28]

The London Book, testament to Jacopo's intellectual fertility, remained in the family for half a century and was passed down from Jacopo's widow Anna to Gentile and then, in 1507, to Giovanni. By 1530 it was in the possession of the connoisseur Gabriele Vendramin, a patron of Titian, who also owned an album that included drawings for or after Mantegna's *Triumphs*. The fate of the Paris Book is less clear, however. Instead of remaining at the core of workshop practice, where its archaic motifs may no longer have been useful, it seems to have been presented to Sultan Mehmet II by Gentile Bellini during his time in Constantinople in 1479–80, perhaps as a cherished example of Venetian artistry. It remained in Turkey until 1728.[29]

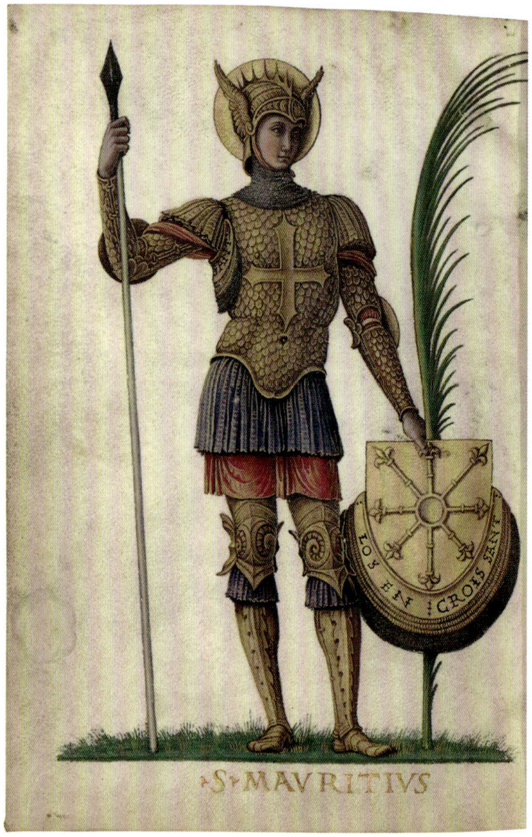

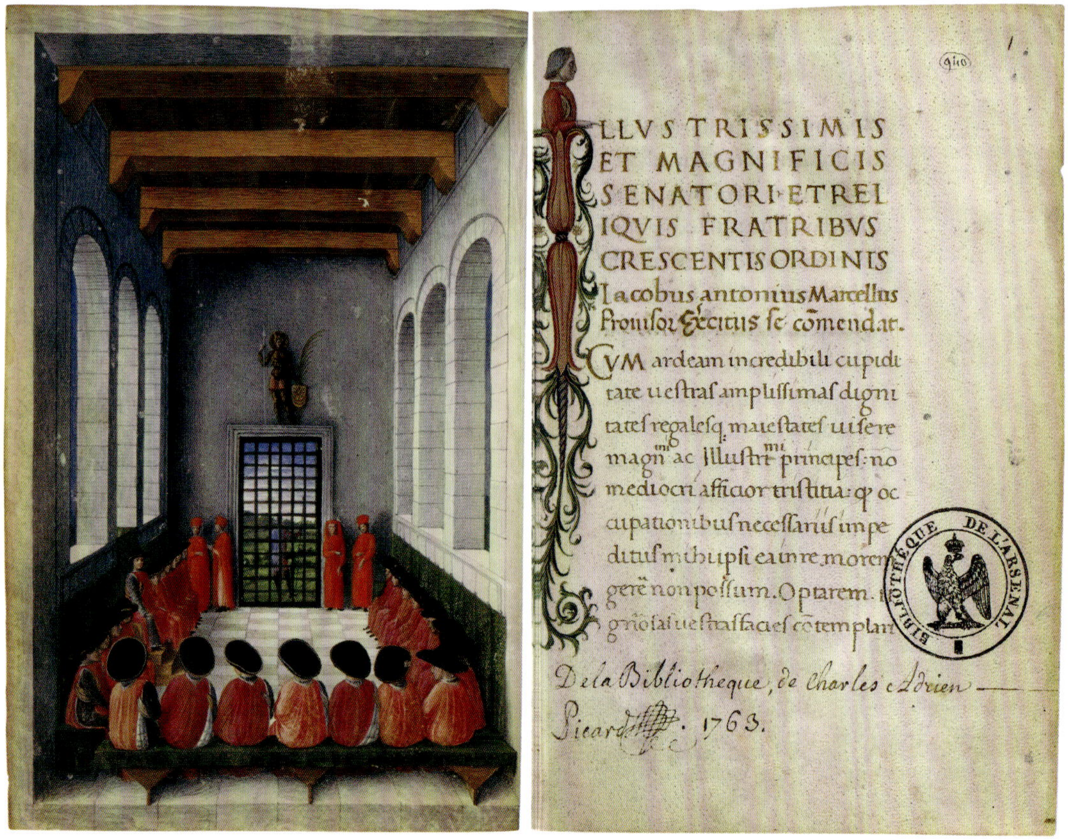

FIG. 94
Attributed to JACOPO BELLINI
Saint Maurice, 1453
Miniature from Jacopo Antonio Marcello, *Passio Mauritii et sotiorum eius*
Tempera, gum or glue on vellum, 18.7 × 14 cm
Bibliothèque de l'Arsenal, Paris (MS 940, fol. 38v)

FIG. 95
Attributed to JACOPO BELLINI
Assembly of the Order of the Crescent, 1453
Miniatures from Jacopo Antonio Marcello, *Passio Mauritii et sotiorum eius*
Tempera, gum or glue on vellum, 18.7 × 14 cm (each page)
Bibliothèque de l'Arsenal, Paris (MS 940, fols Cv-1r)

Miniature painting

As the next generation of the Bellini family grew to manhood, Jacopo could reassure himself that the future of the family workshop was secure. In Gentile and Giovanni, he had two talented painters who could continue the main work of the studio, while he had also managed to add a new side-line in manuscript illumination. This came courtesy of his nephew Leonardo, who had joined the studio as a boy in 1431 and who, after training with Jacopo for 12 years, became a specialist miniaturist.[30] It was a field which seems to have attracted not only his cousin Giovanni but also the young Mantegna.

There has been lively scholarly debate about the role of book illumination in the careers of Mantegna and Bellini, ever since Millard Meiss in 1957 made a claim for 'Mantegna as illuminator'.[31] This is often countered with Mantegna's own much-quoted objection that he 'was unused to painting small figures', reported to the Duke of Milan in 1480 by Federico Gonzaga.[32] However, Federico was in fact referring to small-scale paintings rather than to miniatures, and his sincerity is suspect, for any examination of the works of Mantegna or Bellini demonstrates that both were accustomed to painting on an extremely small scale in the backgrounds of their pictures.[33] There is no doubt that they were both capable of executing miniature works on vellum, even though conclusive proof is lacking. It is likely, however, that their relative approaches would have differed from that of a specialist illuminator such as Bellini's cousin Leonardo.

The discussion of Bellini's involvement in illumination focuses on two important manuscripts of the 1450s, which stand out from the conventions of book illumination in Padua and Venice at the time. Both feature large figures, which fill the page in a way that suggests the spatial awareness of a painter rather a dedicated illuminator.[34] Both were commissioned by Jacopo Antonio Marcello, a patrician, humanist and *provveditore* of the Venetian armies, who was married to a Paduan noblewoman. He is known to have commissioned works from Jacopo Bellini, whose Drawing Books include studies of antiquities at Monselice, Marcello's residence near Padua.[35] Even if neither Jacopo nor Giovanni can be considered manuscript illuminators in the same sense as Leonardo Bellini, it is clear that the family had an interest in the field and we cannot exclude the possibility that they made isolated works in the medium.[36]

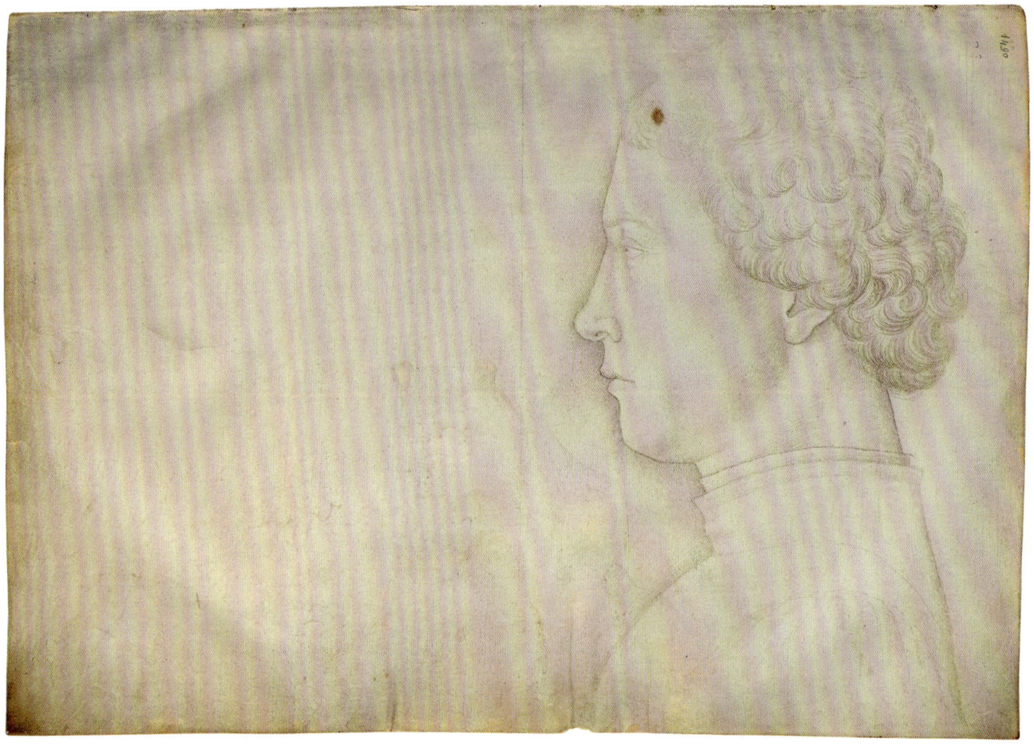

FIG. 96
JACOPO BELLINI
Profile of a young man, from *The Paris Drawing Book of Jacopo Bellini*, about 1455–60
Silverpoint on grey chalk ground, on vellum, 38 × 26 cm
Musée du Louvre, Paris (RF 1490-23 f. 22)

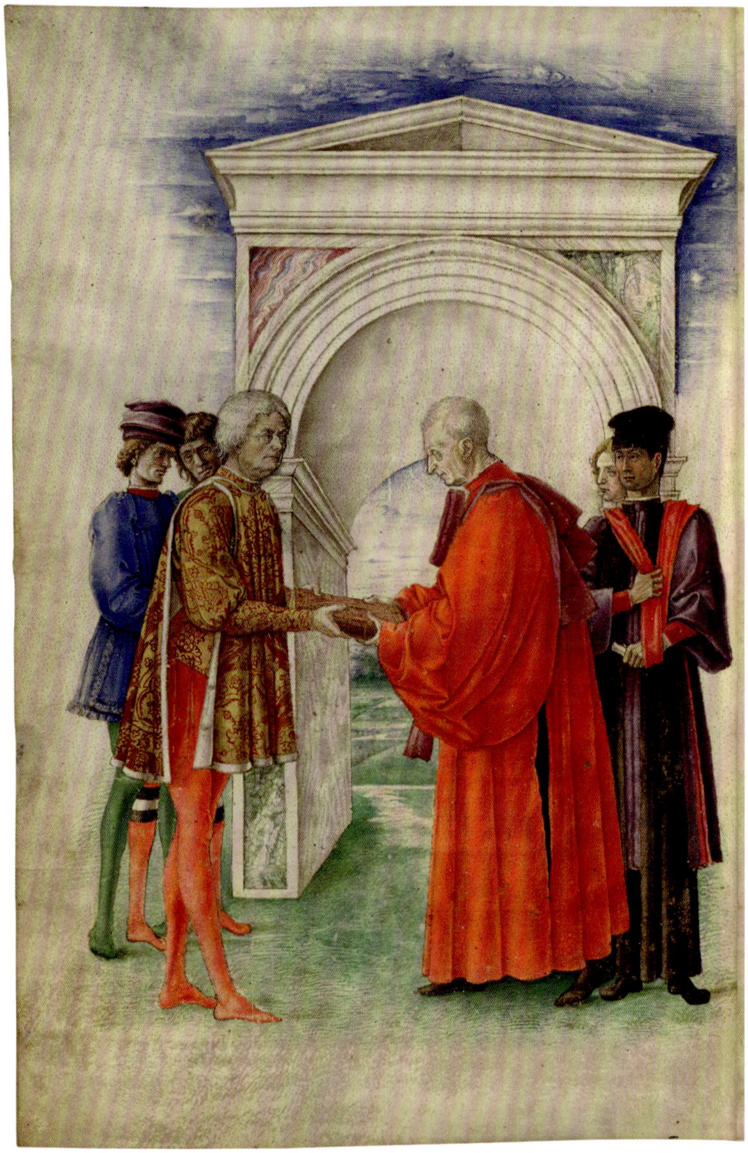

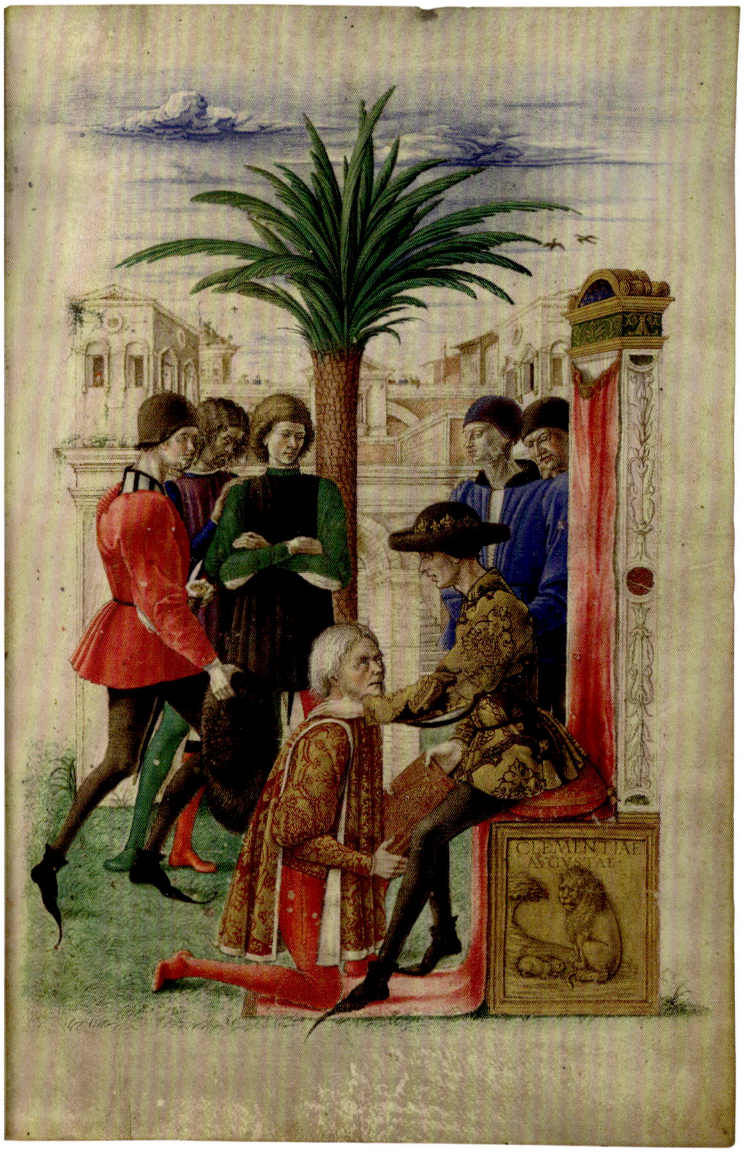

The small *Passion of Saint Maurice*, commissioned in 1453 as a luxurious diplomatic gift, was sent by Marcello to Jean Cossa, councillor of King René of Anjou, as a token of gratitude for his admittance to the chivalric Order of the Crescent in 1449. The text devoted to Saint Maurice, patron of the Order, is accompanied by six miniatures by an unknown Lombard illuminator and four full-page illuminations: an interior with an assembly of the Order (fig. 95, Cv); a profile portrait of Marcello (34v); a standing figure of Saint Maurice (fig. 94, 38v) and an allegorical image of the Venetian Republic (39v).[37] These four pages are distinguished from the six smaller miniatures by their high quality, and their attribution has been much debated.[38] Some scholars, including Andrea De Marchi (elsewhere in this volume), have argued for Giovanni Bellini's authorship, comparing the figure of the saint to that of Christ in the later *Blood of the Redeemer* (fig. 192).[39] However, we and other scholars think that the illuminations can be seen as the work of Jacopo (maybe with the assistance of the young Giovanni as part of his workshop), noting Jacopo's renown as a portraitist, and comparing Marcello's delicately modelled profile to a similar drawing of a head in the Paris Drawing Book (fig. 96); likewise, the perspective used in the *Assembly* scene is close to that seen in some of Jacopo's architectural drawings.[40]

There is similar debate about another extraordinary manuscript commissioned by Marcello: the first Latin

FIG. 97
Attributed to JACOPO or GIOVANNI BELLINI
Guarino da Verona consigns his translation of Strabo to Jacopo Antonio Marcello; Jacopo Antonio Marcello offers the manuscript to René of Anjou, 1459
Miniatures from Strabo, *De situ orbis geographia*
Tempera, gum or glue on vellum
37 × 25 cm
Médiathèque d'Albi-Centre Pierre Amalric, Albi (RES.MS 77, fols 3v–4r)

translation of Strabo's *Geography*, compiled in 1459 as a gift for King René of Anjou (fig. 97). The text was the work of the humanist Guarino da Verona, who had started his translation for Pope Nicholas V and, after the pope's death in 1455, finished it under Marcello's patronage in 1458.[41] Two full-page illuminations depict solemn scenes relating to the book itself: in the first, Guarino presents his translation to Marcello, while in the second the kneeling Marcello offers the book to the King. Yet there is little consensus about the authorship of these fine drawings. Meiss believed them to be by Mantegna, perhaps working in collaboration with Giovanni Bellini, and suggested that the manuscript was the 'operetta' or 'small work' which Mantegna was preparing for Marcello during the first months of 1459.[42] Alternatively and, in our view more plausibly, the illuminations in both Marcello manuscripts have been attributed to Jacopo Bellini and his workshop, implicitly including Giovanni.[43] While the illuminations show a palpable interest in Mantegna's more 'sculptural' style, the delicate expansive landscapes and luminous colours in both manuscripts foreshadow the increasingly personal path that Giovanni would take in his career.[44]

A similar conundrum exists in Paduan book illumination of this period, where a 1450 manuscript of the *Chronicon* by Eusebius shines like a 'lone star'.[45] The ambitious text recounts the history of the world from the time of Abraham until CE 303 and the scribe of this particular copy was Biagio Saraceni of Vicenza, chancellor of Fantino Dandolo, Bishop of Padua (1450–9). Intended for Dandolo, the book was a copy of an older manuscript which recorded Saint Jerome's Latin translation of Eusebius and which had been purchased by Dandolo's predecessor Pietro Donato during his journey to the Council of Basel.[46] Not only did Saraceni's manuscript reproduce the text of this older book, but it also meticulously and reverently copied the layout of the pages and the styles of the scripts.

The most important historical event in the *Chronicon*, the Birth of Christ, is illustrated with an exquisite miniature of the Christ Child in the manger (fig. 98). The swaddled infant (who has sometimes been compared to the child in *The Presentation of Christ in the Temple*, fig. 128),[47] the grass and the wicker basket are rendered with dazzling effects of colour, light and shadow, while touches of gold have been added with the tip of the brush. In showing the child from an elevated viewpoint, with its halo logically positioned under its head, the artist demonstrates his awareness of Donatello's rules of perspective. Mantegna was working on the Ovetari Chapel frescoes at this date and the manuscript, which displays similar preoccupations with colour, volume and perspective, has often been given to him: an attribution which is widely, though not universally, accepted.[48] However, the subtle rendering, the passionate attention to detail, and the integration of the image within the classicised inscription, whose letters rotate to face the image on each side, make him a very plausible candidate.[49] Beyond the questions of attribution, manuscript illumination seems to have played an important role in the formation of both artists, introducing to them the world of humanist learning and patronage.

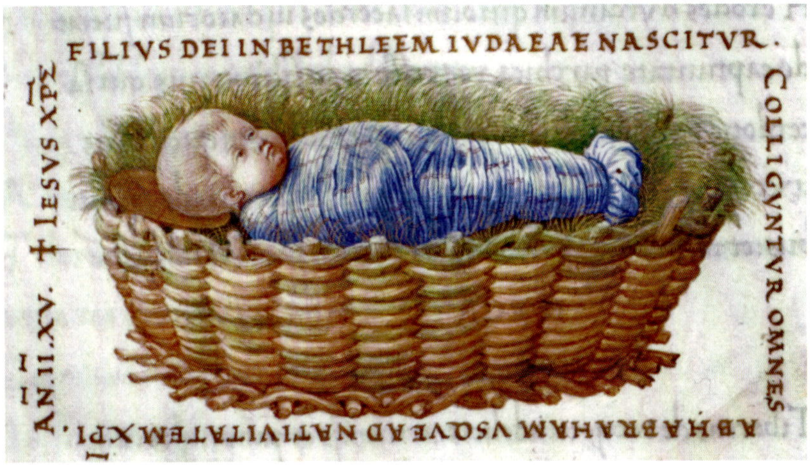

FIG. 98
Attributed to ANDREA MANTEGNA
Child in the manger, 1450
Miniature from Eusebius, *Chronicon*
Tempera, gum or glue on vellum, 27.3 × 18.3 cm
Biblioteca Nazionale Marciana, Venice (Cod. Lat. IX, 1 (3496), fol. 133v)

In Close Artistic Dialogue

DAGMAR KORBACHER

Mantegna's artistic interaction with the Bellini family began at the latest in 1453, the year of his marriage to Nicolosia, the sister of Giovanni and daughter of Jacopo. Clearly the art of Mantegna made an especially strong impression on Giovanni, yet it would be wrong to assume that this artistic influence was limited primarily to the imitation of individual motifs or that it only went in one direction, from Mantegna to Bellini.[1] Its precise course, however, is difficult to delineate due to our lack of knowledge concerning the early phase of Giovanni Bellini's work.

Mantegna's small panel for the predella of the *San Zeno Altarpiece* (fig. 101), for example, painted around 1456–9, shows the crucifixion of Christ in spectacular perspective. Illuminated by an almost glaring light, the

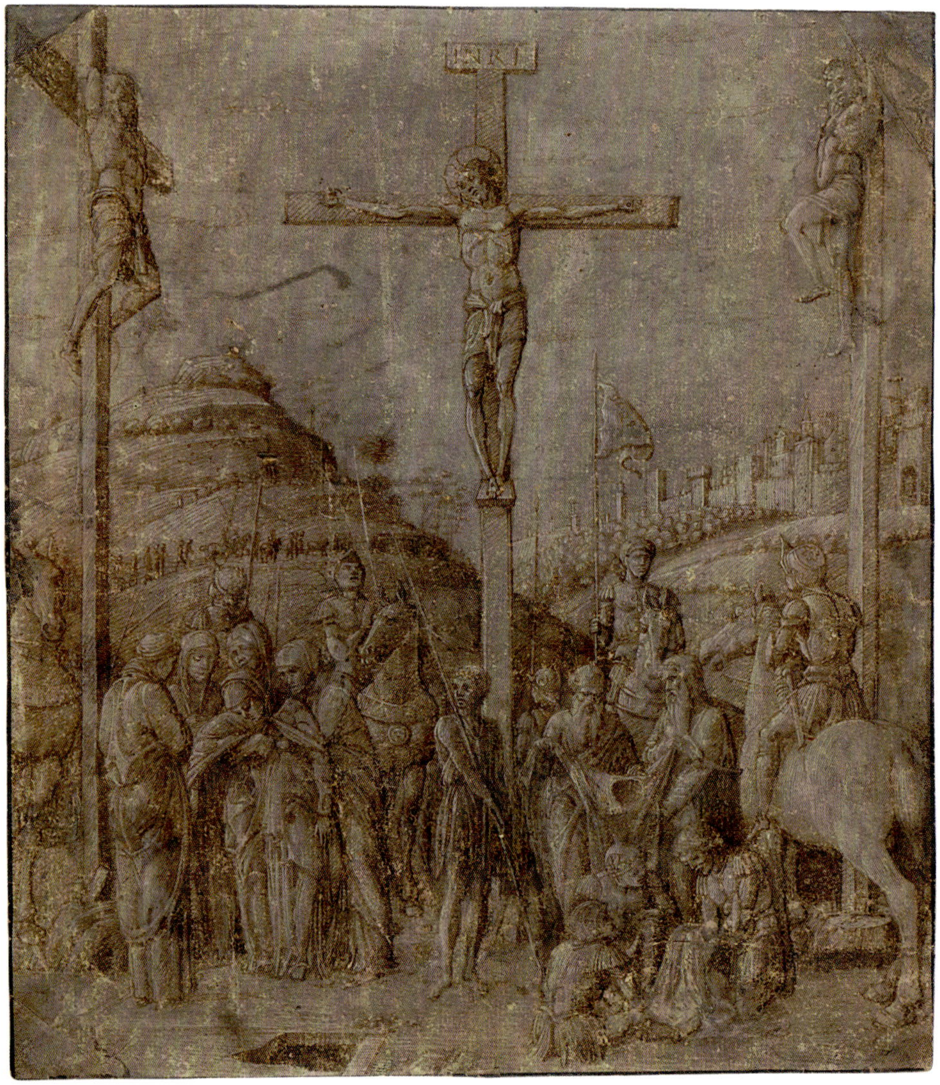

FIG. 99
Attributed to GIOVANNI BELLINI
The three crosses, about 1456–7
Pen and brown ink on grey prepared paper, 24 × 21.5 cm
The British Museum, London (Pp,1.22)

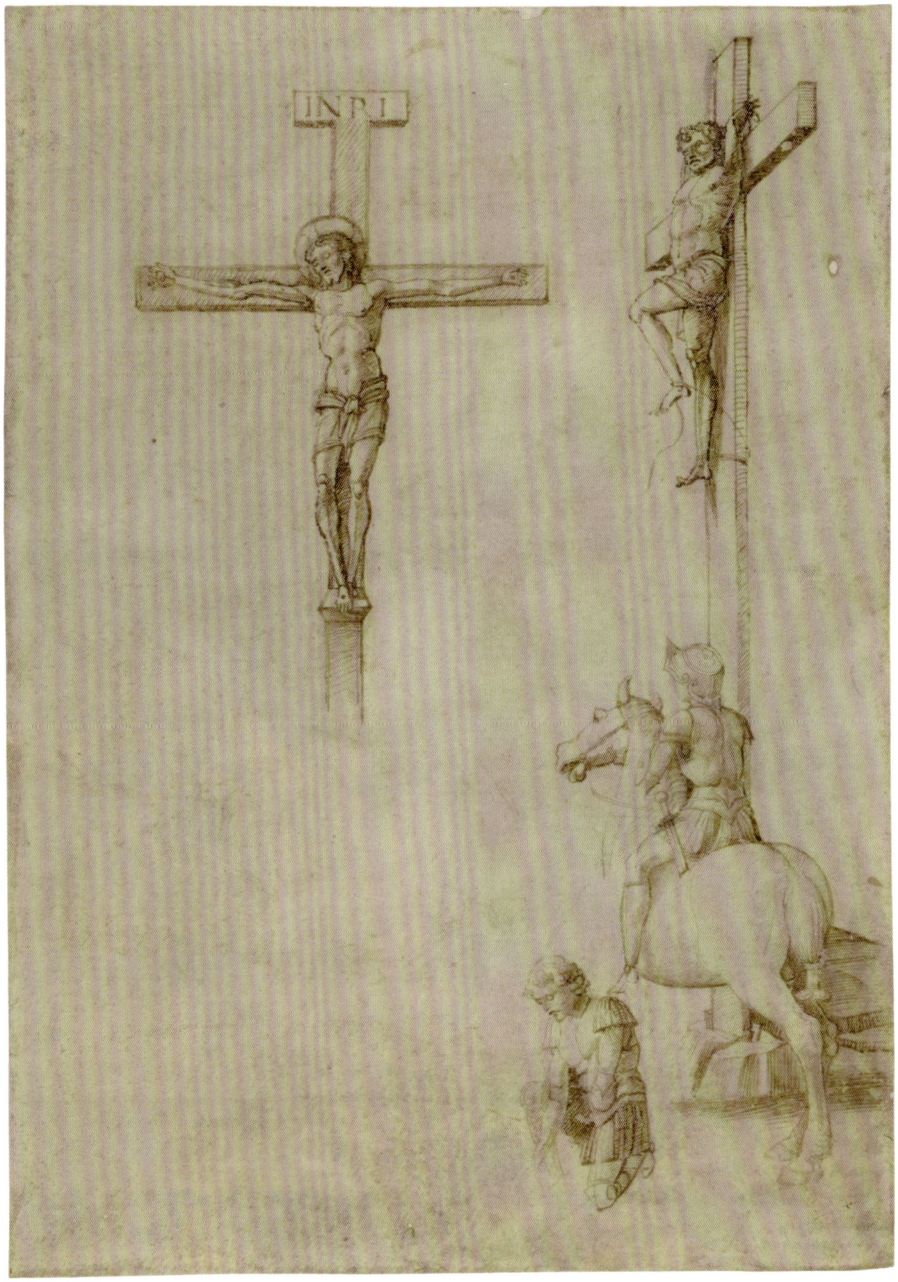

FIG. 100
Circle of
GIOVANNI BELLINI
The Crucifixion, about 1460
Pen and brush and brown ink on vellum, 27.4 × 19.6 cm
Kupferstichkabinett, Staatliche Museen zu Berlin (KdZ 1364)

event transpires as if on a stage against the backdrop of the dark cliffs in the middle ground, which in turn open onto a lighter landscape in the background. This dramatic effect is very similar to the landscape and perspective in the small panel of the *Crucifixion* painted by Giovanni Bellini in the Museo Correr (fig. 14). The slight curvature of the rocky ground beneath the Cross and the agonised faces of the bystanders are also very similar in Bellini's image, of which the exact date remains uncertain between the end of the 1450s and the first half of the following decade.[2] The somewhat archaic forms of the lamenting cherubim above the Cross, as well as the lack of organic relationship between the landscape and the foreground, suggest that the work falls early in Bellini's oeuvre. Contact between the two artists seems to have been especially intense in 1458–9, when Mantegna was painting the panels for the *San Zeno Altarpiece* (fig. 252) and Bellini was staying in Padua with his father and brother Gentile to work on the *Gattamelata Altarpiece*.[3] At that time Giovanni was probably also at the end of his training; thus his encounter with the art of his brother-in-law would have represented a genuine

FIG. 101
ANDREA MANTEGNA
The Crucifixion, 1456–9
Egg tempera on panel, 76 × 96 cm
Musée du Louvre, Paris (368)

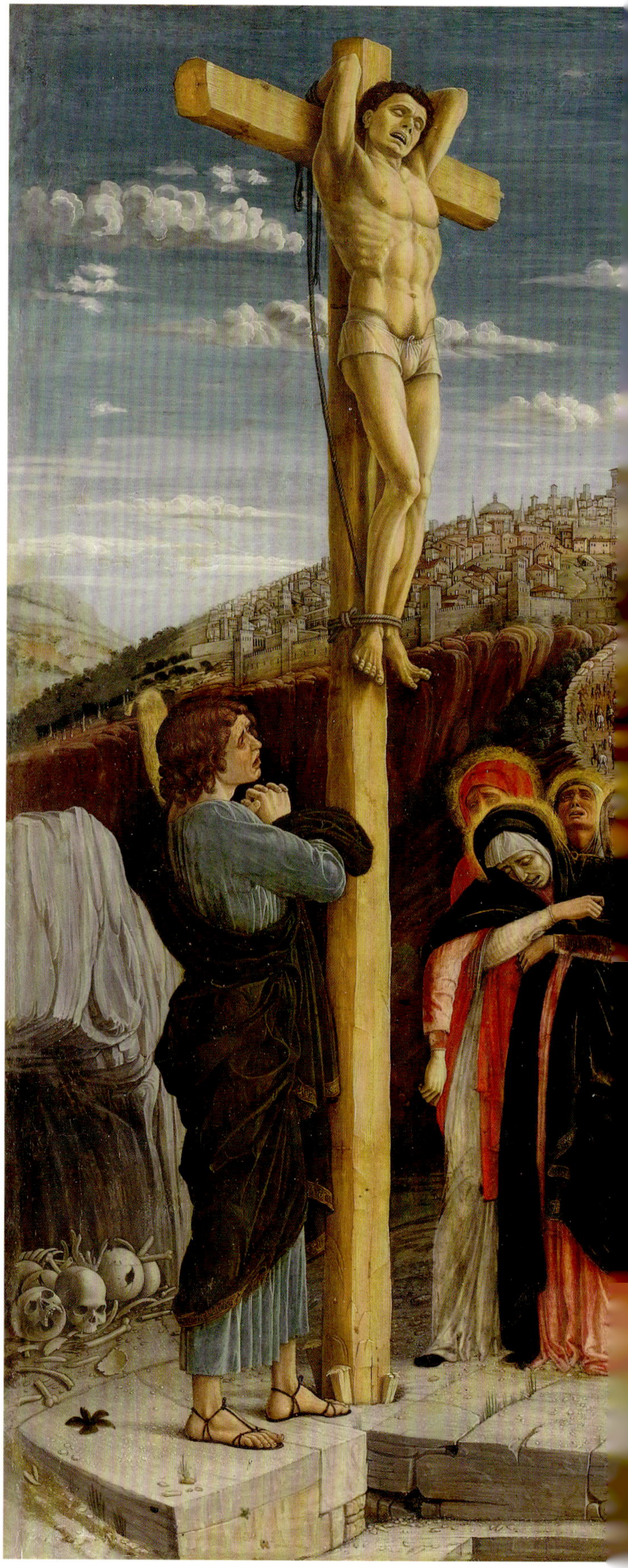

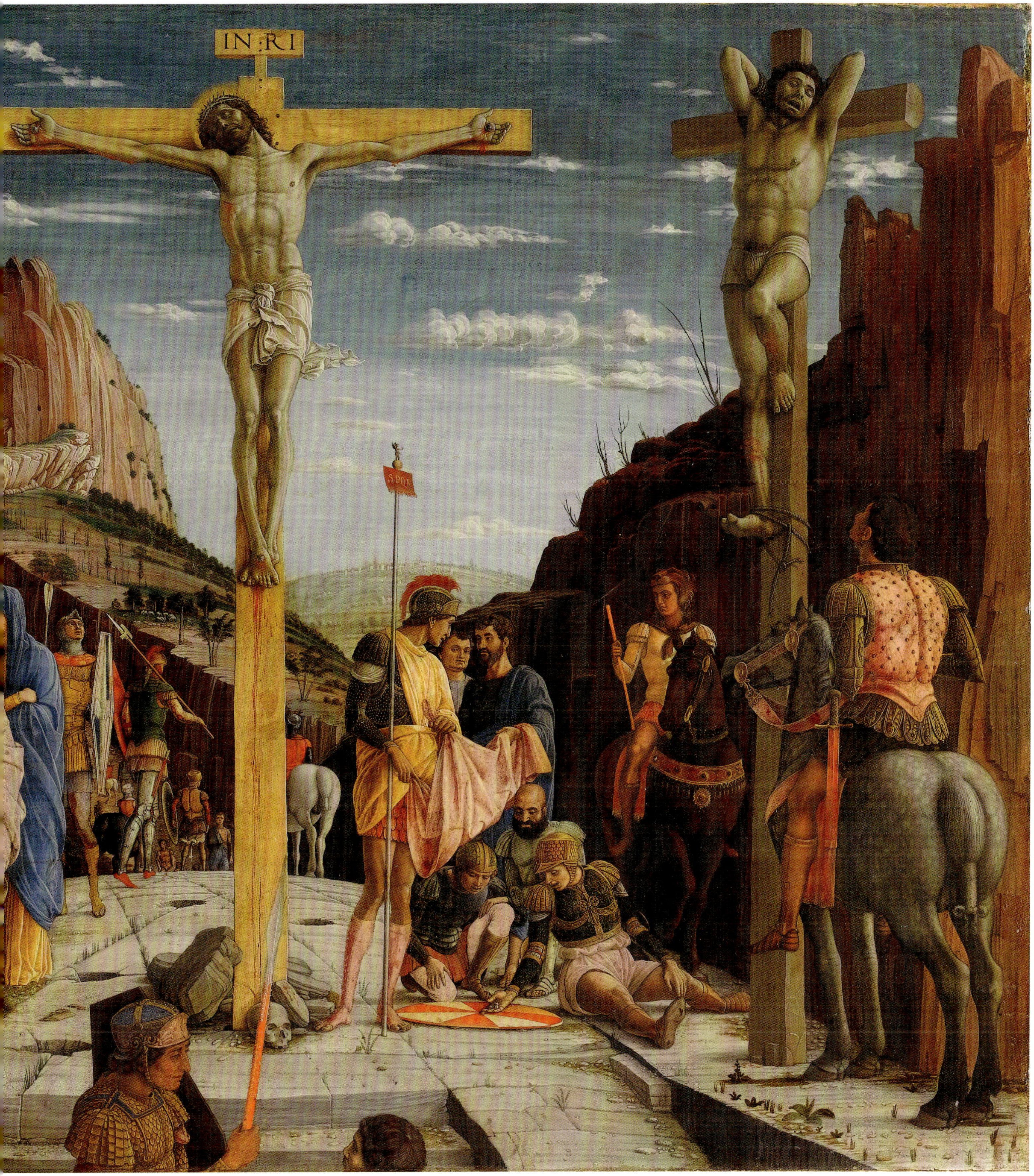
IN·RI

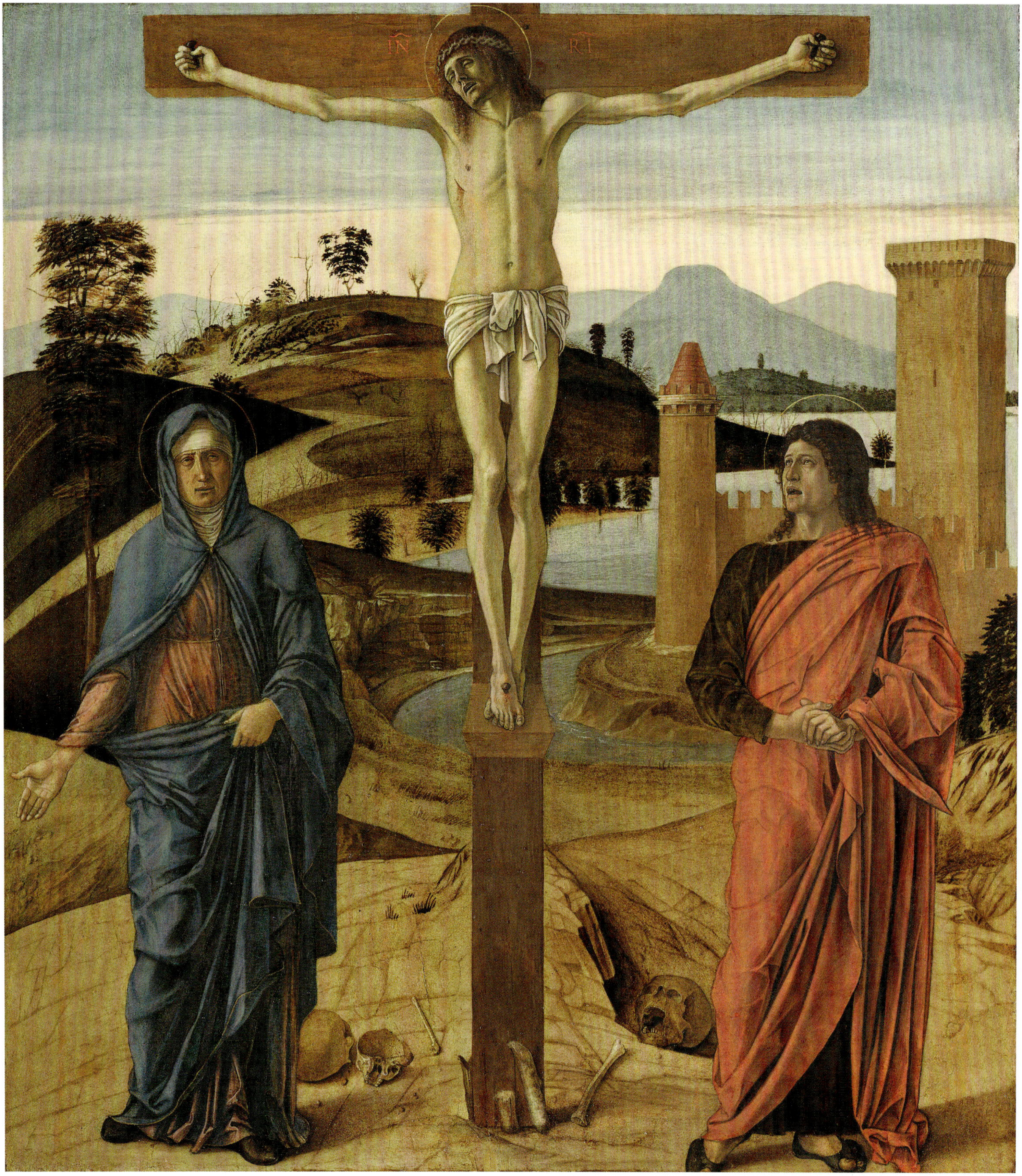

FIG. 102
GIOVANNI BELLINI
The Crucifixion, about 1465
Oil or egg tempera on panel, 71 × 63 cm
Musée du Louvre, Paris (RF 1970-39)

turning point in his artistic development, enabling him to break free of the influence of his teacher and father Jacopo.[4] A drawing of *The three crosses* (fig. 99), now in London, could also have been made during Giovanni's artistic encounter with the pictorial innovations and style of Mantegna. The identity of the drawing's creator has been much discussed,[5] and the work was long attributed to Mantegna himself. The Netherlandish collector and artist Philips Koninck, who owned the drawing in the seventeenth century, even attested in an inscription on the old mount that the work was by Mantegna, and that whoever disagreed did not deserve to live as an art lover.[6] It was only in the twentieth century that the drawing, executed in pen and ink on grey-toned paper with white highlights applied with the brush, was recognised as having clear Bellinesque features.[7] This reassessment may have been based not only on the work's painterly execution and the delicate modelling of the figures and landscape in light and shadow, but also on the similarity of the faces to other, somewhat later drawings by Bellini.[8] If the attribution to Giovanni Bellini can be more firmly established, then this drawing probably bears witness to the young artist's intensive study of the *Crucifixion* painted by Mantegna for the San Zeno predella – countering the spectacular perspective of the painted scenery with a more moderate, realistic solution. Several of the figures also recur in a somewhat simpler drawing in the Kupferstichkabinett in Berlin (fig. 100); here, the hesitant quality of some of the lines and the indifferent, multidirectional hatching suggest that the piece is a copy, most likely created in Bellini's milieu.

Perhaps only a few years later, Bellini returned to the same theme in a *Crucifixion* that may have been painted around 1465 (fig. 102). Here he once again found his way to a pictorial language of his own, particularly in the diverse yet harmonious interaction of the landscape in the background with the figures in the foreground and their generally softer facial features, further enlivened by the gentle illumination of the scene and the lucid rendering of the body of the crucified Christ. Mantegna's influence remains visible only in the clear contours of the figures and the drapery partially clinging to their legs. The panel was probably executed for the altar of Saint John the Evangelist in Santa Maria della Carità in Venice.[9] A predella, now owned by the Wittelsbacher Ausgleichsfonds in Munich, with *Three Stories of Drusiana and Saint John the Evangelist* (fig. 103) certainly belonged to the altarpiece and can also be dated to around 1465. An infrared image of the back of the predella (fig. 104)[10] shows a sketch of the loincloth and legs of the crucified Christ, demonstrating the artist's contemporaneous exploration of the Crucifixion motif; the front of the predella, on the other hand, shows three episodes divided by pilasters, with multiple figures appearing within a cityscape strongly reminiscent of Mantegna's frescoes in the Ovetari Chapel.[11] To the right, Drusiana is carried to the grave; in the middle, the Evangelist John raises her from the dead by commanding her to arise, return home and prepare him a meal – which then occurs in the left-hand field. The progression of the narrative from right to left – the reverse of the usual direction – was dictated by the altarpiece's position in relation to the high altar of the church.[12] Since Roberto Longhi had recognised the predella as the work of Giovanni Bellini as early as 1927, before the connection between it and the *Crucifixion* was made, it was generally assumed that the latter work dated to the 1450s, a period when Bellini was working in close proximity to Mantegna and both painters were strongly influenced by Donatello's works in the Santo. The revised dating to the mid-1460s, now considered likely, clearly indicates that the artistic relationship between the two painters continued beyond their time together in Padua.

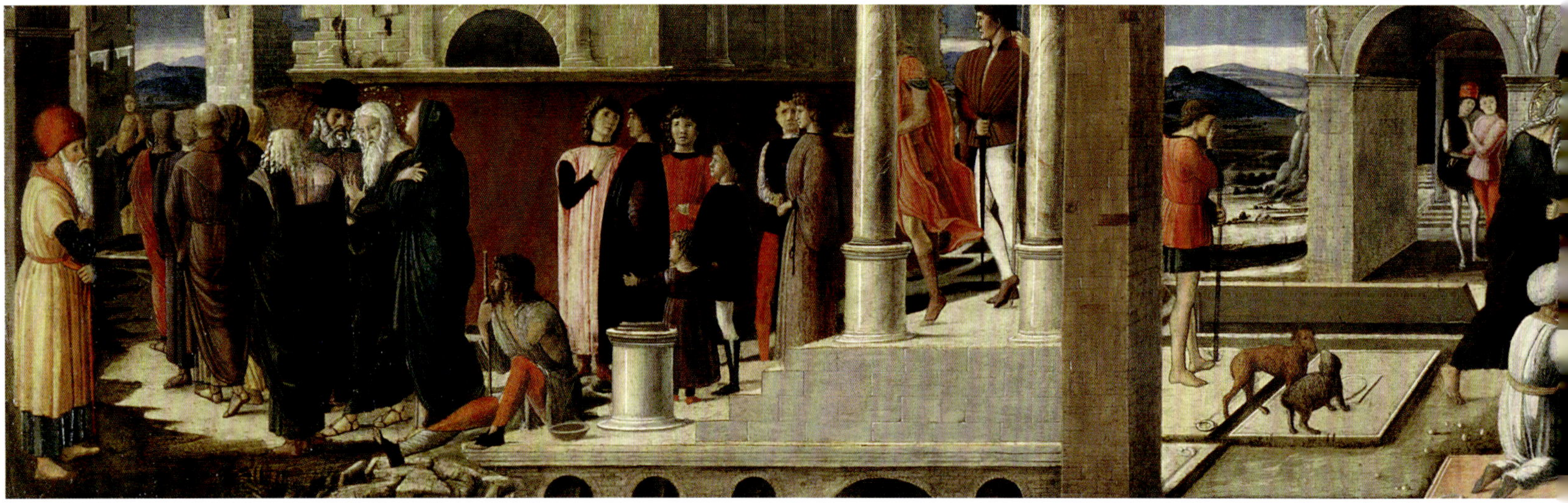

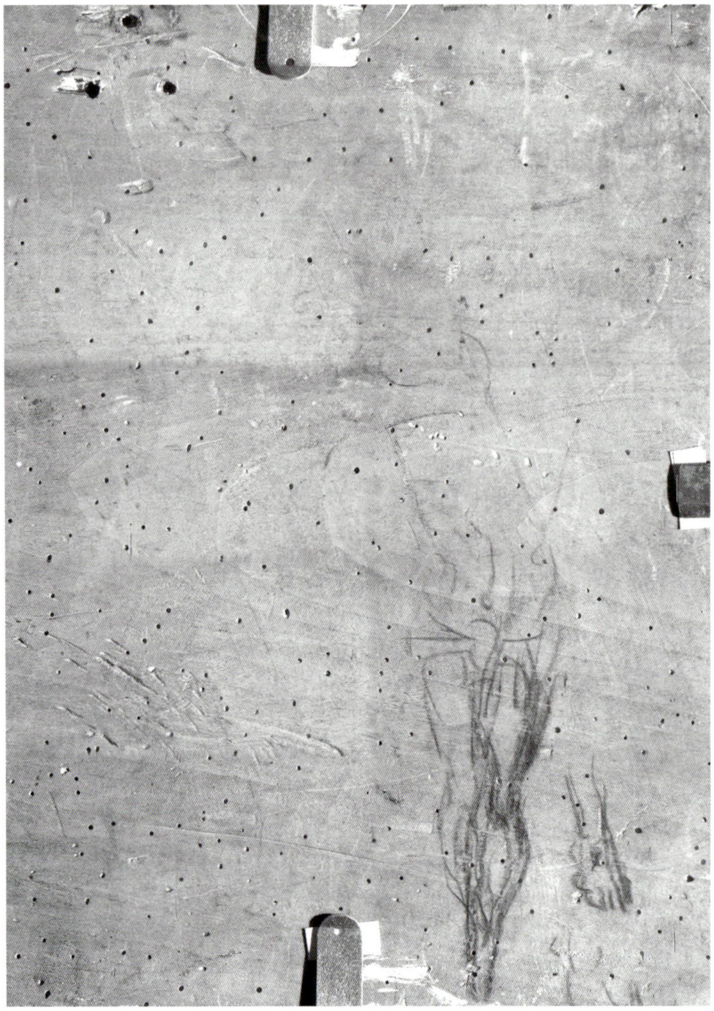

FIG. 103
GIOVANNI BELLINI
Three Stories of Drusiana and Saint John the Evangelist, about 1465
Oil or egg tempera on panel, 32 × 202 cm
Wittelsbacher Ausgleichsfonds, Munich (BI 34)

FIG. 104
GIOVANNI BELLINI
Infrared reflectogram image of the back of the panel [FIG. 103] showing a sketch related to the Crucifixion
Wittelsbacher Ausgleichsfonds, Munich

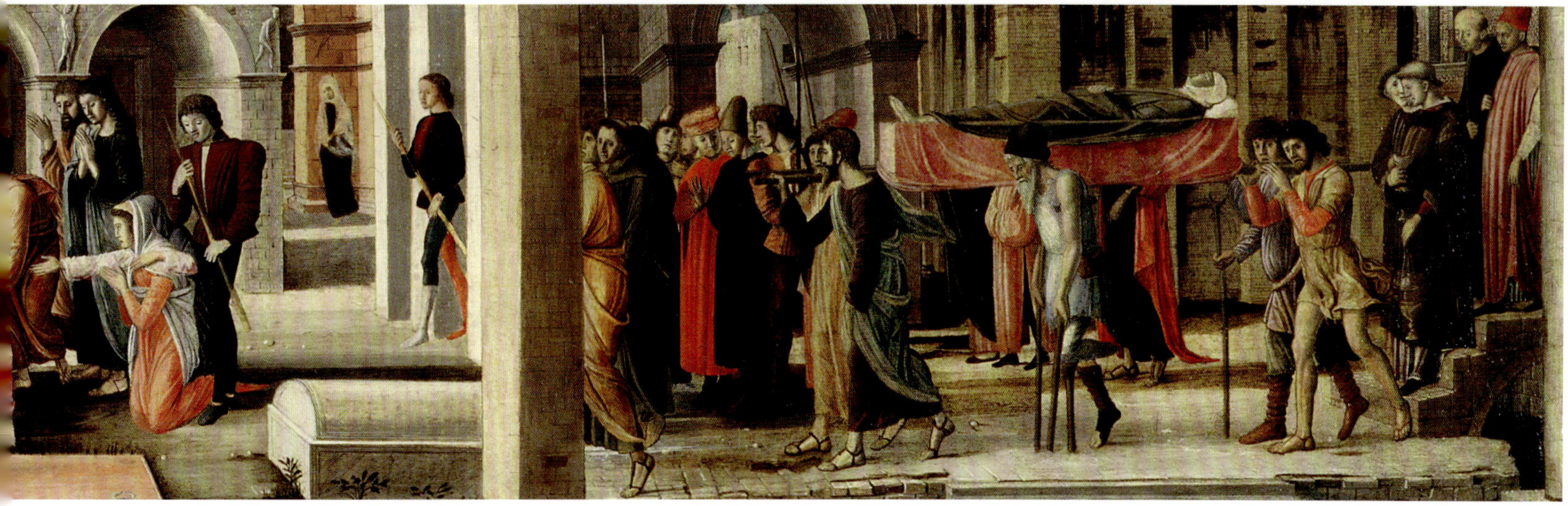

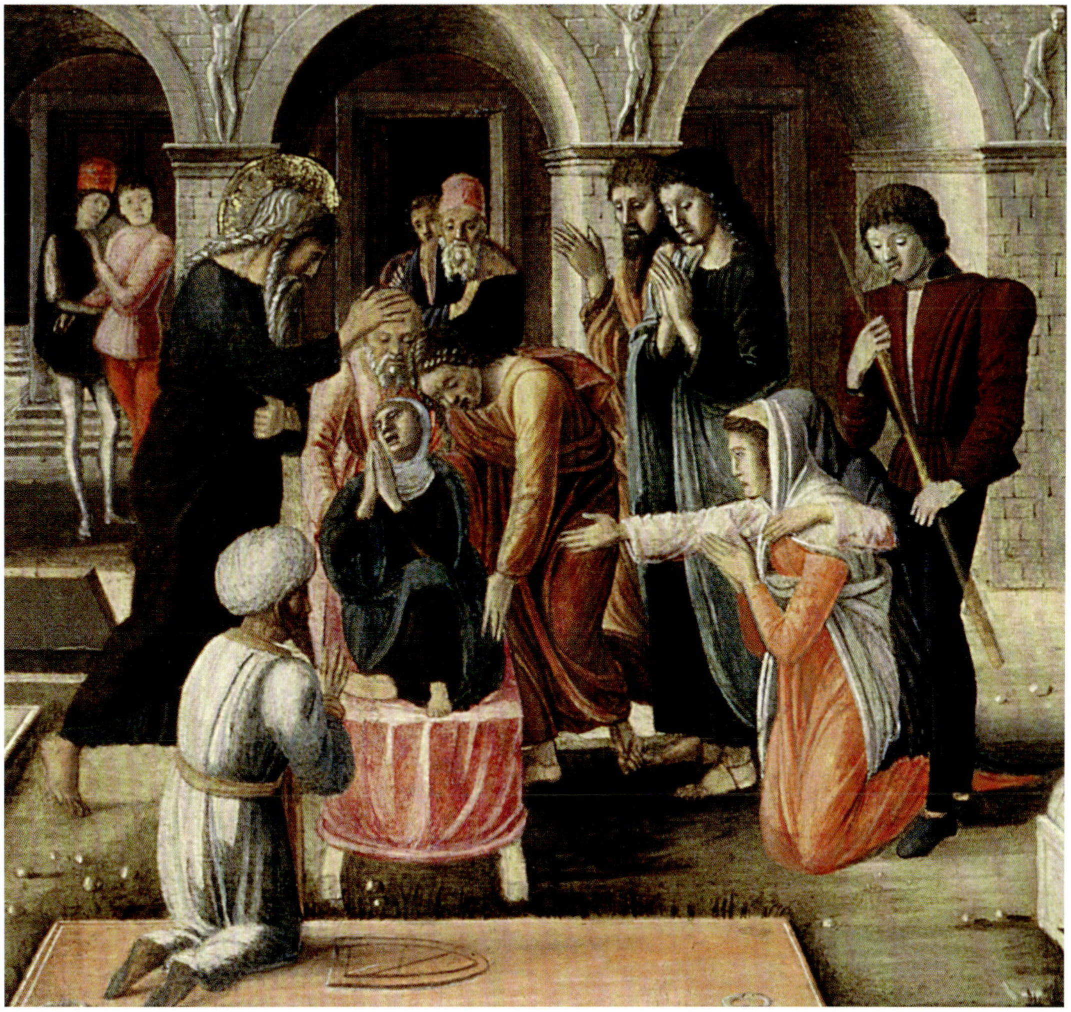

GIOVANNI BELLINI, detail from *Three Stories of Drusiana and Saint John the Evangelist* (FIG. 103)

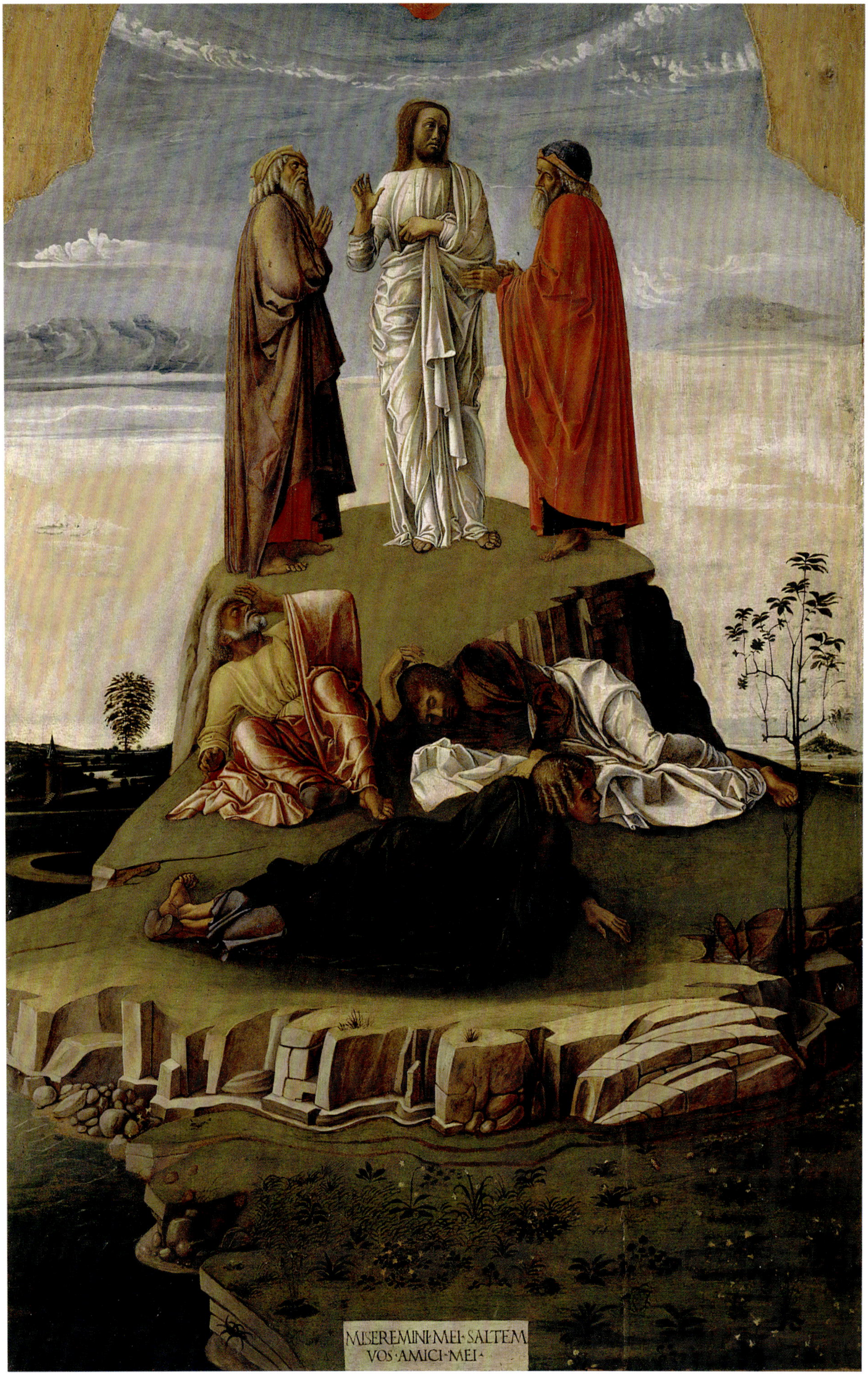
MISEREMINI·MEI·SALTEM
VOS·AMICI·MEI·

FIG. 105
GIOVANNI BELLINI
The Transfiguration of Christ, about 1458–60
Egg tempera and oil on panel, 133 × 90.3 cm
Museo Correr, Venice (27)

A prime example of the reciprocal artistic influence of Mantegna and Bellini in this early period is Bellini's altarpiece of *The Transfiguration of Christ* in the Museo Correr of 1458–60 (fig. 105).[13] The scene represents an episode from the New Testament[14] in which Jesus leads his disciples Peter, James and John to a high mountain to pray. The panel, which has been trimmed at the top, was probably originally part of an altarpiece for a church in Venice. The figures of Jesus and the prophets stand out clearly against a glowing sky that supports the attribution to Bellini, as does the view into the landscape, for which the young Giovanni could have looked to Netherlandish models. Bellini took into account the low vantage point of the worshipper at the altar, who gazes upward towards figures that are slightly foreshortened, especially the head of the left-hand prophet. The device of foreshortening and the lively poses of the apostles betray familiarity with the work of Mantegna. Not surprisingly, this panel was long attributed to the latter,[15] and in fact the faces, and especially the drapery with its firm, pronounced folds, strongly recall his work. A very specific reference to Mantegna, though not yet supported by a conclusive chronology of the exchange, also appears in the foreground: the rocks in the painting exactly correspond to those in Mantegna's drawing of *The Descent of Christ into Limbo* (figs 15, 16).[16]

Another drawing, this time depicting *Saint Jerome and the lion* (fig. 106), likewise connects the two brothers-in-law. In 1937, Fiocco considered it a work by Bellini; since then, however, it has come to be viewed as Mantegnesque, an opinion already espoused by Kristeller in the early twentieth century.[17] Yet the work seems to be, not an alternative design made in preparation for Mantegna's panel in São Paulo (fig. 116), but a further and much later development of the figure of the reading saint, based on Bellini's philosopher-like depictions of Jerome from the 1480s. The use of black chalk, unusual for Mantegna, would support this conjecture. Although the drawing is comparable to the underdrawing of Mantegna's *Virgin and Child with an angel* (fig. 107), which was apparently traced from a prototype,[18] in the latter work the artist used pen and ink to develop the drawing from the traced contour lines, whereas here the figures are rendered entirely in black chalk.

The two painters also engaged in artistic dialogue with respect to devotional images of the Virgin, a genre that was to play a prominent role for Giovanni Bellini in particular throughout his entire career. The subject was an extraordinarily popular motif in Padua as early as the mid-fifteenth century.[19] Giovanni's father Jacopo Bellini and Francesco Squarcione and his pupils, notably Marco Zoppo,[20] all took on the artistic challenge of representing the Virgin with the Christ Child as both a saint to be venerated and a loving, human mother.

Mantegna's *Virgin and Child with Saints Jerome and Louis of Toulouse* in the Musée Jacquemart-André (fig. 108), painted around 1455, is entirely indebted to this Paduan tradition. The mother of God stands directly behind a parapet, between the two saints and a little in front of them. With both hands she holds the Christ Child, who gazes upward, standing on a cushion on the parapet. While Roberto Longhi favoured an attribution to Giovanni Bellini, scholarly consensus has now assigned the work to Mantegna.[21] Its close relationship to the latter's *San Zeno Altarpiece*, created around the same time or shortly thereafter, is especially visible in such elements as the red garment of the Virgin, the haloes and the round arch decorated with a garland of fruit, with similarities extending even to the development of details.[22]

Comparison of this work with Giovanni Bellini's *Virgin and Child* in the Gemäldegalerie in Berlin (fig. 109),[23] probably painted only a few years later around 1460, shows that although Bellini's formal approach to

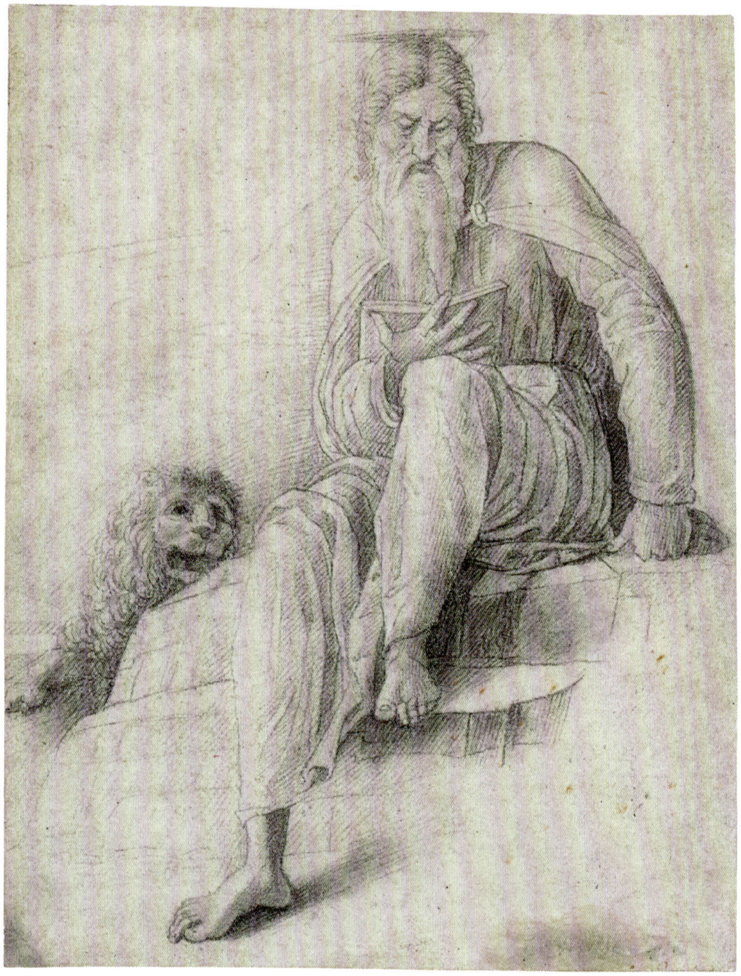

FIG. 106
Attributed to ANDREA MANTEGNA
Saint Jerome and the lion, 1480s
Black chalk on paper, 17.3 × 13.6 cm
Kupferstichkabinett, Staatliche Museen zu Berlin (KdZ 5114)

the motif is similar to that of his brother-in-law, the spirit of the two works is entirely different. Here, as in Mantegna's work, Mary holds the Christ Child, who stands on a parapet and gazes up at her. Now, however, we no longer see the saints who served to elevate the scene to another realm, withdrawing it from the worshipper. Bellini also shows a landscape stretching into the distance, which to a certain extent also locates the event within the realm of earthly reality. The entire scene seems more human, the movements and interactions of the hands more natural, and the relationship between mother and child more intimate.

Another early painting by Giovanni Bellini, the so-called *Lehman Madonna* of around 1459 (fig. 175), likewise reveals the artist's familiarity with the work of his brother-in-law, above all in the figure types and the garland of leaves and fruit. Derived from antique sarcophagi, garlands were especially popular in Squarcione's workshop (fig. 79) and Giovanni probably took the motif from Mantegna, who had employed it in the painting discussed above as well as in the *San Zeno Altarpiece*. The landscape, on the other hand, may have been inspired by Netherlandish or Flemish art: in this context, Mauro Lucco has called attention to the landscape in *The Entombment* by Dirk Bouts in the National Gallery, London, a painting that could have been present in Venice already shortly after its creation in the 1450s.[24] The idea of establishing an even stronger connection between the realm of the Virgin and the sphere of the faithful by depicting her left hand reaching out over the parapet was probably also observed by Bellini in Netherlandish works of this period.

Both panels are closely related to the *Davis Madonna* in New York, which was probably also painted around 1460 (fig. 111)[25] but whose surface is unfortunately heavily damaged. Here, too, the Virgin and Child appear in front of a landscape; now, however, the mother of God worships the sleeping Child lying on the parapet, a motif

FIG. 107
ANDREA MANTEGNA
The Virgin and Child with an angel, about 1485
Pen and brown ink with brown wash on paper, 19.6 × 13.9 cm
The British Museum, London (1858,0724.3)

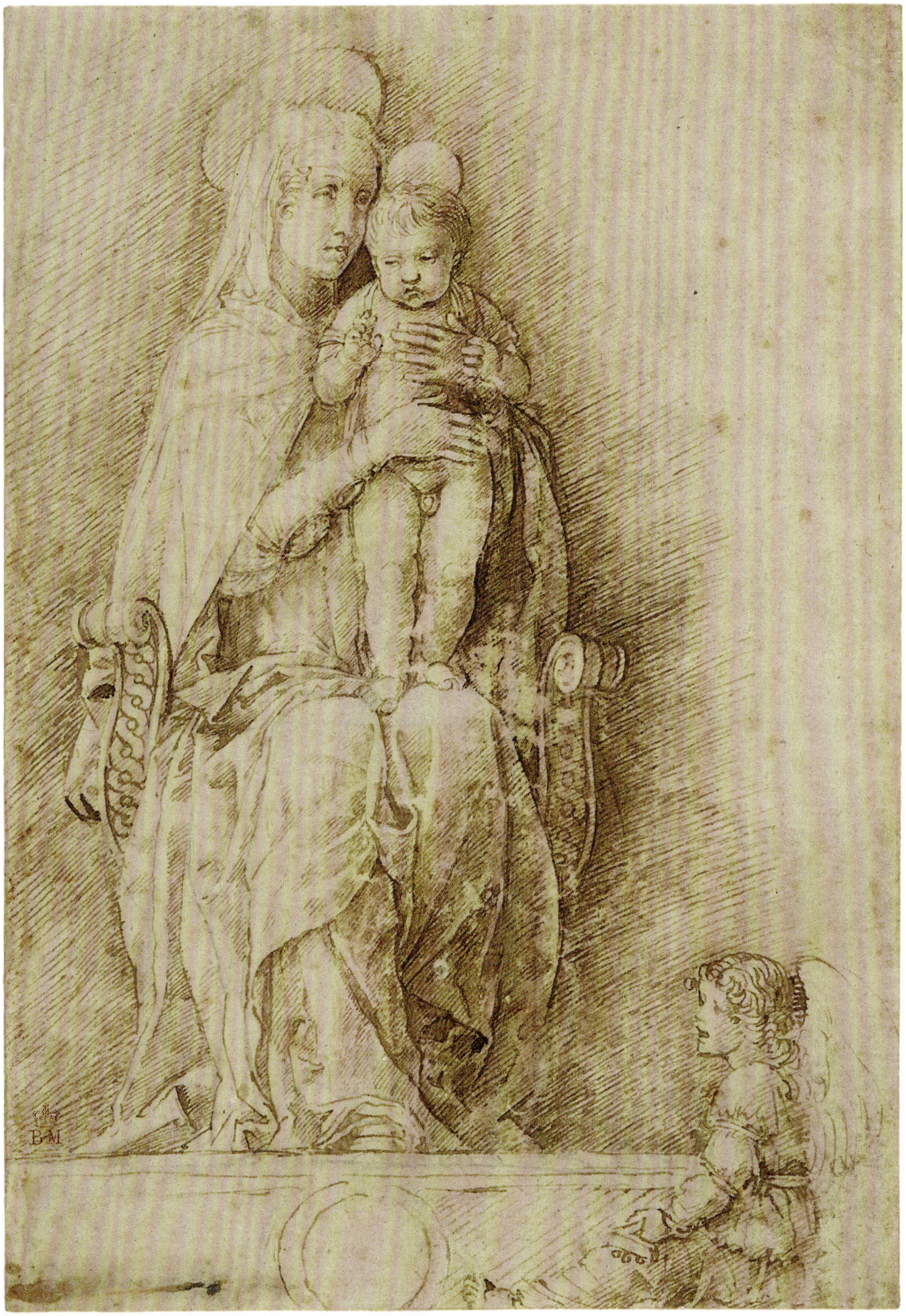

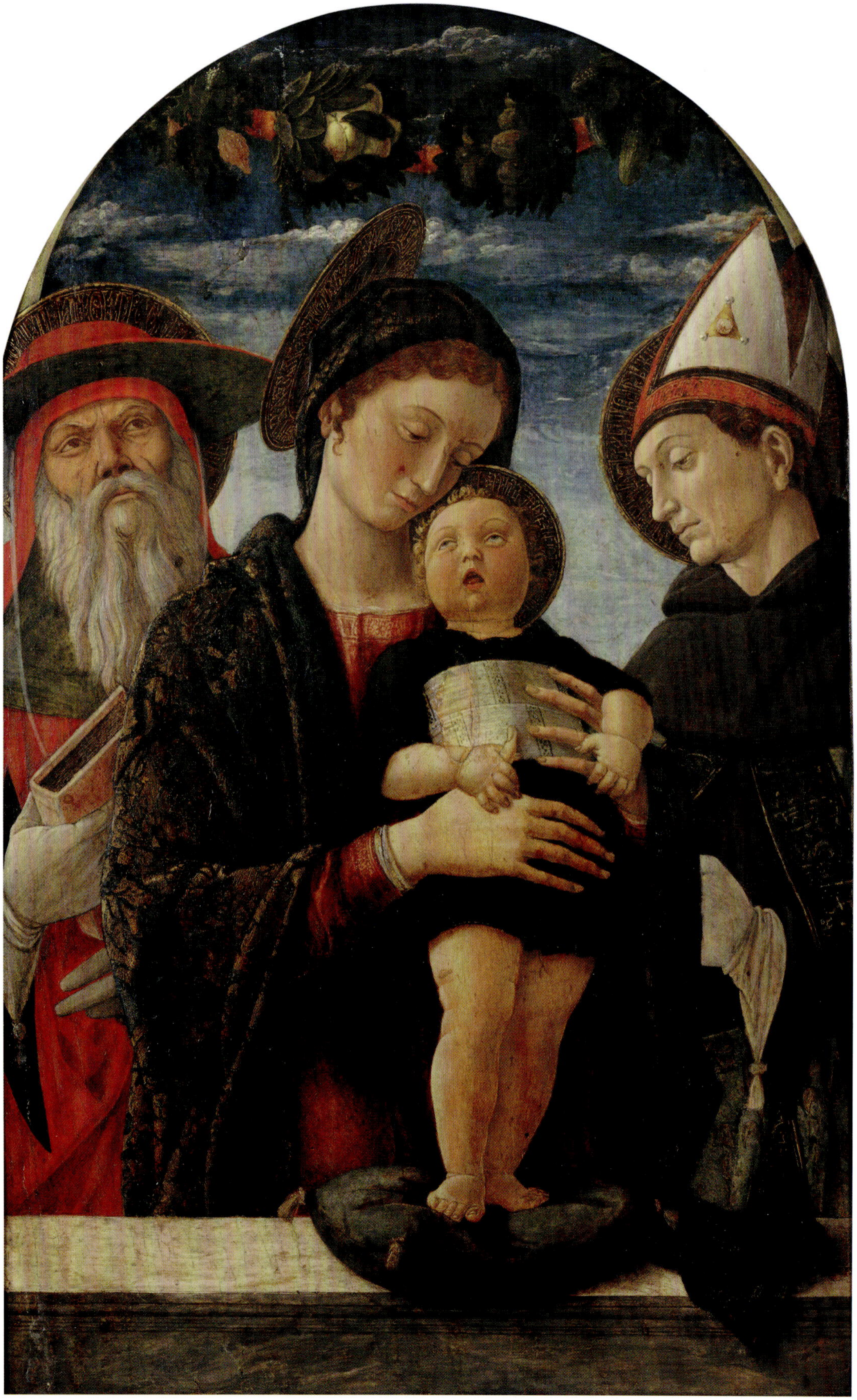

FIG. 108
ANDREA MANTEGNA
The Virgin and Child with Saints Jerome and Louis of Toulouse, about 1455
Egg tempera on panel, 69.4 × 44.5 cm
Musée Jacquemart-André, Paris (MJAP-P2184)

FIG. 109
GIOVANNI BELLINI
The Virgin and Child, about 1460
Egg tempera on poplar, 66.3 × 48.6 cm
Gemäldegalerie, Staatliche Museen zu Berlin (1177)

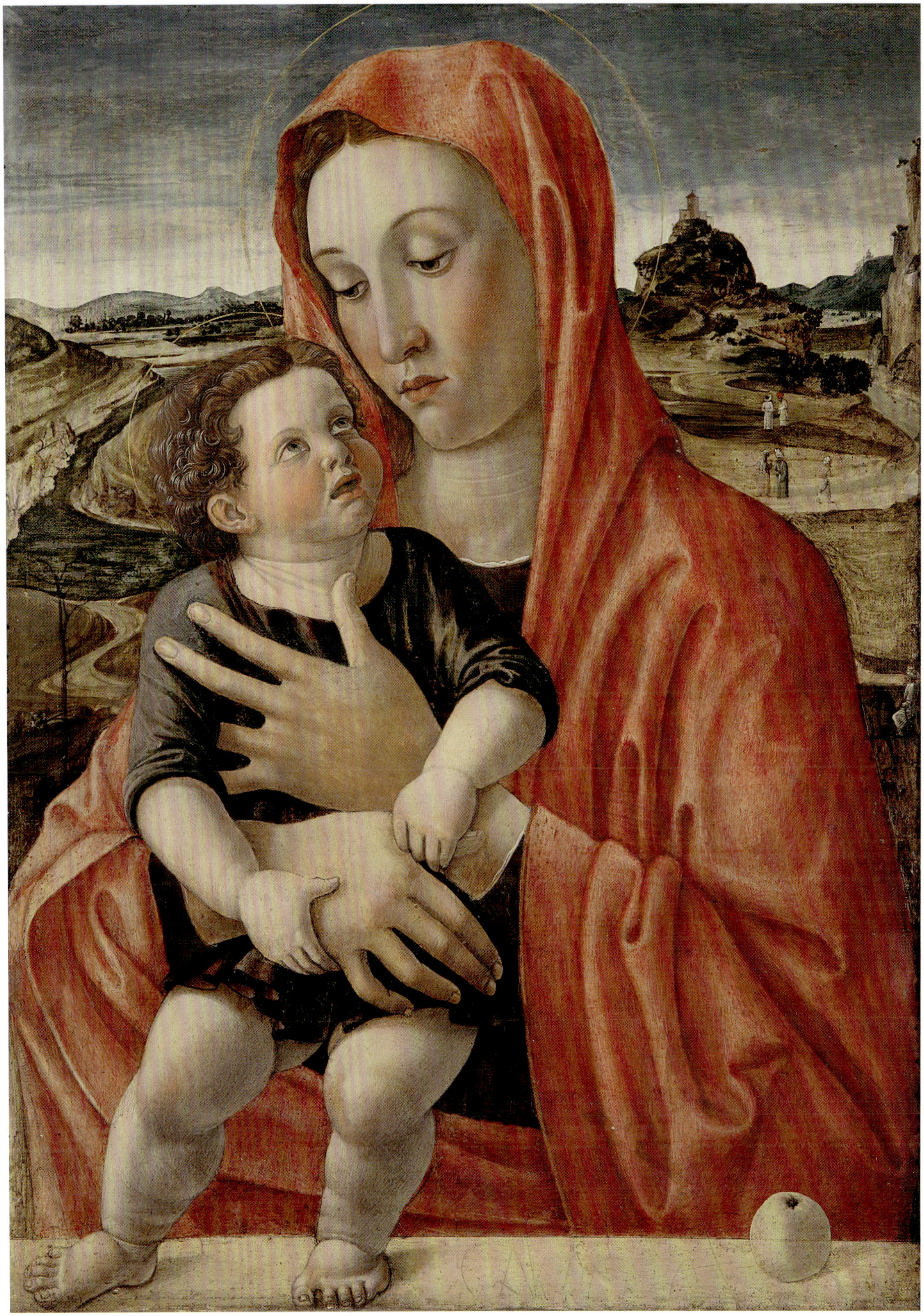

FIG. 110
ANDREA MANTEGNA
Madonna della Vittoria, 1495–6
Egg tempera on canvas, 285 × 168 cm
Musée du Louvre, Paris (369)

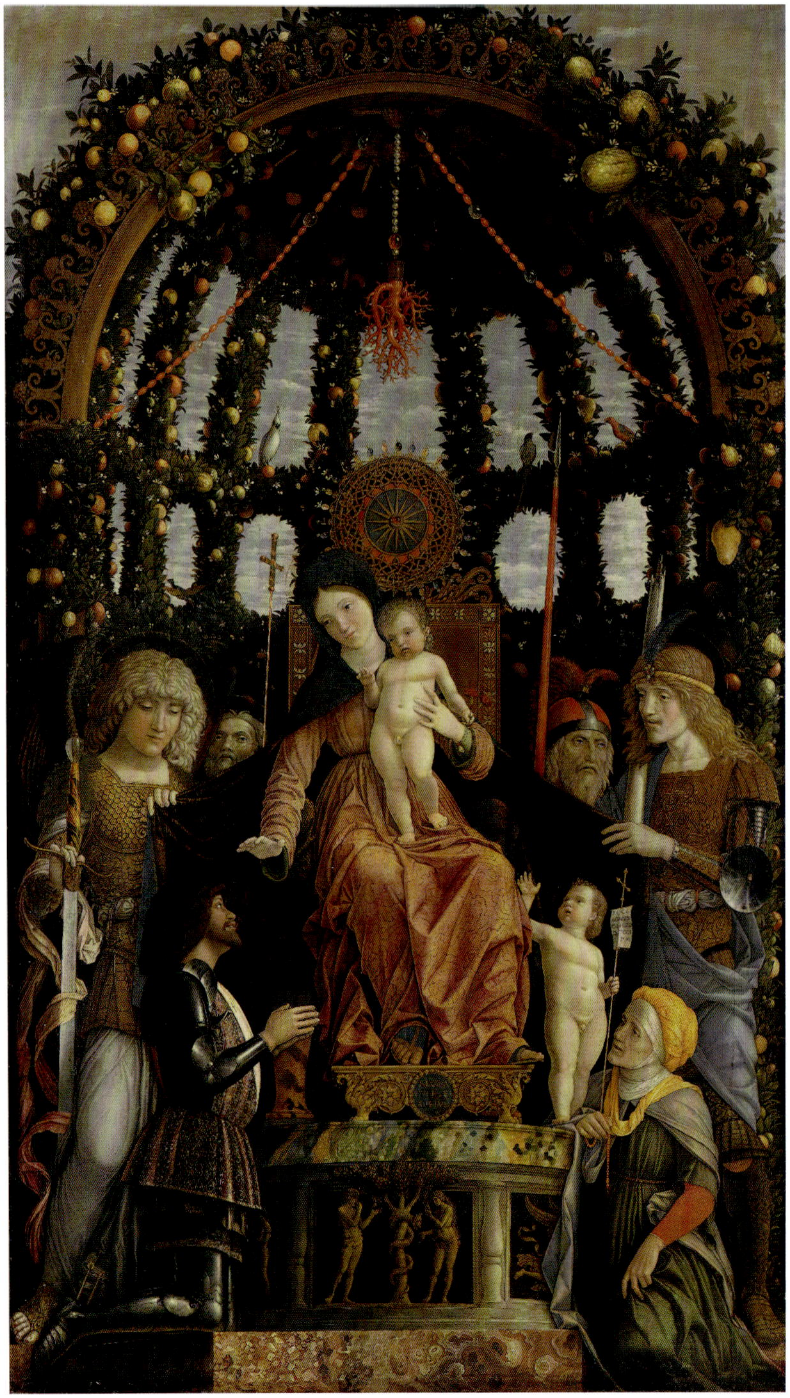

considered a prefiguration of the death of Christ and the Pietà. The linear contours of the figures and the heavy folds of the Virgin's drapery show the influence of Mantegna, reinforced by his familiarity with the Paduan works of Donatello. Influences from Mantegna's art are also discernible in the landscape background, with antique ruins to the left and a row of trees receding in perspective to the right. Thus in dialogue with his brother-in-law, Bellini developed a pictorial language of his own, increasingly distinguished by the remarkable intensification of the figures' physical presence, the concentrated mood and the tranquil landscape.

Mantegna likewise produced images of the Virgin and Child throughout his entire career, though with differing emphases. Several decades after he painted the enthroned Virgin on the central panel of the *San Zeno Altarpiece*, he revisited the motif in such works as the *Madonna della Vittoria* of 1495–6, now in the Louvre (fig. 110), and the *Virgin and Child with the Magdalen and Saint John the Baptist* (fig. 173) painted between 1490 and 1505. Also significant in this context is a drawing that further develops the motif of the Virgin seated on an antique throne with the standing Christ Child and an angel (fig. 107, also discussed on p. 117), probably created between 1480 and 1490. The detailed execution of the figures over an underdrawing in black chalk,[26] enhanced by a flat background of dense parallel hatching, suggests that this work was intended as a kind of *modello* that could be shown to a patron (or perhaps to an engraver). Here Mantegna combines a strong formal composition supported by elements from classical antiquity with sensitive observation of the loving touch of the hands of mother and child. On the whole, Mantegna probably drew inspiration not only from his own previous works, but also from the contemporaneous production of Giovanni Bellini, whose *San Giobbe Altarpiece* painted during the 1480s (fig. 20) shows a very similar structure.

FIG. III
GIOVANNI BELLINI
The Virgin and Child
(*Davis Madonna*), about 1460
Egg tempera on panel,
72.4 × 46.4 cm
The Metropolitan Museum of Art,
New York (30.95.256)

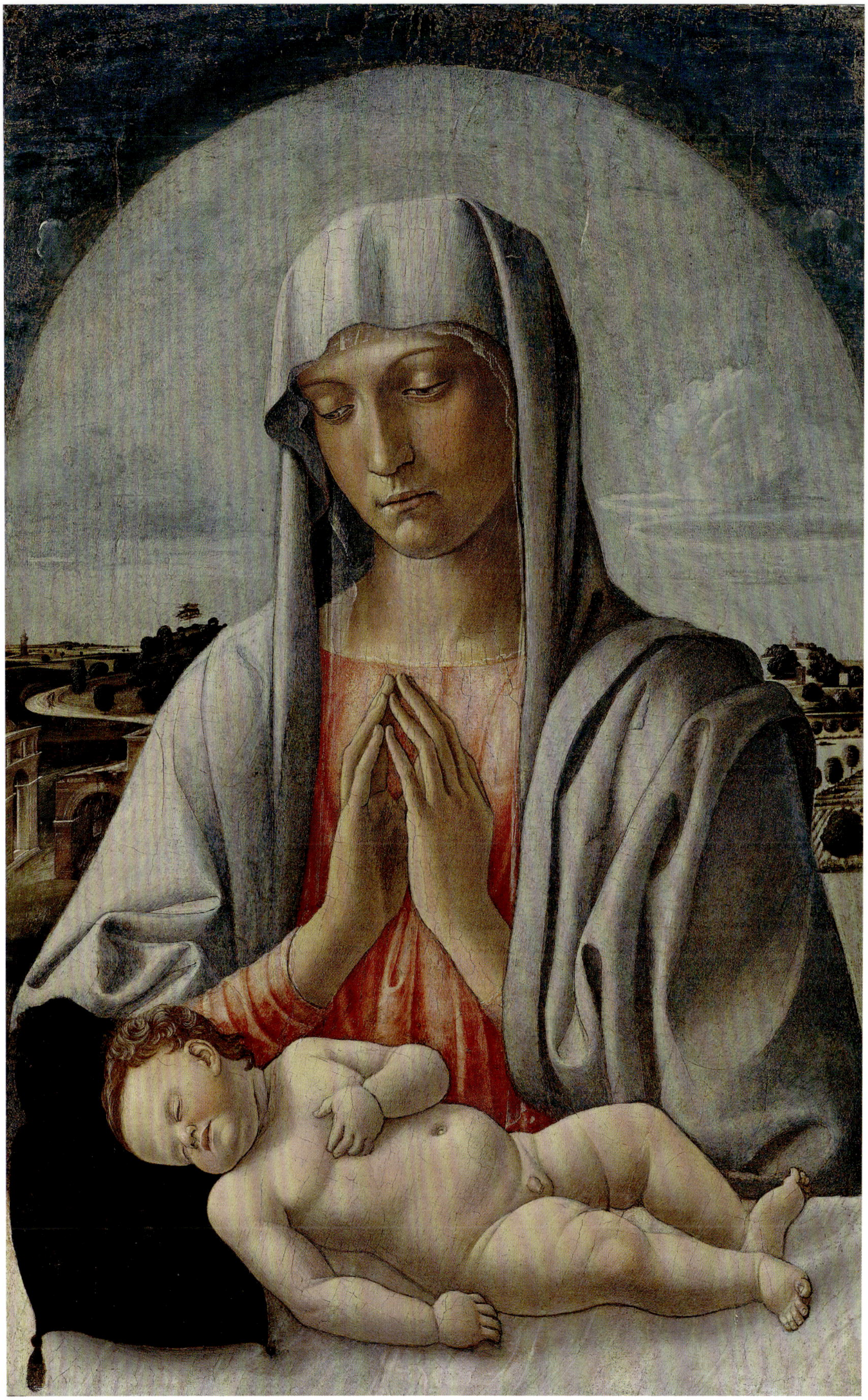

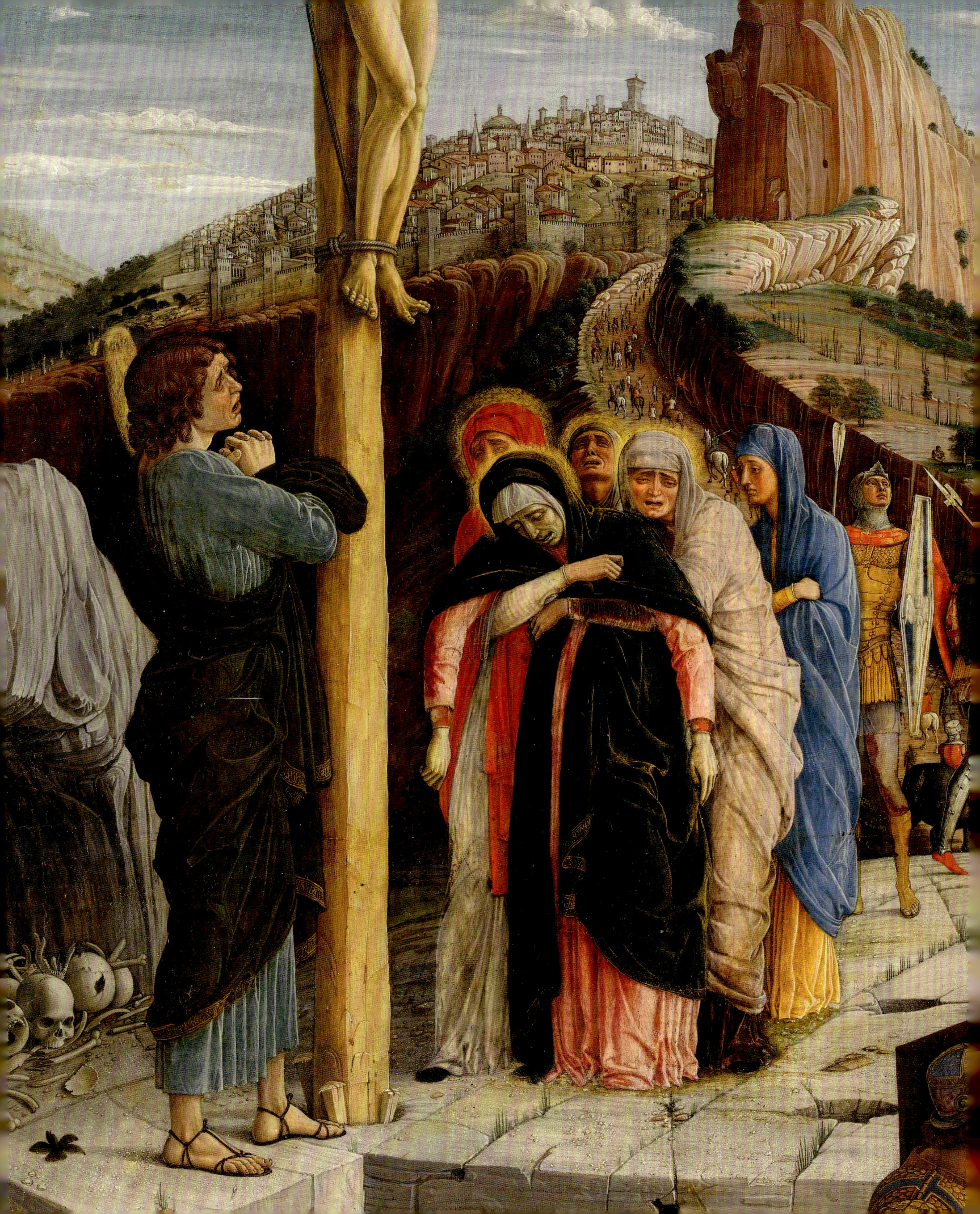

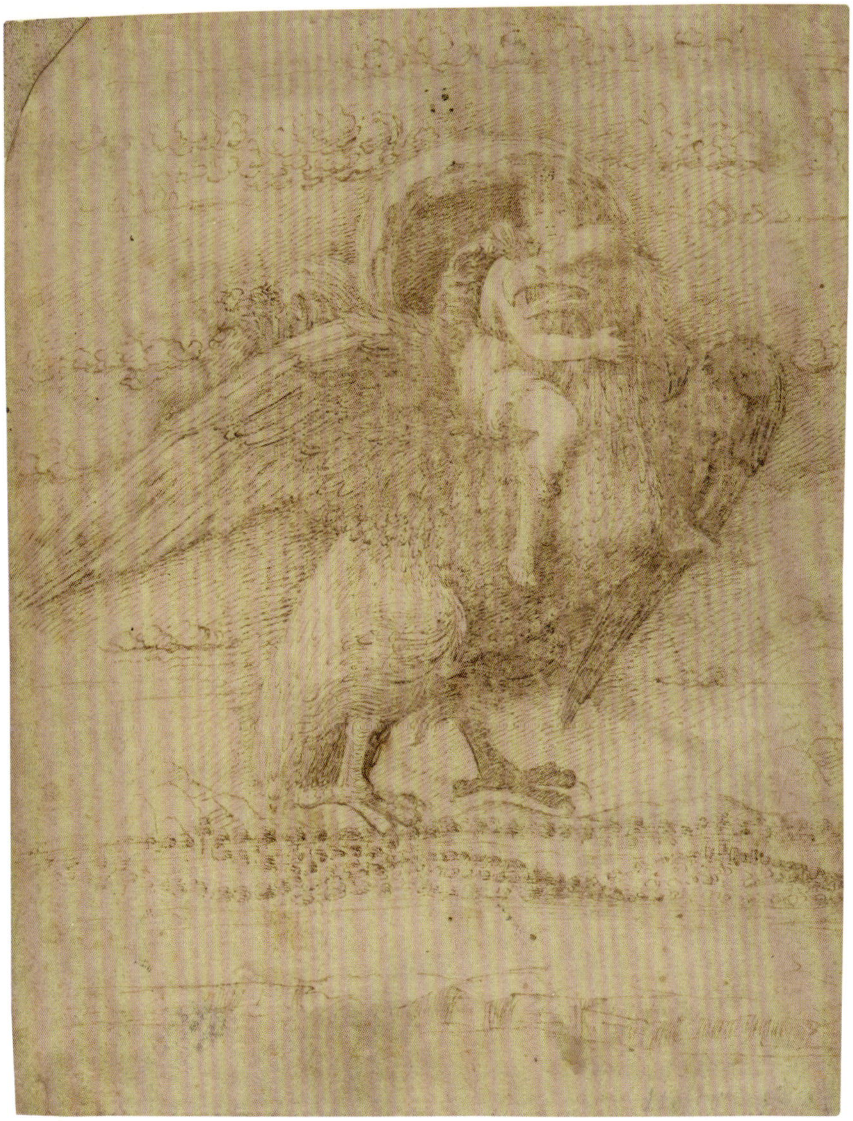

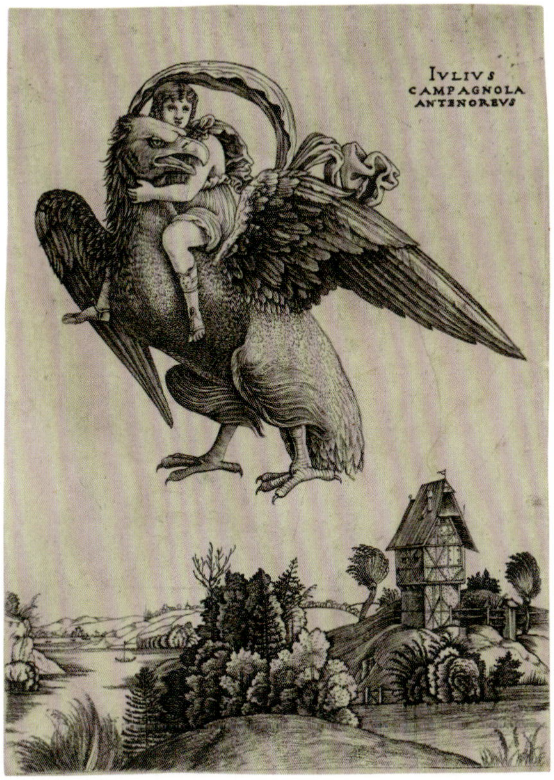

FIG. 112
Attributed to
ANDREA MANTEGNA
Jupiter and Ganymede, 1490s
Pen and brown ink on laid paper, the two figures incised, 15.2 × 11.9 cm
National Gallery of Art, Washington DC (1996.11.1)

FIG. 113
GIULIO CAMPAGNOLA, after ANDREA MANTEGNA
Jupiter and Ganymede, about 1500–5
Engraving, 16.7 × 12.4 cm
Kupferstichkabinett, Staatliche Museen zu Berlin (52-1886)

An engraving is our only concrete point of reference for a drawing of *Jupiter and Ganymede* in Washington (fig. 112). According to the most recent discussion by Andrew Robison, the attribution of the drawing remains undecided between Mantegna and Bellini.[27] The composition, which shows Jupiter in the form of an eagle abducting Ganymede, is reproduced in reverse in an engraving signed by Giulio Campagnola (fig. 113). Campagnola, however, could not have been the author of the drawing, due to differences in quality and misunderstandings in the translation from drawing to print. We would suggest returning to the attribution to Mantegna once advocated by the Tietzes, since the parallel and cross hatching of the drawing is stylistically very similar to the *Virgin and Child with an angel* in the British Museum (fig. 107). In addition, only in Mantegna's oeuvre do we find fully developed drawings of this kind associated with engravings. The young Campagnola, considered a child prodigy in Padua for his skill with burin and plate, also employed various motifs by Mantegna in two other prints, and may have been in direct contact with the artist;[28] thus it makes sense to identify Mantegna as the author of the Washington drawing. The landscape bears his hand, particularly in the rocky cliffs near the lower edge; yet in terms of the whole, he probably also had in mind the atmospheric landscapes familiar from Giovanni Bellini's representations of the Crucifixion and the Virgin and Child.[29]

ANDREA MANTEGNA, detail from *The Crucifixion* (FIG. 101)

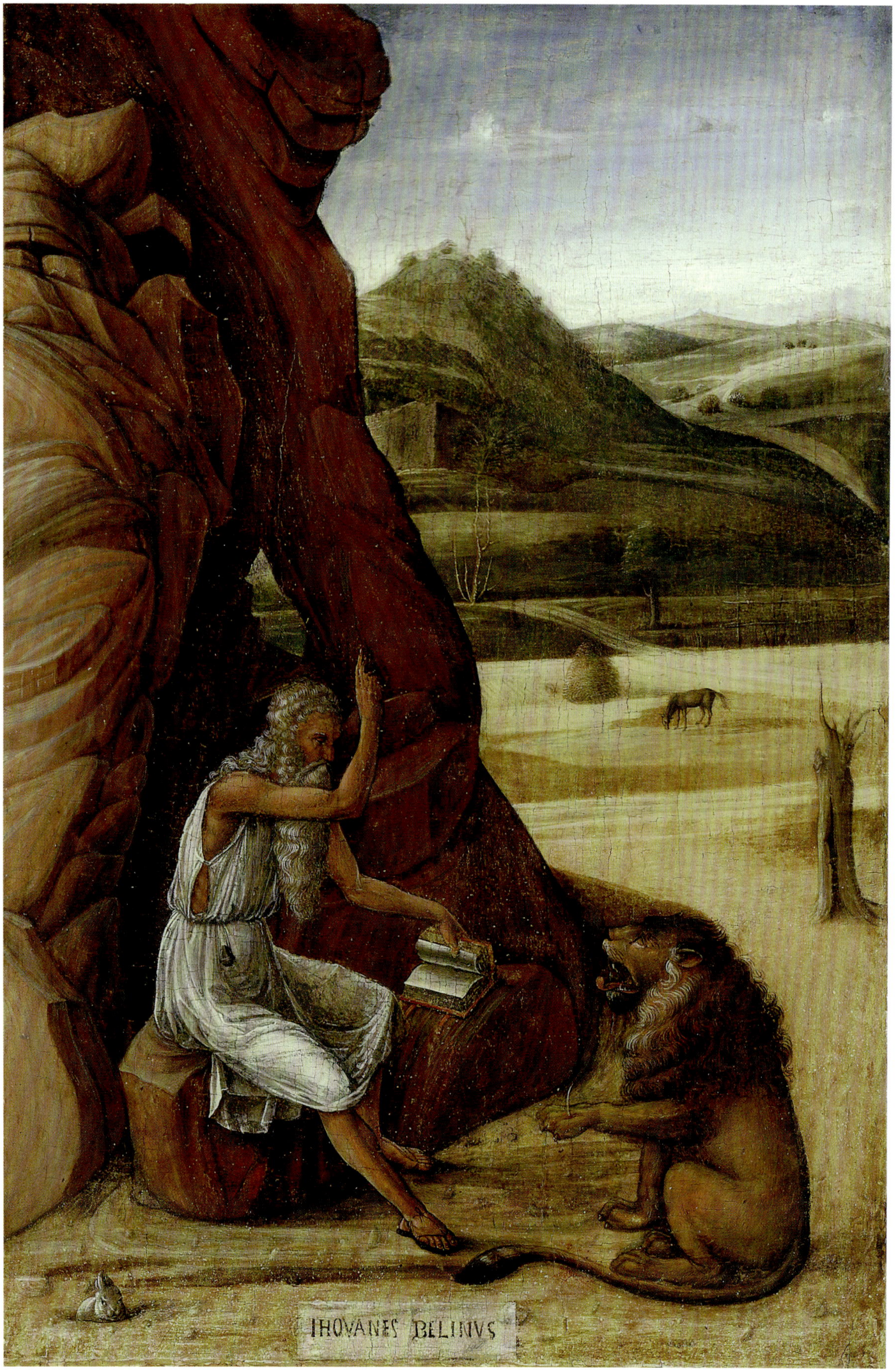

FIG. 114
GIOVANNI BELLINI
Saint Jerome in the Wilderness, probably 1453–5
Egg tempera on panel, 44.2 × 30 cm
The Barber Institute of Fine Arts, Birmingham (49.1)

Saint Jerome

SARAH VOWLES

Giovanni Bellini's earliest surviving painting is generally identified as the small *Saint Jerome* in Birmingham (fig. 114), dating from the early 1450s. A little earlier, perhaps around 1448–51, Mantegna tackled the same subject in a painting now in São Paulo (fig. 116), whose attribution, although contested, has met with growing critical acceptance in recent years.[1] The two panels have much in common, but already display subtle differences between the young artists' aesthetic approaches.

Jerome was a popular saint in Northern Italy, traditionally represented in cardinal's robes as a Father of the Church, emphasising his status as the translator of the Bible into the Latin Vulgate. By the time of Mantegna and Bellini, however, these forms were giving way to a new iconography focusing on Jerome's penitence in the wilderness. Pisanello seems to have been the first to adopt this concept in the north of Italy, but it also inspired Jacopo Bellini, who explored it in his Drawing Books and in a painting.[2]

Both Bellini and Mantegna situate the hermit saint in a rocky fastness surrounded by wilderness, but neither depicts him in active penitence as Jacopo did. Instead they show him holding a weighty book of scripture, accompanied by his familiar lion, whom he had tamed when extracting a thorn from its paw.

Bellini's painting is more immediately narrative, a quality more traditionally associated with Mantegna. While earlier representations of Jerome had often shown him holding an open book, inscribed with the opening of a famous passage in which he stressed the need to conquer both rage and the desires of the flesh, Bellini shows the sentiment in action. Jerome preaches serenity to the wounded lion but ignores the rabbit, symbol of lust, which skulks in its burrow at lower left.[3] The unified whole disguises Bellini's assembly of motifs from different sources: the lion, for example, derives from one in Jacopo's Drawing Book in the Louvre (fig. 115).[4]

For Mantegna, the creation of a mood seems to have been more important than explicit narrative. Drawing on the earlier tradition of the saint as scholar, he shows a frowning Jerome in a rocky shelter. Small details allude to study, seclusion and solitary worship, such as the rosary and the curious wooden object mounted on the wall, perhaps a simantron, used in Orthodox monasteries to call monks together for prayer.[5] Jerome's silent communion with God is presented as a path to wisdom, symbolised by the owl perched on the pinnacle of the cave.

The painting is neither signed nor dated, which has exacerbated the question of its authorship. While there is no evidence to conclusively exclude the possibility of the *Saint Jerome* being by a close collaborator, such as Niccolò Pizzolo, it seems most likely to be by Mantegna himself: the draperies and the ornate rock formations are

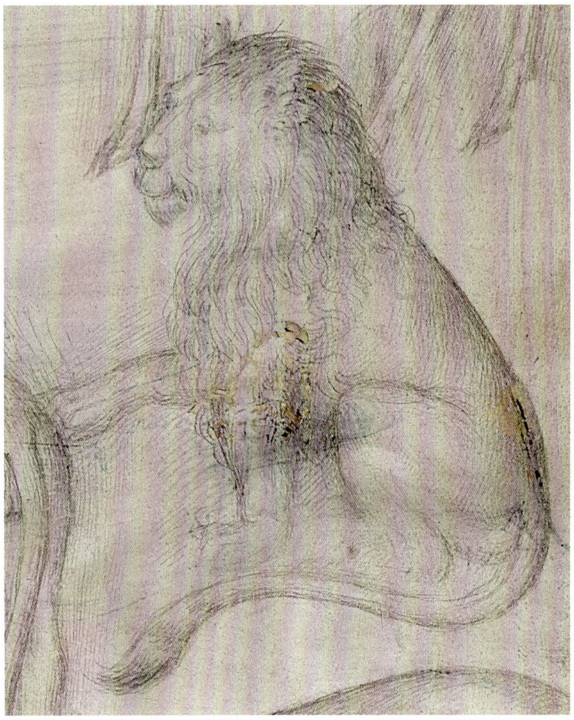

FIG. 115
JACOPO BELLINI, detail of *Studies of seven lions and three deer*, from *The Paris Drawing Book of Jacopo Bellini* (FIG. 91)

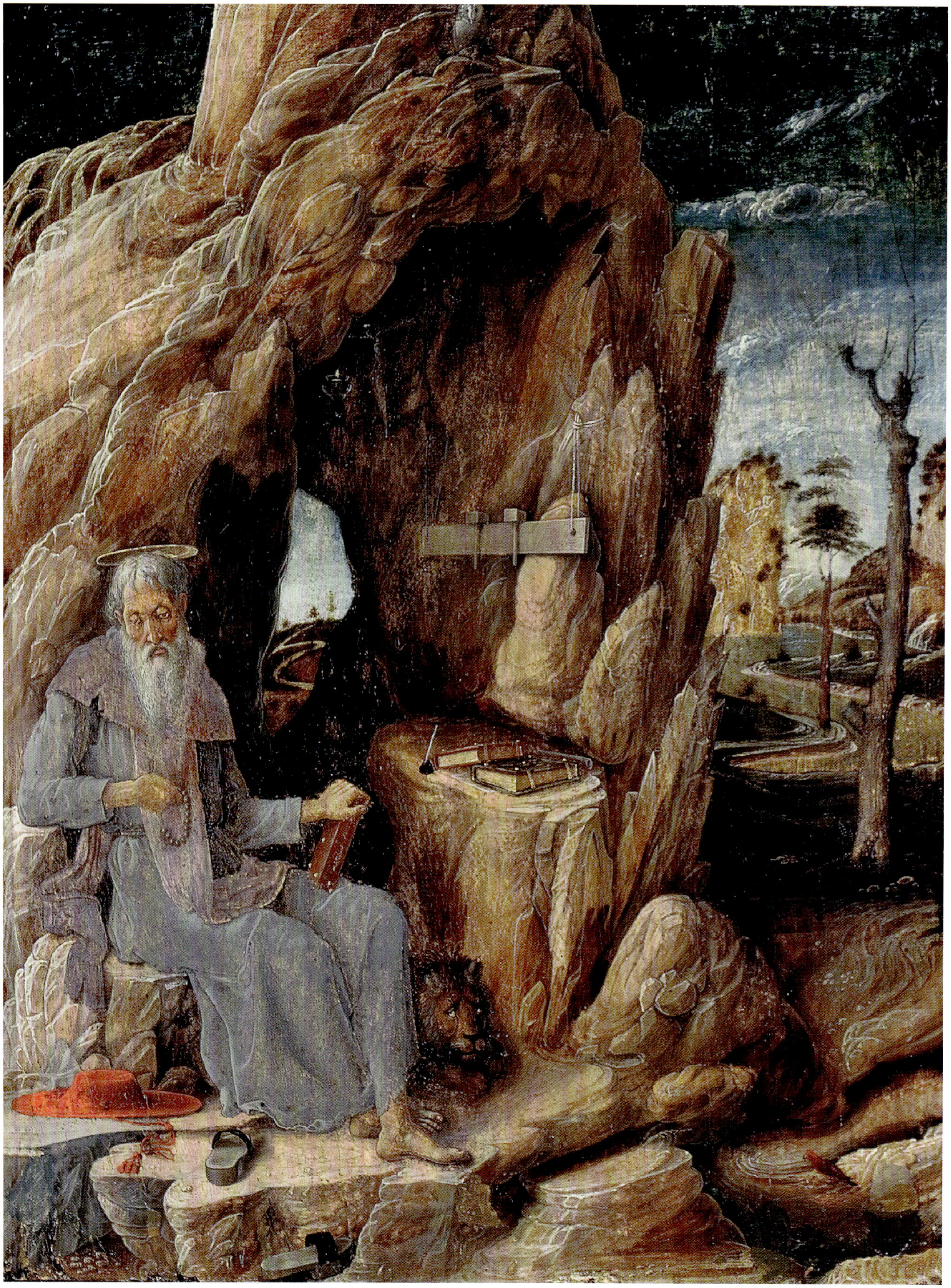

FIG. 116
ANDREA MANTEGNA
Saint Jerome Penitent in the Desert, 1448–51
Egg tempera on panel, 51 × 40 cm
Museu de Arte de São Paulo Assis Chateaubriand (MASP.00015)

FIG. 117
GIOVANNI BELLINI
Saint Jerome reading in a Landscape, about 1480–5
Oil on panel, 46.8 × 33.8 cm
The National Gallery, London (NG 281)

similar to comparable features in the Ovetari frescoes and Jerome's physiognomy is close to that of the figures in the *San Zeno Altarpiece* (see fig. 252).[6] Whether this attenuated and austere figure pre- or post-dates the more typically Mantegnesque *Saint Mark* in Frankfurt (fig. 77) remains uncertain.

There has been much less debate about Bellini's painting, signed using an otherwise unknown form of his signature: 'IHOVANES BELINVS'.[7] Other details, such as the use of gold and silver paint for highlights, a technique which disappeared from his later works, support its status as the work of a young artist still influenced by his workshop training. This sits alongside an already sophisticated understanding of the role of natural light as a unifying factor in a picture. While Mantegna also floods his picture with light, his illumination tends towards starkness, throwing deep shadows which shape the rocks as crisply as the furrows on Saint Jerome's face. Bellini, on the other hand, already employs the softer, more diffused radiance that would characterise his mature paintings.

Although Mantegna did not return to the subject, Bellini painted three further Saint Jeromes: in around 1480 (Uffizi, Florence, Contini Bonacossi collection, no. 25), around 1480–5 (National Gallery, London, fig. 117) and around 1505 (National Gallery of Art, Washington, 1939.1.217). Over time, he became increasingly interested in the landscape element, moving the saint towards the edge of the composition to allow for increasingly elaborate views beyond. The sentiment, however, does not change. Even as a young artist, Bellini had conceived a sensitive, serene vision of Saint Jerome which continued to inform his work for the rest of his life.

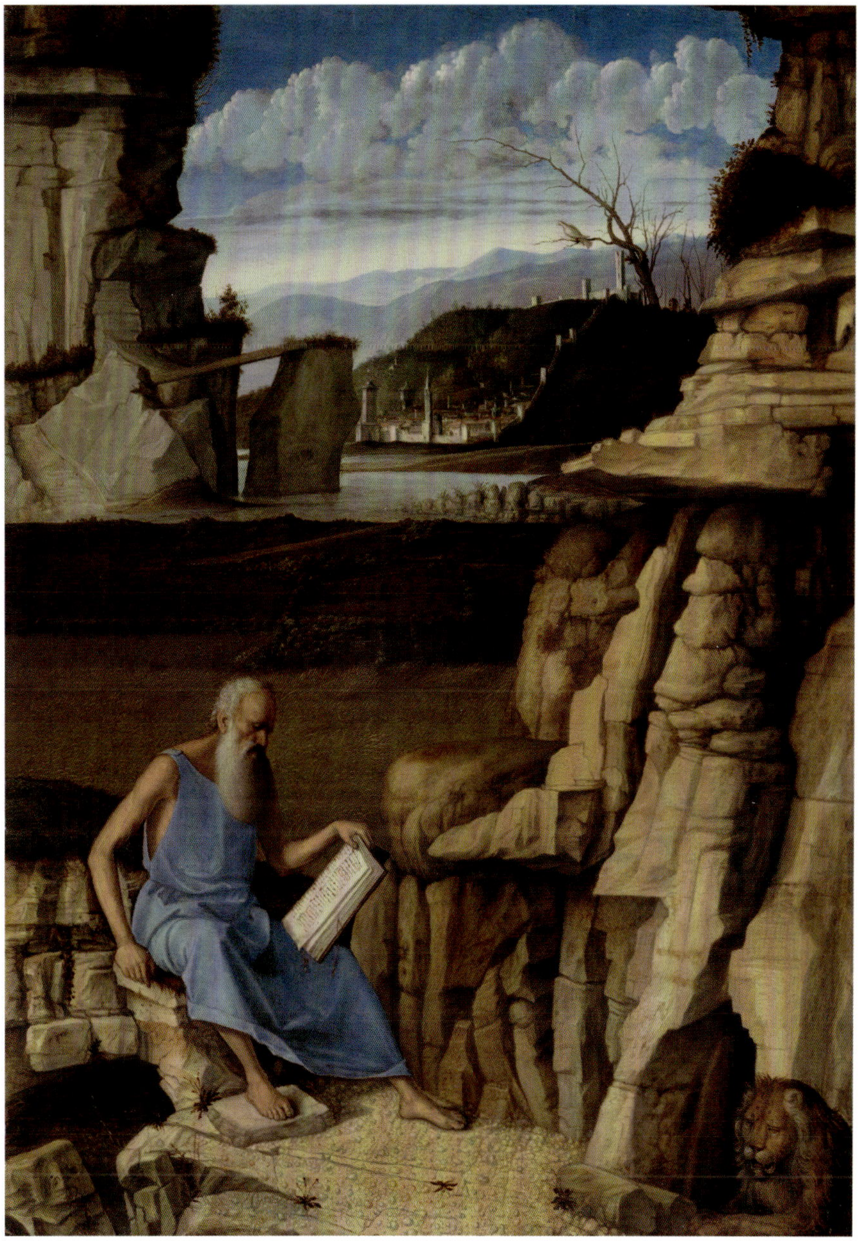

Standing Saints: The Young Mantegna and Bellini as Draughtsmen

SARAH VOWLES

All Renaissance artists expected to represent saints. They appeared in every altarpiece, although the manner of their representation changed radically during Mantegna's and Bellini's careers. Both artists trained in a world where saints usually appeared as isolated figures, placed against a gold background on their own separate panel, as in the *Saint Sebastian Triptych* for the Church of the Carità (fig. 84). Mantegna wished to unify space within these multi-panelled altarpieces, using a common background and light source to connect the separate sections of his *San Zeno Altarpiece* (fig. 252). Bellini, for his part, mastered the *sacra conversazione*, an artistic genre which showed the Virgin and Child accompanied by several saints in a single painting. These could be either monumental, as in his *San Zaccaria Altarpiece* (fig. 257), or strikingly intimate, as in his *Virgin and Child with Saints Catherine and Mary Magdalene* (fig. 187). The compositional drawings that Mantegna and Bellini made in relation to altarpiece commissions in the years around 1460 – the moment of their closest connection – reveal these intrinsic artistic differences.

As a young master, Bellini and his assistants worked on four triptychs (including figs 84, 120) for the Carità during the 1460s.[1] Two small drawings of *Saint Louis of Toulouse* (figs 118, 119), apparently connected to the representation of this saint in the *Madonna Triptych* (fig. 120), show successive stages in his development of a single figure. Both saints wear the same costume, with drapery across the chest fixed by a large oval brooch set with four round jewels. The looser handling and more experimental quality of *Saint Louis of Toulouse holding a book* (fig. 118) means it is probably the earliest. By contrast, *Saint Louis of Toulouse holding a staff* (fig. 119) was drawn with greater care. Firmer pen-lines and more hatching define the shadows of the saint's cloak; his hand is raised in blessing; and the crozier, which

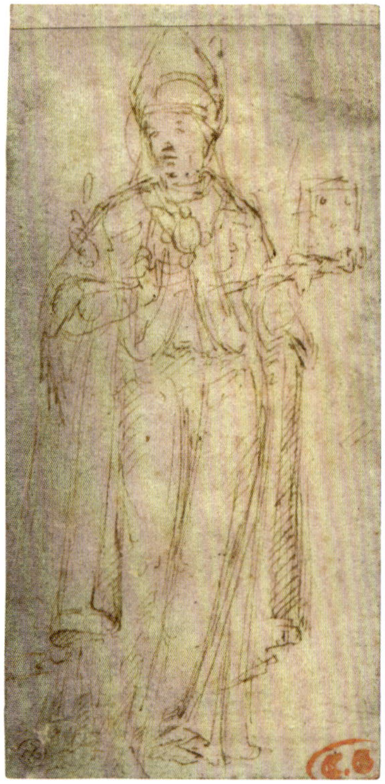

FIG. 118
GIOVANNI BELLINI
Saint Louis of Toulouse holding a book, early 1460s
Pen and brown ink over stylus on paper, 9.8 × 5 cm
National Gallery of Art, Washington DC (1997.40.2)

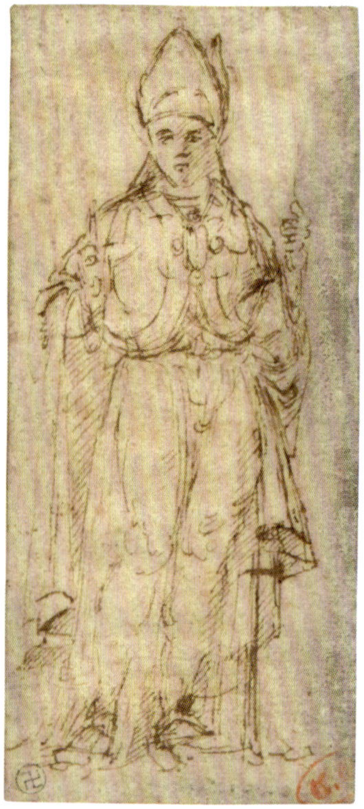

FIG. 119
GIOVANNI BELLINI
Saint Louis of Toulouse holding a staff, early 1460s
Pen and brown ink over stylus on paper, 9.8 × 4.4 cm
National Gallery of Art, Washington DC (1997.40.1)

FIG. 120
GIOVANNI BELLINI and studio
Saint Louis of Toulouse (panel of the *Madonna Triptych*, from the Church of Santa Maria della Carità, Venice), 1462–4
Egg tempera on panel, gold background, 127 × 48 cm
Gallerie dell'Accademia, Venice (621c)

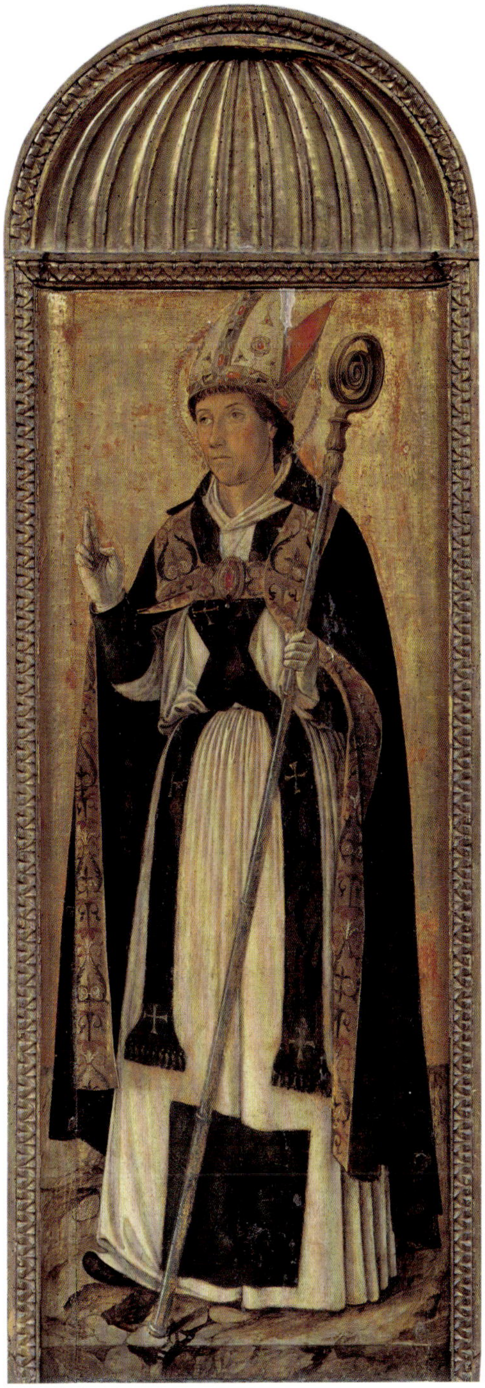

replaces the book, has been sketched in. The painted figure – although different – evidently derives from these drawings.[2]

Meanwhile, Mantegna was settling in as court painter in Mantua. One of his first commissions there seems to have been an altarpiece featuring a group of saints, among them Saint Andrew, to whom the city's basilica was dedicated.[3] The painting – if it was ever completed – is now lost, but three drawings can be connected with it. Their broad strokes, drawn with a thick nib, match other drawings from the early 1460s, as does the characteristic treatment of the hair, curling over the foreheads and around the sides of the faces.

The *Three standing saints* (fig. 62) in fact shows only two: the saint holding the book is depicted twice. The largest figure – on the left – seems to have been drawn first; Mantegna then added Saint Andrew, whose cross shows changes testifying to the complexity of its foreshortening. On the right, Mantegna redrew the saint with the book, this time cradling it in his arm. The two saints on the right seem to have been conceived as a pair, as they share the same scale and stand upon the same decorative cornicing. However, Mantegna was clearly unsatisfied with the reading saint, whom he left unfinished, and tried out for a third time in a British Museum drawing (fig. 123). Here he blocked out a more satisfactory pose, using thicker, more confident lines, indicating the book with the shorthand of a folded page. Another drawing, formed from two joined sheets (fig. 121), testifies to Mantegna's development of this project. It shows figures drawn by Mantegna himself on the left, where he has made two quick studies of a Saint John the Baptist, and studies by an assistant or follower on the right-hand side. Among these less sophisticated drawings are copies of a Saint Andrew, as well as a saint with a book. This may reflect another idea for the reading saint on the Morgan and British Museum sheets.

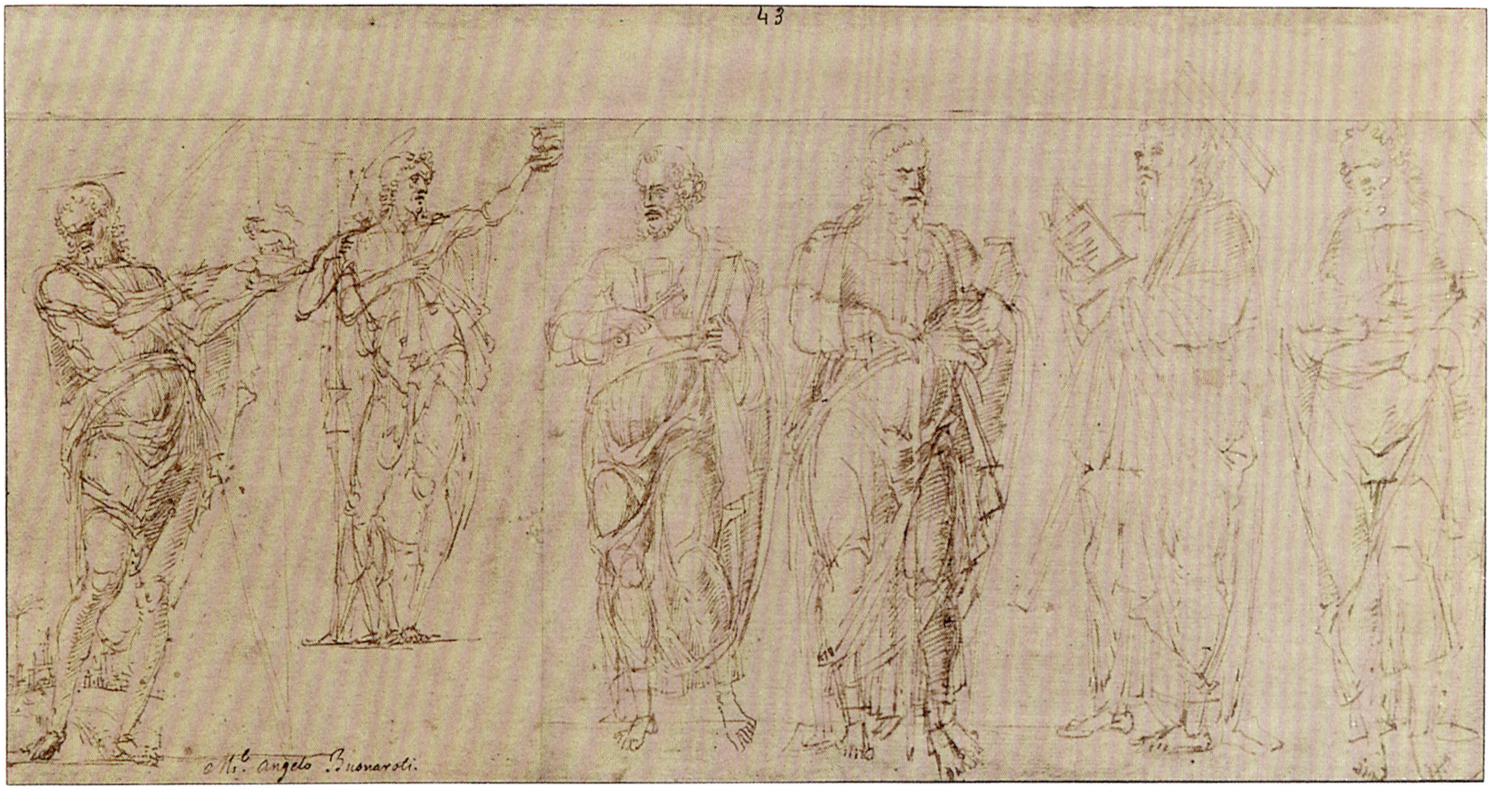

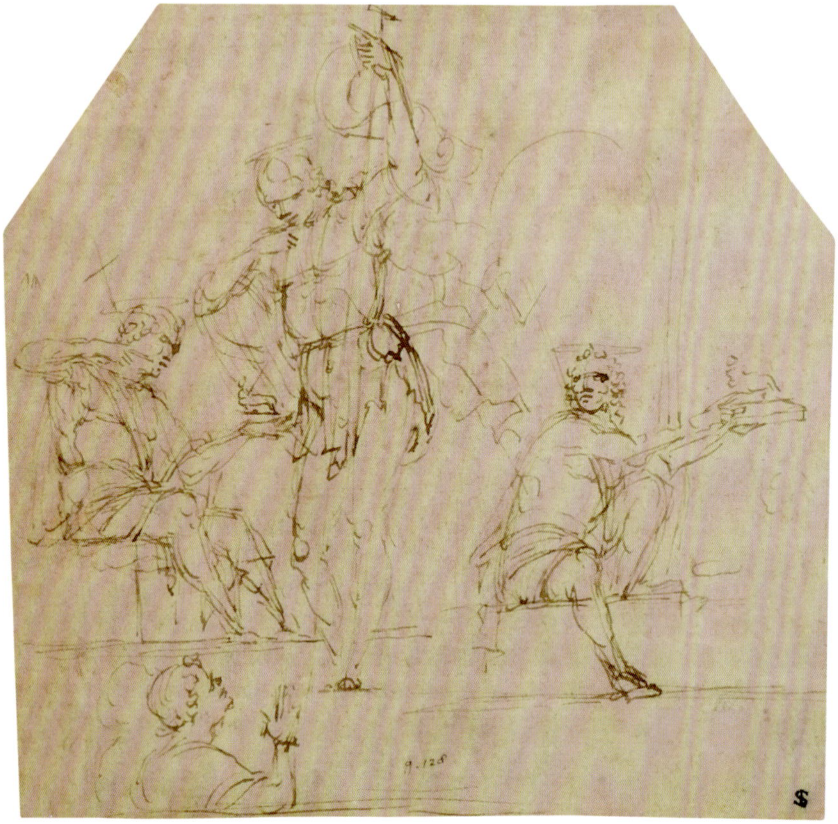

FIG. 121
ANDREA MANTEGNA and studio
Standing saints, about 1460
Pen and ink on two sheets of paper fastened together, 17.1 × 40.3 cm
Formerly in the Koenigs collection. RKD Nederlands Instituut voor Kunstgeschiedenis, The Hague (I. 487)

FIG. 122
ANDREA MANTEGNA
Three studies for Saint John the Baptist, about 1490
Pen and brown ink on pale pink prepared paper, 17.4 × 18.5 cm
Walker Art Gallery, Liverpool (WAG 1995.324)

FIG. 123
ANDREA MANTEGNA
Reading saint, 1460s
Pen and brown ink on pink prepared paper, 17.4 × 6.9 cm
The British Museum, London (1895,0915.780)

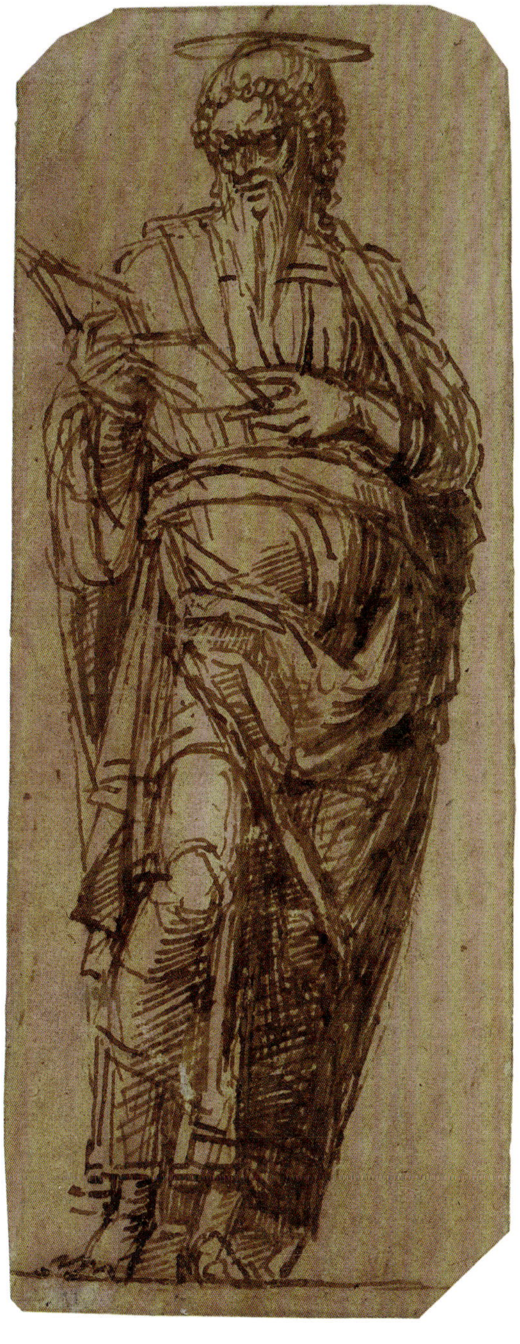

A sheet of studies for a painting of Saint John the Baptist (fig. 122), which has – like the British Museum and Morgan sheets – been considered a first idea for a work of the early 1460s, seems instead to date around 1490.[4] While the subject is similar to these drawings, the pen-work is light and fluid, without the bold weight of Mantegna's early draughtsmanship, and the human form is represented in a more fluidly dynamic way (for instance, Saint John's drapery flutters rather than hanging in careful angular folds). Yet the abbreviated use of horizontal and vertical lines for the facial features, and the tapering limbs, are sure signifiers of Mantegna's hand.

Comparison of Mantegna and Bellini's early drawings reveals two artists pursuing similar graphic styles, but driven by different aesthetic concerns. Parallel hatching is always of paramount importance for Mantegna, unlike Bellini. Bellini's draperies show a lighter touch; they fall in graceful folds, as opposed to Mantegna's stiff creases. The two artists construct faces in different ways. Mantegna's figures habitually have their features sketched in using the graphic shorthand of a T-shape to indicate eyebrows and nose. Yet Bellini, even at his most brisk, as in the *Saint Louis holding a book*, describes facial features individually, with short dashed horizontal lines. He is less concerned with volume than Mantegna, and more interested in the softening qualities of light. This tendency, evident in early paintings including the *Saint Jerome* (fig. 114) as well as drawings, is Bellini's *leitmotif*.

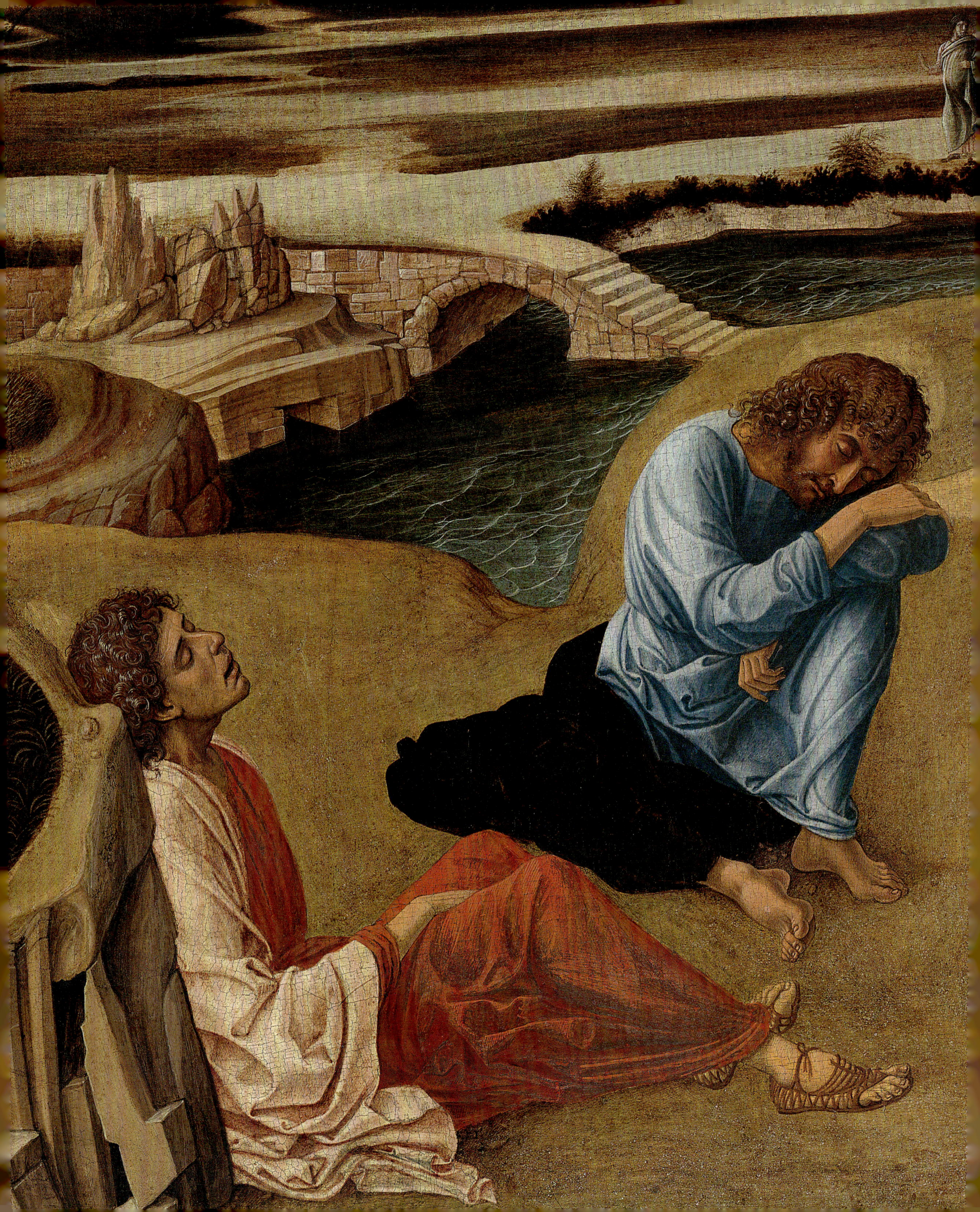

The Agony in the Garden

CAROLINE CAMPBELL

In the decade between 1450 and 1460 the artistic and personal relationship between Andrea Mantegna and Giovanni Bellini was at its most intense.[1] The first of Mantegna and Bellini's related works were the two *Saint Jeromes* (figs 114, 116).[2] More original, and more significant were their three related depictions of Christ's vigil in the Garden of Gethsemane, *The Agony in the Garden* (figs 124, 125, 126), two of which have hung side by side in the National Gallery since 1893.[3] Mantegna's *Agony*, with its elaborate, antiquarian-inspired details,[4] and Bellini's, a landscape suffused with the light of dawn, exemplify the characteristics of each artist and their essential differences. The relationship of these pictures, and their connection to Mantegna's left-most predella panel for the *San Zeno Altarpiece* of *The Agony in the Garden* (fig. 124), has been much studied.[5] Thanks to this research, particularly the recent studies of Jill Dunkerton, Babette Hartwieg and Marika Spring,[6] we can establish a satisfactory chronology for these three works, reflecting a sustained period of artistic dialogue between Mantegna and his wife's family.

Mantegna's first *Agony* is the painting now in the National Gallery (fig. 125), as it – like Giovanni Bellini's picture – is indebted to Jacopo Bellini's drawing of the

GIOVANNI BELLINI, detail from *The Agony in the Garden* (FIG. 126)

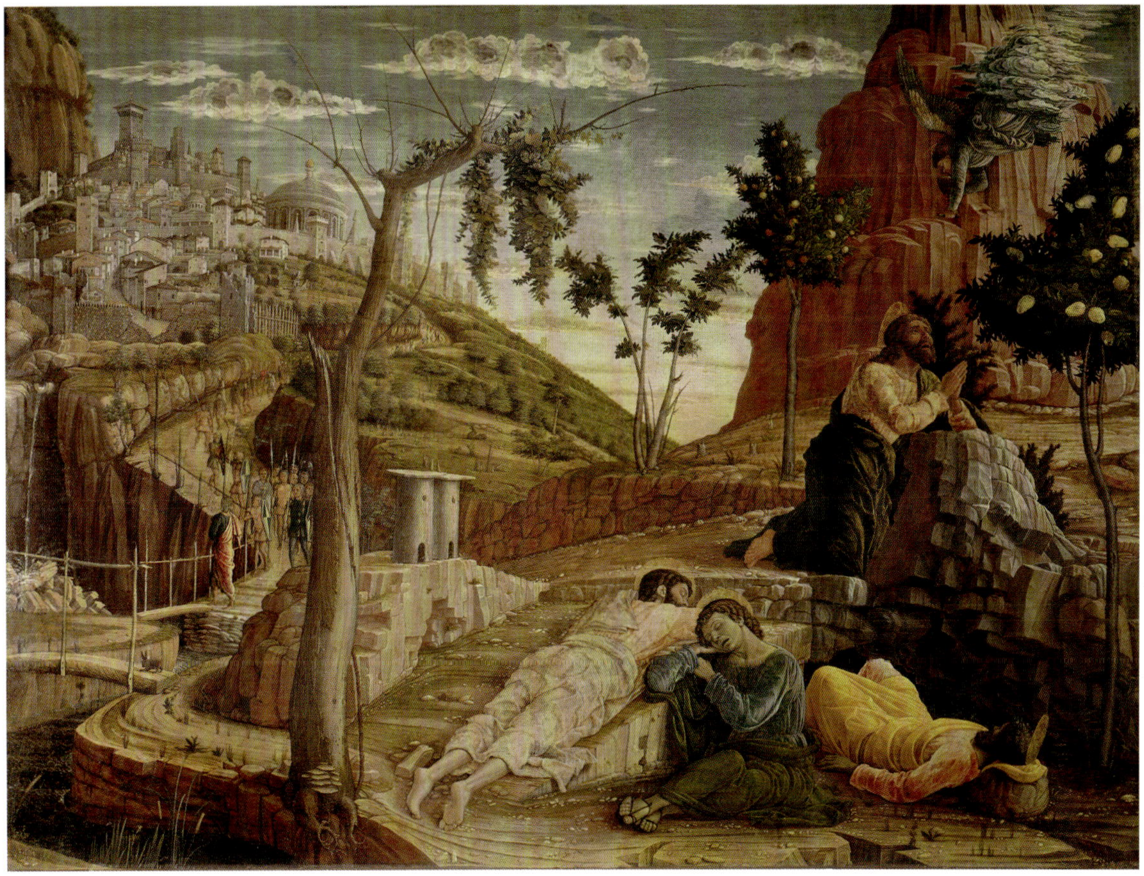

FIG. 124
ANDREA MANTEGNA
The Agony in the Garden, 1456–9
Oil on panel, transferred to canvas, 71.1 × 93.7 cm
Musée des Beaux-Arts de Tours (1803-1-24)

FIG. 125
ANDREA MANTEGNA
The Agony in the Garden,
about 1455–6
Egg tempera on panel,
62.9 × 80 cm
The National Gallery, London
(NG 1417)

subject in the British Museum Drawing Book (fig. 215).[7] Other aspects of Mantegna's *Agony* recall sheets in Jacopo's Louvre Drawing Book.[8] Mantegna's painting cannot predate his marriage to Nicolosia Bellini in 1453, as it is unlikely that the artist would have had sustained access to Jacopo's albums before this moment. The miniaturist style of this *Agony* – seen, for instance, in the gnarled roots of the tree-trunk bridge and the bricks of the city wall – resembles other paintings by Mantegna of the early 1450s, particularly *The Adoration of the Shepherds* (fig. 221). It lacks, however, the emotional connection between landscape and figures evident in the predella scenes for the *San Zeno Altarpiece* (figs 101, 124, 252), painted between 1456 and 1459 at the instigation of Gregorio Correr, the learned Venetian aristocrat who was Abbot of this Benedictine foundation.[9] This characteristic, relatively rare in Mantegna's work,[10] was the result of exposure to Giovanni Bellini's paintings. In the *Agony* for San Zeno (fig. 9), the figure of Christ is more integrated into the landscape. The clouds no longer scud aimlessly in the sky but have been organised to draw attention to the vanishing point on the horizon, from where the sun begins to rise.

Bellini's *Agony* must have been made at a time – or shortly after – when Bellini had close access to Mantegna and his studio.[11] Although it is not a copy of either of Mantegna's *Agonies*, it is impossible not to see it in relationship to these works. The figural composition is based on Mantegna's National Gallery *Agony*, and the foreshortening of Saint Peter shows Bellini's awareness of Mantegna's studies of the human body, whether from drawings of the mid-1450s such as *Three studies for the Dead Christ* (fig. 163), or paintings such as the San Zeno *Agony* (fig. 124). There are also technical features that recall Mantegna's working methods.[12] The stones and pebbles in the foreground are composed of carefully applied spatters of paint – a technique that Mantegna used often, but Bellini never employed it again.[13] A sign of the artists' shared technical innovation is their use of shell gold for Christ's drapery folds and haloes in each of the National Gallery *Agonies*. This method, in which particles of powdered gold (allegedly kept in a shell) were applied as if they were conventional paint, was commonly employed by manuscript illuminators (an area in which both painters experimented; see figs 94, 95, 97, 98),[14] but not by many easel painters at this date.[15] Again, Mantegna used this throughout his career, but it is found very rarely in Bellini's work.

For whom and for what reason were the two National Gallery *Agonies* made? They are too long and too wide to have been part of a predella. Their function must have been, in part, to stimulate prayer and meditation. Although the Agony in the Garden was a regular episode in narrative cycles of Christ's life, such as the mosaics in the Basilica of San Marco in Venice,[16] Mantegna and Bellini's pictures are among the very first stand-alone representations of this subject in paint.[17] This is related to contemporary Christian practice. Christ's Agony in the Garden was commonly described and illustrated in psalters, devotional texts and miscellanies of the later Middle Ages,[18] and the subject was important above and beyond its role at Easter. The 'Way', or Stations of the Cross, a devotional practice that began in the twelfth and thirteenth centuries, generally commenced with Christ's lonely prayer on the Mount of Olives (the traditional site of the Garden of Gethsemane).[19] Influential texts, such as the Pseudo-Bonaventure's *Meditations on the Passion of Christ*,[20] argued that Christians had to meditate on the Agony to understand Christ's sacrifice.[21] As the Franciscan mystic Angela of Foligno (1248/9–1309) wrote: 'Place this mirror [Christ in the Garden] before your eyes and apply yourself to it as often as you have to, because with it he prayed for you, not for himself.'[22]

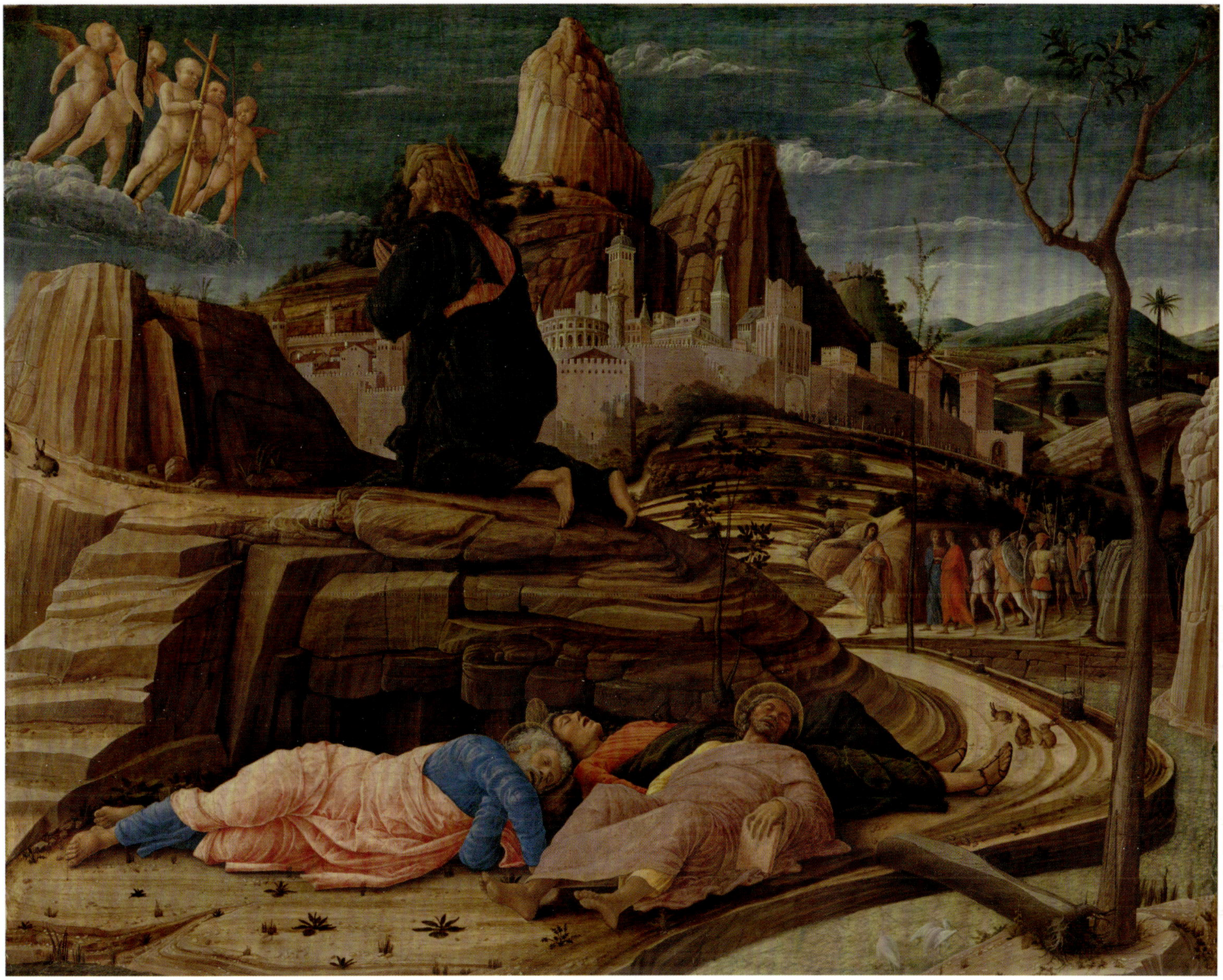

Bellini and Mantegna's paintings, however, cannot simply have been made as devotional aids. Presumably they were commissioned by clients who valued how the artistry and innovation of the painter would have deepened their spiritual meaning.[23] It has been suggested that Mantegna's *Agony* was destined for a Ferrarese courtly patron,[24] and that it was the 'little work' on which Mantegna was engaged for Jacopo Antonio Marcello in 1459,[25] but we know nothing of the history of Bellini's *Agony* before the eighteenth century.[26] Both paintings must have been intended for a private individual, whether a cleric or a layperson, someone with the intellectual interests and erudition of a Ferrarese courtier, a Jacopo Marcello or a Gregorio Correr. It is possible, of course, that the two pictures were made for the same person, who wished to compare their connections and differences as we do today. Their different histories, however – one painting first recorded in Venice; the other probably from Ferrara – make this attractive hypothesis unlikely.[27]

FIG. 126
GIOVANNI BELLINI
The Agony in the Garden, about 1458–60
Egg tempera on panel, 80.4 × 127 cm
The National Gallery, London
(NG 726)

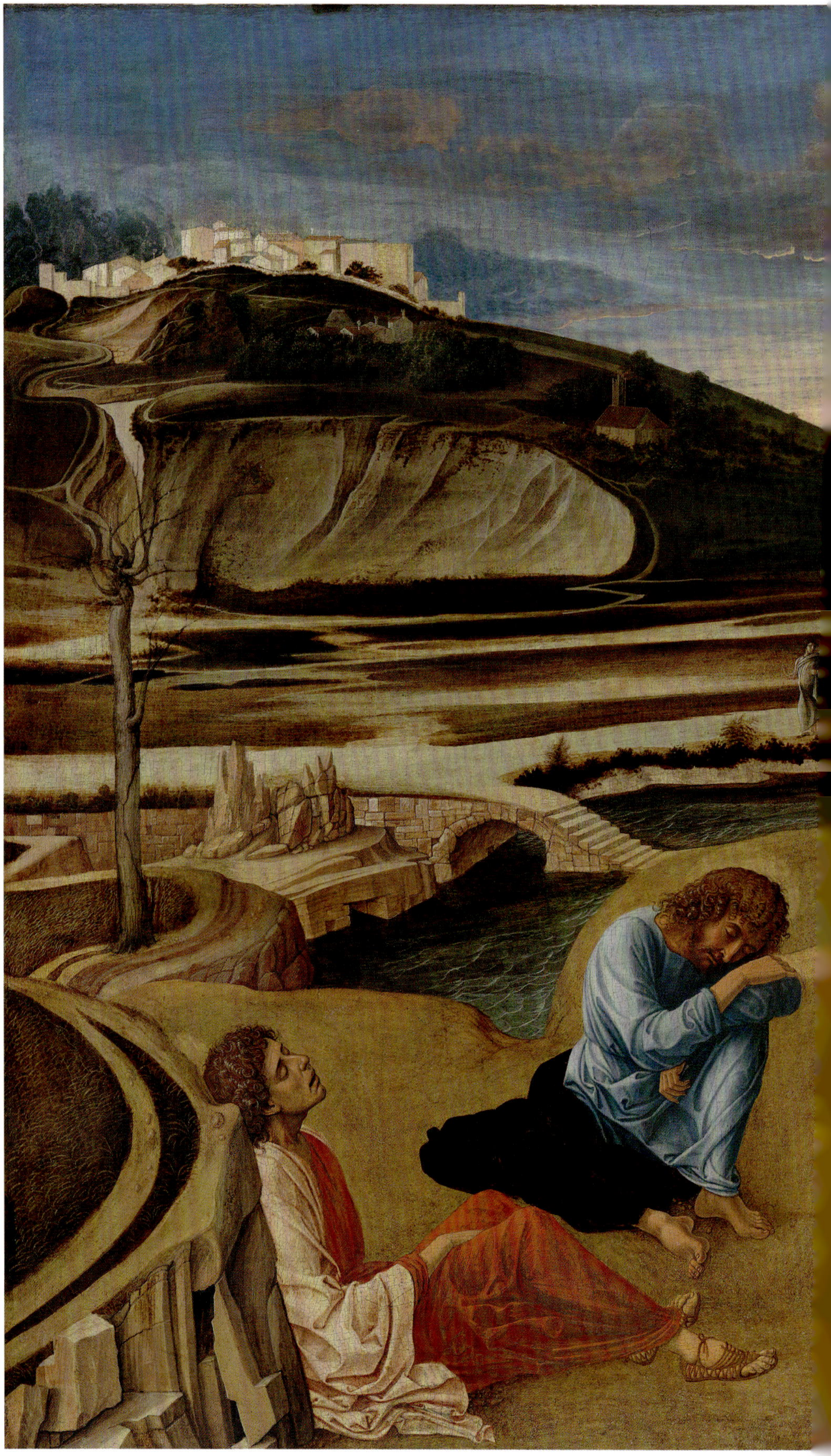

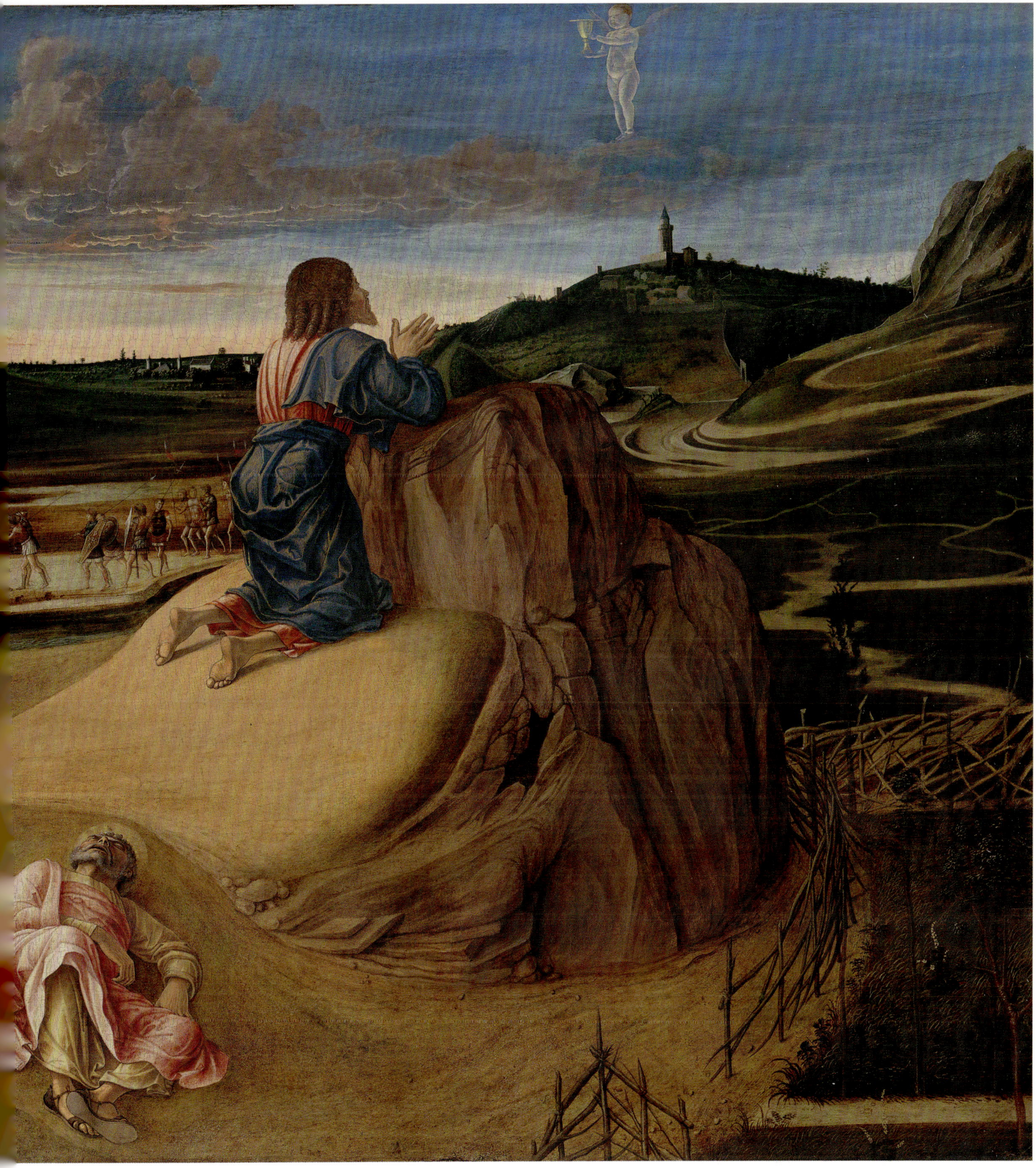

When Bellini *traced* Mantegna: Two Paintings of the Presentation of Christ in the Temple

NEVILLE ROWLEY

The Presentation of Christ in the Temple is narrated in the Gospel of Saint Luke (2: 21–39). Soon after his birth, Jesus was brought to the Temple in Jerusalem by his parents, Mary and Joseph. The reason for this journey is not entirely clear, except that it was a Jewish ritual: were they accomplishing the circumcision of the Child, his consecration to the Lord (as first-born male), or the ritual purification of his mother after giving birth?[1] In any case, says Saint Luke, Joseph and Mary brought with them a pair of turtle doves (or two young pigeons) for sacrifice. In the temple, a wise elder named Simeon took the Child in his arms, recognising him as the Messiah, while Anna, an old prophetess, proclaimed the miracle. At the beginning of the fourteenth century, Giotto painted a notable version of the scene in the Scrovegni Chapel in Padua (fig. 127): the architecture of the temple is symbolised by the canopy over the altar, before which the sacred story takes place. Mary has just left her Child in the arms of Simeon, to the left of her, Joseph holds the sacrificial doves, while at the far right an old woman holds a scroll – this can only be the prophetess Anna. To involve the beholder in the narrative, Giotto added two figures to the scene, a flying angel and a woman at the far left, thus uniting heaven and earth as witnesses to the sacred event.

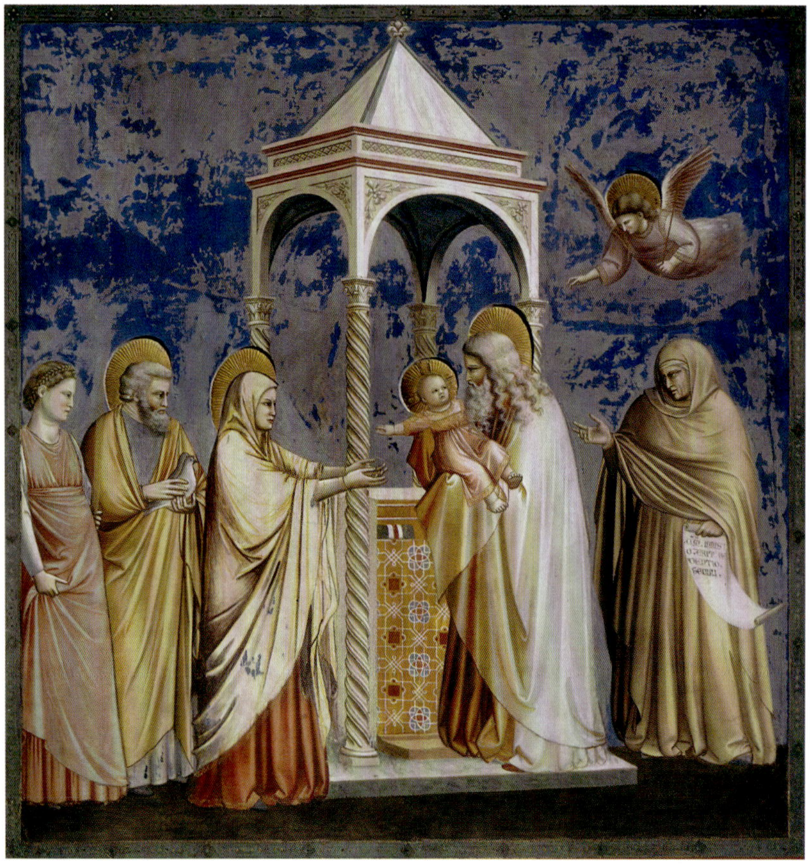

FIG. 127
GIOTTO
The Presentation of Christ in the Temple, about 1303–5
Fresco, 200 × 185 cm
Scrovegni Chapel, Padua

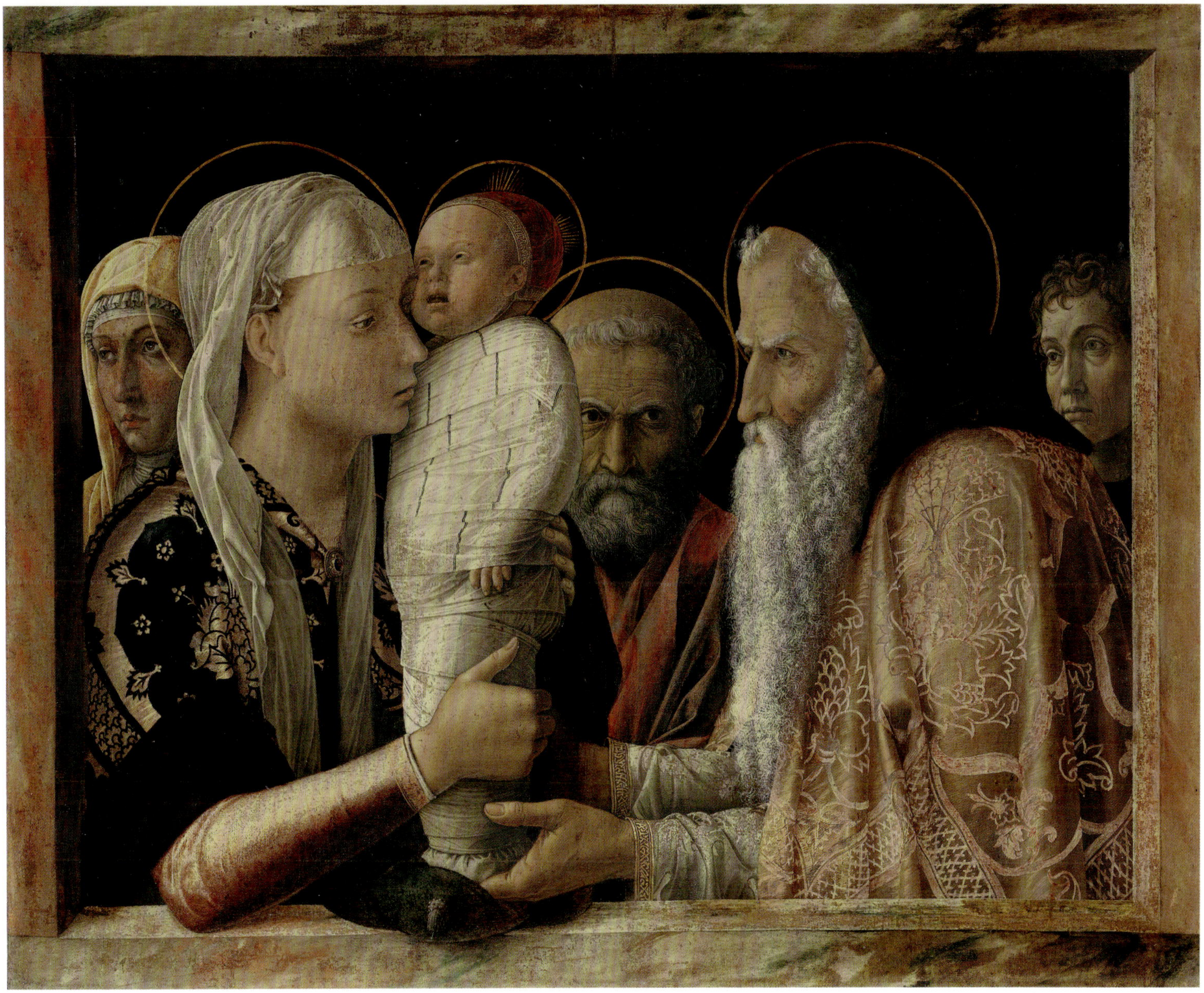

FIG. 128
ANDREA MANTEGNA
The Presentation of Christ in the Temple, about 1454
Egg tempera on canvas, assembled on wooden construction, 77.5 × 94.4 cm
Gemäldegalerie, Staatliche Museen zu Berlin (29)

For any artist working in Padua in the fifteenth century, this model was canonicial. Mantegna's interpretation (fig. 128), however, makes a decisive departure from Giotto's example. He includes neither temple, altar nor doves; there is no place for anecdote. The figures are not seen standing, as Giotto had them, and as any painter was bound to do in representing a religious scene: Mantegna *cuts* his figures, half-length, to show as close as possible what is happening – to the extent that beholders might feel that the painted protagonists are encroaching on the real world. This is especially true of the most important figure, Jesus Christ, standing up on a cushion placed on the lower edge of the marble window framing the scene. Like the *Saint Mark* in Frankfurt (fig. 77), the Virgin has placed her elbow on the frame. This is a sign in the direction of the onlooker as well as a point of support. Mary does not want to release her child, held firm in both hands, while Simeon seems to seize him from her grasp. We are far from the silent miracle described by Giotto. Mantegna's baby Jesus cries out as he will on the Cross, his tight swaddling clothes prefigure his shroud, and the marble parapet on which he stands announces his tomb.[2] Behind these players in the drama, three secondary figures appear: Joseph, seen

FIG. 129
ANDREA MANTEGNA
Saint Maximus, detail from the *Saint Luke Polyptych*, 1453–4
Egg tempera on panel, 66 × 37 cm (panel)
Pinacoteca di Brera, Milan (176)

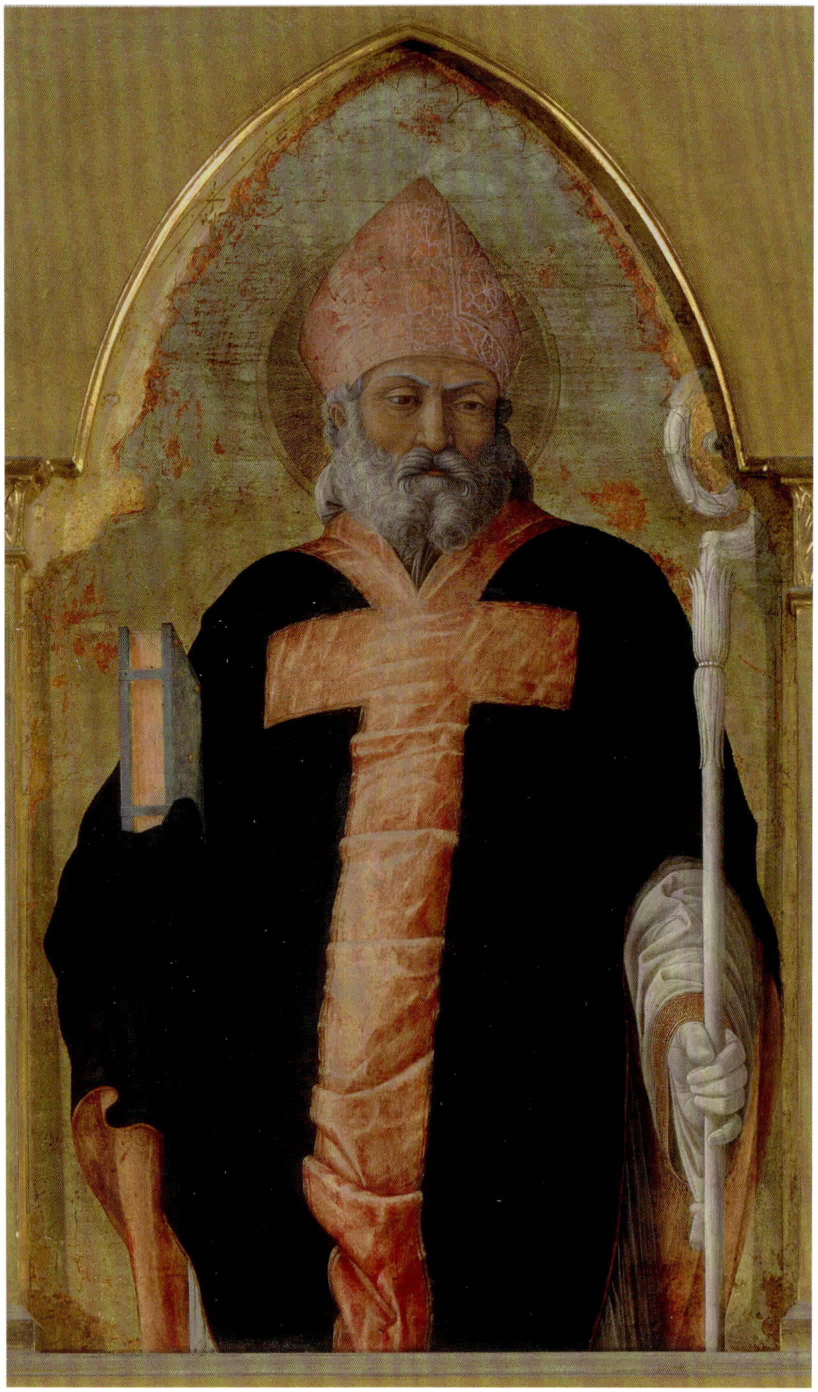

frontally, a woman at the far left, and a man on the far right, both without haloes.[3] The woman is too young to be Anna, described by Saint Luke as being 84, and she is not looking at what is going on. As for the man, he has a surprisingly absent stare.

Mantegna's *Presentation of Christ in the Temple* has often been compared to the one of the key works of Florentine art, Donatello's *Pazzi Madonna* (fig. 130).[4] This marble relief represents the first appearance in Renaissance art of a frame in fictive perspective that serves to mediate the image, while the tender, sad manner in which the Virgin places her forehead on that of her son seems to anticipate the attitude depicted by Mantegna. Since the *Pazzi Madonna* was created in about 1420 for a Florentine patron, it is hardly likely that it could have served as a direct model for Mantegna[5] – but Donatello was incessantly productive, and the painter could have seen a similar work created by the sculptor during his Paduan sojourn. Moreover, Mantegna would have had plenty of time for close study of the bronze reliefs of the Santo altar, in one of which – *The Miracle of the Newborn Child* – Donatello included a Virgin holding her Child with all her might (fig. 131).[6] The X-radiograph of the Berlin painting shows that Mantegna reduced the distance between the Virgin and Child, in order to pit himself a little closer against Donatello's invention (fig. 41). Donatello had established a clear distinction between scenes with half-length figures, representing iconic and meditative subjects such as the Virgin and Child or the Man of Sorrows, and narrative scenes, which show figures in full-length poses. In his *Presentation of Christ in the Temple*, Mantegna combines these two typologies: he thus draws us closer, in an unprecedented way, to the holy figures and to the sacred narrative.[7]

In the 1520s, the Venetian nobleman Marcantonio Michiel recorded a *Circumcision* with half-length figures by Mantegna in his friend Pietro Bembo's Paduan

FIG. 130
DONATELLO
Pazzi Madonna, about 1420
Marble, 74.5 × 73 × 6.5 cm
Skulpturensammlung und Museum für Byzantinische Kunst, Staatliche Museen zu Berlin (51)

FIG. 131
DONATELLO
The Miracle of the Newborn Child (detail), 1446–50
Bronze, 57 × 123 cm
Basilica of Sant'Antonio, Padua

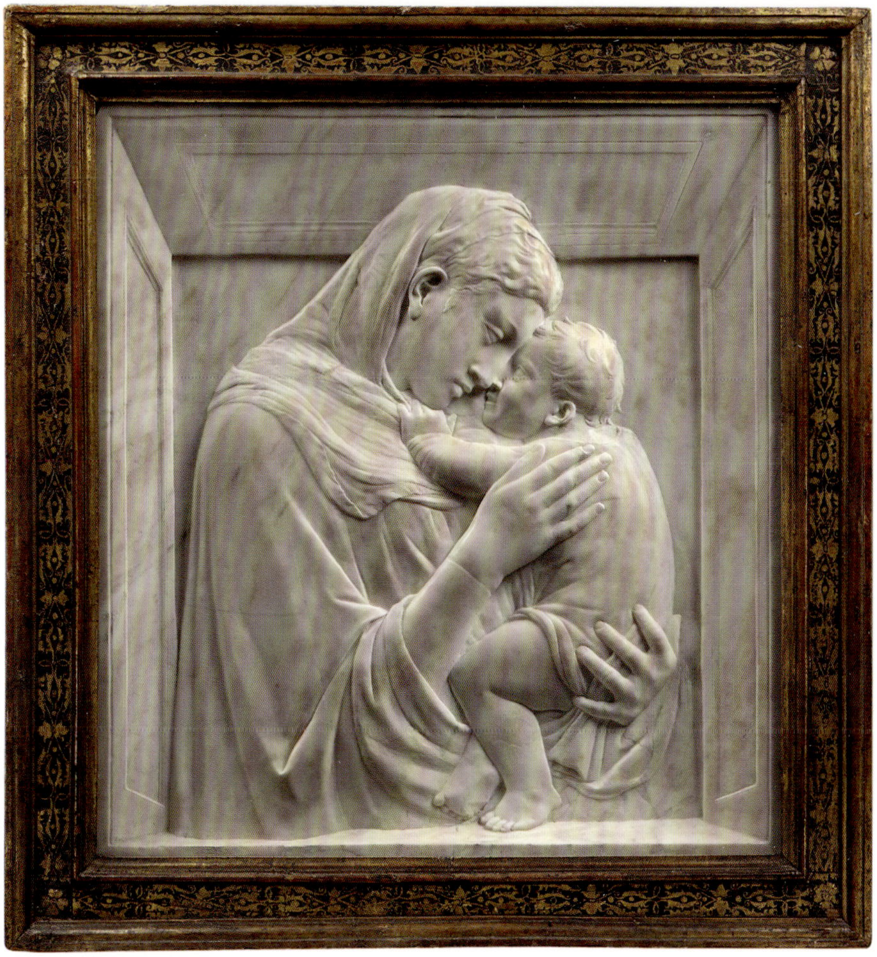

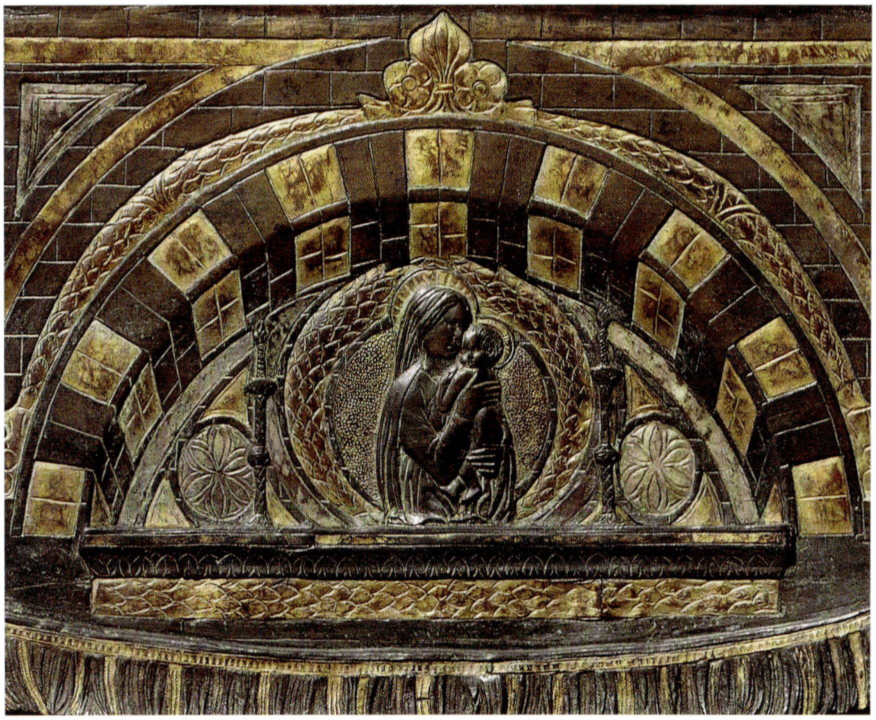

FIG. 132
GIOVANNI BELLINI
The Presentation of Christ in the Temple,
about 1470–5
Oil on panel, 80 × 105 cm
Museo della Fondazione Querini Stampalia,
Venice (2/29)

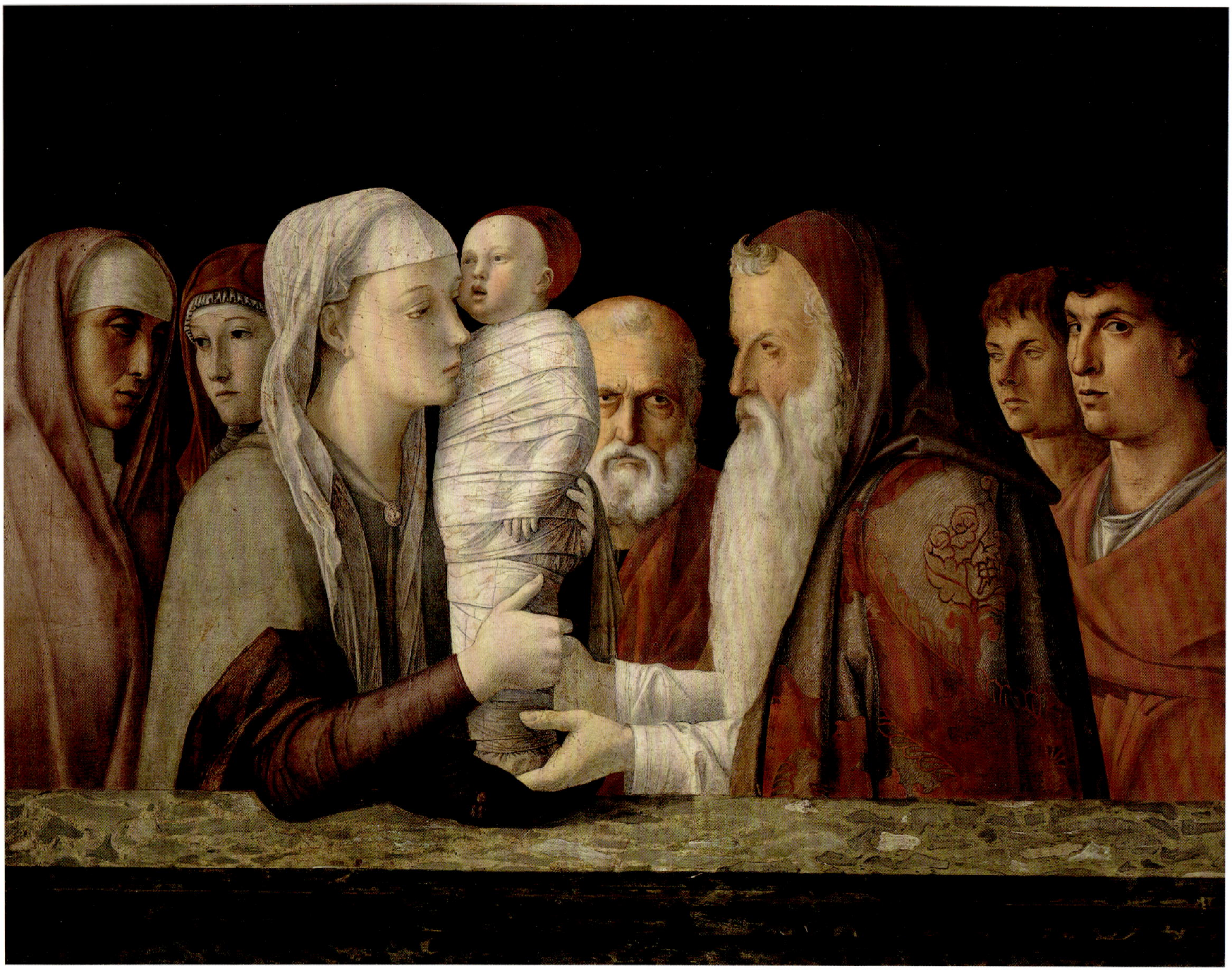

FIG. 133
Attributed to JACOPO DA VALENZA
Portrait of a Young Man, about 1475–80
Oil on panel, 33.7 × 27.5 cm
Accademia Carrara, Bergamo (81LC00148)

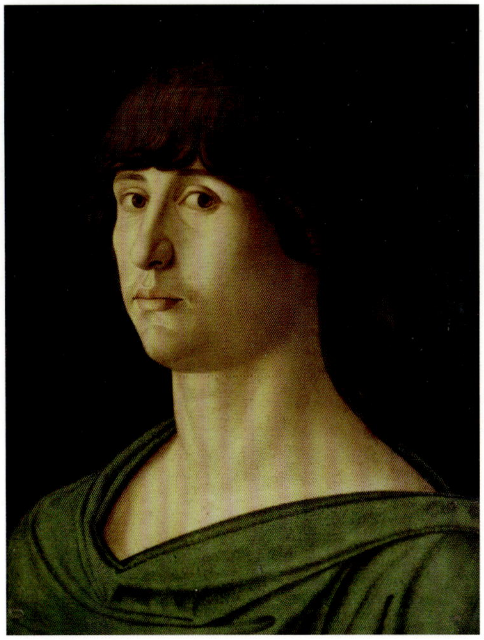

palazzo.[8] As Michiel, a noted connoisseur, specified that this was painted on wood, it has been doubted that this could refer to the canvas by Mantegna now in Berlin. Another *Presentation of Christ in the Temple* is housed in the Fondazione Querini Stampalia in Venice (fig. 132); painted on panel, it bears the name of Mantegna inscribed on its back. This has led some to identify it as the one in the Palazzo Bembo, even if the odds are that this was actually the Berlin picture.[9] The *Presentation* in the Fondazione Querini Stampalia has suffered a great deal, some areas of pigment being irreversibly lost, showing only the preparatory stage (as in the mantle on the Virgin's shoulder, or the right hand of Simeon, reduced to a ghost-like presence).[10] The condition of the painting has not made the task of attribution any easier, even if Mantegna's authorship has long been dismissed.[11] The best-preserved parts nonetheless reveal exceptional pictorial virtuosity: the face of the woman just behind the Virgin, deep in thought, or the white sheets bundled around the Christ Child. This virtuosity (likewise visible in the underdrawing: see fig. 49) directly recalls works painted by Giovanni Bellini in the mid-1470s, beginning with the *Coronation of the Virgin* altarpiece in the Musei Civici in Pesaro (fig. 255).[12]

The X-radiograph of Mantegna's painting shows some pentimenti, absent from Bellini's version. The latter is thus a derivation from the former. Stylistic dating of the two works reveals a certain gap in time: Mantegna's canvas is close to his work from the mid-1450s, notably the *Saint Luke Polyptych* (fig. 129), while Bellini's panel is close (as we have seen) to the mid-1470s.[13] New research has cast light on a remarkable feature: Bellini's version is actually *traced* from that of Mantegna.[14] It remains to be seen why, a number of years after the creation of Mantegna's *Presentation*, Giovanni Bellini felt the need to mechanically reproduce his brother-in-law's work, while being unable to stop himself from changing its content in singular ways: expressions have become less violent, colours are more tonal and shadows more subtle, while the marble framing has disappeared, yielding to a simple parapet. And the lateral figures have increased from two to four.

Since the early nineteenth century, the figure on the right in the Berlin *Presentation* has been identified as a portrait of Mantegna (fig. 51); and it is true that it resembles the head painted in grisaille above the frescoes in the Ovetari Chapel in Padua, unanimously agreed to be the painter's likeness of himself.[15] For reasons of symmetry, the female figure on the left of the Berlin picture was then identified as Nicolosia Bellini, Mantegna's wife; and since their marriage was celebrated in 1453, the work could date from that year, or even from 1454, as the subject could allude to the birth of a first child.[16] As for the portraits in Bellini's painting, scholars have lost themselves in conjecture: if the figure on the right, gazing at us, were a self portait of the artist, how can we explain the fact that his features are so different from those we know of him?[17] How can the identity of the

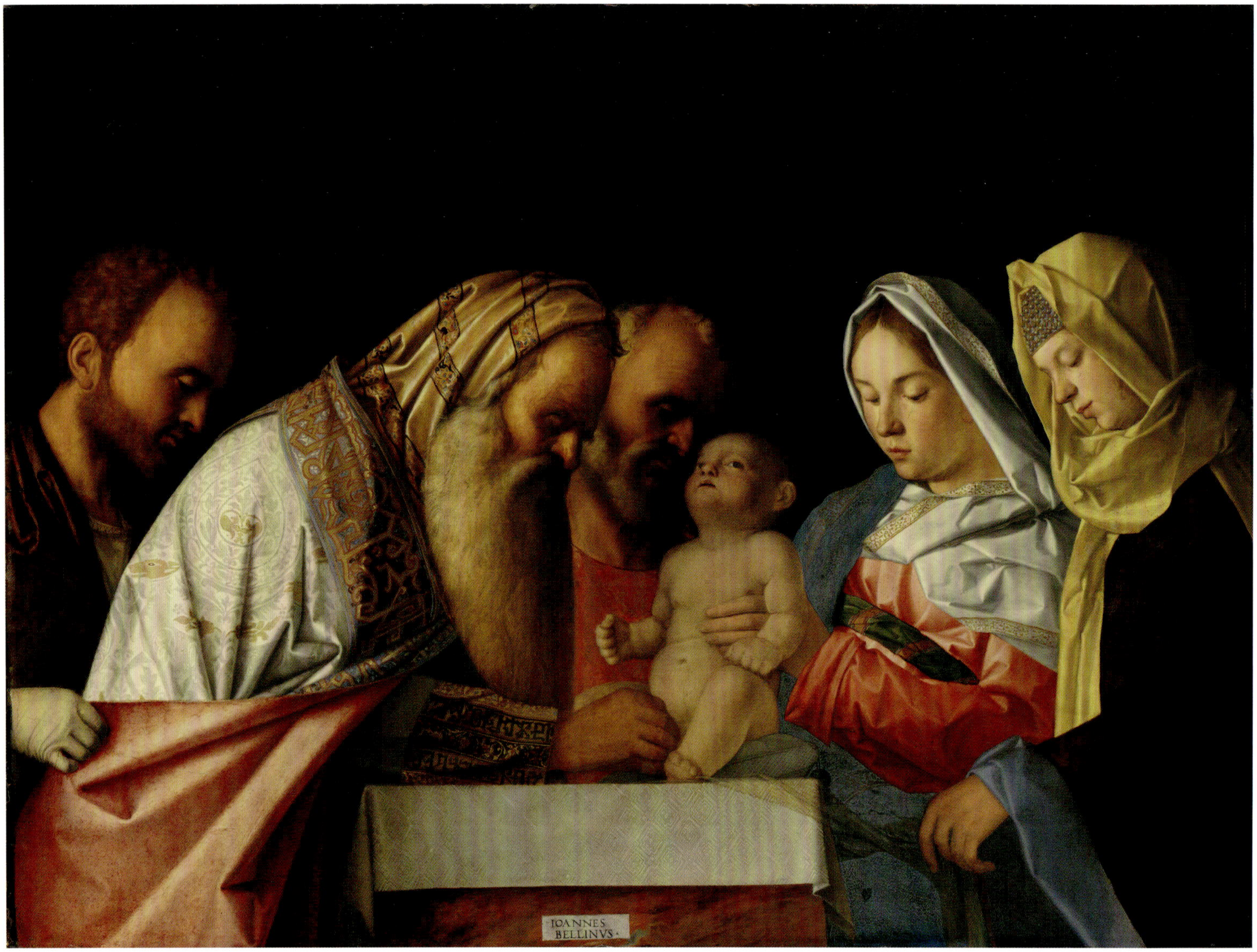

FIG. 134
Studio of
GIOVANNI BELLINI
The Circumcision, about 1500
Oil on panel, 74.9 × 102.2 cm
The National Gallery, London
(NG 1455)

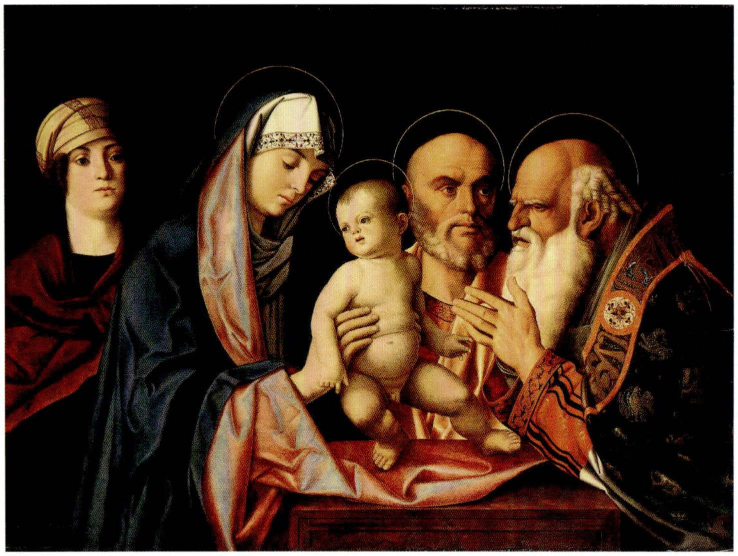

FIG. 135
Studio of
GIOVANNI BELLINI
The Presentation of Christ in the Temple, 1480–5
Oil (?) on poplar, 74.5 × 104.2 cm
Gemäldegalerie, Staatliche Museen zu Berlin (36)

other three figures be understood, given the highly problematic question of Giovanni's birth – indeed given his likely illegitimacy?[18] In our current state of knowledge, it makes sense to remain very prudent on this topic.[19]

Passing from Mantegna to Bellini, the subject of the Presentation of Christ in the Temple was to enjoy a striking fortune. Bellini painted two similar compositions, with half-length figures and against a dark background, widely disseminated by his studio. The first represents the same scene of the *Presentation* (fig. 135), in which the Christ Child no longer has his swaddling clothes, his nudity underlining his condition as 'Word made flesh', whereas the second is a more direct depiction of the episode of the *Circumcision* (fig. 134).[20] Mantegna, on the other hand, refused to repeat himself – that could be done through engraving. He only returned once to a close-up narrative composition. The pretext on this occasion was an *Adoration of the Magi* (fig. 136), a work in which the brilliance of the colours indicates how much the Berlin *Presentation* must have glowed.[21] Having invented the half-length narrative composition, Mantegna hardly ever made use of this pictorial device, whereas his brother-in-law Bellini could not help but multiply it, giving it a central importance for the development of Venetian painting. The subject of the Presentation of Christ in the Temple thus became the stage for enacting the deep and complex relationship between Mantegna and Bellini.

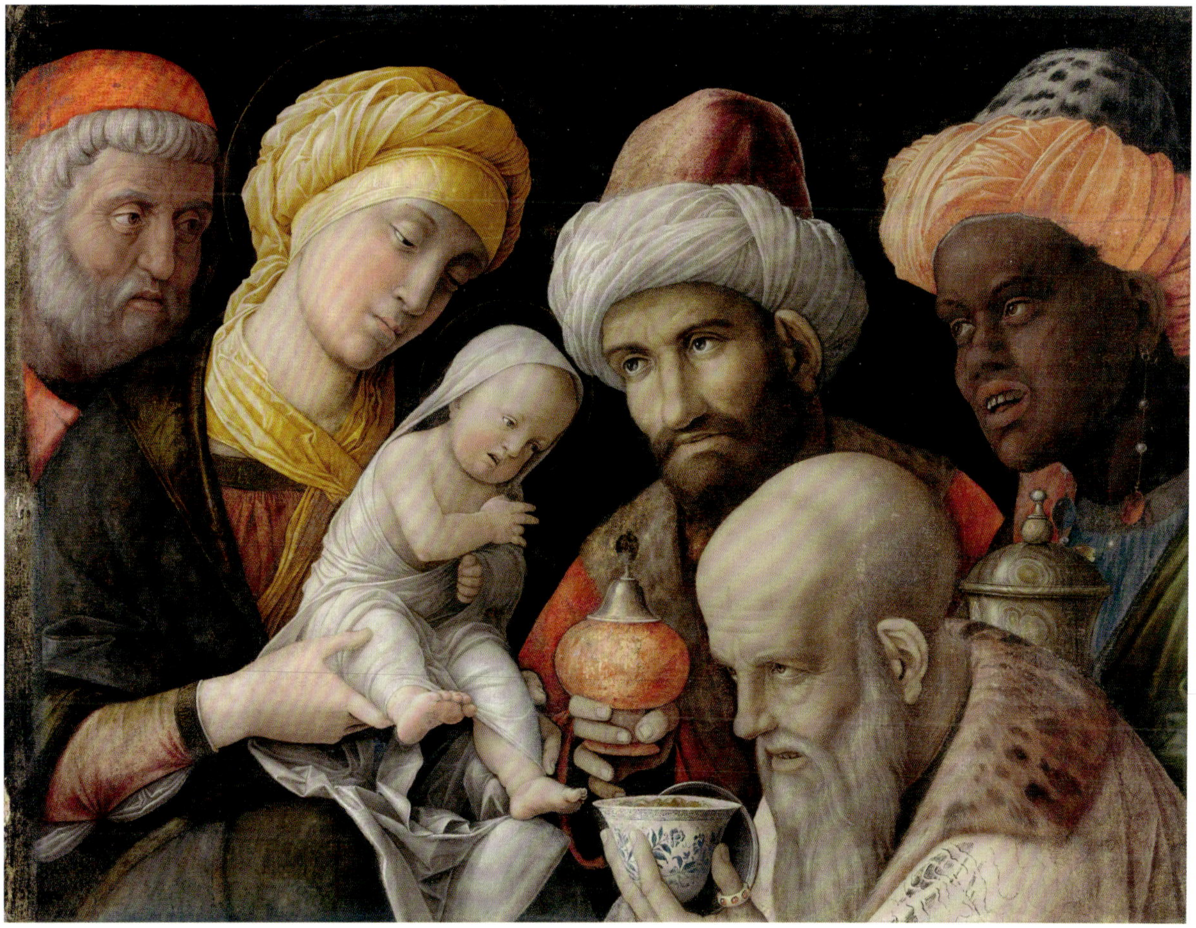

FIG. 136
ANDREA MANTEGNA
The Adoration of the Magi, about 1495–1505
Glue size on canvas, 48.6 × 65.6 cm
The J. Paul Getty Museum, Los Angeles (85/PA.417)

The Descent of Christ into Limbo

DAGMAR KORBACHER

The motif of the Descent of Christ into Limbo occupied both Mantegna and Giovanni Bellini for decades – for Bellini, mainly in dialogue with the corresponding pictorial inventions of his father Jacopo and his brother-in-law Mantegna.

Although Christ's descent into hell is not recorded in the New Testament, it is reported in the *Legenda Aurea* (Golden Legend) of Jacobus de Voragine and was an established element of Christian faith in the fifteenth century. According to this legend, during the time between Christ's burial following his death on the Cross and his Resurrection, he descended into the region known as Limbo, the resting place of the souls of the righteous. After shattering the gates of hell, he liberated them in his triumph over death and evil.

Jacopo Bellini explored this pictorial subject in the early 1450s. Slightly different versions of the scene occur in both the Paris (fig. 137) and the London Drawing Books, where the event occurs against the backdrop of a massive mountain range whose cliffs are populated by demons. A horizontal version of the narrative with motifs from both drawings appears on a small panel, probably from the predella of the *Gattamelata Altarpiece* in the Santo in Padua (fig. 87), signed in 1459 or 1460 by Jacopo along with his sons Gentile and Giovanni.[1]

Mantegna may have drawn inspiration for his handling of the subject from Jacopo Bellini but also from Donatello's bronze relief for the north pulpit of

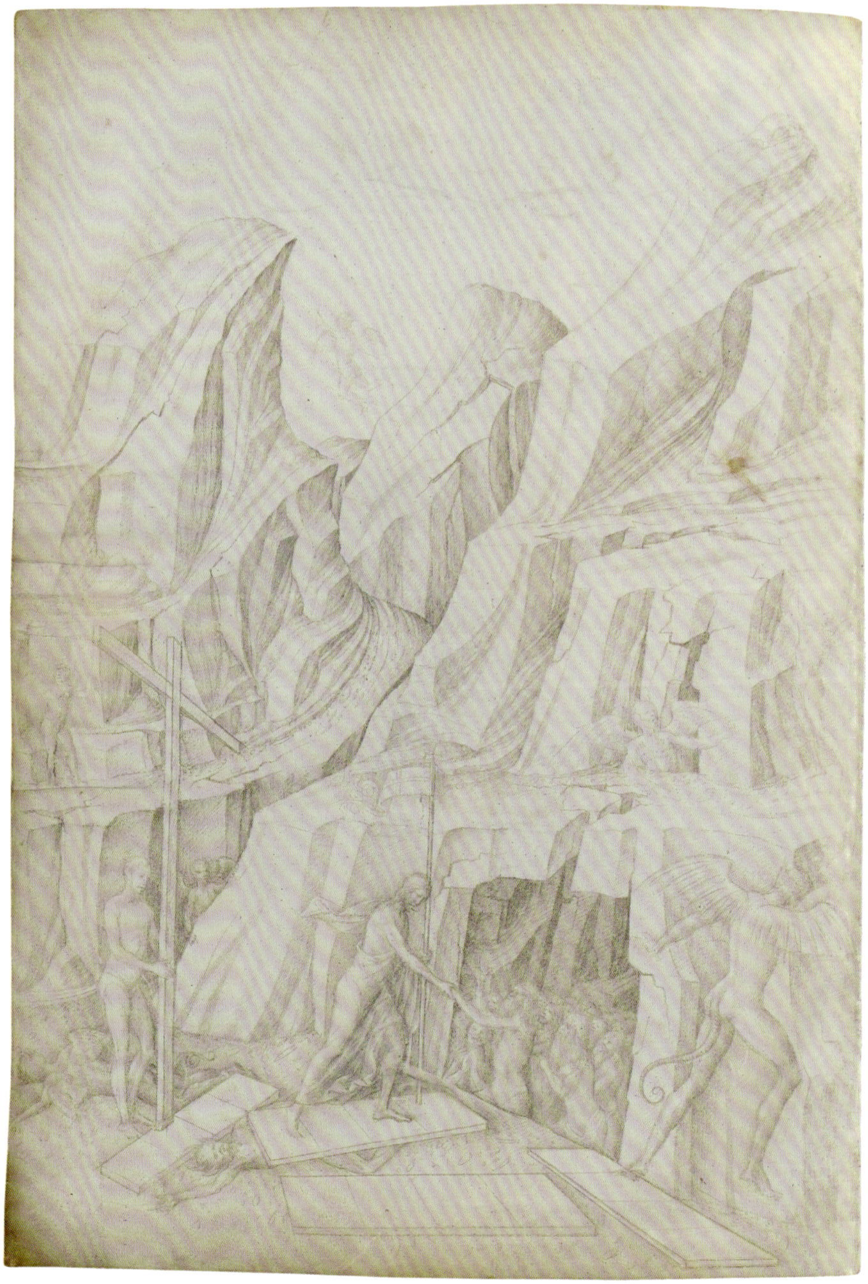

FIG. 137
JACOPO BELLINI
The Descent of Christ into Limbo, from *The Paris Drawing Book of Jacopo Bellini*, about 1455–60
Metalpoint on vellum, 38 × 26 cm
Musée du Louvre, Paris
(RF 1489-22 f. 21v)

FIG. 138
DONATELLO
The Descent of Christ into Limbo, detail from the *Resurrection Pulpit*, about 1460–5
Bronze relief, 75 × 108.5 cm
Church of San Lorenzo, Florence

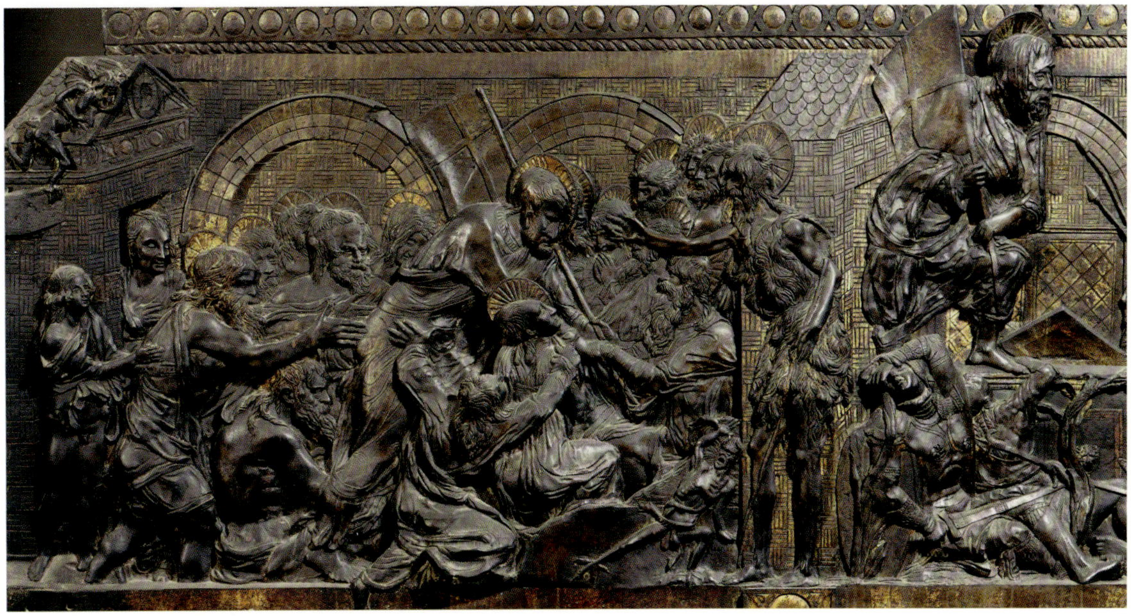

San Lorenzo in Florence (fig. 138), which he could have seen in 1466.[2]

In 1468, Mantegna himself worked on a painting telling the story of Limbo[3] for the Marquess Ludovico III Gonzaga of Mantua, which is now lost. Thus we can only surmise that its composition was closely related to Mantegna's surviving representations of the motif. Viewed from behind, Christ stands in the middle of the image directly in front of the open entrance of hell, with protesting demons above him and the shattered gates at his feet. This spectacular, even radical visual strategy has often been interpreted as an artifice inspired by an anecdote from Alberti's treatise on painting, in which the artist Timantes of Cyprus left the face of a desperate man to the viewer's imagination, since his pain could not be represented.[4] However, such an interpretation is not entirely convincing, especially since Mantegna used the motif of a figure viewed from behind as a repoussoir and a dramatising compositional element in other works as well.[5]

The chronological order of Mantegna's surviving representations of Christ in Limbo is not easy to reconstruct. In our opinion, the drawing in the Lehman Collection in the Metropolitan Museum in New York (fig. 139) is the earliest, even if it remains difficult to determine the exact place of the work in Mantegna's oeuvre or even to unequivocally attribute it to him. Although some areas were apparently retraced by another hand in reddish-brown ink and the page may have been slightly trimmed on both the top and the bottom edge, its quality is still apparent. In view of a few small uncertainties in the execution, a more cautious interpretation might identify the drawing as a copy by a workshop assistant after a lost original by Mantegna. Despite the oft-noted compositional similarity to a late painting from a private collection (fig. 141), an early date for the drawing is more plausible, especially since the composition concentrates less on a balanced overall form than on individual details such as Christ's banner, which is curled into an S-shape for *Salvator* (Saviour), or the grotesque demons whose agitated gestures seem like a reversal of the angels lamenting the Dead Christ in Giotto's fresco in the Scrovegni Chapel in Padua.[6]

A large drawing on vellum (fig. 143), probably created a little later near the end of the 1460s and now in Paris, is of particular interest for the motif of Limbo. Although parts of the work are strongly abraded, the quality of the surviving drawing suggests an attribution to Mantegna himself. The unfinished appearance of certain areas, especially the head and upper body of the female figure (Eve), is probably not due to the disappearance of an original delicate underdrawing in these areas.[7] Rather, the drawing seems to have never been finished,[8] as is also the case with the Munich drawing of the Resurrected Christ (fig. 63), whose dimensions correspond closely to this one and which likewise served as the point of

FIG. 139
Attributed to ANDREA MANTEGNA
The Descent of Christ into Limbo,
about 1465–70
Pen and brown ink, brown wash
on paper, 26.9 × 20 cm
The Metropolitan Museum of Art, New York.
Robert Lehman Collection (1975.1.274)

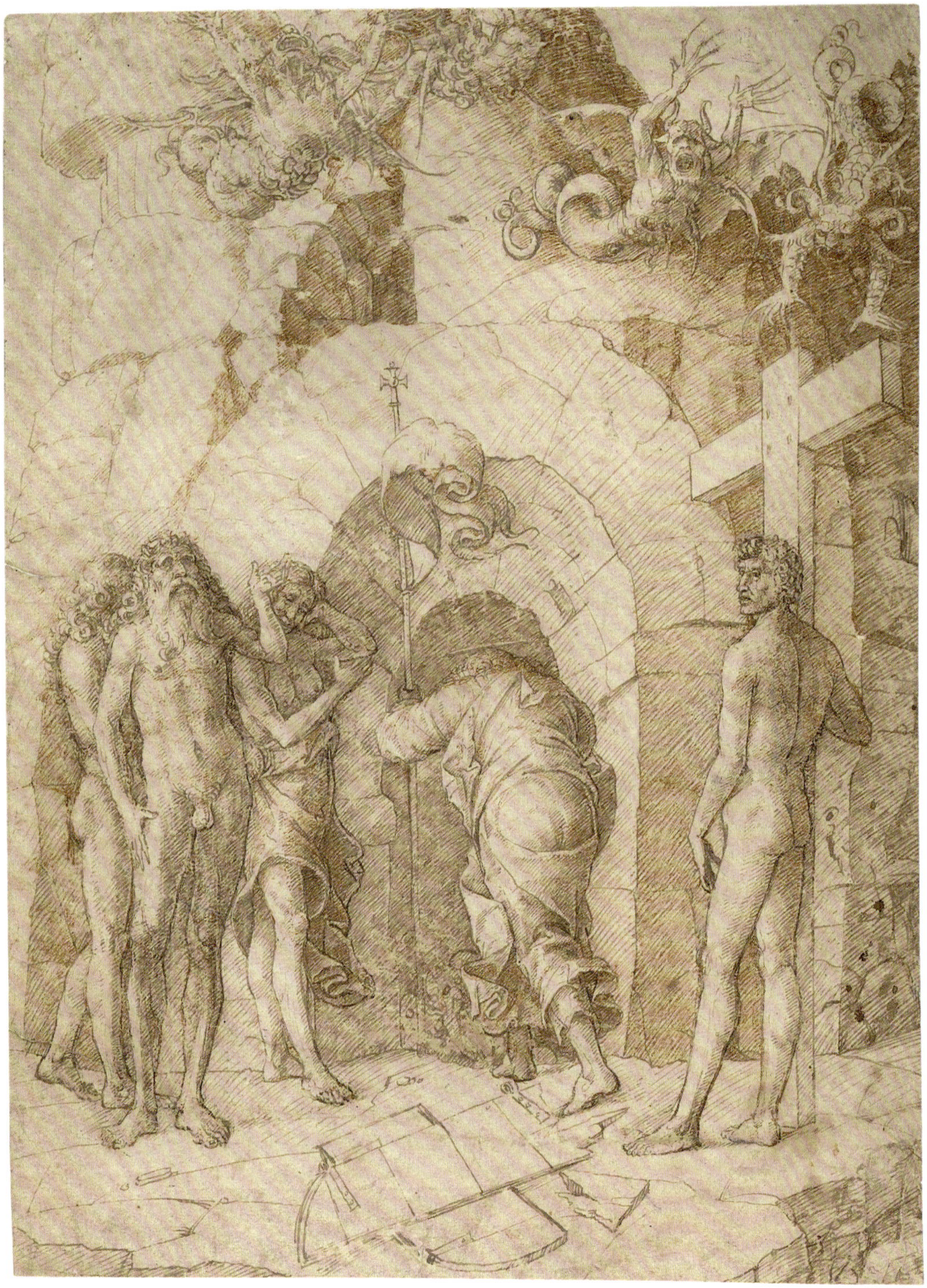

FIG. 140
Attributed to ANDREA MANTEGNA
The Resurrection of Christ, about 1492
Egg tempera on panel, 48.6 × 37.7 cm
Accademia Carrara, Bergamo (81LC00169)

FIG. 141
ANDREA MANTEGNA
The Descent of Christ into Limbo,
probably about 1492
Egg tempera and gold on panel,
38.8 × 42.3 cm
Private collection

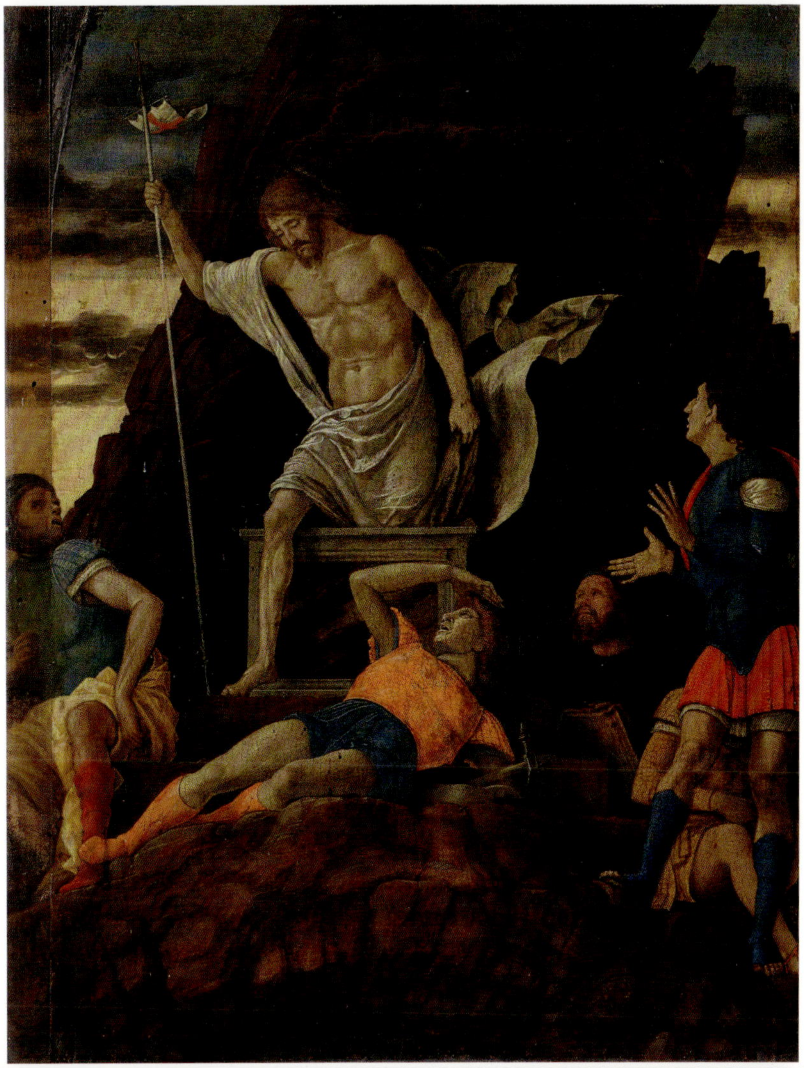

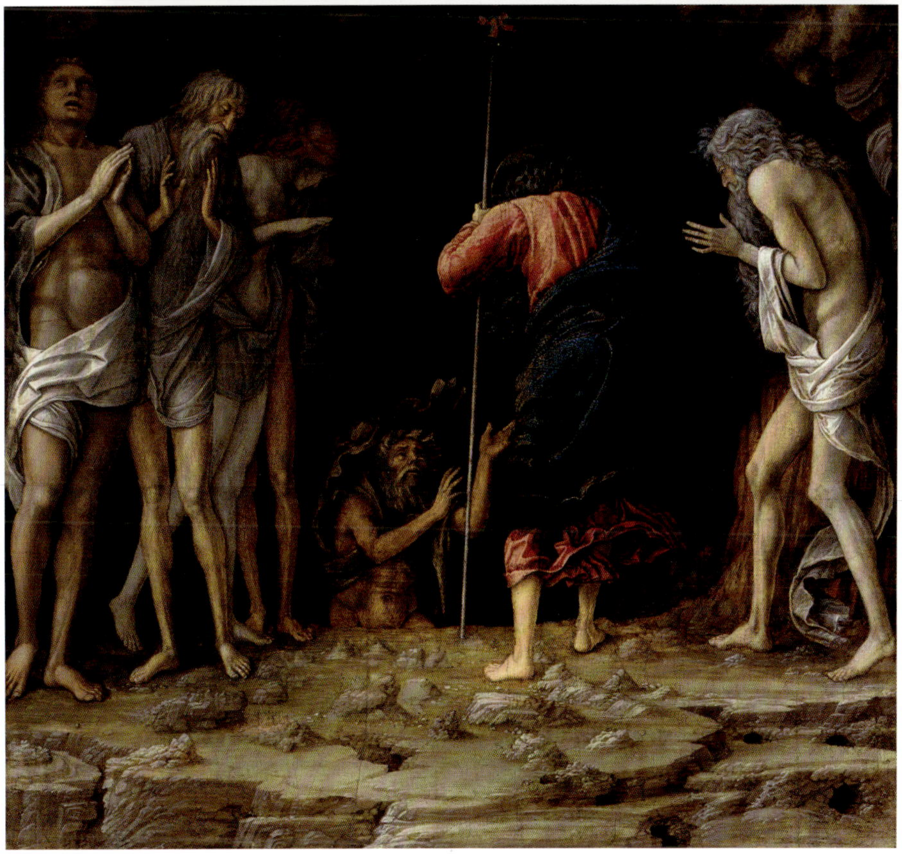

departure for an engraving. Overall, these areas bear witness to a certain openness and may indicate that the motif was not yet fully conceived; however, the generally well-developed execution and its vellum support suggest that the work was intended as a presentation drawing, perhaps even for the Bellini family, as Luke Syson has conjectured.[9] In any case, Antonio Mazzotta and Mauro Lucco have demonstrated a close connection between the drawing and another work by Giovanni Bellini: the shallow rock formations in the foreground recur in exactly the same form in the latter's painting of *The Transfiguration of Christ* (figs 15 and 16).[10]

The Paris drawing served as the point of departure for a closely related engraving (fig. 142); the contours of most of the figures, the shattered doors and the arch in the print correspond exactly to those in the drawing. However, not every detail of the drawing was developed precisely enough to have served as orientation for a professional engraver. One must assume that another, more exact drawing was prepared for the print, or that, if Mantegna did not engrave the plate himself,[11] he worked closely with the engraver to transfer the image to the plate. The undeveloped face and upper body of Eve in the drawing were completed as those of an old woman, while the hidden profile of a jester in the masonry of the arch to the left of the keystone was also added.

The Paris drawing is not only closely related to the engraving, it also bears a striking resemblance to a painted version of the theme in Bristol. Although the composition is clearly derived from Mantegna, the painting, executed in oil on vellum, is the work of Giovanni Bellini and dates to around 1475–80 (fig. 145). The work attests to an ongoing artistic exchange between the two painters, which continued long after Mantegna had moved to Mantua. Previously described as a painting with a clear underdrawing, in actuality it consists of a pen drawing on vellum[12] – incomplete in some areas – and may be a slightly altered copy of the Paris drawing executed by a workshop assistant of Mantegna. Under unknown circumstances, it was acquired by Giovanni Bellini, who then added colour and completed it, particularly in the areas of rock and landscape in the right background as well as the plants in the foreground.[13] The regular hatching visible beneath the thin layer of paint would have been used for finished drawings, rather than for underdrawings. Thus, as Jennifer Fletcher has suggested, the vellum, which is mounted on a small wooden panel, fits most plausibly within the context of the Venetian preference for coloured engravings, and is in no way comparable to manuscript illumination.[14] Here, Eve is young and beautiful, whereas in the Paris drawing this area is missing and in the engraving she seems old and haggard. Also added is a book with a striking silver binding lying beneath the shattered doors, as well as a tiny empty *cartellino*. As in the engraving, a caricature-like head is hidden in the rocks, though in a different location. What differs most, however, is the landscape in the

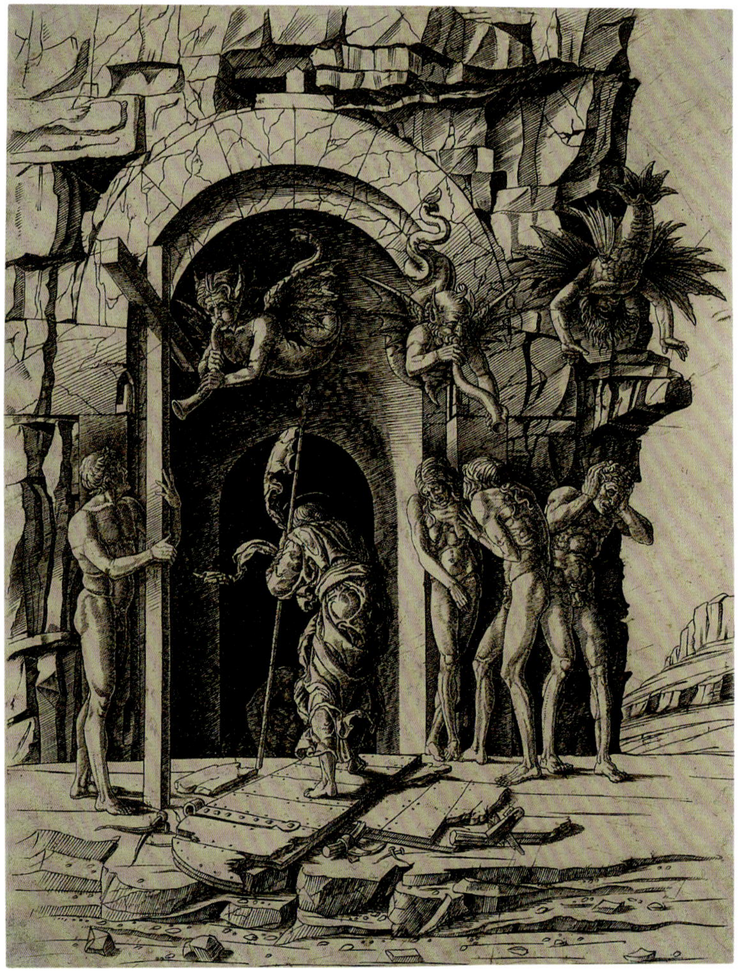

FIG. 142
Circle of ANDREA MANTEGNA
The Descent of Christ into Limbo, about 1480–5
Engraving, printed in brown ink, 42.9 × 33.7 cm
Kupferstichkabinett, Staatliche Museen zu Berlin (840-21)

FIG. 143
ANDREA MANTEGNA
The Descent of Christ into Limbo, about 1468
Pen and brown ink, brown wash on vellum, 37.2 × 28 cm
École Nationale Supérieure des Beaux-Arts, Paris (EBA189)

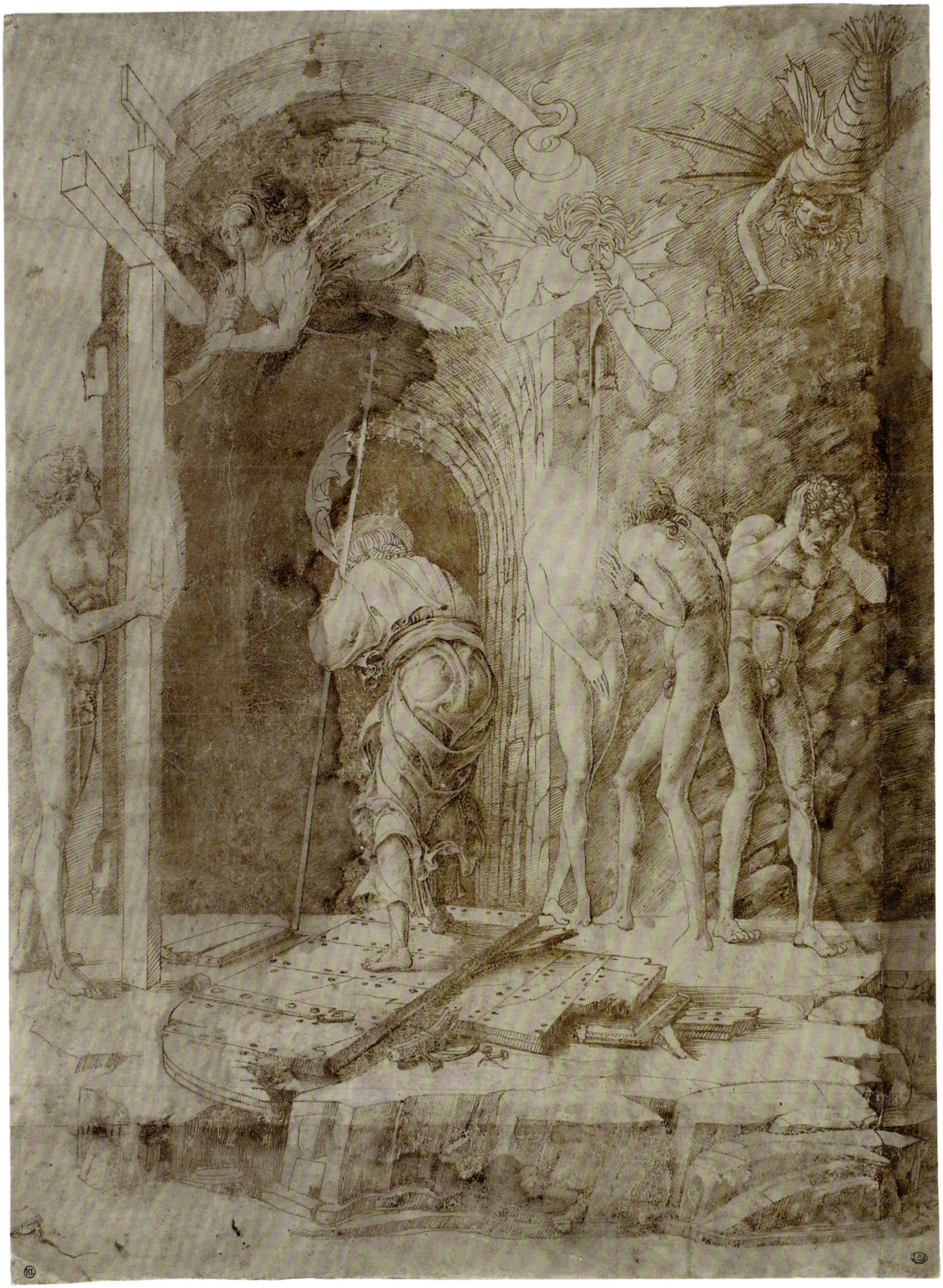

FIG. 144
Studio of ANDREA MANTEGNA
The Descent of Christ into Limbo,
about 1490
Brush in dark brown and grey with white heightening on blue prepared paper, 28.3 × 20.1 cm
Kupferstichkabinett, Staatliche Museen zu Berlin (KdZ 622)

FIG. 145
GIOVANNI BELLINI
The Descent of Christ into Limbo,
about 1475–80
Oil on vellum on panel, 51.8 × 37.3 cm
Bristol City Museum and Art Gallery (K.1654)

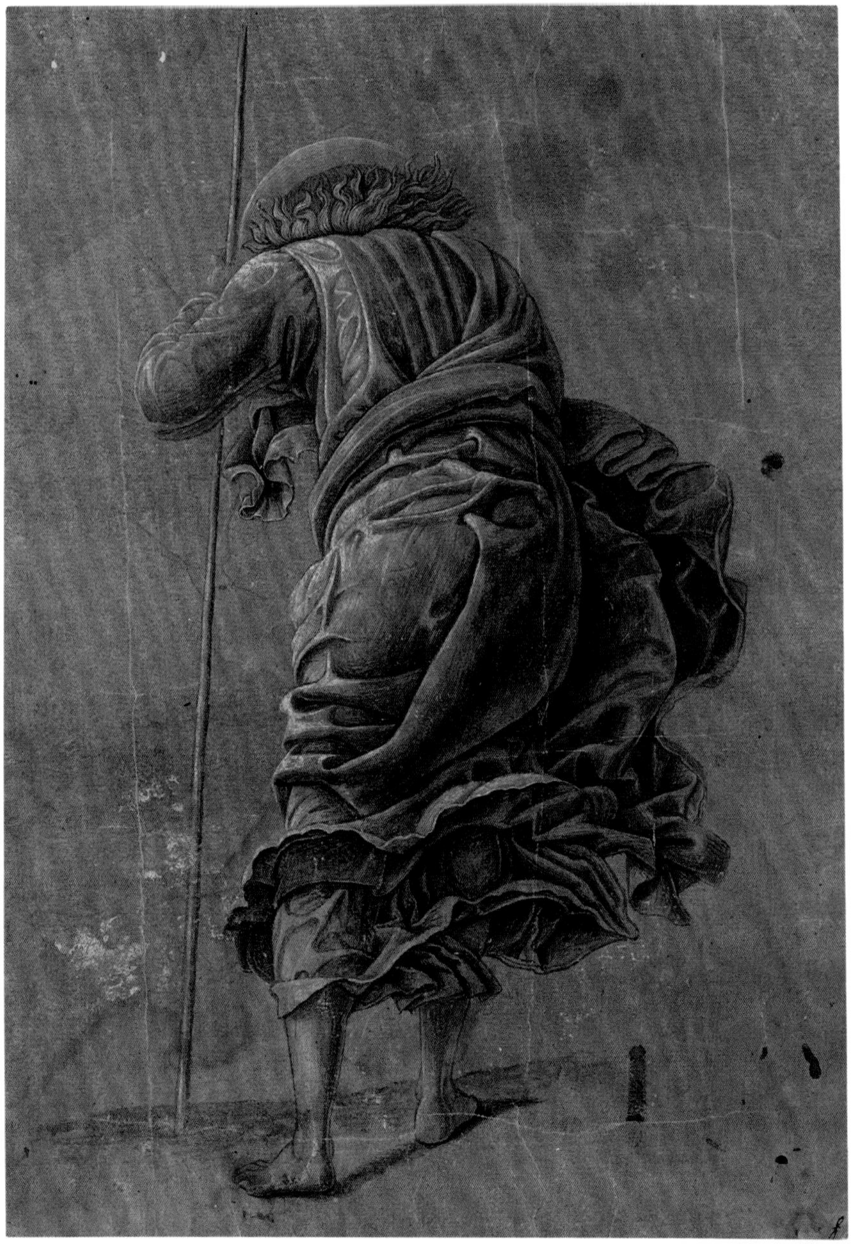

background with rocks and a bright blue sky; these elements, which are not present in the drawing, clearly indicate the painterly hand of Bellini.

Another painting by Mantegna with this pictorial motif is also known (fig. 141); while its upper and left edges have been trimmed, it was probably always characterised by a simpler composition, whose drama is accentuated by a blast of air from the cave causing Christ's hair and garment to billow in the wind. Recently Giovanni Valagussa discovered a panel representing the Resurrection of Christ in the Accademia Carrara in Bergamo (fig. 140). The detail at the lower margin of this panel confirms that the panels belong together: the tiny cross appears to be the crest of the staff Christ is holding in the *Descent into Limbo*. We do not know why Mantegna returned to this theme in the 1490s.[15] This version of the motif proved to be one of the most successful, as evidenced by the existence of two painted copies as well as four later printed reproductions.[16] The drawing in Berlin (fig. 144), which shows only the figure of Christ from the rear with the mere suggestion of the entrance to hell, was probably also made in the late fifteenth century; here the white highlights on the mantle exactly match the golden highlights in the corresponding areas of the painting. The drawing is probably a kind of *ricordo*, executed by an assistant in Mantegna's workshop.

The repetition, continuing development and copying of the motif of the Descent of Christ into Limbo over a period of decades clearly demonstrate that the theme was of particular interest not only to Bellini, but especially to Mantegna. In his last painted version of the subject (fig. 141), Mantegna clearly invoked the formal language of classical antiquity in the figures of the saved; finally, in his engraving of the *Virtus Deserta* (fig. 228) with its figures beneath a round arch being pulled out of the depths by an energetic rescuer, he transposed the entire motif from a Christian context to a humanistic level of interpretation.[17]

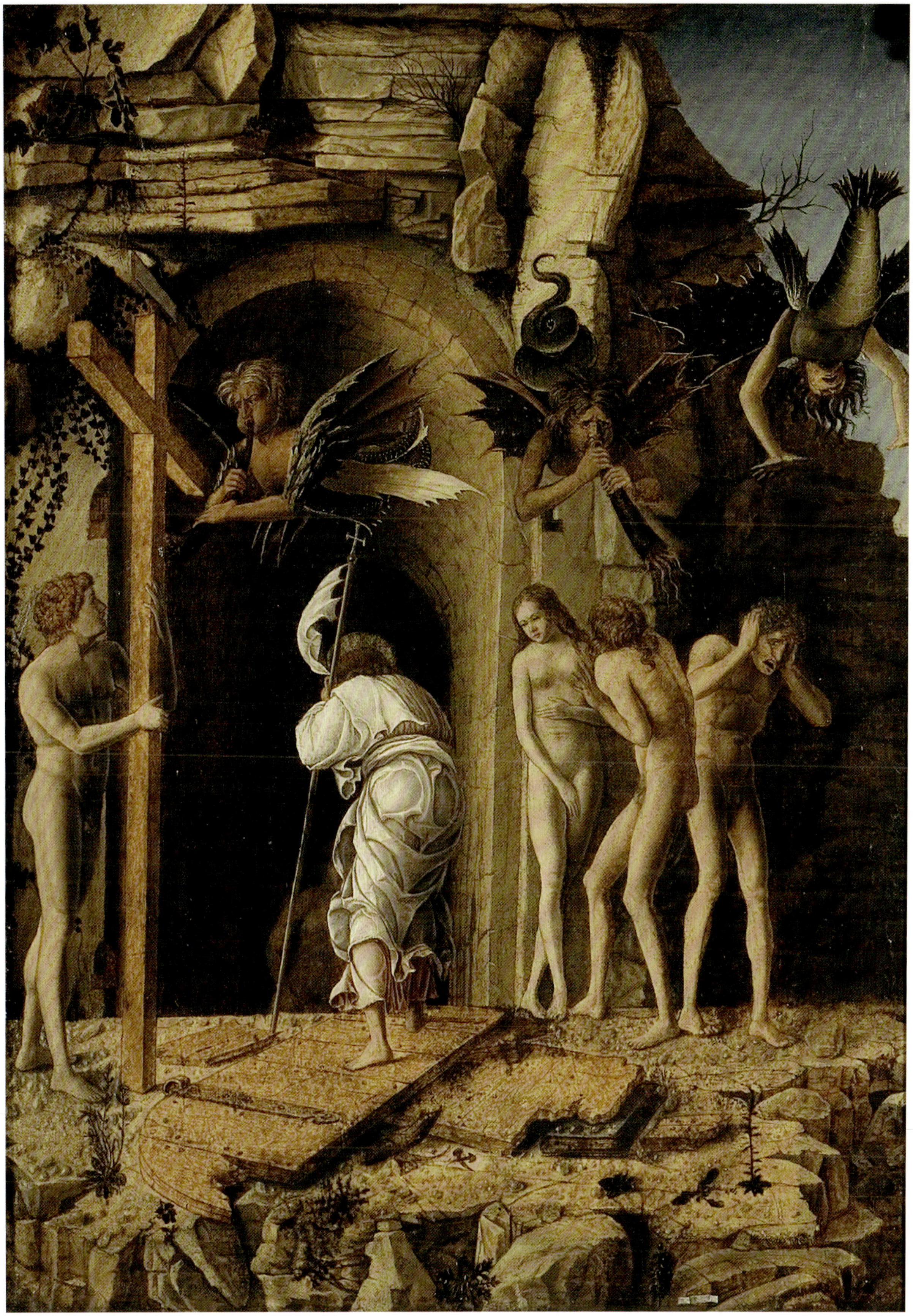

Between Suffering and Redemption: The Motif of the Dead Christ

KATHARINA WEICK-JOCH

Mantegna and Bellini produced numerous drawings and paintings showing Christ between his Deposition from the Cross and Resurrection. Such representations of the Resurrection, which were widespread in Renaissance Italy,[1] had been associated with the iconography of the Man of Sorrows or Ecce Homo since the fourteenth century. In their depictions of the Dead Christ, Mantegna and Bellini place the figures in the foreground, cropped to fill the entire frame. These 'close-up' views of Christ arose from a Byzantine pictorial formula that had found its way to Italy, derived directly from icon painting.[2]

The vertical composition typically used for Italian representations of the Lamentation, with a seated Christ accompanied by standing figures, can be explained in terms of this pictorial tradition.[3] Mantegna and Bellini's depictions originate from two designs in Jacopo Bellini's Paris Drawing Book. In *The Lamentation* (fig. 146), Christ appears as a seated figure, his body half-obscured by the

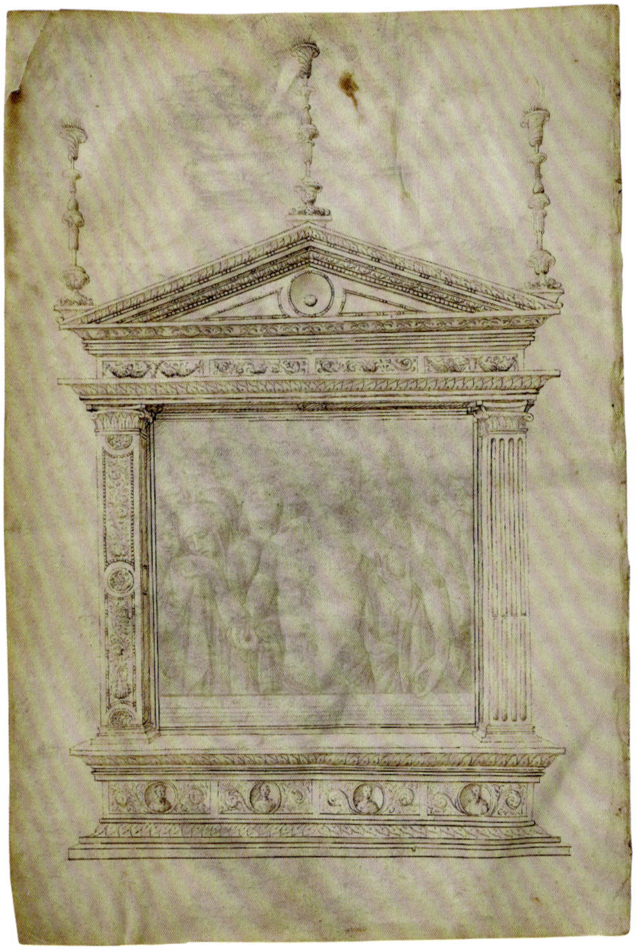

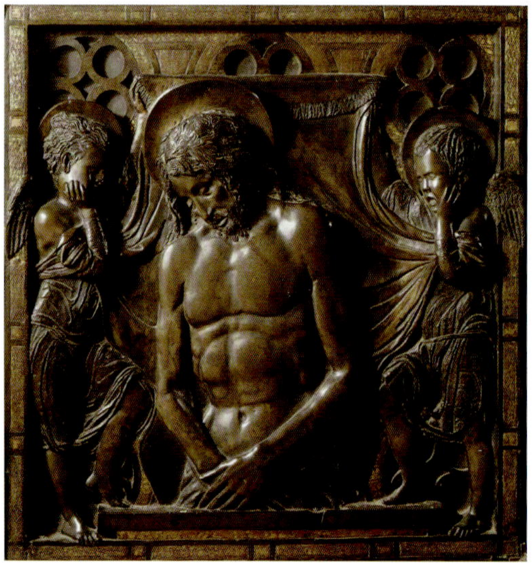

FIG. 146
JACOPO BELLINI
The Lamentation over the Dead Christ, from *The Paris Drawing Book of Jacopo Bellini*, about 1455–60
Metalpoint, pen and brown ink on vellum, 38 × 26 cm
Musée du Louvre, Paris (RF 1475-3 f. 7v)

FIG. 147
DONATELLO
The Dead Christ with Two Angels, 1446–50
Bronze, 58 × 56 cm
Basilica of Sant'Antonio, Padua

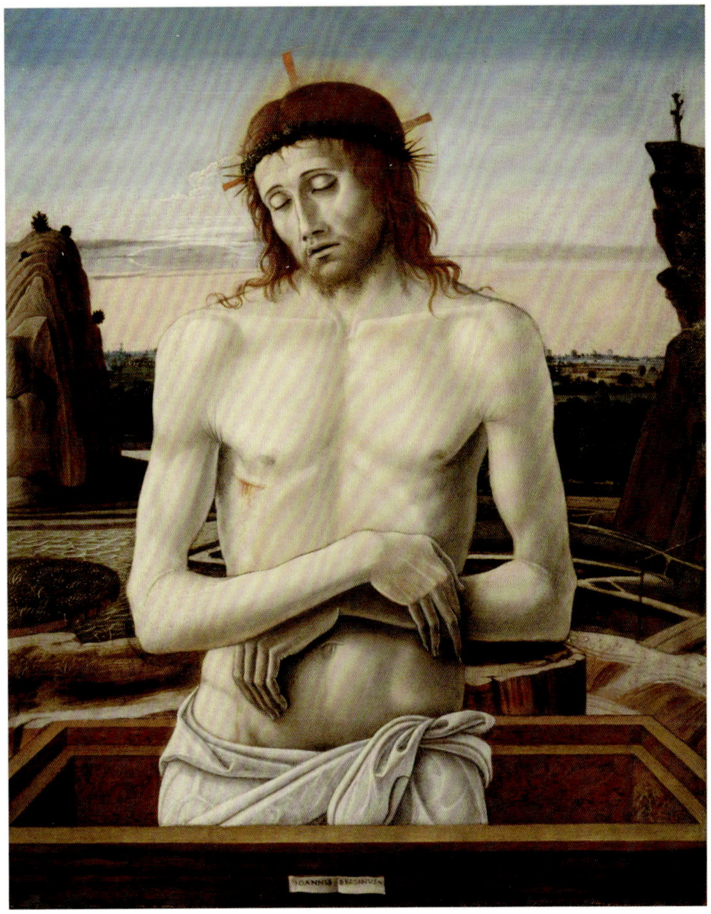

FIG. 148
GIOVANNI BELLINI
Pietà, about 1457
Egg tempera on panel,
50.5 × 40.4 cm
Museo Poldi Pezzoli, Milan (1587)

sarcophagus.[4] Mary supports her son's body to the right, while Saint John on the left holds Christ's hand.

Donatello was the other key inspiration for Mantegna and Bellini's Lamentations. Both artists must have known his relief of Christ in half-length accompanied by two angels on the high altar of the Santo in Padua (fig. 147). A marble relief ascribed by some scholars to Donatello, now in the Victoria and Albert Museum (fig. 149), also depicts Christ seated on the edge of his tomb.[5]

While Bellini's representations of Christ in half-figure throughout his career rarely diverged from the pictorial models he had learnt while working with his father, Mantegna endlessly reinterpreted this theme, first in drawing and then in paint. An early painting by Bellini, the *Pietà* in the Museo Poldi Pezzoli in Milan (fig. 148), reveals the variety of influences informing the young artist.[6] While the motif of Christ in half-length rising from a sarcophagus is clearly borrowed from his father, and the hesitant use of colour and the imprecise handling of light bear witness to Bellini's search for a style of his own, the painting also shows Mantegna's influence. The mountains in the landscape background, for example, parallel those in Mantegna's *Adoration of the Shepherds* (fig. 221), created shortly after 1450.[7] In his *Lamentation over the Dead Christ, with Saints Mark and Nicholas of Bari* of about 1457–9 (fig. 26) Bellini further develops the motif, while maintaining a connection to Jacopo's invention.

A major late work by Mantegna, *The Dead Christ supported by Two Angels* (fig. 150), clearly borrows from Bellini's compositions, in combination with the icon-like motif of the figure of Christ oriented parallel to the picture plane, originally derived from Donatello.[8] Similarities include the depiction of the body of Christ with a loincloth, the position of the tormented Saviour's hands and the overall structure, with a main figure and two angels. Mantegna's painting is indebted to Bellini's two versions of *The Dead Christ supported by Two Angels* (figs 151, 153), made some years apart.[9] In both, Christ appears to be seated and is supported by two angels whose small hands exert a powerful effort to hold his

FIG. 149
Attributed to DONATELLO
The Dead Christ tended by Angels, about 1430–5
Carved marble in low relief, 80.5 × 114.3 × 6 cm
Victoria and Albert Museum, London (7577-1861)

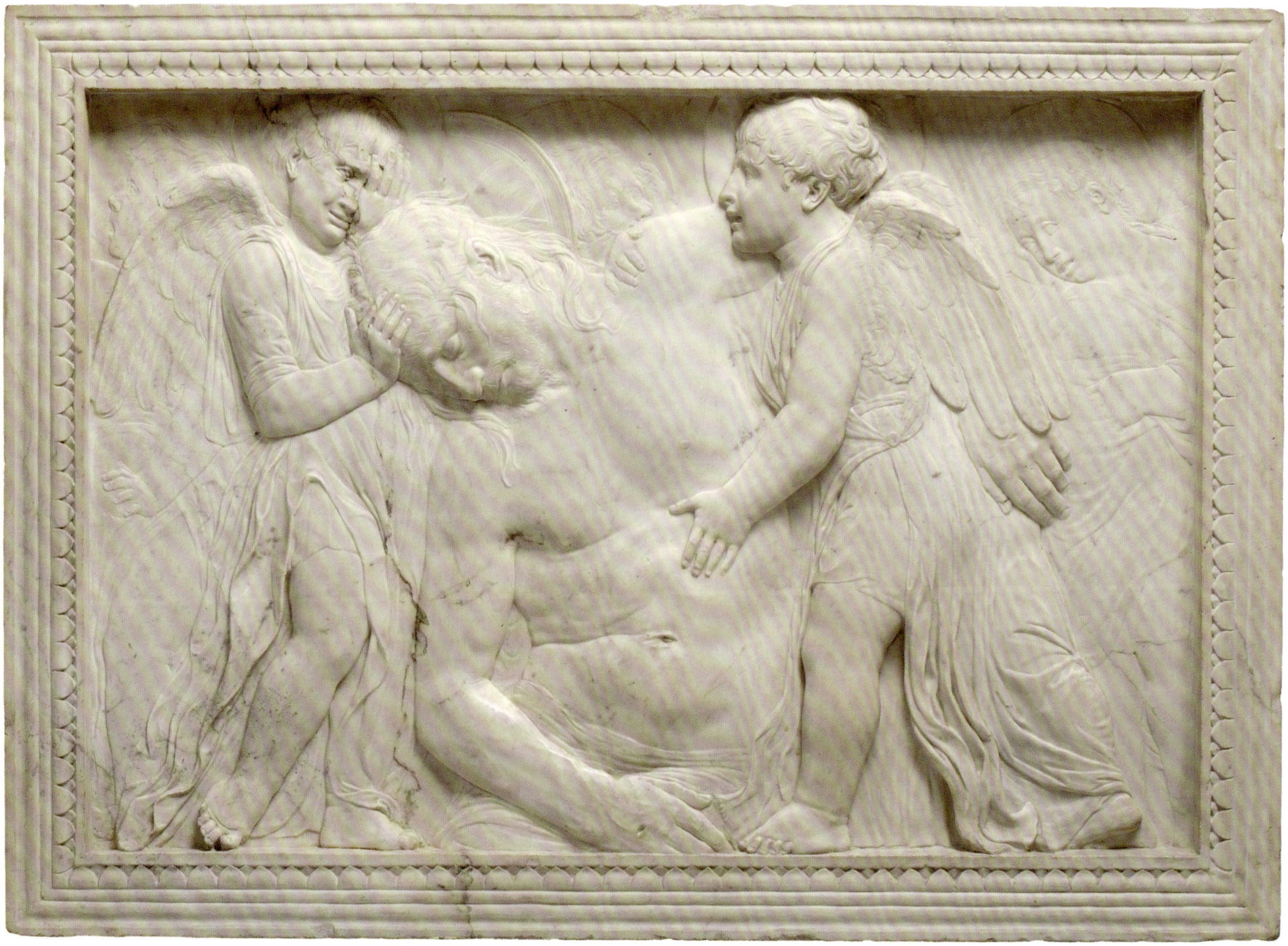

arms. This wounded figure of Christ, supported by angels, requires neither additional explanatory elements such as the Instruments of the Passion or *Arma Christi* (the symbols of Christ's suffering and death) nor a landscape setting with tomb or cross. In both versions, the mournful gazes of the angels serve to elicit empathy in the viewer while the close-up focus on the figures removes the subject from the earthly realm. Bellini uses the composition itself to effect an intimate dialogue between viewer and devotional image.

Mantegna first explored the motif of the Dead Christ in a series of studies, which bear witness to his interest in figure drawing and the study of anatomy. In a drawing now in Venice, dated to 1460–5 (fig. 153), the figure of Christ in half-length is taken directly from Bellini. David Ekserdjian has pointed out that this is the only case of such a borrowing;[10] yet Mantegna's drawing style is recognisable in the characteristic use of dense parallel hatching.

The fundamental difference between the two artists in their mode of representation is evident when we compare this drawing with Bellini's study of the *Pietà* on the recto of a sheet in the British Museum (fig. 162). Compositionally, the work by Bellini is closely related to another of his drawings, of the same subject in Rennes (fig. 154). In both examples, the lifeless body of Christ weighs heavily against the Virgin, who lays her right hand on her son's chest – a gesture derived from Jacopo's Drawing Book. This same gesture also appears in another drawing in the Louvre in which Giovanni ventures to interpret the motif in a horizontal format (fig. 155).

While Giovanni continued to represent the Virgin holding the Dead Christ in an upright position, Mantegna experimented with other perspectival orientations for this subject. The process by which he developed his ideas is clear in two drawings, one from a private collection and the other in the British Museum (fig. 163). The first (fig. 159) was discovered in 2013 and is valuable for an assessment of Mantegna's work.[11] The verso shows the seated Virgin cradling her dead son in her lap and holding his hand in a tender gesture. On the recto is a Lamentation, with Christ laid on the ground and mourned by his mother, Mary Magdalene and Saint John. Beneath this scene an additional figure of the Dead Christ is presented in an unusual perspective, with the head at the lower edge of the picture. The drawing in the British Museum (fig. 163) shows three representations of Christ's body from different perspectives on the recto, and two studies of women on the verso.

The approach to line in these drawings is very similar to a drawing of *The Deposition of Christ* in Brescia (fig. 158), datable to around 1460. Here Mantegna adopts the horizontal composition developed by Donatello (and which was followed by many artists active in Padua),[12] with Mary Magdalene and Saint John laying the body of Christ into the grave with a cloth while the Virgin bends over him in prayer. Once again, Mantegna presents the supine body in a foreshortened view. The perspectivally foreshortened figure of Christ is further developed in the study of *A man lying on a stone slab* (fig. 198), produced somewhat later. All these drawings were presumably made around the time of his famous painting of the Dead Christ in an extreme foreshortened view (fig. 199).[13] Thus it becomes clear that Mantegna experimented extensively, above all in the perspectival representation of the figure.

The drawings and paintings of the Pietà and the Lamentation by Mantegna and Bellini demonstrate how each artist used familiar half-length models introduced by Donatello and Jacopo Bellini to develop their own individual manners. While Giovanni relied above all on emotion, Mantegna emphasised perspective. Both artists developed different compositional concepts for the Pietà that were further developed by their followers.

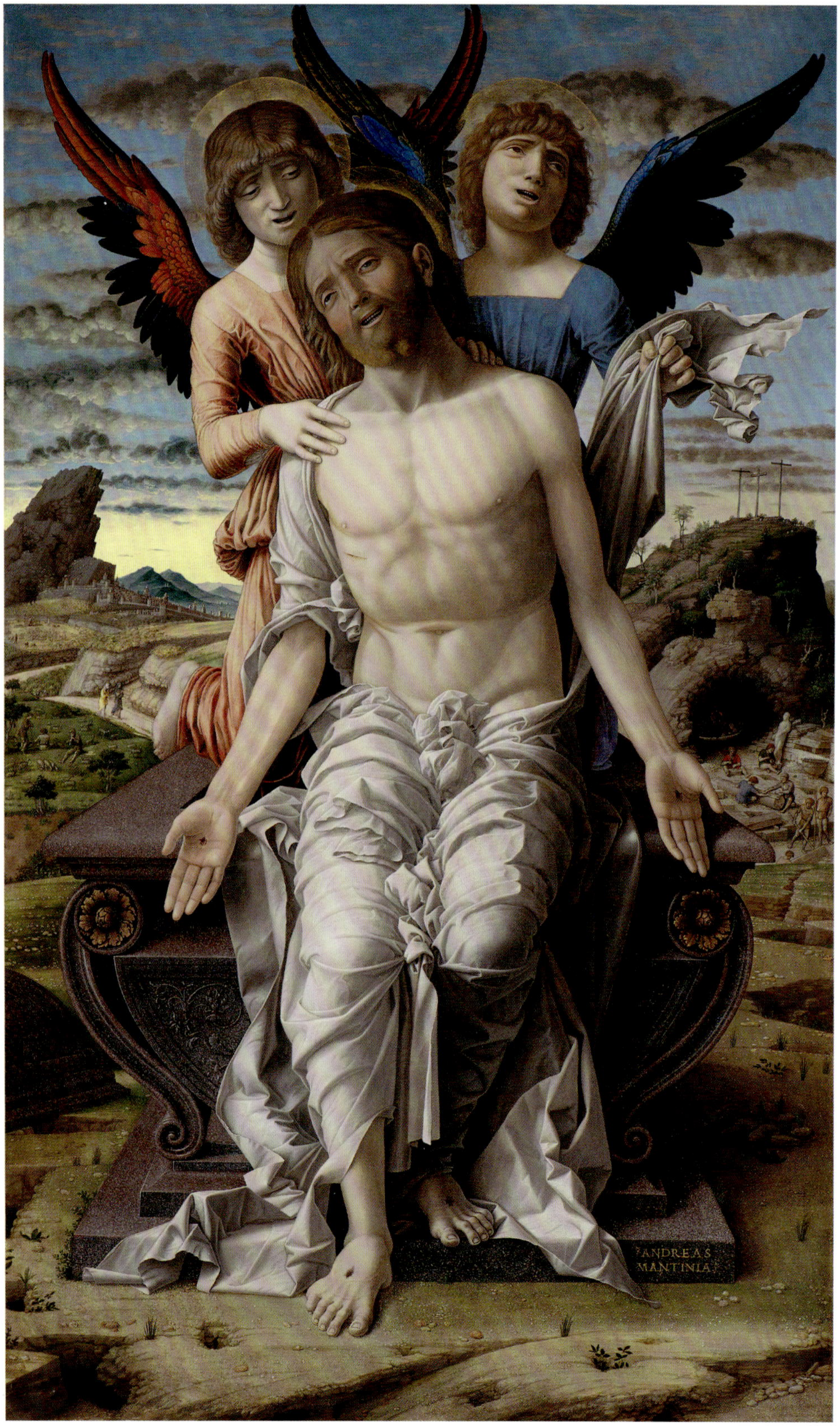

FIG. 150
ANDREA MANTEGNA
The Dead Christ supported by Two Angels,
about 1485–1500
Egg tempera on panel, 78 × 48 cm
Statens Museum for Kunst, Copenhagen
(KMSsp69)

FIG. 151
GIOVANNI BELLINI
The Dead Christ supported by Two Angels,
about 1465–70
Oil on panel, 95 × 71.7 cm
The National Gallery, London (NG 3912)

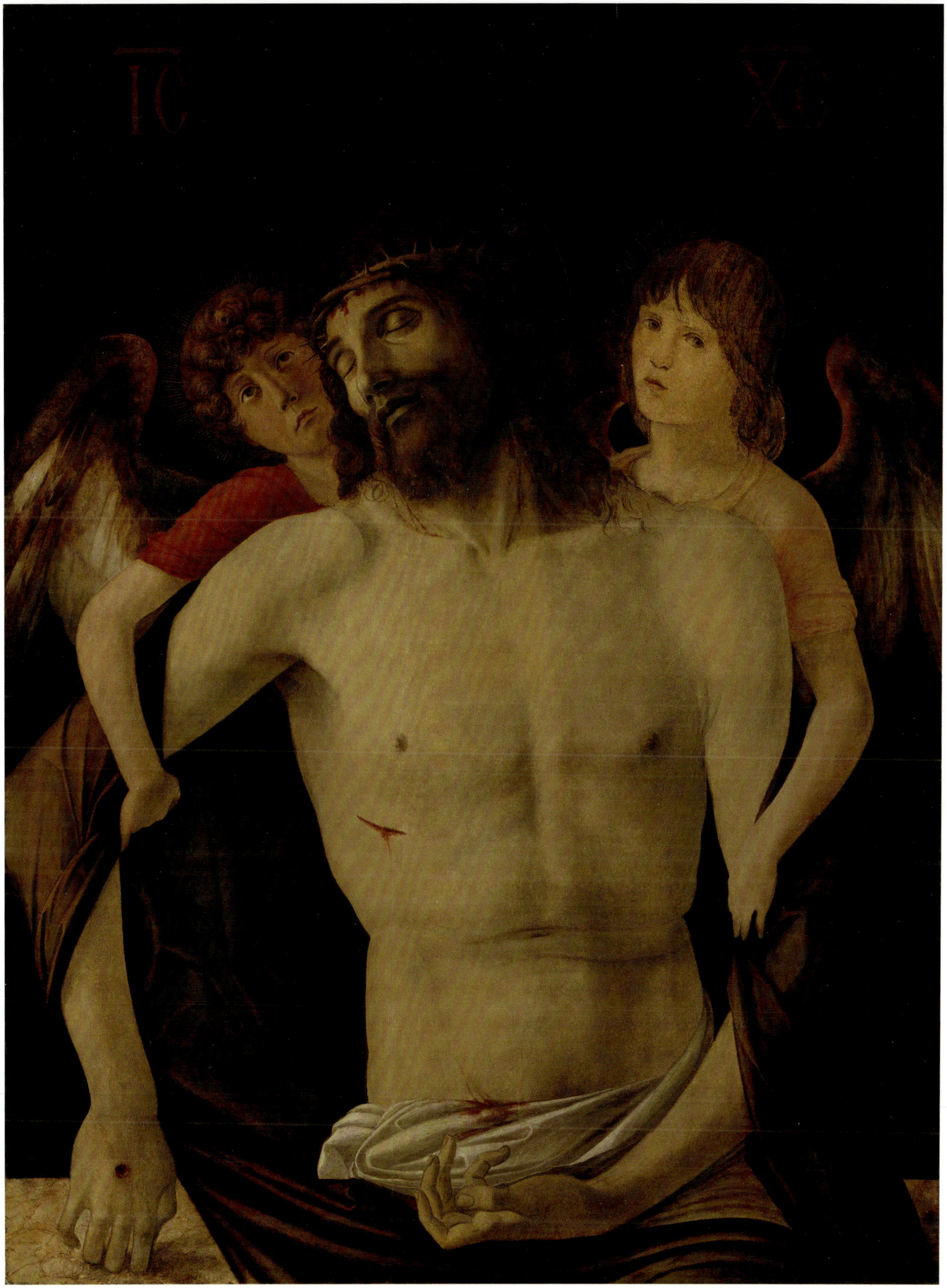
IC
XC

FIG. 152
GIOVANNI BELLINI
The Dead Christ supported by Two Angels, about 1470–5
Egg tempera on poplar, 82.9 × 66.9 cm
Gemäldegalerie, Staatliche Museen zu Berlin (28)

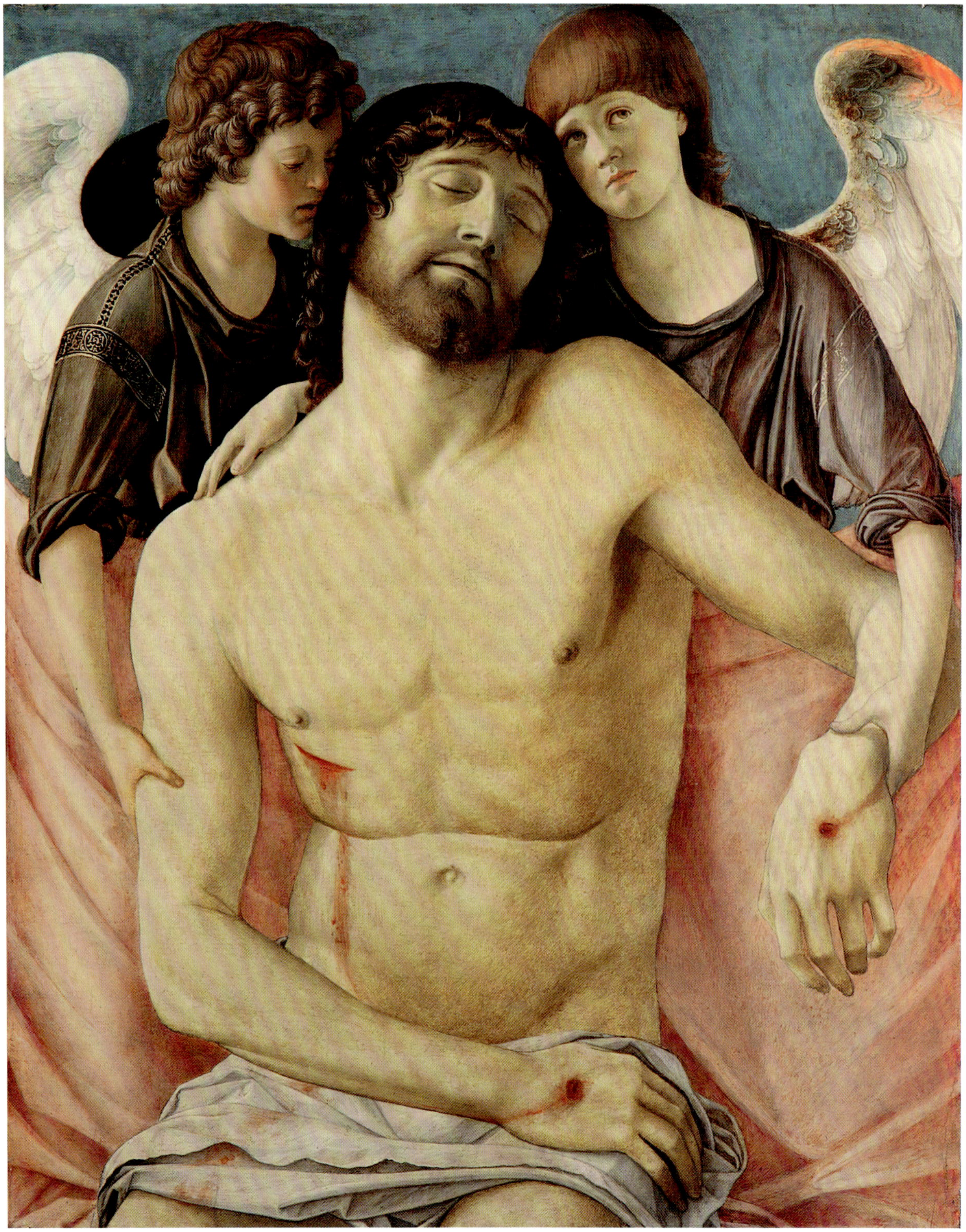

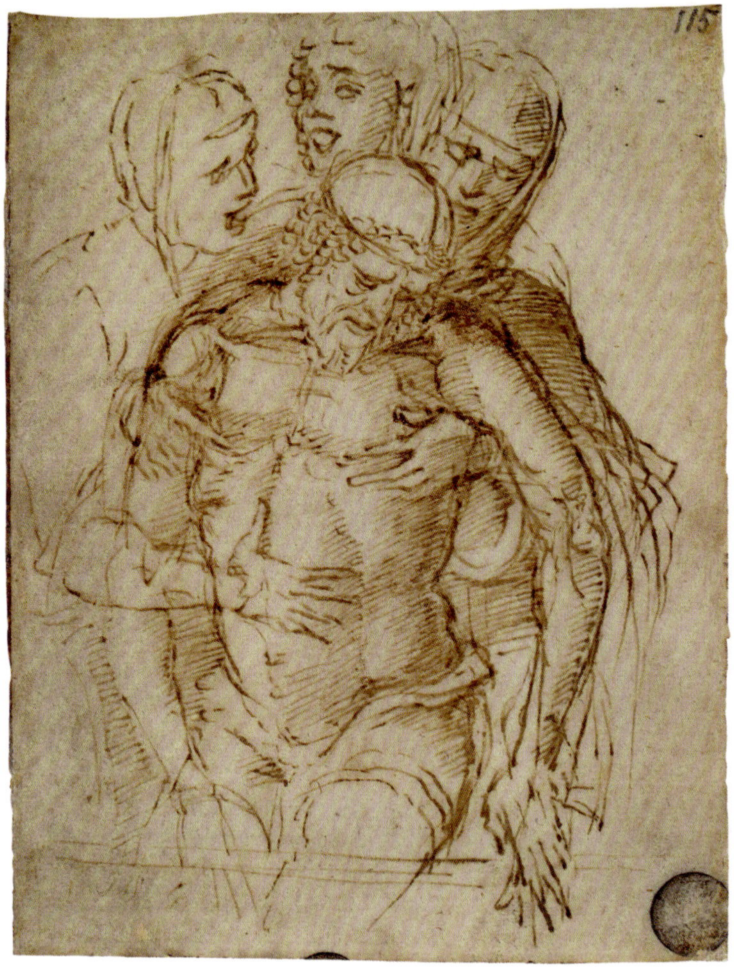

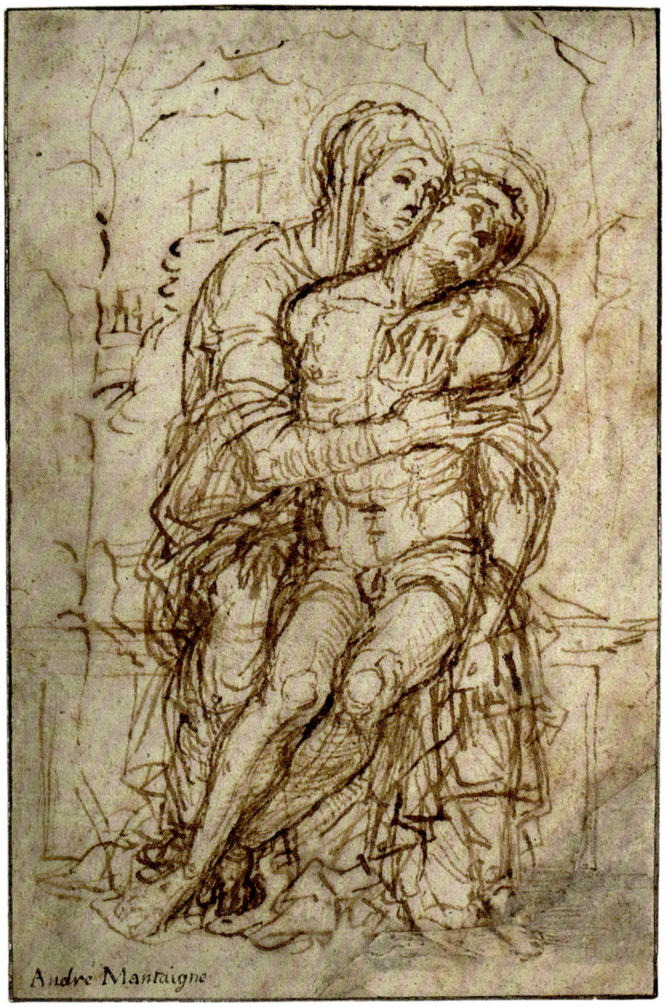

FIG. 153
ANDREA MANTEGNA
Pietà, about 1460–5
Pen and brown ink on paper,
12.7 × 9.8 cm
Gallerie dell'Accademia, Venice (115)

FIG. 154
GIOVANNI BELLINI
Pietà, about 1465–70
Pen and brown ink on paper,
13.2 × 9 cm
Musée des Beaux-Arts, Rennes
(794.1.2503)

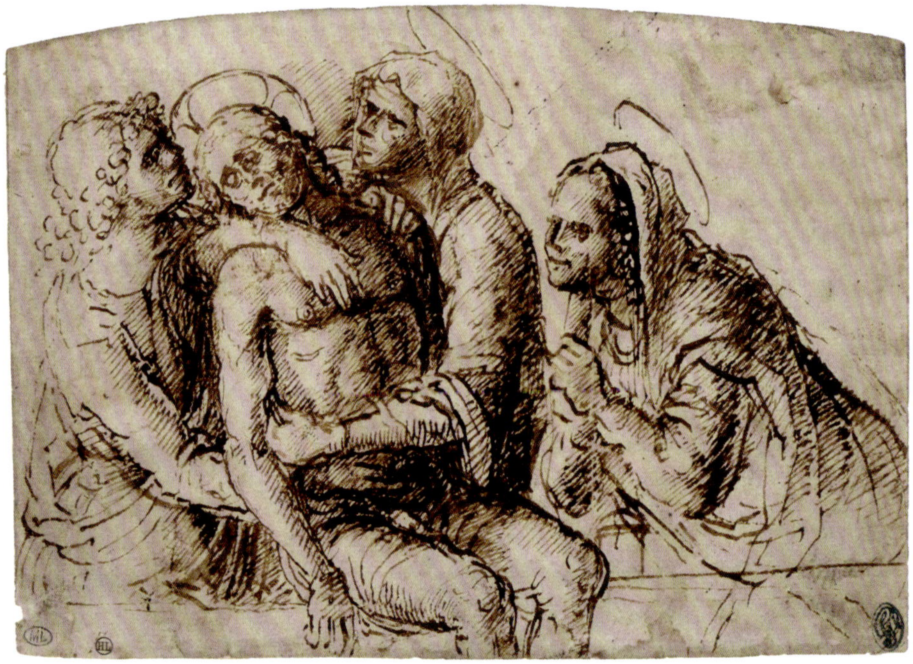

FIG. 155
GIOVANNI BELLINI
The Lamentation over the Dead Christ, about 1490
Pen and brown ink on paper, 12 × 19 cm
Musée du Louvre, Paris (RF 436)

FIG. 156
GIOVANNI BELLINI
The Dead Christ supported by Four Angels, about 1470
Egg tempera (?) on wood, transferred to fibreglass panel, 80.5 × 120 cm
Museo della Città "Luigi Tonini", Rimini (18 PQ)

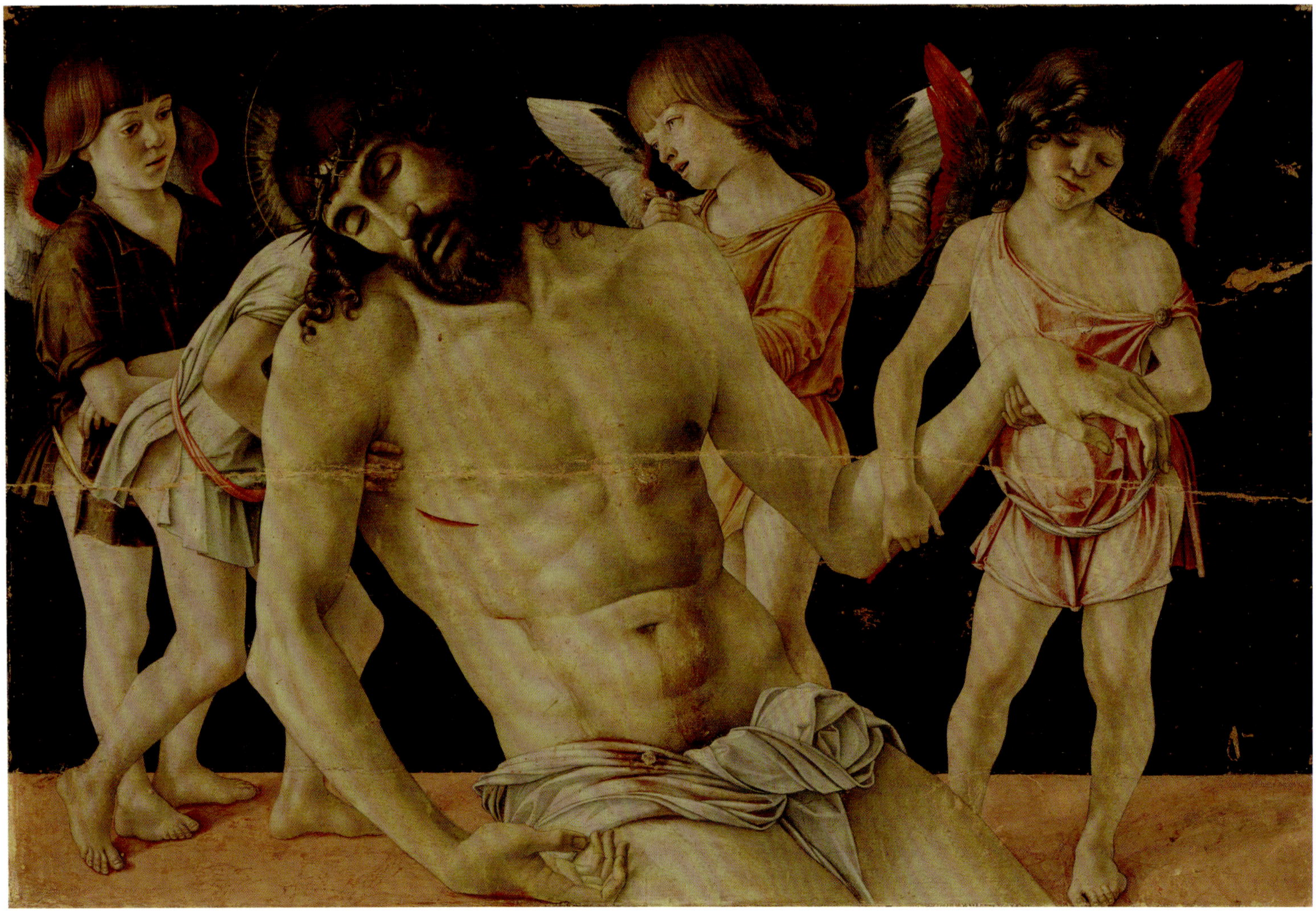

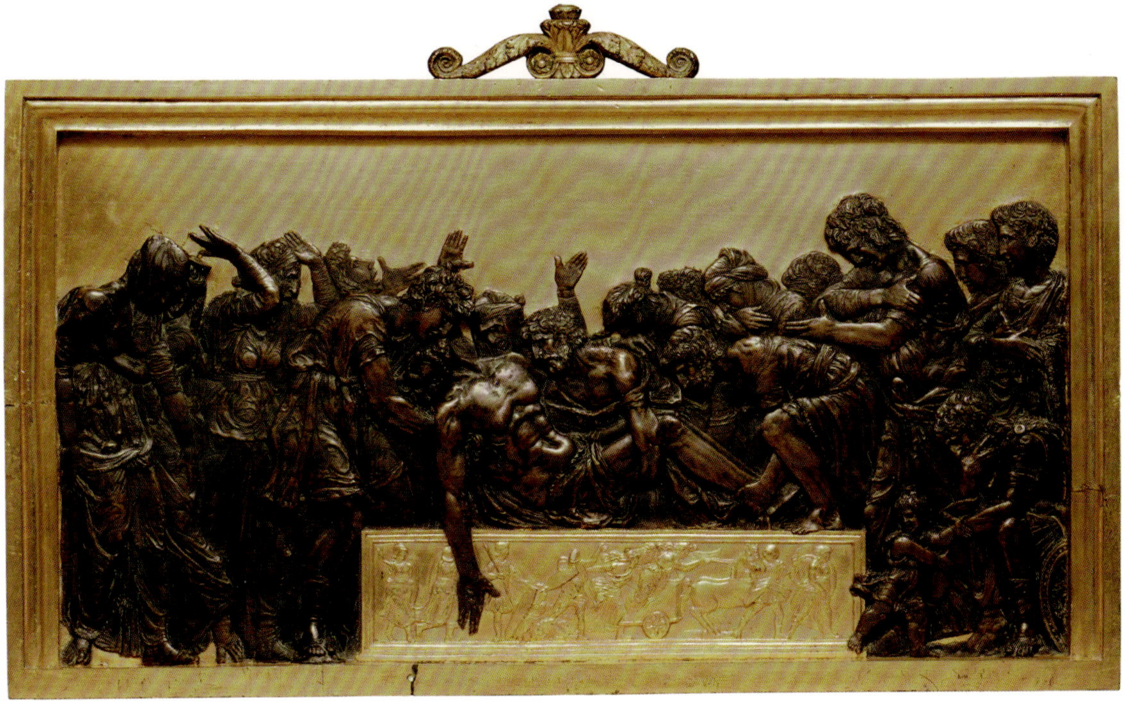

FIG. 157
Circle of
ANDREA MANTEGNA
The Entombment,
about 1470–80
Bronze, partially gilded silver,
24.4 × 44.9 × 2 cm
Kunstkammer, Kunsthistorisches Museum, Vienna (KK 6059)

For instance, artists in Padua, Venice and Mantua made variants on the relief sculpture of *The Entombment* (fig. 157). The example displayed here shows Christ being laid into the grave by several mourning companions.

Bellini's grisaille *Lamentation* in the Uffizi (fig. 161) underscores the close relationship between painting and the graphic arts. Once again Christ is in the centre, but in contrast to other works by Bellini, his body seems light rather than flaccid: his head is almost upright and his right arm is outstretched. The striking position of his knee at the lower edge serves to articulate the spatial perspective and foreshorten the figure of Christ, though here Bellini is much less daring than his brother-in-law and still props his main figure upright in the traditional manner. Christ is supported by the Virgin and Saint John and surrounded by five other figures. In contrast to the more intimate devotional pictures discussed above, the scene is placed at a certain distance and appears removed from the viewer. Bellini thus adopts a mode of representation that stands in fundamental contrast to Mantegna's approach in the Brera painting (fig. 199). While Mantegna presents the striking and frightening illusion of a dead body, Bellini creates a 'well-tempered' figural scene.

Bellini's painting of *The Dead Christ supported by Four Angels* in Rimini (fig. 156) may serve to summarise the way in which the two artists mutually inspired one another. Here the influence of Mantegna's linear approach is clear: in this work, Bellini no longer primarily uses areas of colour to develop the plasticity of his figures, as was the case above all in the Berlin painting of the *Dead Christ* (fig. 152), but rather employs line and contour to an equal extent. Bellini includes a compositional ambiguity in his Rimini *Dead Christ* (fig. 156): the overlapping of forms results in the placement of a feathered angel wing, reminiscent of a halo, directly behind Christ's head, lending the scene a heavenly aspect and pointing to the Resurrection to come.[14] While in his Brera painting (fig. 199), Mantegna elicits a sense of shock with his convincing representation of Christ's corpse reduced to earthly matter, Bellini uses allegorical signs to proclaim redemption. Suffering and redemption – which, in Christological terms, are inseparable – thus constitute fitting categories to describe the related, yet contrasting, artistic approaches of Mantegna and Bellini.

FIG. 158
ANDREA MANTEGNA
The Deposition of Christ, about 1460
Pen and brown ink on paper,
13 × 9.5 cm
Pinacoteca Tosio Martinengo, Dipartimento Disegni e Stampe, Brescia (147r)

FIG. 159
ANDREA MANTEGNA
Two studies of the Lamentation (recto, right); *Studies of the Pietà* (verso, left), early 1460s
Pen and brown ink on paper,
15.1 × 10 cm
Private collection, Milan

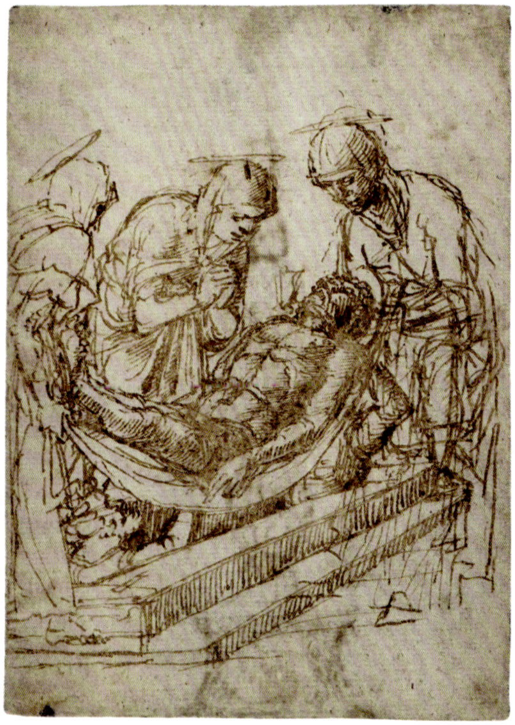

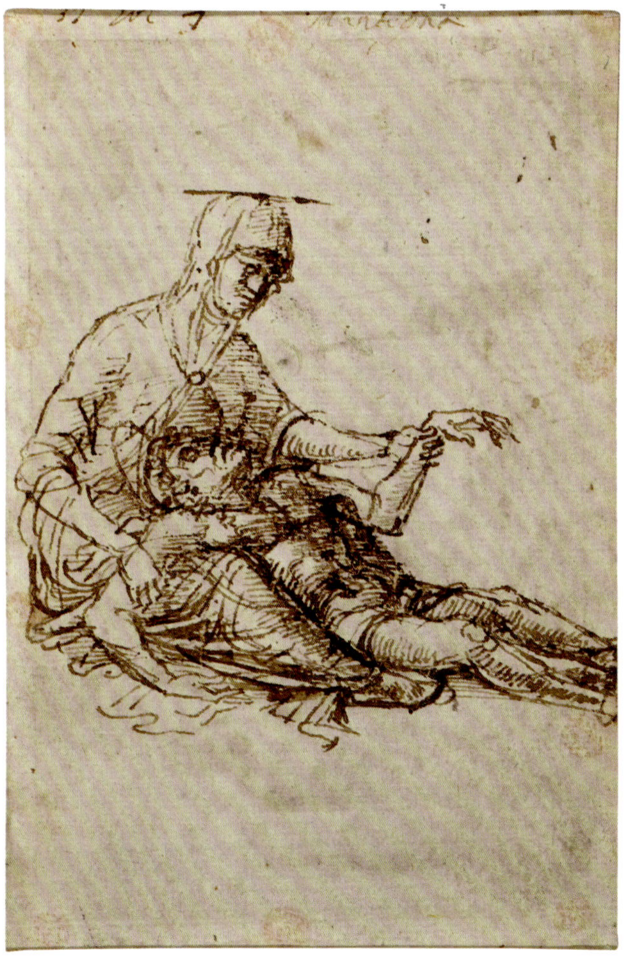

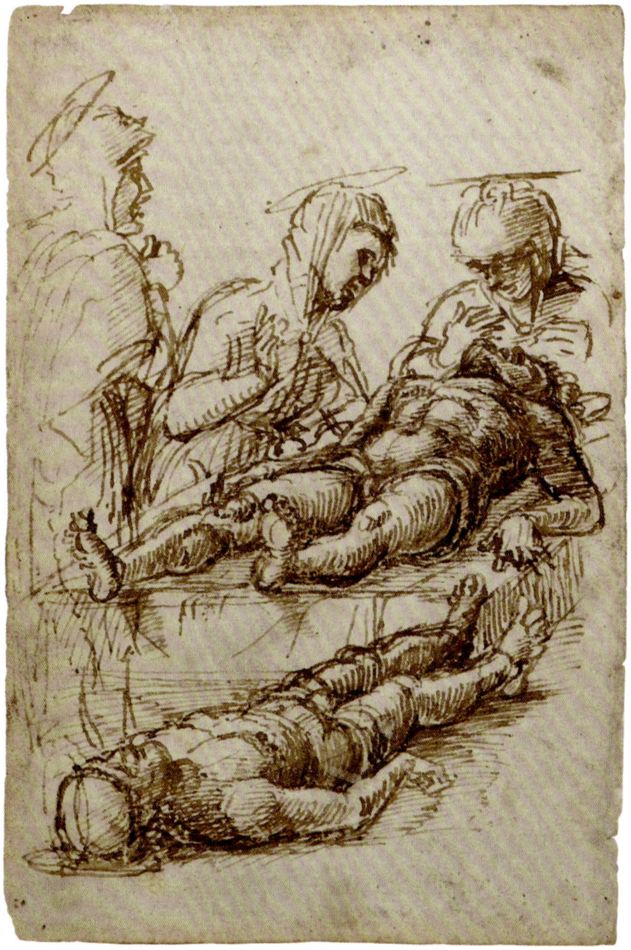

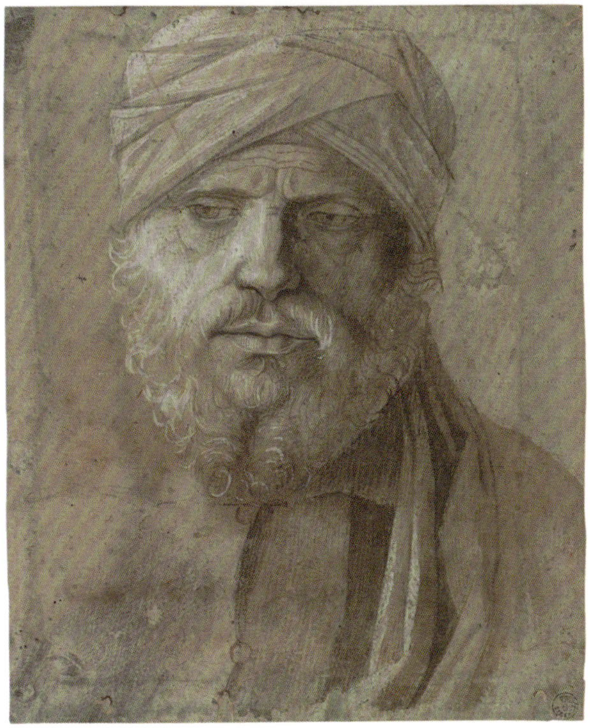

FIG. 160
GIOVANNI BELLINI
Head of a man in a turban, about 1490
Pen and brush and brown ink, white heightening, black chalk on faded blue paper, 30 × 25 cm
Gabinetto dei Disegni e delle Stampe, Galleria degli Uffizi, Florence (595 E)

FIG. 161
GIOVANNI BELLINI
The Lamentation over the Dead Christ, about 1490
Ink brush on a lead white imprimatura on panel, 74 × 118 cm
Galleria degli Uffizi, Florence (1890 no. 943)

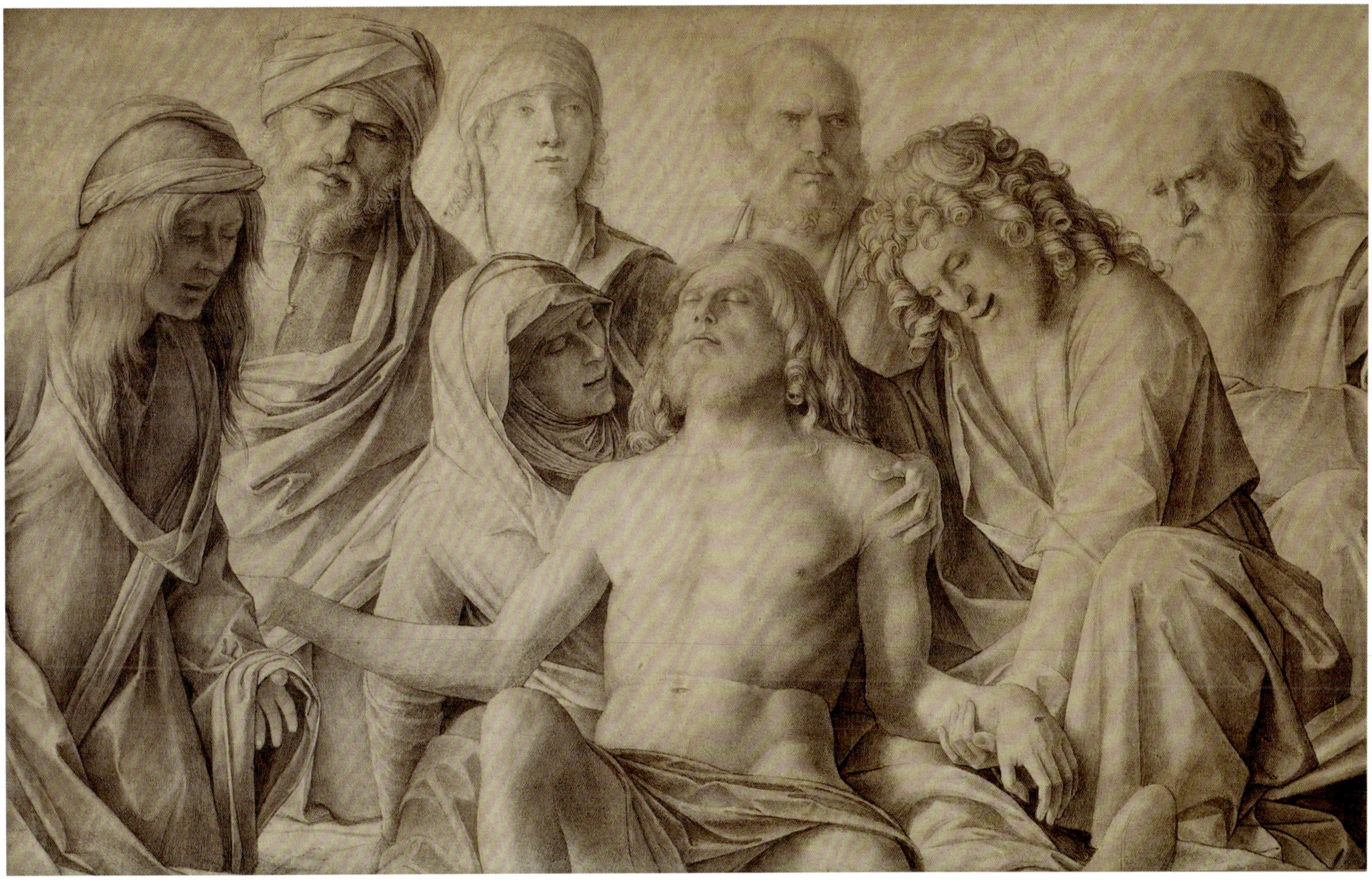

FIG. 162
GIOVANNI BELLINI
Pietà (recto); *Studies of putti* (verso), 1465–70
Pen and brown ink, brown wash on paper, 12.9 × 9.2 cm
The British Museum, London (1895,0915.791)

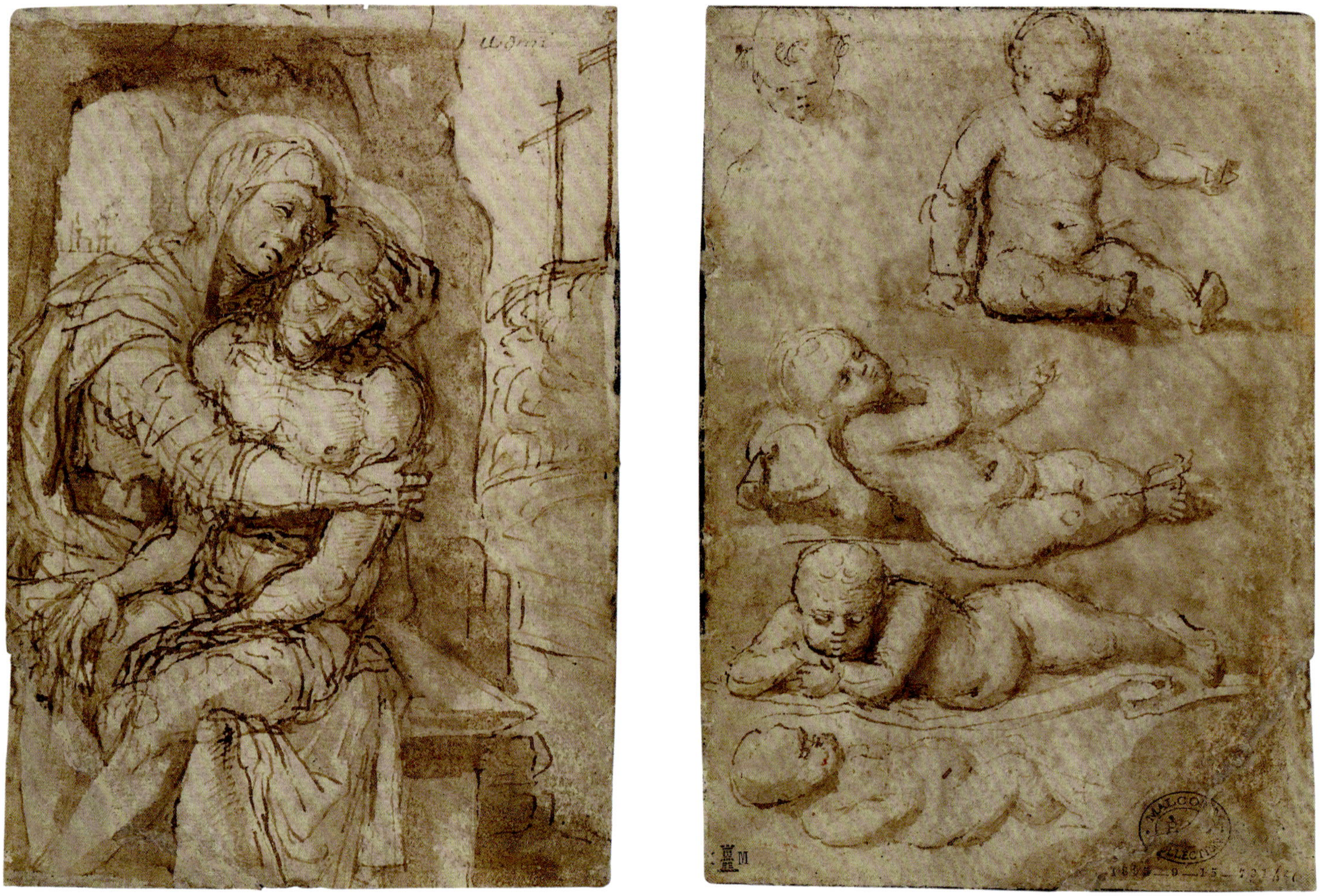

FIG. 163
ANDREA MANTEGNA
Three studies for the Dead Christ (recto);
Two studies of women (verso),
about 1455–65
Pen and brown ink on paper,
12.2 × 8.8 cm
The British Museum, London
(1909,0406.3)

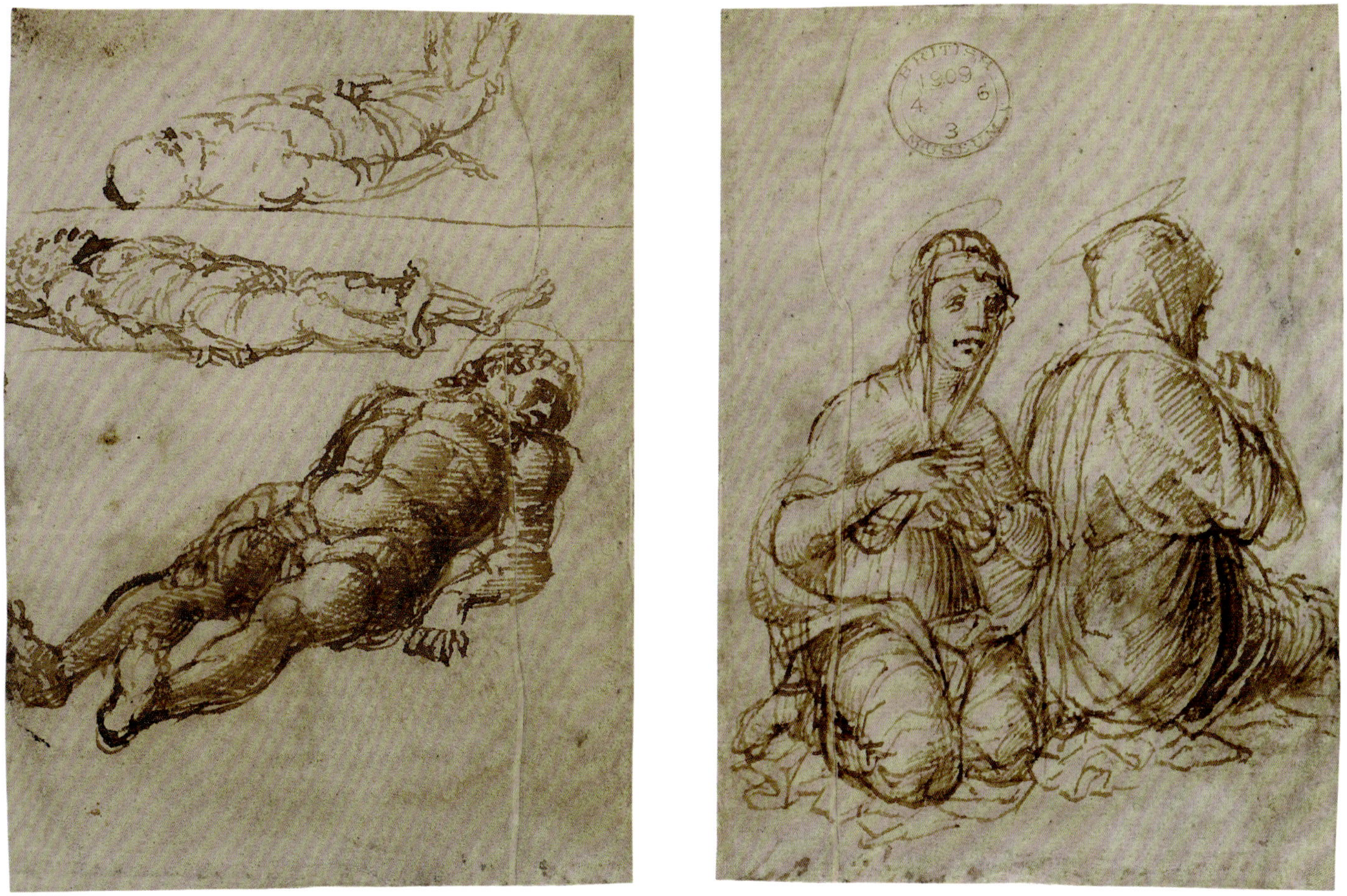

Between Mantegna and Bellini: Marco Zoppo and the Invention of the *sacra conversazione*

NEVILLE ROWLEY

The *Severed Head of Saint John the Baptist* in the Musei Civici in Pesaro (fig. 164) is one of the most terrifying works of fifteenth-century Italian art. A head, oozing blood, appears to emerge from this round painting into the space of the beholder, as seen through an oculus window. Its eyes have not yet had time to close, the mouth seems to be still crying out in pain – and inside the mouth, one can even see the tongue, apparently about to be swallowed, *post mortem*. Blood drips in rivulets from the freshly severed neck, echoing the locks of hair, like live snakes, of the executed man. Hair, beard, mortal wound: all attributes which could be associated with Holofernes, the Old Testament tyrant, were it not for the fact that he is almost never represented without his courageous executioner Judith. No: the individual depicted here belongs to the New Testament, and is the last of the prophets, John the Baptist, who lived a life of penitence in the wilderness, recognised and baptised Christ, and then denounced the incestuous union between the ruler of Galilee Herod Antipas and his niece and half-sister Herodias. One evening, during a banquet, the latter convinced the beautiful Salome to dance for her father

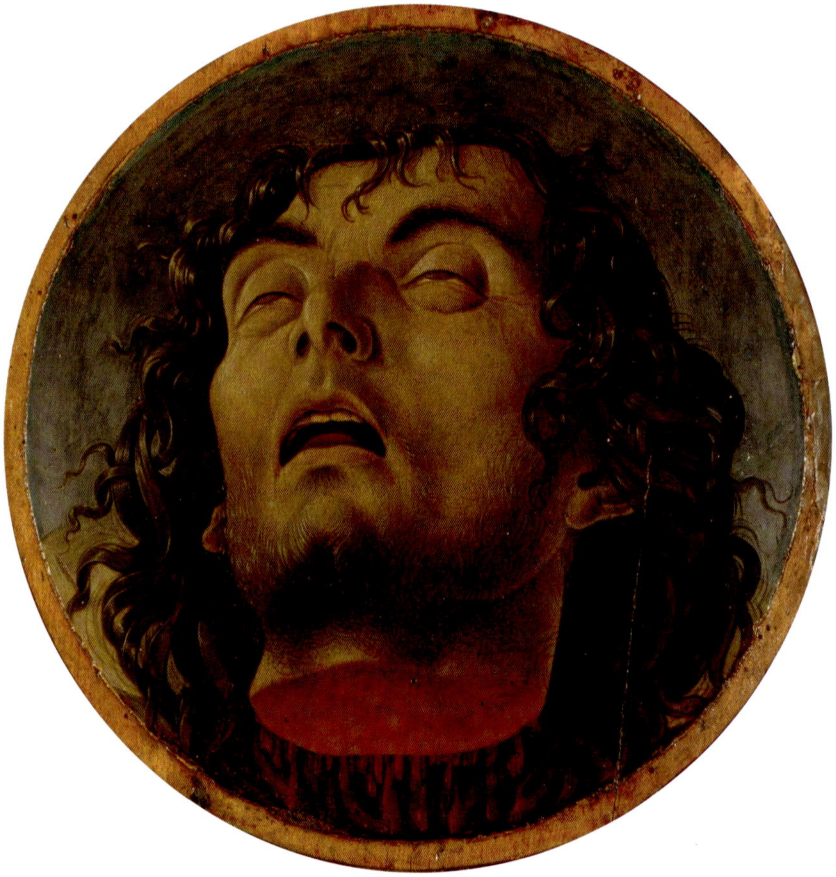

FIG. 164
MARCO ZOPPO
The Severed Head of Saint John the Baptist, about 1470
Egg tempera on panel, 28 cm (diameter)
Musei Civici, Pesaro (4545)

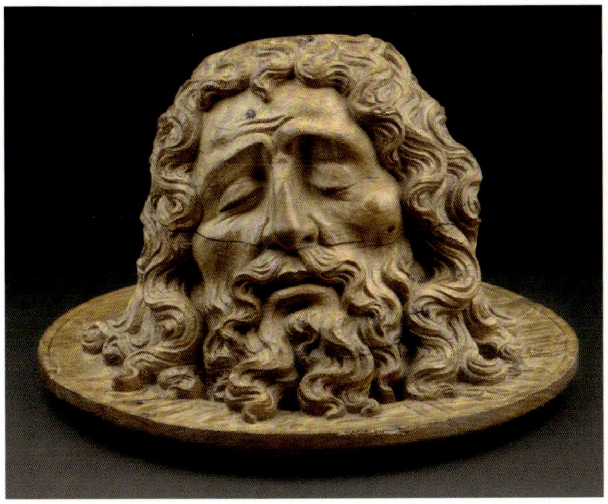

FIG. 165
SOUTH NETHERLANDISH (Tournai?)
Johannesschüssel, about 1430
Oak, 22.5 × 36 × 34.5 cm
Skulpturensammlung und Museum für Byzantinische Kunst, Staatliche Museen zu Berlin. Property of the Kaiser Friedrich Museumsverein (M 268)

FIG. 166
Attributed to ERHARD ALTDORFER
The Adoration of the Johannesschüssel
(detail from a polyptych), 1511
Oil on spruce, 106 × 86 cm (each panel)
St. Johannis Kirche, Gutenstetten

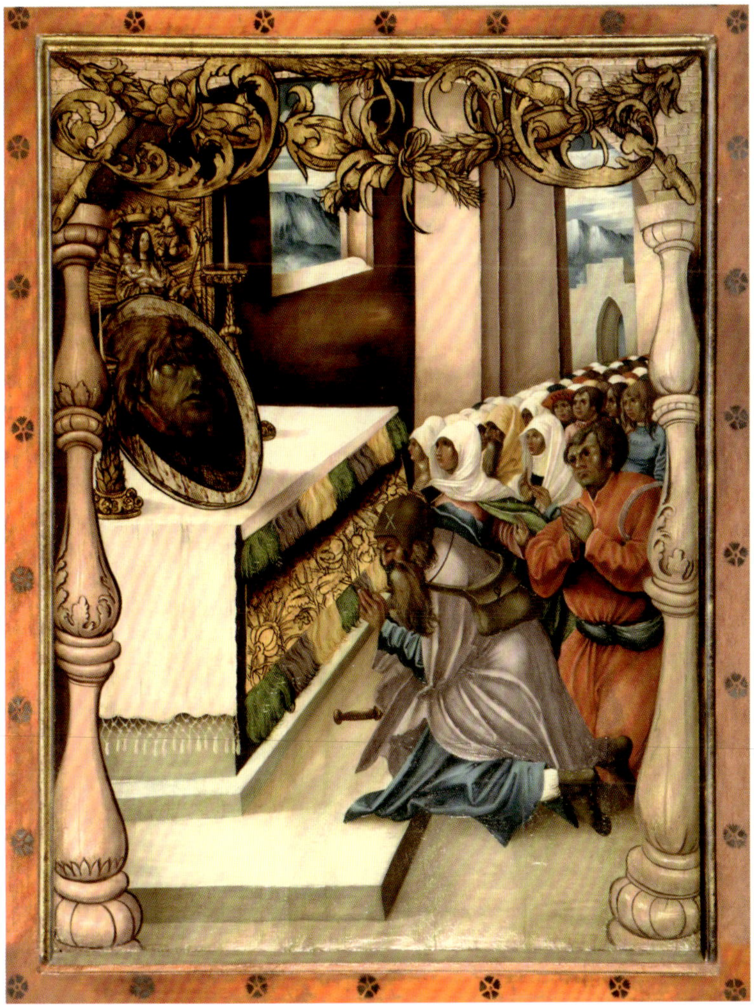

Herod in order to obtain in exchange the head of the Baptist, which was brought out on a platter, even before the end of that banquet. It is this vision of horror we are forced to witness as we look at this painting.[1]

At the end of the Middle Ages, the representation of the Baptist's head spread above all through Northern Europe, where the iconography was known as the *Johannesschüssel* – 'John's platter'. In about 1430, an artist from the southern Low Countries carved an exemplary version of it in wood (fig. 165): the life-size proportions induce the faithful to think of it as an actual severed head, enabling them, once their shock had passed, to meditate on the sufferings of John the Baptist, and by extension, of Christ and the saints – sufferings for which sinners should feel responsible, just as Herod was responsible for the killing of the Baptist.[2] The *Head* in the museum in Pesaro is also a *Johannesschüssel*: the blue ground – representing the sky – only fills the upper part of the background; the lower part is a light brown colour which could represent the platter on which the Baptist's head has been brought to Herod's feast. It has thus recently been supposed that this *Head* was originally mounted independently on an altar, in a similar arrangement to that shown in a German painting of the early sixteenth century (fig. 166). The inclined angle of the picture could allow one to better understand that the head is not floating, as might be imagined when seeing it face on, but that it does indeed rest on a platter.[3]

The attribution of the Pesaro *Head* has posed serious problems for art historians. While traditional historiography attributed the painting to Marco Zoppo – on the basis of a description by Marcello Oretti dating from 1777, when the work was still in the sacristy of the church of San Giovanni Battista in Pesaro – in the 1920s Roberto Longhi profoundly altered scholarly consensus by judging the work to be by Giovanni Bellini.[4] Longhi's authority and his exceptional connoisseur's eye were

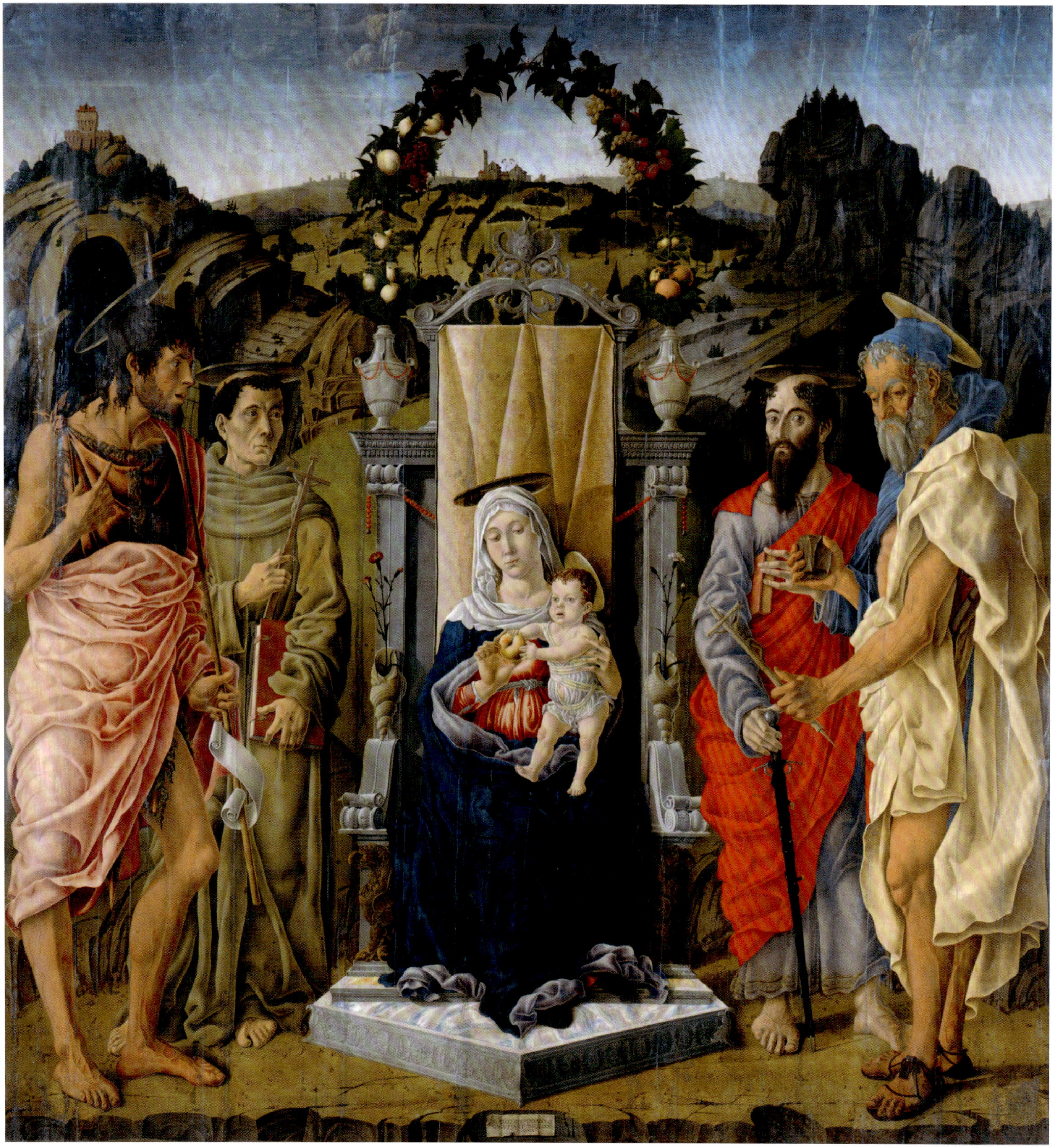

FIG. 167
MARCO ZOPPO
The Virgin and Child between Saints John the Baptist, Francis, Paul and Jerome, also known as the *Pesaro Altarpiece*, 1471
Egg tempera on poplar, 268 × 258 cm
Gemäldegalerie, Staatliche Museen zu Berlin (1170)

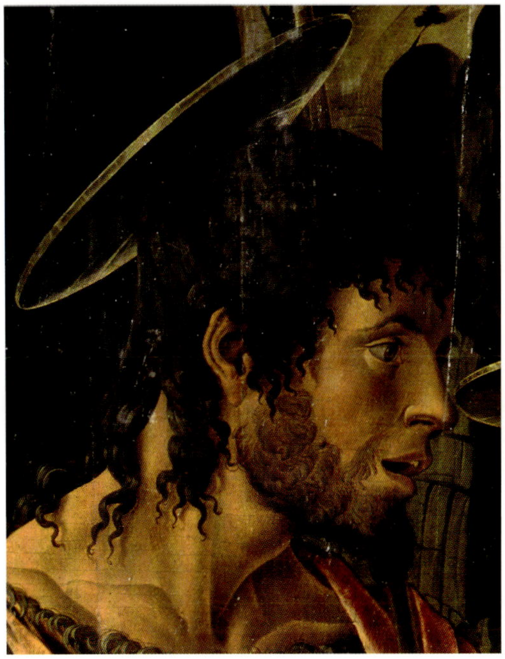

FIG. 168
MARCO ZOPPO, detail from the *Pesaro Altarpiece* (FIG. 167)

persuasive, and the attribution was soon accepted: the *Head* was exhibited as by Bellini in the great monographic exhibition held in the Doge's Palace in Venice after the end of the Second World War.[5] A dozen years later, the work reappeared in another fundamental exhibition of the post-war age, dedicated to Andrea Mantegna, in the Ducal Palace in Mantua. For Giovanni Paccagnini, who had curated both exhibitions, the Pesaro *Head* was an illustration of the period in which Giovanni Bellini had been greatly influenced by his brother-in-law Mantegna, even if the attribution itself did not seem so certain.[6] In the present exhibition, *The Severed Head of Saint John the Baptist* is no longer displayed as a work by Bellini but as a creation of Marco Zoppo – thus following the old eighteenth-century attribution, which a number of scholars accept today.[7] Its presence here might therefore seem incongruous if, beyond the possibility of confirming the attribution through juxtaposition with works by both Zoppo and Bellini, the point of this loan were not also to show that the relationship between Mantegna and Bellini was not solely a conversation between two voices, but was likewise conditioned by the evolution of some of their contemporaries. Trained in Padua by Francesco Squarcione (like Mantegna), and then working as an innovative painter in Venice (like Bellini), Zoppo is an intermediary figure between the two protagonists considered here.

The Berlin iteration of this exhibition will also provide a unique opportunity to draw parallels between the *Severed Head of the Baptist* and a work with which it has always been compared, the altarpiece of the *Virgin and Child between Saints John the Baptist, Francis, Paul and Jerome*, also known as the *Pesaro Altarpiece* from its city of origin (fig. 167), now housed in the Gemäldegalerie in Berlin.[8] The altarpiece poses no attributional problems: it is signed 'Marco Zoppo of Bologna, painted [this work in] 1471 in Venice'. When one compares the head of Saint John the Baptist in the altarpiece (fig. 168) with the *Severed Head*, it is difficult not to accept the attribution to Zoppo for the latter work.[9] In 1777, the altarpiece was in the same church as the *Head*, San Giovanni Battista in Pesaro, next to a *Dead Christ supported by Two Angels* now in the Musei Civici there (fig. 169). Early sources indicate that the altarpiece came from the old church of San Giovanni Battista, occupied by Observant Franciscans and built shortly after 1465 as a mausoleum for the reigning Sforza dynasty, which explains its destruction in the century that followed, when the family was overthrown. It is thus possible that the altarpiece by Marco Zoppo was a direct commission from the ruler of Pesaro, Alessandro Sforza.[10] The *Dead Christ* was certainly the original crowning element, while the predella at its base has only come down to us in one fragment, *Saint Francis receiving the Stigmata*, now in the Walters Art Museum in Baltimore (fig. 170).[11] Some art

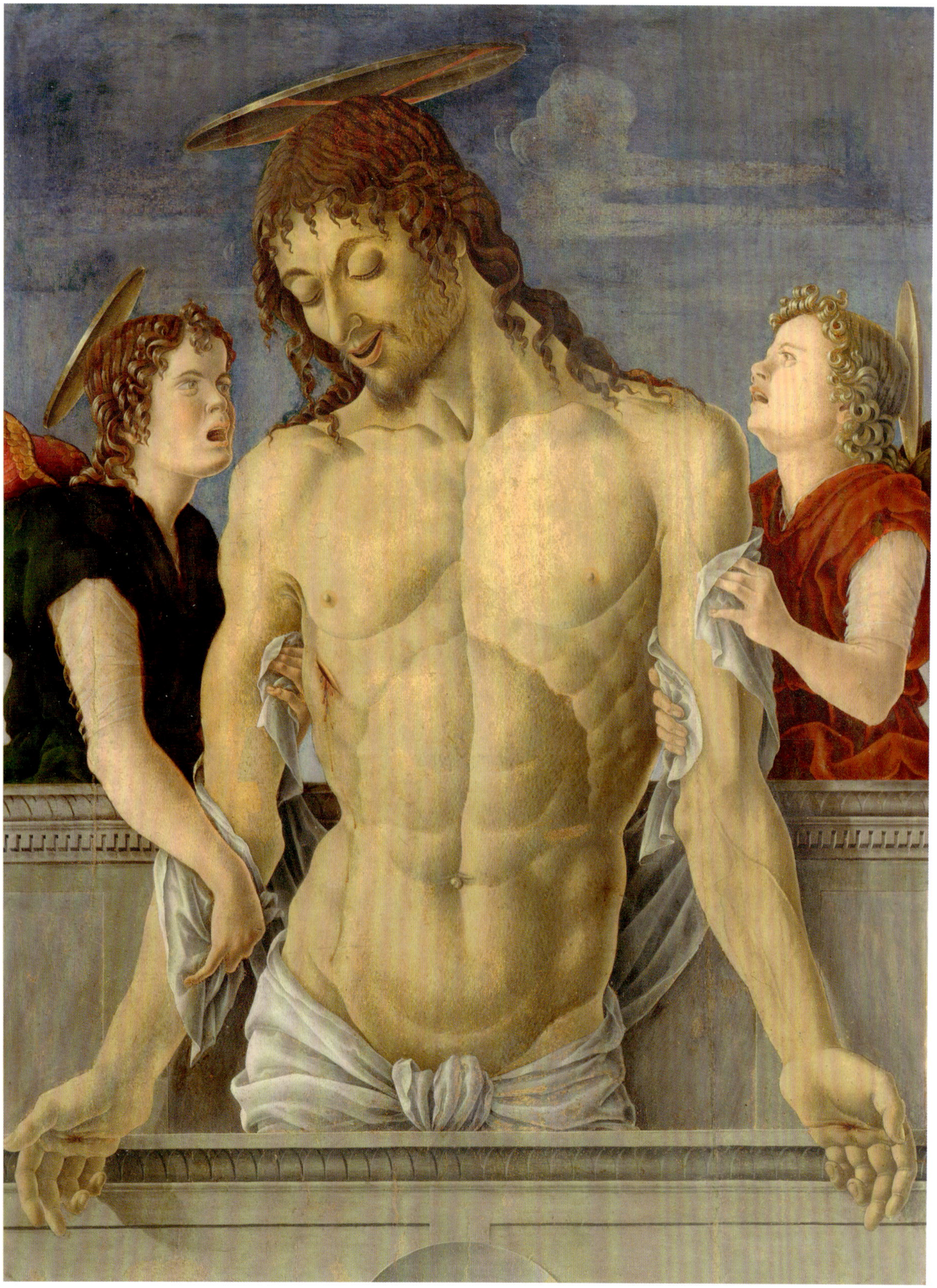

FIG. 169
MARCO ZOPPO
The Dead Christ supported by Two Angels, 1471
Egg tempera on poplar, 102 × 74 cm
Musei Civici, Pesaro (4546)

historians have suggested that the *Severed Head* was originally set in the middle of the predella, although this appears to be contradicted by early sources. It is more likely to have been an independent work, commissioned at the same time as the altarpiece for San Giovanni Battista, perhaps also by Alessandro Sforza.[12]

In 1470, a year before the completion of Zoppo's altarpiece, Alessandro Sforza had sought to acquire a painting by Mantegna;[13] it is therefore especially significant to note that the Pesaro *Head* is not without an echo of one of Mantegna's masterpieces, painted in the mid-1470s: the *Dead Christ* in the Brera in Milan (fig. 199). It is not certain that Zoppo was aware of this work, which probably dates from the mid-1470s and remained in Mantegna's studio until his death, even if there exists a similar combination of drama and extreme foreshortening – as if the brutal perspective allowed the horror of the scene to enter the heart of the faithful more directly.[14] In any case there can be no doubt that the great painter was a vital model for Zoppo, ever since his true artistic beginnings around 1454 in Padua. Donatello had just left the city, and Mantegna's career had taken on an entirely new shape through his marriage to Nicolosia Bellini the year before. Zoppo was then a little over 20, almost Mantegna's age, but lagging considerably with respect to artistic evolution. Born in Cento, between Bologna and Ferrara, he was unable to benefit from the inventions of Donatello and the other Florentines during his adolescence. Once in Padua, Zoppo followed the same steps as his model Mantegna, who was then completing – alone – the frescoed decoration of the Ovetari Chapel. Initially the pupil of Squarcione, Zoppo soon became his master's adoptive son, just as Mantegna had a decade earlier.[15] At this point Squarcione was a bachelor of almost 60, thus making the young painter the potential heir of his workshop, which included a rich collection of drawings, reliefs and ancient inscriptions. From an artistic point of view, Zoppo was already a good painter; above all, he was an outstanding draughtsman, largely influenced by Mantegna, to whose work he responded with exceptional sensitivity, which manifested itself through increased graphic restlessness (fig. 171).[16] But soon thereafter Squarcione married, and his wife became pregnant, putting an end to any dreams of inheritance. Zoppo left Padua for Venice, and his style gradually distanced itself from that of Mantegna, approaching that of Bellini.

FIG. 170
MARCO ZOPPO
Saint Francis receiving the Stigmata, 1471
Egg tempera on panel, 35.1 × 46.7 cm
The Walters Art Museum, Baltimore, MD (37.544)

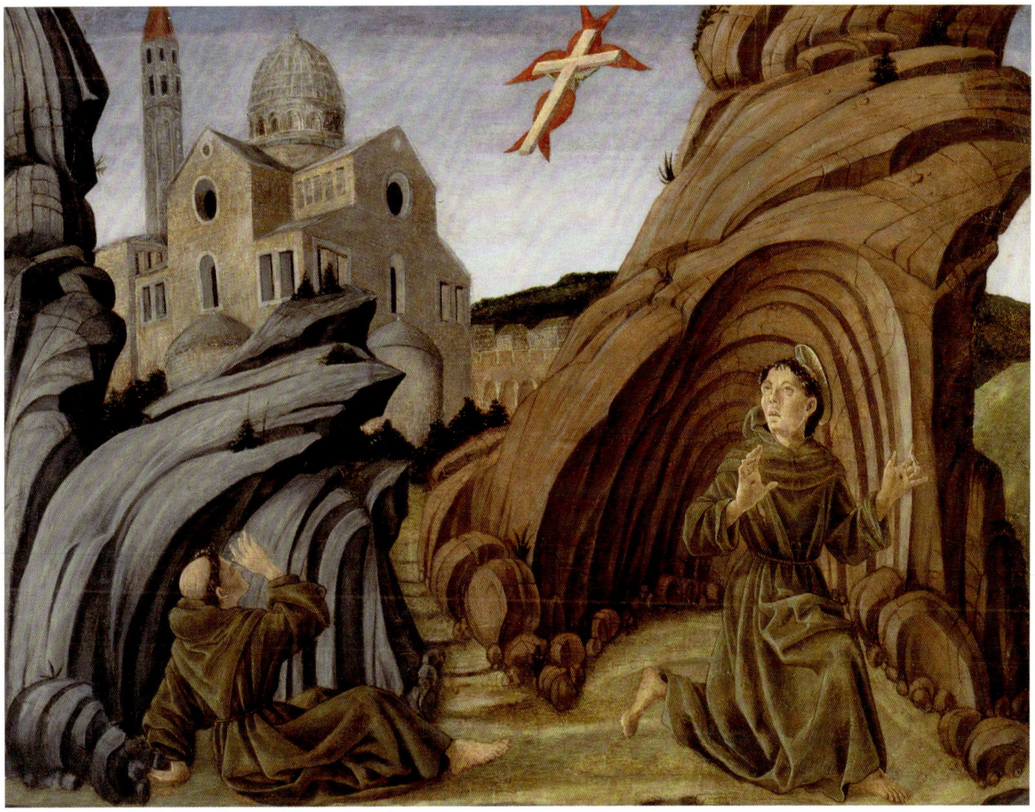

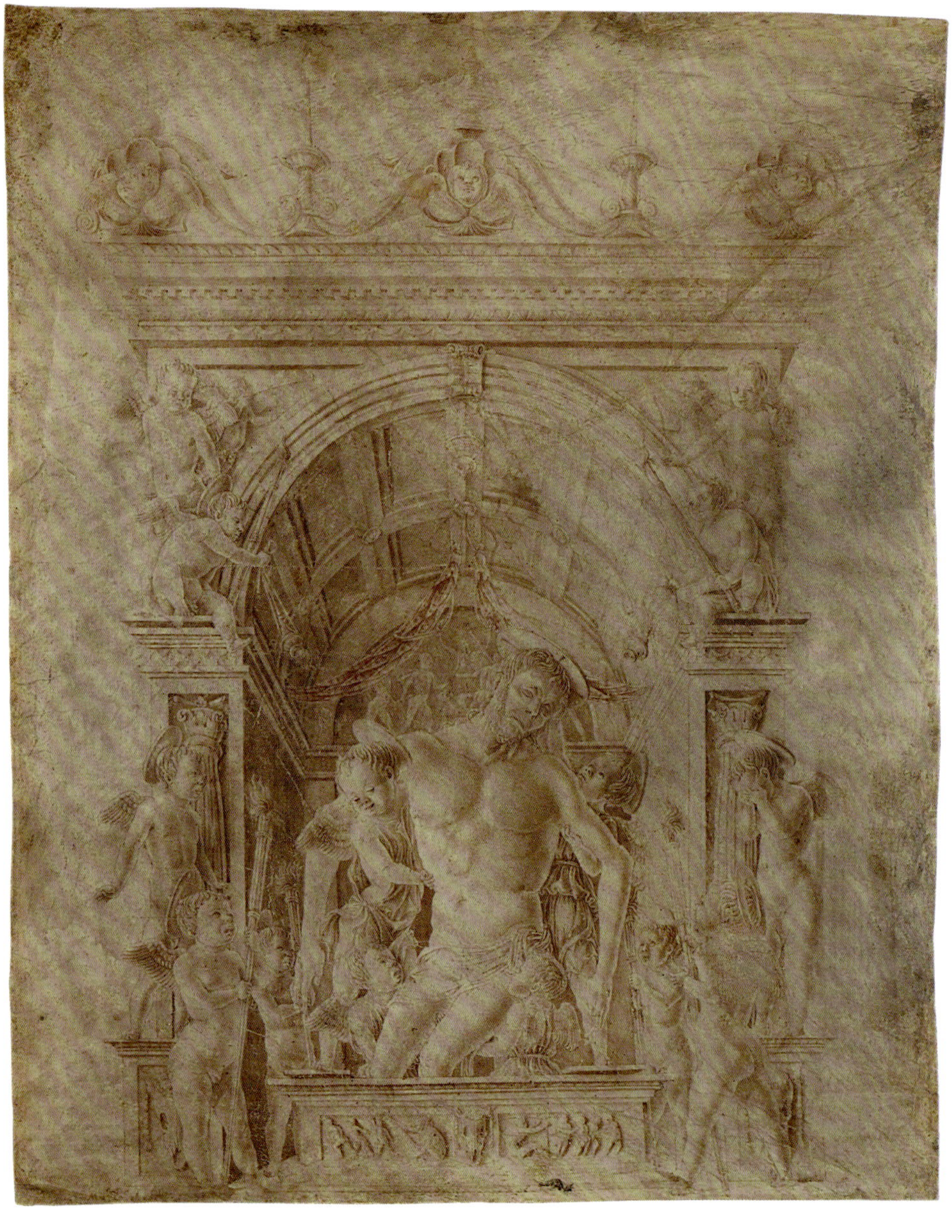

FIG. 171
MARCO ZOPPO
The Dead Christ supported by angels, about 1455–7
Pen and brown ink, brown wash on vellum, 35 × 28 cm
The British Museum, London (1995,0506.7)

The *Pesaro Altarpiece* (fig. 167) represents the outcome of this evolution, with the petrified forms of the saints and the throne of the Virgin – but also the landscape behind them – merging into a more atmospheric luminosity.

The *Pesaro Altarpiece* is certainly Zoppo's masterpiece; the work also marks a vital step in the evolution of the altarpiece form, and one cannot merely reduce it to representing a middle stage between Mantegna and Bellini. Ever since Donatello's arrival in Padua, the typology of the church altarpiece had been uppermost in the minds of artists in the Veneto. In the era of polyptychs with multiple registers and numerous separate panels, the high altarpiece made by Donatello for the Santo (fig. 2) constitutes an unprecedented example of uniting the Virgin and Child and the saints flanking them within one space; this was a model, inherited from Florentine painting, that would be referred to as a 'sacra conversazione' – literally, a holy or sacred conversation.[17] The terracotta altarpiece of the Ovetari Chapel in the Church of the Eremitani in Padua (fig. 250) adhered to this type, and indeed its concept has even been attributed to Donatello, who had taught the artist who executed it, Giovanni da Pisa.[18] There is no doubt that the young painters active in the chapel, Niccolò Pizzolo and Mantegna, would have been profoundly influenced by this example. At the end of the 1450s, in his *San Zeno*

Altarpiece (fig. 252), a work made for the high altar of the eponymous church in Verona, Mantegna adopted a type that unified the space between the Virgin and saints, even though the archaic triptych structure was still present. In Venetian painting, the unification of the principal panel would be achieved by a painter little known for his modernist propensities, Bartolomeo Vivarini, in an altarpiece dated 1465 now in Capodimonte in Naples (fig. 172). At that point, Giovanni Bellini still showed himself to be very close to what Mantegna was doing (fig. 253). As for Zoppo, having formerly adopted the separated structures of the polyptych, the Pesaro commission gave him the opportunity of creating a unified altarpiece with a composition set before a landscape background. In those years, this was an undeniable innovation.

In the early 1470s, Giovanni Bellini received a commission for the high altarpiece of the church of San Francesco in Pesaro. For the Conventual Franciscans – rivals of the Observant Franciscans who were in charge of the church of San Giovanni Battista, where Zoppo's altarpiece had recently been erected – this was a model to imitate, but also to outdo. Bellini thus created a work of almost identical dimensions, tackling the unified altarpiece type for the first time and organising the saints around *The Coronation of the Virgin* as if it were a *sacra conversazione* (fig. 255). From Zoppo Bellini thus took the type, which included a *Lamentation* as crowning element, but also the decision to assign a substantial role to landscape, yet ultimately achieving a far more miraculous balance between space, colour and light.[19] After this commission, Bellini was to assert himself as one of the greatest painters of *sacra conversazione* altar-pieces in Venice (for example figs 20, 257), expanding the inventions of Donatello, seen through the lens of Mantegna and renewed with the arrival on the scene of Antonello da Messina. Within this evolution, the role played by Marco Zoppo cannot be forgotten, even if he never had occasion to respond to further commissions as important as his *Pesaro Altarpiece*: he died a few years later aged only 45.

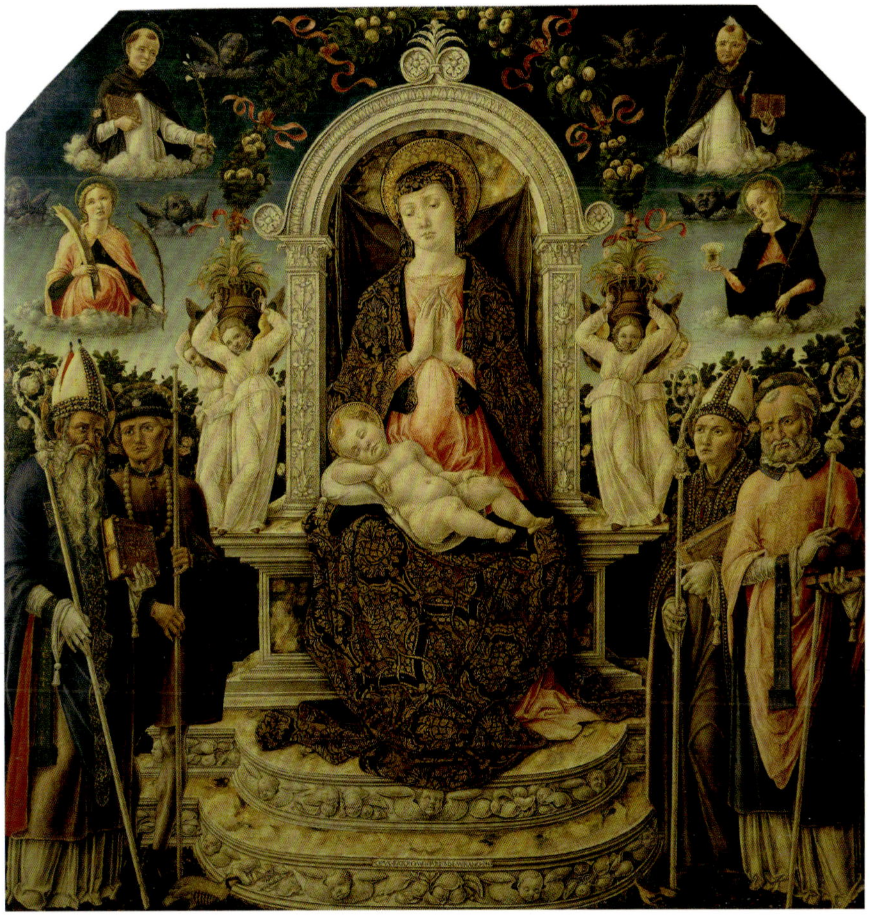

FIG. 172
BARTOLOMEO VIVARINI
The Virgin and Child Enthroned with Saints, 1465
Egg tempera on panel,
118 × 118 cm
Museo Nazionale di Capodimonte, Naples (Q. 66)

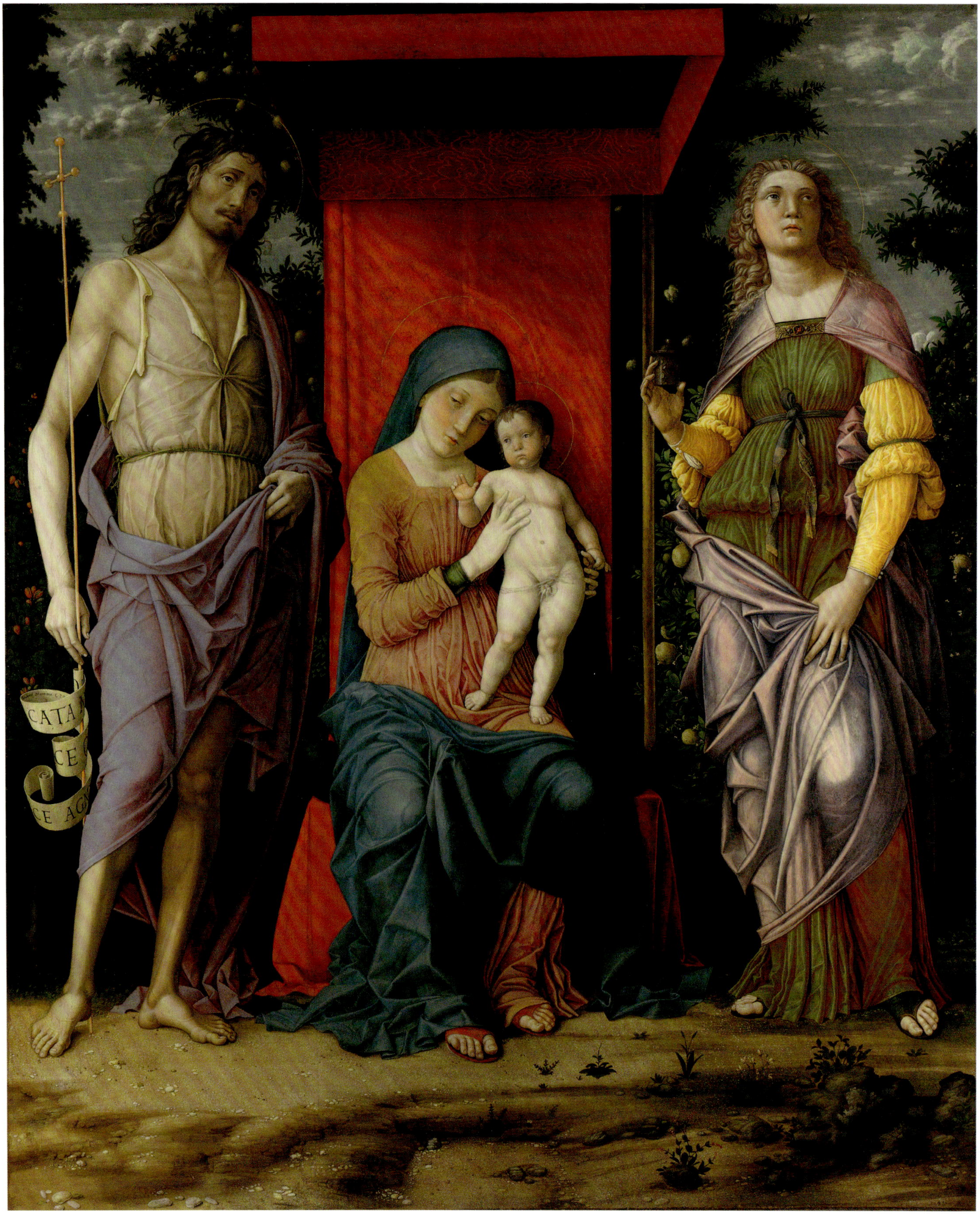
CATA
CE
CE AGN

FIG. 173
ANDREA MANTEGNA
The Virgin and Child with the Magdalen and Saint John the Baptist,
about 1490–1505
Egg tempera on canvas, 139.1 × 116.8 cm
The National Gallery, London (NG 274)

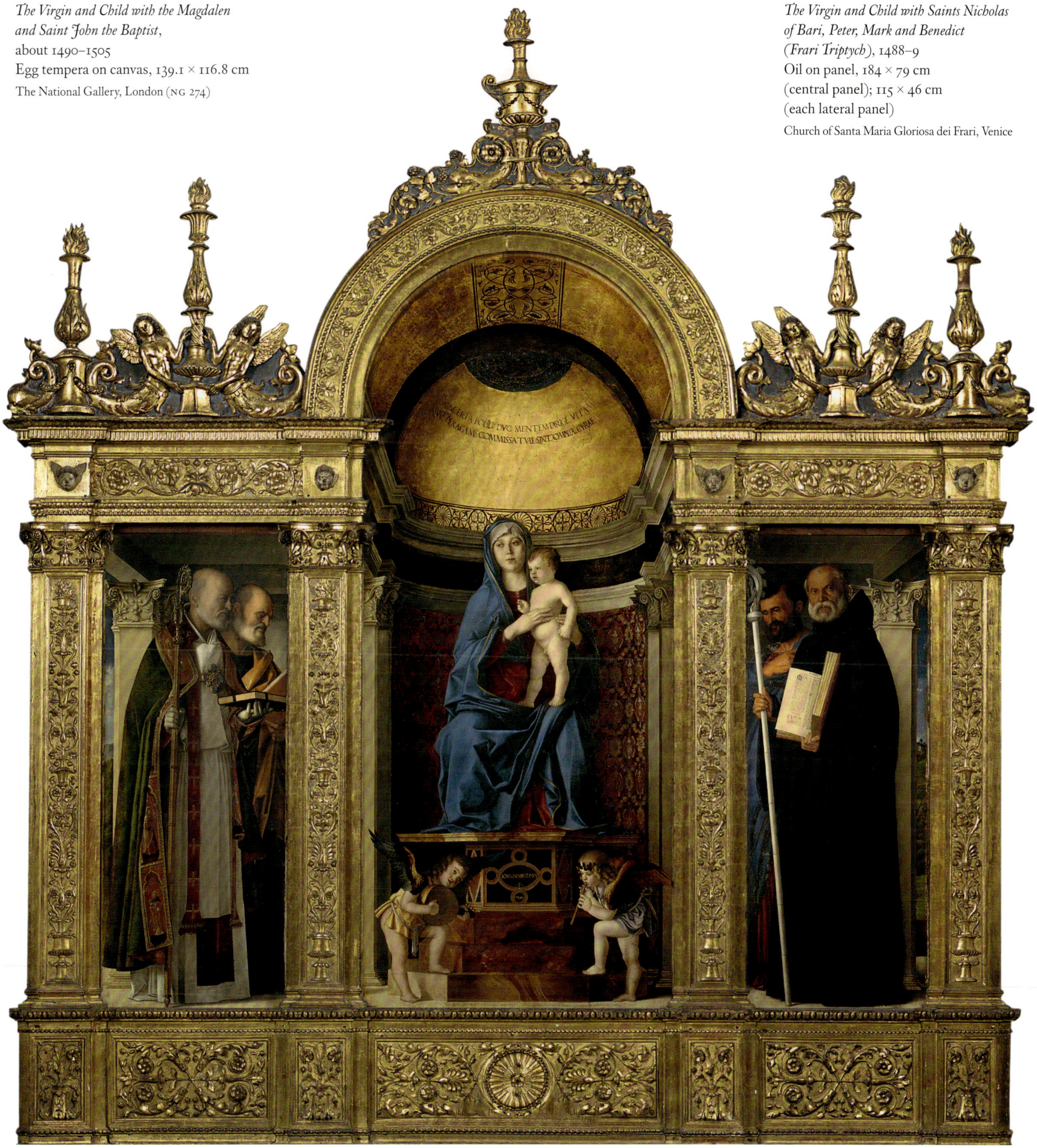

FIG. 174
GIOVANNI BELLINI
The Virgin and Child with Saints Nicholas of Bari, Peter, Mark and Benedict (Frari Triptych), 1488–9
Oil on panel, 184 × 79 cm (central panel); 115 × 46 cm (each lateral panel)
Church of Santa Maria Gloriosa dei Frari, Venice

The Virgin and Child: Small-Scale Devotional Works

CAROLINE CAMPBELL

Every fifteenth-century artist – be they a painter or a sculptor, and whether they worked in a court or a Republic such as Venice – expected to produce multiple images of Christian subjects. Representations of the Virgin and Child, in particular, were to be seen everywhere in Christendom. They were found at the centre of most altarpieces, on the high altars and private chapels of churches, in the shared spaces of monasteries and confraternities, on the outside of buildings and even on street corners. Many more of these images, meanwhile, were intended for the domestic setting of the home or for private contemplation. It was widely believed that they ultimately derived from a prototype drawn by the Evangelist Saint Luke himself, to whom Mary and the infant Christ had appeared in a vision.[1]

Artists such as Mantegna and Bellini consciously used the very familiarity of this subject as a means of demonstrating their abilities. By departing from the familiar, particularly when creating paintings for a domestic setting, they could display their technical and compositional skills, as well as their powers of observation.

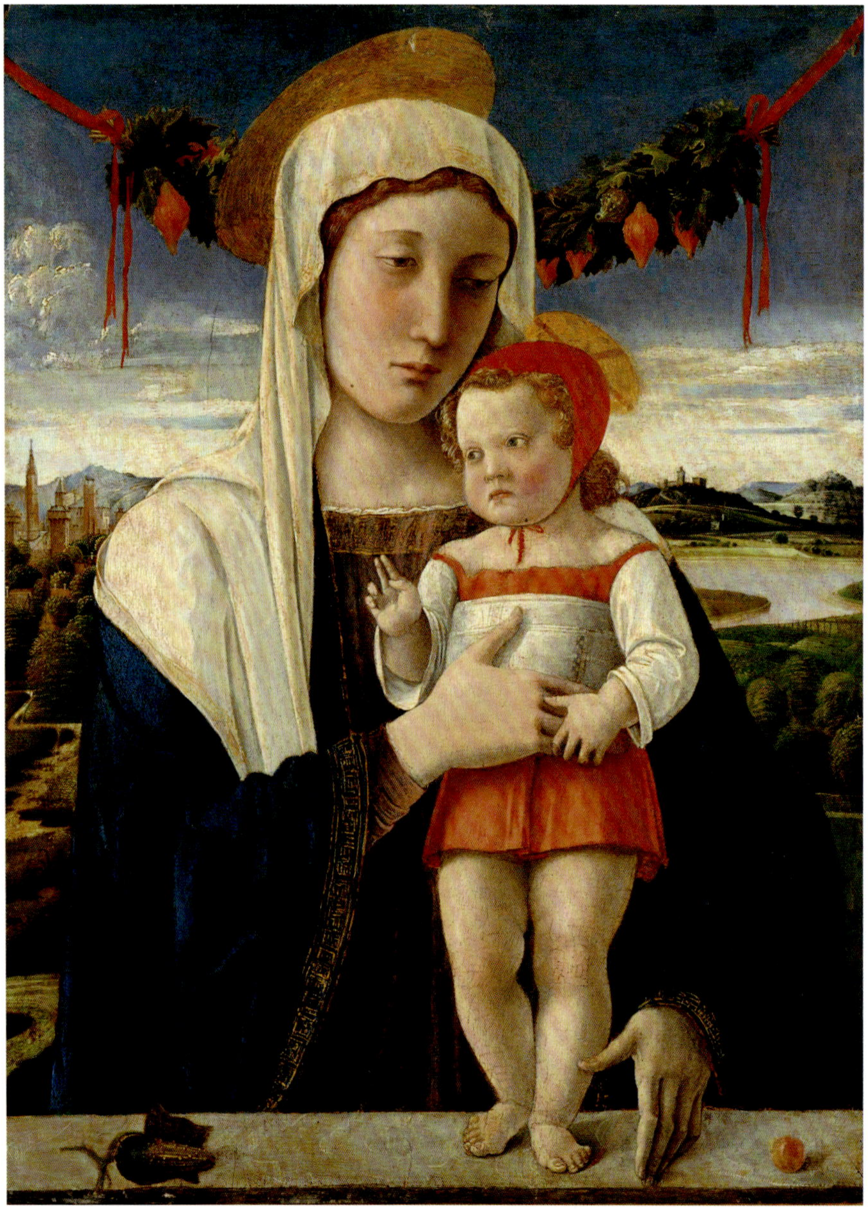

Bellini: innovation within tradition

We know little for certain about Bellini's personal faith. He certainly had strong connections with ecclesiastical and humanistic circles. He was observant, a parishioner at San Lio and subsequently Santa Marina in the *sestiere* (district) of Castello, and a member of several confraternities.[2] Fra Teodoro, the Dominican theologian whom Bellini portrayed as Saint Dominic in one of his final portraits (fig. 210), and who is documented in the monastery of Santi Giovanni e Paolo,[3] was possibly his spiritual adviser. Ultimately Bellini chose to be buried in the same church, clothed either in the simple robes of the Scuola Grande di San Marco or of a tertiary (a lay

FIG. 175
GIOVANNI BELLINI
The Virgin and Child (Lehman Madonna), about 1459
Egg tempera, oil and gold on panel, 53.9 × 39.9 cm
The Metropolitan Museum of Art, New York. The Robert Lehman Collection (1975.1.81)

associate of a monastic order).[4] The minutiae of detail in his many devotional paintings (whether altarpieces or paintings for a more private context), the seriousness of the images and his desire at the end of his life to be properly buried all suggest that Bellini had a strong, and probably very orthodox, faith. This undoubtedly informed his artistic production, but how it did so is impossible to reconstruct with any certainty.

What is clear, however, is that like other painters in Venice, he focused enormous energy on creating Christian art for a domestic setting. Venetian art of the fifteenth century was in some respects very traditional, its iconographic and visual conventions deeply indebted to Byzantine precedent. Yet, within the limited compositional range imposed by this connection,[5] no one painted the Virgin and Child with more variety or more often than Giovanni Bellini. Indeed, in purely statistical terms, the largest number of his surviving works are small-scale paintings of the Virgin and Child intended for use and display in the home.[6] To look at Bellini's Madonnas together, however, is not to look at a series of copies or repetitious work. Instead, it is to see a strikingly varied group of images, whose full interest and ingenuity is only apparent through close inspection and reflection.

What attracted patrons to Bellini was probably the combination of tradition in format and iconography, and a sophisticated execution. His images of the Virgin and Child are incredibly simple. The majority consist of Mary and her son, placed on or behind a parapet or an arch, sometimes in front of a cloth of honour and often with a landscape behind them. Sometimes this landscape is continuous, across the picture plane, but more commonly it exhibits significant differences on either side of the holy figures. Bellini's adherence to the visual traditions of Venice and his exposure to Byzantine images in paintings or in mosaic – including cult images such as the *Virgin Praying* on the south façade of the Basilica of San Marco and the icon of the *Madonna Nicopeia*, ('Victory'), looted from Constantinople in the Fourth Crusade of 1204 and kept in the chapel bearing her name in the left transept of the Basilica as well as contemporary paintings in the Byzantine style – enabled him to see how variety could be created within an apparently limited template.[7]

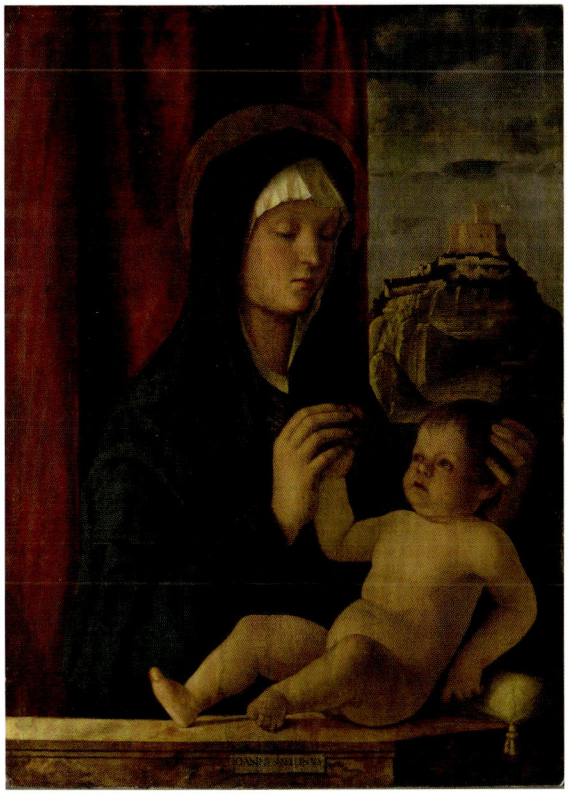

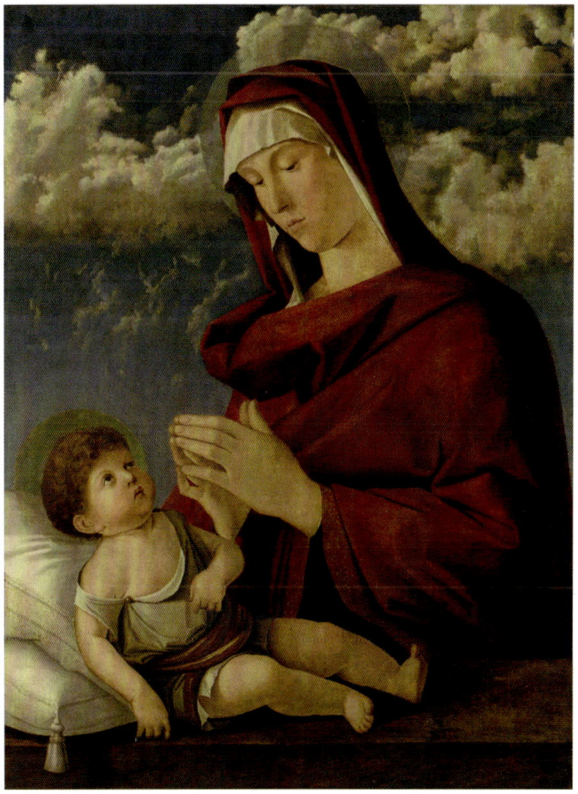

FIG. 176
GIOVANNI BELLINI and studio
The Virgin and Child, probably 1480–1500
Oil on panel, 78.7 × 58.4 cm
The National Gallery, London (NG 3913)

FIG. 177
Studio of GIOVANNI BELLINI
The Virgin and Child, perhaps about 1475
Oil on panel, 81.9 × 62.2 cm
The National Gallery, London (NG 2901)

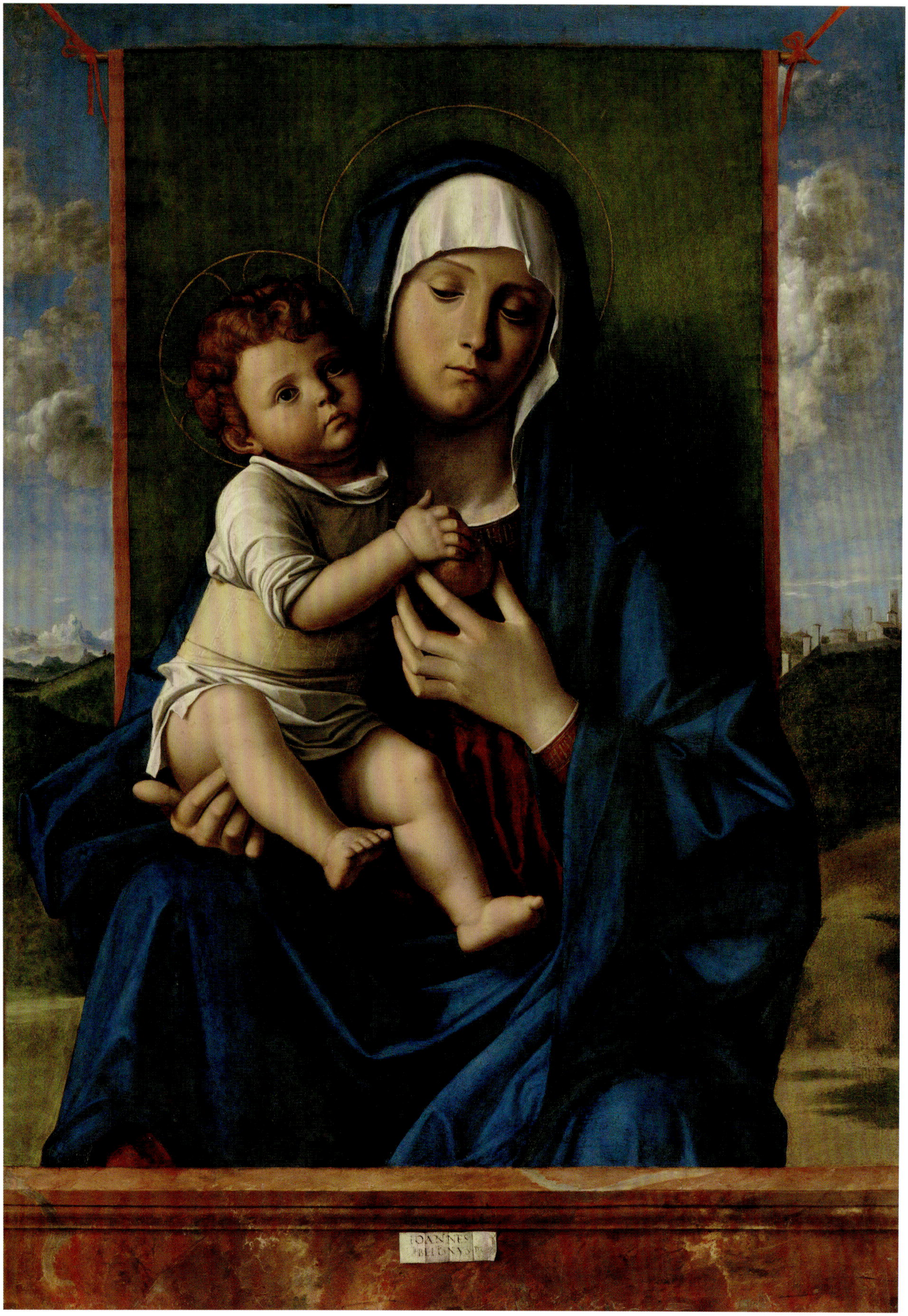

FIG. 178
GIOVANNI BELLINI
The Virgin and Child
(*'The Madonna of the Pomegranate'*),
possibly 1488–9
Oil (?) on poplar, 91.3 × 65.3 cm
The National Gallery, London (NG 280)

FIG. 179
GIOVANNI BELLINI
The Virgin and Child, about 1475
Oil on poplar, 76 × 54.2 cm
Gemäldegalerie, Staatliche Museen
zu Berlin (10A)

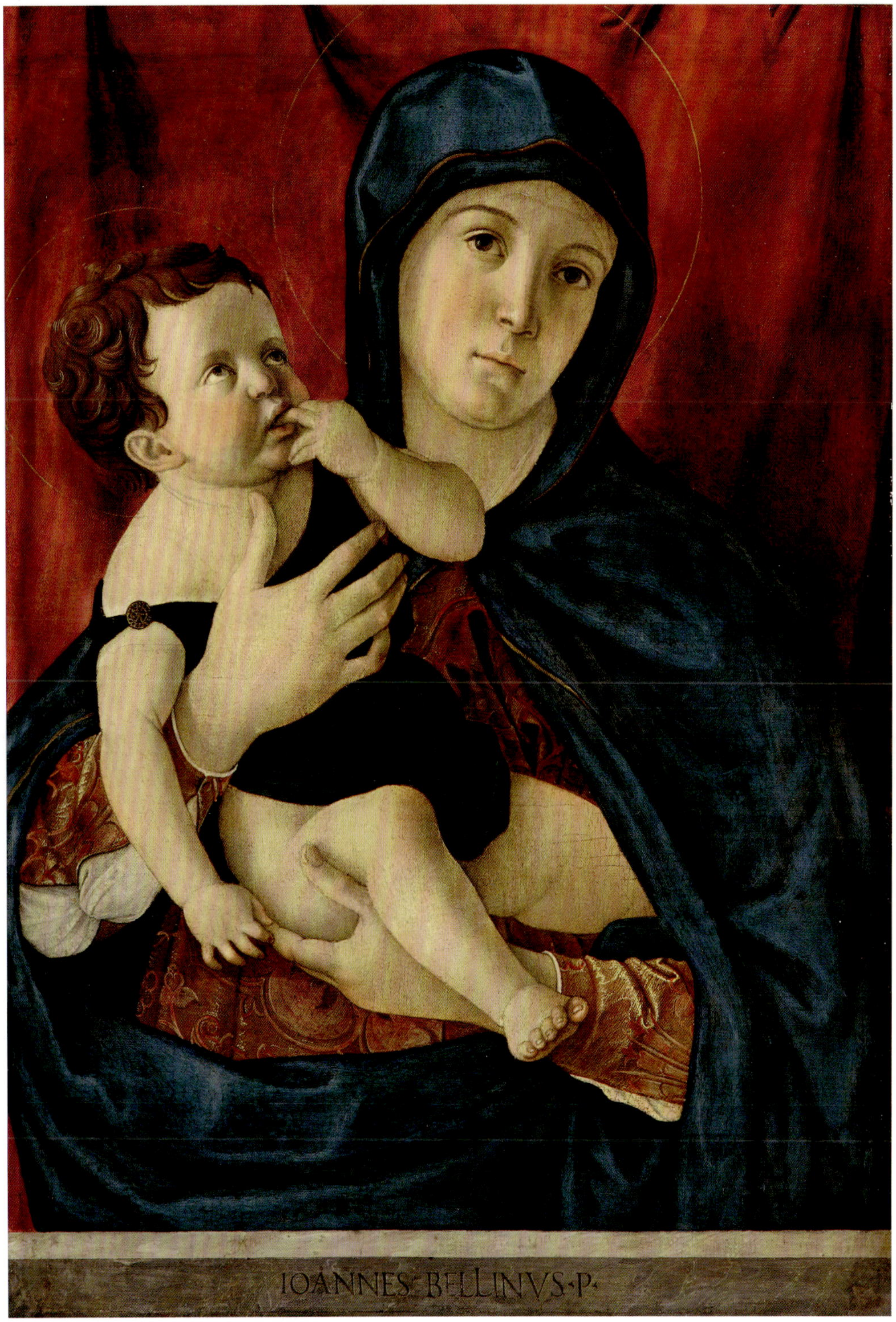

FIG. 180
GIOVANNI BELLINI
Madonna of the Meadow, about 1500–5
Oil on synthetic panel, transferred from wood, 66.5 × 85.1 cm
The National Gallery, London (NG 599)

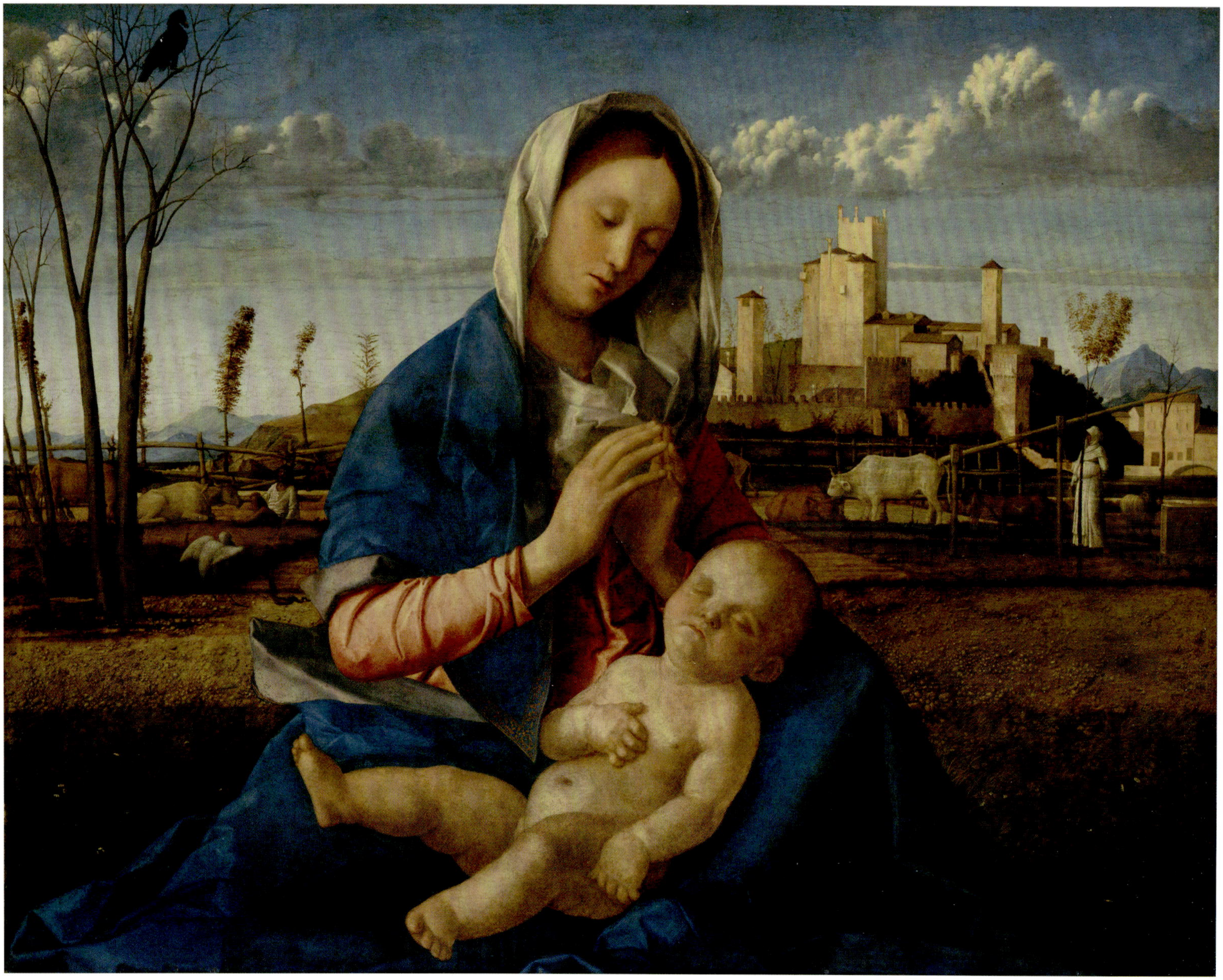

Giovanni's first paintings of the subject are indebted not just to the Byzantine tradition that inspired all Venetian painters, but also to the artists that surrounded him, including his father Jacopo, his brother Gentile and his brother-in-law Mantegna (fig. 186). Although most of the small-scale devotional works that Jacopo painted and devised have been lost, those few surviving pictures, such as the *Virgin and Child* in the Accademia, Venice emphasise the personal relationship and emotional connection between Mary and her son; in this instance she places her left hand on his shoulder, and her right hand on his knee. We can see the impact that this, or a closely related composition, had on Giovanni Bellini in his *Lehman Madonna* (fig. 175), which shows the Christ Child on a parapet, to the right of his mother.

Mantegna's images of the Virgin Mary also made an impression on Bellini – even though he worked relatively little in this genre. In Bellini's *Lehman Madonna*, the arched garland above the Virgin's head recalls Mantegna's master Squarcione, and Mantegna's own *San Zeno Altarpiece* (fig. 252).[8] Bellini's *Davis Madonna* (fig. 111) is yet more deeply indebted to Mantegna. The linearity of the figures, the clarity of the cold, even light (atypical of Bellini's subsequent work) and the drapery folds of the Virgin's cloak are all indicative of Mantegna's impact on the younger painter.[9]

Giovanni Bellini combined iconographic conservatism with sophisticated execution. His Virgins may follow a traditional form, but they have weight and gravitas. They are often very strongly lit and placed against Arcadian landscapes,[10] and were endlessly copied: no one, perhaps, in the field of Christian images for private consumption, was as much replicated as Bellini in the fifteenth century, within Venice and her domains, including by artists still active in the 'Greek' manner.[11] Bellini's pupils were unusually loyal to him, and often signed their paintings as such, many years after they had started to work as independent artists. As a result,

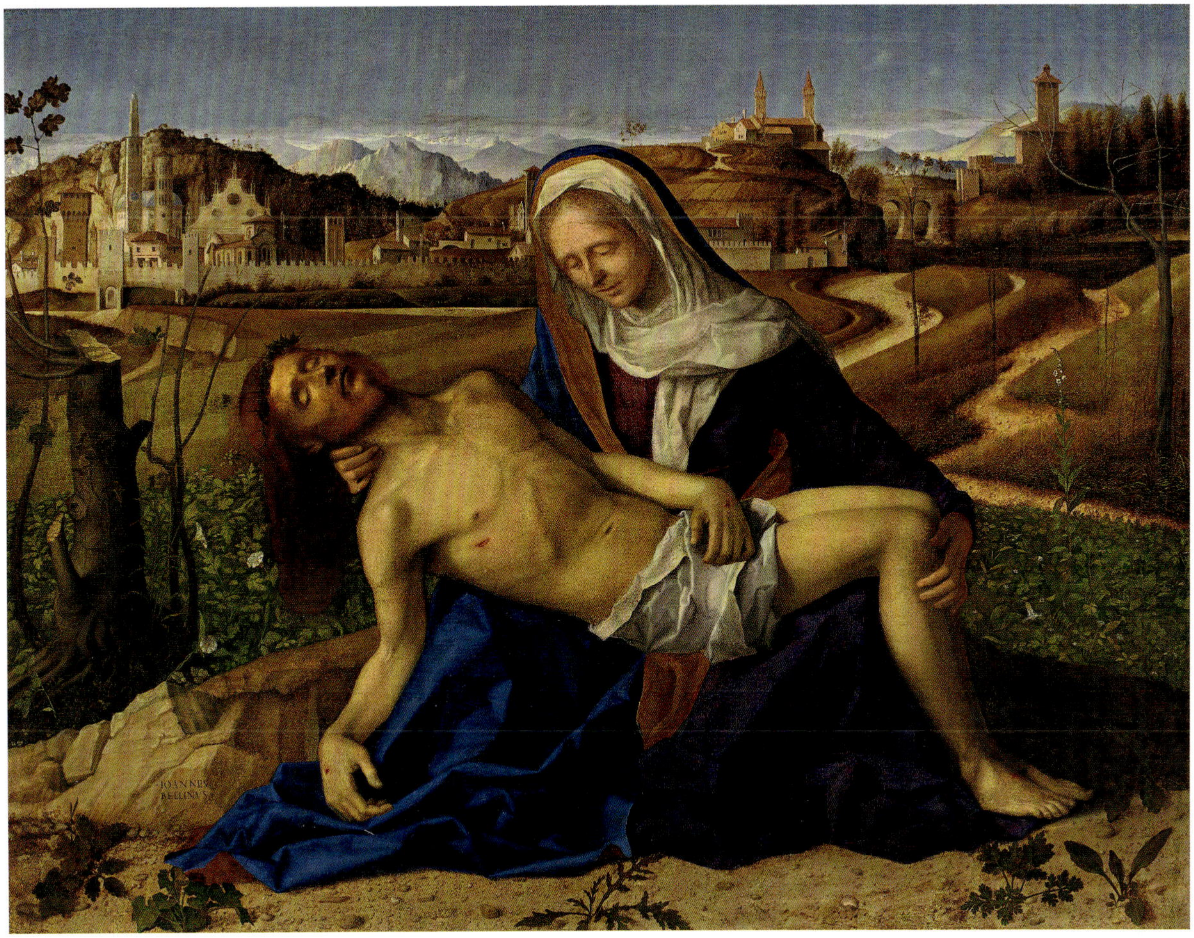

FIG. 181
GIOVANNI BELLINI
Pietà (*Pietà Donà dalle Rose*), about 1505
Oil on panel, 65 × 87 cm
Gallerie dell'Accademia, Venice (883)

GIOVANNI BELLINI,
detail from *Madonna of the Meadow* (FIG. 180)

a variety of artistic manners can be associated with the inscription 'made by Giovanni Bellini'.[12]

It can be very difficult to attribute many of the small-scale Madonnas which proclaim that they are the work of Giovanni Bellini, as many are not – at least according to modern conceptions of authorship – straightforwardly by him, but paintings made in his workshop, under his supervision. For instance, a *Virgin and Child* in the National Gallery (fig. 178) has often been said to be a work of the studio, because of its relationship to a lost full-length painting of *The Virgin and Child Enthroned* (a copy, by the Bellini assistant Francesco Tacconi, is also in the National Gallery's collection).[13] In fact its high artistic quality and costly pigments, and the small but significant changes that were made to the composition during the course of painting, suggest that Bellini was at least intimately involved in its making, if not its sole painter.[14]

Despite the apparent similarity of paintings of the Virgin and Child by Bellini and his workshop, what is often surprising is their difference. Two paintings of the same iconography in the National Gallery's collection, one by Bellini, the other by an associate, make this point.[15] Both depict a toddler Christ reclining on pillows, on the edge of a marble parapet, behind which his mother contemplates her child, her eyes closed as if in prayer. But here the similarity ends. In one painting (fig. 177) Mary is praying, she is dressed in red, the child is in contemporary clothing and the scene is placed before a backdrop of a blue sky with scudding clouds. The same formula is used to different effect in the other painting (fig. 176): Mary, in deep ultramarine blue, stands before a red curtain, partly drawn back to reveal a landscape with a rocky crag. This is topped by a castle, but a large tomb has been hewn out of the rock, which opens immediately above Christ's head. Each of these works seem subtly distinct because of these different elements, the clever and considered use of colour and light and a sophisticated illusionism, as well as the depth of the relationship between the Virgin and Child. Bellini's infants – as in most of his works – are solemn rather than playful, and through their pose, their nakedness or their placement on cold stone, remind the viewer of Christ's ultimate fate on the Cross. Even in paintings such as figs 109 and 179 – which, superficially, are difficult to distinguish from a number of similar works by Bellini – every movement of the Virgin or Child, each interaction and pose, has significance and potential symbolic meaning.[16] While Mantegna's genius lay in his ability to make antiquity and complex intellectual ideas seem believable, that of Bellini was connected to his skill to make the quotidian appear special – even divine – by the power of his brush.

The *Madonna of the Meadow* (fig. 180), one of Bellini's greatest paintings of the early sixteenth century, is a highly typical work in its exceptional beauty and complexity, even if everything looks straightforward at the first glance. Mary, seated directly on the ground in the persona of the Madonna of Humility, cradles her sleeping son in her lap. Although he is alive, and a baby, there is some ambiguity as to whether he is dead and (because of his relative size) almost an adult. The world might be changing, yet life continues as it always has: cows rise and are taken to the fields by herders, water is drawn from the well and a bird scares off a snake that is twice its size. There is something calming about this continuity, even in the face of a deep sleep that resembles death.[17]

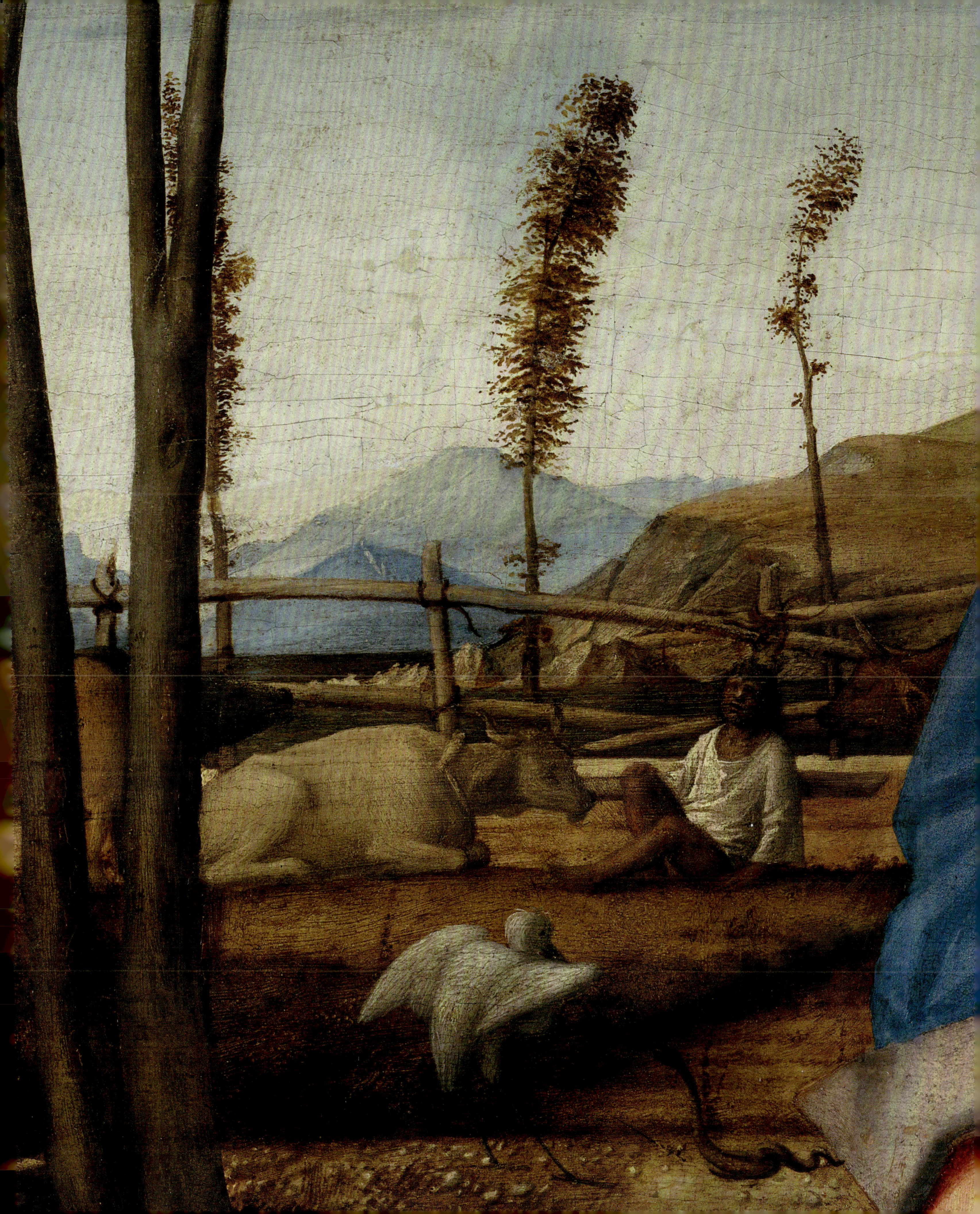

Mantegna: an infrequent painter of Madonnas

Mantegna would have learnt to make devotional images of the Virgin and Child in the Paduan workshop of his master, Francesco Squarcione. Remarkably few paintings by Squarcione survive – suggesting that he was more an impresario than a practising artist – but those that have, along with the many works by his pupils, are unusually consistent in their typology. Of all the 'Squarcionesque' compositions, that of the Virgin and Child is the most common. Squarcione's *Virgin and Child* in Berlin (fig. 79) shows the sacred figures in profile, positioned behind a parapet.[18] A foreshortened piece of fruit attempts to convey the illusion that this is real, rather than merely represented. A candelabra in the classical style at the far left, and festoons of ribbons, fruit and foliage placed, like an arch of honour, around the Virgin and Child are details that are replicated in the production of many of Squarcione's pupils, including Marco Zoppo (fig. 167) and Carlo Crivelli, many decades after they had left his 'Academy'.

It is possible that Mantegna, whose break with Squarcione was acrimonious, purposely avoided this subject because of its association with his master. Certainly, there are fewer surviving Madonnas by Mantegna than by practically any other Renaissance artist. But the more likely explanation for this is that, as an artist working first in a university city, and secondly at a court, the demands on his time were somewhat different to those on his brother-in-law in the Republic of Venice. As an artist who was recognised from a young age as an innovator, rather than a representative of a pictorial tradition, those patrons who commissioned small-scale paintings from him sought works that emphasised his salient qualities of innovation and invention. If Bellini's genius was in the reinterpretation of conventional formulae so that they seemed both respectful of tradition and in keeping with the modern age, Mantegna's was in the creation of new subjects and motifs.

Given that Mantegna was 'saved' from Squarcione by his association with the Bellini family and their circle, it is perhaps not surprising that his only surviving Paduan Madonna, *The Virgin and Child with Seraphim and Cherubim* (fig. 186), which must date shortly after his marriage to Nicolosia Bellini, is very Bellinian in its appearance. Mary's encirclement by arches of angels is paralleled in two paintings by Jacopo Bellini of a similar date. Yet the painting also shows characteristics that Mantegna was to develop further in later works, notably a considerable originality and depth of feeling. These qualities reflect a starting point from the sculptural reliefs

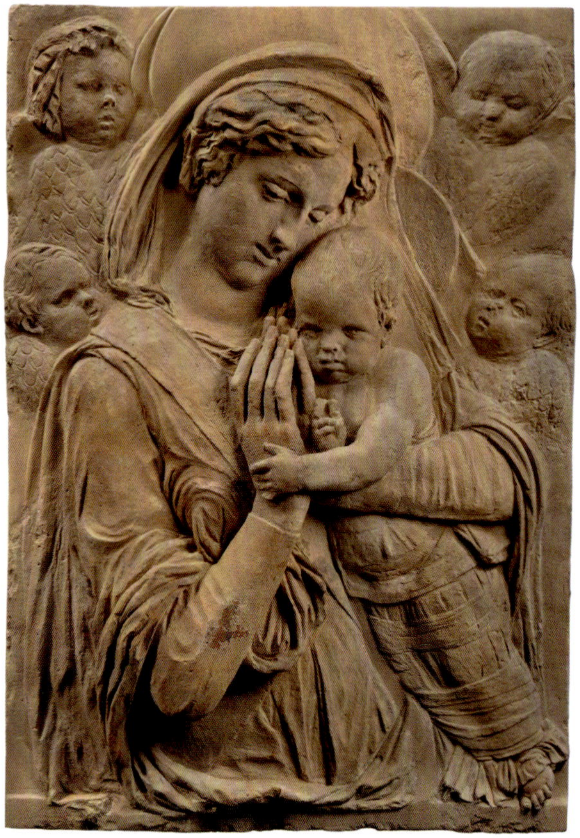

FIG. 182
DONATELLO
The Virgin and Child with Four Angels, about 1435–40
Terracotta, 99 × 69 × 20 cm
Skulpturensammlung und Museum für Byzantinische Kunst, Staatliche Museen zu Berlin (54)

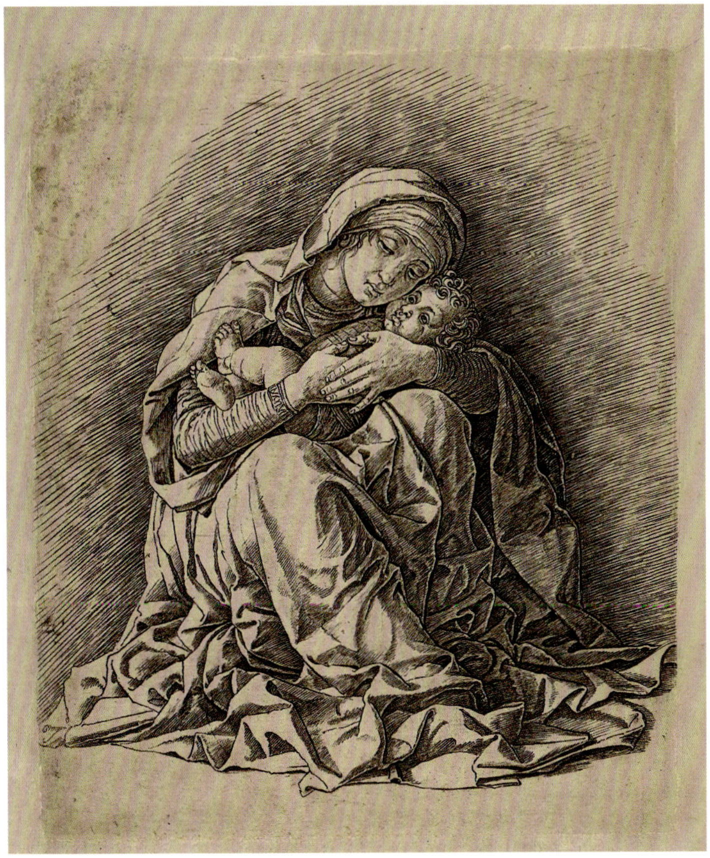

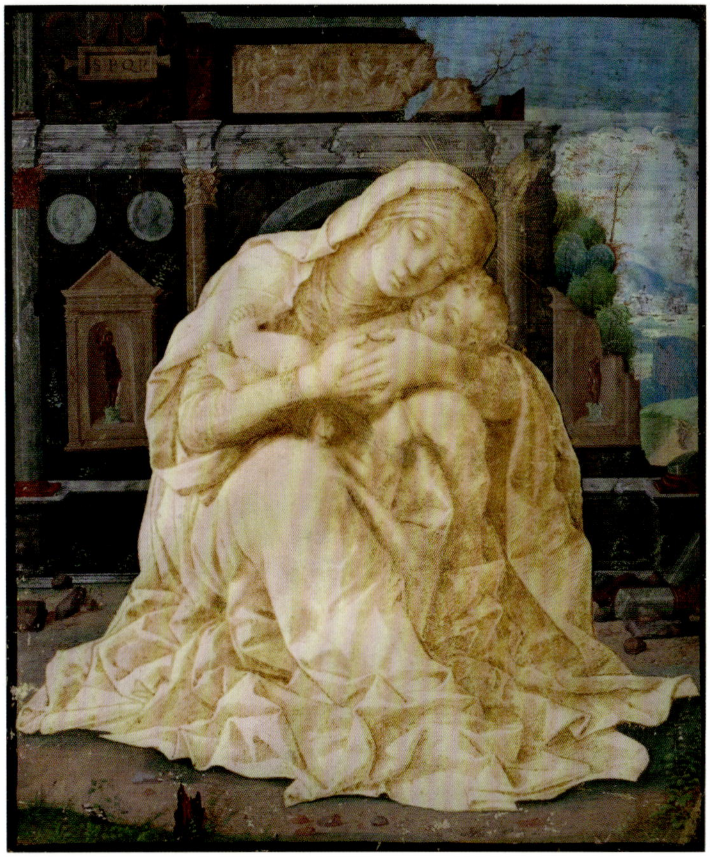

FIG. 183
Studio of ANDREA MANTEGNA
The Virgin and Child, about 1480–5
Engraving, 24.7 × 21 cm
The British Museum, London (1856,0712.1072)

FIG. 184
ANDREA MANTEGNA and FRANCESCO MARMITTA
Madonna of Tenderness, 1491
Egg tempera on panel, 24 × 22 cm
Private collection, on loan to the Musei Civici di Padova

of Donatello.[19] The close relationship between mother and son in many of Donatello's Paduan works of the 1440s and 1450s inspired Mantegna to attempt a similar naturalism and emotional engagement. Donatello's terracotta of *The Virgin and Child with Four Angels* in the Skulpturensammlung in Berlin (fig. 182), or a derivation of it, was another powerful model for this painting, although Mantegna has reversed the composition. As in Mantegna's probable, Donatellian model, the child is partially naked, and his feet are placed illusionistically on the parapet in the foreground, where (in the painting) they cast a small shadow.

Mantegna's depictions of the Virgin and Child are striking for their originality. The most significant was not a painting but an engraving (fig. 183), which David Landau has called 'one of the most touching depictions of the Virgin and Child in the history of art'.[20] The sensitive and sophisticated modulation of light and shade, achieved through a full understanding of the possibilities of dry-point and of engraving, is exceptional. Here, Mantegna responds to the Byzantine iconic type of the Madonna of Tenderness, and Christ and his mother's cheeks touch. But this Virgin is sitting on the ground, as a Madonna of Humility (Mantegna was no doubt aware of Jacopo Bellini's painting of this subject for the Este court in Ferrara),[21] as she cradles her son. Christ is partially swaddled, but his legs are moving and his eyes are open. It is likely that this image can be identified with the 'quadretino' or 'little picture' that Mantegna mentioned in a letter of 1491 to the Marquess of Mantua, Francesco Gonzaga.[22] In 1510, the post-mortem inventory of Ludovico III Gonzaga mentions 'uno stampo de rame cum la effigie de la Madona suso cum el putino in brazo', which must be the plate for this print.[23] This was certainly the most directly copied of Mantegna's devotional works. A partially autograph variation on vellum, discovered in the early 2000s (fig. 184), has also been identified as the 'little picture' of Mantegna's letter

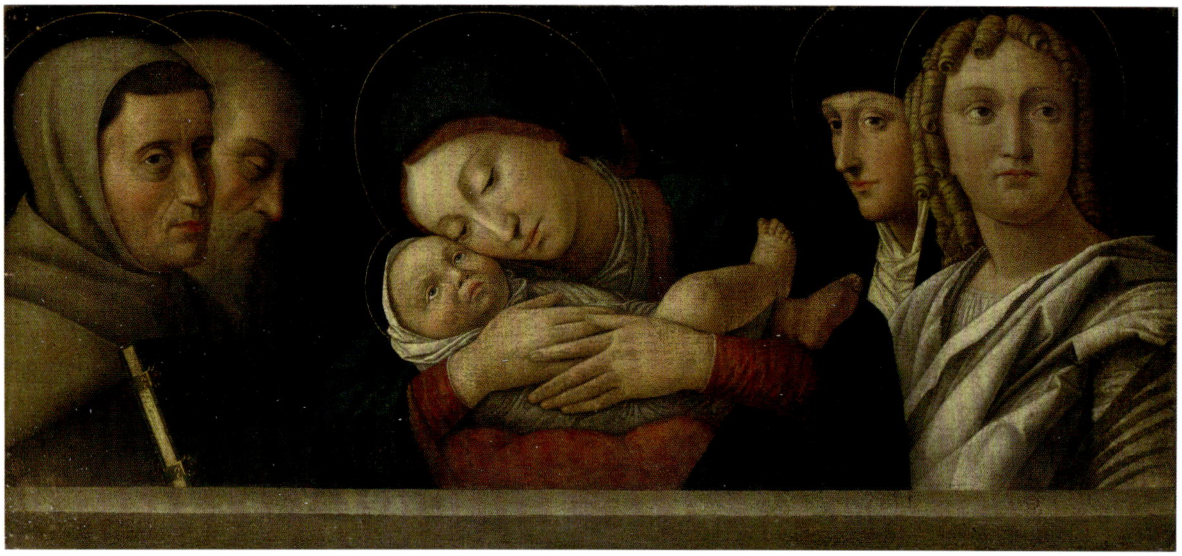

FIG. 185
FRANCESCO BONSIGNORI
The Virgin and Child with Four Saints, about 1490–1510
Oil on canvas,
48.3 × 106.7 cm
The National Gallery, London
(NG 3091)

of 1491. The background, however, which shows a classical architectural fantasy, based on the Arco di Gavi and the Colosseum, may not be by Mantegna, but the work of a miniaturist working under his direction.[24]

A frieze-like picture of four saints and the Virgin and Child by the Veronese painter Francesco Bonsignori (fig. 185), active in Mantua from at least 1492, but which probably dates from after Mantegna's death, directly copies Mantegna's print (although, strangely, the hands of the Virgin are not reversed, unlike the rest of the engraving). It is highly likely also that Bellini knew Mantegna's invention. Its emotional tenor, and the motif of the Virgin sitting both regally and humbly on the bare ground, finds a neat parallel in two of Bellini's most original devotional works of the early sixteenth century – the *Madonna of the Meadow* (fig. 180) and the *Pietà Donà dalle Rose* (fig. 181). In no sense are these paintings 'copies' of Mantegna; yet it seems likely that Bellini reached his pictorial solutions in part from the stimulus of Mantegna's composition.

A work that is even more touching in its simplicity is the small *Virgin and Child* (*Simon Madonna*; fig. 188)[25] in which Mantegna emphasises the melancholy of the mother, who knows that her son will die young. One senses in this picture Mantegna's truthful observation of a mother with her baby, oblivious to the world, and absorbed (or just resigned) to her infant's sleep, not wishing to do anything that might wake him from his slumbers. There is no halo to identify the mother as the Virgin Mary, and indeed it is only prior knowledge of Christian iconography that enables the observer to convert this image of mother and child into a sacred subject. The painting functions, therefore, both as a depiction of a mother and child, and as a devotional picture. The close-up view means that we focus on Mary's face, as she tenderly encircles and protects her sleeping child, who nestles on her front, his head abutting her chin. At the same time, Mary looks pensive and thoughtful, as if she knows the fate that will befall her son, enabling the viewer (if they wished) to simultaneously contemplate Christ's passion and death.

Where Mantegna and Bellini both experimented in the years around 1500 was in the development of small-scale, multi-figural and non-narrative compositions of the Virgin and Child or the Holy Family, sometimes accompanied by saints, and sometimes at specific moments in the Christological story (including figs 134, 135, 136, 187, 189, 190). These pictures often melded together familiar motifs from other works by each artist, meaning that they could be easily identified as in Mantegna or Bellini's manner. For example, the slight twist in the body of the Christ Child in fig. 190 is indebted to a three-dimensional young male figure Mantegna had already invented, recorded in the small bronze of a *Standing Boy* by a follower of Mantegna in the Metropolitan Museum of Art, New York.

These 'sacra conversazioni' became commonplace in North Italian paintings of the early sixteenth century.[26] A celebrated Bellinian composition of Christ's

Circumcision, of which the most likely candidate to be even close to Giovanni himself is the version in the National Gallery (fig. 134), has a formal relationship to Mantegna's and Bellini's earlier paintings of *The Presentation of Christ in the Temple* (figs 128, 132), although in this case no ledge or frame divides the viewer from the sacred figures. The connection with the *Presentations* is unsurprising because the Circumcision follows this story in the New Testament. Bellini's *Circumcision* – relatively unusually for him – takes place against a monochrome background. This is a much more common characteristic of Mantegna, and it is particularly reminiscent of the more or less contemporary *Adoration of the Magi* (fig. 136), in which a similar absence of a framing device encourages us to see the scene as taking place in our world.[27] In Mantegna's painting, the oldest king's body is cut off, and we look into the picture at his level. Bellini adopted a pictorial device that also brings the viewer into the picture's space, in the action of the priest's assistant drawing up Simeon's cloak.

Mantegna's *Adoration* and Bellini's *Circumcision* are not formally connected – unlike the earlier *Presentations* – but their analogous monumental and solemn figural compositions, and their inter-connection of temporal and sacred space – suggest more than a chance relationship. This had, however, developed from the artists' earlier years, as neither felt any longer any requirement to copy or mimic the work of his brother-in-law. While Mantegna's final private devotional paintings, such as the two Holy Families with saints (figs 189, 190), are intentionally flat and matt, those of Bellini, including *The Virgin and Child with Saints Catherine and Mary Magdalene* (fig. 187), reflect his interest in the glossy, rich and artificial colour that oil paint could provide. Age, apparently, had brought an artistic relationship which both understood and valued difference. Mantegna and Bellini's final private devotional works exemplify their intrinsic artistic qualities, no longer made in a spirit of competition – implicit or otherwise – but in an appreciation of what made them distinctive and unique.

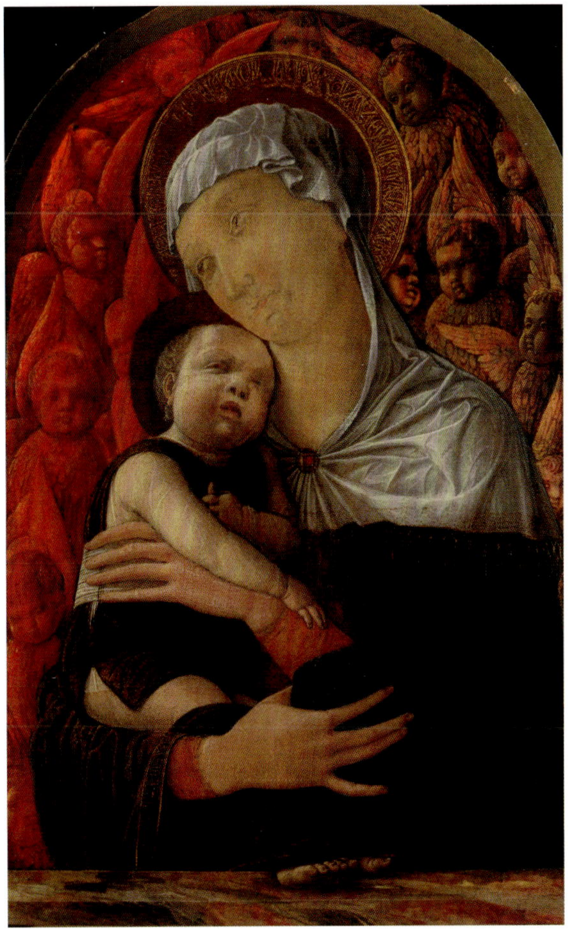

FIG. 186
ANDREA MANTEGNA
The Virgin and Child with Seraphim and Cherubim (Butler Madonna), about 1454
Egg tempera and gold on panel, 44.1 × 28.6 cm
The Metropolitan Museum of Art, New York. The Friedsam Collection, Bequest of Michael Friedsam, 1931 (32.100.97)

FIG. 187
GIOVANNI BELLINI
The Virgin and Child with Saints Catherine and Mary Magdalene, about 1490
Oil on panel, 58.8 × 108 cm
Gallerie dell'Accademia, Venice (613)

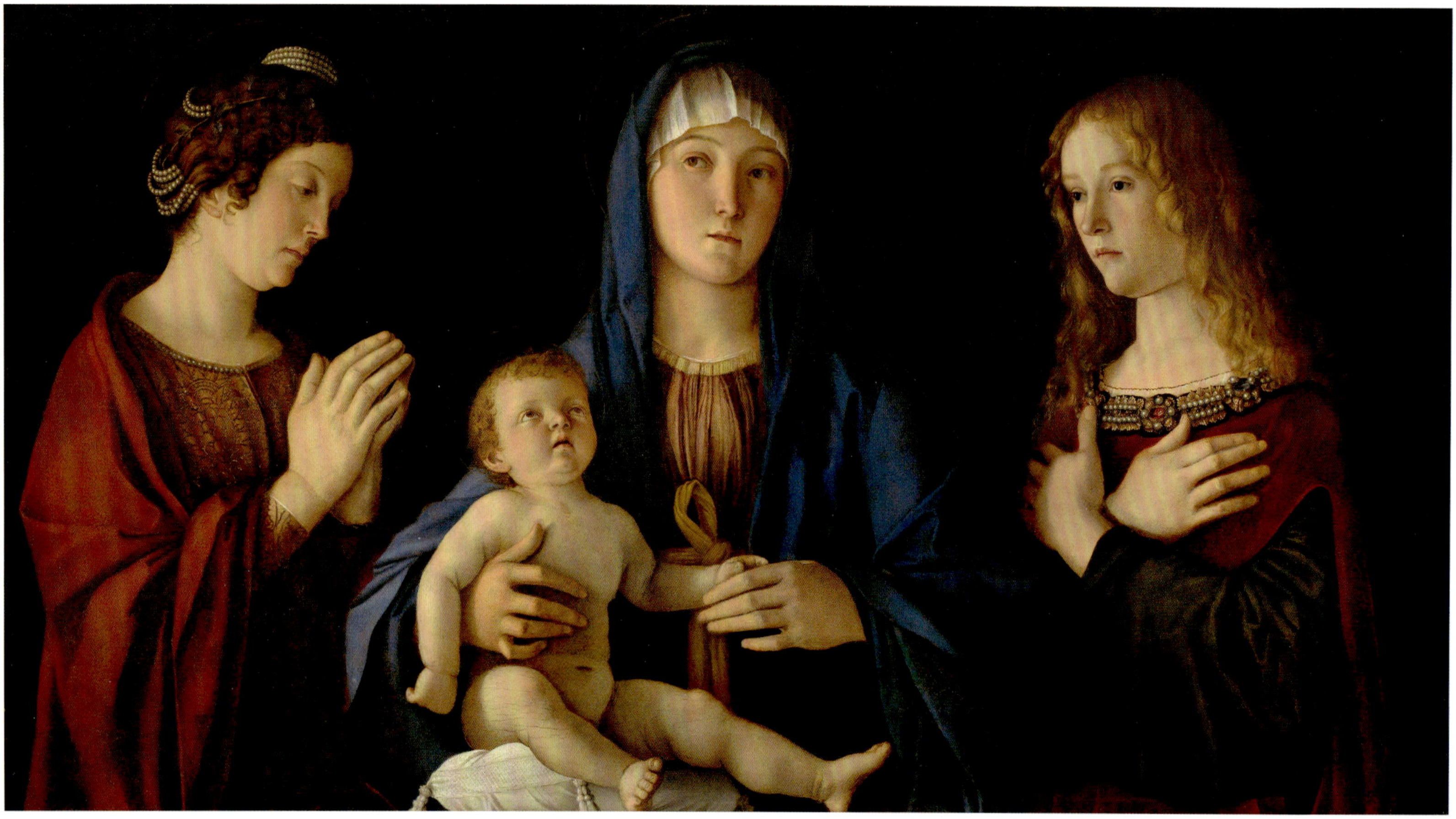

FIG. 188
ANDREA MANTEGNA
The Virgin and Child (Simon Madonna), about 1455–60
Glue size on canvas, 48.4 × 32.2 cm
Gemäldegalerie, Staatliche Museen zu Berlin (s 5)

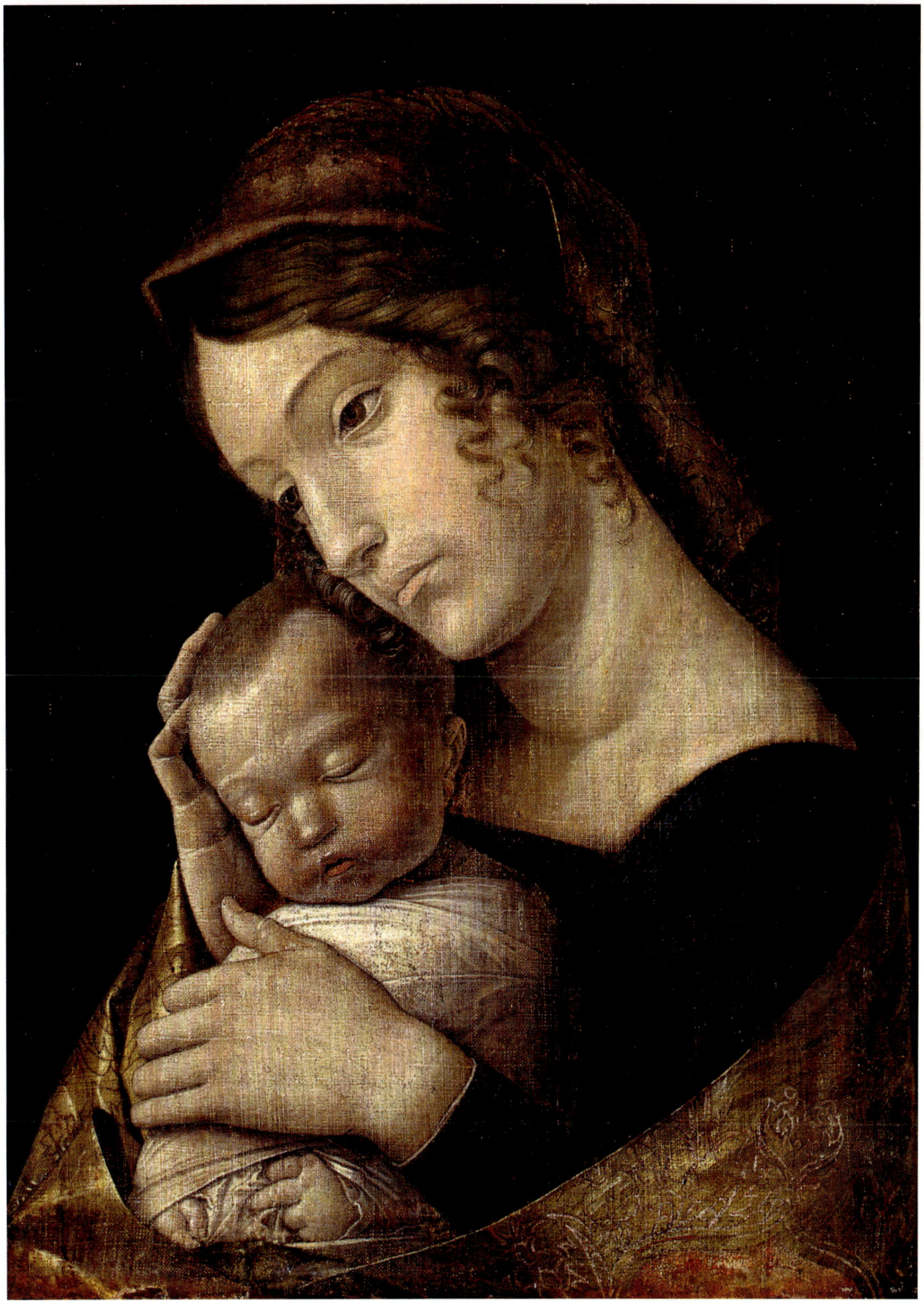

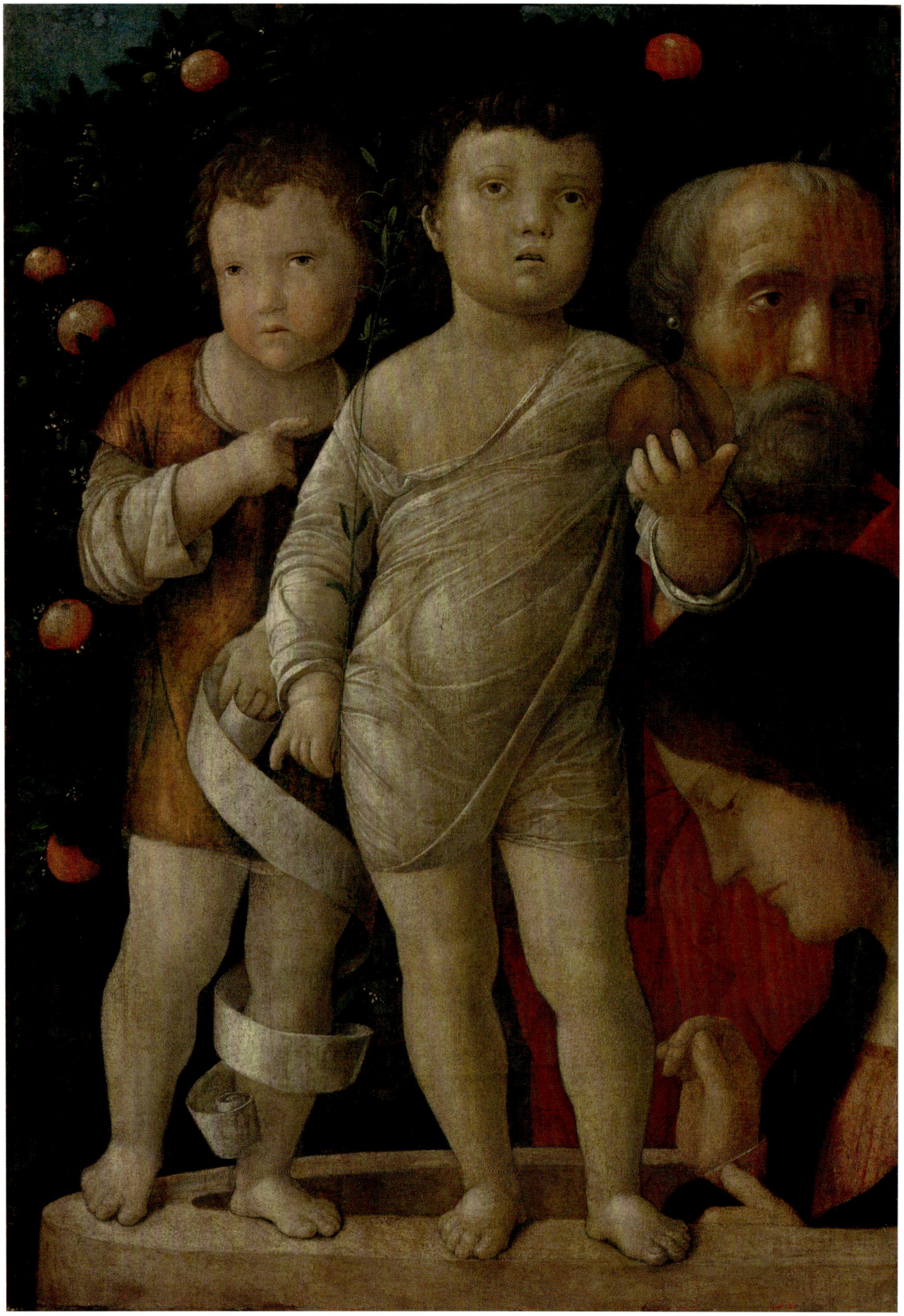

FIG. 189
ANDREA MANTEGNA
The Holy Family with Saint John the Baptist, about 1500
Glue size on canvas, 71.1 × 50.8 cm
The National Gallery, London (NG 5641)

FIG. 190
ANDREA MANTEGNA
The Holy Family, about 1490–1500
Egg tempera with some oil on canvas, 75 × 61.5 cm
Gemäldegalerie Alte Meister, Staatliche Kunstsammlungen, Dresden (51)

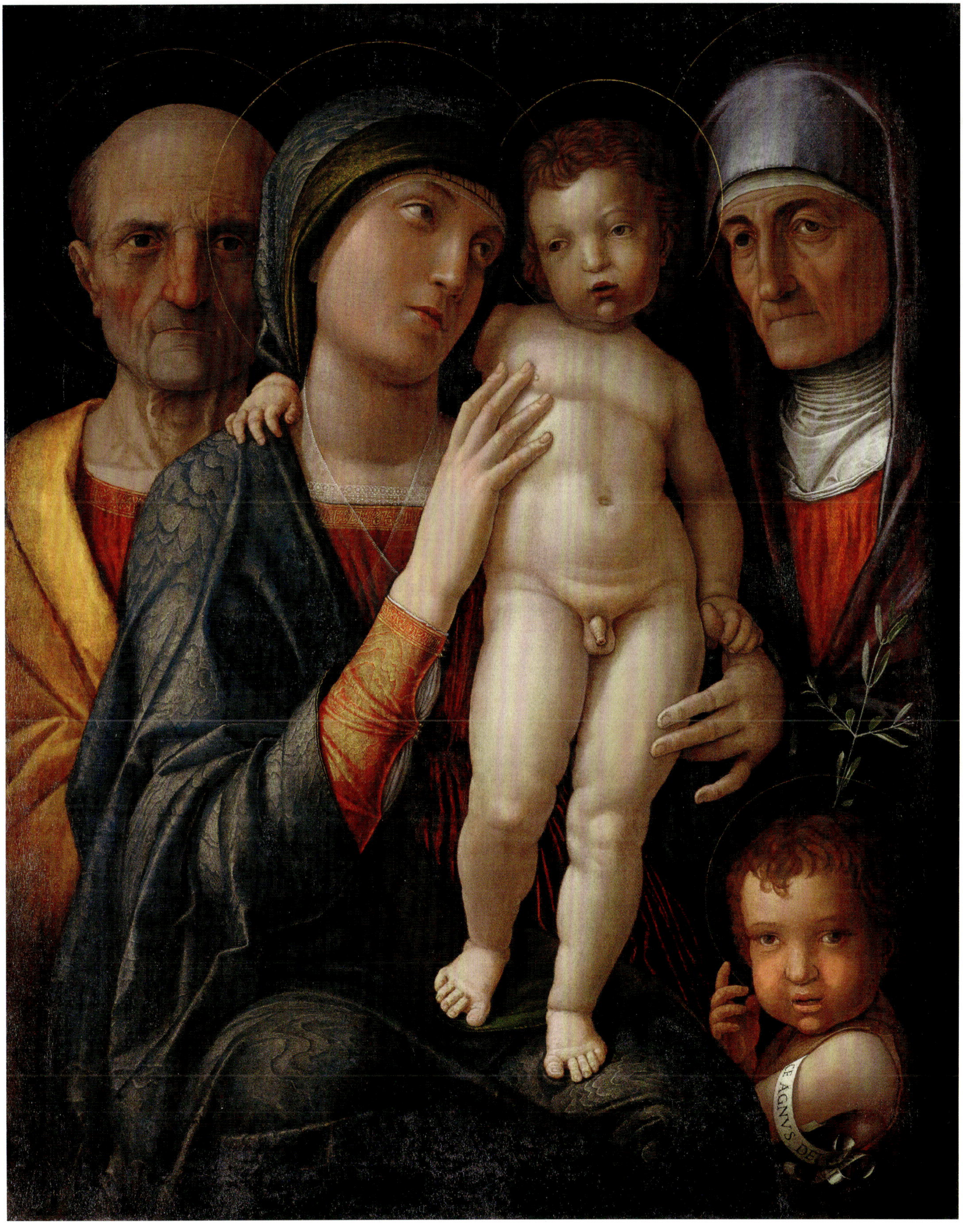
CE AGNVS DE

Shaping Sacrifice: The Body in the Work of Mantegna and Bellini

SARAH VOWLES

In the years around 1460, both Mantegna and Bellini produced works which placed the isolated, exposed human body at centre stage. In Bellini's *Blood of the Redeemer* of about 1465 (fig. 192) and Mantegna's *Saint Sebastian* of about 1459–60 (fig. 193), the young artists confronted the prevailing conventions of anatomy and began to explore its potential in very different ways, growing nonetheless from the same source.

There are marked similarities between *The Blood of the Redeemer* and *Saint Sebastian*. Both show the main figure at full length, exposed to the gaze of the viewer to emphasise the nature of bodily sacrifice. Both subjects are shown in a state of martyrdom and yet also in a state of triumph: Mantegna's Sebastian is riddled with the arrows, which have as yet failed to kill him, while Bellini's Christ is shown triumphant over death, pressing the blood from his pierced side into a chalice to become the wine of the Mass. Both artists seek to move away from the tradition of showing religious figures at full-length against a plain or gold ground, which at this date was still used in polyptych panels such as those in the Church of the Carità altarpieces (fig. 84), which Bellini must have been working on at much the same time. Instead, they situate the body within nature, without fully integrating it into the landscape. Both present the sacred scene staged upon a chequered paved platform, bordered with a low wall, and both emphasise the triumph of Christianity over the antique, which nevertheless offers the chance to include erudite references to classical iconography.

The dating of *The Blood of the Redeemer* is least problematic, as it is demonstrably an early work in which Bellini's anatomy shows the marked influence of the Paduan tradition. Although he drew on an already established iconography of the Holy Blood, his representation of the scene introduces new elements drawn from other sources.[1] The emaciated figure with its marked horseshoe-shaped ribcage and defined stomach muscles, its wiry arms and legs and awkward contrapposto, is of a very similar type to Mantegna's *Saint Sebastian* and indicates a form of exchange between the two artists at this period. Giles Robertson has argued that Christ's face, which appears gaunt and austere in comparison to Mantegna's heads of the same period, represents Bellini's awareness of Northern European painting, in particular that of Rogier van der Weyden and his studio.[2]

Nevertheless, clear differences between the pictures show that the two young artists already had different aesthetic priorities. Mantegna describes every detail of the scene, from the rocky wall lining the road in the left background to the streaks of marble in the column. He even includes the fanciful figure of a knight appearing from one cloud, which may be an erudite allusion to the writings of the humanist, Leon Battista Alberti, or the Roman poet Lucretius (fig. 191).[3] On the contrary, Bellini uses sweeps of paint to evoke rather than describe

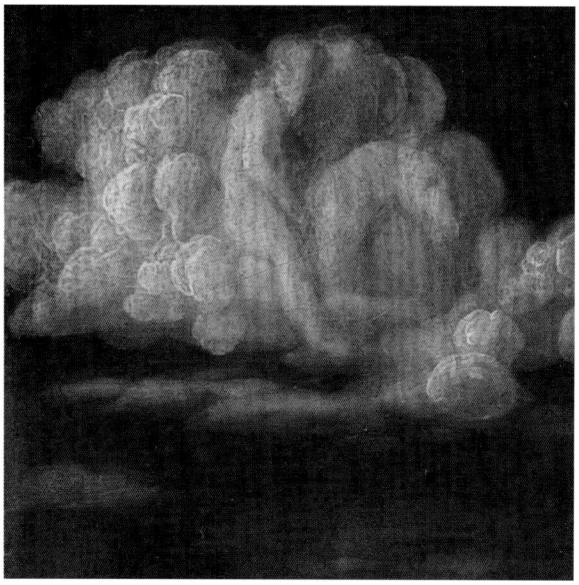

FIG. 191
ANDREA MANTEGNA,
detail from *Saint Sebastian* (FIG. 193)

FIG. 192
GIOVANNI BELLINI
The Blood of the Redeemer, about 1465
Egg tempera on panel, 47.6 × 35.2 cm
The National Gallery, London (NG 1233)

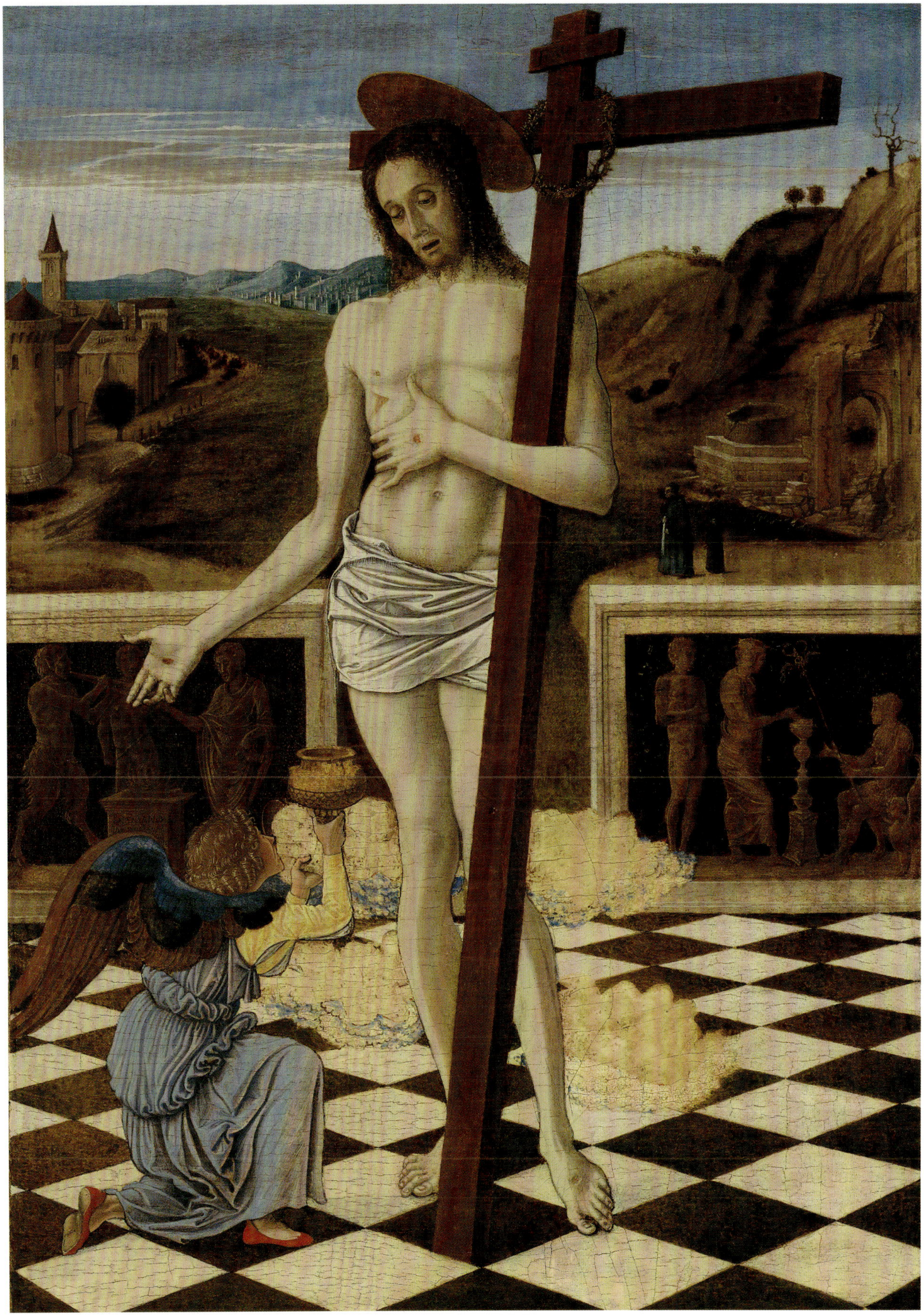

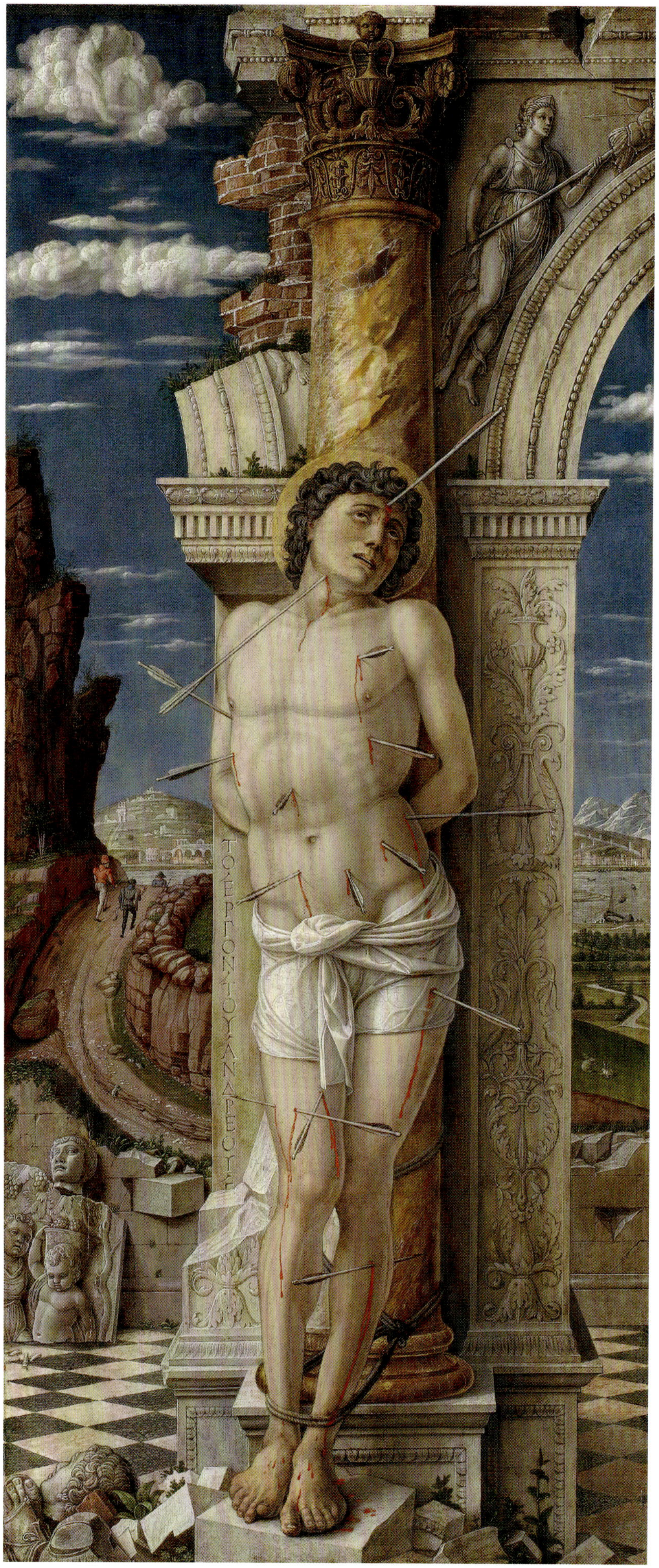

FIG. 193
ANDREA MANTEGNA
Saint Sebastian, about 1459–60
Egg tempera on poplar,
68 × 30 cm
Gemäldegalerie, Kunsthistorisches
Museum, Vienna (GG 301)

FIG. 194
GIOVANNI BELLINI
Saint Sebastian, early 1460s
Brush drawing in brown ink, with touches of pen and ink, heightened with white (mostly oxidised), on pink-red prepared paper, 18.6 × 5.8 cm
The British Museum, London (1895,0915.800r)

landscape, as can best be seen in comparing his treatment of the rocky mountains with those of Mantegna, or his way of painting clouds. Even his handling of more detailed areas, such as Christ's drapery, contrasts with the intricate detail of Sebastian's loincloth, which already shows the 'wet drapery' effect Mantegna would use throughout his career. The contrast between the style of the foreground Christ and the background, which hints at the kind of light-suffused landscapes that would become characteristic of Bellini as a mature painter, does indicate a conscious decision to juxtapose two styles. The difference may be deliberate in order to emphasise Christ's otherworldly nature: neither he nor the angel cast shadows, unlike the corporeal figures of a priest and his assistant seen in the background.

At first glance the tonal range of the two pictures seems very different, with the colours in *Saint Sebastian* appearing much fresher and brighter. Indeed, the cool tones of *The Blood of the Redeemer* have been cited as further proof of Bellini's Northern influences. However, the pigments of Bellini's picture have altered more than those of Mantegna and the pigments have entirely flaked away in the region around Christ's lower legs. Here, once-blue clouds originally contained vermilion heads of cherubs, whose traces can still be seen in the faint underdrawing.

At much the same time as these two works, Bellini himself was exploring the subject of Saint Sebastian, perhaps with a view to preparing the figure for the *Saint Sebastian Tripytch* for the Carità, now in the Accademia (fig. 84). A drawing in the British Museum shows his ideas (fig. 194). The respective dating of this in relation to the Mantegna *Saint Sebastian* (fig. 193) cannot be ascertained with certainty, but it is clear that the two are connected. Bellini's Sebastian stands in a very similar pose, although Mantegna's effortful contrapposto has been simplified: the absence of any arrows suggests that Bellini

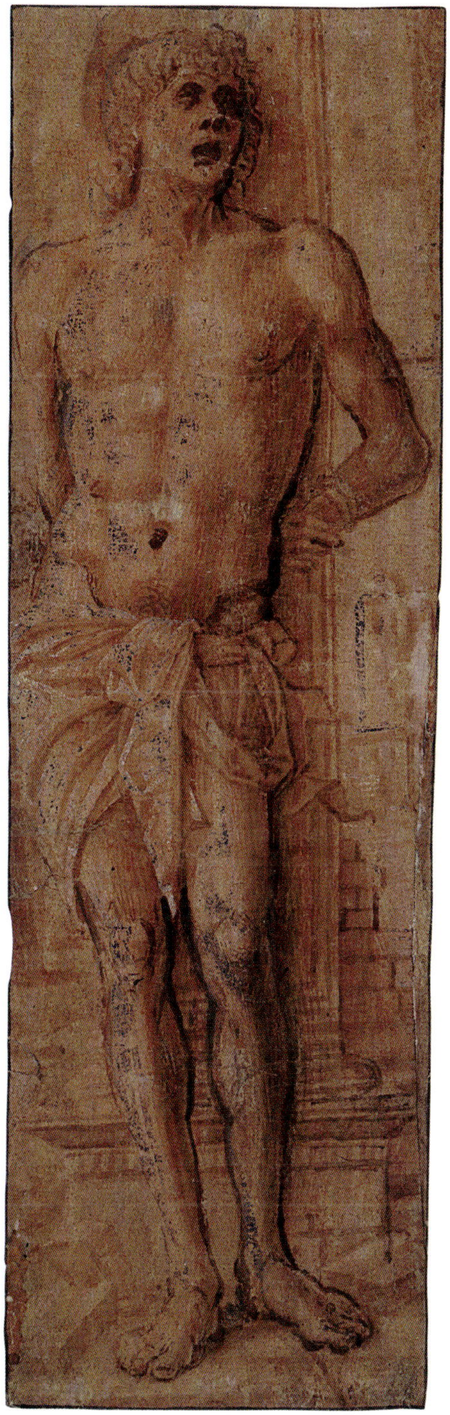

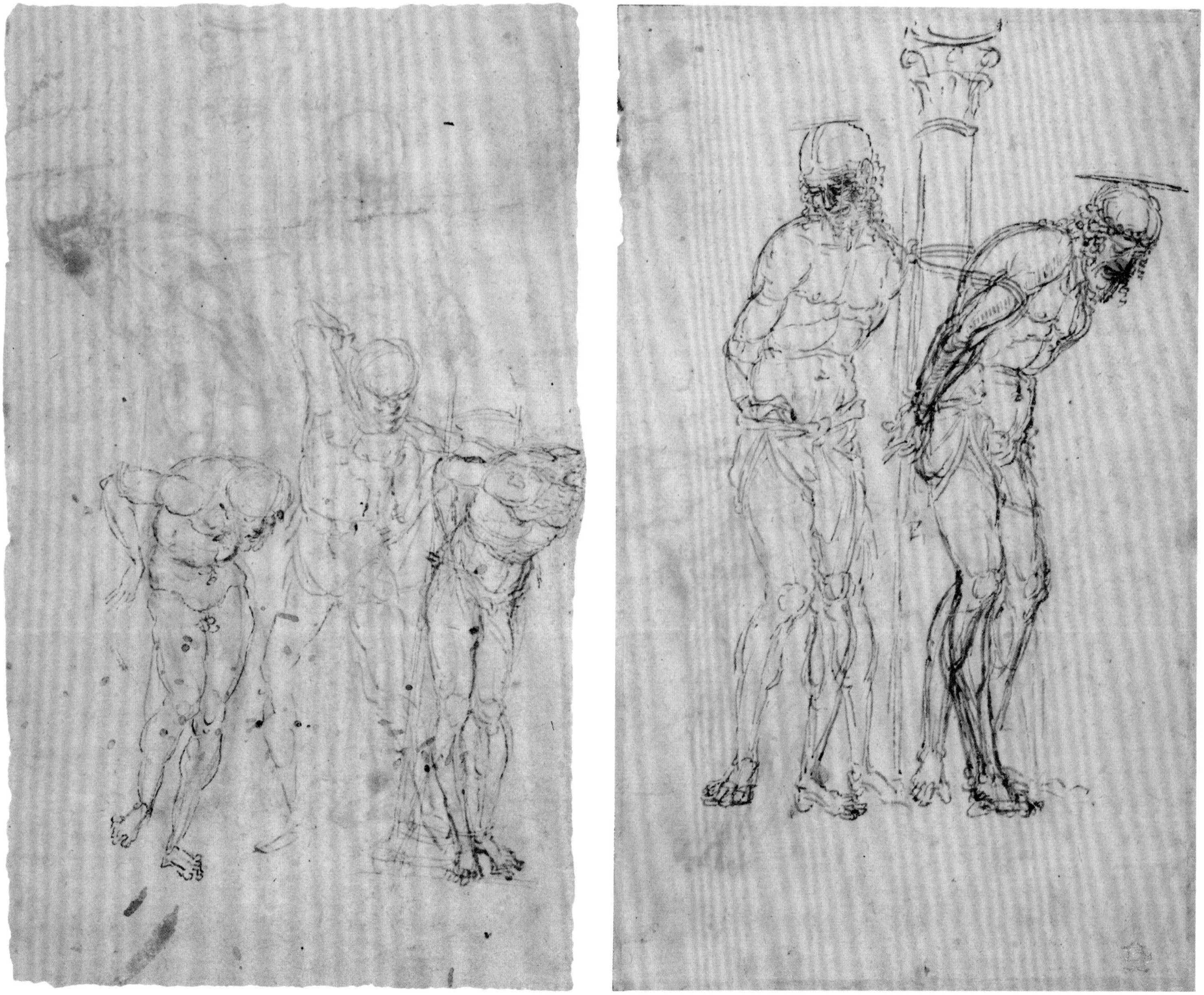

FIG. 195
ANDREA MANTEGNA
Studies for Christ at the column
(verso and recto), 1460–5
Pen and brown ink on paper,
23.7 × 14.5 cm
The Courtauld Gallery, London
(D.1978.PG.345)

may have been drawing from a model set in the same pose. The position of the arms is much the same and the use of a classical pilaster with a broken brick revetment visible behind it, as well as a pedestal with classical toothed cornicing, is common to both. Of the two, it seems that Bellini's drawing must be later: the form of this body is already moving away from the geometrical quality of Mantegna's anatomy, towards a smoother and more robust interpretation of the ribcage and pectorals – though the strongly marked pelvic bone remains the same. Bellini's drawing shows an attempt to replicate – not entirely successfully – the raised left shoulder and prominent tendons in the neck of Mantegna's Sebastian and, using white lead (now discoloured), he emphasises the modelling of the body through light.

The two artists' approach to anatomy continued to develop in tandem, most noticeably in their graphic works. Indeed, the debate over the attribution of these works testifies to the way that both artists continued to take inspiration from each other well into their maturity. The Courtauld's *Studies for Christ at the column* (fig. 195) is a case in point. Long attributed to

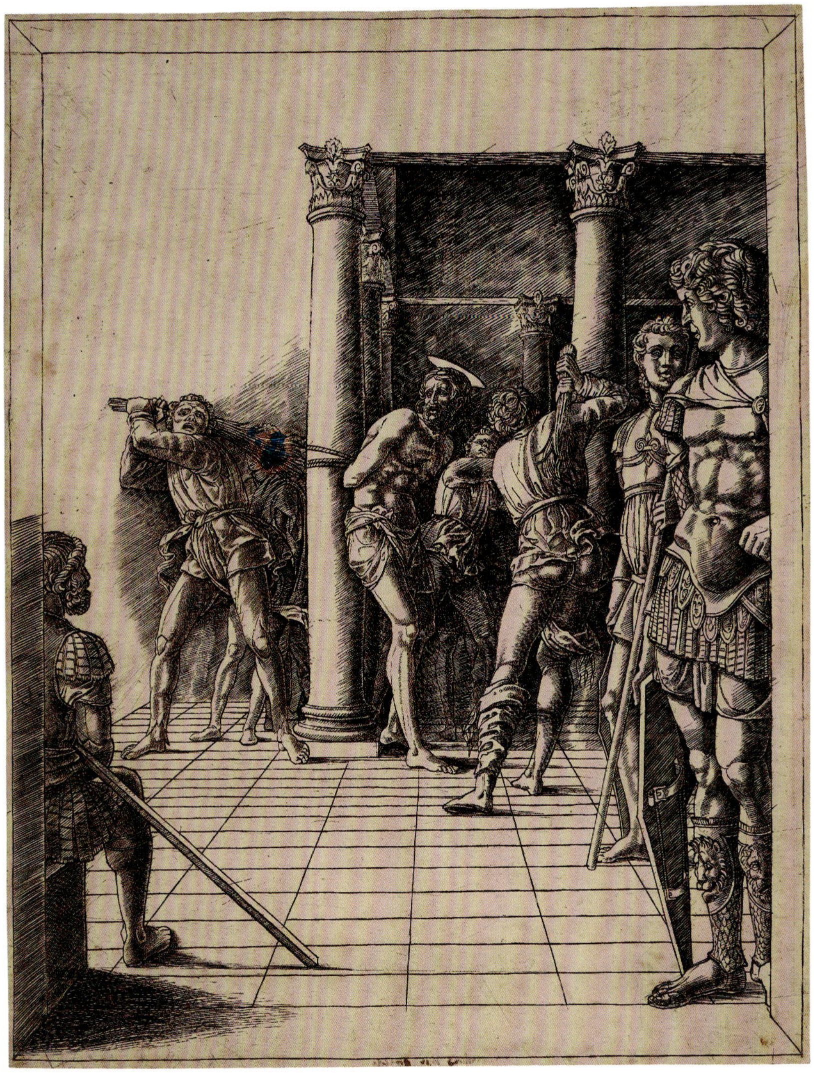

FIG. 196
Circle of ANDREA MANTEGNA
The Flagellation, about 1470–80
Engraving, 40.5 × 31.8 cm
The British Museum, London
(1845,0825.594)

Bellini, it was first linked to Mantegna in 1930, at the time of the *Italian Art* exhibition at the Royal Academy, due to its connection to the print of *The Flagellation* (fig. 196), which was recognised as being a Mantegnesque composition.[4]

Thereafter given again to Bellini, it was returned to Mantegna in 1958 when, with the revelation of its verso, its connection to the print became ever clearer.[5] Indeed, it must be a preparatory drawing for the print: the size of the figures on the recto match that of Christ in the print, and a clear developmental process can be followed on both sides of the sheet. The exploratory verso came first and then Mantegna turned the sheet over to refine two different ideas of Christ: one upright and defiant, the other bent and suffering. The final figure used in the print combines the hunched posture of the figure on the right with the upraised head of that on the left. It is not surprising that so many scholars have believed this to be by Bellini, for the concentration on sweeping lines and the almost complete absence of hatching (save on Christ's right arm in the figure to the right) are far from our understanding of Mantegna's graphic technique. The geometrical assembly of the body is, however, still very apparent even though Mantegna has virtually abandoned the horseshoe ribcage of his earlier works. The construction of kneecaps, shins and feet, as well as that of the abdomen, is essentially carried out through assemblies of shapes, something which becomes even more visible on the verso. Here the figure with the scourge demonstrates Mantegna's draughtsmanship at its most expressive and fluid: his legs taper to points, with only the faintest suggestion of a foot.

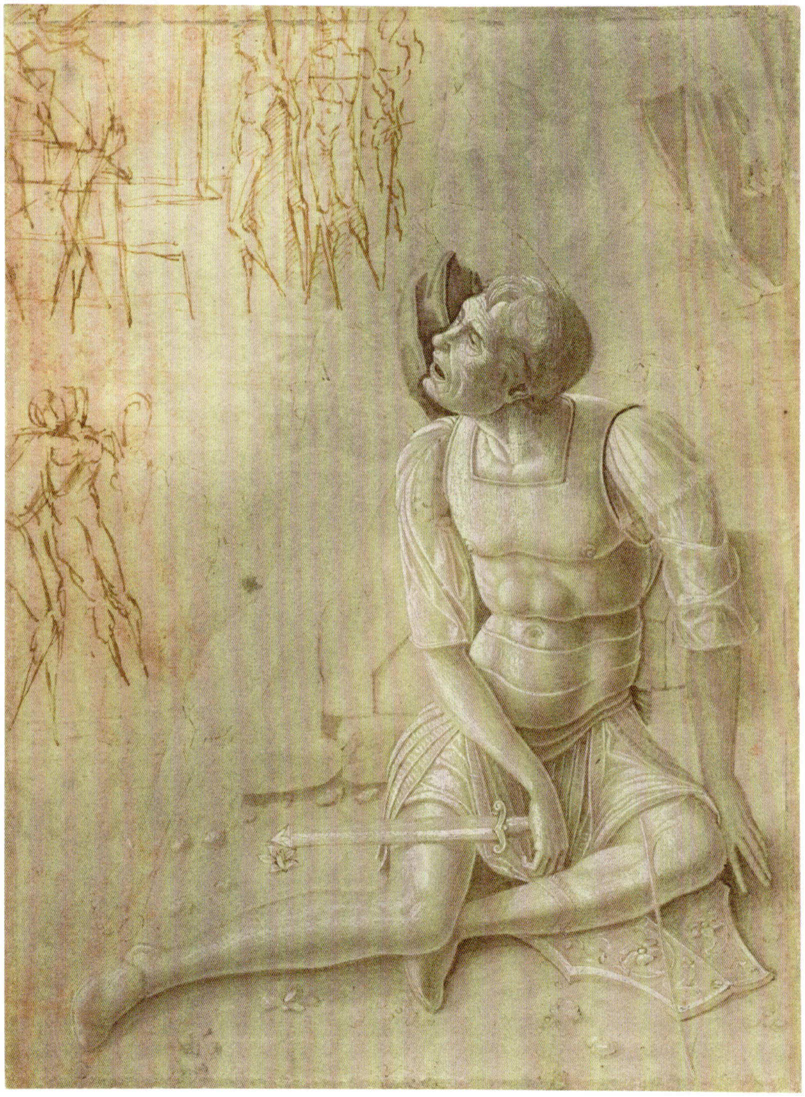

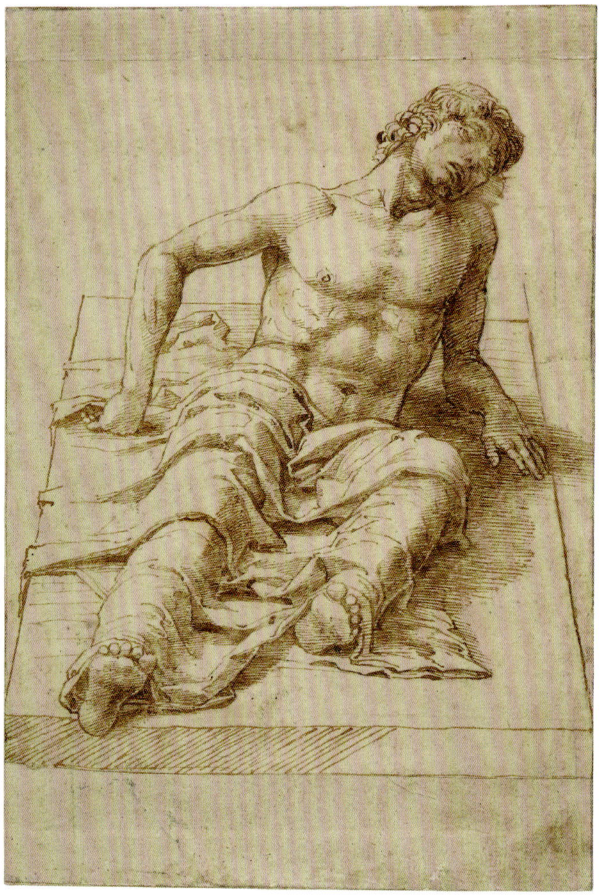

FIG. 197
Studio of ANDREA MANTEGNA
Study for a soldier of the Resurrection and other figures, about 1455–65
Pen and light brown ink on orange-brown prepared paper, 25 × 18.8 cm
The Royal Collection Trust / HM Queen Elizabeth II (RCIN 912795r)

FIG. 198
ANDREA MANTEGNA
A man lying on a stone slab, late 1470s
Pen and brown ink over traces of black chalk on paper, 20.3 × 13.9 cm
The British Museum, London (1860,0616.63)

This brisk and geometrical approach to anatomy raises the question of a drawing at Windsor (fig. 197) that is, correctly, regarded as a product of Mantegna's studio. There is no doubt that the seated soldier in the foreground is by an assistant of Mantegna rather than by the master himself, and it has the air of a fair copy made for study or as a *ricordo*. It is similar in type to the Roman soldiers in the *Crucifixion* and the *Resurrection* of the *San Zeno Altarpiece* (fig. 252), suggesting a date for the sheet in the mid-1450s. The figures in the upper-left corner, however, may be due closer inspection. Formerly dismissed as un-Mantegnesque, they in fact show much the same conception of form as the searching drawing of the executioner. The Windsor sheet is probably somewhat earlier than the *Christ at the column* and its figures at upper left are of the elongated, attenuated type seen in more finished form in *Saint James led to martyrdom* (fig. 83). These very quick sketches, made to capture an idea rather than to explore it, have a better claim than previously accepted to be by Mantegna himself.

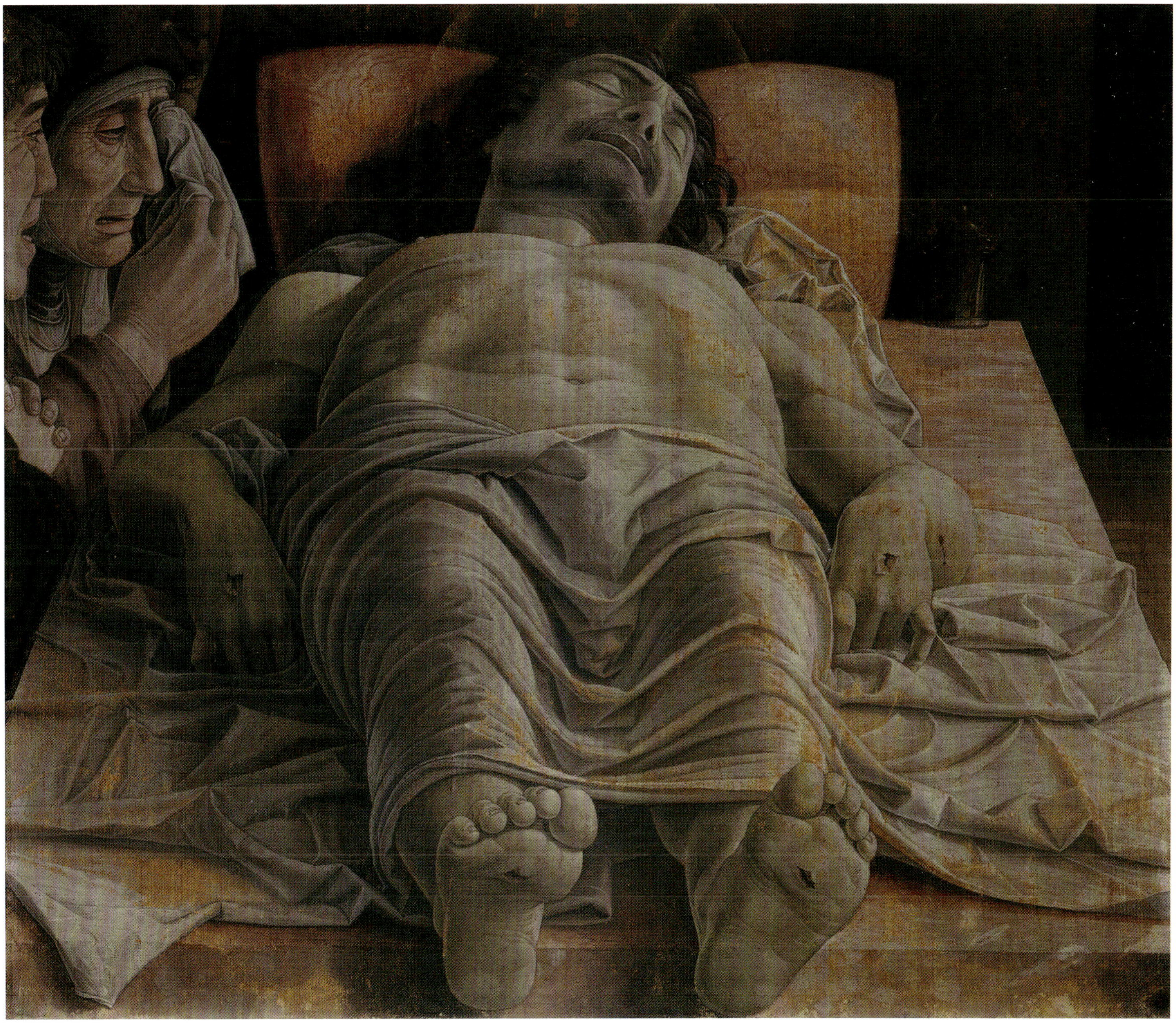

FIG. 199
ANDREA MANTEGNA
The Dead Christ with the Virgin Mary and Saint John the Evangelist, mid-1470s
Egg tempera on canvas, 68 × 81 cm
Pinacoteca di Brera, Milan (352)

Mantegna had always been more interested than Bellini in the dramatic potential of anatomy and the effect of unusual viewpoints. While Bellini had experimented with foreshortened figures in his early *Agony in the Garden* (fig. 126), his later works dispense with effortful positions, favouring more serene figures. Mantegna, however, was fascinated by the challenges of such extreme perspectives and the foreshortened body became a constant in his work, finding its apogee in his explorations of the *Dead Christ* theme, both in his drawings (fig. 155) and in the splendid picture in the Brera (fig. 199). The drawing of *A man lying on a stone slab* (fig. 198) in the British Museum extends this exploration of foreshortening, although it cannot, as was argued by earlier scholars, be a preparatory drawing for the *Dead Christ*. As first noted by Popham and Pouncey, it shows a living figure who raises himself up on his elbows. The figure has been tentatively identified with other scenes showing a figure raised from the dead, such as the Raising of the Widow's Son and the Raising of Lazarus, but neither interpretation has gained widespread acceptance. While it is tempting to see the figure as a Dead Christ supported and displayed by angels, I find this hard to credit, as the highly finished figure does not have stigmata or wounds, nor does he hold his hands in a position that would render them visible. This is not a preparatory study but a finished drawing: similarly, the absence of supporting angels or women argues against this interpretation. The drawing has alternatively been interpreted as a study from life inspired by classical statuary, though this too seems unlikely due to the length of time that such a careful drawing would take, and the consequent demands on the model.[6] Its purpose thus remains enigmatic. We still lack a full understanding of Mantegna's graphic work and it may be that, like Jacopo Bellini before him, he collected careful records of poses and ideas that could be compiled into a source of intellectual property for his studio. While the subject cannot be identified, the technique is demonstrably Mantegnesque and is a fine example of his later work, with the fine hatching used to emphasise the volume of limbs and drapery, set off by sharp highlights achieved by the use of blank paper.

It is striking, however, that even at a late stage in his career, Mantegna's ideal body remains of the type that appeared in his *Saint Sebastian* so many years before: with the arched horseshoe-shaped ribcage, the marked musculature of ribs and abdomen, and the use of prominent bones and tendons to show the attachment of neck to collarbone. While Bellini increasingly swathed the body in graceful draperies, using elegant forms to convey an aura of calm introspection, Mantegna continued to give the body an active role in his paintings: a dramatic, strained, sometimes tortured role, which articulated the intense emotionality of his themes in the wiry play of bone, muscle and flesh. The expressive quality of his bodies remained influential for future generations, as can be seen in the little-known terracotta relief of *The Blood of the Redeemer* from the Victoria and Albert Museum (fig. 200). Stylistically, this sculpture has been associated with both Padua and Venice, but its significance for this exhibition lies in its combination of Mantegnesque anatomy with a more purely classical taste, similar to that of Tullio Lombardo and his workshop. Christ's body, the draperies of the saints and the style of the architecture all continue Mantegna's quest to recover the antique nobility of body and form.

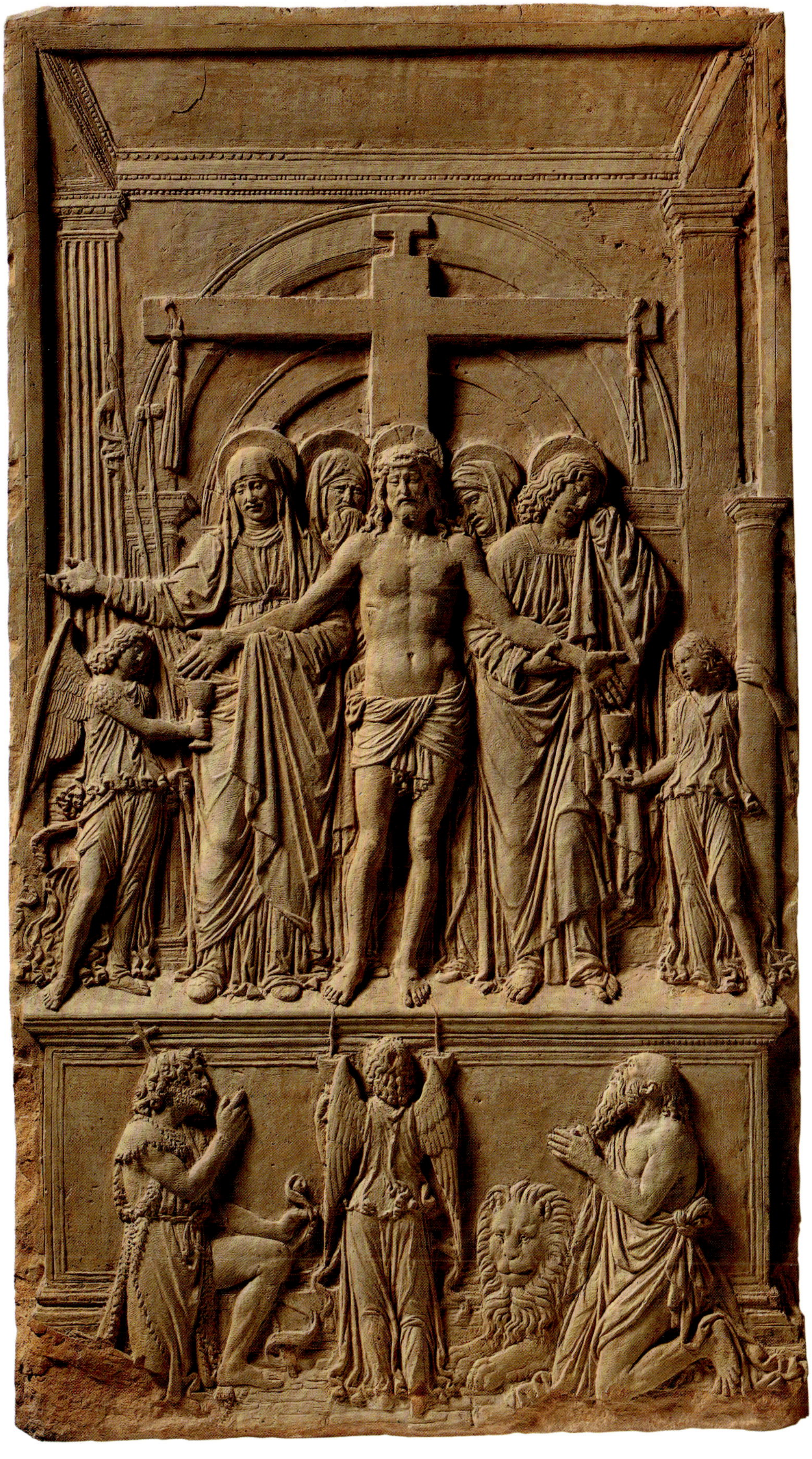

FIG. 200
VENETIAN SCHOOL
The Blood of the Redeemer, about 1500
Terracotta, 80 × 45.7 cm
Victoria and Albert Museum, London
(1195:1-1903)

‘Truly Lifelike and Real’: The Portraits of Mantegna and Bellini

SARAH VOWLES

In 1449, at the age of 18, Mantegna was commissioned to paint a double-sided portrait of the Marquess of Ferrara, Leonello d’Este, and his chamberlain.[1] He followed in the footsteps of his future father-in-law, Jacopo Bellini, who had painted Leonello in 1441, apparently in competition with Pisanello.[2] Little documentary evidence survives for that contest, but a sonnet by the Venetian poet Ulisse degli Aleotti praises Jacopo’s portrait for its verisimilitude. To be lifelike, to render the absent present, was the greatest compliment that could be given to a Renaissance portrait.[3] Mantegna himself earned a tribute from Aleotti in 1452, the year before he married Jacopo’s daughter Nicolosia. The poet noted a portrait that Mantegna had painted of a young nun, so evocative that it appeared ‘truly lifelike and real’.[4] Six years later, he was the subject of another poem, this time by the humanist Janus Pannonius, who had commissioned a double portrait of himself and his friend Galeotto Marzio da Narni and who celebrated Mantegna’s ability to ‘make our faces live for centuries, though the earth cover the bodies of us both’.[5] None of these pictures survives, but their naturalism can be deduced from the contemporary *Portrait of an Old Man* (fig. 201), in which old age is sensitively rendered through loose skin, sunken lips and drooping ears.

It is clear that Mantegna was an experienced and accomplished portraitist before he married into the Bellini family. He must, however, have drawn inspiration from Jacopo’s expertise in this field and from the growing reputations of his brothers-in-law. Gentile, initially regarded as the leading portraitist among the Bellini, was employed to paint the official portraits of new doges from the 1460s until 1501 and was also selected to travel to Constantinople in 1479–80 to paint Sultan Mehmet II (National Gallery, London, NG3099). Giovanni also made his name in the field: the humanist Raffaele Zovenzoni wrote an epigram celebrating the ‘living likeness’ of his

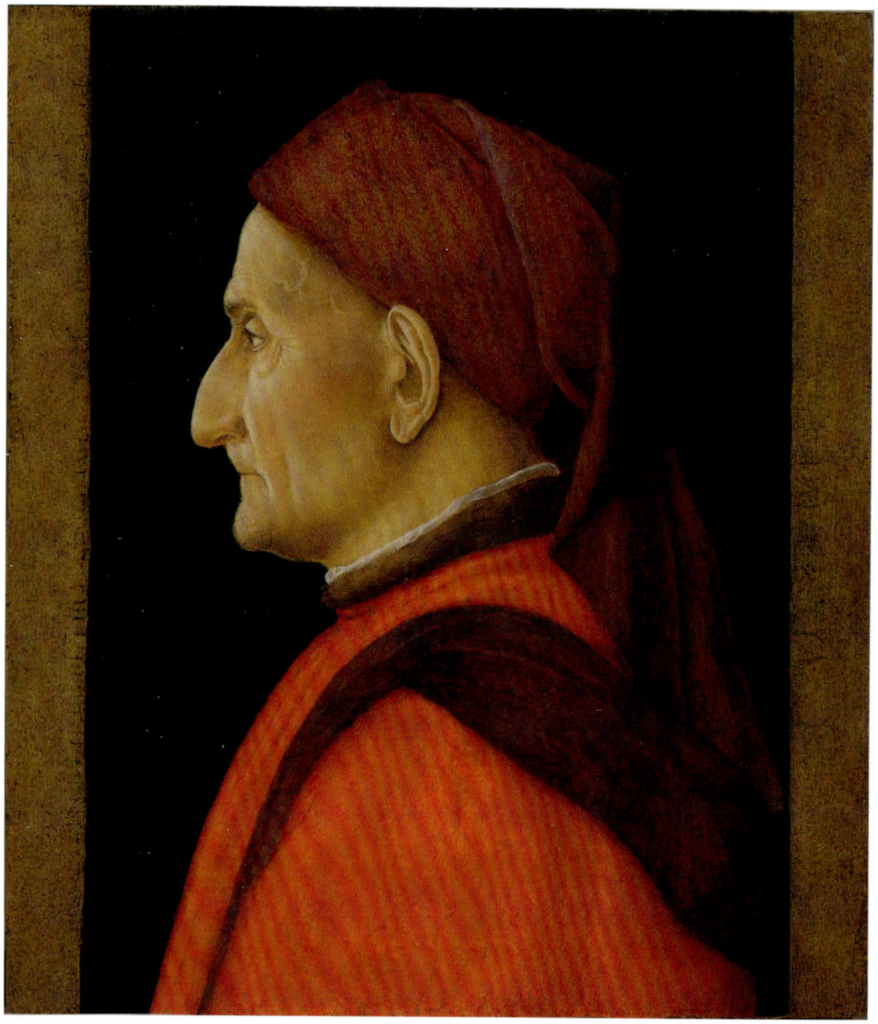

FIG. 201
ANDREA MANTEGNA
Portrait of an Old Man, about 1450
Egg tempera on panel, 32.3 × 28.8 cm
Museo Poldi Pezzoli, Milan (1592)

FIG. 202
Attributed to NICOLÒ DI GIOVANNI BARONCELLI and DOMENICO DI PARIS
Portrait of a Soldier, possibly Ludovico III Gonzaga, about 1453
Bronze, 37 × 29 × 28 cm
Skulpturensammlung und Museum für Byzantinische Kunst, Staatliche Museen zu Berlin (52)

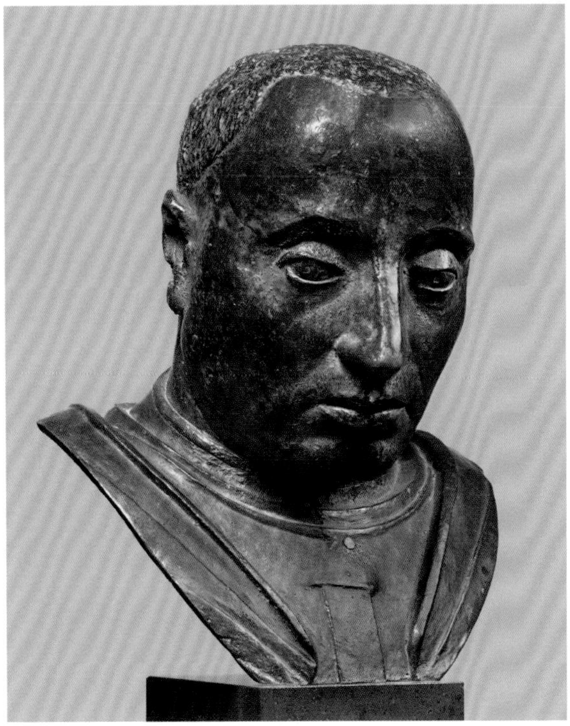

portraits and commissioned his own image in 1474, apparently in miniature format to illustrate his poem *Istrias*.[6] There were plenty of other opportunities for the young artist: portraiture was particularly popular in Venice, where many members of mercantile families worked abroad for years at a time. The nobility also commissioned portraits of their sons when they began their official careers in the Venetian Senate. By the 1520s, when the connoisseur Marcantonio Michiel recorded the pictures owned by his fellow patricians, portraits made up a disproportionately large proportion of Venetian collections.[7]

Mantegna and Bellini both started their careers at a time when portrait conventions were changing dramatically. Until the mid-fifteenth century, most Northern Italian portraits were derived from Franco-Netherlandish models, such as those which inspired the influential Pisanello in the 1430s.[8] By the 1460s, however, portraits by followers of Jan van Eyck and Hans Memling could be seen in Venice, and in 1474 the arrival of the Sicilian artist Antonello da Messina introduced another influential aesthetic, inspired by the Northern works he had seen in Naples.[9] Bellini drew on both styles, adopting the parapet used by Northern painters, on which he habitually added a fictive label bearing his signature, and emulating the strong side-lighting which added volume to a sitter's features. He was interested in Antonello's psychological acuity and the richer colours afforded by his use of oil paint, but adapted these elements to suit his own style. His backdrops are lighter, usually blue, and his sitters tend to maintain an elegant disconnect, eschewing the direct eye contact of Antonello's works.

Bellini was more responsive to new influences than either his father or brother: his 1474 depiction of the German banker Jörg Fugger in the Norton Simon Art Foundation, Pasadena, was one of the first Venetian portraits to adopt the three-quarter view, as well as one of the earliest to use pigments bound in oil. Although Gentile remained responsible for official ducal portraits, Giovanni was sometimes approached to paint their votive pictures, such as that of Doge Agostino Barbarigo (1488; San Pietro Martire, Murano). He also worked with Gentile on larger commissions, most notably the scenes from Venetian history painted in the Ducal Palace in the late 1470s and later destroyed by fire in 1577, which would have included numerous portraits.

Mantegna would never become as closely associated with portraiture as his brother-in-law, although it formed an important branch of his work. One of his first acts in Mantua, in 1461, was to paint a profile portrait of his new patron's son Francesco, on his return from studying in Pavia (fig. 208).[10] Like the Bellini, he was accustomed to including portraits in large-scale decorative or religious commissions. In *The Martyrdom of Saint Christopher* in the Ovetari Chapel he had painted a group of Paduan humanists among the bystanders and he embarked on an even more demanding scheme of this type in Mantua. The Camera Picta (fig. 203), commissioned by Ludovico III Gonzaga and painted between 1465 and 1474, includes two informal depictions of court life, populated by the Gonzaga family with their officials, allies, servants and pets. Similar cycles were planned or executed in Milan, Pavia and Ferrara, although the Camera Picta is the only

FIG. 203
ANDREA MANTEGNA
The Family and Court of Ludovico III Gonzaga, fresco, Camera Picta, 1465–74
Ducal Palace, Mantua

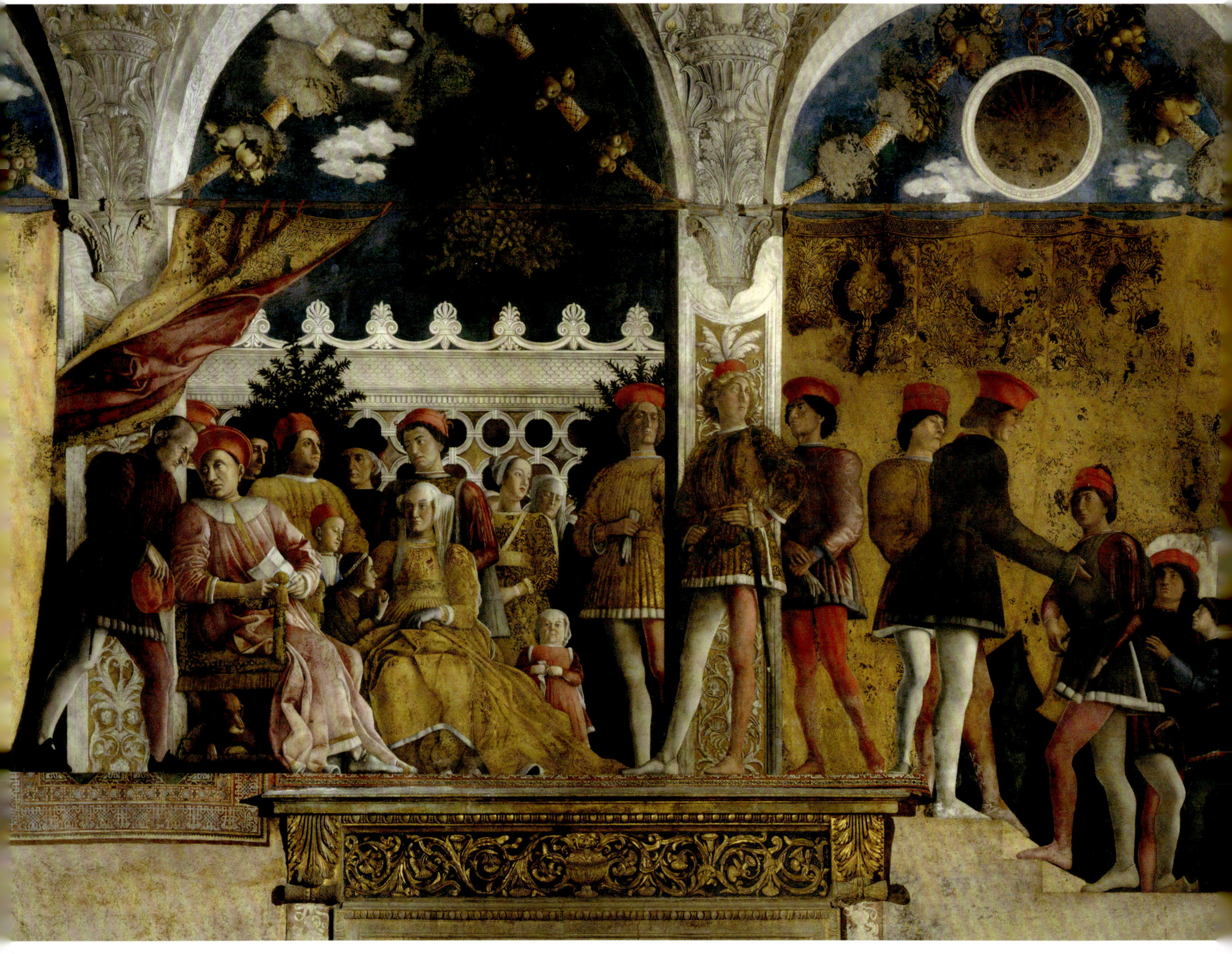

example to remain in good condition.[11] The two scenes were not intended to record actual events but to serve as visual assertions of the Gonzaga dynasty and their powerful family connections. This explains the presence of both the King of Denmark (Barbara of Brandenburg's brother-in-law) and the Emperor Frederick III, who were not in Mantua at the same date.[12] Mantegna seems to have worked not only from life but also from earlier portraits of his patron: Ludovico's profile in the Camera Picta is very close to that of a bronze bust, now in the Skulpturensammlung, Berlin (fig. 202), which has formerly been associated with Donatello and Leon Battista Alberti, but in fact probably dates from the early 1450s.[13]

In 1475, shortly after this immense work was completed, Ludovico III Gonzaga wrote to his Milanese ambassador, Zaccaria Saggi, dismissing Mantegna's talents as a portraitist: 'It is true that Andrea is a good master in other things, but in portrait painting he could have more grace, and doesn't do so well.'[14] This should not be taken at face value: five years earlier, a delighted Ludovico had invited the Duke of Milan's ambassadors to compare two of his daughters to their painted likenesses.[15] Now the duke was offended at having been omitted from the Camera Picta and so Ludovico was trying to defuse an awkward diplomatic situation. Ludovico's own opinion of Mantegna's talents remained high, and he continued to commission portraits from him, sometimes in an offhand fashion that left the artist deeply exasperated. In 1477 Mantegna wrote: 'if you wish to have these portraits so quickly, I do not understand how I am to make them, whether just as drawings or coloured on panel or on canvas and what size.'[16] After Ludovico's death, Mantegna continued to make portraits of the Gonzaga family. The black-chalk portrait of a man from the National Gallery of Ireland (fig. 204) has been persuasively identified as Francesco II, whose broad features and bulging eyes are similar to those in a terracotta bust made by Gian Cristoforo Romano around 1497–1500 (fig. 205).[17] Francesco's direct gaze makes it a powerful and strikingly intimate image, but the artist's frankness was not always welcome. Francesco's wife, the notoriously demanding Isabella d'Este, turned down a portrait that Mantegna had painted in 1493, claiming 'the painter has done it so badly, that it does not resemble us in the least'. Considering that she made the same complaint about two other portraits by different artists at the same date, it seems that her vanity rather than the likeness was at fault.[18]

Representations of power: Trevisan and Loredan

At the heart of this section are two great images of power: Mantegna's early *Cardinal Ludovico Trevisan* (fig. 206) and Bellini's *Doge Leonardo Loredan* (fig. 207). Both blend naturalism and a deft handling of light and shadow with psychological insight.

Mantegna's *Ludovico Trevisan* was probably painted during the Congress of Mantua, an ecclesiastical gathering convened by Pope Pius II between 27 May 1459 and 8 February 1460 to propose a new crusade against the Turks. Trevisan was a forceful opponent of the project, a humanist and a collector of antique medals and gems.[19] He may have known Mantegna before the Congress, as he had owned land near the Arena in Padua since 1451 and is said to have been an admirer of Francesco Squarcione. The portrait could have been painted either in Padua before the Congress, or in Mantua at its very end, when Mantegna returned from supervising the erection of the *San Zeno Altarpiece* (fig. 252) at the end of January 1460.[20] It is one of the first surviving three-quarter portraits painted in Italy, presenting the viewer with the full impact of Trevisan's

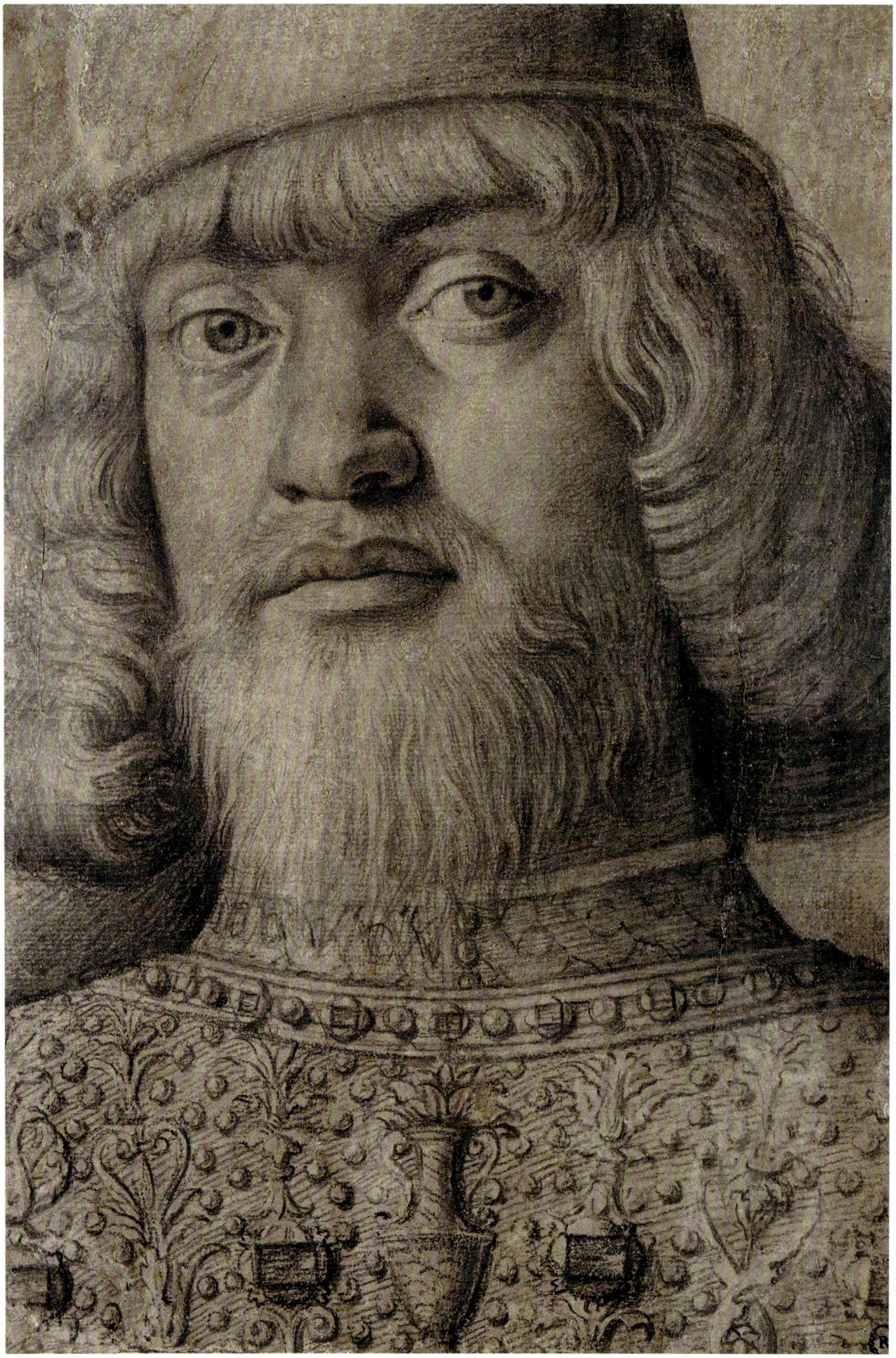

FIG. 204
ANDREA MANTEGNA
Francesco II Gonzaga, 1490s
Black chalk, highlighting with brush, and white gouache on greenish paper, 34.8 × 23.8 cm
National Gallery of Ireland, Dublin (NGI.2019)

FIG. 205
GIAN CRISTOFORO ROMANO
Portrait Bust of Francesco II Gonzaga, about 1497–1500
Terracotta, 70 × 56 × 30 cm
Museo della Città, Palazzo San Sebastiano, Mantua (11969)

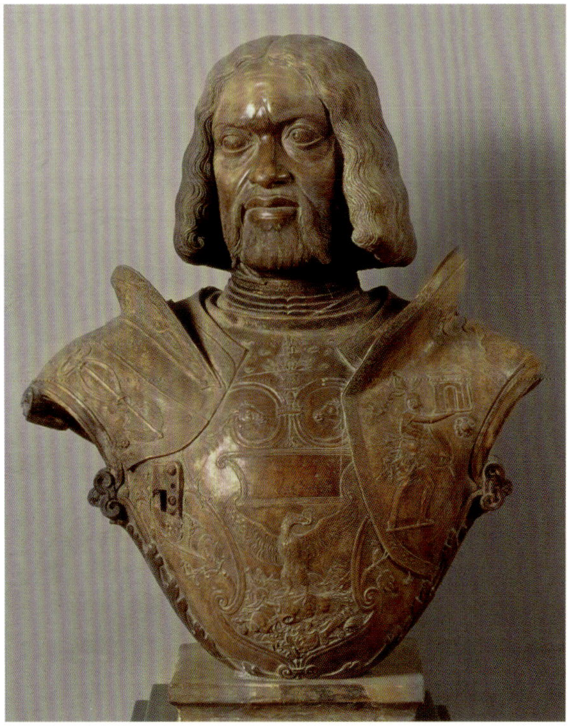

FIG. 206 (page 212)
ANDREA MANTEGNA
Cardinal Ludovico Trevisan, 1459–60
Egg tempera on poplar, 45.5 × 34.8 cm
Gemäldegalerie, Staatliche Museen zu Berlin (9)

FIG. 207 (page 213)
GIOVANNI BELLINI
Doge Leonardo Loredan, about 1501–2
Oil on poplar, 61.4 × 44.5 cm
The National Gallery, London (NG 189)

personality while he gazes, dignified and resolute, off to the viewer's left. The format may reflect Mantegna's knowledge of Northern prototypes, but it is also likely to have been inspired by his familiarity with classical portrait busts. Indeed, the choice of a format with antique allusions may have been down to Trevisan as much as to Mantegna: the artist reverted to the traditional profile format for his near contemporary portrait of Francesco Gonzaga, now in Naples (fig. 208), and his work in the Camera Picta uses a mixture of profile and three-quarter portraits, the former sometimes more confident than the latter. By the mid-1460s, he again chose to use a three-quarter format for his portrait of *Carlo de' Medici* (Galleria degli Uffizi, Florence), and in the late portrait drawing of *Francesco II Gonzaga* attributed to Mantegna (fig. 204), the sitter is presented in an even more uncompromising, almost frontal pose.

Giovanni Bellini's *Leonardo Loredan*, painted some 40 years later, poses an equally daring challenge within the highly conservative tradition of doges' portraits. Due to the 1577 fire in the Ducal Palace, the official portraits of Loredan and his fellow doges have been lost, but Gentile Bellini's replica of his portrait of *Doge Pasquale Malipiero*, from around 1460–2, records their appearance (fig. 209).[21] These profile formats, which must have appeared old-fashioned by the first decade of the sixteenth century, suited the consciously archaic tendencies of the Venetian state and made for easy translation into other, often three-dimensional media. A splendid portrait medal of Loredan, attributed to Vettor di Antonio Gambello and datable to around 1505–10 (British Museum, London), may well have been based on Gentile's lost official portrait but, in its attention to detail, forms a valuable juxtaposition with Giovanni's painting. Loredan is immediately recognisable, with his gaunt face and wrinkles minutely rendered; he also wears the damask mantle, fastened with ball-shaped buttons known as *campanoni d'oro*, and the horned *corno ducale*. On the reverse of the medal stands the allegorical figure of Equity, bearing scales to indicate Loredan's justice and integrity as ruler.

For both Mantegna and Bellini, these portraits of high-profile figures provided an opportunity to demonstrate their technical skills. Mantegna suggested the faint hint of Trevisan's red robes seen through the fine linen of his surplice using a blend of lead white and red lake, and employed a strong shaft of light to sculpt the cardinal's features. Bellini, likewise, used bright light falling from the left to add character to his sitter's face, subtly altering Loredan's expression to suggest the twin aspects of his role as doge. On the left side of his face, strongly illuminated, the doge's features are stern, displaying his readiness to

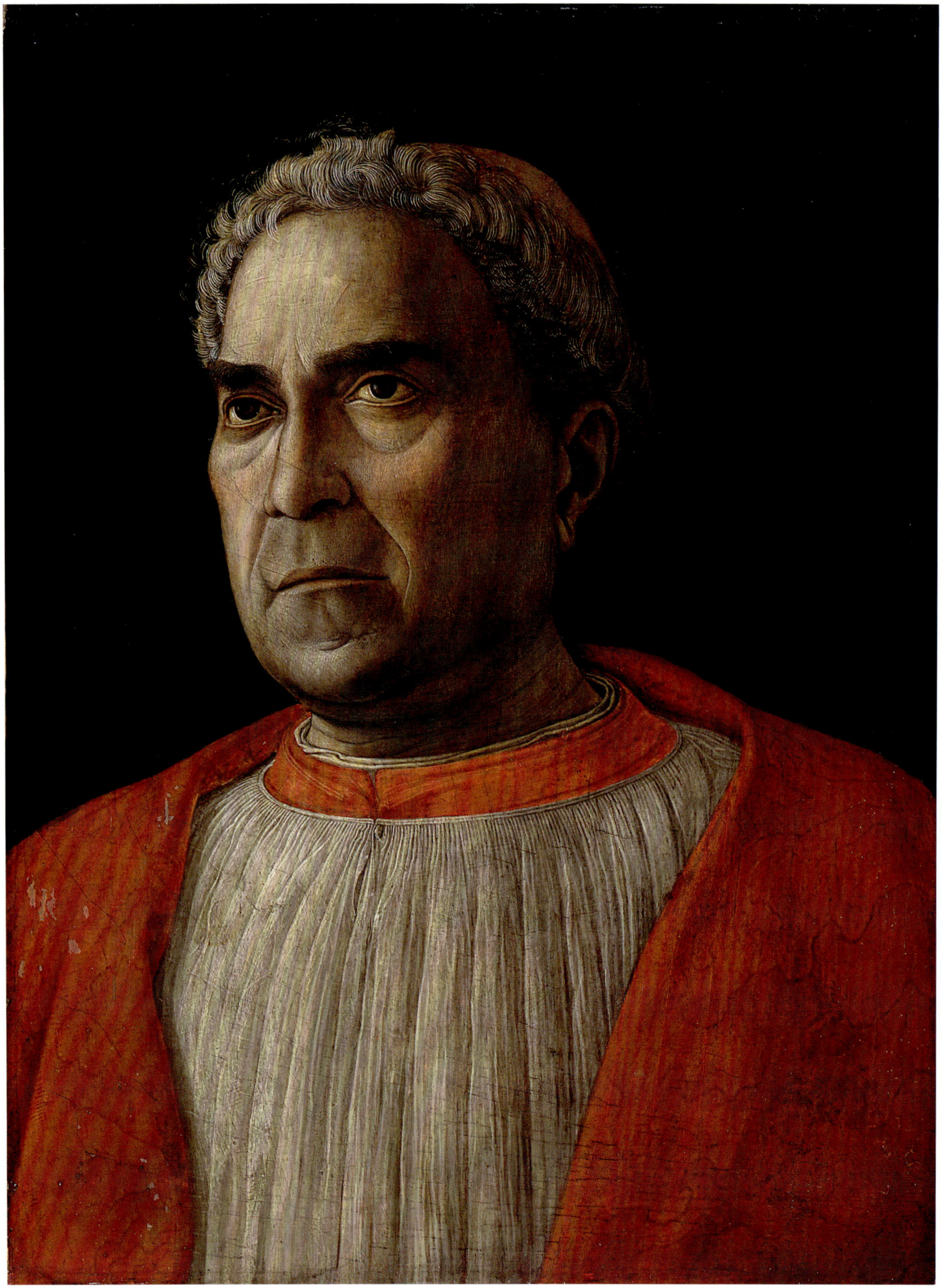

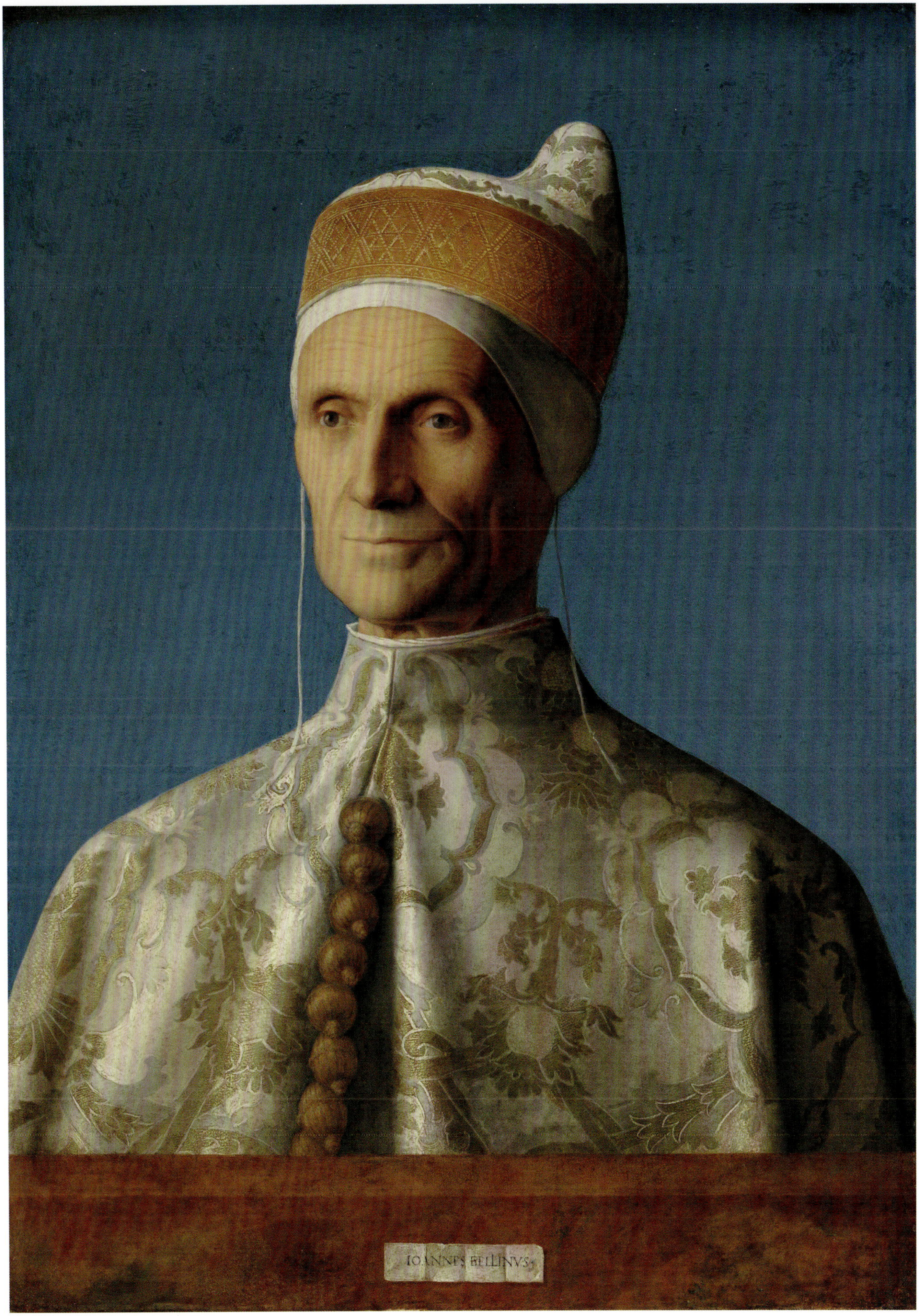
IOANNES BELLINVS

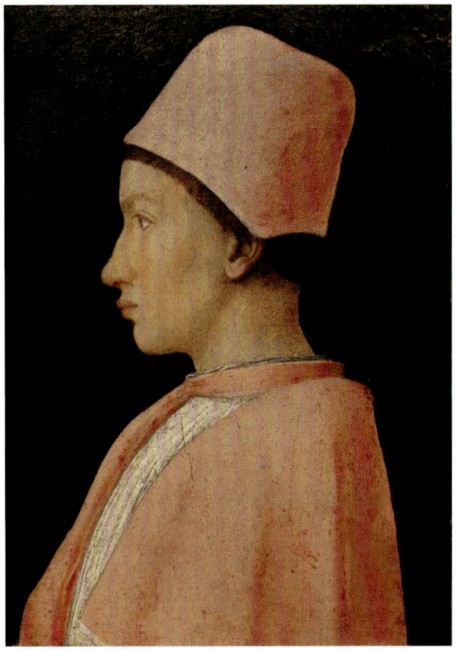

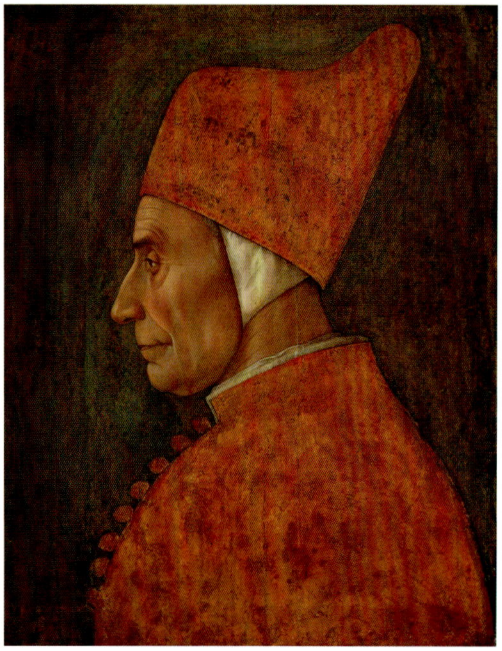

FIG. 208
ANDREA MANTEGNA
Francesco Gonzaga, about 1461
Egg tempera on panel, 30.5 × 20.9 cm
Museo Nazionale di Capodimonte, Naples (Q. 60)

FIG. 209
GENTILE BELLINI
Doge Pasquale Malipiero, 1460–2
Egg tempera on panel, 53.3 × 42.5 cm
Museum of Fine Arts, Boston (36.934)

FIG. 210
GIOVANNI BELLINI
Portrait of Fra Teodoro of Urbino as Saint Dominic, about 1515
Oil on canvas, 62.9 × 50.8 cm
Victoria and Albert Museum, London
On long term loan at the National Gallery, London (L1115)

act as a just lawgiver while, on the right, soft shadows reveal the faintest hint of a smile, indicating his innate compassion. With this psychological sleight of hand, Bellini imbues his sitter with all the virtues recommended to contemporary statesmen. His expressive use of paint suggests rather than describes the details of Loredan's features, and confident sweeps of impasto give texture to the patterns on his damask garments.[22]

In these two portraits, two powerful men are captured for posterity, not only as representatives of their positions, but as individuals. Although privately commissioned, they demonstrate that sitters increasingly wanted portraits which focused less on symbolism and more on the viewer's ability to recognise the sitter.

Fantasy as portrait / Portraits as fantasy

The pursuit of naturalism was also becoming increasingly important in the 'portraiture' of saints during this period. It began with the representation of modern holy men, who were portrayed by artists who had known them, for a public who would remember them. One of the first to be depicted in a naturalistic fashion was Saint Bernardino of Siena, who had preached in Venice and was represented in a posthumous portrait that has been attributed both to Jacopo and Giovanni Bellini (fig. 12).[23] Jacopo himself had probably attended Bernardino's sermons; the original patron of the portrait had almost certainly seen the saint in person. The striking three-quarter view of the saint, which shows him open-mouthed as if in the midst of speaking, must have been intended to arouse memories of his inspiring homilies.[24] Another portrait of Bernardino was recently attributed to Mantegna and dated to around 1450 (Accademia Carrara, Bergamo)[25] and Gentile Bellini painted an imposing grisaille portrait of the Blessed Lorenzo Giustiniani in 1465 (Gallerie dell'Accademia, Venice), showing the first Patriarch of Venice in profile but with an equal attention to his strong, emaciated features.

Perhaps as a result of this fashion for portraits of contemporary holy figures, artists also began to individualise historical saints. Two surviving drawings attributed to Bellini seem to have been made from living models as studies for painted heads. The *Head of an old man* at Windsor (fig. 211), datable to about 1460–6, cannot be related to a known work, but was probably intended for an apostle or a hermit saint in a *sacra conversazione*. The man's direct stare, unusual for a conventional portrait, would be more appropriate for a saint looking out from his liminal space between image and worshipper. Even at this early date, Bellini used light to add sophistication and volume to the figure: his careful modelling is especially evident in the man's beard, where strokes of white heightening and brown ink are alternated to depict the sheen of light falling from the left. The much later

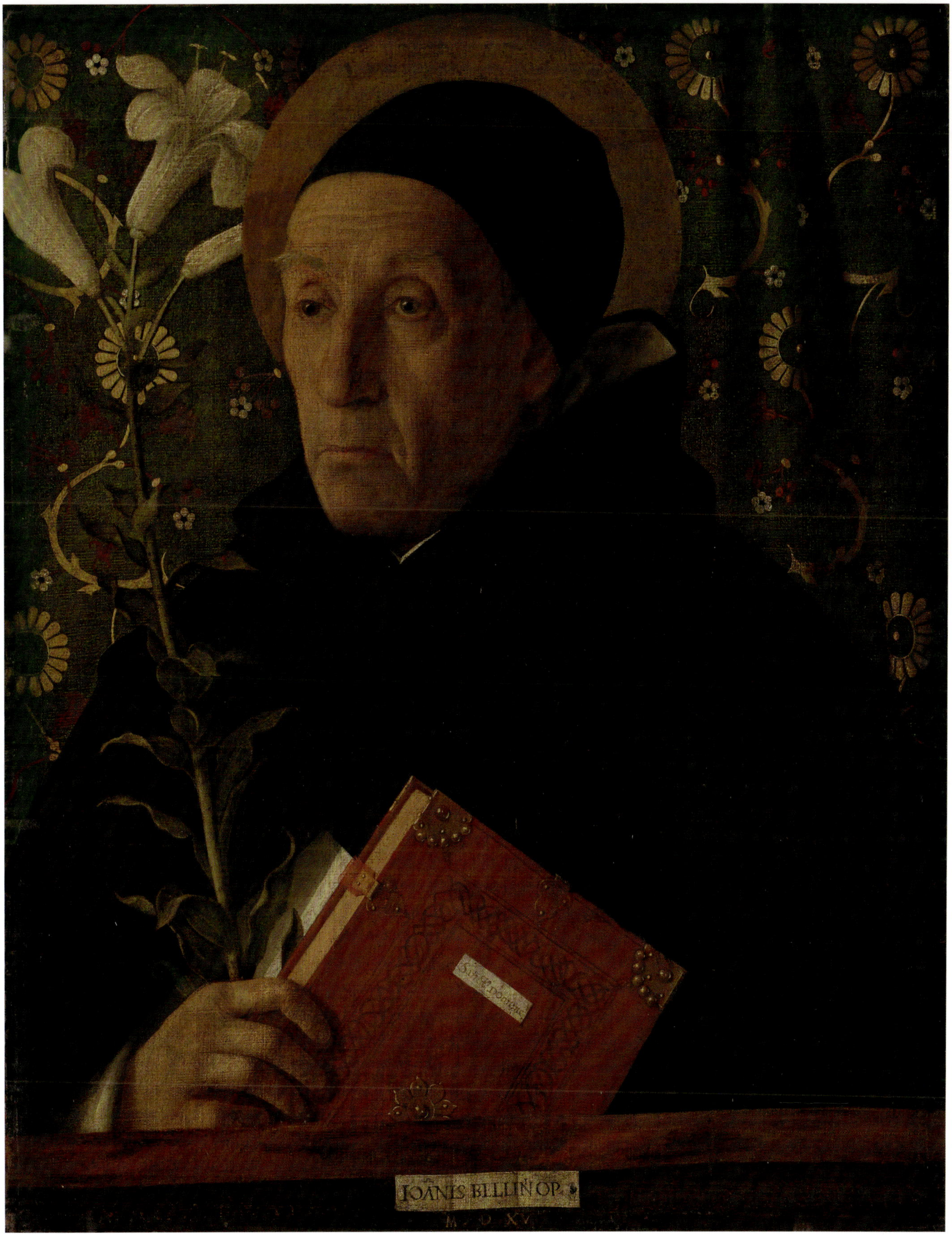
IOANIS BELLIN OP.
M D XV

Head of a man in a turban (fig. 160) can be linked to Bellini's grisaille *Lamentation* (fig. 161). It has sometimes been regarded as a workshop copy after the painting but, while some of the features appear somewhat hard, the overall understanding of light and shade can be favourably compared to the Windsor head. The delicate, if more painterly, representation of the hairs in the beard has even been achieved with the same alternation of lead white and brown ink.[26]

As saints and other imaginary figures became increasingly individualised, portraits could also draw on an air of fantasy. Bellini had sometimes represented donors in the guise of their patron saints, which may be the case with the figure of Saint George in his *Virgin and Child with Saints Paul and George* (Gallerie dell'Accademia, Venice).[27] Yet this fashion is taken to its extreme in his stand-alone *Portrait of Fra Teodoro da Urbino as Saint Dominic* (fig. 210). Even if this picture, painted at the very end of Bellini's life in 1515, was intended as a 'portrait' of the saint himself, the naturalistic representation of the model suggests that Fra Teodoro's features were meant to be recognised by his contemporaries, in an audacious self-identification with his order's founder. A similarly striking fantasy portrait shows a man crowned with laurel leaves and dressed in an antique mantle (fig. 212). The identity of both artist and sitter has been much debated, but the picture is now generally accepted as a work by Bellini from the end of the fifteenth century. The sitter is usually identified as a humanist, but Giovanni Agosti has recently revived a nineteenth-century tradition identifying the picture as a portrait by Bellini of Mantegna.[28] This tantalising suggestion rests on one's ability to see physiognomic parallels with Mantegna's funerary bust in Sant'Andrea, Mantua (fig. 242), and on his earlier self portrait in the decorative border of the Camera Picta. Although it would certainly be a strange portrait to have been commissioned by one of Bellini's usual patrons, there is an intriguing link to Bellini's 1474 portrait of *Jörg Fugger*, where the sitter is also shown wearing a wreath, this time of berries. Whether or not we can accept the Milan sitter as Mantegna himself, the portrait testifies to Bellini's contacts in a literary world generally associated with his brother-in-law. Mantegna and his friends diverted themselves by imagining themselves as ancient scholars, and Bellini's portrait indicates that such aspirations to antique virtue were not restricted to the written word, but could be embodied in ambitious, innovative portrait forms.[29]

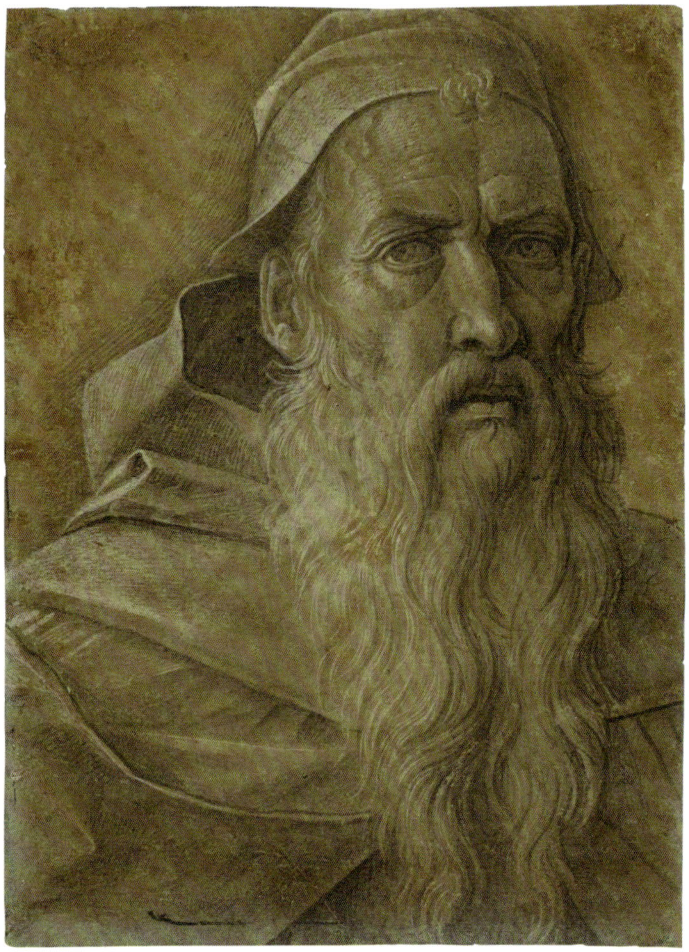

FIG. 211
GIOVANNI BELLINI
Head of an old man (Saint Anthony Abbot), about 1460–6
Brush and ink with white body colour on paper, 26 × 19 cm
The Royal Collection Trust / HM Queen Elizabeth II (RCIN 912800)

FIG. 212
Attributed to GIOVANNI BELLINI
Portrait of a Humanist (Andrea Mantegna?), about 1475–80
Oil on board, 35 × 28 cm
Pinacoteca del Castello Sforzesco, Milan (249)

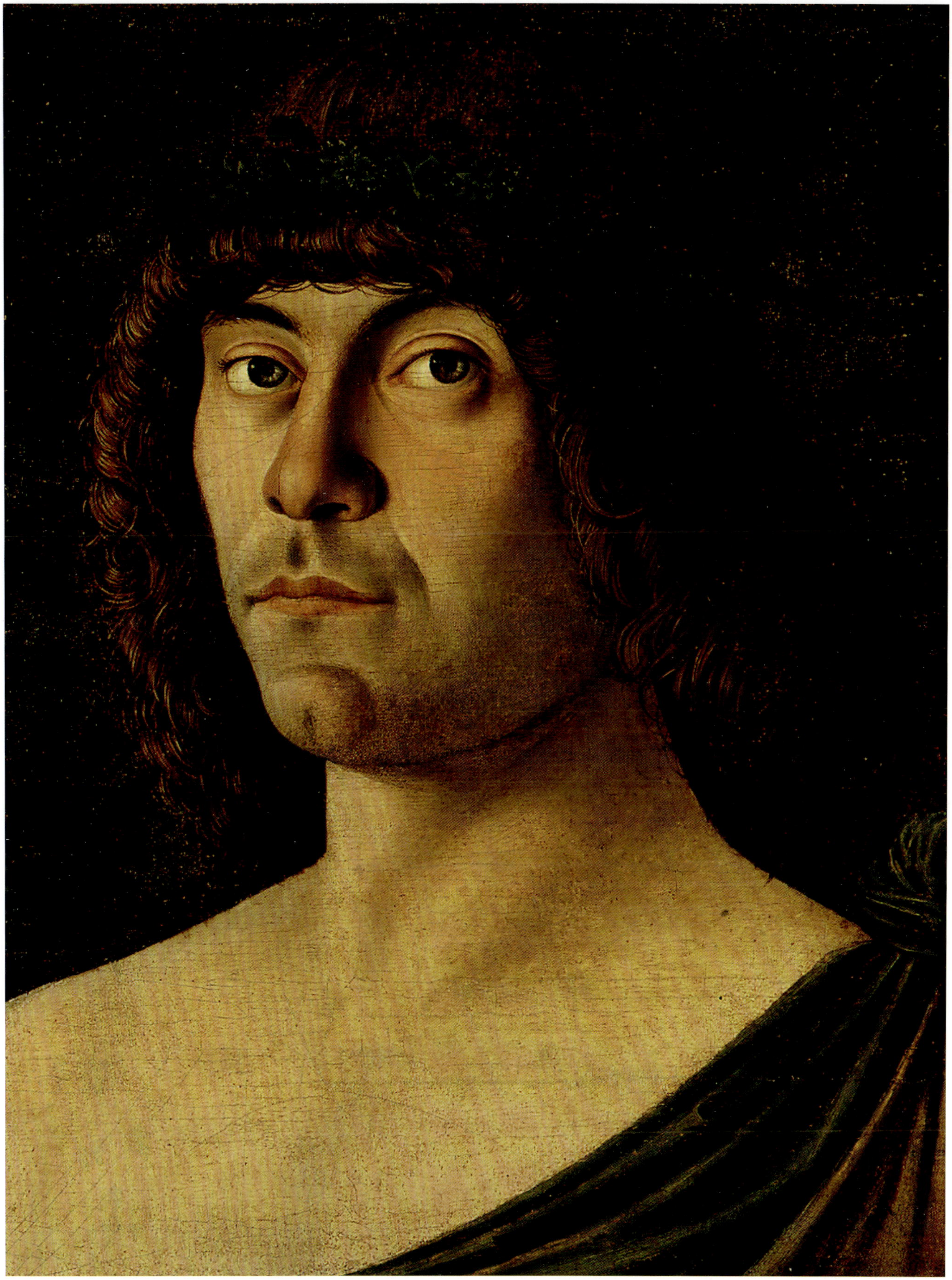

Landscape

CAROLINE CAMPBELL AND
DAGMAR KORBACHER

Landscape was an important element of Italian painting from at least the early fourteenth century. It was used, for example, in cycles of narrative painting, such as Giotto's frescoes in the Scrovegni Chapel (fig. 127), in order to give stories set in the Christian past or the classical world a believable sense of place. In the fifteenth century, however, the role of landscape moved from the background to the foreground. Landscape became a key part of many painters' repertoires, as a way of demonstrating powers of invention and of independent creation, by improving on nature and rendering it perfect.[1]

No artist developed their skills as a painter of atmospheric and evocative landscapes more deliberately, or more influentially, than Giovanni Bellini, who is justly characterised as one of the first true painters of landscape.[2] Mantegna, however, was also an accomplished and innovative landscapist – one of the handful of fifteenth-century Italian painters who portrayed 'real' landscapes in a topographically accurate way. *The Death of the Virgin* (fig. 214, painted in the early 1460s for the Chapel in the Ducal Palace at Mantua (reunited here with its companion panel, *Christ with the Virgin's Soul*, fig. 213),[3] depicts the lake at Mantua, as it would have been seen from the Castle, with Borgo San Giorgio discernible on the far shore.[4] For both painters, landscape was a means of making pictures not just credible, but capable of playing on their viewer's heart strings. Even more importantly, painting landscapes became a powerful means for Mantegna and Bellini to demonstrate their virtuosic skills, particularly (in the case of the latter) using the medium of oil. Technical innovation in oil painting, as John Berger has noted, has repeatedly been connected to the depiction of landscape.[5]

An essential stimulus for both artists' development as landscape painters in their own unique manners was the presence of works in North-East Italy by the contemporary Netherlandish painters Jan van Eyck and Dirk Bouts. These works were highly valued by patrons and by artists for their creation of convincingly real illusionistic worlds. In Bouts's *Entombment* in the National Gallery, London, for instance, painted in the 1450s directly for the export market to Venice, no parapet or architectural device separates the sacred space of Christ and his followers from the secular world of the beholder.[6] The landscape encourages the viewer to visualise the act of mourning over Christ's body in a world like theirs, with green fields and distant rolling hills. Van Eyck's ability

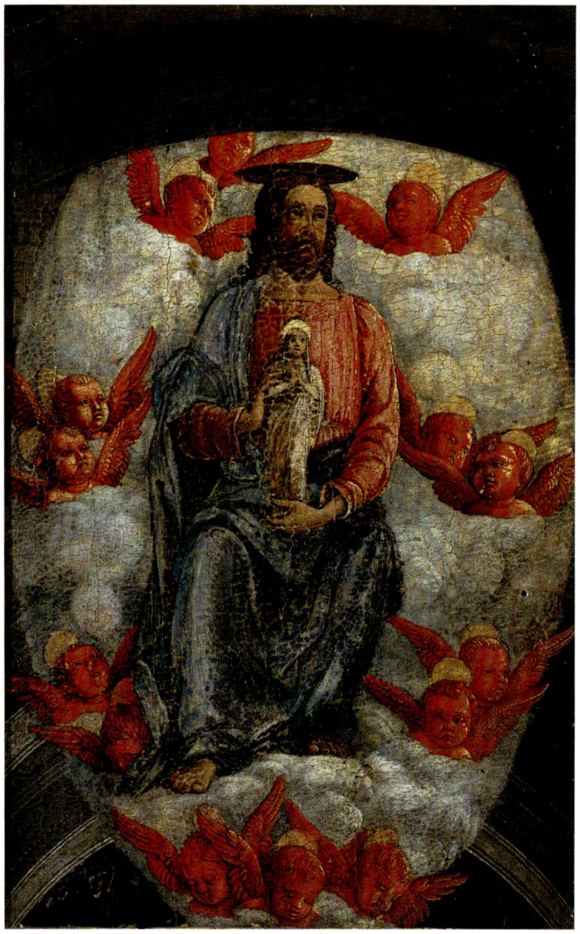

FIG. 213
ANDREA MANTEGNA
Christ with the Virgin's Soul, about 1460–4
Egg tempera on panel, 27.5 × 17.5 cm
Pinacoteca Nazionale, Ferrara (333)

FIG. 214
ANDREA MANTEGNA
The Death of the Virgin, about 1460–4
Egg tempera on panel, 54.5 × 42 cm
Museo Nacional del Prado, Madrid (P00248)

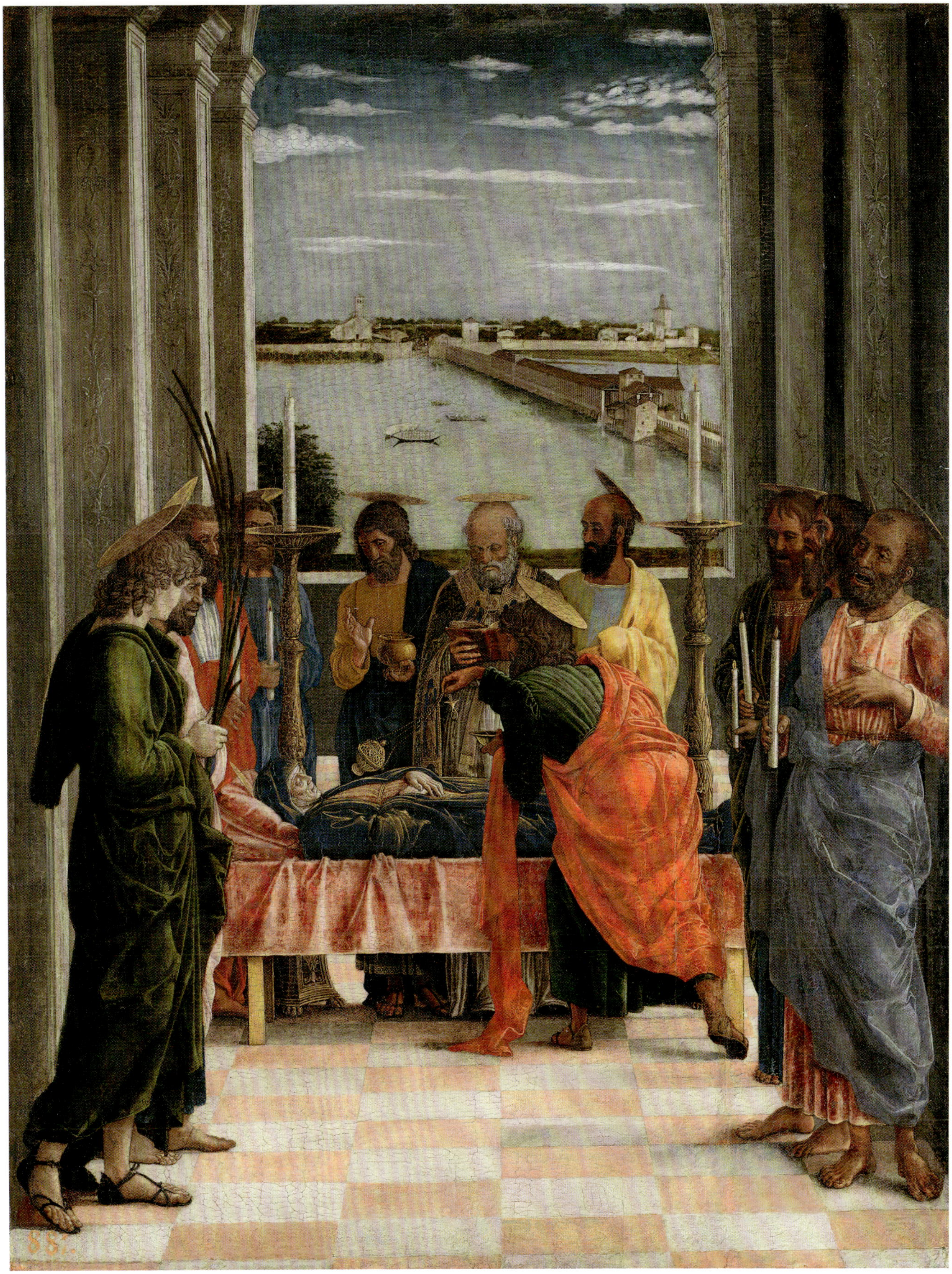

FIG. 215
JACOPO BELLINI
The Agony in the Garden,
from *The London Drawing Book of Jacopo Bellini*, 1440–70
Leadpoint on paper,
41.5 × 33.5 cm
The British Museum, London
(1855,0811.43r)

FIG. 216
Attributed to
GIOVANNI BELLINI
The Nativity, about 1480
Pen and brush and brown ink on laid paper,
21.1 × 21.1 cm
The Courtauld Gallery, London
(D.1978.PG.79)

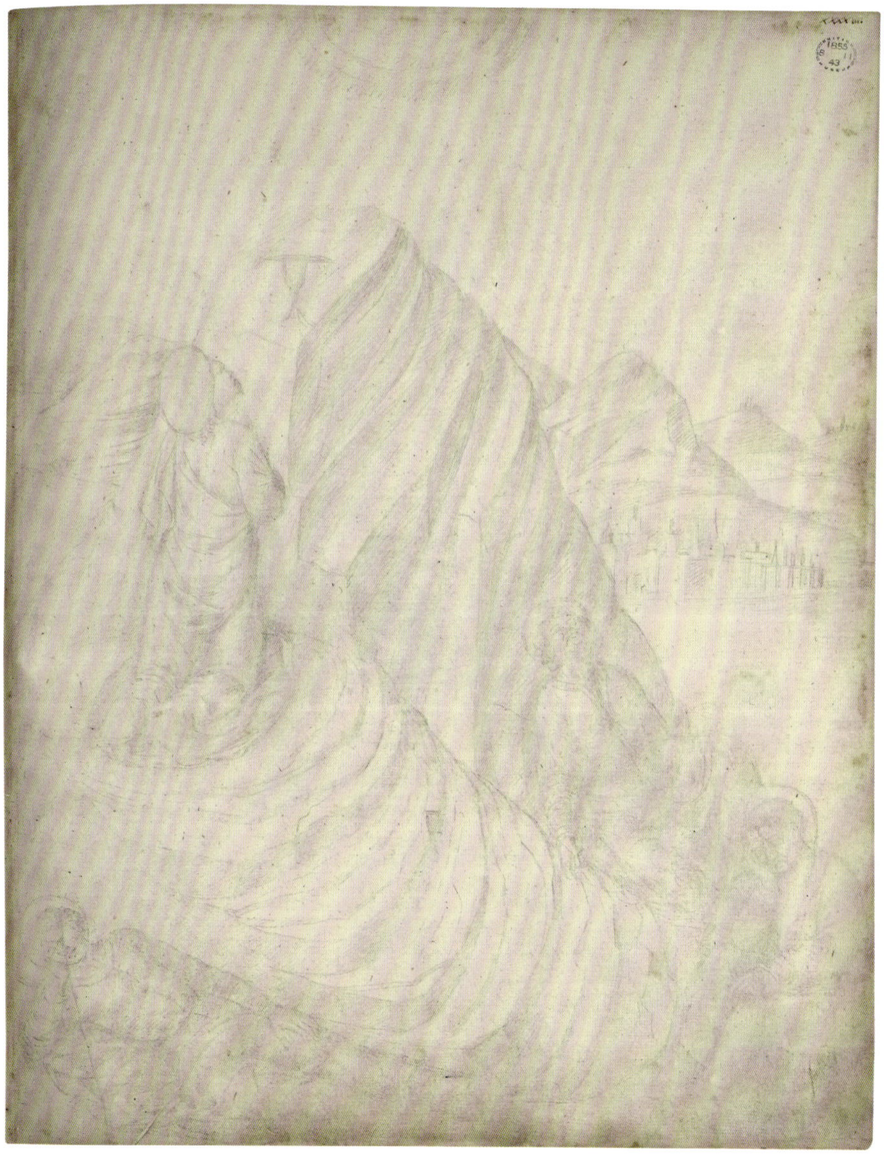

to convey the changing effects of light on different surfaces, and in different environmental conditions, was supremely influential for Northern Italian painters.

The greatest impact upon Mantegna's and Bellini's development as landscapists, however, was closer to home, in the person of Jacopo Bellini, whose innovatory land- and townscapes reflect his wide intellectual interests, particularly in mathematics and perspective. The majority of drawings in Jacopo's Drawing Books (including figs 89, 90, 215) are scenes from the New Testament and from his imagination, set among townscapes of interconnected buildings and panoramic landscapes.[7] Many of Jacopo's most ambitious compositions, such as *The Agony in the Garden* (fig. 215), are conceived over a two-page spread. The form of Christ in prayer, on the right-hand side of the opening, is framed (and dwarfed) by the rocky outcrop on which he kneels. Three of his apostles sleep at the foot of the rock, while at the left, Judas and the Roman soldiers who will arrest Christ are making their way along a winding path from the walled city representing Jerusalem. A large tree, and a statue of an idol on a column (soon to be toppled by Christ) frame the composition. Jacopo's drawing must have been the main influence for Mantegna and Giovanni's closely related paintings of the same subject (figs 125, 126). Today this sort of composition perhaps seems unremarkable, because there are thousands of examples of such 'framing' details in Western landscape painting, yet this precisely underlines Jacopo's innovation.

It was, however, in the hands of his younger son Giovanni, that painting the natural world took on a life of its own.[8] The strong Venetian tradition of landscape painting, ranging from the pastoral and Arcadian fantasies of the early sixteenth century to the eighteenth-century view paintings (*vedute*) of Canaletto and Guardi, is rooted in the art of Giovanni Bellini.[9] Marco Boschini

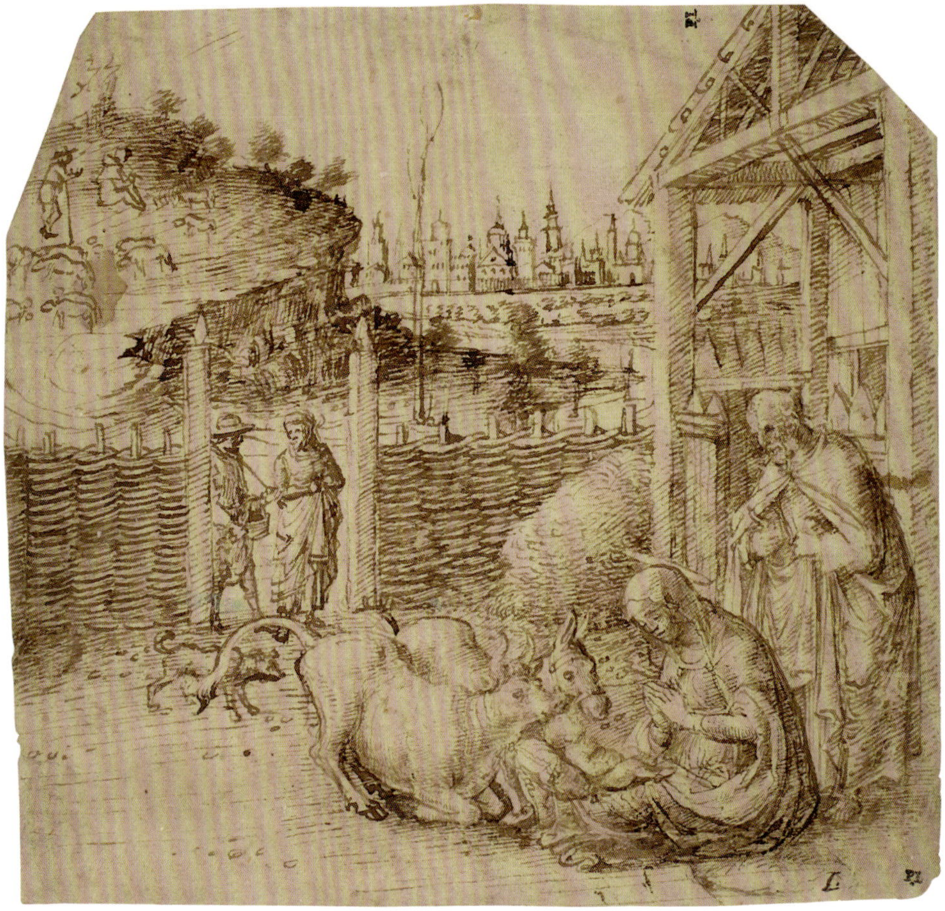

wrote in the *Carta del navegar pitoresco* (the first comprehensive study of Venetian painting, first published in 1660): 'Giovanni Bellini could be called the spring of the whole world, in the art of painting / because from him derives all greenery / and without him art would be an icy winter.'[10] In Bellini's hands, landscape moved from being an element of painting to being the feature that conveyed the principal message of his works. A sensibility to light, to the sky and to landscape, became the *leitmotif* of his production, and the quality that distinguished him from his contemporaries and rivals. This can be seen from his earliest works, such as the *Saint Jerome* (fig. 114) to his latest, *The Drunkenness of Noah* (fig. 247) and *The Feast of the Gods* (fig. 226).

Mantegna's views, as mentioned above, excel in giving a definite sense of place, and his abiding interest in perspective means that they make strong connections between the real and the imagined world. For instance, in *Saint James led to Martyrdom* in the Ovetari Chapel (fig. 251), painted before Mantegna had reached his mid-twenties, contemporary town houses, including castellated structures, jostle with an *all'antica* vaulted arch. A surviving drawing for this composition (fig. 83) is remarkable for the strong, unnatural effects of light and shadow, and for giving a direct architectural focus to the central episode of the scene, Saint James healing the paralytic. In the Camera Picta, devised and painted in the late 1460s, Mantegna represents the meeting in early 1462 between Duke Ludovico, his court and his sons (fig. 203) – which took place at the small settlement of Bozzolo, on the Lombard plains – before an idealised view of Rome as the Eternal City. Rome, conveniently and spectacularly inaccurately shown on a single hillside, is a combination of actual monuments and imagined structures in the ancient style, celebrating the Gonzaga family's connections with the Papacy and the current pope, Pius II.[11]

We have nothing in Bellini's work to compare directly with the illusionistic vistas Mantegna devised for the Ovetari Chapel and the Camera Picta: most of Bellini's paintings on such a scale were destroyed in the 1577 fire in the Doge's Palace. Yet several surviving drawings

FIG. 217
Attributed to GIOVANNI BELLINI
Saint Mark healing Ananias, about 1485
Pen and brown ink on paper, 18.4 × 17.2 cm
Kupferstichkabinett, Staatliche Museen zu Berlin
(KdZ 1357r)

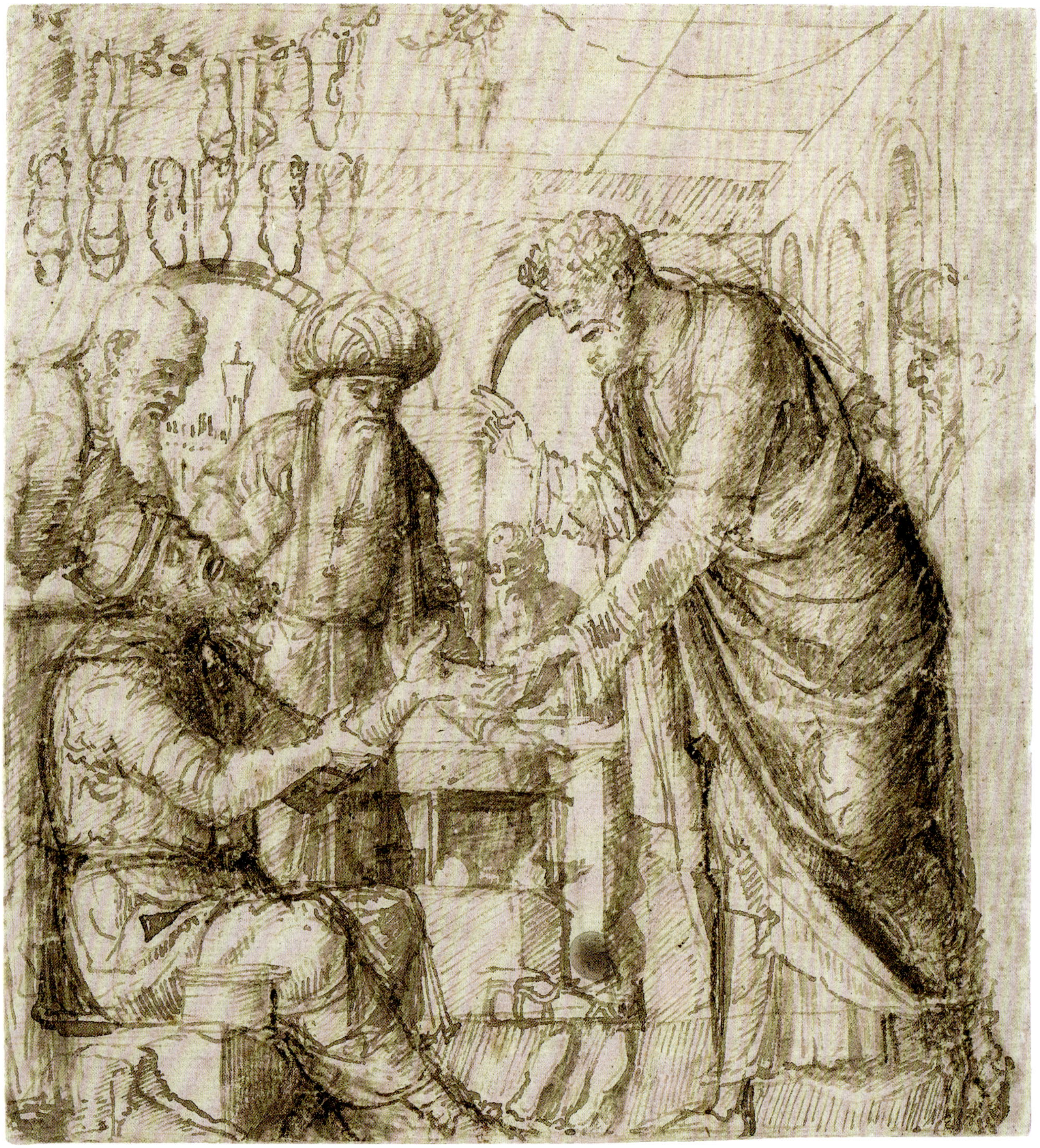

reflect his need to invent landscapes and townscapes as settings for telling stories. The compositional study for *The Nativity* (fig. 216), tentatively dated to around 1480[12] and loosely related to the *Pesaro Altarpiece* (fig. 255), sets the episode of the birth of Jesus in a landscape that recalls Jacopo's Drawing Books. The carefully drawn main figures are juxtaposed with a roughly conveyed landscape, with cursory shapes indicating shepherds, their flocks and a distant town. The unusual pose of mother and child, with the Virgin sitting on the ground and the Christ Child propped up by her feet, may be drawn from Giovanni Bellini's Northern Italian legacy. A small drawing by the Veronese draughtsman and painter Artemio, from the Badile Album in Munich, shows an elderly woman in a similar position.[13] Stylistically related to the Courtauld drawing is a slightly later compositional study in Berlin (fig. 217). It depicts an episode from the life of Saint Mark showing the saint healing the wound of the cobbler Ananias, who has injured his hand while mending Mark's shoe. The scene takes place inside Ananias's shop, but an archway opens up to the Venetian townscape, ensuring that the miracle is witnessed by several bystanders.[14]

Bellini's altarpieces, however, provide compelling evidence of the unity that landscape, as well as architecture,[15] gave to his paintings, enabling him to bring together the separate panels of the traditional polyptych (for example in the *Carità Altarpiece*, fig. 84, and the *Saint Vincent Ferrer Altarpiece*, figs 23, 253) into one pictorial space – the so-called *sacra conversazione*, where Christ and the Virgin Mary are depicted in the same environment as their saintly companions (such as the *Pesaro Altarpiece*, fig. 255, and the *San Giobbe Altarpiece*, fig. 20). The altarpiece of *The Resurrection of Christ* (fig. 218) that Bellini painted around 1475–9 for the Zorzi family chapel in San Michele in Isola is one of his most impressive examples of landscape as narrative.[16] While some of the figures of the soldiers still convey his knowledge of his brother-in-law's Ovetari Chapel frescoes (figs 249, 251),[17] both the depiction of the landscape and its importance in the composition indicate a new and very 'Bellinian' development. The sky – shown on a typical spring morning, appropriately for Easter Sunday[18] – appears to be the main subject of the painting, embracing the narrative element of Christ rising from his tomb. The role of landscape goes far beyond simply providing a passive natural setting for the biblical episode, and even beyond establishing the biblical episode in the context known to the viewer: the Venetian Terraferma.

The contemplative, atmospheric landscape is closely related to the subject, and the rising morning sun is a striking and symbolically charged analogy to Christ's resurrection from the tomb. The landscape is populated, but its idyllic tranquillity is not disturbed by human action – described memorably by Anchise Tempestini as the 'true poetics of silence' transformed into painting.[19] The shepherd with his flock is not part of the biblical narrative of the Resurrection. His earthy colours and quiet, background presence in Bellini's *Resurrection* suggest that he is included as an attribute of the landscape to reinforce its peaceful character. This apparently incidental figure, which may have been inspired by pastoral poetry, demonstrates Bellini's pioneering role in the development of the Arcadian imagery that dominated Venetian painting in the early sixteenth century, and made it so influential far beyond Venetian territory.[20]

Recognition and appreciation of the very special nature of Bellini's landscapes, led to the development of what could almost be called 'pure' landscapes in which Bellini could indulge his desire to 'wander at will in painting', as Pietro Bembo put it,[21] creating both distant views (*lontani*) and fantasies (*fantasie*), which dazzled his patrons and contemporaries, even if the subjects

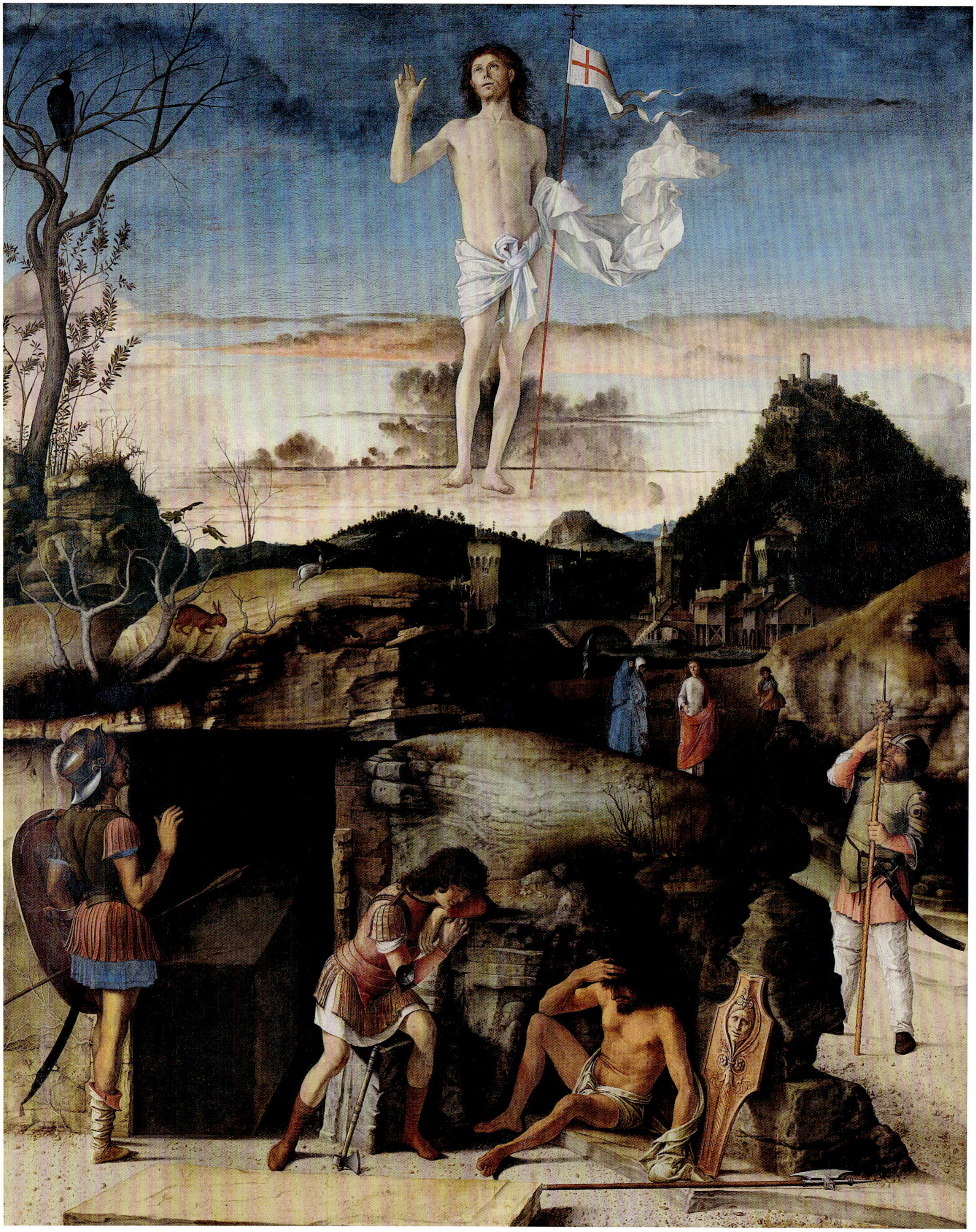

FIG. 218
GIOVANNI BELLINI
The Resurrection of Christ, 1475–9
Oil on canvas, transferred
from panel, 148 × 128 cm
Gemäldegalerie, Staatliche Museen
zu Berlin (1177A)

FIG. 219
GIOVANNI BELLINI
Saint Francis in the Desert,
about 1476–8
Oil on panel, 124.6 × 142 cm
The Frick Collection, New York
(1915.1.03)

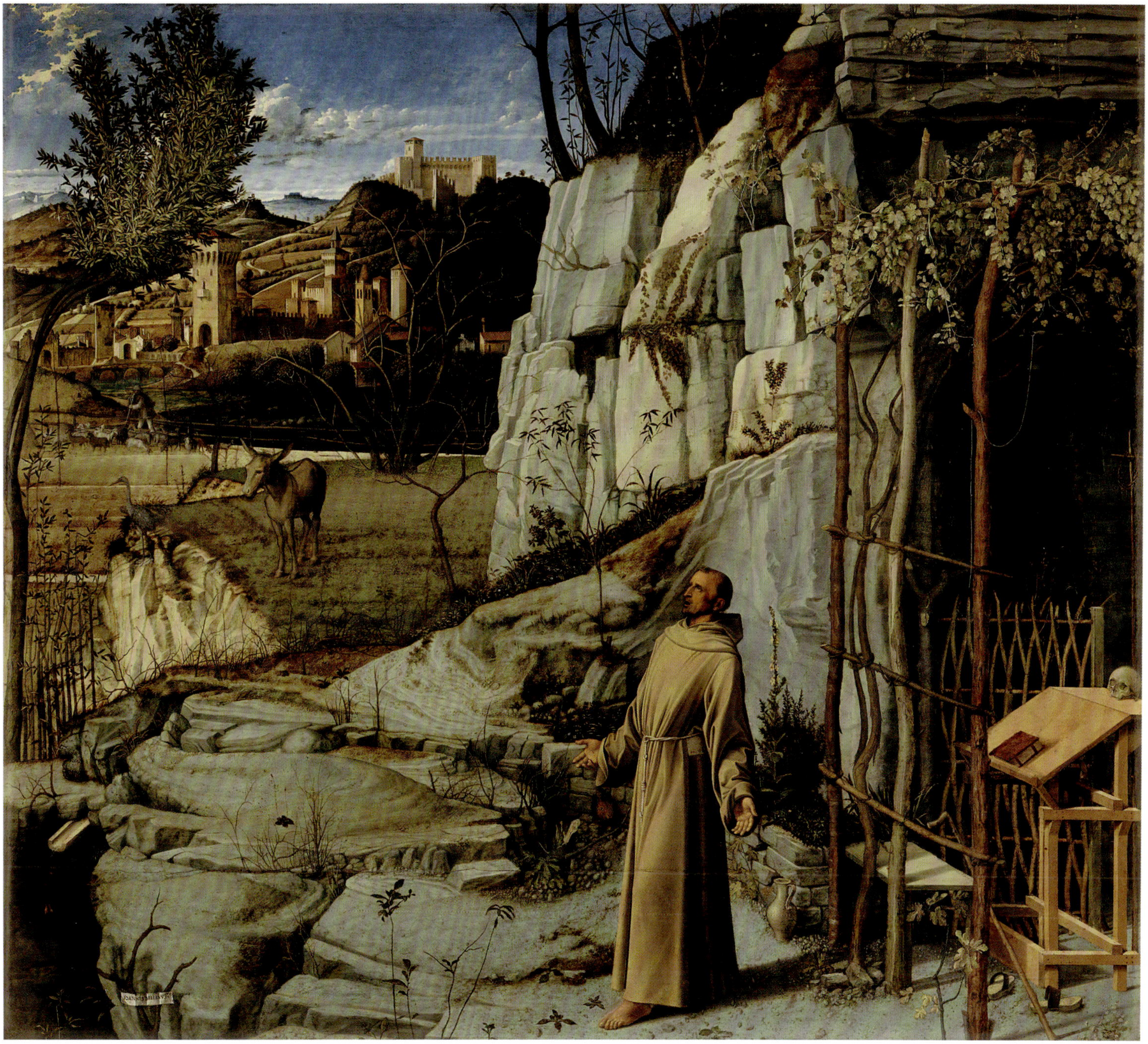

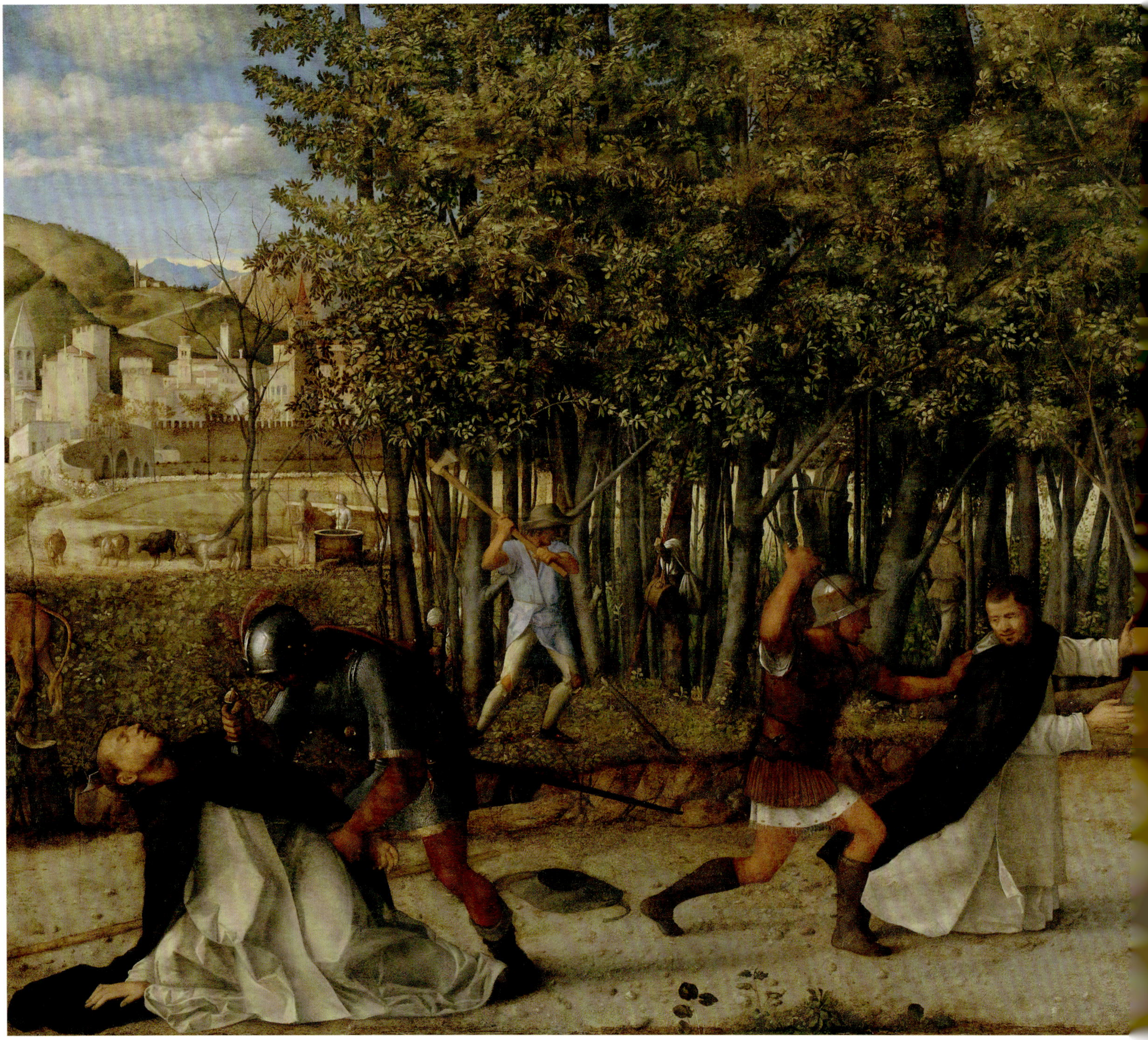

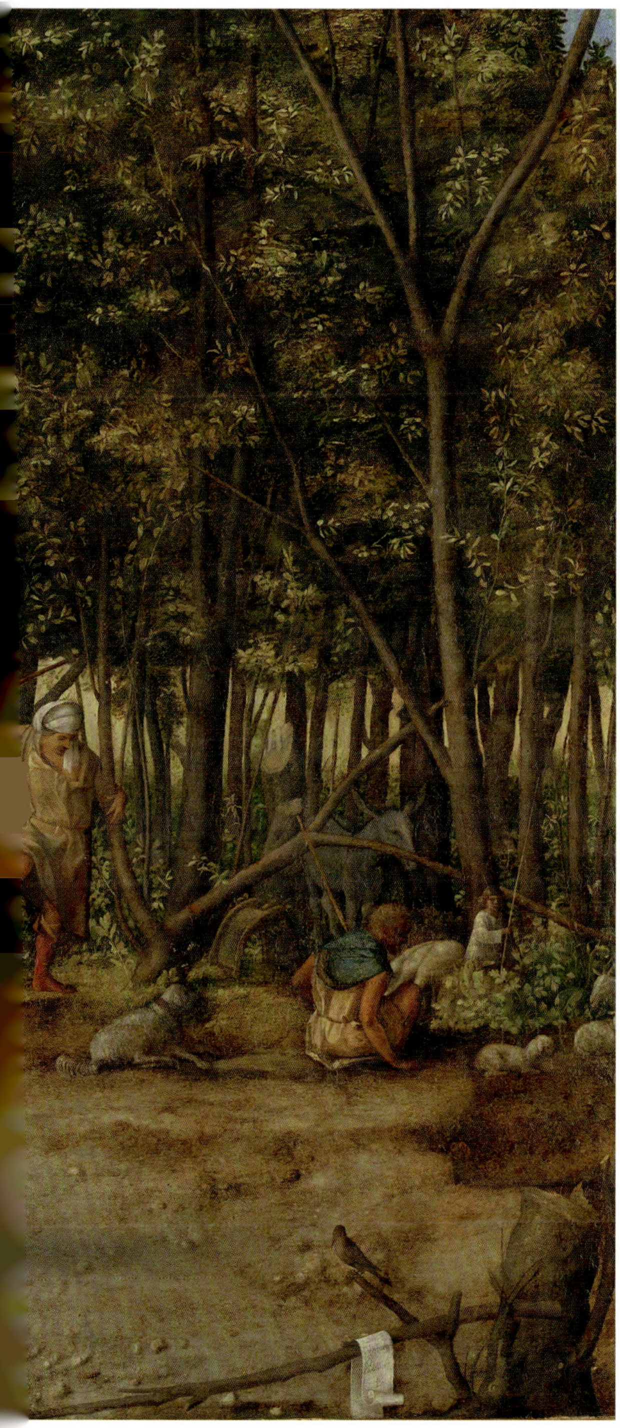

FIG. 220
GIOVANNI BELLINI
The Assassination of Saint Peter Martyr, about 1505–7
Oil on panel, 99.7 × 165.1 cm
The National Gallery, London (NG 812)

themselves were quite conventional. *Saint Francis in the Desert* (fig. 219), made for Bellini's neighbour Zuan Michiel in the late 1470s, shows the saint receiving the stigmata,[22] or wounds of Christ, in an expansive landscape, notable both for close-up details, such as the pebbles and weeds in the foreground, and the 'blue remembered hills'[23] stretching away into the horizon. As Keith Christiansen has noted, this picture created a 'new type of meditational image',[24] in which the landscape itself becomes the true subject of the painting.

The same can be said of another unusual painting of a well-known subject, *The Assassination of Saint Peter Martyr* (fig. 220), in which Bellini infuses every natural element with meaning.[25] The animals and shepherds going about their everyday business in the quiet of the dawn, in a wooded landscape on the edge of a town, contrast with the unnatural violence inflicted on the saint (even the trees bleed in sympathy with Peter, in a brilliant visual example of 'pathetic fallacy'). The *Saint Francis* is first recorded in a private home in Venice (that of Taddeo Contarini), in 1525,[26] and although it is often assumed that it was made for a non-public setting, we know nothing concrete about its original location, or that of *The Assassination of Saint Peter Martyr*. The potential for these 'landscape' pictures (neither altarpieces, nor small-scale private devotional works) to be displayed publically, as well as in private, is demonstrated by *The Transfiguration of Christ* (fig. 222), which despite having overall dimensions and proportions similar to those of the Frick *Saint Francis*, was almost certainly painted for the funerary chapel of Archdeacon Fioccardo in Vicenza Cathedral.[27]

Small pictures made for the homes of their patrons for private devotion offered Mantegna and Bellini the opportunity to develop further the artistic potential of landscape painting, although this could take very different directions. Paintings by Mantegna in which landscape plays an important role were special commissions for particularly erudite or literary patrons, often made within a courtly context. *The Adoration of the Shepherds* (fig. 221), probably painted for Borso d'Este, Duke of Ferrara, is one of Mantegna's earliest works in this genre. It takes on an intellectual challenge posed by the Duke's half-brother Leonello in *De politia litteraria*, a literary dialogue by their court humanist Angelo Decembrio.[28] Leonello praises miniature paintings which reproduce the effects of nature, but doubts that painters can surpass poets in this regard. Miniaturistic details in the *Adoration*, such as the wattle fence and the gourd hanging over the fence, constitute Mantegna's combative response to this challenge. Command of such exquisite naturalism can be found in small-scale paintings throughout his career. Mantegna's *Agony in the Garden* (fig. 125), full of carefully observed details such as the fallen tree trunk which acts a bridge, or the rabbits on the path, must have been commissioned by a patron with as strong intellectual interests as the Benedictine Abbot Gregorio Correr, patron of the *San Zeno Altarpiece* (fig. 252) or Jacopo Antonio Marcello, for whom the tiny *Saint Sebastian* (fig. 193), complete with an illusionistic cloud shaped as a bearded horseman (fig. 191), was possibly made.

Working in the protected bubble of the Mantuan court, however, Mantegna was never required to mass-produce private devotional paintings – the bread and butter of his Venetian brother-in-law. The exigencies

FIG. 221
ANDREA MANTEGNA
The Adoration of the Shepherds, about 1450–2
Egg tempera on canvas, transferred from panel, 40 × 55.6 cm
The Metropolitan Museum of Art, New York (1932.130.2)

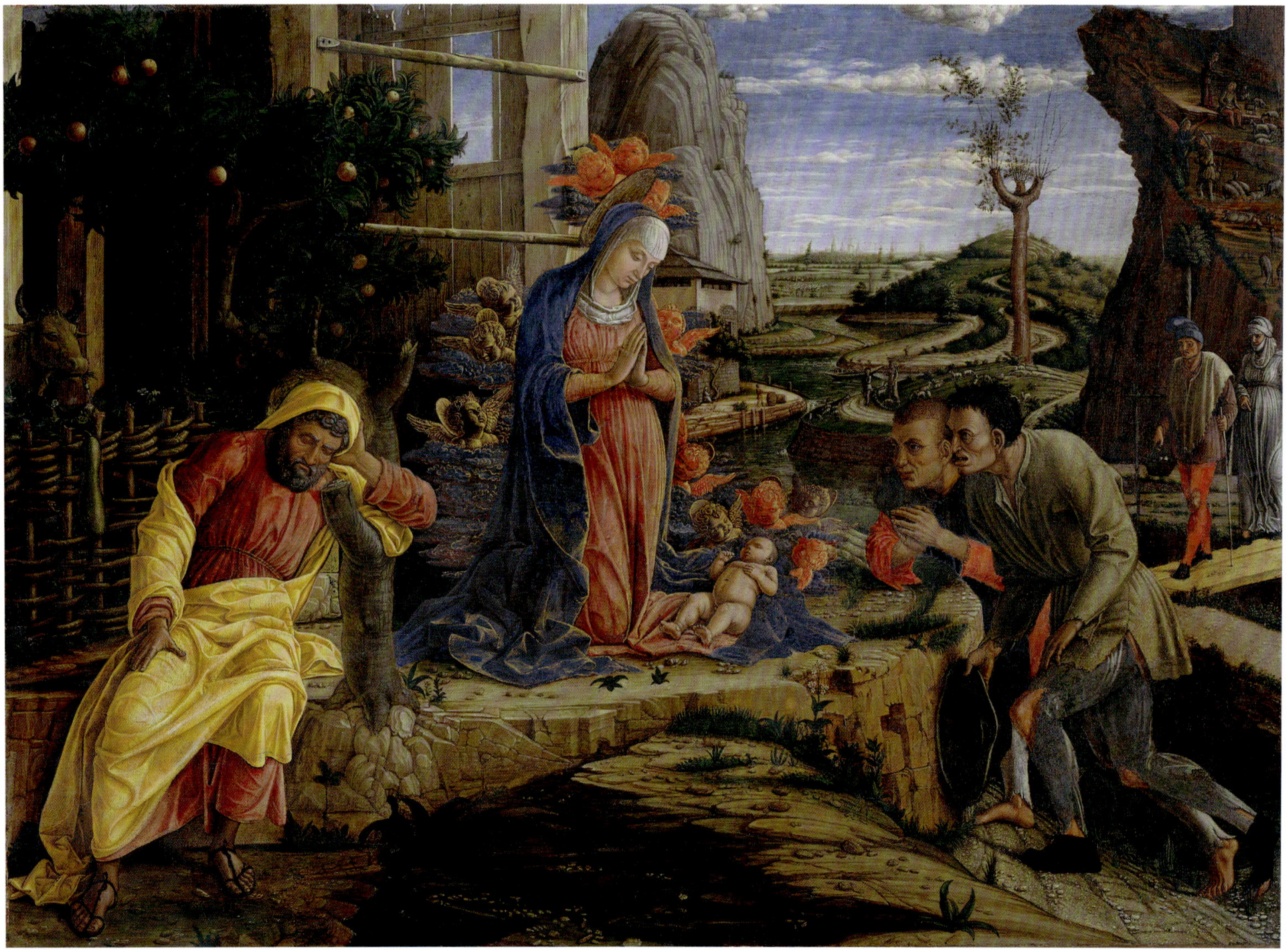

FIG. 222
GIOVANNI BELLINI
The Transfiguration of Christ, 1478–9
Oil on panel, 115 × 152 cm
Museo Nazionale di Capodimonte, Naples (56)

of this market, in the sophisticated context of Venice, where 'paesi' or landscapes were particularly valued by discerning collectors, and where Bellini belonged to humanist circles,[29] encouraged the painter to develop a genre of small-scale religious paintings which derived meaning from their use of landscape and of light. We can observe this tendency in the numerous and diverse pictures of two subjects that Bellini painted throughout his career, the Virgin and Child[30] and Saint Jerome. A version of *Saint Jerome in the Wilderness* (fig. 114) is Bellini's earliest independent work, and many pictures of this subject survive by the master and his workshop, including fig. 117 and a painting in the Uffizi, Florence (Contini Bonacossi collection).[31] While Saint Jerome himself does not change much from painting to painting, the artist continually re-invented the surrounding landscapes.[32] These are never hostile wildernesses but calm natural settings, which accord with Jerome's serene appearance. Certain individual elements have been discussed as conveyors of religious symbolical meaning,[33] but these paintings cannot simply be seen as an 'anthology of symbols'.[34] Saint Jerome's solitude is distant from human civilisation yet –as with any Arcadian retreat described by Petrarch, Boccaccio and

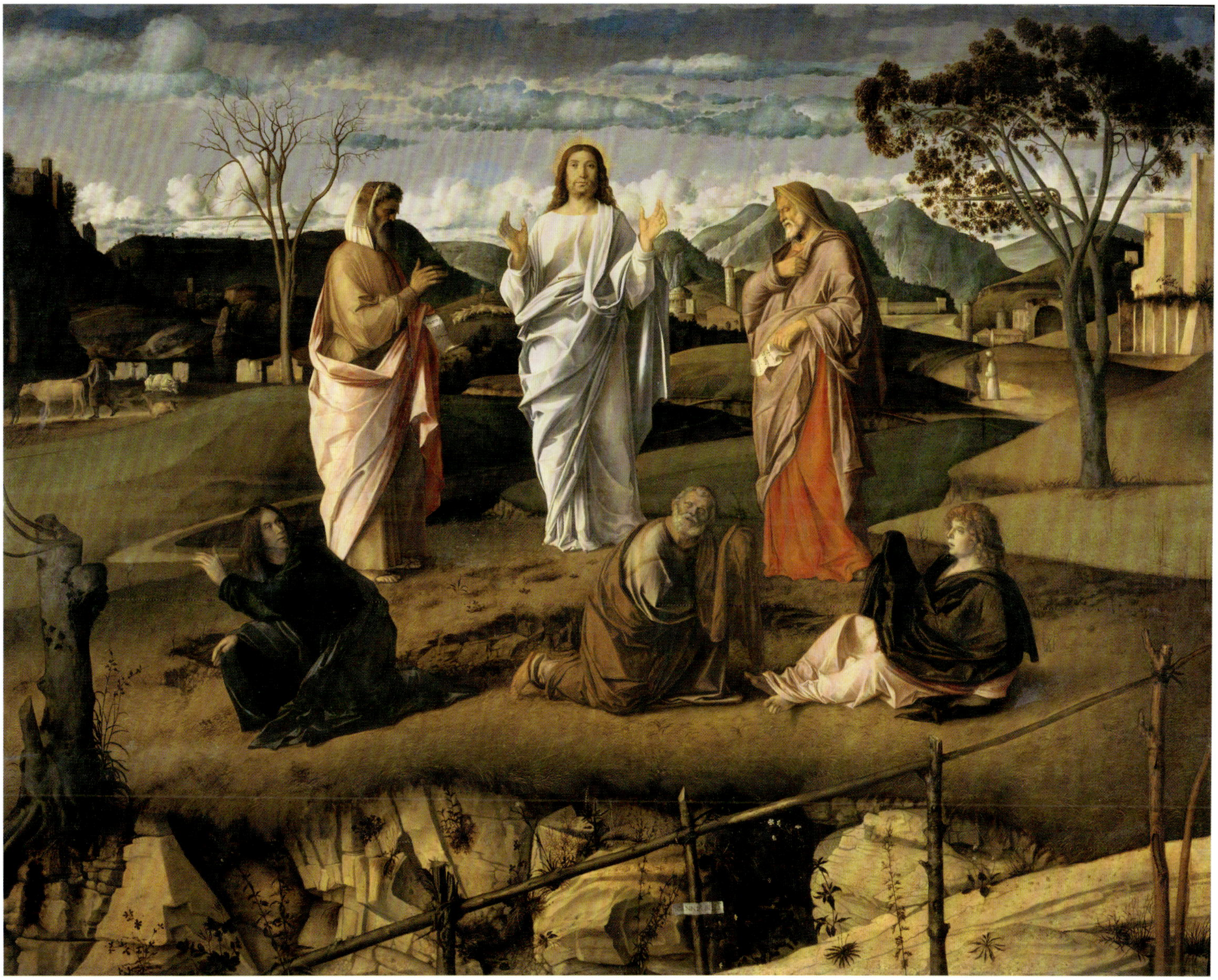

Sannazaro – inconceivable without it. The cityscape in the background is an ideal synthesis of motifs. As in Bellini's pictures, it is not the portrait of a real place, even if it is clearly inspired by Venetian towns and cities of the Terraferma.

While the very subject of Saint Jerome in the wilderness could be argued to require a landscape setting, this was not the case for depictions of the Virgin and Child. In Bellini's hands, this subject was very rarely separated from landscape. In fact the two became intimately related, to the extent that landscape was never just the setting for the sacred figures. In this context Bellini's *Madonna of the Meadow* (fig. 180) provides an excellent example of how landscape provided a narrative which enhanced the meaning of Bellini's devotional images. The seated Virgin is shown in adoration of her sleeping son, laid across her lap in a pose which is a presentiment of his dead body on the lap of his mother in the Pietà. The Virgin sits in front of the landscape rather than in it;[35] her closeness to the viewer/worshipper is enhanced by the familiar Venetian landscape in the background.[36] The melancholic atmosphere is also symbolically charged by details of the landscape. To the left of the Virgin a crane is attacking a snake, perhaps symbolising the battle between good and evil,[37] while the vulture in the tree may be a symbol of death, a role it plays in other works by Mantegna and Bellini, from the earliest period of their acquaintance (figs 125, 126).

Just as Bellini recognised Mantegna as a master of intellectual narratives,[38] the visual evidence of several works by Mantegna suggests his admiration for his brother-in-law's use of landscape and light to convey meaning. In Mantegna's *Virgin and Child with the Infant Saint John the Baptist and Female Saints* of about 1495, in the Isabella Stewart Gardner Museum, Boston,[39] quite possibly painted for Isabella d'Este, we can see the sort of carefully constructed landscape that Isabella was hoping to receive from Giovanni Bellini.[40]

It seems a fitting reflection of Mantegna's admiration of his brother-in-law's work that his most striking small-scale landscape is also his most Bellinian and his least typical. The *Dead Christ supported by Two Angels* (fig. 150), painted in the last 15 years of the fifteenth century, perhaps for the Mantuan Valenti family,[41] shows Christ returning to life. His face is suffused with colour, while his body, up to his neck, remains in the stony pallor of death. It is the moment of daybreak, and the sky is divided between the glow of the sun, which we can imagine rising just behind the rocky outcrop with the three crosses on the right, and the dark blue of the departing night. Under the mound of Golgotha, in front of a long tunnel, we see stonemasons at work, one of whom is carving a marble statue. The motif of the tunnel disappearing directly into the hill may recall the connection between nature and artifice seen in *The Descent of Christ into Limbo* (fig. 145), and Christ's tomb in Bellini's *Resurrection of Christ* (fig. 218). In the countryside, meanwhile, the shepherds working in the fields suggest peace and the continuity of ordinary life through the defining event of the Passion of Christ. Landscape here is not simply a backdrop to the scene depicted, but a foil that sets off and enhances its meaning.

GIOVANNI BELLINI,
detail from *The Resurrection of Christ* (FIG. 218)

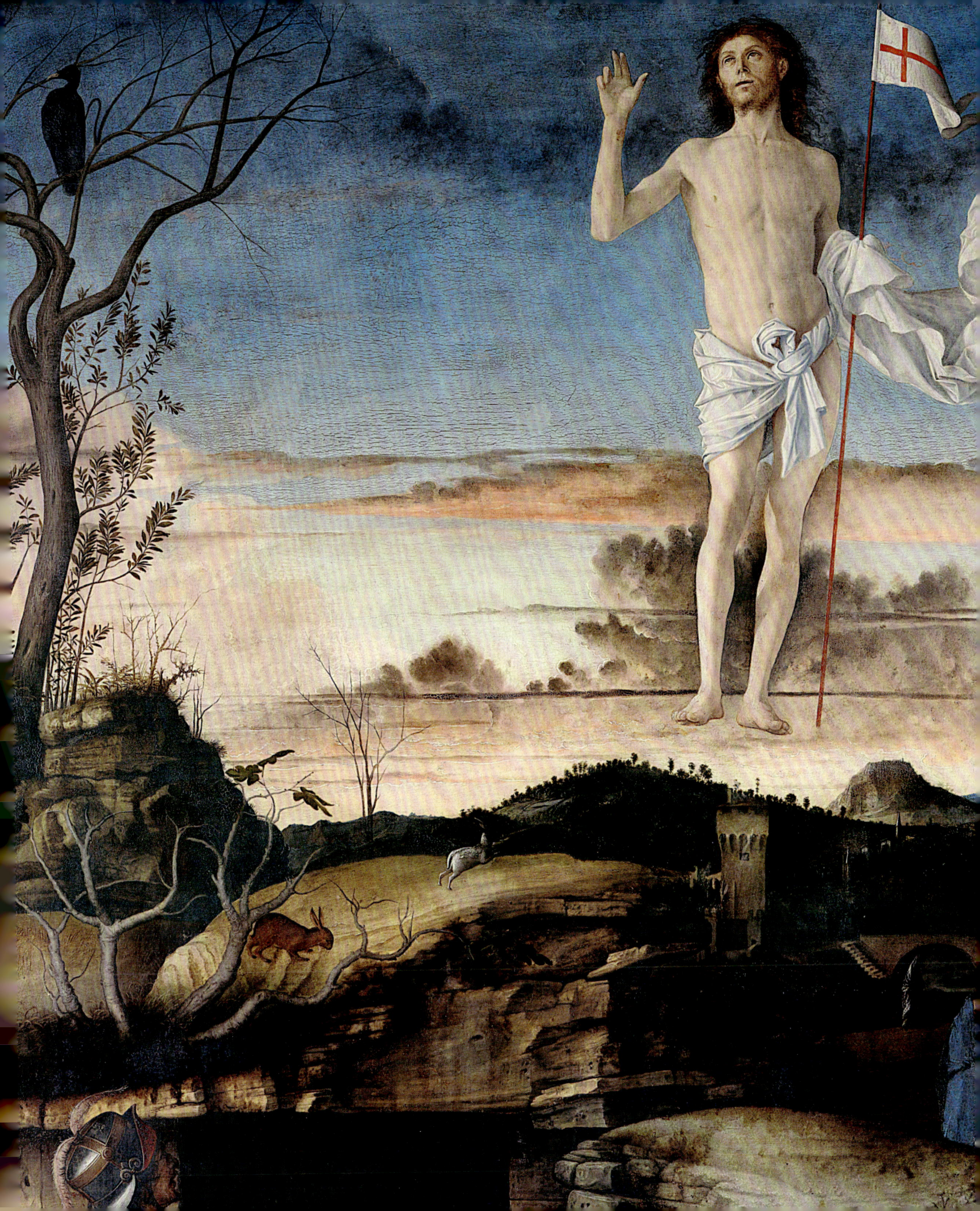

Mantegna, Bellini and Antiquity

SARAH VOWLES AND CAROLINE CAMPBELL

On 23 February 1483 Lorenzo de' Medici visited Mantegna's house in Mantua, where he admired 'certain heads in relief and many other antique things' in the artist's collection.[1] Eleven years earlier, the artist had also been invited to visit Cardinal Francesco Gonzaga to discuss 'cameos, bronze statuettes and other antiquities'.[2] Contemporaries evidently regarded him as a discerning collector, who appreciated antiquities not just as artistic models but as classical relics.[3]

Since his boyhood in Padua, Mantegna had moved in circles which explored, studied and identified with the classical past.[4] When he arrived in Mantua in 1460, he found an equally enthusiastic culture of classicism encouraged by his noble patron Ludovico III Gonzaga. Ludovico had studied with the humanist Vittorino da Feltre and retained his admiration for classical authors and culture throughout his life.[5] His court attracted like-minded men, among them Mantegna's friend, the Veronese poet Felice Feliciano, who dedicated two volumes of antique inscriptions to the artist in January 1463, praising him for being 'ever most prompt and partial to the investigation of antiquities of this sort'.[6] Evidence for such investigations comes from Feliciano's famous but probably fictitious account of a trip to Lake Garda with Mantegna and other friends in search of antique inscriptions.[7] Mantegna's interest in such relics suggests that he had sufficient Latin to appreciate them, an unusual accomplishment in an artist of this period.

Although Venice had no classical history of its own,[8] the young Bellini was surrounded by humanists and classical scholars.[9] Feliciano, for instance, was as much his friend as he was Mantegna's.[10] Giovanni's father Jacopo collected antiquities, and made numerous studies of classical themes in his Drawing Books, including Roman inscriptions from Jacopo Antonio Marcello's country property.[11] His brother Gentile had a small collection of ancient sculpture,[12] and apparently the Bellini studio housed a torso of Venus (probably the source for the *Woman with a Mirror* of 1515, now in the Kunsthistorisches Museum in Vienna) and a bust of Plato.[13] Infamously, Giovanni and their other brother Nicolò attempted to sell this heavily restored bust to Isabella d'Este in 1512.[14] As with much of Giovanni Bellini's life, we can draw inferences from his paintings, and from his family and friendship circles, but we have little firm evidence of what he actually thought.

The republican context of Venetian life prompted a set of priorities, in literary scholarship and art collecting, very different from those in insular, courtly Mantua.[15]

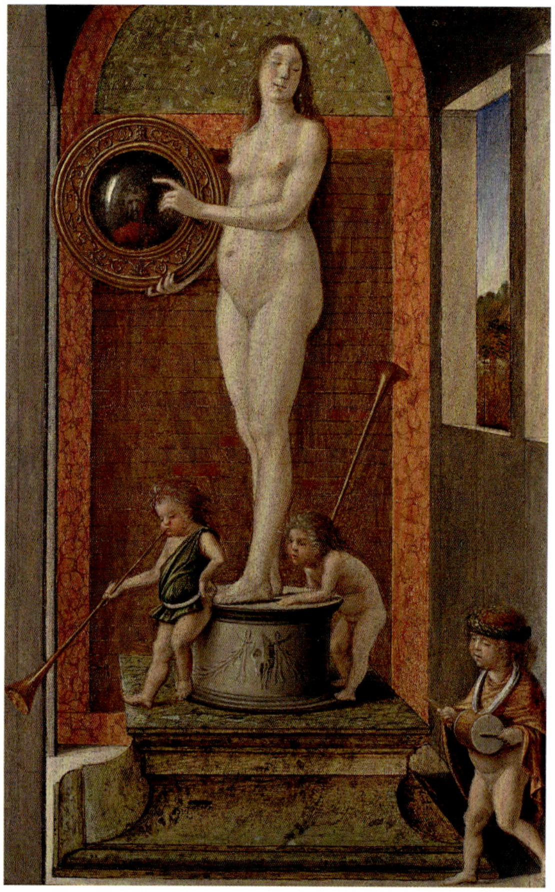

FIG. 223
GIOVANNI BELLINI
Allegory of Vanity, about 1490
Oil on panel, 34 × 22 cm
Gallerie dell'Accademia, Venice (595c)

Relatively few Venetian citizens and noblemen had any desire for the elaborate classical painted allegories commissioned by the Gonzaga.[16] Most of Bellini's surviving paintings are of Christian subjects, and he rarely painted 'pure' antique narratives. The pictures in which he comes closest to Mantegna's spirit in this regard are the *Allegories of Virtues* from the Accademia in Venice (fig. 223), which were probably made to be set into furniture,[17] and the *Sacred Allegory* now in the Uffizi (fig. 224). Moreover, his surviving paintings on classical themes – including *The Continence of Publius Cornelius Scipio* (fig. 246) and *The Feast of the Gods* (fig. 226) – all date from the final years of his life. They rarely follow a clear textual source: Bellini was resistant to following the 'humanist programme' so beloved of Isabella d'Este, and indeed of twentieth-century Warburgian scholars such as E.H. Gombrich.

Unlike Mantegna, Bellini did not incessantly quote classical and classicised architecture and sculpture (although such antique allusions can be found in his works,[18] and presumably more would have been included in the now destroyed history paintings he and Gentile made for the Ducal Palace in Venice). Yet it is evident that he was motivated by classical ideas – and Renaissance reinterpretations of them – about the philosophical purposes of painting, and the individual agency of the painter.[19] For instance, Bellini's development of 'tonal' painting – one of his key artistic innovations – was deeply indebted to Pliny's *Natural History*.[20] And Bellini's pictures, including those of resolutely Christian subjects,[21] assert the status of painting as an art form analogous to poetry itself, following the classical trope 'ut pictura poesis' ('as is painting, so is poetry'), as much as those of later Venetian painters including Giorgione and Titian.

The classical interests of Bellini and his patrons can be discerned, subtly, from the references found in his paintings: such as in *The Dead Christ supported by the Virgin and Saint John* (fig. 11), where an adaptation of one of Propertius's elegies inscribed on the *cartellino* asserts:

FIG. 224
GIOVANNI BELLINI
Sacred Allegory, about 1490
Oil on panel, 73 × 119 cm
Galleria degli Uffizi, Florence (1890 no. 903)

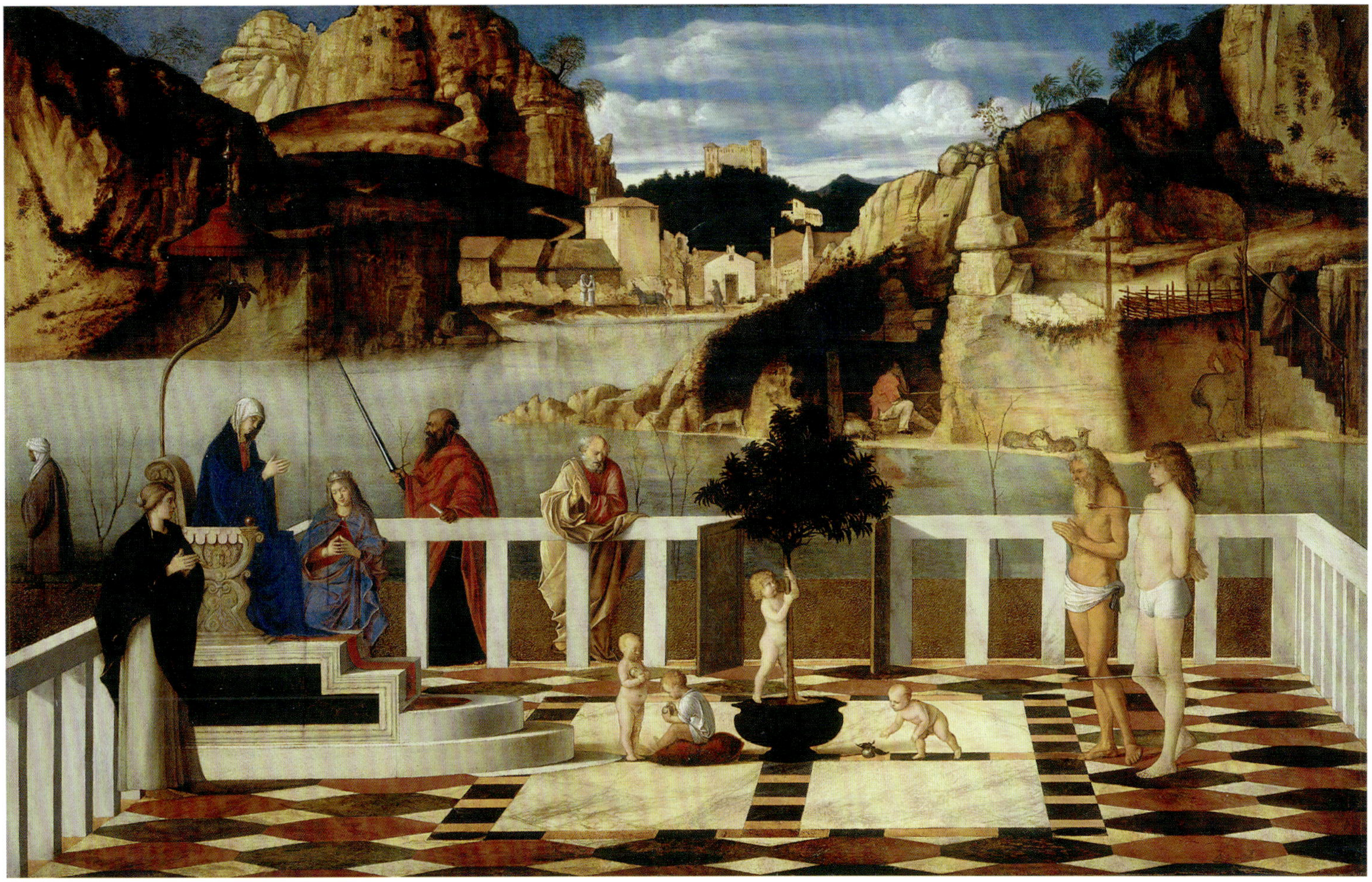

FIG. 225
ANDREA MANTEGNA
Minerva expelling the Vices from the Garden of Virtue, about 1500–2
Egg tempera on canvas,
159 × 192 cm
Musée du Louvre, Paris (371)

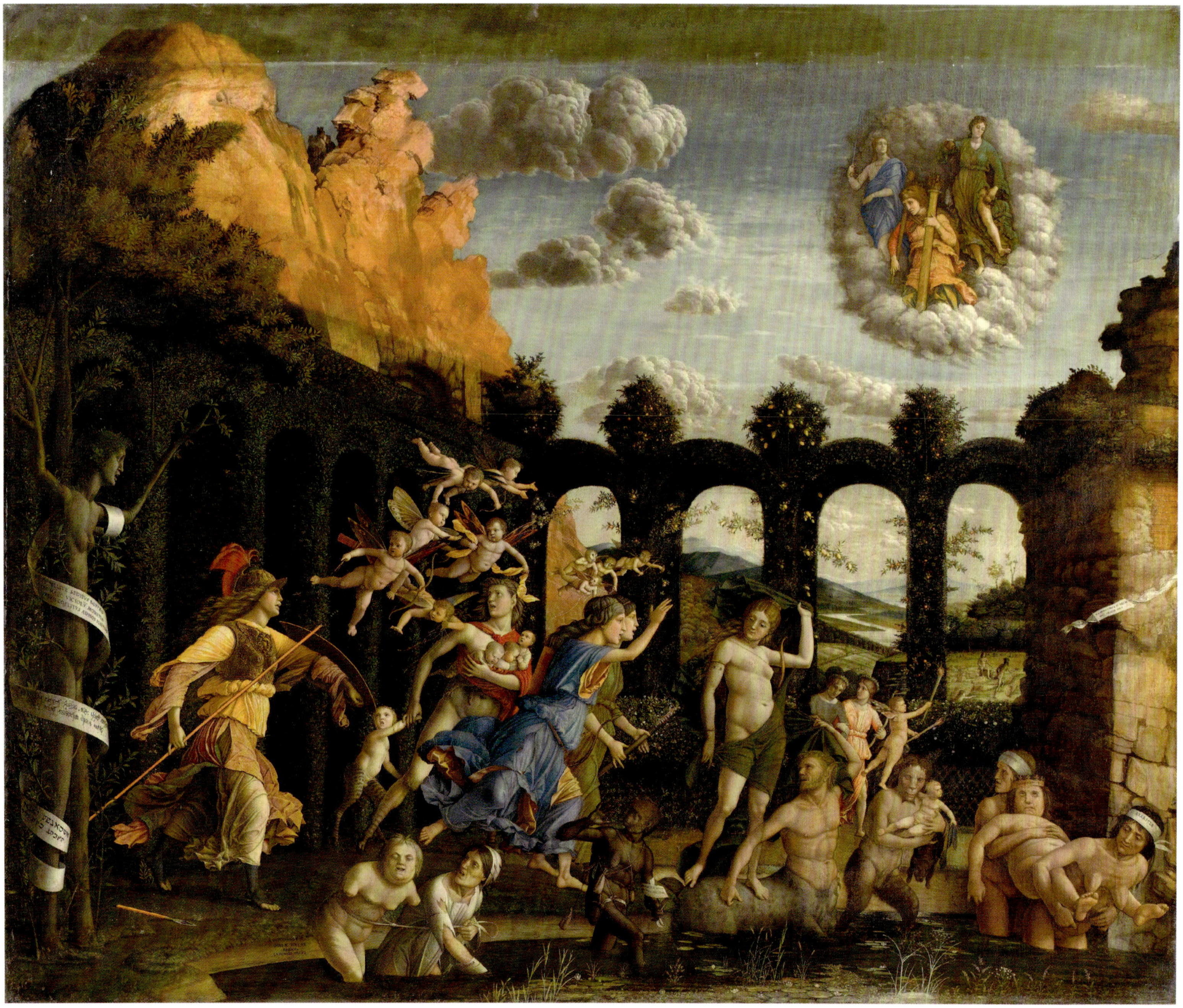

FIG. 226
GIOVANNI BELLINI, with
later additions by DOSSO DOSSI
and TITIAN
The Feast of the Gods, 1514–29
Oil on canvas, 170.2 × 188 cm
National Gallery of Art, Washington DC
(1942.9.1)

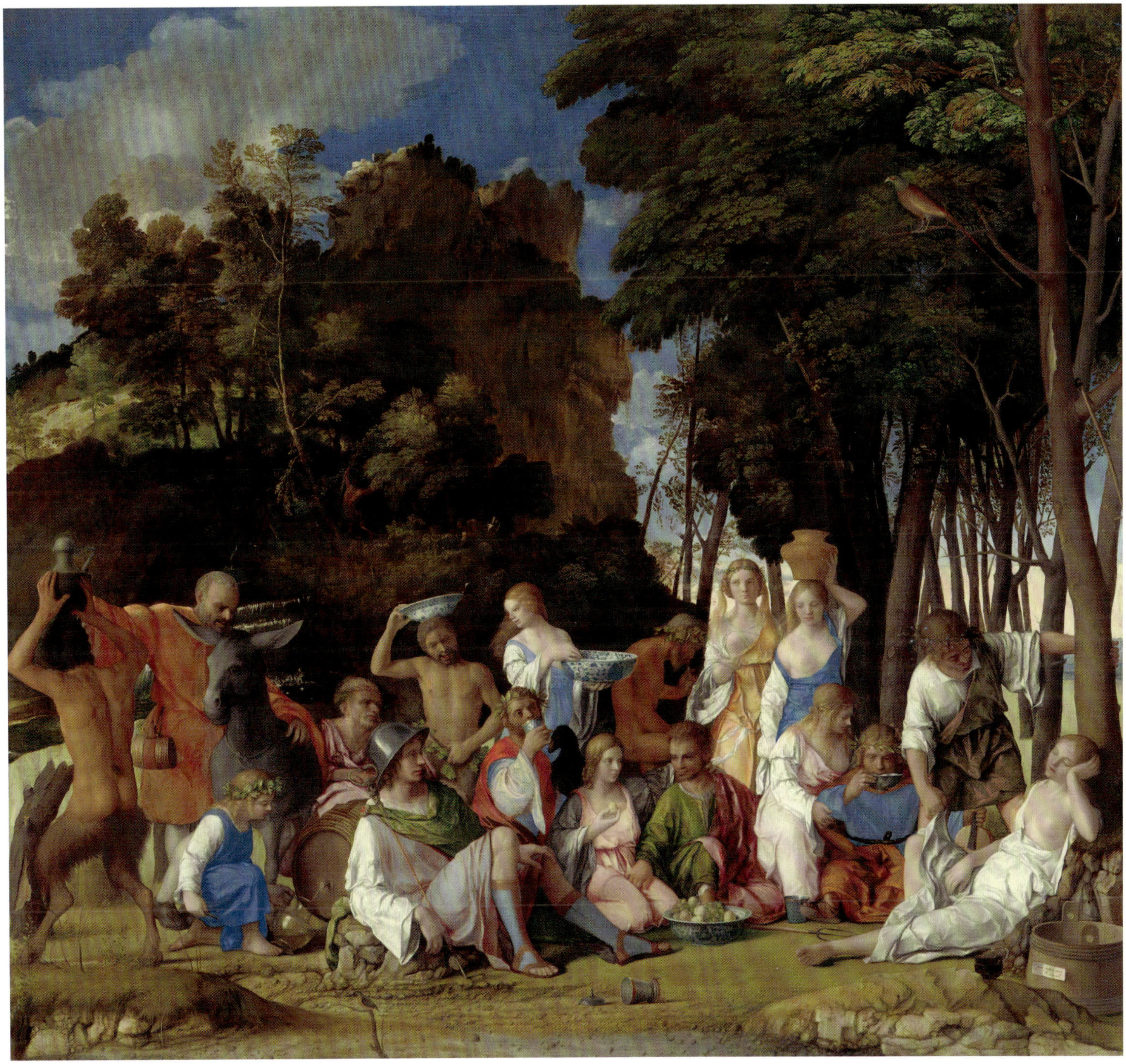

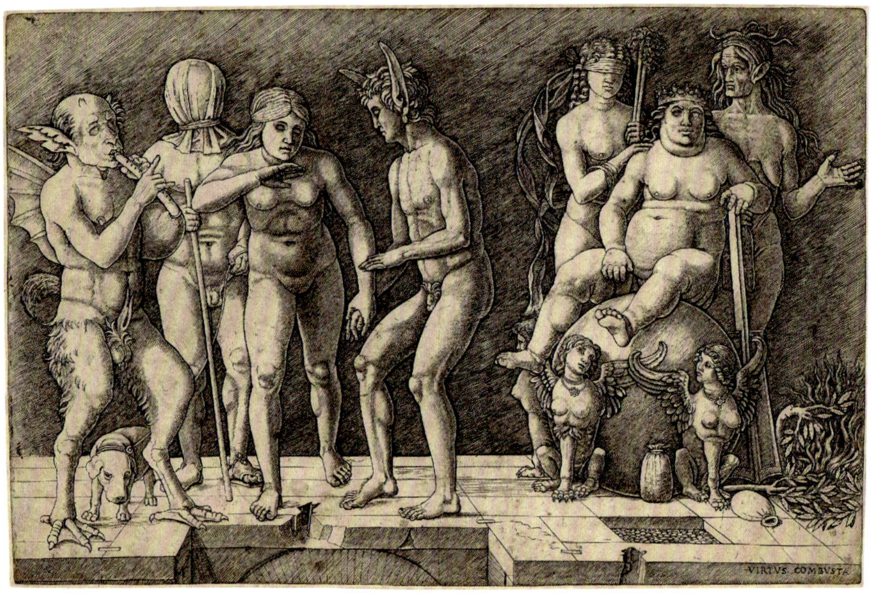

FIG. 227
GIOVANNI ANTONIO DA BRESCIA,
after ANDREA MANTEGNA
Virtus Combusta, about 1490–1506
Engraving, 27.9 × 42.4 cm
The British Museum, London
(1845,0825.673)

'When these swelling eyes bring forth groans, this work of Giovanni Bellini will be able to shed tears',[22] or the *Woman with a Mirror* in Vienna, which reflects Bellini's understanding of ancient sculpture, but which defies being tied to an all-defining 'source' or 'sources'.[23] An awareness of classical, or classically inspired, poetry can also be understood in the elegiac and pastoral moods of many of Bellini's devotional works,[24] whether paintings for a private house, such as the *Madonna of the Meadow* (fig. 180), altarpieces for the more public setting of a church, such as *The Resurrection of Christ* (fig. 218), or paintings of unusual iconography, like *The Drunkenness of Noah* (fig. 247).[25]

Bellini, Mantegna and the studioli

Isabella d'Este – who had arrived in Mantua from Ferrara in 1490 as the 16-year-old bride of Francesco Gonzaga – was one of the most demanding of Renaissance patrons and often personally defined the programmes for her artists to follow.[26] For many years, her energies were concentrated on the decoration of her apartments in the south-east corner of the Castello San Giorgio, particularly her 'little study' (*studiolo*) and 'grotto' (*grotta*). Isabella's plans upset Mantegna, for she not only intended to limit his artistic freedom by requiring that he follow an 'invention' (*invenzione*) devised by her adviser(s),[27] but she also wished to include works by other renowned artists in her *studiolo*. She desired – as her brother Alfonso did some years later – to acquire a cycle of paintings on ancient themes by the most celebrated painters active in Italy.[28] Mantegna was ultimately to deliver two substantial narrative compositions: the *Parnassus* (fig. 57) , finished by 1497,[29] and *Minerva expelling the Vices from the Garden of Virtue* (fig. 225), along with two small paintings in imitation of bronze reliefs[30] for the *studiolo*. Mantegna's genius in *Parnassus* and *Minerva* was to translate into paint complex iconographic schemes which provided fruit for discussion by the erudite,[31] but whose general tenets could be also understood by viewers with limited knowledge of classical and humanistic texts. In *Minerva*, for instance, the meaning is clear from the representations of the Vices, including Ignorance, Lust and Idleness, accompanied by satyrs, who flee before the armed goddess of Wisdom. The subject seems to have been suggested by Isabella's adviser, Paride Ceresara,[32] but it must have been left up to Mantegna how to interpret the advice he received for both pictures, as similar characters appear in other works by him. Ignorance, who is personified as an obese, crowned woman in *Minerva* appears in both *Virtus Combusta* (fig. 229) and *The Calumny of Apelles* (fig. 230),[33] while the female figures in the coloured drawing of *Three deities* (fig. 231) echo the stances of Venus and one of the Muses in the *Parnassus* (fig. 57).[34]

A third large work, the *Comus*, was left incomplete at Mantegna's death.[35] Other artists, however, were less obliging than the Mantuan court painter. Isabella disliked the *Combat between Love and Chastity* that she commissioned from Pietro Perugino,[36] and she was never able to satisfy her desire for an allegory in the ancient style from Bellini. In 1506, after a decade of negotiations,[37] the Marchioness was still waiting for her picture.[38] At this juncture she would have been happy to receive 'any history or ancient story', or even any subject invented by Bellini on an ancient theme.[39]

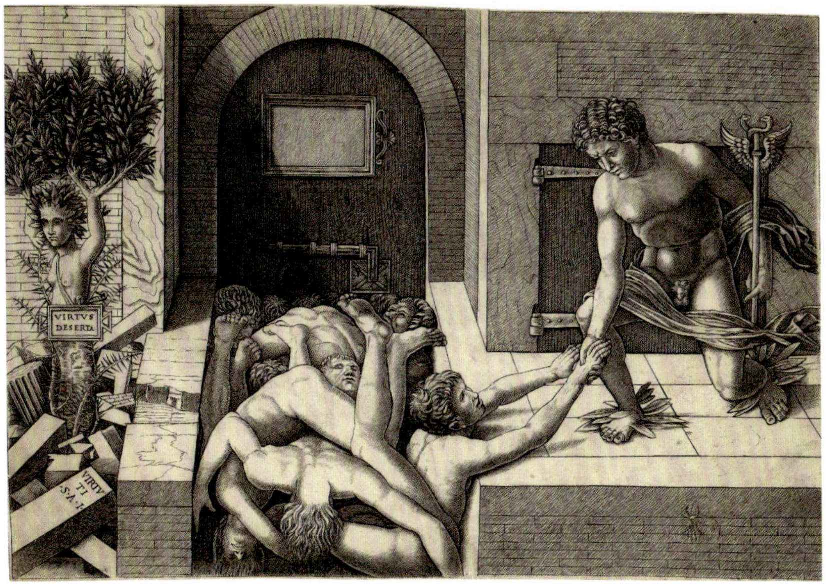

FIG. 228
GIOVANNI ANTONIO DA BRESCIA, after ANDREA MANTEGNA
Virtus Deserta, about 1490–1510
Engraving, 30 × 43.3 cm
The British Museum, London
(1845,0825.672)

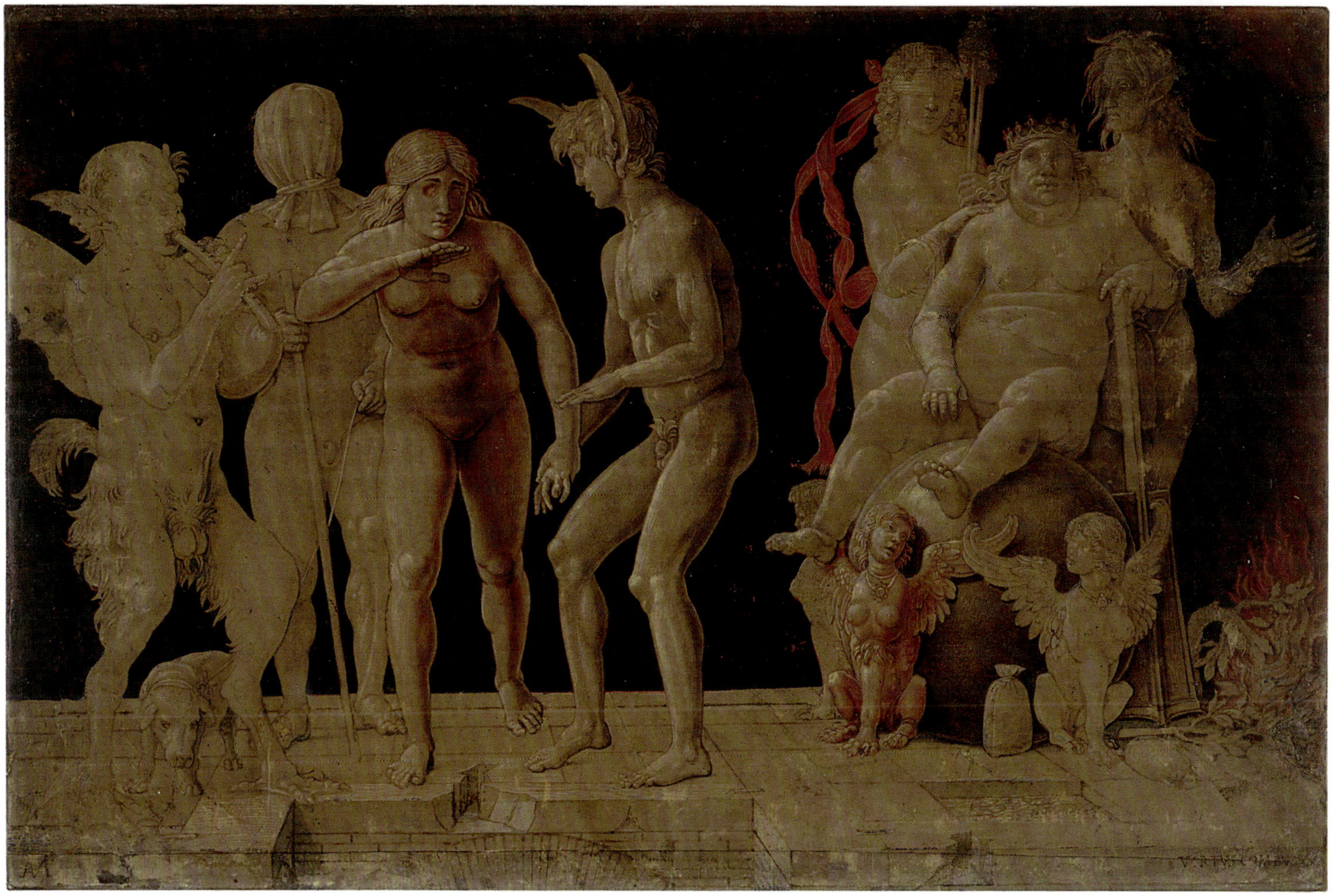

FIG. 229
ANDREA MANTEGNA
Virtus Combusta, 1490s
Pen and brown ink and point of the brush on a brown ground, heightened with white, the black background over red, on paper, 28.6 × 44.1 cm
The British Museum, London
(Pp,1.23)

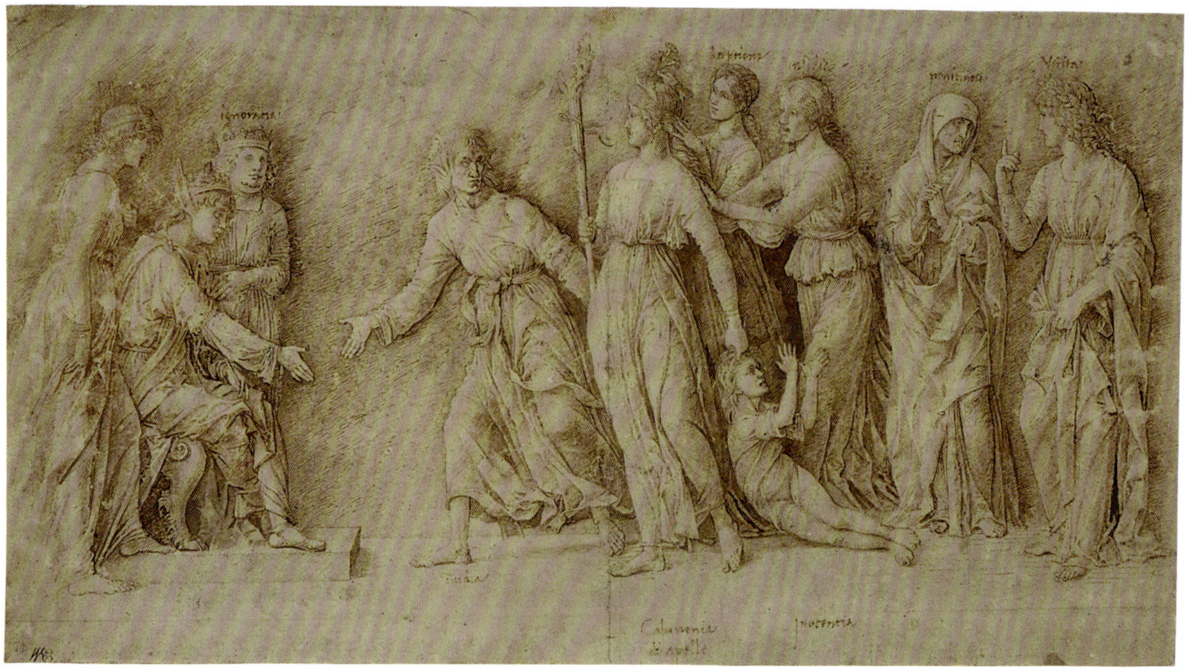

FIG. 230
ANDREA MANTEGNA
The Calumny of Apelles,
1505–6
Pen and three shades of brown ink with some white heightening, in part oxidised, on paper, 20.6 × 37.9 cm
The British Museum, London (1860,0616.85)

Would the picture that Isabella sought have looked anything like *The Feast of the Gods* (fig. 226), which Bellini delivered to her brother Alfonso for his private *studiolo*-like space in his Castle in Ferrara, the *Camerino d'alabastro*, in 1514? This is a type of painting, in terms of subject and size, which is far from Bellini's norm. There are resonances between Bellini's *Feast of the Gods* and Mantegna's *Parnassus* (fig. 57) and *Minerva expelling the Vices* (fig. 225), even though the *Feast* was painted around 15 years after Mantegna's works, long after his death. In these works by Mantegna and Bellini it is striking how the divine and semi-divine creatures are ranged in horizontal rows, within a unified landscape, and placed in the foreground. Looking at Mantegna's *Minerva* and Bellini's *Feast* together, it is hard to believe that Bellini was ignorant of Mantegna's large-scale secular compositions for Isabella's *studiolo*, which were, after all, among the most celebrated paintings of the early sixteenth century.[40] There is no evidence that Bellini ever visited Mantua, but we know of Bellini's close scrutiny of other Mantuan compositions by Mantegna, including *The Descent of Christ into Limbo*;[41] in addition, his brother Nicolò was a regular traveller to the city in the years that Mantegna was working on Isabella's *studiolo* paintings.[42]

The patron as well as the painter of *The Feast of the Gods* must have had Isabella's *studiolo* – as well as that of her and Alfonso's mother – in mind, but the genesis of Alfonso's private room is unfortunately far less well documented than his sister's commissions in Mantua.[43] Bellini's painting for the *Camerino d'alabastro*, the first to be commissioned and to be delivered,[44] is based on a description in Ovid's poem of the Roman calendar, or *Fasti*, of a meeting between a number of the Roman gods including Apollo, Neptune and Jupiter in a sylvan glade.[45] The harmonious mood is spoilt by Priapus, god of fertility, who attempts to remove the clothing of the sleeping nymph Lotis. A second later, we are to imagine, Silenius's donkey brays, Priapus's evil act is noticed, and the moment of misadventure has passed. The quiet, contemplative mood of *The Feast of the Gods* is close to several landscape compositions by Bellini from the first decade of the sixteenth century, including the *Madonna of the Meadow* and *The Assassination of Saint Peter Martyr* (fig. 220). The painting has often been criticised for its static nature, at least in its original state before Dosso Dossi and Titian had altered it.[46] This, however, is to misunderstand Bellini's intention. Rather than being viewed as a staid forerunner of Titian's mythological poems in paint, from *Bacchus and Ariadne* for Alfonso d'Este to *The Death of Actaeon* for Philip II of Spain,[47] *The Feast of the Gods* demands to be recognised as among the very earliest of Venetian large-scale paintings of classical antiquity – a pictorial genre which had a lasting impact on the development of Western art.

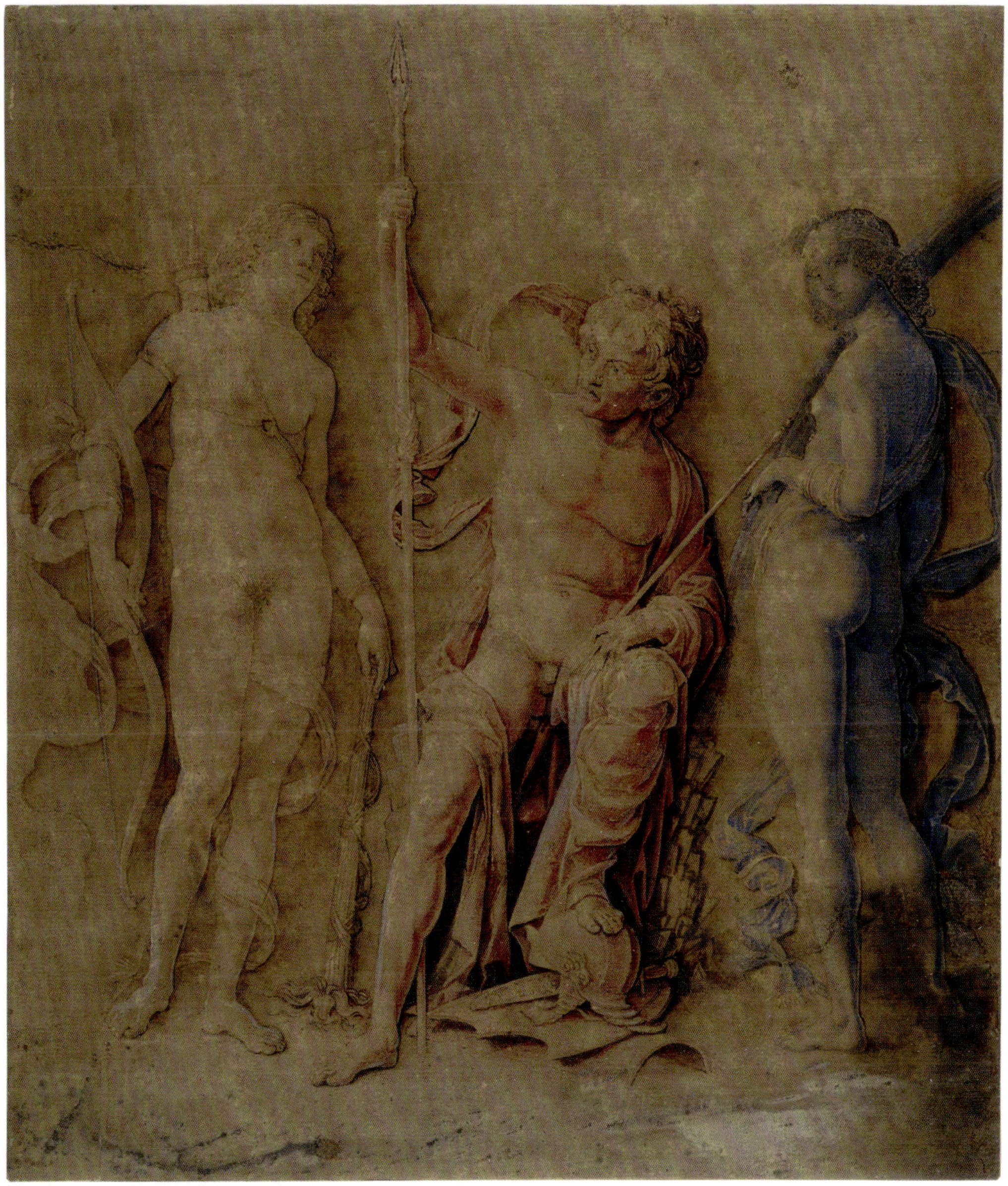

FIG. 231
ANDREA MANTEGNA
Three deities, 1490s
Pen and brown ink with brown, red and blue wash, heightened with white, on paper, 36.3 × 31.6 cm
The British Museum, London (1861,0810.2)

Mantegna, invention and the antique

Mantegna usually turned to antiquity to spur his own visual imagination. However, two studies of birds – *A bird catching a fly* (fig. 233) and *Bird on a branch* (fig. 232)[48] – may be directly copied from antique sources,[49] while the *Orange tree* (fig. 234) seems to be Mantegna's invention, drawn in an antique style. Perhaps they were made for study in the workshop, rather than as working drawings.

To emulate and to visibly complete with the great artists of antiquity, Mantegna developed a series of complex allegories on paper, as well as the paintings discussed above. These autonomous drawings and prints are works of staggering innovation, in terms of their illusionism and their iconography.[50] For instance, the *Virtus Combusta* (fig. 229) and the *Three deities* (fig. 231) use a limited palette of colour to achieve sculptural effects very different to Mantegna's fictive bronzes and marbles such as *The Introduction of the Cult of Cybele at Rome* (fig. 245) and *Judith and Abra* (fig. 58).

In *The Calumny of Apelles* (fig. 230) Folly, with ass's ears, is enthroned with Suspicion and Ignorance at his side. Calumny approaches the throne, preceded by Envy

FIG. 232
ANDREA MANTEGNA
Bird on a branch, about 1480
Pen and brown ink on
laid paper, 10.5 × 11.5 cm
National Gallery of Art,
Washington DC (1976.33.1)

FIG. 233
ANDREA MANTEGNA
A bird catching a fly, about 1480
Pen and brown ink on paper,
12.8 × 8.8 cm
The British Museum, London
(1946,0713.7)

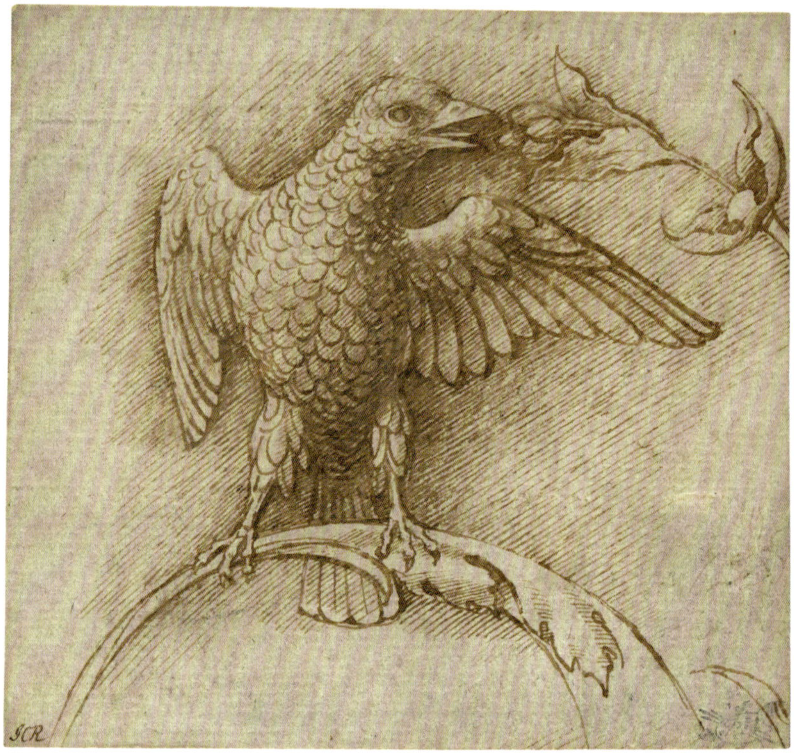

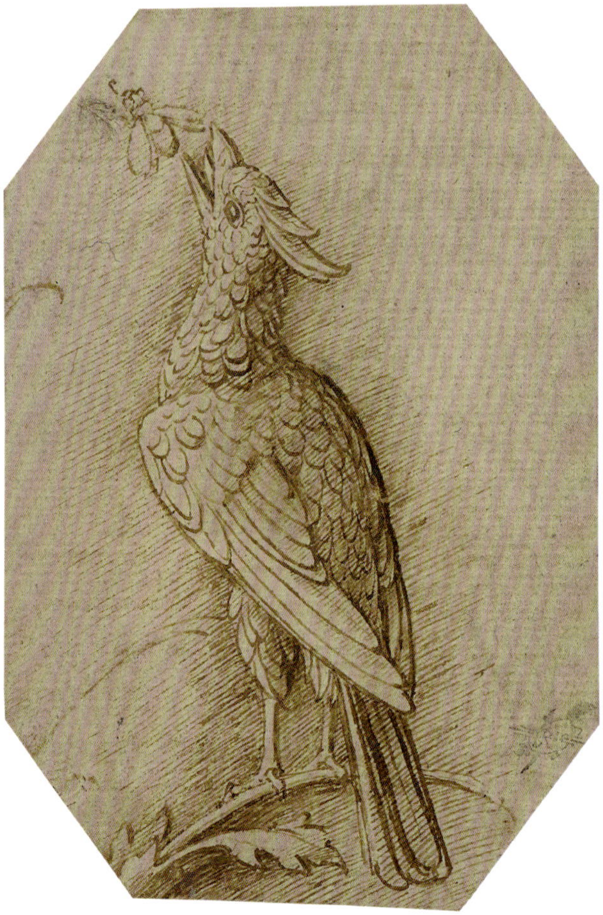

and accompanied by her handmaidens Treachery and Deceit, dragging Innocence by the hair.[51] Repentance and Truth follow behind, each figure carefully identified by an inscription by Mantegna.[52] The subject, drawn from the Greek author Lucian's *On Calumny*, describes a painting by the celebrated artist Apelles. The fifteenth-century architect and theorist Leon Battista Alberti had recommended the *Calumny* as an ideal *istoria*, or visual narrative, for artists to emulate:[53] Mantegna's was not the first, but it was the most influential.[54] The *Three deities* is harder to understand, but it is most likely a sort of moral allegory, like the Choice of Hercules.[55] Diana holds a bow and quiver, and an upturned torch, whose guttering flame represents her power to extinguish earthly lusts. Her male companion, who is armed but holds a sceptre, may represent Hercules,[56] while the puzzling winged figure on the right is most likely to be Venus.[57]

Virtus Combusta (fig. 229) was even challenging for contemporary viewers.[58] Ignorance is enthroned on a globe, holding a rudder – symbols of instability. Her chair is supported by sphinxes, also representing Ignorance, while laurel branches – symbols of Virtue – burn nearby. Behind Ignorance stand blindfolded Ingratitude and Avarice, while a blind woman representing Humanity teeters towards a precipice.[59] Evil advisers – satyr-shaped Lust, ass-eared Folly and a hooded man leading a dog (Deceit or Fraud)[60] – confuse her. As in the *Calumny* (fig. 230), this dense allegory probably reflects a knowledge of Lucian, although there is no single classical source.[61]

Virtus Combusta, like the paintings for Isabella's *studiolo* may have been conceived as a visual representation of a moral problem: in this case, humanity's enslavement to Ignorance. A more optimistic coda is offered by Giovanni Antonio da Brescia, who engraved *Virtus Combusta* around 1490–1506 (fig. 227) and added a pendant, *Virtus Deserta* (fig. 228),[62] in which Mercury, god of knowledge, is shown rescuing Humanity from its pit of error. Mantegna may also have designed this; certainly, this motif is described by Alberti in his pastiche of Lucian, the *Dialogo della Virtù contro la Fortuna*.[63]

These allegories – even if they were later disseminated in prints – were made to be admired in their own right, to stimulate discussion among courtiers and scholars. The popularity of classical themes at the Mantuan court meant that certain figures could easily be reused by Mantegna and by his associates. Diana from the *Three deities* was represented in a fictive bronze by a follower of Mantegna, while the drawing of a *Dancing muse* in Berlin (fig. 56) was copied from the dancer at the extreme right of *Parnassus*.[64]

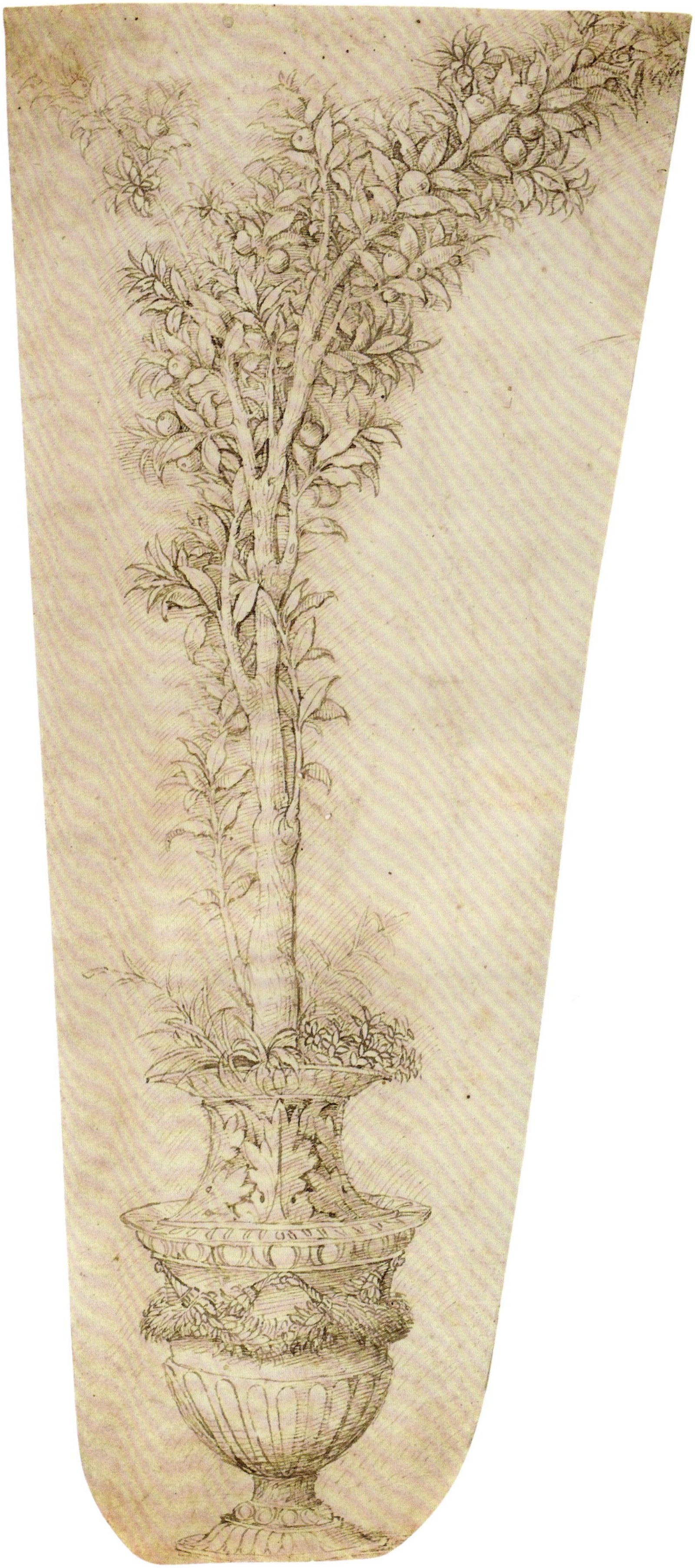

FIG. 234
ANDREA MANTEGNA
Orange tree, about 1490
Pen and brown ink on paper, 31.2 × 14.2 cm
Musée du Louvre, Paris (776 DR)

FIG. 235
ANDREA MANTEGNA
The Triumphs of Caesar II: The Standard-Bearers and Siege Equipment, mid-1480s – before 1506
Egg tempera on canvas,
270.3 × 281.1 cm
The Royal Collection Trust / HM Queen Elizabeth II (RCIN 403959)

Mantegna's Triumphs of Caesar

The most significant of Mantegna's antique compositions are *The Triumphs of Caesar*, painted between 1486 and his death in early 1506.[65] The artist himself remarked, with some restraint, to Francesco Gonzaga '... in truth I am not ashamed of having made them',[66] and Francesco considered them, together with the chapel and the Camera Picta in the Ducal Palace, to be Mantegna's most remarkable works. The *Triumphs* – three of which are exhibited here (figs 235, 236, 237) – are among those very few works of art that have always been regarded highly: for instance, they were the only artworks from Charles I's collection that were not sold following his execution in 1649.[67]

In the *Triumphs*, Mantegna showed that he was the equal of any historian. There is no single literary source for Julius Caesar's *Triumphs*, and Mantegna found inspiration in the account of triumphs by the ancient writers Suetonius, Plutarch, Appian and Livy: perhaps compiled in a more modern book that sadly no longer survives, written by his friend Giovanni Marcanova.[68] Mantegna must have made use of at least two other fifteenth-century sources, Roberto Valturio's *De re militari* (first published in Latin in 1472),[69] but most pertinently Flavio Biondo's *Roma triumphans* (first published in Mantua in about 1472).[70] It seems scarcely possible that Mantegna would not have utilised Biondo's text, which helpfully cites his sources, and provides a valuable compendium of the 'last word' in studies of Roman triumphs in the last quarter of the fifteenth century.[71] He used his substantial understanding of the ancient Roman world – further developed, no doubt, by his Roman sojourn between 1488 and 1490[72] – to meld these dry textual details into a visually convincing account of Julius Caesar's *Triumphs*.

The *Triumphs* evolved, as Mantegna worked on them, into a group of nine canvases, which functioned as a single work of art.[73] Many questions remain about the evolution of this series, including the role that drawings played in the genesis both of the cycle, and its individual components. Several surviving drawings have been connected to the *Triumphs*, but the sheet which is most plausibly Mantegna's own work is a recently discovered, highly finished drawing (fig. 65), closely related to *Triumph II: The Standard-Bearers and Siege Equipment*.[74] There must have been other autograph drawings, which are now lost.[75] It is also unclear who initiated the *Triumphs*. The most likely patron is Francesco Gonzaga,[76] but as the subject could hardly have offered a better vehicle for Mantegna's talents, and his ability to convey the ancient world imaginatively as well as accurately, it is possible that Mantegna himself was responsible for the genesis of the cycle.[77] Today they remain, as he called them in 1489, emphatically 'my triumphs'.[78]

FIG. 236 (page 244)
ANDREA MANTEGNA
The Triumphs of Caesar IV: The Vase-Bearers, mid-1480s – before 1506
Egg tempera on canvas,
269.5 × 280 cm
The Royal Collection Trust / HM Queen Elizabeth II (RCIN 403961)

FIG. 237 (page 245)
ANDREA MANTEGNA
The Triumphs of Caesar V: The Elephants, mid-1480s – before 1506
Egg tempera on canvas,
270 × 280.7 cm
The Royal Collection Trust / HM Queen Elizabeth II (RCIN 403962)

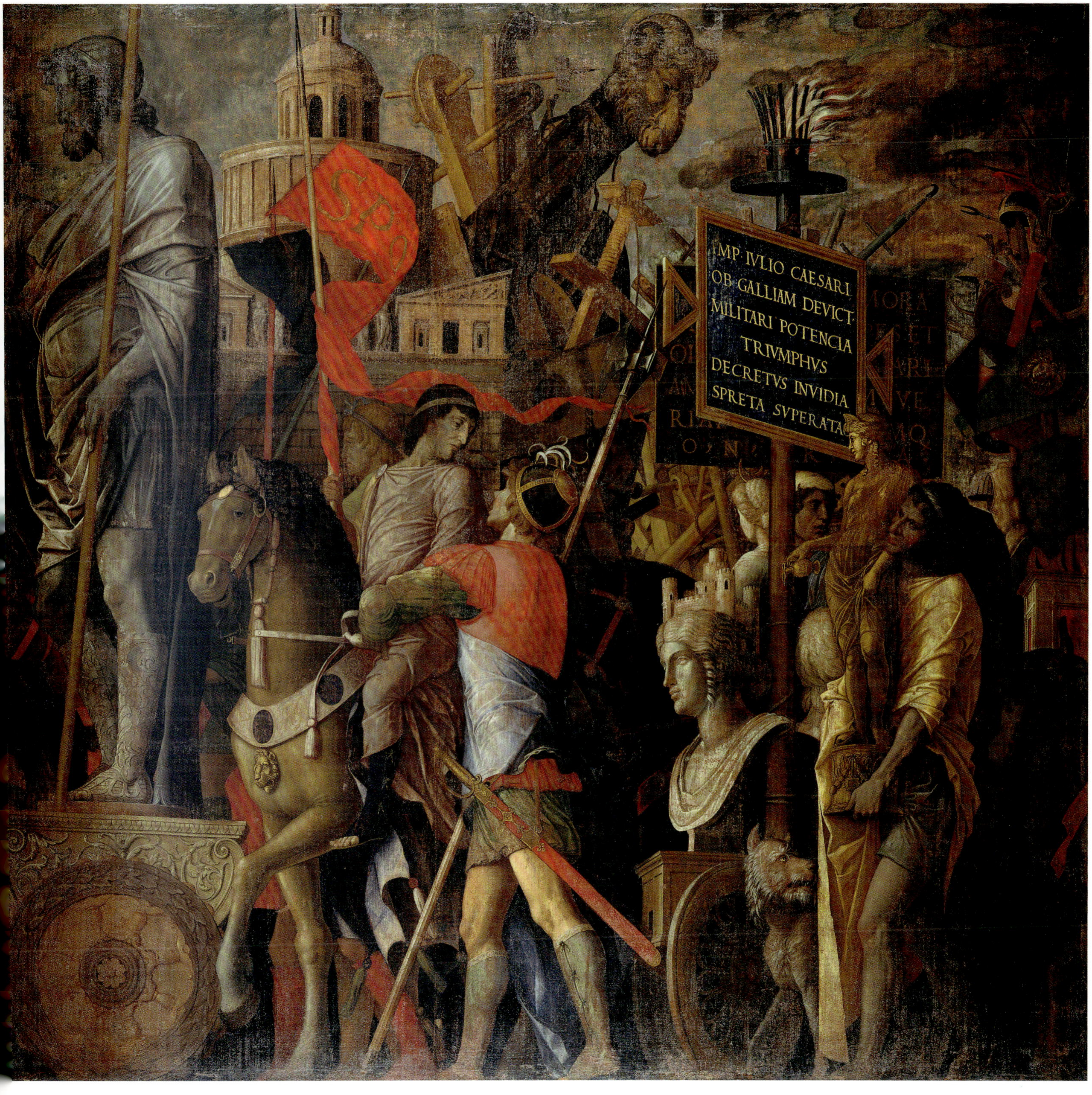
IMP IVLIO CAESARI
OB GALLIAM DEVICT
MILITARI POTENCIA
TRIVMPHVS
DECRETVS INVIDIA
SPRETA SVPERATA

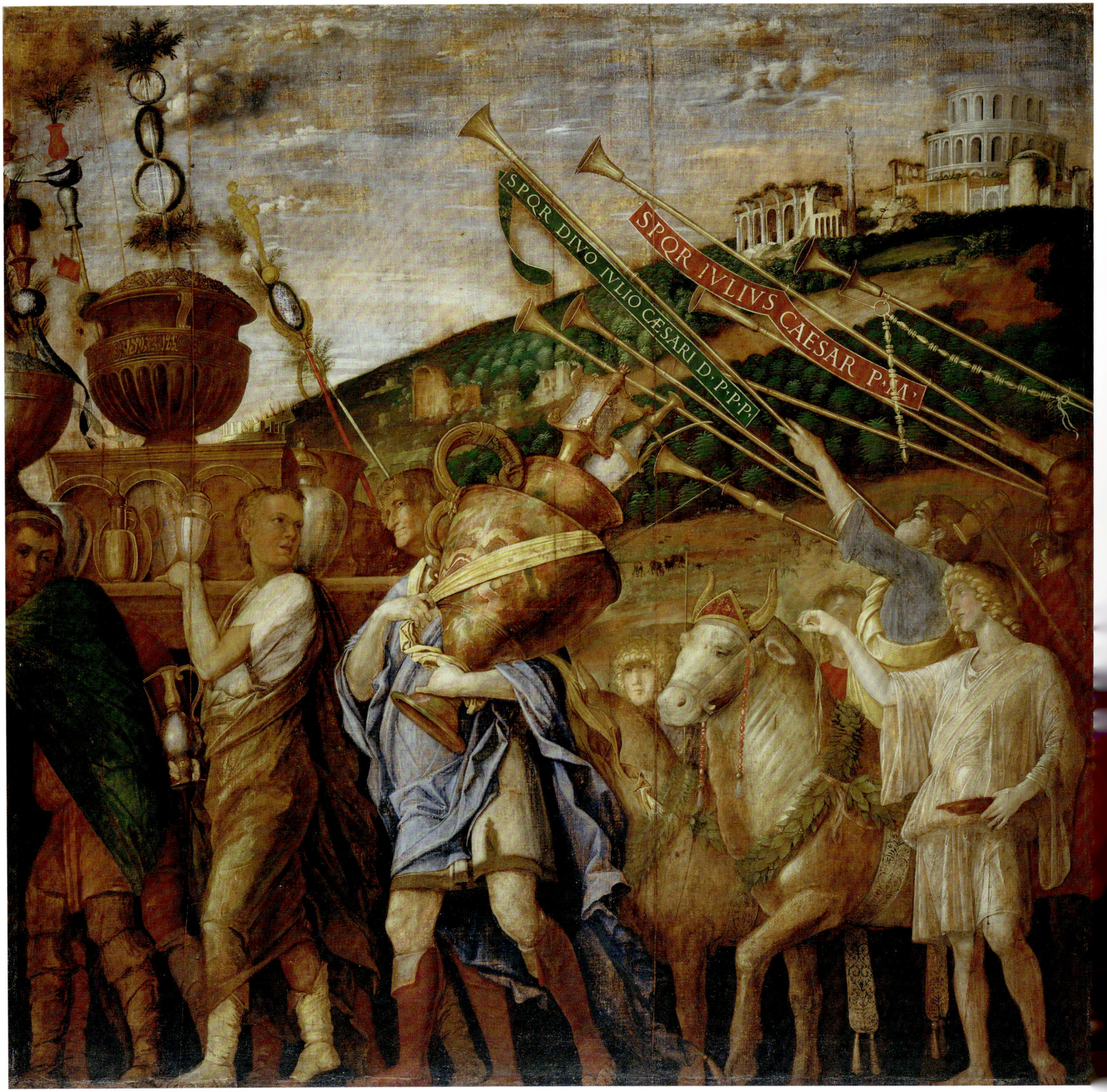
SPQR DIVO IVLIO CÆSARI D·P·P·P·
SPQR IVLIVS CAESAR P·M·

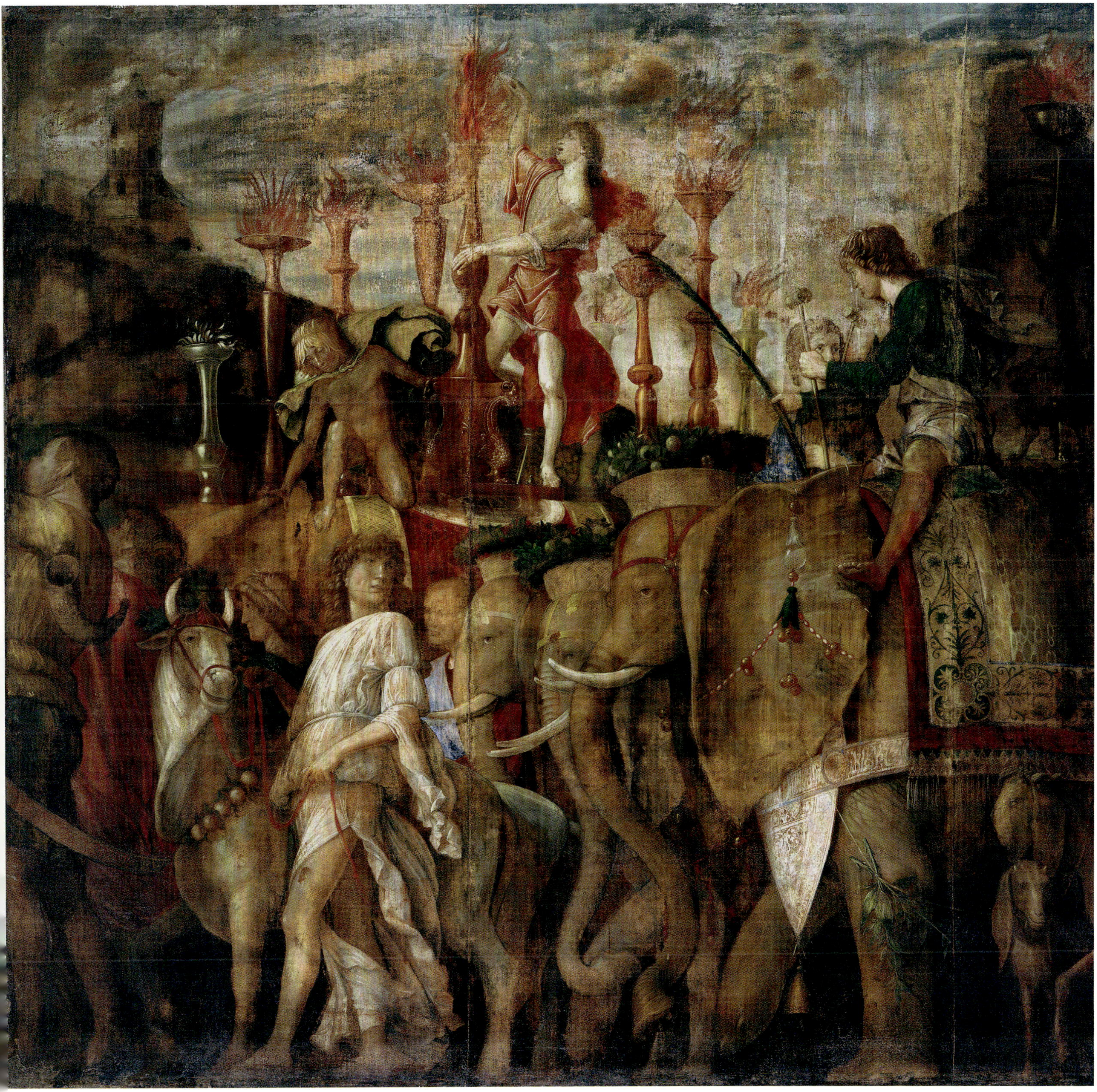

FIG. 238
ANDREA MANTEGNA
Samson and Delilah, about 1500
Glue size on canvas, 47 × 36.8 cm
The National Gallery, London (NG 1145)

Mantegna's and Bellini's grisailles

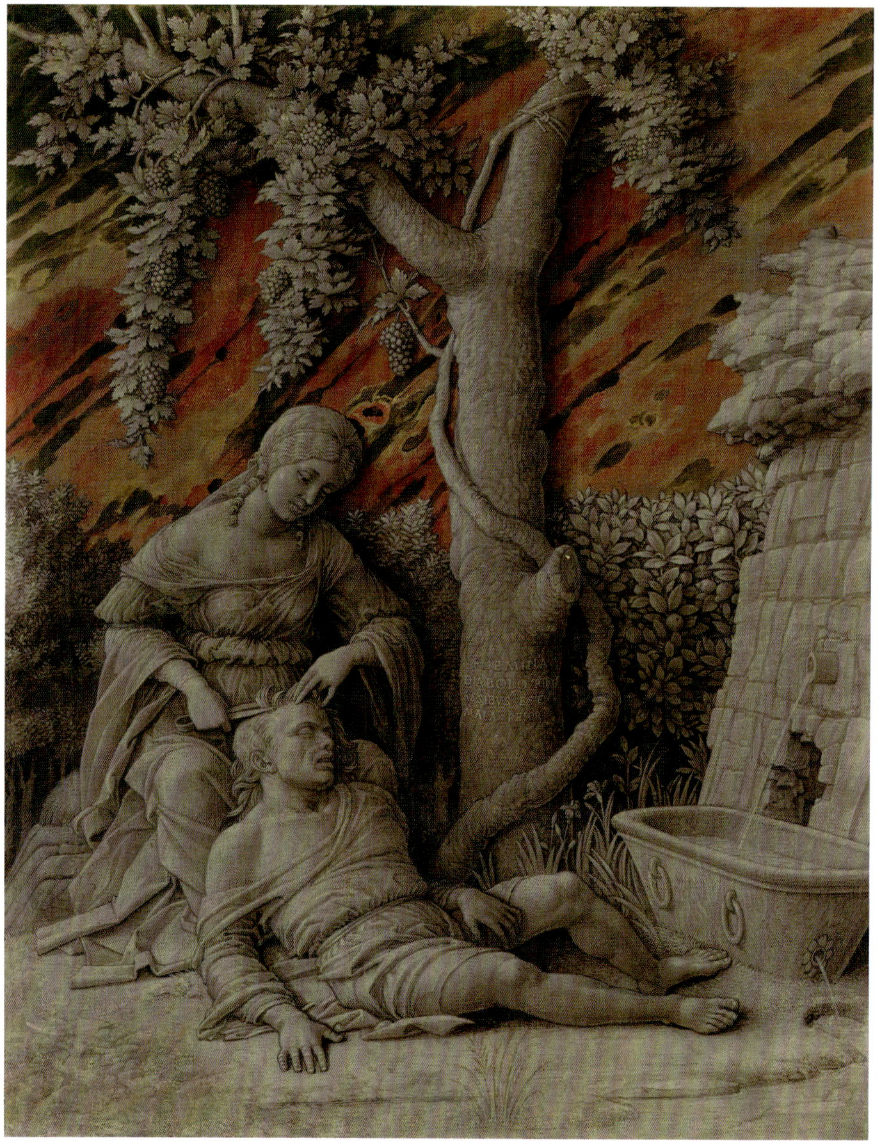

What became the quintessential debate of the High Renaissance of the sixteenth century, the *paragone*, or comparison between sculpture and painting, was highly significant for Mantegna and Bellini, but in very different ways. Essentially Mantegna was a painter who thought in sculptural terms. His pictures, whether monumental altarpieces including that for San Zeno in the 1450s (fig. 252), whose piers are decorated with sculpted medallions, and the *Madonna della Vittoria* of 1495–6 (fig. 110), or small-scale works such as the *Saint Sebastian* (fig. 193) and *Samson and Delilah* (fig. 238), demonstrate how pictorial invention could create sculptural illusions more effectively than sculpture itself.[79] Bellini, who was always open to novelty, used sculpture, as well as the example of Mantegna, to create his own style in the late 1450s and early 1460s.[80] And throughout his career sculptural forms, as well as particular motifs, inspired him to paint conventional subjects such as the Virgin and Child in new ways.[81]

Grisailles, or paintings in a limited palette, often intended to trick the eye (*trompe l'oeil*) and mimic sculptural relief, were an obvious way for painters to show their superiority over sculptors, and indeed also over the painters of the ancient world. So, of course, were prints, an innovative form in which Mantegna excelled.[82] In the 1490s Mantegna and his studio produced a group of stand-alone grisailles representing historical and biblical women,[83] probably commissioned by Isabella d'Este, although some may have been made as gifts.[84] There are two distinct types: fictive marble reliefs painted in glue size on thin linen, such as *Samson and Delilah* (fig. 238), and fictive bronzes painted in egg tempera on panel and heightened with gold, as in *The Vestal Virgin Tuccia with a Sieve* (fig. 240) and *A Woman Drinking / Sophonisba* (fig. 241). The pictures have frequently been divided into sets, based on their subjects,[85]

FIG. 239
GIOVANNI BELLINI
Two men in antique dress, about 1506–8
Grey wash, lead white, pen and black ink on paper, 41.4 × 26.6 cm
Fondation Custodia, Collection Frits Lugt, Paris (4145)

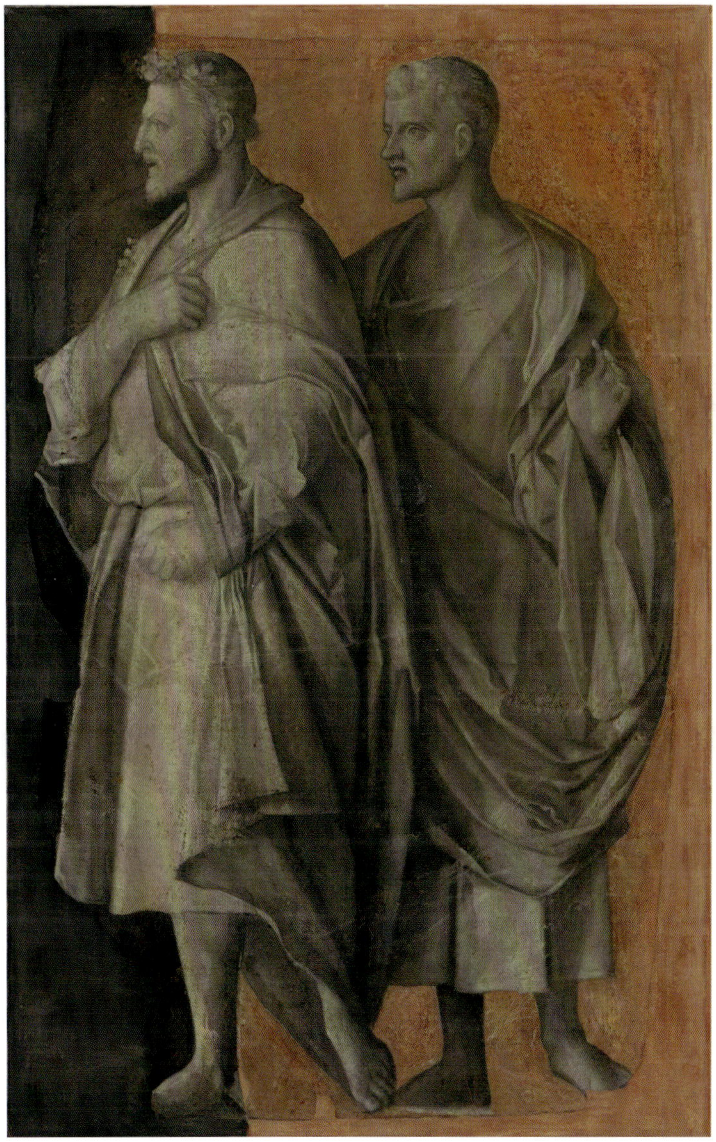

their scale, or the shared colouring of their marble backgrounds: *Tuccia* and *Sophonisba* were probably a pair.[86] *Judith and Abra* (see fig. 58), which is closely linked to these paintings, seems to be a finished work of art in its own right. If Mantegna's grisailles were painted for Isabella's *studiolo*, they belonged to a scheme that prized the interplay of real and fictive.[87] Visibly textured, *Samson and Delilah* – which mimics stone – would have appealed to the sense of touch, as stone itself does. The fluttering ribbons of *Tuccia* and *Sophonisba*, and the flowing water in *Samson and Delilah* demonstrated the greater flexibility of painting over sculpture.

Bellini's only surviving grisaille painting, *The Continence of Publius Cornelius Scipio* (fig. 246), was completed in a posthumous *paragone* of sorts with Mantegna's last documented work, *The Introduction of the Cult of Cybele into Rome* for Francesco Cornaro, discussed below by Neville Rowley (fig. 245).[88] Bellini here competes not just with his recently deceased brother-in-law, but with sculpted cameos (much admired by collectors of the period) rather than reliefs.[89] Three further grisaille studies of standing men in classical costume by Bellini survive, one in the Fondation Custodia, Paris (fig. 239), another at the Archdiocesan Museum Kroměříž in Olomouc and a third in a private collection.[90] Rather than being connected to Bellini's *Scipio*, it is likely that these are copies by Bellini of figures from the two final pictures of the Cornaro commission, which are now lost.[91] With their orange-brown backgrounds, they recall the *rosso antico* stone which Bellini simulates in the background of his *Scipio*.[92] Superficially, these four works resemble Mantegna's *Introduction of the Cult of Cybele*, but they serve to remind us that by this point, at the end of Mantegna's life, the art of the two brothers-in-law was worlds apart.

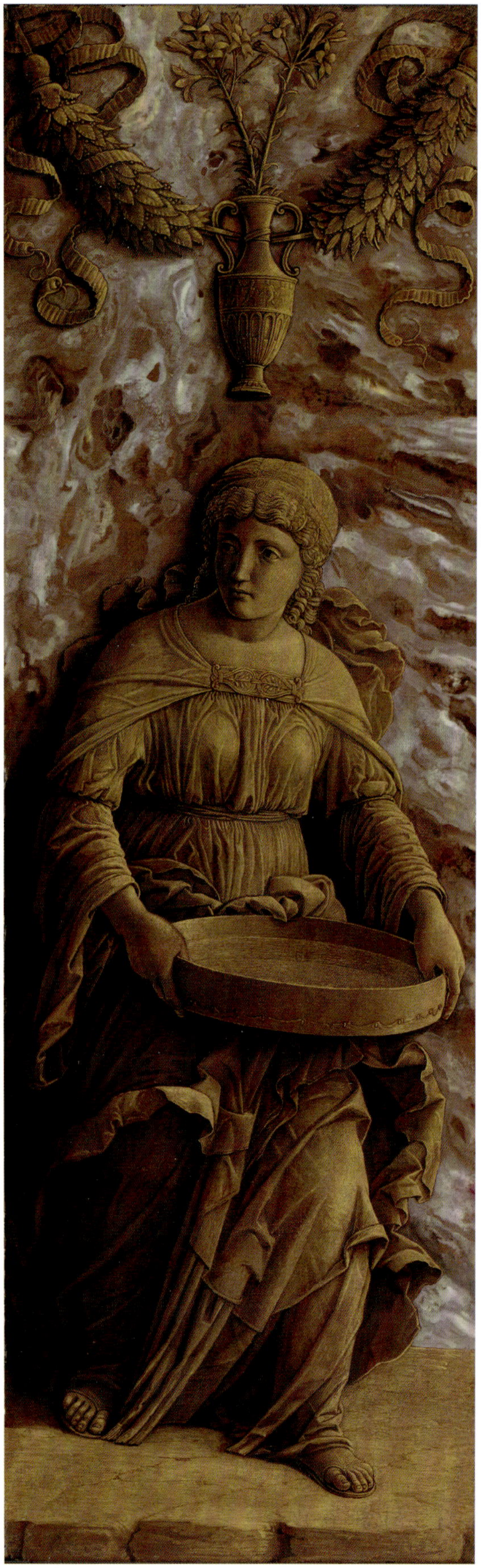

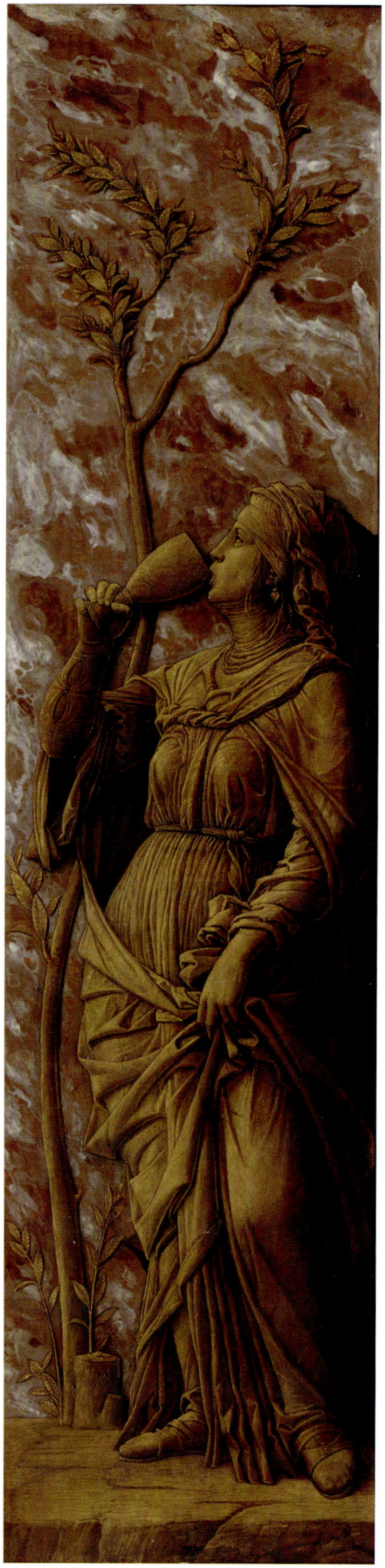

FIG. 240
ANDREA MANTEGNA
The Vestal Virgin Tuccia with a Sieve, about 1495–1506
Egg tempera on poplar, 72.5 × 23 cm
The National Gallery, London (NG 1125.1)

FIG. 241
ANDREA MANTEGNA
A Woman Drinking, about 1495–1506
Egg tempera on poplar, 71.2 × 19.8 cm
The National Gallery, London (NG 1125.2)

The Last Works

NEVILLE ROWLEY

FIG. 242
Attributed to
ANDREA MANTEGNA
Self Portrait,
late 15th century
Bronze, porphyry and Istrian stone, height 47 cm (bust); diameter 70 cm (roundel)
Basilica of Sant'Andrea, Mantua

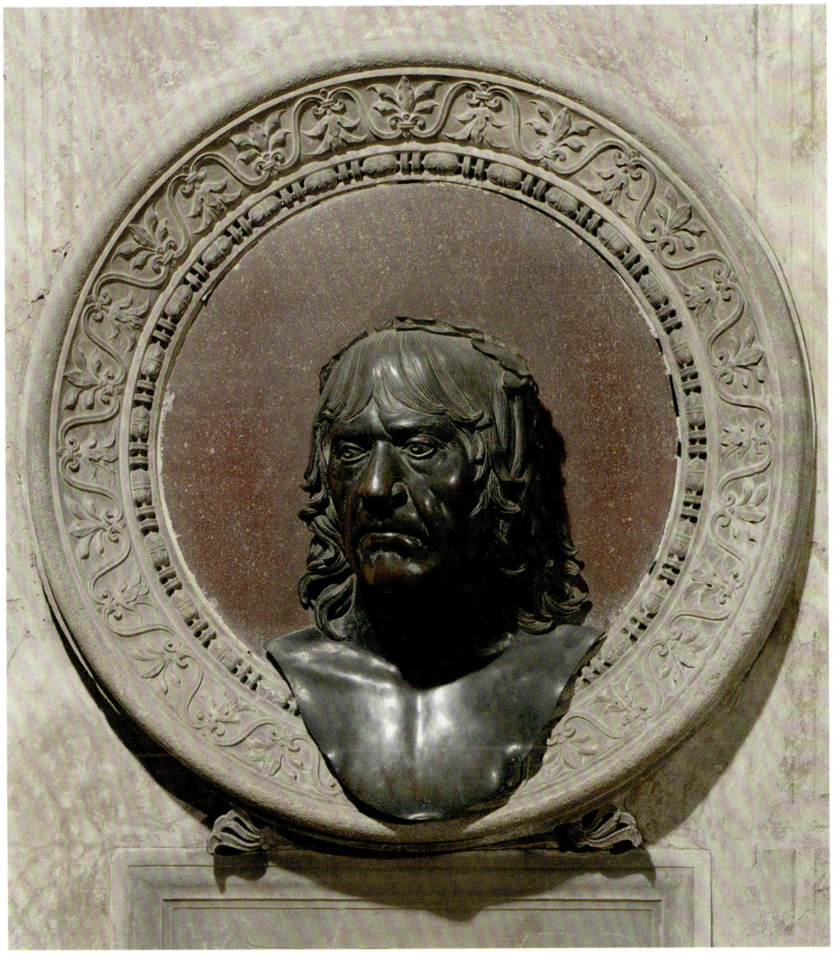

After several decades of work at the Mantuan court, Mantegna had become an individual of considerable importance: he had earned the title of Count Palatine and drawn up the antique-inspired plans of his house, where he received the great people of his world and showed them his archaeological collection. He had sought to shape his posterity in two ways, training his sons in the painter's profession and obtaining the patronage rights to a funerary chapel in a church designed by the great humanist Leon Battista Alberti, Sant'Andrea in Mantua. With age, hardships began to accumulate: a weakened body, waning finances and offspring failing to acquire the expected talent. His house had to be sold, and he was even forced to face the soul-destroying loss of an ancient bust of the Empress Faustina, a work that meant so much to Mantegna but which the Marchioness of Mantua, Isabella d'Este, ended up buying from him. Only one goal remained: the completion, at all costs, of the decoration of his tomb chapel.

The chapel is still there: to the left of its entrance, a bronze bust representing the painter (fig. 242) indicates where he is buried, while the two lateral walls have pictures on canvas connected with the life of Saint John the Baptist and frescoed decoration.[1] The murals are the work of Mantegna's pupils, especially the most brilliant among them, the young Correggio, while one of the three canvases, a *Visitation*, was painted over half a century after Mantegna's death, in 1560. As for the two other paintings, representing *The Holy Family with the Family of Saint John the Baptist* (fig. 243) and *The Baptism of Christ* (fig. 244), they are mostly autograph, even if their presence in the painter's workshop when he died indicates they were completed by other hands.[2] In the *Baptism*, the ageing Mantegna does not entirely succeed in defining the forms with his customary crispness, which gives the work a poignant character that is lacking in most of his earlier pictures, with their perfect handling. In the anatomically hesitant Christ, the gaunt-faced Baptist, the wingless angel on the left who stares at us with a melancholy gaze, not to mention the curious onlooker on the right, holding a bucket, we witness the sincerity of an artist seeking to convey his talent one last time, conscious of his own limitations.[3] The chromatic alteration over time certainly reinforces the work's crepuscular character, which calls to mind to the last canvases by Titian or Rembrandt.

FIG. 243
ANDREA MANTEGNA
The Holy Family with the Family of Saint John the Baptist, about 1504–6
Egg tempera on canvas, 40 × 169 cm
Basilica of Sant'Andrea, Mantua

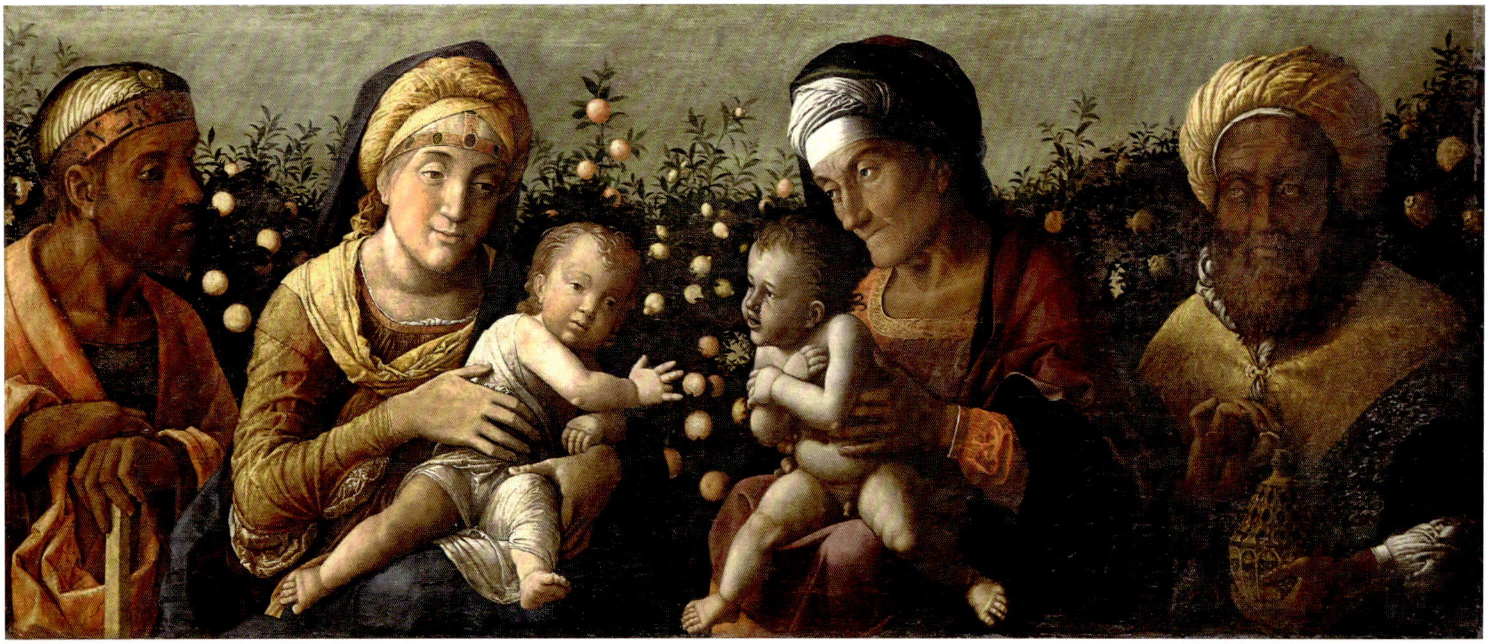

On 13 September 1506, Mantegna died, and it took his heirs a decade – not a year, as he had stipulated – to execute his will and install these pictures in the funerary chapel.

As is often the case, the workshop of a vanished genius soon becomes coveted, and in this case a *Dead Christ* and a *Saint Sebastian* also vanished.[4] As for a painting in grisaille, nearly nine feet (2.73 metres) across, it was sold by one of Mantegna's sons to the brother of the Marquess of Mantua, the powerful Cardinal Sigismondo Gonzaga. The Venetian nobleman Francesco Cornaro, who had commissioned it, succeeded in securing the picture for his palazzo in Venice after lodging a complaint. Of the cycle requested from Mantegna in 1505 – a series of images narrating the exploits of the *gens Cornelia*, the Roman patrician clan from whom he claimed descent – Francesco Cornaro (whose family name often appears as Cornelio or Corner) only obtained one finished painting, with a highly original subject, since the event had never been represented (and never would be again): *The Introduction of the Cult of Cybele at Rome* (fig. 245).[5]

The scene combines several ancient sources, including Livy, Ovid and Appian. In 204 BCE, the Italian peninsula had been occupied for about 15 years by the army of Hannibal, and Rome itself was threatened. As in every grave crisis, the Romans consulted the Sibylline Books, compilations of prophecies that would tell them what to do to ensure success. On this occasion, they were instructed to go to Mount Dindymon in Anatolia to transfer the cult of the mother goddess Cybele to Rome. A young man, Publius Cornelius Scipio Nasica, was given the signal honour of receiving the goddess (or rather, a statue of her), but it failed to reach its destination as the ship carrying it became stranded near the port of Ostia. Only the intervention of a Roman matron, Claudia Quinta, whose chastity had been unjustly doubted, finally enabled the ship to find its haven. Mantegna depicts the moment in which the statue of the goddess makes its triumphal arrival at the gates of Rome, passing along the Via Appia before two pyramidal structures, the tombs of Scipio Nasica's father and uncle.[6] The procession is greeted by Roman dignitaries, one of whom must be

FIG. 244
ANDREA MANTEGNA
The Baptism of Christ, about 1504–6
Egg tempera on canvas, 230 × 176 cm
Basilica of Sant'Andrea, Mantua

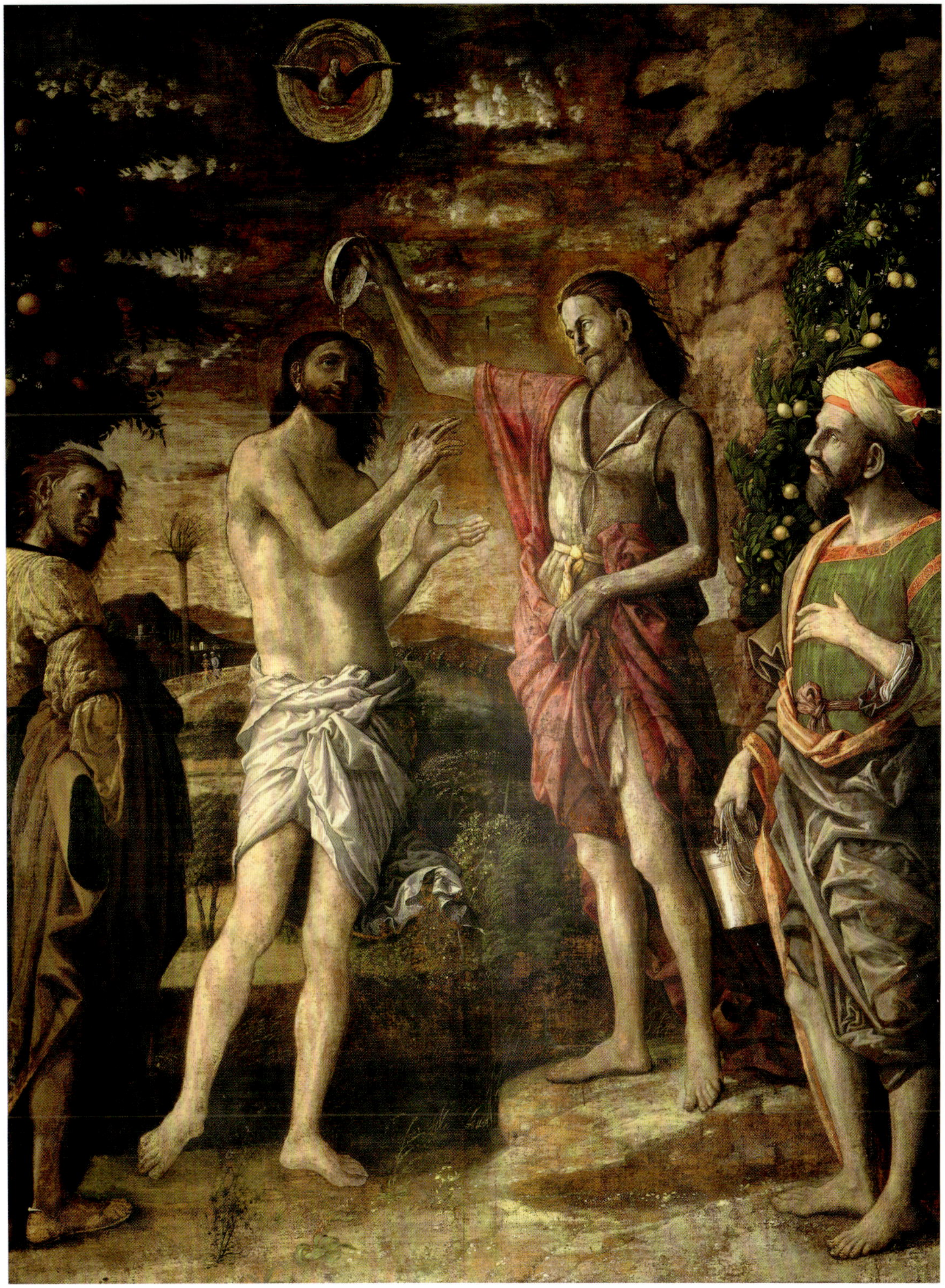

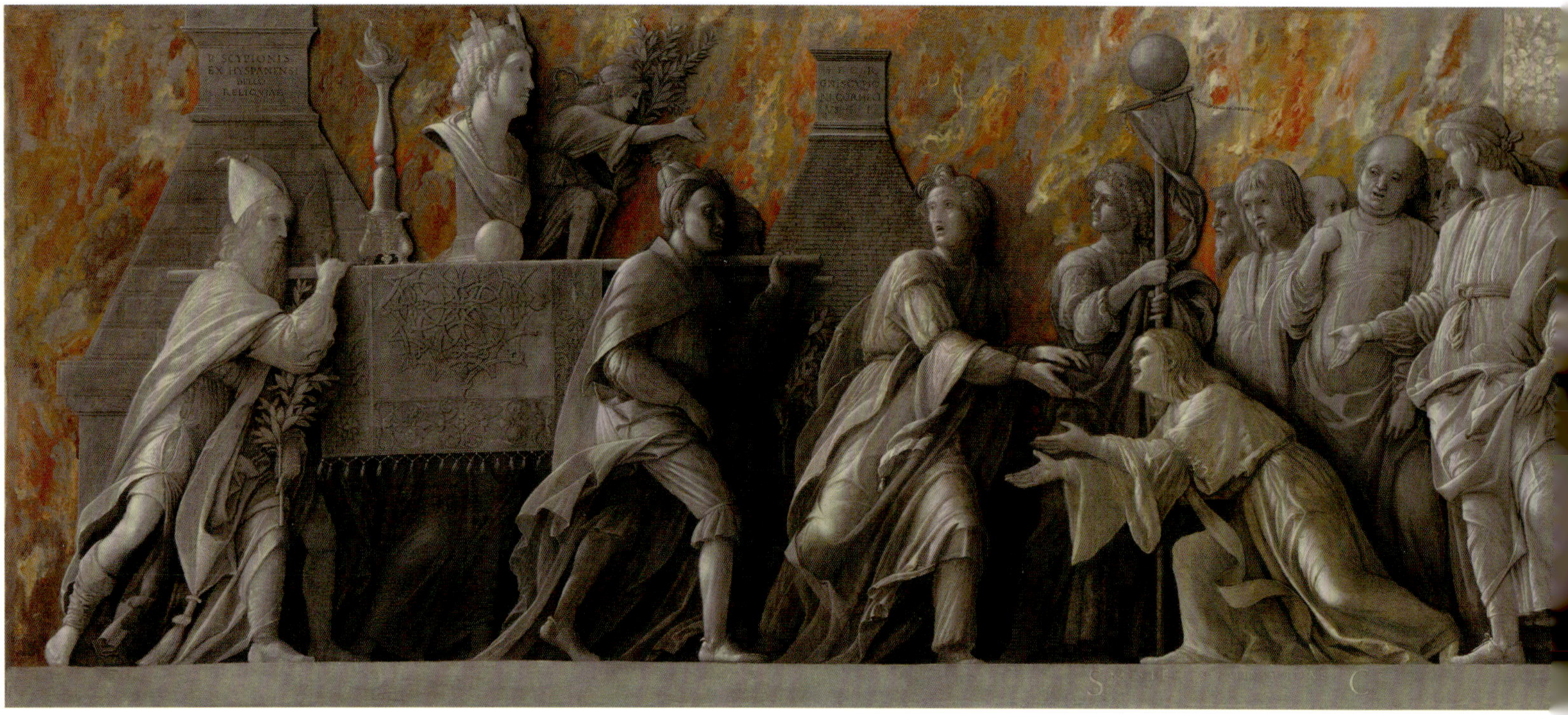

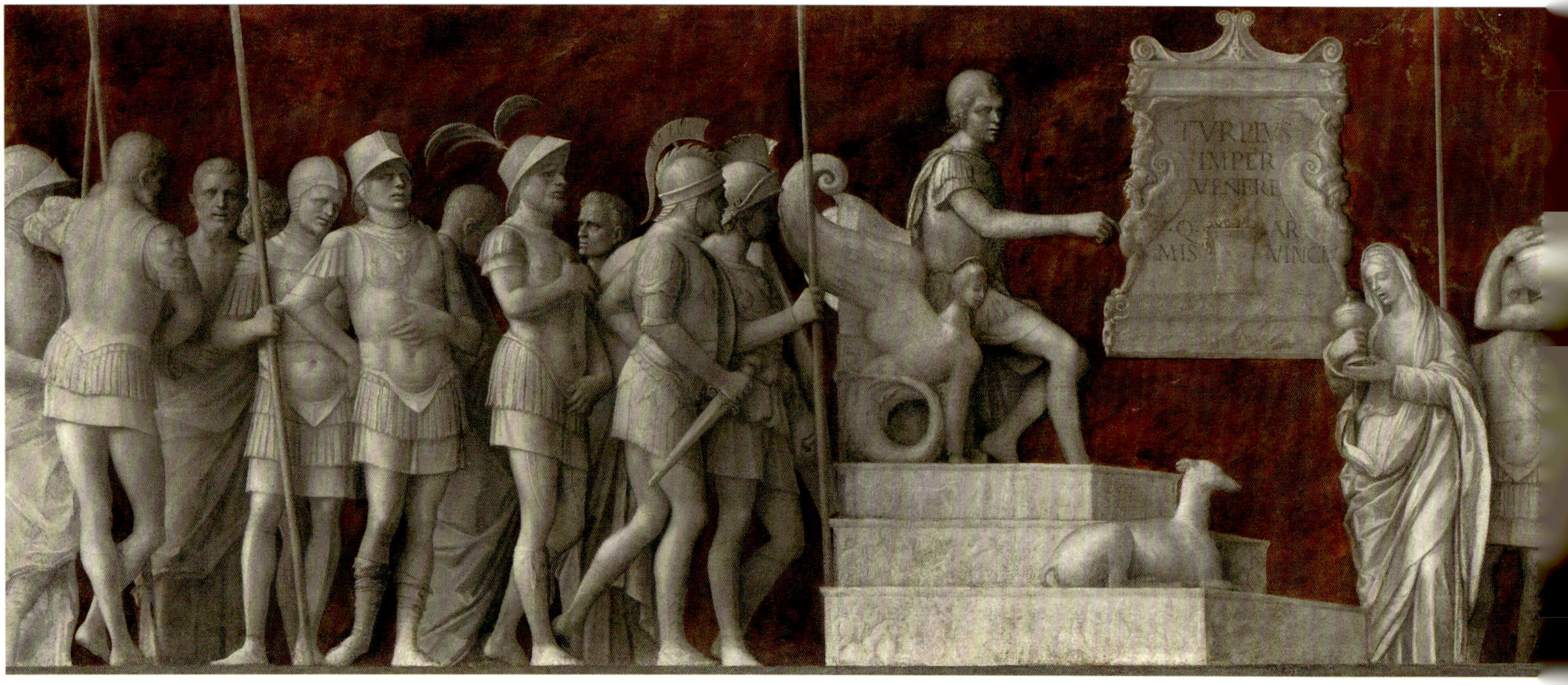

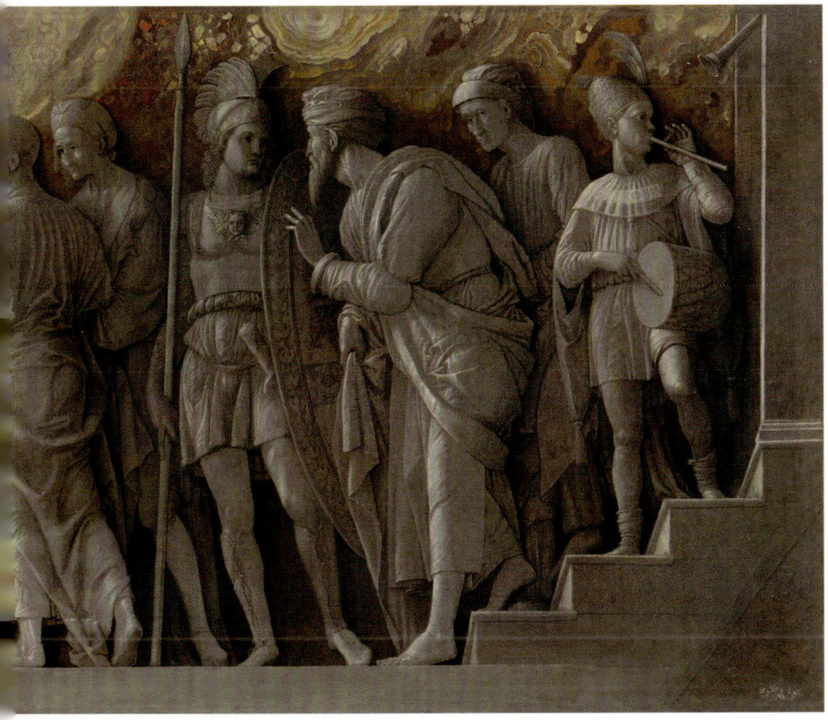

FIG. 245
ANDREA MANTEGNA
The Introduction of the Cult of Cybele at Rome, 1505–6
Glue size on canvas, 76.5 × 273 cm
The National Gallery, London
(NG 902)

FIG. 246
GIOVANNI BELLINI
The Continence of Publius Cornelius Scipio, about 1506–8
Oil on canvas, 74.8 × 356.2 cm
The National Gallery of Art, Washington DC (1952.2.7)

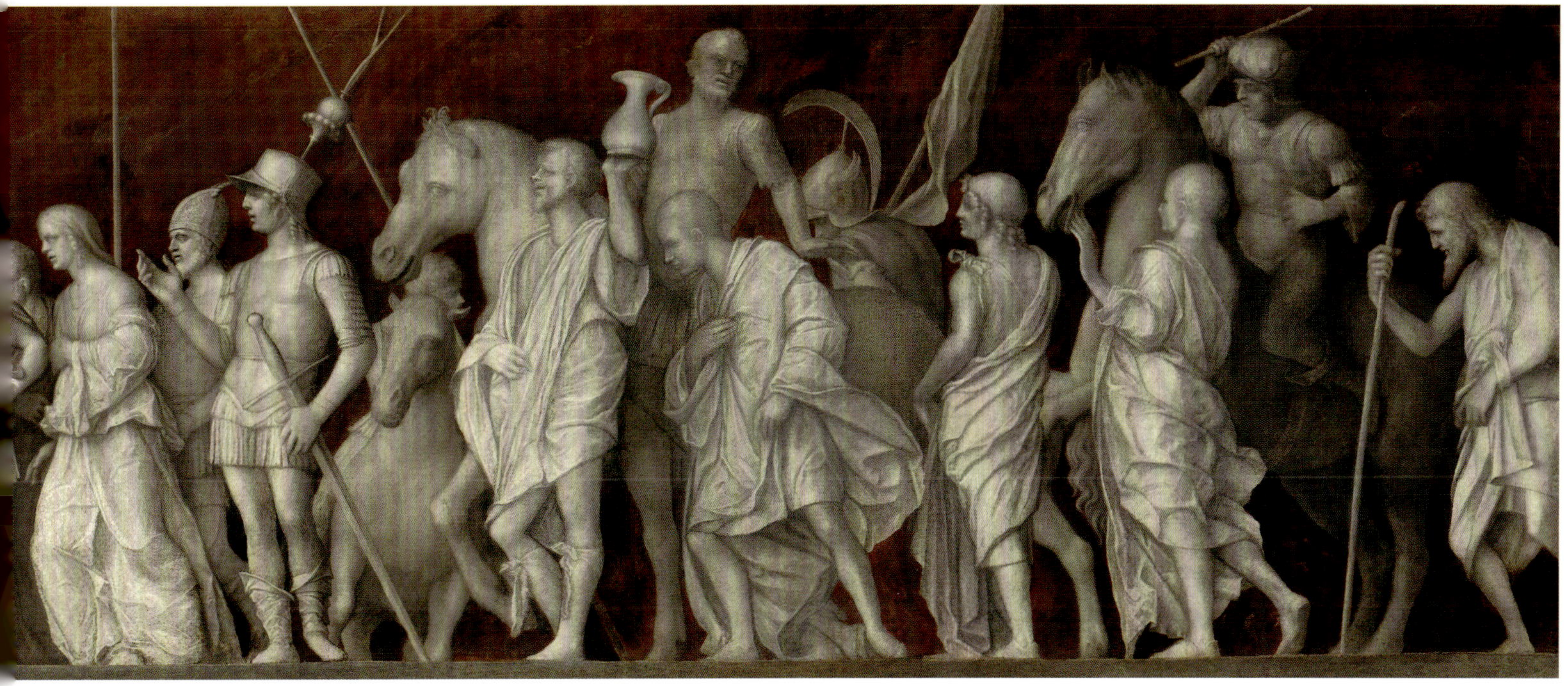

FIG. 247
GIOVANNI BELLINI
The Drunkenness of Noah, about 1515
Oil on canvas, 103 × 157 cm
Musée des Beaux-Arts et d'Archéologie, Besançon (896.1.13)

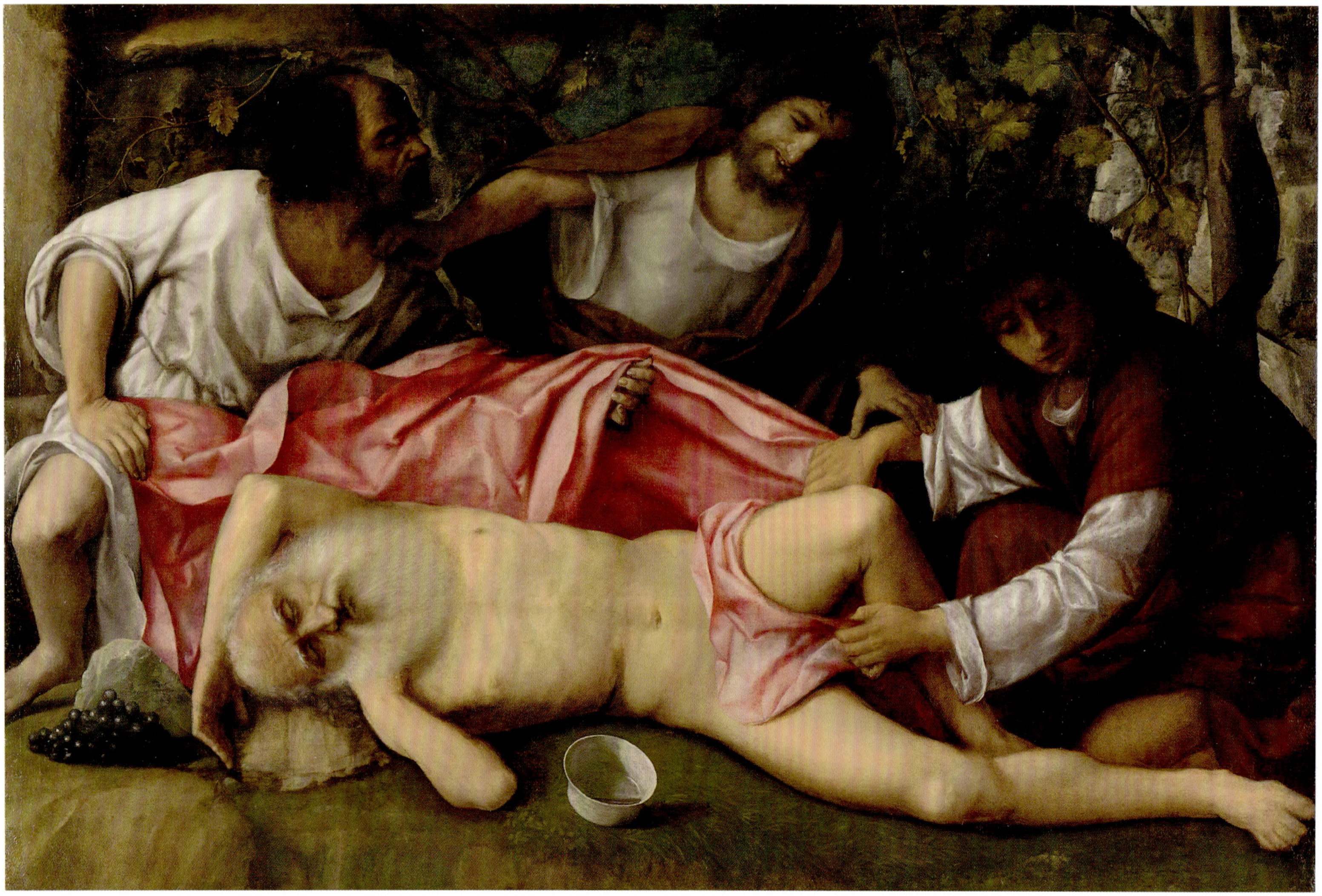

Scipio himself, though there is no consensus as to whether he is the figure kneeling in fervent welcome before it, or the man standing further to the right, gesturing with his right arm.[7] The scene shows Mantegna displaying his archaeological flair one last time, each of his figures seeming to have emerged directly from a marble sarcophagus, set against coloured plaques of a startling realism.[8]

Once he had recovered his painting, Francesco Cornaro could think of completing the decoration of his *camerino*. Scipio Nasica was not enough – one absolutely had to represent his homonymous first cousin, Publius Cornelius Scipio, who led the Romans to the final victory of the Second Punic War at Zama in 202 BCE, thereby earning the nickname Scipio Africanus. In order to represent the great deeds of his illustrious presumed ancestor, Cornaro significantly turned to the elderly Giovanni Bellini, known for not readily accepting commissions involving antique subjects. Had Bellini not feared in 1501 to be 'judge[d] in comparison with the work of Master Andrea [Mantegna]' for an ancient *istoria* that was asked to him by Isabella d'Este, Marchioness of Mantua?[9] In this instance, Mantegna did indeed begin the project, but, alas, he was now no longer alive, and the history painter of the Bellini family, Gentile, had died soon after. Giovanni thus agreed to the completion of this decorative cycle for the Cornaro *camerino*, and in measuring himself one last time with his brother-in-law, he paid a final tribute to a painter to whom he was deeply indebted.

The painting by Bellini, now in the National Gallery of Art in Washington (fig. 246), shows Scipio Africanus in what might seem an unexpected attitude: not so much the military strategist, but a man who can spare his victims and establish peace. In 209 BCE, after the Romans conquered the Spanish city of New Carthage (Cartagena), the victorious general is offered its most beautiful young maiden. However, Scipio refuses both the carnal gift and the treasure gathered by the poor woman's parents to buy her back, on condition that her fiancé (to whom she has been returned) works towards reconciling Romans and New Carthaginians. The Latin inscription provides the moral for this fable, which is known as *The Continence of Publius Cornelius Scipio*: 'For a victorious general, it is more shameful to be vanquished by Venus than by arms.'[10] As with his earlier works painted after Mantegna – *The Agony in the Garden* (fig. 126), *The Presentation of Christ in the Temple* (fig. 132) and *The Descent of Christ into Limbo* (fig. 145) – Bellini is never entirely faithful to his brother-in-law's paintings: his much subtler manner lends a pastel tone to the grisaille, playing on different levels of depth that are absent in the pendant picture in London. Thus the horse in the middle right area seems to leap out of the background into the space of the beholder (fig. 55). Mantegna had painted a fictive relief, whereas Bellini cannot help but give life to his figures.[11]

The older he grew, the freer his handling became: Giovanni's very last picture may have been *The Drunkenness of Noah* in Besançon (fig. 247), where Noah – inebriated, naked, asleep – is mocked by his son Ham, placed centrally behind him, while his two other sons, Shem and Japheth, modestly cover the body of their father without daring to gaze at him.[12] Noah was the only man chosen by God to survive the Great Flood, yet he was unable to resist the temptation to get drunk, thus demonstrating the fallibility of the human race and its intrinsically sinful nature, likewise visible in the action of the mocking son. Looking at this bony old man, it is hard not to see a self portrait of Bellini, a painter who knows his end is near but who can express himself with a freedom of handling inspired by the recent works of Giorgione and Titian, curiously also recalling the *Baptism* in Mantegna's funerary chapel (fig. 244). On 29 November 1516, Giovanni Bellini died. The dialogue between the two brothers-in-law had lasted over 60 years.

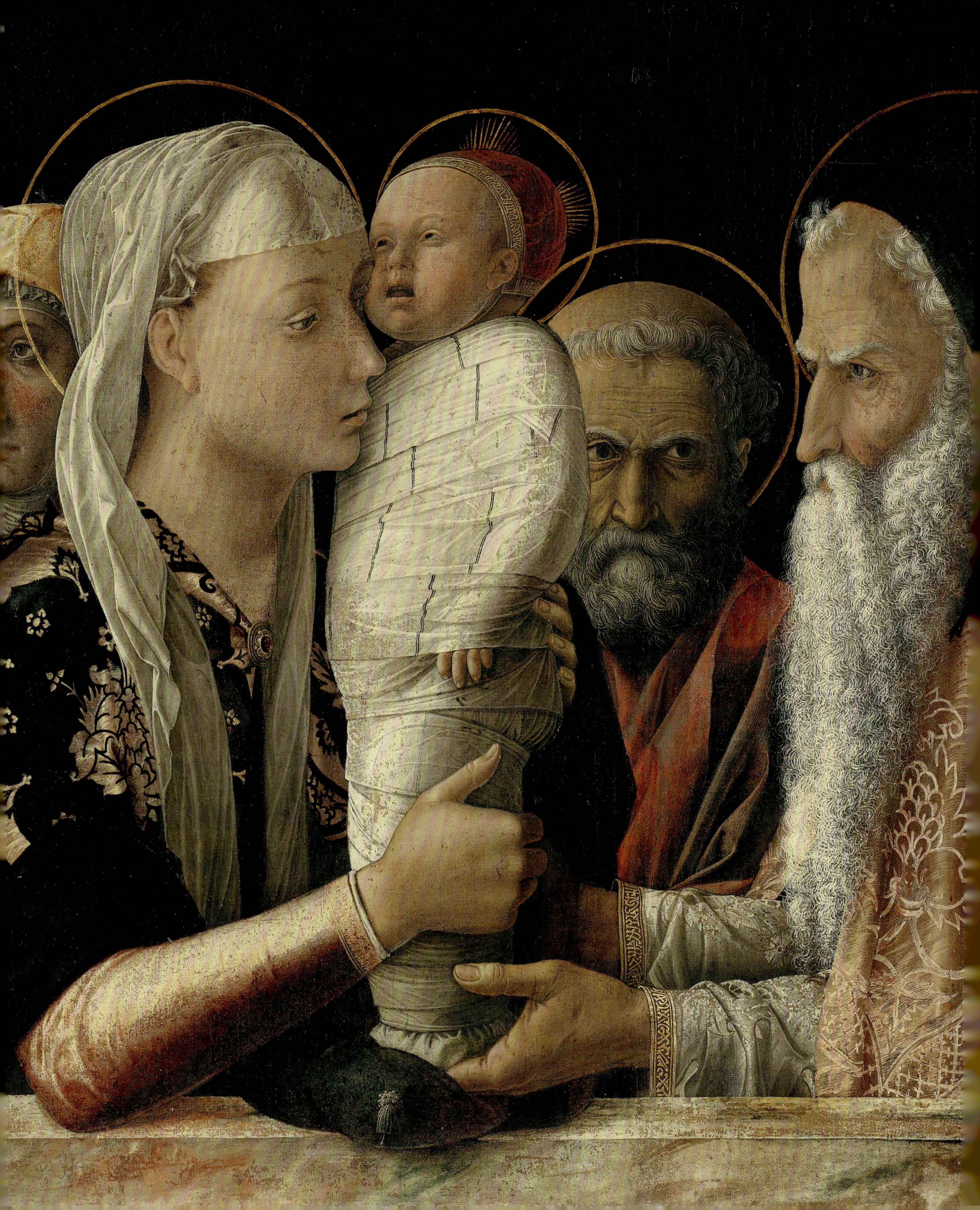

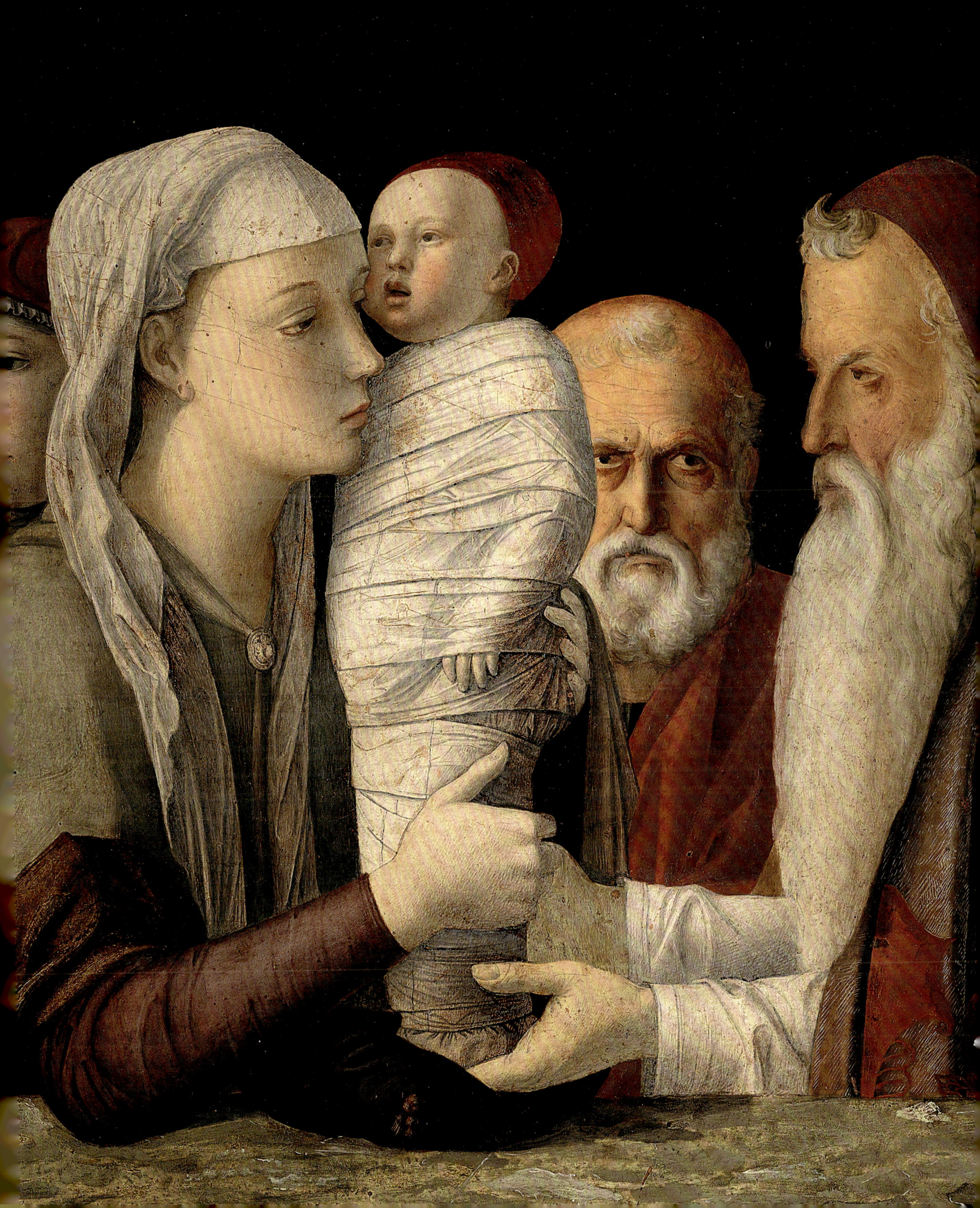

Appendix of non-exhibited works

Some key works by Mantegna and Bellini are illustrated here; some are shown *in situ*, others survive in partial reconstructions, or are now lost.

Ovetari Chapel, Church of the Eremitani, Padua, 1448–57
Black and white photographs taken before Allied bombing on 11 March 1944

FIG. 249 (below left)
ANDREA MANTEGNA
Saint James before Herod Agrippa, 1451

FIG. 250 (below right)
View of the Ovetari Chapel showing Mantegna's *Assumption of the Virgin* (fig. 82) behind the altar carved by GIOVANNI DA PISA, photographed by Osvaldo Böhm
Archivio Naya-Bohm, Venezia. Special collections, Fine Arts Library, Harvard University (172 P138 2E(i)1 Bohm 6480)

FIG. 251 (facing page)
ANDREA MANTEGNA
Saint James led to Martyrdom, 1453–7

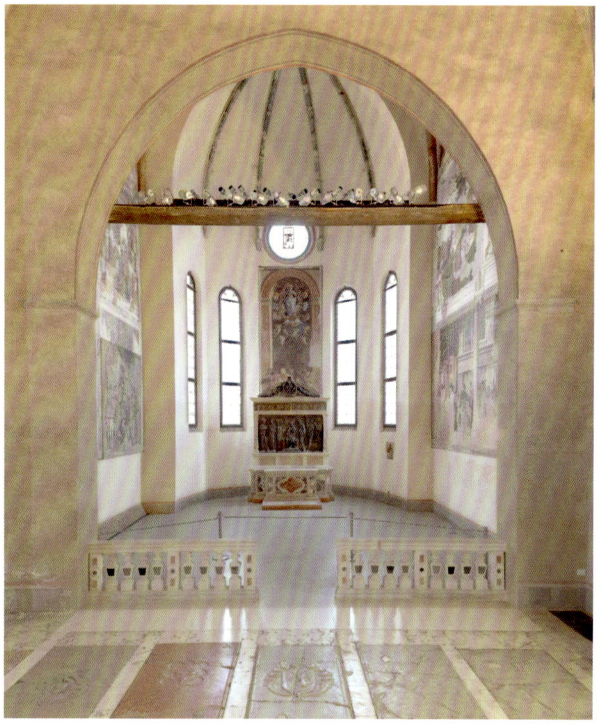

FIG. 248
View of the Ovetari Chapel

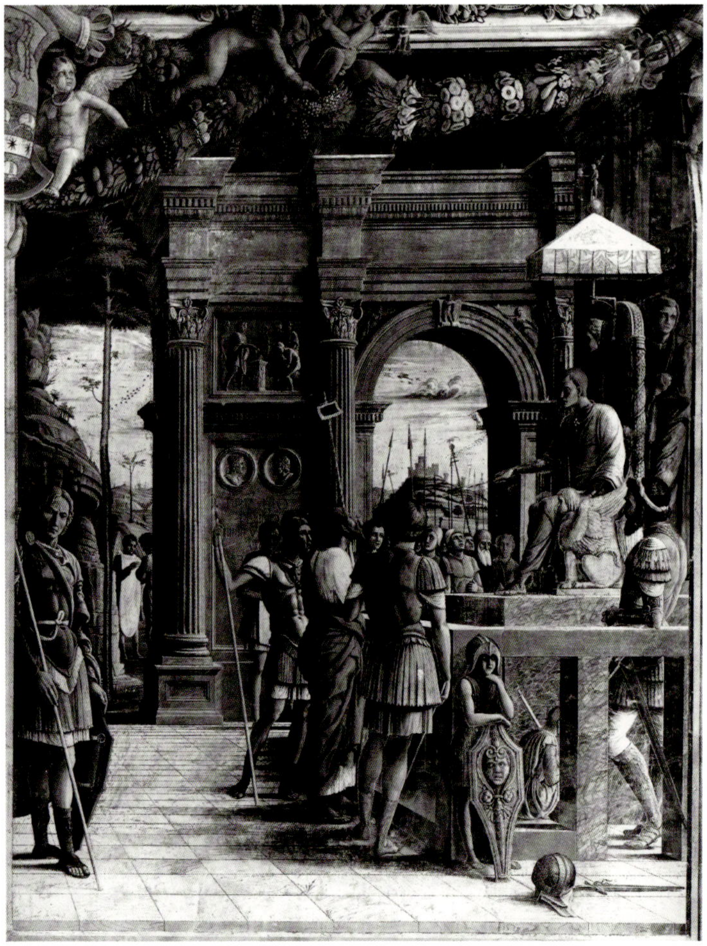

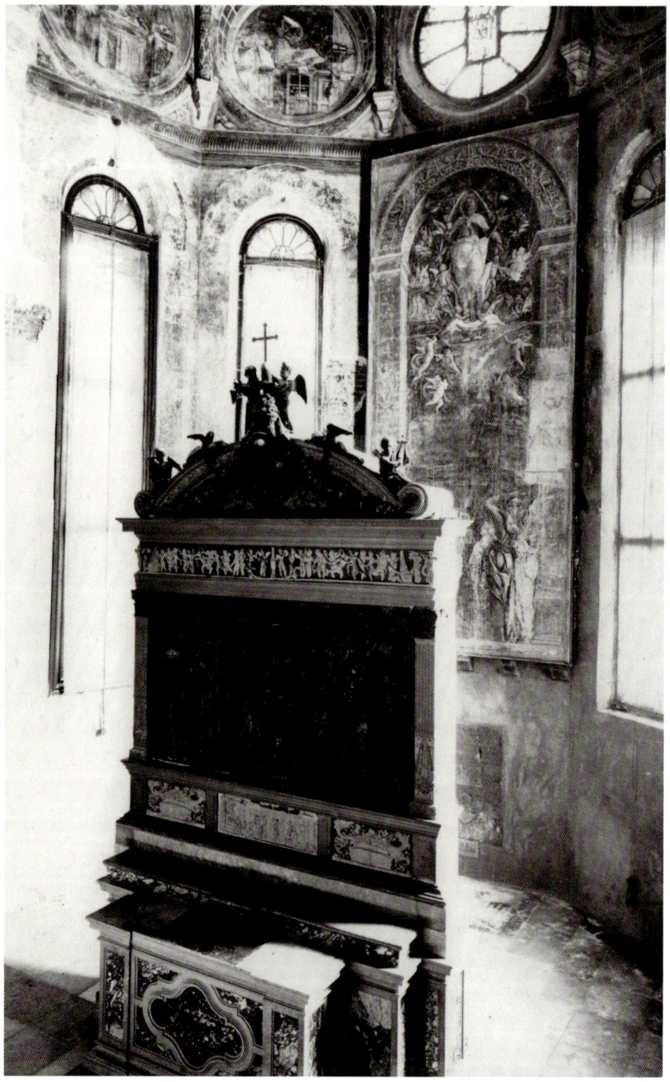

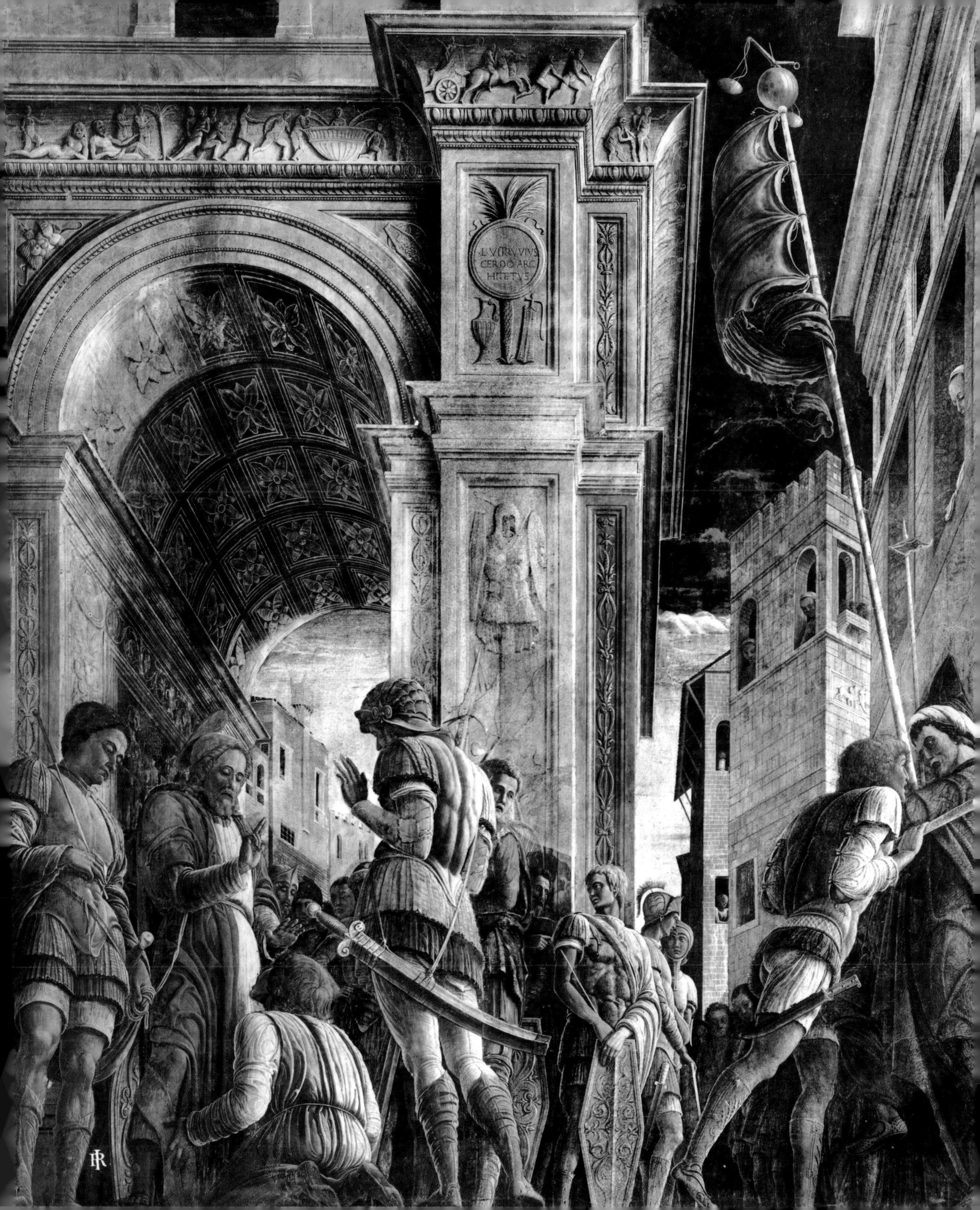
L·VITRVVIVS
CERDO·ARC
HITETVS

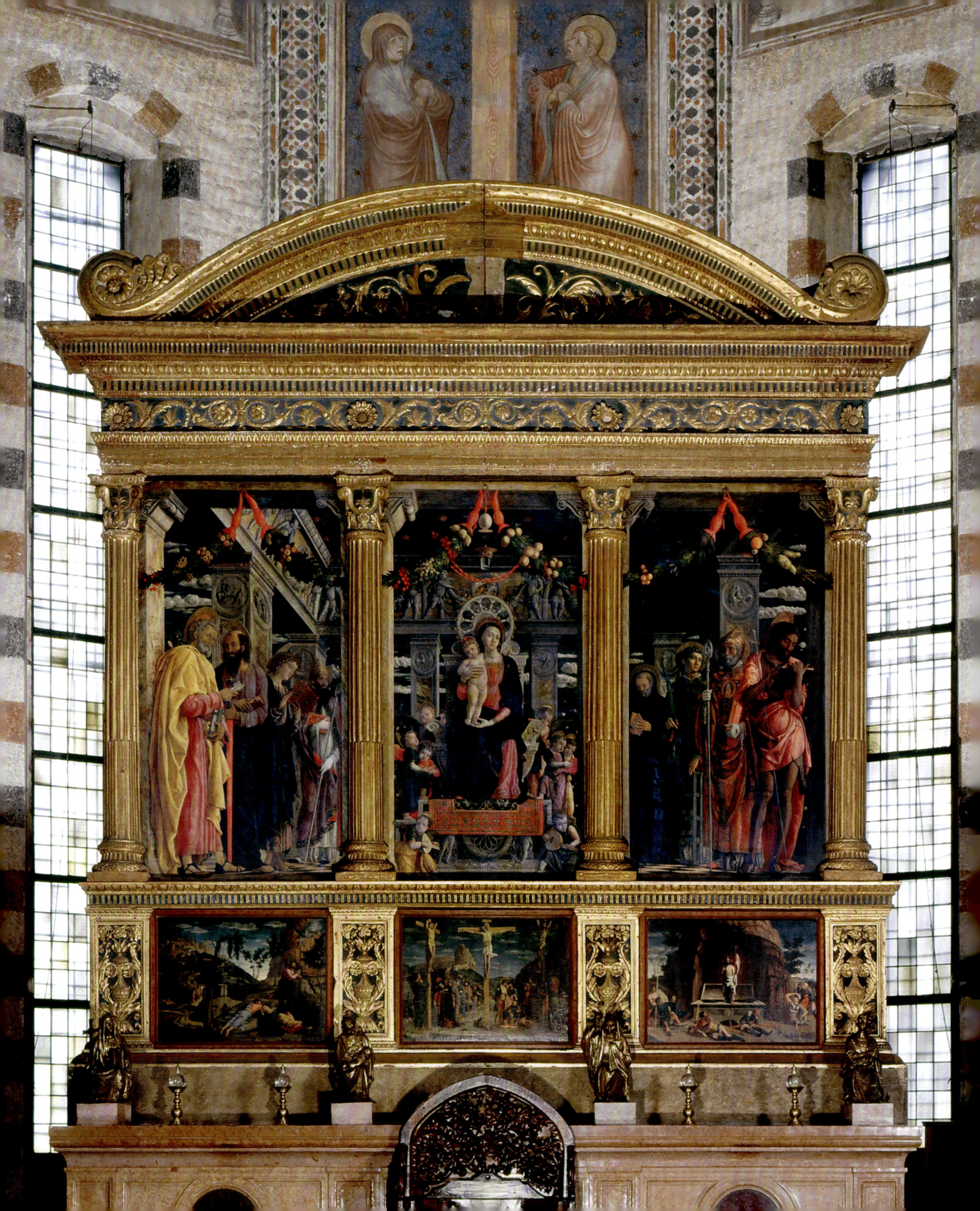

FIG. 252 (left)
ANDREA MANTEGNA
San Zeno Altarpiece, 1456–9
Egg tempera on panel,
480 × 450 cm
Church of San Zeno, Verona
The predella panels are copies of the original now in the Musée des Beaux-Arts, Tours, and the Musée du Louvre, Paris

FIG. 253 (right)
GIOVANNI BELLINI
Saint Vincent Ferrer Altarpiece, about 1467
Egg tempera on panel,
width of each panel 67 cm
Church of Santi Giovanni e Paolo (San Zanipolo), Venice

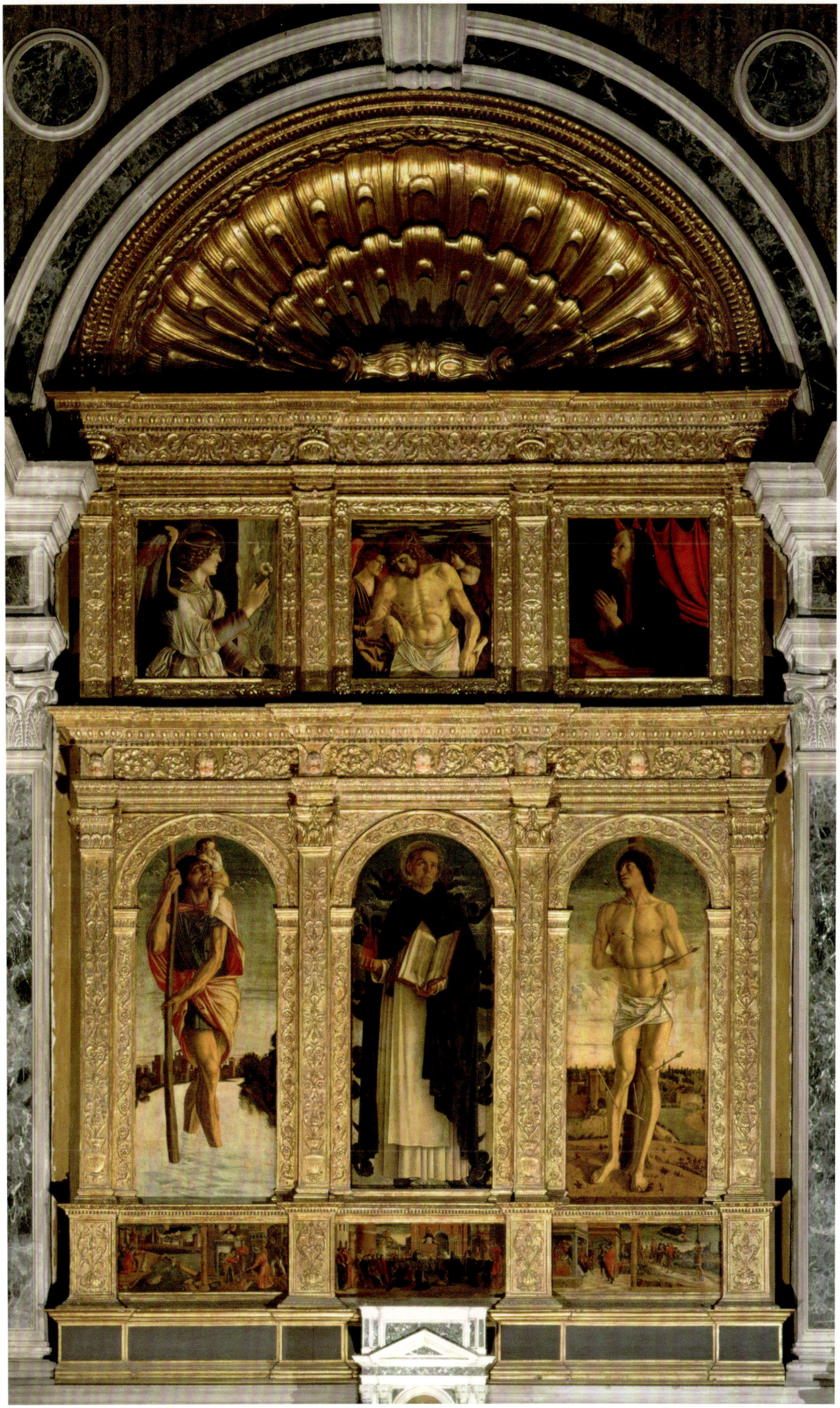

FIG. 254
ANDREA MANTEGNA
Camera Picta, 1465–74
Ducal Palace, Mantua

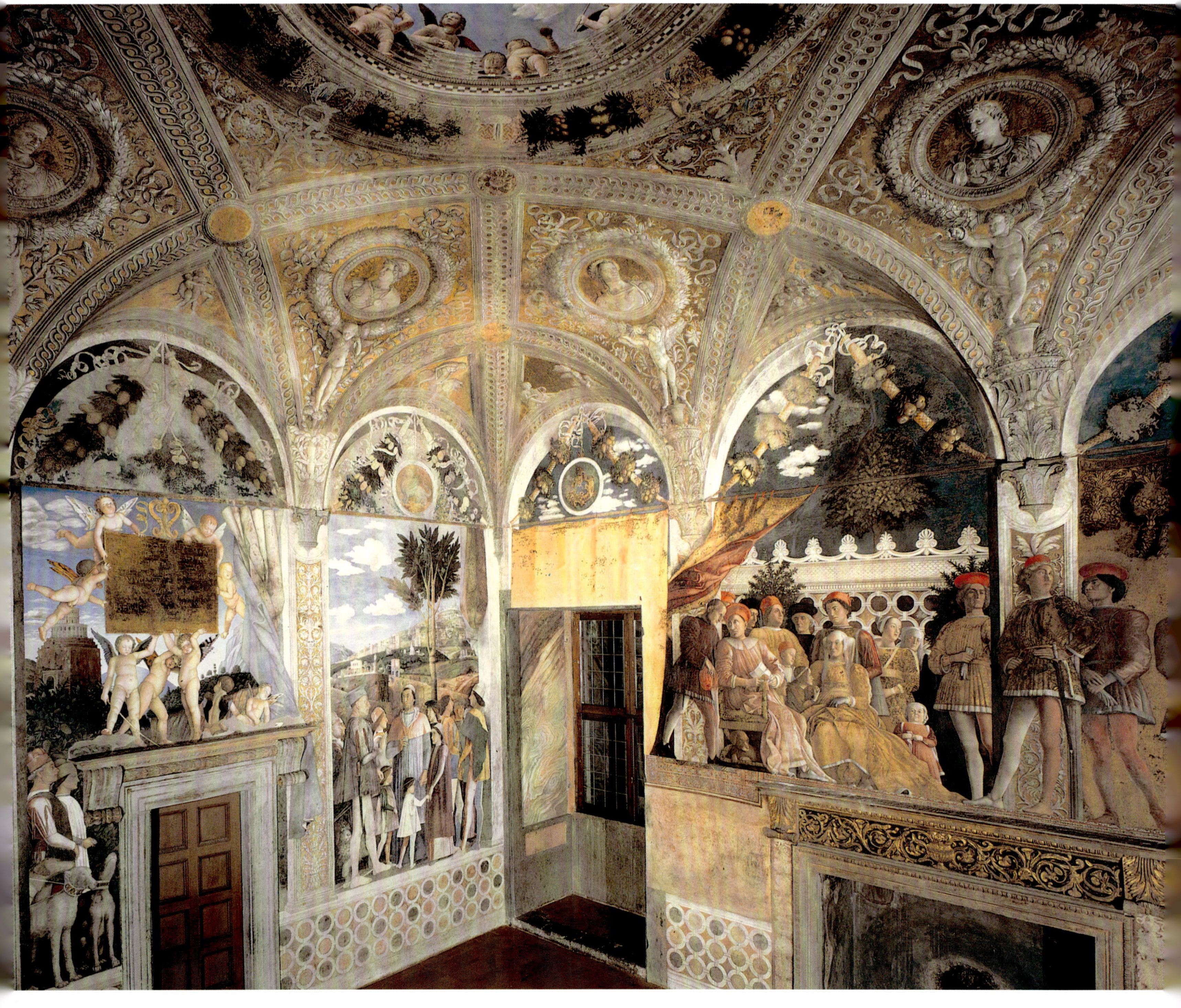

FIG. 255
GIOVANNI BELLINI
The Coronation of the Virgin, known as the *Pesaro Altarpiece*, about 1475
Oil on panel, 262 × 240 cm
Musei Civici, Pesaro

This reconstruction shows the *Lamentation over the Dead Christ*, which once crowned the altarpiece and is now preserved in the Pinacoteca Vaticana

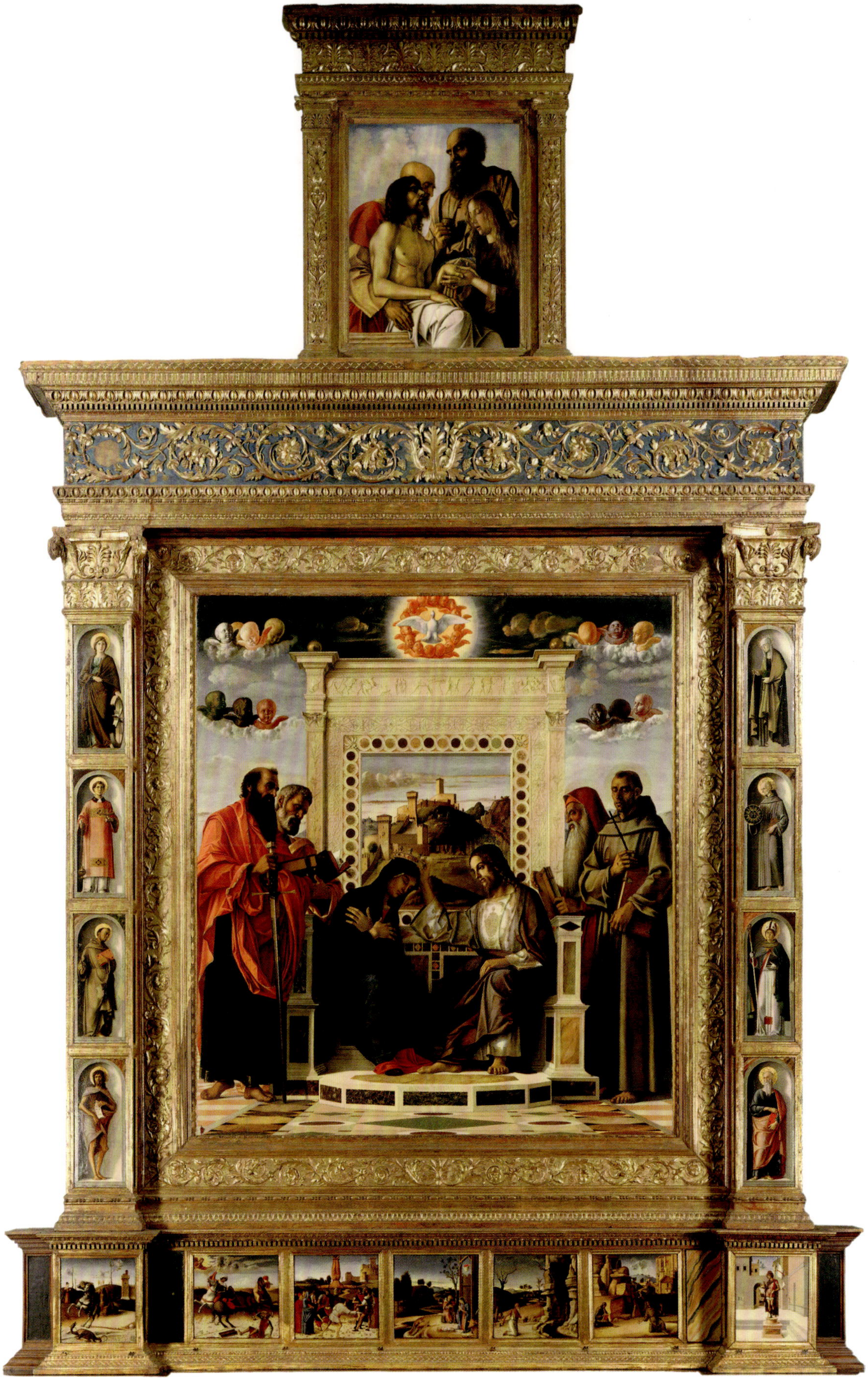

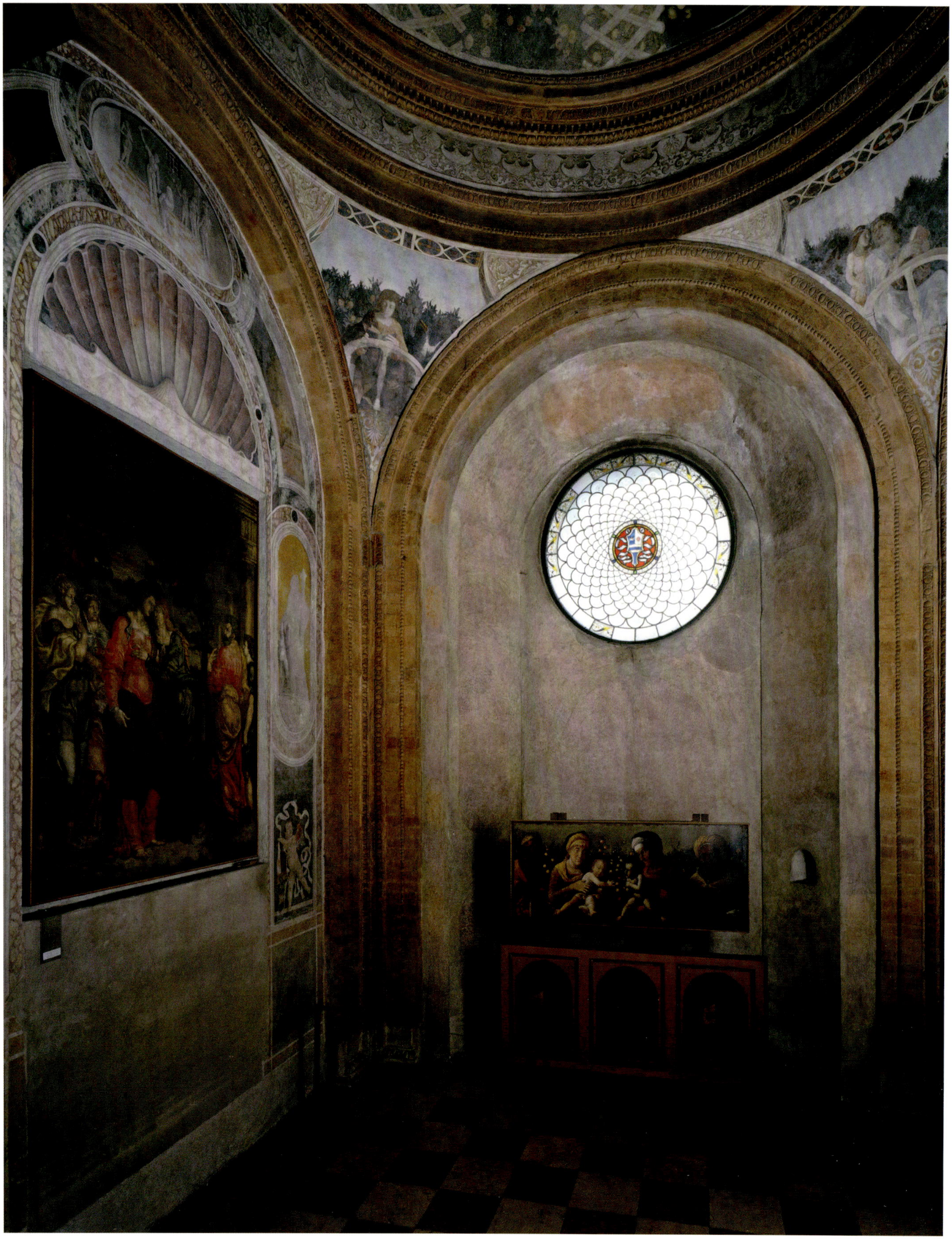

FIG. 256 (left)
View of the funerary chapel of ANDREA MANTEGNA, in the Church of Sant'Andrea, Mantua, completed long after Mantegna's death

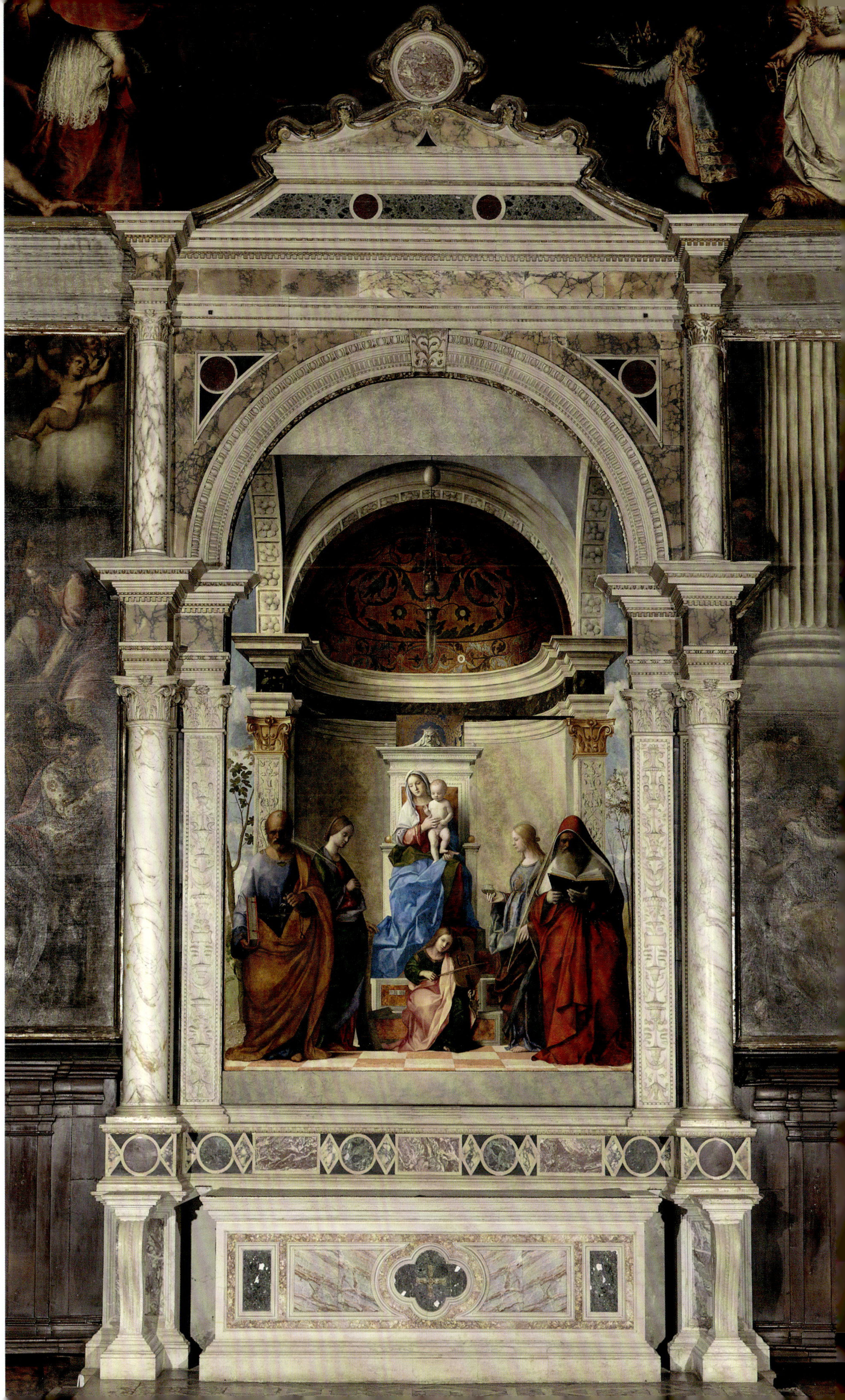

FIG. 257 (right)
GIOVANNI BELLINI
San Zaccaria Altarpiece, 1505
Oil on panel, 500 × 235 cm
Church of San Zaccaria, Venice

Notes

The attributions and dating of works discussed in these texts represent the views of the named authors.

I A TALE OF TWO ARTISTS AND TWO CITIES: MANTEGNA, BELLINI; PADUA, VENICE

This essay is dedicated to Jennifer Fletcher in celebration of her 80th birthday – beloved teacher and mentor.

1 'He is very old and still the best in painting' ('Er jst ser alt vnd jst noch der pest jm gemoll'). Quoted in Robertson 1968, p. 1.
2 'Ma de quela istoria li à datto vostra signoria non si poria dire quanto la fa male volontieri perché sa il iudizio di vostra signoria e poi va al parangone de quele opera de messer Andrea e, per tantto, lui in questa opera vole fare quanto saperà e dize che in questa istoria non pole far chose che stia bene, né che abia del buon...' Letter of 25 June 1501 from Michele Vianello in Venice to Isabella d'Este. Barausse 2008–9, p. 345, doc. 64.
3 'E questa matina sono stato con Giovane Belino e pù e pù volte unde che l'ha finito el quadro che non li mancha niente, e invero l'è bela cosa, à fato melio de quelo che me credeva; so che el piacerà a la ecelencia vostra e in questo quadro s'è molto sforcato per l'onore, masime per respeto de messer Andrea Mantegna.' Letter of 6 July 1504 from Lorenzo da Pavia in Venice to Isabella d'Este. Barausse 2008–9, p. 350, doc. 88.
4 The late fifteenth-century Milanese pilgrim, Don Pietro Casola, recounts leaving Padua after dinner on the evening of 20 May 1494, and arriving at Venice by water the same evening, at the 23rd hour. Casola 1907, p. 122.
5 Pincus 2017, pp. 45–6.
6 Blake McHam 2007, p. 213.
7 See, most recently, Blass-Simmen 2017, p. 4.
8 For a summary of Donato's career, see King 1986, pp. 370–2; for his patronage see Holgate 2002.
9 This account of Mantegna's life and career is indebted to the following fundamental sources: Kristeller 1902; Lightbown 1986; London and New York 1992; De Nicolò Salmazo 2004; Agosti 2005; Paris 2008–9; Christiansen 2009.
10 Vasari 1568 (1996), vol. 1, pp. 557–8.
11 Kristeller 1902, p. 448, doc. 1.
12 Kristeller 1902, pp. 493–5, doc. 12.
13 Kristeller 1902, pp. 489–90, doc. 4; Lightbown 1986, pp. 459–60.
14 Scardeone 1560, p. 371.
15 Lightbown 1986, pp. 28, 457–8.
16 For the formal arbitration process that ended Mantegna and Pizzolo's collaboration, see Rigoni (1948–9) 1970, pp. 17–20, doc. VI.
17 For a summary see De Marchi 2008–9.
18 D. Landau in London and New York 1992, pp. 48–52.
19 For the *Triumphs*, see Martindale 1979; C. Hope in London and New York 1992, pp. 350–6; C. Elam in Paris 2008–9, pp. 363–71.
20 Casola 1907, pp. 125, 129.
21 Lewkenor 1599, sig. A3r, p. 1.
22 See most recently Perry 2016, pp. 18–29.
23 Labowsky 1979, pp. 147–56 (trans. in Englander 1990, p. 150).
24 Ascham 1570, p. 24.
25 Fletcher 2004, p. 29.
26 Fletcher 2004, p. 33; Eisler 1989, pp. 512–13.
27 This account of Giovanni Bellini's life is indebted to Robertson 1968; Goffen 1989; Pächt 2003; the contributions in Humfrey 2004: particularly Fletcher 2004; Bätschmann 2008; Rome 2008–9.
28 For the arguments concerning Giovanni's birthdate, see De Marchi in this volume; Maze 2017–18, pp. 39–41; Lucco 2008–9, pp. 21–3. The question will also be addressed in P. Humfrey's, M. Lucco's and G.C.F. Villa's forthcoming monograph on Giovanni Bellini.
29 This account of Jacopo Bellini's life and work is indebted to Eisler 1989. It has been suggested that Giovanni Bellini was not the son of Jacopo, but his half-brother. See Maze 2013. Giovanni and Gentile had a third brother, Nicolò, who was not a painter, and was a member of the household of the Corner family by at least the early sixteenth century. See Fletcher 2004, pp. 28, 31.
30 See Mazzotta 2018a.
31 The key scholarly work on Gentile is Meyer zur Capellen 1985. See also Boston and London 2005–6.
32 See Barausse 2008–9, p. 339, doc. 36.
33 See Barausse 2008–9, p. 354, doc. 105.
34 In contrast, Gentile held office both as the Vicario and Guardian del Matin of the Scuola. See Fletcher 2004, pp. 21–4.
35 A trip to Pesaro seems highly likely; otherwise he is unlikely to have travelled further from Venice than Padua.
36 Fletcher 2004, p. 15.
37 Barausse 2008–9, p. 334, doc. 16.
38 Boskovits and Brown 2003, p. 18 note 17.
39 Fletcher 2004, p. 26.
40 Rutherglen and Hale 2015.
41 Barausse 2008–9, p. 345, doc. 64.
42 Nicolosia gave birth to at least four sons: one boy, who was dead in 1480; Girolamo (d. 1484); Francesco (d. after 1517) and Ludovico (d. 1510).
43 Nicolosia is not mentioned in the will of Anna Rinversi, Jacopo Bellini's wife, dated 25 November 1471 (see Barausse 2008–9, p. 338, doc. 31), which may mean that she was dead by this date.

II MANTEGNA / BELLINI: INVENTION VERSUS POETRY

1 See Christiansen 2004b.
2 Some examples cited in Lucco 2008–9, pp. 34–5.
3 As independently noticed by Raimondo Callegari (1996, p. 29) and Giovanni Agosti (2005, p. 20).
4 Venice 2018.
5 The observation was made by Keith V. Shaw (see K. Christiansen in Milan 1991, vol. 1, p. 309). On this work see A. Di Lorenzo in Milan 2012–13, no. 4, pp. 56–9.
6 Thus Pietro Bembo writing from Venice to the 'marchesana' on 1 January 1505, having met the painter: 'La invenzione, che mi scrive V. S. che io truovi al dissegno, bisognerà che s'accomodi alla fantasia di lui che l'ha a fare, il quale ha piacere che molto signati termini non si diano al suo stile, uso, come dice, di sempre vagare a sua voglia nelle pitture che, quanto è in lui, possano sodisfare a chi le mira' (Gaye 1839–40, vol. 2, pp. 71–4, doc. XXII; Fletcher 1981–2, pp. 51–63; Barausse 2008–9, p. 352, doc. 99).
7 See Letter from Michele Vianello to Isabella d'Este, 25 June 1501, cited in the essay by Campbell in this volume, p. 15 note 2. Brown and Lorenzoni 1982, p. 159, doc. VIII; Barausse 2008–9, p. 345, doc. 64.
8 Belting 2017–18, p. 30.
9 Musée du Louvre, Paris, RF 1489, f. 19v: see Gasparotto 2017–18, pp. 15–16.
10 Gasparotto 2017–18, p. 15.
11 'prima bizantino e gotico, poi mantegnesco e padovano': Longhi 1946 (1978), p. 12.
12 See Longhi 1949 (1978), p. 102.
13 See De Marchi 2014.
14 See Bellosi 2008–9, pp. 104, 119–21.
15 See Lucco 2008–9, who hypothesises a date of birth of about 1438–40.
16 On Giovanni Bellini's belated fortune in the literature, with respect to that of Mantegna, see Vinco 2014.
17 Shaw with Boccia-Shaw 1989 thought that the Latin inscription 'Andreas Mantinea Pat[avinus] ann[os] septem et decem natus sua manu pinxit M.CCC. XLVIII', recorded by Scardeone, was the result of manipulation (as opposed to Christiansen 1992a, p. 112 note 38; and De Nicolò Salmazo 1993, pp. 26–7).
18 The relic of the blood of Christ, housed in Sant'Andrea in Mantua and already recognised by Imperial Privilege granted by Charles IV in 1368, prompted a heated debate, in September 1459, on the very legitimacy of such a relic, and on its consequent cult; on this occasion the Franciscan Francesco della Rovere (the future Pope Sixtus IV) prevailed over the Dominican Juan de Torquemada. These Mantuan events provide a context for Bellini's painting, which I believe was carried out at the end of 1459, at the conclusion of this dispute. Pius II attributed his recovery from the gout that struck him in Mantua to his invocation of the relic of the Holy Blood

and he instituted a confraternity bearing its name (Donesmondi 1612–16, vol. 2, pp. 11–19).

19 Mantegna could artfully shelter behind a commission which he had in fact passed on (or would pass on) to his brother-in-law, engaged as he was during those months in completing the San Zeno triptych, which was erected in July of that year; the Strabo was sent to King René in September (see De Marchi 2008–9, pp. 156–7).

20 The closest parallel is with the *Three Marys and other mourners at the empty tomb of Christ* (Musée du Louvre, Paris, RF 1520, f. 57r).

21 Meiss 1957.

22 De Marchi 1992, pp. 218 and 220. Bearing an attribution to Jacopo, first proposed by David Carritt, the panel was published by Christiansen 1987, p. 172, and by Eisler 1989, pp. 15, 516.

23 K. Christiansen in Berlin and New York 2011–12, p. 324.

24 See Shaw and Boccia-Shaw 1996.

25 The particularly close similarity, suggesting a date around 1459 for the Correr *Crucifixion*, was also noticed by Christiansen (2004a, pp. 57–8).

26 As was independently noted by Mauro Lucco (in Rome 2008–9, no. 6, pp. 148–50) and Antonio Mazzotta (see M. Servi in Paris 2008–9, no. 68, pp. 196–8).

27 See L. Bellosi in Paris 2008–9, no. 33, pp. 124–7; M. Lucco in Rome 2008–9, pp. 156–9; M. Vinco in Los Angeles 2017–18, no. 3, pp. 70–5. I have already given detailed reasons for my opinion on the dating of the predella with *Drusiana and Saint John* and the chronology of Giovanni Bellini's youthful work, in general, see De Marchi 2009, p. 21 note 15.

28 See Fogolari 1924.

29 Thus too Lucco (2004, pp. 78–80), as opposed to Bellosi 2008–9, pp. 106–7.

30 This merits in-depth analysis, supported by precise comparisons. I suspect Alvise's collaboration can most clearly be perceived in the triptych of the *Nativity*, in the Saint Francis and in the lunette; and that of Lazzaro in the *Saint Sebastian*, especially in the lunette (his authorship was already suggested by Christiansen 2004a, p. 68, for the triptych dedicated to the Virgin Mary).

31 See Humfrey 1990; and Vinco 2018 (forthcoming).

III 'BELLINI STANDS HIGHER … THAN MANTEGNA'

1 Thiébaut 2008–9, p. 22.

2 For these two works see the chapter on the Presentation of Christ in the Temple in this volume.

3 According to the archives of Gemäldegalerie, Berlin, the Paris exhibition initially hoped to bring together Mantegna's Berlin *Presentation* and the one by Bellini in Venice.

4 Mantegna's date of birth has also been debated, but what was put forward by Shaw with Boccia-Shaw 1989 has not resonated (except with the authors themselves: Shaw and Boccia 2016).

5 M. Lucco in Rome 2008–9, pp. 156–8. See also p. 113 in this volume.

6 Bellosi 2008–9, p. 105; L. Bellosi in Paris 2008–9, p. 124.

7 Agosti 2008–9, p. 34 (trans. from the Italian edition of Paris 2008–9, p. 37).

8 Lucco 2008–9, p. 37 note 12.

9 Longhi 1914 (1961). For a biographical summary of Longhi, see Facchinetti 2005.

10 Berenson 1907, p. 86.

11 Berenson 1913 (1916).

12 Longhi 1914 (1961), pp. 90–4.

13 Berenson 1907, p. 86.

14 On the relationship between Longhi and Berenson, see Garboli and Montagnani 1993, and more specifically regarding the case of the *Saint Giustina* in the Museo Bagatti Valsecchi in Milan, see G. Agosti in Bertelli 2006, pp. 176–82; and Calogero 2016.

15 On this altarpiece see p.95 in this volume.

16 Fiocco 1927 (the volume is dated the year after its publication); Longhi 1926 (1967).

17 Fiocco 1927, pp. 223–38; Longhi 1926 (1967), pp. 85–6. Longhi 1934 (1968) would later recognise that the fragment in question, at that time in the Vendeghini collection in Ferrara and now in the Pinacoteca Nazionale there, formed the uppermost part of the *Death of the Virgin* by Mantegna in the Prado (fig. 214). The attribution of the cartoons for the mosaics in the Mascoli Chapel remains unresolved: see pp. 269–70 note 26 in this volume.

18 On the maxim about connoisseurship that nurtured Longhi ('first connoisseurs, then historians'), see Romano 1998, p. 14.

19 Longhi 1926 (1967), p. 93 (trans. by S.J. Campbell in Campbell and Koering 2015, p. 221).

20 Longhi 1927 (1963).

21 Fiocco 1926a; Longhi 1926 (1967), pp. 97–8. On the ambiguous language used by Fiocco during the fascist period, see Tomasella 2002, p. 389. Longhi was not entirely unsympathetic towards facism; see recently De Marchi 2017, pp. 25–31.

22 Longhi 1949 (1978), p. 102.

23 M. Lucco in Rome 2008–9, p. 148; for Mantegna's letter, see Kristeller 1902, p. 525, doc. 39.

24 Lucco 2008–9, pp. 28–30.

25 Longhi 1927 (1963), pp. 146–7, had himself admitted the lack of maturity in his essay, even if he was always to defend its substance.

26 See Agosti 1999, p. 70; and G. Agosti in Milan 2002–3, pp. 54–9. In 2009, the art historian published a vitriolic review of the Bellini exhibition at the Scuderie del Quirinale (Agosti 2009a).

27 Bellosi's first book, dedicated to a painter forgotten by all, Buonamico Buffalmacco, author of the frescoes of the *Triumph of Death* in the Camposanto in Pisa, stands as an emblematic example of his method (Bellosi 1974).

28 Bellosi 2008–9, p. 103.

29 See pp. 104–7 in this volume.

30 M. Servi in Paris 2008–9, p. 198 (trans. from the Italian edition, p. 200), citing the point made by Antonio Mazzotta.

31 The opponents in the 2008 debate both found agreement on the influence of Piero on Bellini in the *Storia dell'arte italiana* published by Einaudi: see Bellosi 1980, pp. 33–4 and Lucco 1983, pp. 447–8. How Italian scholars received Longhi's thesis merits an article of its own; beyond Italy, the influence of the *Montefeltro Altarpiece* on the *Pesaro Altarpiece* was emphasised from Robertson 1968, pp. 68–9, to Bätschmann 2008, p. 162. The Franciscan connection between Piero and Bellini was recently underlined by Rutherglen 2015, p. 45.

32 Suffice it to cite the two reviews published in *The Burlington Magazine*. Luke Syson's, on the Paris exhibition, is an assault on Longhi's positions: the miniatures of the Bibliothèque de l'Arsenal (figs 94, 95) are given to Jacopo Bellini, the *Saint Vincent Ferrer Altarpiece* (fig. 253) to Alvise Vivarini, the predella with *Drusiana and Saint John* (fig. 103) to an assistant of Giovanni Bellini, the *Presentation of Christ in the Temple* (fig. 132) in Venice is likewise withdrawn from Bellini, and the *Virgin and Child* in the Musée Jacquemart-André (fig. 108) is given to Lazzaro Bastiani (Syson 2009, pp. 532–3 and 535 note 36). My own review of the Rome exhibition maintained that Bellini could have seen (lost) works by Piero in Ancona (Rowley 2008); I would now prefer to underline the words 'this must certainly remain an open question'.

33 See, respectively, Brown and Pizzati 2014; and Maze 2013 (argued once again in Maze 2017–18, pp. 39–41).

34 Mazzotta 2018b. See also Mazzotta 2018a for another attribution following Longhi's views.

35 In the case of the predella with *Drusiana and Saint John* (fig. 103), M. Vinco (in Los Angeles 2017–18, p. 74) noted that the dates 1468–71 should simply regarded as a *terminus ante quem*. See also the essay by De Marchi in this volume, p. 37.

36 M. Lucco in Rome 2008–9, no. 12, pp. 172–4; Bellosi 2008–9, p. 106.

37 See, respectively, Longhi 1949 (1978), p. 104 and Longhi 1925–6 (1995), p. 372.

38 See the impressive analyses by Keith Christiansen and Andrea De Marchi, although they leave some questions unanswered: the *Lamentation* in the Doge's Palace is dated to either 1472 (Christiansen 2004a, p. 71) or nearly a decade earlier (De Marchi 2009, p. 21 note 15; and De Marchi 2012–13, p. 27).

39 This phase can also be seen in Gentile Bellini, who in 1465 painted the organ shutters for the Basilica of San Marco in Venice in a style showing direct loyalty to Mantegna's *San Zeno Altarpiece* (see Christiansen 2004a, p. 68).

40 Longhi 1961, p. VIII.

41 On this question of altered perception, see Rowley 2010, I, pp. 243–93.

IV MANTEGNA AND BELLINI: CONTRASTING APPROACHES TO TECHNIQUE

1 For the technique and restoration of the *Saint Luke Polyptych* see Bandera Bistoletti 1989, pp. 63–87.

2 For aspects of the technique of the Carità triptychs see Venice 2000, pp. 34–5.

3 Christiansen 1992b, p. 68 and p. 78 note 3.

4 For Giovanni's likely participation in this series see Mazzotta 2018a.

5 For more detailed discussion of the technique of Mantegna's version, see Dunkerton 1993, pp. 28–30, and Billinge and Spring 2009, pp. 12–14; for Bellini's see Dunkerton 2004, and Dunkerton and Spring 2018 (forthcoming).

6 It was evidently Mantegna's usual practice to establish his designs in considerable detail at the underdrawing stage. Extensive underdrawing with significant alterations has been found on the *San Zeno Polyptych*. The approach to drawing varies from figure to figure: some are drawn with schematic outlines alone, others are more worked up with some hatched shading. See Bracco, Sartiani and Toso 2009, pp. 125–80, esp. pp. 129–40. For more examples of detailed underdrawings on panel paintings see Christiansen 1992b, pp. 67–78, and Ravaud et al. 2009a, pp. 74–81, esp. p. 77, and Oberthaler 2009, pp. 99–105, esp. p. 103.

7 A similar linear underdrawing has been found on the panels of the Carità Triptych; see Venice 2000, p. 34. For further discussion of this point see Dunkerton and Spring 2018 (forthcoming).

8 Dunkerton and Spring 2018 (forthcoming).
9 For a more detailed discussion of the support and technique see Hartwieg 2018, pp. 75–84; and also Rothe 1992, pp. 82–3.
10 The complex development of this painting has also been studied using Hyperspectral Imaging (NIR) and Fiber Optic Reflectance Spectroscopy (FORS) point analysis by John Delaney and Francesca Gabrieli, National Gallery of Art, Washington DC, Scientific Research Department, see Hartwieg 2018, p. 80.
11 Pigment analyses were carried out using Micro-X-ray-fluorescence (μXRF) analysis by Sabine Schwerdtfeger and Ina Reiche, Rathgen Research Lab, Staatliche Museen zu Berlin. Further results were provided by Delaney and Gabrieli (see note 10).
12 Rothe 1992, pp. 80–2.
13 Most notably the *Ecce Homo* in the Musée Jacquemart-André, a late canvas that had previously been held up as the best preserved of all Mantegna's glue-size paintings: see Ravaud et al. 2009b, pp. 27–34, esp. p. 31. This study confirmed that egg tempera is the principal medium used for the large canvases, the *Madonna della Vittoria* and the *Saint Sebastian* (both Musée du Louvre, Paris).
14 Identification of egg was possible especially in the flesh tones through spectral analysis using NIR and FORS, carried out by Delaney and Gabrieli (see note 10).
15 Rothe 1992, p. 84, reported analysis that suggested the unlikely medium of casein for the *Saint Mark*. The paint layer is substantial and not soluble in water. In addition, pentimenti have been observed. This all points to egg tempera as the most likely medium.
16 It has been suggested that this was the case with the *Virgin and Child* in the Accademia Carrara, Bergamo. See Bellucci and Frosinini 2009, pp. 21–6, esp. p. 26.
17 For an excellent account of the properties of the glue-size medium see Carr 1997, pp. 3–4.
18 Campbell 1998, pp. 42–4.
19 For the technique and restoration of Gentile Bellini's canvas see Manieri Elia 2010, pp. 86–99.
20 See Dunkerton and Spring 2018 (forthcoming).
21 Published examples from some his most celebrated works include the Frick *Saint Francis in the Desert* (Rutherglen and Hale 2015, pp. 81–131, esp. p. 84) and the *Frari Triptych* (see Poldi and Villa 2008, pp. 125–51).
22 See, for example, Dunkerton and Spring 2018 (forthcoming).
23 For the analysis of the binding medium of the *Pietà*, which appears to be egg see Frezzato 2014, pp. 107–10, esp. p. 109; and for the underdrawing see Borghese, Carini and Scatragli 2014, pp. 111–25, esp. pp. 113–15.
24 See Dunkerton 2004, p. 206. That the making of such monochromes using a hatched modelling technique like a drawing was the practice in Venice is confirmed by a panel attributed to Mansueti showing *The Supper at Emmaus* (Sam Fogg Ltd).
25 B. Hartwieg was able to prove this for the first time at the Querini Stampalia Museum in July 2014. She presented the results of her studies in a lecture 'Andrea Mantegna's and Giovanni Bellini's "The Presentation of Christ in the Temple." The Genesis, Correspondence, and Difference of Two Paintings in Berlin and Venice' at the conference of the Renaissance Society of America in Berlin on 28 March 2015.
26 The authors examined the surface of the painting in Venice in June 2017, using a stereo-binocular microscope. The suggestion made by G.C.F. Villa in Villa 2017, p. 83, that the men's heads are 'the result of successive additions that are in complete disagreement with the rest of the pictorial portrayal', has to be rejected.
27 Analysis of a few fibres by FTIR microscopy confirmed that they contained protein and the support is therefore vellum.
28 Even when working on a large scale as in the main tier panels of the *San Zeno Altarpiece* Mantegna persisted in using egg tempera; see Andreotti, Colombini and Degano 2009, pp. 313–18, esp. pp. 315–16. The only exception might be the *Madonna dei Cherubini* in the Brera, Milan. This panel is in problematic condition but its oil technique is anomalous for a panel by Mantegna. The panel may be a copy of a lost Mantegna, probably painted in Venice and possibly even in the Bellini workshop. It has not been accepted by all scholars and was questioned most recently by Lightbown who judged it 'very doubtful' (Lightbown 1986, pp. 477–8).
29 Roy 2009, pp. 88–92, and Filtenborg 2009, pp. 93–8.
30 Schölzel 2009, pp. 106–13, esp. p. 112.
31 Mantegna mentions this in a letter from 6 July 1477 to Marquess Ludovico, transcript in Kristeller 1902, pp. 534–5, doc. 69.
32 For the technique of the *Trivulzio Madonna*, very probably yet another egg tempera painting, see Beccaria 2008, pp. 163–75, esp. p. 173.
33 Rothe 1992, p. 84, listed these as distemper. However, samples had been analysed in 1974 at the National Gallery, showing that the medium was egg tempera; see Dunkerton 1993, p. 37.
34 For discussion of Mantegna and varnishes see Dunkerton 1993, pp. 37–8.
35 Billinge and Spring 2009, p. 16.
36 For the technique of this canvas see Poldi and Villa 2008, pp. 103–23. For discussion of Bellini's paintings in oil on canvas see Dunkerton 2004, pp. 213–15.
37 For an account of the technique of Bellini's later works with special emphasis on those in the National Gallery, and also *The Drunkenness of Noah* and the *Portrait of Fra Teodoro of Urbino as Saint Domenic*, see Dunkerton and Spring 2018 (forthcoming).

V DRAWING CONCLUSIONS: THE GRAPHIC WORK OF MANTEGNA AND BELLINI

1 Cited in Romano 1981 (1994), pp. 400–1.
2 Vasari 1568 (1996), vol. 1, pp. 489, 560, 564.
3 Vasari 1568 (1996), vol. 1, pp. 487, 558; London 1998, pp. 29–30. According to Vasari, Squarcione made available 'casts taken from ancient statues and ... pictures painted upon canvas which he caused to be brought from diverse places, particularly from Tuscany and from Rome': Vasari 1568 (1996), vol. 1, p. 558. See the essay by Campbell and the chapter on Jacopo Bellini and the formation of Giovanni in this volume.
4 Villa 2008, pp. 78–80. They were first published by Fogolari 1932. The authenticity of Bellini's sketches on his panels were doubted by the Tietzes, who dismissed them as 'spurious ... scrawls'. Tietze and Tietze-Conrat 1944, p. 73. Villa also mentions drawings that are hidden in plain sight, such as grotesque caricatures in rock or marble structures.
5 For more details, see p. 38 in this volume.
6 Cennino Cennini writes about this work. See Cennini 2015, chapters 30 (pp. 50–1) and 122 (pp. 158–9).
7 Such as *The Resurrected Christ with Saints Andrew and Longinus* (fig. 63) and *The Descent of Christ into Limbo* (fig. 143), which both have related engravings.
8 The *Judith* is very probably the drawing which was in Vasari's collection: see Vasari 1568 (1996), vol. 1, p. 563; Faietti 2010, p. 24.
9 Heinemann 1962–91, vol. 1; Goldner 2004.
10 D. Ekserdjian in London and New York 1992, no. 63, p. 251, considered these to be by a studio hand. Martin Clayton suggested that the studies may be by Mantegna, in conversation with the authors (2017).
11 See the chapter on the Motif of the Dead Christ in this volume.
12 Byam Shaw 1979, no. 34b, p. 17, and Lightbown 1986, pp. 481–2, date the Morgan Library sheet to the late 1450s, but D. Ekserdjian in London and New York 1992, no. 23, p. 173, argues that they are closer to works of the early 1460s. See the chapter on Standing Saints in this volume.
13 For the subject of the *Man lying on a stone slab*, see the chapter on the Body in this volume.
14 A. Mazzotta in Paris 2008–9, no. 94, p. 258.
15 See, for example, Pisanello's *Three courtiers* (British Museum, London, 1846,0509.143); the copy after an ancient statue of the *River Tigris* (Kupferstich-kabinett, Berlin, KdZ 1359); or the *Two naiads riding sea monsters* (Museum Boijmans Van Beuningen, Rotterdam, I.523 verso); London 2001–2, pp. 73, 92, 144.
16 Since its rediscovery the drawing has been the subject of two investigations. A technical examination was made by Eva Hummert, Berlin, with the input of Irene Brueckle, Staatliche Akademie, Stuttgart, and Georg Josef Dietz, Staatliche Museen zu Berlin and art-historical expertise was provided by Mauro Lucco. Lucco is inclined to date the drawing to the earliest period of work on the Triumphs shortly after the conclusion of work on the Camera Picta, around 1474.
17 The Louvre drawing is given to Mantegna by Martindale 1979, p. 164, D. Ekserdjian in London and New York 1992, fig. 99 and nos 116, 119, 125, pp. 352, 373–4, 379–80, 389, and C. Loisel in Madrid and Paris 2004–5, no. 10, p. 126. C. Elam in Paris 2008–9, no. 161, pp. 382–3, presents the *Trumpeters* as a studio work. Paul Joannides published another workshop drawing for the *Triumphs*, also related to Canvas II, in Hamburg 2008, no. 2, pp. 20–1.
18 First suggested by Agosti 1993, p. 67 notes 25–6, and p. 78; repeated in Agosti 2005, pp. 110–11 notes 31–2, and p. 135. A date in the 1490s was also accepted by X. Brooke in Liverpool and London 1998–9, no. 36, pp. 80–2, and by I. di Maio in Paris 2008–9, no. 182, p. 413.
19 Christiansen 2009, p. 49.
20 For Marcantonio and Raphael, see Landau and Parshall 1994, pp. 120–31. For a summary of the discussion see Boorsch 2010.
21 Cited by Christiansen 2009, p. 48.
22 Christiansen 2009, pp. 49–50.
23 Letter from Lancillotto de Andreasis to Federico Gonzaga, 1483, cited in Baxandall 1974, p. 12.

24 See Whistler 2016, pp. 158, 160; Bätschmann 2008, p. 39.

25 Given to Bellini in full by H. Chapman in London and Florence 2010–11, p. 18, but catalogued as 'Attributed to Giovanni Bellini' by C. Campbell in London and New York 2012–13, no. 5, p. 52.

26 Christiansen 2004b, pp. 10, 21; For Bellini's underdrawings see Dunkerton 2004, p. 6; Villa 2008; Zgraja 2015; Whistler 2016, p. 105.

27 Schmidt Arcangeli 1996.

28 Bätschmann 2008, p. 19.

29 Date suggested by C. Campbell in London and New York 2012–13, p. 54. A. Mazzotta dates the *Nativity* to about 1470 and *Saint Mark* to about 1475 (Los Angeles 2017–18, no. 4, pp. 76–81).

30 Dated by A. Mazzotta in Paris 2008–9, nos 45–6, pp. 147–50, to around 1480. See also M. Vinco in Milan 2014, nos 16–17, pp. 166–7.

31 A drawing of *The Funeral Procession of the Virgin* (Fogg Museum, Harvard, 1932.275) forms a tempting bridge between the stiffness of early drawings like the *Saint Sebastian* (and, perhaps, *The three crosses*) and the greater fluidity of the *Saint Louis of Toulouse* studies. Rearick 2004, p. 299, and A. Robison in Venice 2014–15, p. 32, give it to Giovanni Bellini.

32 Parker 1928, p. 19 and pl. 21; Popham and Wilde 1949, no. 2, p. 171.

33 Robertson 1968, p. 119; Goldner 2004, p. 254; and P. Humfrey in Rome 2008–9, p. 230, under no. 27, considered it a workshop drawing.

34 Goldner 2004, p. 249, notes but does not reproduce the private collection work.

35 Goldner 2004, p. 249.

36 Villa 2008, p. 77.

37 'n'anco disegnare le tavole con tanta istrema diligenza, componendo il tutto di chiaro e scuro, come usava Giovan Bellino, perch'è fatica gettata, avendosi a coprire il tutto con li colori.' Pino 2000, p. 109.

38 Whistler 2016, p. 105. See also Dunkerton 2004.

39 See the essay by Dunkerton and Hartwieg in this volume.

40 See the chapter on the Descent of Christ into Limbo in this volume.

41 London and New York 1992, no. 27, p. 179. The same inscription exists, trimmed, on the upper edge of the verso of Mantegna's *Three Studies for the Dead Christ* in the British Museum (fig. 163).

42 Goldner 2004, p. 231.

43 The portrait of *Francesco II Gonzaga* from Dublin (fig. 204), the *Portrait of a man* from Christ Church Picture Gallery, Oxford; and two *Portraits of men* in the Musée des Beaux-Arts, Besançon. A fifth drawing, a *Portrait of a man* from the Albertina in Vienna, sometimes added to this group, is a preparatory study for the painting of the same sitter by Francesco Bonsignori (National Gallery, London, NG736). See G. Goldner in Berlin and New York 2011–12, nos 153–8, pp. 349–54.

44 See Pisanello's two portraits of Emperor Sigismund of Luxembourg (1433; 2479, 2339) and his black-chalk portraits, preparatory for medals, of Filippo Maria Visconti and Niccolò Piccinino (2483, 2482), all in the Louvre; Berlin and New York 2011–12, nos 62–3, 94, 96, pp. 194–5, 244–6, 248–50.

45 See Berlin and New York 2011–12, no. 159, pp. 357–9.

46 See the chapter on Portraits in this volume.

47 See G. Goldner in Berlin and New York 2011–12, no. 158, pp. 353–4.

48 See London and New York 1992, no. 1, p. 477.

49 Other comparably accomplished black-chalk drawings from the same period and region are the *Portrait of a young man* attributed to Alvise Vivarini (Staatliche Museen, Berlin, KdZ 5050): see D. Korbacher in Berlin and New York 2011–12, no. 165, pp. 368–9; and the *Young man looking up* (Städelsche Kunstinstitut, Frankfurt, 453), given to Venetian School, about 1500 (Frankfurt and Paris 2006–7, no. 9, p. 44).

CATALOGUE

'Sculpting in paint': Mantegna's Training in Padua

1 Vasari 1966–97, vol. 3, p. 548: 'pare fatta da un vecchio ben pratico e non da un giovanetto' (1568 edition). The signature was recorded by Scardeone 1560, p. 372: 'Andreas Mantegna Pat. an. septem & decem natus, sua manu pinxit, M.CCCC. XLVIII'. This inscription has been doubted by Shaw with Boccia-Shaw 1989, for reasons which have left scholars unconvinced (see Christiansen 1992a, p. 112 note 38).

2 On Mantegna's interest in ancient script, see Zamponi 2006–7. The authenticity of the signature on the *Saint Mark* has also been unjustly contested; see instead the technical analyses in Sander 2004, p. 34, and A. Galli in Paris 2008–9, pp. 70–2.

3 On Mantegna's peculiar painting technique, see the essay by Dunkerton and Hartwieg in this volume. On the presence of Flemish paintings in the Veneto during the fifteenth century, see Campbell 1981 and Lucco 2004.

4 Paolo Uccello sojourned in Venice between 1425 and 1427, and then in Padua in about 1445; Filippo Lippi came to Padua between 1432 and 1437; and Andrea del Castagno worked in Venice in 1442. The importance of Filippo Lippi's Paduan sojourn has been studied by De Marchi 1996b.

5 In 1423, Ghiberti delivered his first pair of bronze doors, begun in 1403. This soon earned him a similar commission, largely accomplished by 1443 but only completed in 1452; Michelangelo nicknamed it the Gate of Paradise ('Porta del Paradiso').

6 In the mid-Quattrocento, the principal model for a bronze equestrian monument was the statue of Marcus Aurelius near the Lateran in Rome, now in the Capitoline Museums. However, one should also remember the statue of the *Regisole* in Pavia (destroyed in 1796) and the Quadriga of San Marco in Venice, brought there by the Venetians after the Sack of Constantinople in 1204.

7 On the influence of Donatello on the frescoes in the Ovetari Chapel, see Dunkelman 1980, even if the young Mantegna's journey to Florence posited by the author need not have taken place.

8 On the spread of this motif, see Kokole 1990.

9 On these words by the poet Ulisse degli Aleotti ('scolpì in pictura propria viva et vera'), see Kristeller 1902, p. 488, doc. 1.

10 On Squarcione, see De Nicolò Salmazo 1999.

11 Squarcione later had other adoptive sons, notably Marco Zoppo (see the chapter on Zoppo in this volume).

12 The break between Mantegna and Squarcione became formal in January 1448. Until the end of the fifteenth century, some (whether ignorant or ill-intentioned) still referred to Mantegna as 'Andrea Squarcione' (Cavazzini and Galli 2008–9, p. 60 note 2).

13 On this work see Schmidt Arcangeli 2015, pp. 383–9.

14 Lucco 2013, p. 58.

15 See Christiansen 1992a, pp. 97–8; H. Chapman in London 1998, pp. 27–31; and De Nicolò Salmazo 2006–7, p. 9.

16 In November 1448, a certain Luca, native of Puglia, stated to Pizzolo that he wished to work with him 'in order to paint in the latest manner' ('ut disceret pingere in recenti'): Rigoni 1948–9 (1970), pp. 32, 39, doc. V. On Pizzolo's activity in the Santo, see Vinco 2015, p. 370, usefully reviewing the existing documentation and ruling out his oft-supposed sculptural intervention. Whereas Squarcione also collaborated with Donatello in the Santo (in 1449: De Marchi 1996b, p. 22 note 62), Mantegna was only active there in 1452, decorating the lunette over the main portal, now in the Basilica's Museo Antoniano. The work, representing *Saints Anthony of Padua and Bernardino of Siena presenting the Monogram of Christ*, has been very damaged by weathering and later repainting.

17 In 1568 Vasari 1966–97, vol. 3.1, p. 548 (Vasari 1996, vol. 1, p. 558) believed that the commission for the chapel was given to Mantegna and Pizzolo through the intervention of Squarcione, but this is questionable.

18 On the controversy between Mantegna and Pizzolo, settled by an agreement in July 1449, see Rigoni 1948–9 (1970), p. 42, doc. X. On the presence of Marchigian artists in Padua (Ansuino da Forlì, Giovanni Boccati, Giovanni Angelo d'Antonio and Girolamo di Giovanni), see De Marchi 2002b, pp. 53–5.

19 Lightbown 1986, p. 392.

20 In 1435, Leon Battista Alberti mentions such a precept in his *De Pictura* (II, 36).

21 On the iconographic hesitations in this drawing, as well as the mysterious (and awkward) head brushed on its verso, see D. Ekserdjian in London and New York 1992, pp. 135–8.

22 In *Du côté de chez Swann* (1913), Proust describes 'a strapping great lad in livery [who] stood musing, motionless, statuesque, useless, like that purely decorative warrior whom one sees in the most tumultuous of Mantegna's paintings, lost in dreams, leaning upon his shield, while all around him are fighting and bloodshed and death', Proust 1913 (2005), p. 390. Other soldiers with large shields appear in the Ovetari frescoes, including the one on the left of the *Saint James before Herod Agrippa*, which has often been identified as a self portrait of Mantegna.

23 On the conservation of the chapel see De Nicolò Salmazo, Spiazzi and Toniolo 2006.

24 The portrait is now lost (Lucco 2013, pp. 76–7). From these years one should especially mention, apart from the *Saint Jerome* in the Museu de Arte in São Paulo (fig. 116), the *Saint Luke Polyptych*, painted between 1453 and 1454 for the convent of Santa Giustina in Padua, now in the Brera in Milan (fig. 129), and the *Saint Euphemia*, signed and dated 1454, painted for the Church of Santa Maria Assunta in Montepeloso, now in the Museo di Capodimonte in Naples.

25 The marriage date can be deduced from the loan contracted by Jacopo on 25 February 1453 to finance his daughter's dowry.

26 Even before his marriage, Mantegna could certainly have had Venetian patrons, as Fletcher 1993, p. 21 suggested was the case for the *Saint Mark* in Frankfurt (fig. 77), while M. Boskovits (in Boskovits and Brown 2003, p. 88) took up the hypothesis of Mantegna's participation, alongside Jacopo Bellini, on the cartoons for the mosaic in the Mascoli Chapel

in the Basilica of San Marco in Venice (fig. 24). De Marchi 1996a, pp. 64–5 thought of Pizzolo's authorship.

27 Sufficient to notice that the preparatory drawing for the Ovetari Chapel (fig. 83) has also frequently been attributed to the young Giovanni Bellini, copying the frescoes by his brother-in-law (Fiocco 1933; and, for a summary of this controversy, De Nicolò Salmazo 1993, p. 121 note 389).

Jacopo Bellini and the Formation of Giovanni

1 Giovanni Bellini, son of Jacopo, has sometimes been identified with the Giovanni Bellini who was the illegitimate half-brother of Jacopo. See Maze 2013. This, however, seems implausible given the absence of works before around 1450 and in the hesitant quality of the earliest surviving works by Giovanni. Judging by Giovanni's later innovation, sensitivity and adaptability, these cannot be regarded as mature works by him (which is necessary if we wish to see Giovanni as Jacopo's half-brother). See further the essays by Campbell and De Marchi in this volume.

2 For Jacopo's competition with Pisanello to paint the portrait of Leonello d'Este, see the chapter on Portraits in this volume, p. 206.

3 Bätschmann 2008, p. 34.

4 This signature is now lost, but was recorded in a description in 1590: 'Jacobi Bellini Veneti Patris ac Gentilis et Joannis Natorum Opus MCCCCIX'. The last two characters 'IX' may be interpreted either as 'LX' or 'LIX'. The chapel's structure and tombs were complete by 1458: Eisler 1989, p. 517.

5 Jacopo Bellini and studio, 1990.118.1.

6 Padua 2006–7, nos 69–71, pp. 290–5.

7 D. Tosato in Milan 2014, no. 8, pp. 161–2. The mason Jacopo da Milano was contracted to work on the choir in 1462, at which point it was described as 'tutto a lantiga'.

8 See, for example, Eisler 1989, pls 239–41.

9 Robertson 1960, pp. 50–1, sees saints Sebastian and Anthony Abbot as Giovanni's. Keydel 1969, pp. 68–70, is only prepared to accept Sebastian as being from his hand. For Giovanni's likely involvement in the later *Madonna Triptych* and the related drawings in Washington, see the chapter on Standing Saints in this volume.

10 Bätschmann 2008, pp. 20–1.

11 Bätschmann 2008, p. 23; see also Lightbown 1986, no. 1, pp. 387–400.

12 'Jacobus haec pinxit, tenui quantam attigit artem / Ingenio Bellinus. Idem praeceptor et illi. Gentilis veneto fama celeberrimus orbe Quo Fabriana viro praestanti urbs patria gaudet'. Cited in Eisler 1989, p. 525 (trans. I. Gumb and M. McGann).

13 It was destroyed in 1759. See Eisler 1989, p. 525.

14 P. Humfrey in Berlin and New York 2011–12, p. 49.

15 Eisler doubts this, but Bätschmann points out that one of the documents upon which Eisler bases his argument is misdated. Eisler's other contention, that the court documents name this Jacopo's father as 'Piero', is also challenged by Fletcher's point about the unreliability of legal documents: Bätschmann 2008, p. 33; Eisler 1989, pp. 26–7; Fletcher 1998, p. 134. See also the essay by De Marchi in this volume.

16 Eisler 1989, p. 510. He follows the dating of Zeri 1971, pls 239–40.

17 For the shell-niche motif, see Eisler 1989, p. 510.

18 British Museum, London, 1855,0811.22.

19 Jacopo Bellini, *Dead Christ with Angels* (Musée du Louvre, Paris, RF 1475, 3, f. 7v); see Eisler 1989, pl. 219. For Donatello's bronze, see M. Pizzo in Padua 2006–7, no. 5.

20 Jacopo Bellini, London Drawing Book, rectos of ff. 62–5.

21 Eisler 1989, p. 510. He compares the panels to drawings, his plates 239–41.

22 For a thorough analysis of the albums, see Elen 1989.

23 Jacopo Bellini, *Studies of lions* (Musée du Louvre, Paris, RF 1540, 91, f. 72v).

24 Eisler 1989, p. 469, as Louvre f. 77v.

25 London and Florence 2010–11, p. 122.

26 H. Chapman in London and Florence 2010–11, p. 127.

27 See the chapter on Saint Jerome in this volume.

28 H. Chapman in London and Florence 2010–11, pp. 122–3 believes that both the Paris drawings and some of the London sheets have been reinforced by later hands: 'more likely his heirs' than Jacopo himself. See Eisler 1989, Appendix E, p. 533, for Gentile offering in 1493 to retouch with pen a drawing by Jacopo offered for sale to Francesco II Gonzaga.

29 London and Florence 2010–11, p. 122.

30 Eisler 1989, pp. 530–1: docs 1431, 1443 record the beginning and end of Jacopo's apprenticeship in the studio.

31 Meiss 1957.

32 Cited in London and New York 1992, p. 133; Lightbown 1986, p. 494.

33 Eisler 1989, p. 534; London and New York 1992, p. 133.

34 For painters working in books see Alexander 2016, p. 97.

35 See L. Armstrong in London and New York 1994–5, no. 29, p. 90, and Eisler 1989, pp. 534–5.

36 The miniature portrait in the Biblioteca Trivulziana, supposedly that of Raffaele Zovenzoni depicted by Giovanni Bellini in 1474 should, in our opinion, be excluded from the oeuvre of Giovanni Bellini due to its poor quality. See the chapter on Portraits in this volume, note 6.

37 Thus the miniatures address the major challenges of art at the time: the representation of interiors, humanist portraits, *all'antica* figures and allegorical images. See Mariani Canova 2009, p. 335.

38 See the essay by De Marchi in this volume. While Millard Meiss (Meiss 1957) gives them to Mantegna, Robertson argues in favour of the authorship of the young Giovanni Bellini (Robertson 1981, pp. 17–18).

39 L. Bellosi in Paris 2008–9, no. 30, pp. 119–20.

40 Syson 2009, p. 532–3.

41 The Albi manuscript is the second copy of this translation. The first is in the Bodleian Library in Oxford, ms. Can. Class. Lat. 161.

42 This idea was taken up by Conti and De Marchi, while others have identified this 'small work' with the *Saint Sebastian* in Vienna (fig. 193). See L. Bellosi in Paris 2008–9, nos 31–2, pp. 122–3; but also the chapters In Close Artistic Dialogue, note 22, and The Agony in the Garden, note 25, in this volume.

43 It dates from the same period as the family's work on the *Gattamelata Altarpiece.*

44 Joost-Gaugier 1979.

45 Mariani Canova 1999, p. 26: 'stella isolata'.

46 The source manuscript is now at Merton College, Oxford, ms. 315. It was probably copied out in Reichenau during the Carolingian period. For copies, see London and New York 1992, no. 7, pp. 123–5.

47 See A.C. de La Mare and D. Ekserdjian in London and New York 1992, no. 7, p. 125.

48 Alternative attributions have included an artist from the circle of Squarcione (Meiss 1957) and Nicolò Pizzolo (Marcon 1987, pp. 254–6). De Nicolò Salmazo (in Padua 1999, no. 92, pp. 91–2), is also sceptical about an attribution to Mantegna, noting that the minute description of surfaces can be linked back to late Gothic taste, while the apparently weightless Child is very different in spirit from the 'weighty plasticity' of the figures in the Ovetari Chapel.

49 Compare the signatures on Mantegna's painting of *Saint Sebastian* (fig. 193) and his drawing of *Judith and Abra* (fig. 58).

In Close Artistic Dialogue

1 See Christiansen 2004a, p. 66.

2 A. De Marchi in Paris 2008–9, no. 52, p. 164, and L. Bellosi, ibid., p. 106, favour an early date.

3 The *Gattamelata Altarpiece* was completed in 1459–60, but we may assume that Jacopo had already been to Padua somewhat earlier, perhaps in order to view the work's intended location or sign a contract. See Christiansen 2004a, pp. 56–7.

4 See Prochno 2006, p. 79, who asserts that Giovanni Bellini 'practised by imitating a foreign style, namely that of his brother-in-law Mantegna, in order in to gain an artistic profile of his own'.

5 Popham and Pouncey 1950, vol. 1, no. 15, pp. 9–10.

6 The inscription by Philips Koninck (1619–1688) reads: '*dit is montanges hant, wie hier noch tegen streeft / en is niet weert dat hij als kunstbeminner leeft / p. ko—.*'

7 Beginning with Tietze and Tietze-Conrat 1944, no. 312, pp. 87–8.

8 See the essay by Vowles and Korbacher in this volume.

9 See Los Angeles 2017–18, no. 3, pp. 70–5.

10 Villa 2008, p. 74.

11 L. Bellosi in Paris 2008–9, no. 33, p. 124.

12 See Los Angeles 2017–18, no. 3, p. 73, citing an observation by A. De Marchi.

13 Tempestini 2000, no. 7, p. 194.

14 Luke 9: 28–36, as well as Mark 9: 2–9 and Matthew 17: 1–8.

15 This attribution was also supported by the initials A.M. on a stone to the right in the picture, mentioned by Zanetti in 1733 (see M. Lucco in Rome 2008–9, no. 6, p. 248).

16 See the essay by De Marchi and the chapter on The Descent of Christ into Limbo in this volume.

17 See D. Ekserdjian in London and New York 1992, no. 4, p. 117, and A. Mazzotta in Paris 2008–9, no. 40, pp. 138–9. Ekserdjian does not rule out the possibility of an attribution to Mantegna himself, and dates the drawing to around 1448–9, while Mazzotta associates it with Mantegna's followers and assumes a date of around 1500.

18 The tracing of the contour lines would also explain the strange difference in line quality between the stiff contours and the looser elaboration.

19 See Christiansen 2004a, p. 52.

20 See the chapter on Marco Zoppo in this volume.

21 Mostly since Agosti 1999.

22 G. Agosti in Paris 2008–9, no. 28, p. 116; see the essay by Rowley in this volume.

23 M. Lucco in Rome 2008–9, p. 140, also with discussion of the related picture in the Rijksmuseum in Amsterdam (A 3287).

24 See M. Lucco in Rome 2008–9, no. 4, p. 144.

25 Christiansen 2004a, pp. 66–7. A. De Nicolò Salmazo (in Padua 2006–7, no. 73, p. 298) notes the stylistic affinity to the miniatures of the Guarino da

Verona manuscript of Strabo's *Geography* (fig. 97), which she views as an argument in favour of Giovanni Bellini's authorship and a date of around the same time.

26 See Verri and Ambers 2010, p. 96.

27 See Venice 2014–15, no. 6, pp. 41–4.

28 The two other engravings are Hind 1 (*Tobias and the Angel*) and Hind 12 (*Saint John the Baptist*). On 10 September 1497, Michele de Placiola wrote to Ermolao Bardellino, an adviser of Francesco Gonzaga in Mantua, praising Campagnola as a 'garzone de anni 15' ('boy of 15') who already 'taia de bulino, et anche in calcedonio' ('cut with the burin, even in chalcedony') and attempted to find him a place at court in Mantua so that he could continue his education in painting under Mantegna. Although this presumably did not occur, contact cannot be entirely ruled out. See Safarik 1974.

29 For a discussion of Mantegna's engraving of *The Virgin and Child* (fig. 183) see the chapter on the Virgin and Child in this volume.

Saint Jerome

1 Accepted by K. Christiansen in London and New York 1992, p. 115; N. Ridel Kaplan in Padua 2006–7, no. 19, pp. 176–7; and A. Galli in Paris 2008–9, p. 72; doubted by L. Syson, who proposes an attribution to Niccolò Pizzolo (Syson 2009, p. 531).

2 For the *Saint Jerome* painted by Pisanello in the Malaspina Chapel in around 1440, see London 2001–2, p. 29, fig. I.34. Three of Jacopo Bellini's drawings are in the London Book (see Eisler 1989, pls 272, 273, 275) and two in the Paris Book (Eisler 1989, pls 276, 277). The painting is in the Museo di Castelvecchio, Verona.

3 Bätschmann 2008, p. 15.

4 Jacopo Bellini, *Seven lions and three deer*, f. 72v (Musée du Louvre, Paris, RF 1540, 91); Eisler 1989, pl. 6.

5 Paris 2008–9, p. 74.

6 Borenius 1938, p. 106; London and New York 1992, p. 115; Paris 2008–9, p. 74.

7 The signature is accepted as autograph by virtually all scholars, with the exception of D. Pincus, who regards it as a later addition: Pincus 2008, p. 114 note 17. See also Los Angeles 2017–18, no. 1, pp. 58–63.

Standing Saints: The Young Mantegna and Bellini as Draughtsmen

1 For a longer discussion of these triptychs (now in the Accademia in Venice, whose rooms include the former Church of the Carità for which they were made), see the chapter on Jacopo Bellini and the Formation of Giovanni in this volume.

2 Venice 2014–15, pp. 29–32.

3 Lightbown 1986, p. 482 suggests the figures could have been intended for a fresco cycle, but an altarpiece seems more likely because the frontal poses resemble those found in panel paintings.

4 Agosti 1993, pp. 67 and 78 notes 25–6; Agosti 2005, pp. 111 and 135 notes 31–2; Paris 2008–9, p. 413.

The Agony in the Garden

1 See the essay by Campbell in this volume.

2 See the chapter on Saint Jerome in this volume.

3 For their provenance, see the List of Exhibited Works in this volume.

4 Faietti 2014; De Marchi 2008–9, p. 155; Vickers 1976; Davies 1961, pp. 335–8.

5 See Davies 1961, pp. 58–60, 335–8; N. Penny in Dunkerton et al. 1991, pp. 294–5; De Marchi 2008–9; Lucco 2008–9, p. 25; Gasparotto 2017–18, p. 15.

6 See the essay by Dunkerton and Hartwieg in this volume; Dunkerton and Spring 2018 (forthcoming).

7 Jacopo Bellini, Drawing Book (British Museum, London), 1855,0811.41 v. and 1855,0811.43 r.

8 Jacopo Bellini, Drawing Book (Musée du Louvre, Paris), *Saint Jerome in the wilderness*, f. 18v. and *Saint Christopher*, f. 21r and f. 51v. See Paris 2008–9, p. 158.

9 For the richest documentation on the *San Zeno Altarpiece* see Puppi 1972.

10 See the chapter on Landscape in this volume; also Gasparotto 2017–18.

11 Mantegna was in Mantua by the 21 June 1460. See Dall'Acqua 1980, p. 310. The *Agony* has often been dated to the early 1460s: see Dunkerton et al. 1991, p. 292; Lucco 2008–9, p. 25.

12 See the essay by Dunkerton and Hartwieg in this volume.

13 See Dunkerton and Hartwieg in this volume.

14 See the chapter on Jacopo Bellini and the Formation of Giovanni in this volume.

15 See Bomford et al. 1989, pp. 21–6, 43–8.

16 A. De Marchi in Paris 2008–9, no. 48, p. 158. At this time the Basilica's mosaics were an essential resource for every artist in Venice and the Veneto.

17 The French artist Colart de Laon painted an *Agony in the Garden* as a central panel of a triptych (the other panels are now lost) for Duke Louis d'Orléans, about 1405–8 (Museo del Prado, Madrid, P008106). See Silva Maroto 2013. I am grateful to Gabriele Finaldi for bringing this panel to my attention. Other early autonomous *Agonies in the Garden* include versions by Lo Spagna (around 1500, National Gallery, London, NG1032) and Botticelli (about 1498, Museo de la Capilla Real, Granada), painted for Queen Isabella of Castille.

18 See Hamburger 1997 for an excellent summary.

19 The Stations of the Cross only became fixed in the seventeenth century; they changed again in the late twentieth century.

20 According to the OPVS research project (www.opvs.fr), the *Meditations* were one of the five most 'popular' late medieval devotional texts; translated into five vernacular tongues before the advent of printing.

21 Hamburger 1997, p. 80.

22 Cited in Hamburger 1997, p. 82.

23 See also the essays by Campbell and De Marchi in this volume; also De Marchi 2008–9.

24 It is first recorded in the Aldobrandini collection in Rome in 1603, which was greatly enriched following the Papal annexation of Ferrara in 1598. See K. Christiansen in London and New York 1992, no. 8, p. 126.

25 For a discussion of the other paintings which have also been argued to be this 'operetta', see M. Servi in Paris 2008–9, p. 202.

26 Davies 1961; London 2016, no. 51, p. 81.

27 The best summary of their provenance is given in Davies 1961.

When Bellini traced Mantegna: Two Paintings of the Presentation of Christ in the Temple

1 On this ambiguity in the gospel account, see Greenstein 1992, pp. 110–42.

2 On symbolism in this painting, see above all Ringbom 1965 (1984), pp. 72–7; the other interpretations are summarised by Schmidt Arcangeli 2015, pp. 316–24. Walter 1989, pp. 61–2 usefully cites the fresco by Altichiero da Zevio in the Oratorio di San Giorgio in Padua (painted in 1384), in which Simeon likewise tears the Christ Child from his mother.

3 The haloes currently visible are repaints, which prompts caution when it comes to any interpretation (such as that by Cassegrain 2015, p. 81). The X-radiograph shows that Mantegna had initially thought of depicting the haloes in perspective, but he abandoned the idea when he added the two figures on the sides (see the essay by Dunkerton and Hartwieg in this volume, where it is noted that the background of the picture was originally deep blue, not black, a possible reference to the frescoes by Giotto in the Scrovegni Chapel, according to Blass-Simmen 2017, pp. 16–18).

4 Ringbom 1965 (1984), p. 74; Carr 1997, p. 69; Krüger 2001, p. 64.

5 While the work was certainly executed in Florence, the provenance of the painting from the Palazzo Pazzi is by no means certain: see Rowley 2018a (forthcoming).

6 On Donatello's sojourn in Padua, see the chapter on Mantegna's Training in Padua in this volume.

7 See especially Belting 1981, p. 83, who speaks of a work midway between icon and narrative painting. On his dispute with Ringbom, see Nova 2008–9.

8 Michiel 1800, pp. 17–18: 'El quadro in tavola piccola della nostra Donna, che presenta el puttino alla circoncisione, fu de mano del Mantegna, & è a mezze figure' ('the painting on a small wood panel of Our Lady, who presents the little Child for circumcision, was by the hand of Mantegna, and is in half-length figures'). For the dating of this text to between 1525 and 1528, see Schmitter 2003, p. 571.

9 On these doubts, see especially Morelli 1893, pp. 98–9, and Venturi 1914, p. 204, who attribute the work in Venice to Mantegna, demoting the one in Berlin. According to Rothe 1992, p. 83, the fact that the canvas in Berlin was glued onto a wood support could explain Michiel's confusion. In the eighteenth century the Berlin picture was in the Gradenigo collection in Padua, located in the old Palazzo Bembo, strengthening its identification as the painting noted by Michiel (see Lightbown 1986, p. 405, and Rowley 2018b).

10 The work has even been called unfinished (Robertson 1968, pp. 75–6), which is not the case.

11 See the hesitations expressed by Goffen 1989, pp. 282–4, who considered the work a copy after Giovanni Bellini; followed by Syson 2009, p. 533 note 29.

12 See especially the relevant remarks by Villa 2017, p. 86.

13 For the different proposals about dating, see Schmidt Arcangeli 2015, p. 319 (Mantegna), and B. Trevisan in Rome 2008–9, p. 176 (Bellini).

14 See the essay by Dunkerton and Hartwieg in this volume. The use of a tracing was already assumed by Bagarotto et al. 2000, pp. 188–9.

15 This suggestion was made by Giovanni de' Lazara as early as 1803 (see Campori 1866, p. 351), even if the Eremitani head was not recognised as a self-portrait until the mid-twentieth century. See Rowley 2018b, pp. 57–8.

16 The identification with Nicolosia, made by Bode 1889, p. 116, was developed by Prinz 1962. Lightbown 1986, p. 405, suggested the picture celebrated a birth.

17 According to Villa 2009, pp. 47–8, this portrait on the right side of the Querini Stampalia *Presentation* is essentially the work of the restorer Placido Fabris (1802–1859); see the different view of Dunkerton and Hartwieg in this volume

(p.62). The figure has rightly been compared to a *Portrait of a Young Man* probably by Jacopo da Valenza in the Accademia Carrara, Bergamo (fig. 133), whose attribution to Giovanni Bellini has been debated (see G. Valagussa in Rome 2010–11, pp. 48–9).

18 For example, B. Trevisan in Rome 2008–9, p. 176, suggests that the four lateral figures may be recognised as 'from left to right, Giovanni Bellini himself, his brother-in-law Mantegna, his sister Nicolosia (Mantegna's wife) and the wife (or mother) of Giovanni'.

19 Schmidt Arcangeli 2015, pp. 321–2, considers the Berlin painting to have been directly commissioned by the father of Pietro Bembo, Bernardo, while Gasparotto 2013, p. 55, believes it was made for Jacopo Bellini, who would have passed it on to his friend Bernardo Bembo. One can wonder if the version by Bellini was not executed as a consequence of the death of Jacopo (see Rowley 2018b, p. 59).

20 For a list of works with these two subjects, see Heinemann 1962–91, vol. 1, pp. 41–4.

21 On this work see Carr 1997, as well as Agosti 2005, p. 61 (who notes that the composition is derived from a relief by Donatello known through a workshop replica of about 1440). The *Holy Family with the Family of Saint John the Baptist* (fig. 243), painted by Mantegna for his own funerary chapel, can be regarded as an ultimate reincarnation of this type of composition.

The Descent of Christ into Limbo

1 See the chapter on Jacopo Bellini and the Formation of Giovanni in this volume, p.95.

2 Janson 1957, vol. 2, p. 212; at that time, the relief was not yet mounted on the pulpit, which presumably would have allowed Mantegna to see it at close range. Donatello died in December 1466.

3 '[Q]uadro dove fo la instoria del linbo', in a letter from Mantegna to Ludovico on 28 June 1468; Kristeller 1902, p. 525, doc. 40, quoted in London and New York 1992, pp. 258–9 (David Ekserdjian).

4 D. Ekserdjian in London and New York 1992, p. 258.

5 As seen for example in his painting of the *Death of the Virgin* in the Prado (fig. 214) or the fresco of the *Preaching of Saint James* in the Ovetari Chapel; Alberti 1435 (2004), p. 63.

6 D. Ekserdjian in London and New York 1992, no. 65, p. 261.

7 For this theory, see D. Ekserdjian in London and New York 1992, no. 66, p. 261.

8 A few weaker areas also suggest an attempt by a pupil to complete the master's unfinished drawing.

9 Syson 2009, p. 533.

10 M. Servi in Paris 2008–9, no. 68, p. 198, and M. Lucco in Rome 2008–9, no. 6, p. 150.

11 The other side of the printing plate, which remained in Mantegna's possession his entire life, shows a representation of The Flagellation of Christ with a tiled floor (fig. 196); see D. Landau in London and New York 1992, nos 67a, 67b, p. 265.

12 In her restoration report of June 1978, Kate Lowry noted that the support was parchment rather than paper. We are most grateful to Helen Dowding and Jenny Gaschke for providing us with this information.

13 The plants recall Bellini's painting of *Saint Francis in the Desert* in the Frick (fig. 219).

14 See Fletcher 1993, p. 20; Weston 2009, pp. 49–50. Fletcher suggests Giulio Campagnola as an alternative attribution.

15 This painting may have been commissioned by the Gonzaga. On the Bergamo painting, see Valagusso 2018.

16 The painted copies are found in the Houston Museum of Fine Arts (Sarah Campbell Blaffer Foundation) and the Pinacoteca Nazionale di Bologna. An engraved reproduction from the eighteenth century includes the year 1492, which may have originally appeared with Mantegna's monogram on the painting itself or on the frame.

17 See Franceschini 2017, p. 126.

Between Suffering and Redemption: The Motif of the Dead Christ

1 For the general development of the motif, see Panofsky 1927 (1998); Ringbom 1965 (1984); Belting 1985; Milan 2014.

2 As early as the sixth century, icons of Christ show the head and occasionally also the upper body in a frontal view. The paint is usually applied in flat areas, levelling the corporeality of the subject and embedding the figures into a perspectival, often gilded background.

3 North of the Alps, where the influence of Byzantine art was less evident, vertical compositions, such as the *Vesperbild* (Pietà), are far more common.

4 Ringbom 1965 (1984), p. 109, points out that the second variant of Jacopo, is a sketch not only of a pictorial idea, but also of a framed image with this motif.

5 For this work, including the question of its attribution, see Motture 2013; Pope-Hennessy 1993, esp. pp. 140–2.

6 See Milan 2012–13.

7 See the chapter on Landscape in this volume, p. 220.

8 See the chapter on Landscape in this volume; see Hauser 2000.

9 See Dunkerton 2004, p. 201 for the London painting. For the Berlin *Dead Christ*, see Schmidt Arcangeli 2015, esp. pp. 125–32.

10 See D. Ekserdjian in London and New York 1992, no. 28, p. 181. The drawing was formerly attributed to Bellini (Goffen 1989, pp. 82–3).

11 For further discussion see the essay by Vowles and Korbacher in this volume. The red wax dots for mounting and the inscriptions match those on another double-sided drawing in the Pinacoteca Tosio Martinengo in Brescia (fig. 158).

12 See also the bronze relief (fig. 157) with this composition showing Christ being laid into the tomb.

13 See K. Christiansen in London and New York 1992, fig. 74, pp. 155–6.

14 For this observation and interpretation, see Hills 2004, esp. pp. 183–4.

Between Mantegna and Bellini: Marco Zoppo and the Invention of the sacra conversazione

1 The beheading of John the Baptist is reported by the Gospels of Matthew (14: 1–13) and Mark (6: 16–29).

2 On the head in the Skulpturensammlung, originally polychromed, see Kunz et al. 2018 (forthcoming). On this iconographic type, see Combs Stuebe 1968–9, and Baert 2011, who makes an interesting connection (p. 350) between the Pesaro *Head* and the type of the beheaded Medusa, which might have recalled the serpentine hair of the Baptist.

3 Calogero 2013, pp. 7–8.

4 Longhi's opinion was first cited by Fiocco 1922–3, p. 45. On the quarrels of that period regarding historiography, see my essay in this volume.

5 R. Pallucchini in Venice 1949, no. 37, pp. 62–3.

6 R. Pallucchini in Mantua 1961, no. 63, pp. 90–1.

7 Scholarly opinion is summarised by Giacomo A. Calogero, one of the finest current specialists on Zoppo, whose own view is that the Pesaro *Head* was painted by Giovanni Bellini (see Calogero in Rimini 2012, pp. 26–31, and Calogero 2013).

8 On this altarpiece, see most recently Schmidt Arcangeli 2015, pp. 394–404, and Giardini 2016.

9 Even Longhi 1925–6 (1995), p. 382 could not ignore this resemblance.

10 See Wilson 1977, p. 404.

11 Apart from subject and dimensions, the presence of a church in the background closely resembling the old Church of San Giovanni Battista (known from an image in inlaid wood) supports this provenance. Two other panels were proposed as components of the predella of the altarpiece, a *Penitent Saint Jerome* in the Pinacoteca Nazionale in Bologna and a *Saint John the Baptist in the Wilderness* in the Fondazione Giorgio Cini in Venice, but this reconstruction must now be rejected (see Calogero 2013, p. 6).

12 The idea of fitting the *Severed Head* into the predella was put forward by Schmidt Arcangeli 1990, p. 707, and Lucco 1990b, p. 430 (see also Humfrey 1993a). Calogero 2013, pp. 8–10, usefully recalls that an eighteenth-century inventory mentions that the panel was given to the new church of San Giovanni Battista by the 'SS. [Signori] Duchi', that is, the Della Rovere, Dukes of Pesaro from 1513 to 1631; however, this does not rule out an original commission from Alessandro Sforza (first proposed by Armstrong 1976, p. 384).

13 On this aborted commission, see Lightbown 1986, p. 417, doc. 5.

14 On the provenance of Mantegna's *Dead Christ*, see M. Lucco in Mantua 2006–7, p. 72.

15 See the chapter on Mantegna's Training in Padua in this volume. On Zoppo's Paduan period, see London 1998.

16 Interestingly, the back of the panel with the *Severed Head* in Pesaro bears a freehand drawing of a *Triton*, which has been compared to the manner of Zoppo (Brandi 1949, pp. 288–9). Mantegna and Bellini also had the habit of drawing on the backs of their panel paintings.

17 On its development in the Veneto, see Humfrey 1993b, pp. 163–93.

18 Cavazzini and Galli 2008–9, p. 58.

19 Vinco 2018 (forthcoming) believes that the *Dead Christ supported by Two Angels* surmounting Zoppo's altarpiece (fig. 169) was inspired by the *Crucifixion* now in the Louvre (fig. 102), which could have come from the top of an altarpiece in the Church of Santa Maria della Carità. The disappearance of the main register of this work hinders the reconstruction of the evolution of altarpieces such as the *Saint Catherine Altarpiece* by Giovanni Bellini, a true *sacra conversazione*, painted for the church of Santi Giovanni e Paolo in Venice and destroyed by fire in 1867, but known through prints (see Humfrey 1993b, pp. 184–8).

The Virgin and Child: Small-Scale Devotional Works

1 There is a huge literature on this subject. The key modern work is Belting 1994, pp. 57–77.

2 Fletcher 2004, pp. 15–19, 21–5. Bellini belonged to the Scuola Grande di San Marco and the Scuola Piccolo of San Cristoforo dei Mercanti.

3 See S. Weppelmann in Rome 2008–9, p. 85; Davies 1961, pp. 61–2.

4 Fletcher 2004, p. 42.
5 The classic studies are Goffen 1975 and Christiansen 2004b.
6 Tempestini 2000 lists 36 half-length compositions of the Virgin and Child which he assigns to Bellini himself; 9 half-length compositions of the Virgin and Child with saints, and 31 paintings of this subject that he attributes to Bellini's workshop. See also Tempestini 2004, Heinemann 1962–91.
7 See Goffen 1975.
8 See the chapter In Close Artistic Dialogue in this volume.
9 See the chapter In Close Artistic Dialogue in this volume.
10 See the chapter on Landscape in this volume.
11 See C. Campbell in Boston and London 2005–6, p. 57.
12 Matthews 1998, considers Bellini's signatures in her survey of Venetian painters' inscriptions. For artists' signatures in the Renaissance more widely, see Rubin 2006.
13 Davies 1961, pp. 56–7; Dunkerton, Foister, Gordon and Penny 1991, pp. 68–9.
14 For a full study of this painting, with complete references, see the entry on NG280 in Dunkerton and Spring 2018 (forthcoming).
15 The following paragraph is indebted to discussions with Jill Dunkerton and Marika Spring. The two paintings are studied fully in Dunkerton and Spring 2018 (forthcoming).
16 Schmidt Arcangeli 2015.
17 For the *Madonna of the Meadow*, see Davies 1961, pp. 57–8; Goffen 1989, pp, 62–3; Bätschmann 2008, pp. 199–200; Gasparotto 2017–18, pp. 13–14.
18 See Cavazzini and Galli 2008–9, p. 55.
19 K. Christiansen in London and New York 1992, no. 12, pp. 139–40, 153.
20 D. Landau in London and New York 1992, no. 48, p. 219.
21 Musée du Louvre, Paris, RF 41. See Eisler 1989.
22 D. Landau in London and New York 1992, p. 219.
23 S. Boorsch in Paris 2008–9, no. 114, p. 284.
24 De Marchi 2008.
25 K. Christiansen in London and New York 1992, no. 41, pp. 205–6.
26 Bätschmann 2008, pp. 83–9.
27 The most complete study of this work is Carr 1997, esp. pp. 66–74.

Shaping Sacrifice: The Body in the Work of Mantegna and Bellini

1 Robertson 1981, pp. 34–5. See also the essay by De Marchi in this volume.
2 Robertson 1981, p. 33.
3 Lightbown 1986, no. 10, p. 408.
4 Clark 1930, p. 187. See the section on Mantegna and printmaking in the essay by Vowles and Korbacher in this volume for our conclusions about his role in producing engravings.
5 London and New York 1992, p. 193.
6 Popham and Pouncey 1950, p. 94.

'Truly Lifelike and Real': The Portraits of Mantegna and Bellini

1 Lightbown 1986, no. 64, p. 457; Elam 1981–2, p. 15; Berlin and New York 2011–12, p. 39.
2 The competition is recorded by Angelo Decembrio in *De politia litteraria* and by Ulisse degli Aleotti in his sonnet *Pro insigni certamine*; see translations in Brown 2011–12, p. 32. Warnke 1993, p. 94 note 60, doubts that the competition actually took place; Brown herself notes that such a contest is a trope derived from Pliny the Elder's account of a competition between Timanthes, Zeuxis and Apelles to paint the portrait of Alexander the Great.
3 Alberti noted that painting's 'divine power' was to 'make the absent present', as it also 'represents the dead to the living… Through painting, the faces of the dead go on living for a very long time': Alberti 1435 (2004), p. 60.
4 London and New York 1992, p. 12; Lightbown 1986, no. 65, p. 457.
5 Lightbown 1986, no. 68, p. 459; translation in Brown 2011–12, p. 39.
6 Robertson 1981, p. 13. This portrait was identified by Fletcher 1991 with a cutting in the Biblioteca Trivulziana, Milan, but there is no firm evidence to associate that illumination with Bellini, as noted by Dillon Bussi 1995, pp. 28–9. See M. Vinco in Milan 2014, no. 8, pp. 160–1. For a discussion of miniatures in the work of Mantegna and Bellini, see the chapter on Jacopo Bellini and the Formation of Giovanni in this volume.
7 Humfrey 2011–12, p. 49.
8 Brown 2011–12, p. 31.
9 Humfrey 2011–12, p. 50, notes that one of the first Northern portraits to be seen in Venice was that of *Marco Barbarigo*, painted in 1449 by a follower of Jan van Eyck (National Gallery, London). For Memling and Venice, see ibid., p. 59. See also New York 2013.
10 Berlin and New York 2011–12, no. 89, pp. 234–6.
11 Berlin and New York 2011–12, p. 43. In Ferrara, while the frescoes in the Palazzo Schifanoia do survive, the scenes of Borso d'Este's court have been much damaged and are not as well-preserved as the allegorical figures that accompany them.
12 Elam 1981–2, p. 19.
13 For the critical fortune of the work, and its attribution to Niccolò Baroncelli and Domenico di Paris, see Rowley 2016.
14 Elam 1981–2, p. 19 note 22.
15 Brown 2011–12, p. 43.
16 Kristeller 1901, p. 477, doc. 29; translation in Brown 2011–12, p. 40.
17 For a discussion of the attribution of the drawing, see the essay by Vowles and Korbacher in this volume.
18 Elam 1981–2, p. 19.
19 London and New York 1992, p. 16. The identification of Mantegna's sitter was made thanks to a copy, which bore an inscription with Trevisan's name, as well as the physiognomic similarities with a medal of the cardinal made by Cristoforo di Geremia. See Berlin and New York 2011–12, no. 142, pp. 324–7.
20 London and New York 1992, no. 100, pp. 333–5.
21 Berlin and New York 2011–12, no. 143, pp. 327–8.
22 For a detailed discussion of Bellini's technical mastery, see the essay by Dunkerton and Hartwieg in this volume.
23 See the essay by De Marchi in this volume.
24 Berlin and New York 2011–12, no. 140, pp. 322–4. The portrait has also been attributed to Giovanni Bellini by A. De Marchi in De Marchi 1992, no. 13, pp. 218–20; see also his essay in this volume.
25 S. Facchinetti, in Paris 2008–9, no. 9, pp. 76–7, gives it in full to Mantegna.
26 This question is discussed in more detail in the essay by Vowles and Korbacher in this volume.
27 Robertson 1981, pl. LXXVII.
28 Agosti 2005, p. 225. Dillon Bussi 1995, pp. 28–9, suggests in contrast that the sitter may be Raffaele Zovenzoni.
29 For the excursion to Lake Garda, probably a literary fantasy, see the chapter on Antiquity in this volume.

Landscape

1 For studies of Bellini and landscape, see Gentili 2004; Gasparotto 2017–18. Mantegna and landscape is not the focus of a single study; it has been meaningfully studied by Keith Christiansen, in relation to ekphrasis, or a description that re-creates an experience (see Christiansen 2009, especially pp. 19–26). For more problematised studies of landscape and meaning, see Fermor 1993, and the work of Amanda Lillie, including Lillie 2007.
2 The subject is treated most completely and recently in Gasparotto 2017–18.
3 See Paris 2008–9, nos 60–1, pp. 184–6.
4 An interesting parallel is with the views of Sansepolcro in Piero della Francesca's *Baptism of Christ* (after 1437), and *Nativity* (1470s), both now in the National Gallery, London.
5 Berger 1972, p. 105.
6 Humfrey 1993b, pp. 159–60; Campbell 1998, pp. 42–4.
7 See the essay by Vowles and Korbacher in this volume.
8 Gasparotto 2017–18.
9 This is not the place to discuss Gentile Bellini's parallel contribution to the art of the cityscape: for which see Fortini Brown 1988, pp. 96–7, 143–52, 163–4; Meyer zur Capellen 1985; and Pächt 2003.
10 Boschini 1660 (1966), p. 666. 'Zambelin se puol dire la primavera / Del Mondo tuto, in ato de Pitura: / Perché da lù deriva ogni verdure, / E senza lù l'arte un inverno giera.'
11 Signorini 1985, pp. 152–70; Faietti 2014, p. 136 (and references thereof).
12 See C. Campbell in London and New York 2012–13, p. 54.
13 See H.-J. Eberhardt, in Staatliche Graphische Sammlung München 2010, no. 783, pp. 72–5. The so-called Badile Album is a (dismantled) book of drawings from the early fifteenth to the early sixteenth centuries, which was in possession of the Badile, a Veronese family of painters.
14 Bätschmann 2008, p. 19.
15 The drawing is related to a relief of the same subject, sculpted by Pietro and Tullio Lombardo for the façade of the Scuola Grande di San Marco around 1489 (fig. 70). Bellini was a member of this *scuola* and he was probably involved in planning the relief decoration of the building. See Howard 2004.
16 See M. Lucco in Rome 2008–9, no. 21, pp. 208–10.
17 See M. Lucco with reference to Giovanni Agosti in Rome 2008–9, no. 21, p. 208.
18 See further Gasparotto 2017–18, p. 17; for the inspiration that Bouts's pentaptych (see note 6 above) held for Bellini, see Lucco 2004, p. 82.
19 'la vera poetica del silenzio', see Tempestini 1992, p. 124. For landscapes in Bellini's oeuvre in general see Gentili 2004 and Gasparotto 2017–18.
20 See Korbacher 2012, pp. 23–4; also Gasparotto 2017–18.
21 Barausse 2008–9, p. 352, doc. 99. Letter of Pietro Bembo to Isabella d'Este, 11 January 1506, '… di sempre vagare a sua voglia nella pitture'.
22 See Rutherglen and Hale 2015.
23 A.E. Housman, *A Shropshire Lad*, XL, London 1896.
24 K. Christiansen in Rutherglen and Hale 2015, p. 12.
25 Dunkerton and Spring 2018 (forthcoming).
26 For the fullest account of the history of the picture, see S. Rutherglen in Rutherglen and Hale 2015, p. 47.

27 Goffen 1989, p. 40.
28 Christiansen 2009, pp. 15–18.
29 See Fletcher 2004, pp. 32–41.
30 See the chapter on The Virgin and Child in this volume.
31 See the chapter on Saint Jerome in this volume.
32 See Belting 2017–18, p. 28.
33 Gentili 2004, pp. 167–72.
34 P. Humfrey in Rome 2008–9, no. 32, p. 242.
35 See Grave 2004, p. 22.
36 D. Gasparotto in Los Angeles 2017–18, pp. 13–14.
37 Goffen 1989, pp. 62–3; Bätschmann 2008, pp. 199–200.
38 See the essay by Campbell in this volume.
39 See C. Elam in Paris 2008–9, no. 136, pp. 330–1 (and references thereof). Unfortunately it is in a rather compromised condition. Some scholars have questioned the attribution to Mantegna, although the picture is signed.
40 See C. Elam in Paris 2008–9, no. 136, p. 330.
41 K. Christiansen in London and New York 1992, no. 60, pp. 243–5.

Mantegna, Bellini and Antiquity

1 Transcribed in Kristeller 1901, p. 481, doc. 39: 'la vite cum grande piacere alcune picture desso Andrea et certe teste di relevo cum molte altre cose antique, che pare molto se ne deletti.'
2 Chambers, Martineau and Signorini 1992, p. 18.
3 See the chapter on Last Works in this volume for discussion of the Faustina bust Mantegna was obliged to part with to Isabella d'Este.
4 See the essays by Campbell, and Vowles and Korbacher in this volume.
5 Chambers, Martineau and Signorini 1992, p. 16.
6 Chambers, Martineau and Signorini 1992, pp. 16–17.
7 Chambers, Martineau and Signorini 1992, p. 17. The members of the party were Felice Feliciano, the artist Samuele da Tradate, the engineer Giovanni da Padova and Mantegna himself.
8 See the essay by Campbell in this volume.
9 For the best account of this, see Fletcher 2004, pp. 32–41.
10 Fiocco 1926b, pp. 193–4.
11 Raffaelle Zovenzoni recorded the bust of Plato 'apud Bellinos Venetiis': Eisler 1989, p. 48; Robertson 1981, p. 13. For Jacopo's Drawing Books, see the chapter on Jacopo Bellini and the Formation of Giovanni in this volume. For Jacopo Marcello and Jacopo Bellini see, most recently, King 2009, pp. 127–8.
12 Fletcher 1990, p. 170.
13 Fletcher 2004, pp. 35–6.
14 Brown 1969, pp. 376–7.
15 Fletcher 2004, p. 34.
16 The situation was rather different for sculptors. For an analysis of this, in relation to Bellini, see Pincus 2004, p. 123, and Fletcher 1990.
17 Campbell 2011.
18 Specific quotations from ancient or anciently inspired buildings and sculpture can be found throughout Bellini's work, such as the fictive bronze reliefs in *The Blood of the Redeemer* (fig. 192); the marble pilasters and cornicing of the throne in *The Virgin and Child* in the Accademia in Venice; and the similar marble window frame in *The Coronation of the Virgin* from Pesaro (fig. 255). For the latter two works, see Robertson 1981, pls XLa, XLVI. See also Pincus 2004 and Howard 2004.
19 See the essay by De Marchi in this volume.
20 Blake McHam 2013, p. 43.
21 Christiansen 2004a, p. 70, and Christiansen 2004b.
22 See Milan 2014.
23 Goffen 1991.
24 See the chapter on Landscape in this volume.
25 See the chapter on Last Works in this volume.
26 For a full account of Isabella's *studiolo*, see Campbell 2004a.
27 K. Christiansen in London and New York 1992, p. 423.
28 See the essays by Campbell and De Marchi in this volume.
29 For the *Parnassus*, see C. Pidatella and G. Romano in Paris 2008–9, no. 137, pp. 332–3 (and references thereof).
30 K. Christiansen in London and New York 1992, p. 411, suggests that they must have most resembled the *Judith and Dido* (Museum of Fine Arts, Montreal; nos 133–4 in London and New York 1992).
31 For the scheme behind *Parnassus*, see Gombrich 1963; Lightbown 1986, pp. 191–201; Campbell 2004a, pp. 117–44; Shepherd 2014, pp. 77–84.
32 Lightbown 1986, pp. 190–1.
33 Dated to around 1500, or later. See D. Ekserdjian in London and New York 1992, no. 154, p. 468.
34 D. Ekserdjian in London and New York 1992, p. 449, and M. Faietti in London and Florence 2010–11, no. 22, pp. 140–1. Ekserdjian also notes that the figure on the left of the *Three deities* is close in pose to Saint John the Baptist in *The Virgin and Child with the Magdalen and Saint John the Baptist* in the National Gallery (fig. 173), which is dated around 1490–1505.
35 Both the *Comus* and the *Combat between Love and Chastity* (cited in note 36 below) belong to the Musée du Louvre. See Kristeller 1902, pp. 580–1, doc. 180.
36 See C. Pidatella and G. Romano in Paris 2008–9, no. 149, pp. 352–4.
37 See the essay by Campbell in this volume.
38 Barausse 2008–9, pp. 344–54, docs 58–80, 82–4, 87–100, 103–4.
39 Letter of Isabella d'Este to Michele Vianello, 28 June 1501: 'qualche historia o fabula antiqua, aut de sua invenzione ne finga una che representi cosa antiqua et de bello significato'. Barausse 2008–9, p. 345, doc. 65.
40 G. Romano in Paris 2008–9.
41 See the chapter on The Descent of Christ into Limbo in this volume.
42 Fletcher 2004, p. 31.
43 For a clear summary, see Bayer 1998, pp. 31–40, and Borella 2004.
44 See on the series, M. Falomir in Madrid 2003, nos 11–13, pp. 162–9; on the painting, see Walker 1956 and the essays by J. Anderson, D.A. Brown, D. Bull, J. Manca, J. Plesters and W. Sheard in Manca 2013; J. Anderson in Washington and Vienna 2006–7, no. 32, pp. 172–4. We await David Alan Brown's forthcoming monograph on *The Feast of the Gods.*
45 Ovid, *Fasti*, I, 391–440; VI, 319–48.
46 For the alterations, see essay by D.A. Brown in Manca 2013, pp. 288–99.
47 Both National Gallery, London (NG35 and NG6420). See N. Penny in London 2003, no. 13, pp. 104–5; Penny 2008, pp. 248–59.
48 In this we follow Hirst 1992, pp. 320–1, and Goldner 1993, p. 174. However, Mezzetti 1958, pp. 240–2, 327, dates them to the 1450s; D. Ekserdjian in London and New York 1992, nos 72–3, pp. 277–8, to the 1460s; A. Canova in Paris 2008–9, pp. 265–6, to the 1470s; Popham and Pouncey 1950, vol. 1, no. 160, p. 99, to the 1490s. The 1460s dating has recently been cautiously revived by A. Robison in his excellent entry on the Washington drawing in Venice 2014–15, pp. 33–5.
49 A relief in the Uffizi has similar motifs of birds, although this particular sculpture was not discovered until the sixteenth century, too late to have served as a model for Mantegna.
50 See the essay by Vowles and Korbacher in this volume.
51 Innocence is usually represented as a young man; see, for example, Botticelli's *Calumny of Apelles* as well as later treatments of the subject. However, Mantegna is unusual in showing her as both female and a very young child.
52 The inscriptions read: 'Calumnia / di apelle', 'inocentia', 'i[n]vidia', 'dec[e]ptione', 'insidia', 'penitentia', 'verita', 'sospic[ione]' and 'ignora[n]tia'.
53 As Ekserdjian notes in London and New York 1992, no. 154, pp. 467–8, this would explain why Mantegna shows the scene in reverse to that described by Lucian: Alberti was the only translator who did not specify that the king was seated to the right. The composition cannot be intended for translation into print (though an engraving in the same direction by Girolamo Mocetto does survive), as the various figures gesture with their right hands.
54 Sandro Botticelli's *Calumny of Apelles* (Gallerie degli Uffizi, Florence) probably dates to about 1494–5. It is not clear whether Mantegna visited Florence on his journey to or from Rome in 1489–90 and, even if he did, there is no guarantee he could have seen either Botticelli's *Calumny* or his *Primavera*, both of which are often cited for links to his works of the 1490s. For the influence of Mantegna's composition on future artists, see Agosti 2005, pp. 121 note 65, 141, 295 note 79, 338: the subject was reworked by Jörg Breu the Elder, Pieter Brueghel and Lambert Lombard. Rembrandt also copied the scene in a drawing now in the British Museum (1860,0616.86), and it was adapted into a fictive bronze by the Mantuan artist, Lorenzo Leonbruno (Pinacoteca di Brera, Milan).
55 Lightbown 1986, no. 194, p. 486; A. Mazzotta and V. Romani in Paris 2008–9, no. 143, pp. 342–3. The first published interpretation of the subject, in the Thomas Philipe sale catalogue of 1801 (Metz 1801), was in fact 'Hercules between Vice and Virtue', although by 1861, when the drawing was acquired by the British Museum, it was called 'Mars, Venus and Diana'.
56 He reappears in a painted *Allegory of Mantua* by Mantegna's follower Lorenzo Leonbruno (Paris 2008–9, no. 154, p. 342; Ventura 1995, no. 16, pp. 182–7). The composition was also published as a print by Girolamo Mocetto (British Museum, London, 1839,0413.112), although the seated figure of the man appears in a slightly different pose here.
57 A. Mazzotta and V. Romani in Paris 2008–9, p. 342.
58 S. Boorsch in London and New York 1992, no. 148, pp. 453–6.
59 As identified by S. Boorsch in London and New York 1992, under no. 148, p. 453–6.
60 Deceit, in London and Florence 2010–11, no. 22, pp. 140–1. Fraud in S. Boorsch in London and New York 1992, under no. 148, pp. 453–6.
61 Cited in London and Florence 2010–11, no. 22, pp. 140–1.
62 S. Boorsch in London and New York 1992, no. 148, pp. 453–6.
63 Massing 1990, p. 175. The reference is also cited by S. Boorsch in London and New

York 1992, under no. 148, p. 453, and M. Faietti in London and Florence 2010–11, no. 22, pp. 140–1.

64 For the fictive bronze, see Zimmermann 1965, cited in Christiansen 1992c, p. 399; for the Berlin *Dancing muse*, by a member of Mantegna's studio, see Schulze Altcappenberg 1995, pp. 62–3; Bambach 1999. For another drawing of a *Dancing muse* in Munich, also from Mantegna's studio, see London and New York 1992, no. 137, p. 431.

65 The key work is Martindale 1979. See also Hope 1992 and London and New York 1992, nos 108–15, pp. 357–72; C. Elam in Paris 2008–9, nos 160–7, pp. 362–71; Furlotti and Rebecchini 2018, and London 2018, nos 25–33, pp. 237–8.

66 Kristeller 1902, p. 546, doc. 102.

67 See C. Elam in Paris 2008–9, pp. 366–8 for a clear account of their subsequent reception by artists and writers.

68 It is highly likely that Mantegna used Marcanova's text. For this see Martindale 1979, p. 51 note 1; C. Hope in London and New York 1992, p. 355, C. Elam in Paris 2008–9, p. 364.

69 Martindale 1979, p. 58; C. Hope in London and New York 1992, p. 355.

70 C. Hope in London and New York 1992, p. 355.

71 Martindale 1979, pp. 50, 58; C. Hope in London and New York 1992, p. 355; C. Elam in Paris 2008–9, nos 21, 22, pp. 364, 370.

72 Chambers, Martineau and Signorini 1992, pp. 20–3.

73 As Martindale recounts, in 1506 their display along one wall in the Gonzaga Palazzo di San Sebastiano was being planned, and framing pilasters were carved in Venice. See Martindale 1979, p. 184, doc. 19.

74 For a discussion of this drawing see the essay by Vowles and Korbacher in this volume.

75 A number of workshop drawings for the *Triumphs* survive, including the *Triumph of Julius Caesar* in the British Museum, London (1895,0915.773), the *Trumpeters* in the Louvre, Paris (in our opinion not a work by Mantegna himself; 775 DR), and the *Triumph with Trophies and Weapons* published by P. Joannides in Hamburg 2008, no. 2, pp. 20–1.

76 C. Hope in London and New York 1992, p. 356; C. Elam in Paris 2008–9, p. 363 does not exclude the possibility that the patron was Federico Gonzaga; see also Elam 1981–2; London 2018, pp. 55, 237–8.

77 Campbell 2004b.

78 C. Elam in Paris 2008–9, p. 363 (and references thereof). See Kristeller 1902, p. 546, doc. 102, for Mantegna's 1489 description of 'li trionfi mei'.

79 This subject has been discussed most interestingly by K. Christiansen in London and New York 1992, pp. 394–9.

80 Robertson 1981, pp. 33–5.

81 Bellini and sculpture has been most extensively addressed in Ceriana 2008–9. See also Luchs 1995 for Bellini's adoption of sculptural forms.

82 Blake McHam 2013, pp. 234, 401 note 55 (and references thereof).

83 For the grisaille, see London and Düsseldorf 2017–18. The most comprehensive study of Mantegna's grisailles is Blumenröder 2008. For the 'virago' series, see Christiansen 1992c and Fletcher 2015. The works by Mantegna and his studio include, beyond those mentioned in the main text, *Judith and Abra* in the National Gallery of Ireland, Dublin; *David* and *The Sacrifice of Isaac* in the Kunsthistorisches Museum, Vienna; *Judith* and *Dido* in the Museum of Fine Arts, Montreal; and the *Judith and Abra* in the National Gallery of Art, Washington; and the *Sibyl and a Prophet* in the Cincinnati Art Museum.

84 Fletcher 2015, p. 189; Christiansen 1992c, pp. 395–400. The questionable character of Dido's moral exemplar is discussed in Fletcher 2015. However, her role as one of the most celebrated characters in the *Aeneid*, written by Mantua's most famous son, Virgil, may have overcome qualms about her possible lack of chastity.

85 Fletcher 2015, pp. 190–1.

86 For the marble backgrounds, see Christiansen 1992c. For the size, see M. Lucco in Mantua 2006–7, nos 17–18, p. 106.

87 Christiansen 1992c, pp. 395–9; Fletcher 2015, p. 189. They may well be identical with some of the 'quattro quadri (quarte 2 × 4 l'uno) rappresenta chiari e scuri, la Bella Judith et altre figure di mano del Mantegna', which are listed in the posthumous inventory of Carlo Federico Gonzaga, last Margrave of Mantua, though the dimensions are not reliable enough to judge for certain and some scholars remain unconvinced (as quoted by M. Lucco in Mantua 2006–7, nos 17–18, p. 106).

88 See the chapter on Last Works in this volume.

89 Pincus 2004, pp. 140–2.

90 All six figures have been identified in a painting of *Christ and the Adulteress* (Novara, private collection), made in Bellini's workshop. Goldner notes, but does not reproduce, a third similar painting in a private collection. Goldner 2004, p. 249.

91 Goldner 2004, p. 249.

92 Pincus 2004, p. 140.

The Last Works

1 On the decoration of the chapel (and the façade of the church), see Lightbown 1986, pp. 452–6. The bronze bust was attributed to Mantegna starting in the mid-sixteenth century, although we cannot be certain of its authorship (however, see A.F. Radcliffe in London and New York 1992, pp. 89–90).

2 The reassessment of these two works was made by Christiansen 1994.

3 The motif of an angel gazing at the beholder may have been included as homage to Leon Battista Alberti, who advised in his *De Pictura* of 1435 (II, 42) that an 'admonitor' should be represented in paintings so as to establish contact with the beholder.

4 The *Dead Christ* is now in the Brera (fig. 199, or a copy) and the *Saint Sebastian* is in the Galleria Giorgio Franchetti at the Ca' d'Oro in Venice.

5 On Francesco Cornaro, see Hochmann 1992; on the commission for the *camerino*, see Knox 1978.

6 The tombs of the Cornelii were indeed on the Via Appia near the Porta Capena, the gate through which Ovid says the procession entered Rome (see Panizon 2007, p. 60).

7 The differing interpretations are summarised by Panizon 2007, who identifies the kneeling figure as Claudia Quinta.

8 Knox 1978, p. 84 note 12, noted that the standing man he presumed to be Scipio Nasica was painted at the juncture of the two marble panels in the background, which could have a symbolic significance (fig. 54).

9 Gasparotto 2018, p. 123. In 1505 the intermediary between the Cornaro family and Mantegna was Nicolò Bellini, the son of Jacopo and brother of Gentile and Giovanni.

10 'TURPIVS IMPER[ATORI] VENERE Q[UAM] ARMIS VINCI.' On this reading, given by Salvatore Settis, see A. Tempestini in Rome 2008–9, p. 63; for a different interpretation, put forward by Erwin Panofsky ('To exact love is more degrading than to be aided by the compassion of others'), see Shapley 1979, vol. 1, p. 53 note 1. On the Tuscan origins of this iconography, see Baskins 2002.

11 One should nonetheless read Tressider 1992 for the archaeological inspiration behind Bellini's painting. Four grisaille drawings appear to be closely connected with Bellini's painting in Washington; see the chapter on Antiquity in this volume, p. 247.

12 See G.C.F. Villa in Rome 2008–9, no. 62, pp. 320–2.

Further Reading

ALEXANDER RÖSTEL

The following references are intended to help the reader learn more about the art of Andrea Mantegna and Giovanni Bellini. They touch upon the ideas explored and the works of art illustrated in this book. Priority is given to texts published relatively recently.

ANDREA MANTEGNA

The best short introductions to Andrea Mantegna are Christiansen 2009 (reprinted 2010) and Kenneth Clark's lecture on the artist (Clark 1958). Lightbown 1986 remains one of the most useful surveys of the artist's life and work. Complete with a catalogue of all paintings, drawings and prints, it draws on three fundamental earlier monographs (Kristeller 1901; Fiocco 1937; Tietze-Conrat 1955). More recently, De Nicolò Salmazo 2004 and Lucco 2013 have offered generously illustrated accounts of the artist. Exhibitions in the past decades have widened the scope, exploring the significance of Mantegna's precursors, contemporaries and followers. The catalogue of the exhibition held at the Royal Academy of Arts and the Metropolitan Museum of Art in 1992 (London and New York 1992) is especially useful for a survey of works on paper. The 500th anniversary of Mantegna's death prompted a whole series of exhibitions in Italy, each with comprehensive catalogues, three of which are particularly noteworthy (Mantua 2006–7; Padua 2006–7; Verona 2006–7). The catalogue of the monumental retrospective exhibition staged at the Musée du Louvre between 2008 and 2009 provides essays and detailed information on almost 200 objects, including most of Mantegna's movable works (Paris 2008–9; revised Italian edition 2008). Among the numerous essays on further aspects of Mantegna's career, three collected volumes deserve a special mention (Signorini, Rebonato and Tammaccaro 2010; Campbell and Koering 2015; Agosti 2005). The introduction in the latter provides another valuable primer for the understanding of the art of Mantegna.

GIOVANNI BELLINI

As long as a catalogue raisonné remains a scholarly desideratum – Peter Humfrey's, Mauro Lucco's and Giovanni C.F. Villa's monograph is forthcoming – Robertson 1968 (reprinted 1981) remains the most accessible introduction to Bellini and is the first monograph in the English language since Roger Fry's brief study (Fry 1899). Rona Goffen's more recent monograph groups Bellini's paintings according to genres, from images made for private and public devotion, on to portraiture and mythological scenes (Goffen 1989). Huse 1972 and Bätschmann 2008 (published in German and English respectively) are divided into thematic sections, thereby addressing many of the central issues of the artist's activity. Questions of chronology and attribution are at the heart of Anchise Tempestini's numerous studies (for example Tempestini 1992; Tempestini 2000). Fritz Heinemann's three volumes on the paintings by Bellini and his followers remain an extensive reference (Heinemann 1962–91). The collection of essays edited by Peter Humfrey circumvents the challenges involved in approaching Bellini in monographic format, offering a number of thought-provoking contributions on all aspects of Bellini's career. Further edited volumes – Kasl 2004 and Wilson 2015 – provide useful additions. In-depth discussions of individual paintings can be found in Poldi and Villa 2008; Rutherglen and Hale 2015; and David Alan Brown's forthcoming book on *The Feast of the Gods*. The catalogues published in conjunction with recent exhibitions complement the monographs and essays, making available updated information on the provenance, attribution and date of the works of Bellini and his workshop. Chief among them is the 2008–9 monographic exhibition held at the Scuderie del Quirinale in Rome (Rome 2008–9). Two shows in Milan focused on Bellini's devotional paintings (Milan 2012–13; Milan 2014). Most recently, the first monographic exhibition in America devoted to Bellini was held at the J. Paul Getty Museum (Los Angeles 2017–18).

Bibliography

AGOSTI 1993
G. Agosti, 'Su Mantegna, 2 (All'ingresso della "maniera moderna")', *Prospettiva*, 71 (1993), pp. 66–82

AGOSTI 1999
G. Agosti, 'Piccole osservazioni nell'area dello Squarcione', in De Nicolò Salmazo 1999, pp. 53–78

AGOSTI 2005
G. Agosti, *Su Mantegna I. La storia dell'arte libera la testa*, Milan 2005

AGOSTI 2008–9
G. Agosti, 'Mantegna 2046', in Paris 2008–9, pp. 29–52

AGOSTI 2009a
G. Agosti, 'Al bar delle Scuderie', in Agosti 2009b, pp. 93–194

AGOSTI 2009b
G. Agosti, *Un amore di Giovanni Bellini*, Milan 2009

ALBERTI 1435 (2004)
L.B. Alberti, *On Painting*, trans. C. Grayson, London 2004

AMES-LEWIS AND BEDNAREK 1993
F. Ames-Lewis and A. Bednarek (eds), *Mantegna and 15th-Century Court Culture: Lectures delivered in connection with the Andrea Mantegna exhibition at the Royal Academy of Arts, London 1992*, London 1993

ANDREOTTI, COLOMBINI AND DEGANO 2009
A. Andreotti, M.P. Colombini and I. Degano, 'Caratterizzazione dei materiali organici naturali nel dipinto su tavola "Pala di San Zeno"', in Ciatti and Marini 2009, pp. 313–18

ARMSTRONG 1976
L. Armstrong, *The Paintings and Drawings of Marco Zoppo*, New York and London 1976

ASCHAM 1570
R. Ascham, *The Scholemaster*, London 1570

BAERT 2011
B. Baert, '*He Must Increase, but I Must Decrease*. On the Spiritual and Pictorial Intertwining between the *Johannesschüssel* and the *vera icon* (1200–1500)', in K. Enekel and W. Melion (eds), *Meditatio – Refashioning the Self. Theory and Practice in Late Medieval and Early Modern Intellectual Culture*, Leiden and Boston 2011, pp. 323–66

BAGAROTTO ET AL. 2000
R. Bagarotto et al., 'La tecnica pittorica di Giovanni Bellini', in Venice 2000, pp. 184–94

BAMBACH 1999
C. Bambach, 'Review: *Die italienischen Zeichnungen des 14. und 15. Jahrhunderts im Berliner Kupferstichkabinett. Kritischer Katalog*', *Master Drawings*, 37/1 (1999), pp. 55–62

BANDERA BISTOLETTI 1989
S. Bandera Bistoletti (ed.), *Il Polittico di San Luca di Andrea Mantegna (1453–4) in occasione del suo restauro*, Florence 1989

BARAUSSE 2008–9
M. Barausse, 'Giovanni Bellini. I documenti', in Rome 2008–9, pp. 327–59

BARTSCH 1811
A. von Bartsch, *Le Peintre Graveur*, vol. XIII: *Les vieux maîtres italiens*, Vienna 1811

BASKINS 2002
C.L. Baskins, '(In)famous Men: The Continence of Scipio and Formations of Masculinity in Fifteenth-Century Tuscan Domestic Painting', *Studies in Iconography*, 23 (2002), pp. 109–36

BÄTSCHMANN 2008
O. Bätschmann, *Giovanni Bellini*, London 2008

BAXANDALL 1974
M. Baxandall, *Painting and Experience in Fifteenth Century Italy*, Oxford 1974

BAYER 1998
A. Bayer, 'Dosso's Public: The Este Court at Ferrara', in P. Humfrey and M. Lucco, *Dosso Dossi: Court Painter in Renaissance*, exh. cat., Galleria d'Arte Moderna, Ferrara; Metropolitan Museum of Art, New York; J. Paul Getty Museum, Los Angeles 1998, pp. 27–54

BECCARIA 2008
C. Beccaria, 'Le vicende conservative della Pala Trivulzio', in Pesci and Toniolo 2008, pp. 163–75

BELLONCI AND GARAVAGLIA 1967
M. Bellonci and N. Garavaglia, *L'opera completa del Mantegna*, Milan 1967

BELLOSI 1974
L. Bellosi, *Buffalmacco e il trionfo della morte*, Turin 1974

BELLOSI 1980
L. Bellosi, 'La rappresentazione dello spazio', in Previtali 1980, pp. 5–39

BELLOSI 2008–9
L. Bellosi, 'Giovanni Bellini et Andrea Mantegna', in Paris 2008–9, pp. 103–9

BELLUCCI AND FROSININI 2009
R. Bellucci and C. Frosinini, 'The *Madonna* from the Accademia Carrara', in Menu and Ravaud 2009, pp. 21–6

BELTING 1981
H. Belting, *Das Bild und sein Publikum im Mittelalter. Form und Funktion früher Bildtafeln der Passion*, Berlin 1981

BELTING 1985
H. Belting, *Giovanni Bellini. Pietà: Ikone und Bilderzählung in der venezianischen Malerei*, Frankfurt 1985

BELTING 1994
H. Belting, *Likeness and Presence: A History of the Image before the Era of Art*, Chicago 1994

BELTING 2017–18
H. Belting, 'Poetry and Painting: Saint Jerome in the Wilderness', in Los Angeles 2017–18, pp. 25–35

BERENSON 1897
B. Berenson, *The Central Italian Painters of the Renaissance*, London 1897

BERENSON 1907
B. Berenson, *North Italian Painters of the Renaissance*, New York and London 1907

BERENSON 1913 (1916)
B. Berenson, 'La 'Sainte Justine' de la collection Bagatti-Valsecchi à Milan', *Gazette des Beaux-Arts*, 55 (1913), pp. 461–79, reprinted in B. Berenson, *The Study and Criticism of Italian Art*, vol. 3, London 1916, pp. 38–61

BERENSON 1916
B. Berenson, *Venetian Painting in America: The Fifteenth Century*, New York 1916

BERGER 1972
J. Berger, *Ways of Seeing*, London 1972

BERLIN 2015
J. Chapuis and S. Kemperdick (eds), *The Lost Museum: The Berlin Painting and Sculpture Collections 70 Years after World War II*, exh. cat., Bode Museum, Berlin 2015

BERLIN AND NEW YORK 2011–12
K. Christiansen and S. Weppelmann (eds), *The Renaissance Portrait: From Donatello to Bellini*, exh. cat., Bode Museum, Berlin; Metropolitan Museum of Art, New York 2011–12

BERTELLI 2006
C. Bertelli (ed.), *Restituzioni 2006. Tredicesima edizione. Tesori d'arte ritrovati*, Vicenza 2006

BILLINGE AND SPRING 2009
R. Billinge and M. Spring, 'The Materials and Techniques of Paintings by Andrea Mantegna in the National Gallery, London', in Menu and Ravaud 2009, pp. 11–20

BLAKE MCHAM 2007
S. Blake McHam, 'Padua, Treviso, and Bassano', in P. Humfrey (ed.), *Venice and the Veneto: Artistic Centers of the Italian Renaissance*, New York 2007, pp. 207–51

BLAKE MCHAM 2013
S. Blake McHam, *Pliny and the Artistic Culture of the Italian Renaissance*, New Haven and London 2013

BLASS-SIMMEN 2017
B. Blass-Simmen, 'Cultural Transfer in Microcosm. Padua and Venice: An Introduction', in Blass-Simmen and Weppelmann 2017, pp. 1–18

BLASS-SIMMEN 2018
B. Blass-Simmen, 'Un cartone, due dipinti', in Venice 2018, pp. 35–49

BLASS-SIMMEN AND WEPPELMANN 2017
B. Blass-Simmen and S. Weppelmann (eds), *Padua and Venice: Transcultural Exchange in the Early Modern Age*, Berlin 2017

BLUMENRÖDER 2008
S. Blumenröder, *Andrea Mantegna – Die Grisaillen: Malerei, Geschichte und antike Kunst im Paragone des Quattrocento*, Berlin 2008

BODE 1889
W. Bode, 'La Renaissance au musée de Berlin (septième article)', *Gazette des Beaux-Arts*, 31 (1889), pp. 107–20

BOMFORD ET AL. 1989
D. Bomford et al., *Art in the Making: Italian Painting before 1400*, London 1989

BOORSCH 2010
S. Boorsch, 'Mantegna and Engraving: What We Know, What We Don't Know, and a Few Hypotheses', in Signorini, Rebonato and Tammaccaro 2010, vol. 1, pp. 415–37

BORELLA 2004
M. Borella, 'Lo "Studio de preda marmora fina" sopra la Via coperta di Alfonso III duca', in M. Ceriana (ed.), *Il Camerino di Alabastro: Antonio Lombardo e la scultura all'antica*, Milan 2004, pp. 111–18

BORENIUS 1938
T. Borenius, 'St Jerome in the Wilderness', *The Burlington Magazine*, 72 (1938), pp. 105–7

BORGHESE, CARINI AND SCATRAGLI 2014
P. Borghese, A. Carini and S. Scatragli, 'La "Pietà" di Giovanni Bellini: tecnica pittorica e restauro', in Milan 2014, pp. 111–25

BOSCHINI 1660 (1966)
M. Boschini, *La Carta del navegar pitoresco* (Venice 1660), in a criticial edition by A. Pallucchini, Venice and Rome 1966

BOSKOVITS AND BROWN 2003
M. Boskovits and D.A. Brown, *Italian Paintings of the Fifteenth Century: The Collections of the National Gallery of Art. Systematic Catalogue*, New York and Oxford 2003

BOSTON AND LONDON 2005–6
C. Campbell and A. Chong (eds), *Bellini and the East*, exh. cat., Isabella Stewart Gardner Museum, Boston; National Gallery, London 2005–6

BRACCO, SARTIANI AND TOSO 2009
P. Bracco, O. Sartiani and C. Toso, 'Per te Parte Porto', in Ciatti and Marini 2009, pp. 125–80

BRANDI 1949
C. Brandi, 'La mostra di Giovanni Bellini', *L'immagine*, II, 13 (1949), pp. 287–94

BROWN 2011–12
B.L. Brown, 'Portraiture at the Courts of Italy', in Berlin and New York 2011–12, pp. 26–47

BROWN 1969
C.M. Brown, '*Una testa di Platone antica con la punta dil naso di cera.*' Unpublished negotiations between Isabella d'Este and Niccolò and Giovanni Bellini', *Art Bulletin*, 51 (1969), pp. 372–7

BROWN AND LORENZONI 1982
C.M. Brown and A.M. Lorenzoni, *Isabella d'Este and Lorenzo da Pavia. Documents for the History of Art and Culture in Renaissance Mantua*, Geneva 1982

BROWN 2010
D.A. Brown, 'Giulio Campagnola: The Printmaker as Painter', *Artibus et Historiae*, 31 (2010), pp. 83–97

BROWN AND PIZZATI 2014
D.A. Brown and A. Pizzati, '"Meum amantissimum nepotem": A New Document Concerning Giovanni Bellini', *The Burlington Magazine*, 156 (2014), pp. 148–52

BYAM SHAW 1979
J. Byam Shaw, *Mantegna*, Biblioteca di Disegni, III, Florence 1979, pp. 16–18

CALLEGARI 1996
R. Callegari, 'Opere e committenze d'arte rinascimentale a Padova', *Arte Veneta*, 49 (1996), 49, pp. 7–29

CALOGERO 2013
G.A. Calogero, 'Nuove ricerche sulla pala di Pesaro di Marco Zoppo', *Paragone*, 64 (2013), pp. 3–21

CALOGERO 2016
G.A. Calogero, 'Piero della Francesca tra Bernard Berenson e Roberto Longhi: la nascita di un mito', in Forlì 2016, pp. 37–49

CAMPBELL 2011
C. Campbell, 'When is a *cassone* Painting not for a *cassone*? Towards a History of Furniture Painting in Sixteenth-Century Venice', in J. Harris, S. Nethersole and P. Rumberg (eds), *Una insalata di più erbe. A Festschrift for Patricia Lee Rubin*, London 2011, pp. 11–20

CAMPBELL 1981
L. Campbell, 'Notes on Netherlandish Pictures in the Veneto in the Fifteenth and Sixteenth Centuries', *The Burlington Magazine*, 123 (1981), pp. 467–73

CAMPBELL 1998
L. Campbell, *National Gallery Catalogues. The Fifteenth Century Netherlandish Schools*, London 1998

CAMPBELL 2004a
S.J. Campbell, *The Cabinet of Eros: Renaissance Mythological Painting and the 'Studiolo' of Isabella d'Este*, New Haven and London 2004

CAMPBELL 2004b
S.J. Campbell, 'Mantegna's Triumph: The Cultural Politics of Imitation "all'antica" at the Court of Mantua, 1490–1530', in S.J. Campbell (ed.), *Artists at Court: Image-Making and Identity 1300–1500*, Chicago 2004, pp. 91–105

CAMPBELL AND KOERING 2015
S.J. Campbell and J. Koering (eds), *Andrea Mantegna: Making Art (History)*, Malden 2015

CAMPORI 1866
G. Campori (ed.), *Lettere artistiche inedite*, Modena 1866

CARR 1997
D.W. Carr, *Andrea Mantegna: The Adoration of the Magi*, Los Angeles 1997

CASOLA 1907
P. Casola, *Canon Pietro Casola's Pilgrimage to Jerusalem in the Year 1494*, M.M. Newett (ed.), Manchester 1907

CASSEGRAIN 2015
G. Cassegrain, 'Mantegna the Grammarian', in Campbell and Koering 2015, pp. 77–92

CAVAZZINI AND GALLI 2008–9
L. Cavazzini and A. Galli, 'Padoue, carrefour artistique', in Paris 2008–9, pp. 55–60

CENNINI 2015
C. Cennini, *Cennino Cennini's Il libro dell'Arte*, trans. L. Broecke, London 2015

CERIANA 2008–9
M. Ceriana, 'Bellini e le arti plastiche', in Rome 2008–9, pp. 91–103

CHAMBERS, MARTINEAU AND SIGNORINI 1992
D. Chambers, J. Martineau and R. Signorini, 'Mantegna and the Men of Letters', in London and New York 1992, pp. 8–30

CHRISTIANSEN 1987
K. Christiansen, 'Venetian Painting of the Early Quattrocento', *Apollo*, 125 (1987), pp. 166–77

CHRISTIANSEN 1992a
K. Christiansen, 'Early Works: Padua', in London and New York 1992, pp. 94–114

CHRISTIANSEN 1992b
K. Christiansen, 'Some Observations on Mantegna's Painting Technique', in London and New York 1992, pp. 67–78

CHRISTIANSEN 1992c
K. Christiansen, 'Painting in Grisaille', in London and New York 1992, pp. 394–400

CHRISTIANSEN 1994
K. Christiansen, 'Mantegna's Legacy', in M. Boskovits (ed.), *Studi di storia dell'arte in onore di Mina Gregori*, n.p. 1994 , pp. 79–86

CHRISTIANSEN 2004a
K. Christiansen, 'Bellini and Mantegna', in Humfrey 2004, pp. 48–74

CHRISTIANSEN 2004b
K. Christiansen, 'Giovanni Bellini and the Practice of Devotional Painting', in Kasl 2004, pp. 7–58

CHRISTIANSEN 2009
K. Christiansen, *The Genius of Andrea Mantegna*, New York 2009 (reprinted New Haven and London 2010)

CIATTI AND MARINI 2009
M. Ciatti and P. Marini, *La Pala di San Zeno di Andrea Mantegna. Studio e conservazione*, Florence 2009

CLARK 1930
K. Clark, 'Italian Drawings at Burlington House', *The Burlington Magazine*, 56 (1930), pp. 174–7, 180, 183, 187

CLARK 1958
K. Clark, 'Andrea Mantegna', *Journal of the Royal Society of Arts*, 106 (1958), pp. 663–80

CLERI AND GIARDINI 2016
B. Cleri and C. Giardini (eds), *Arte venduta. Mercato, diaspora e furti nelle Marche in età moderna e contemporanea*, Ancona 2016

COMBS STUEBE 1968–9
I. Combs Stuebe, 'The *Johannesschüssel* from Narrative to Reliquary to *Andachtsbild*', *Marsyas*, 14 (1968–9), pp. 1–16

DALL'ACQUA 1980
M. Dall'Acqua, 'Mecenatismo e collezionismo dei Gonzaga da Ludovico a Isabella d'Este: la nascita dell'esperto e del dilettante', in A. Prosperi (ed.), *La Corte e il 'Cortegiano' II. Un modello europeo*, Rome 1980, pp. 295–319

DAVIES 1961
M. Davies, *The Earlier Italian Schools*, London 1961

DE MARCHI 1992
A. De Marchi, *Gentile da Fabriano. Un viaggio nella pittura italiana alla fine del gotico*, Milan 1992

DE MARCHI 1996a
A. De Marchi, 'Centralità di Padova: alcuni esempi di interferenza tra scultura e pittura nell'aera adriatica alla metà del Quattrocento', in Dempsey 1996, pp. 57–79

DE MARCHI 1996b
A. De Marchi, 'Un raggio di luce su Filippo Lippi a Padova', *Nuovi Studi*, 1 (1996), pp. 5–23

DE MARCHI 2002a
A. De Marchi, 'Pittori a Camerino nel Quattrocento: le ombre di Gentile e la luce di Piero', in De Marchi 2002b, pp. 24–99

DE MARCHI 2002b
A. De Marchi (ed.), *Pittori a Camerino nel Quattrocento*, Milan 2002

DE MARCHI 2008
A. De Marchi, 'Francesco Marmitta tra Roma e Bologna, un florilegio di eleganze all'antica', in *Il Libro d'Ore Durazzo*, Modena 2008, pp. 9–66

DE MARCHI 2008–9
A. De Marchi, 'Autour du triptyque de San Zeno de Vérone', in Paris 2008–9, pp. 153–7

DE MARCHI 2009
A. De Marchi, *Le triptyque de San Zeno de Vérone et sa prédelle*, in Tours 2009, pp. 17–21

DE MARCHI 2012–13
A. De Marchi, '*Im Laufe der Zeit*: la 'Pietà' di Giovanni Bellini', in Milan 2012–13, pp. 17–31

DE MARCHI 2014
A. De Marchi, 'Giovanni Bellini, Andrea Mantegna e la tenerezza della Madre', in Milan 2014, pp. 73–82

DE MARCHI 2017
A. De Marchi, 'Perché vale ancora la pena di fare i conti col *Giudizio sul Duecento*?', in A.M. Ambrosini Massari et al. (eds), *Il mestiere del conoscitore. Roberto Longhi*, symposium papers (Fondazione Federico Zeri, Bologna, 2015), Bologna 2017, pp. 25–57

DEMPSEY 1996
C. Dempsey (ed.), *Quattrocento adriatico. Fifteenth-century Art of the Adriatic Rim*, symposium papers (Florence, 1994), Bologna 1996

DE NICOLÒ SALMAZO 1993
A. De Nicolò Salmazo, *Il soggiorno padovano di Andrea Mantegna*, Padua 1993

DE NICOLÒ SALMAZO 1994
A. De Nicolò Salmazo, 'Per gli anni padovani di Andrea Mantegna: appunti in margine alla mostra del 1992', *Arte veneta*, 46 (1994), pp. 91–102

DE NICOLÒ SALMAZO 1999
A. De Nicolò Salmazo (ed.), *Francesco Squarcione. 'Pictorum gymnasiarcha singularis'*, Padua 1999

DE NICOLÒ SALMAZO 2004
A. De Nicolò Salmazo, *Andrea Mantegna*, Milan 2004

DE NICOLÒ SALMAZO 2006–7
A. De Nicolò Salmazo, 'Andrea Mantegna e Padova 1445–1460', in Padua 2006–7, pp. 3–27

DE NICOLÒ SALMAZO, SPIAZZI AND TONIOLO 2006
A. De Nicolò Salmazo, A.M. Spiazzi and D. Toniolo (eds), *Andrea Mantegna e i maestri della Cappella Ovetari. La ricomposizione virtuale e il restauro*, Milan 2006

DILLON BUSSI 1995
A. Dillon Bussi, 'Due ritratti di Raffaele Zovenzoni', *Libri e Documenti*, 21 (1995), pp. 24–42

DONESMONDI 1612–16
I. Donesmondi, *Dell'historia ecclesiastica di Mantova*, 2 vols, Mantua 1612–16

DRESDEN 2006
A. Henning (ed.) *Andrea Mantegna: die Heilige Familie*, exh. cat., Staatliche Kunstsammlungen, Gemäldegalerie Alte Meister, Dresden 2006

DUNKELMAN 1980
M.L. Dunkelman, 'Donatello's Influence on Mantegna's Early Narrative Scenes', *The Art Bulletin*, 62 (1980), pp. 226–35

DUNKERTON 1993
J. Dunkerton, 'Mantegna's Painting Techniques', in Ames-Lewis and Bednarek 1993, pp. 26–38

DUNKERTON 2004
J. Dunkerton, 'Bellini's Technique', in Humfrey 2004, pp. 195–225

DUNKERTON ET AL. 1991
J. Dunkerton, S. Foister, D. Gordon and N. Penny, *Giotto to Dürer: Early Renaissance Painting in the National Gallery*, London 1991

DUNKERTON AND SPRING 2013
J. Dunkerton and M. Spring, 'Titian's Painting Technique to *c.*1540', *National Gallery Technical Bulletin*, 34 (2013), pp. 4–31

DUNKERTON AND SPRING 2018
J. Dunkerton and M. Spring, with R. Billinge, C. Campbell and B. New, *National Gallery Technical Bulletin: Giovanni Bellini's Painting Technique*, 39 (2018) (forthcoming)

EISLER 1989
C. Eisler, *The Genius of Jacopo Bellini: The Complete Paintings and Drawings*, New York 1989

ELAM 1981–2
C. Elam, 'Mantegna and Mantua', in London 1981–2, pp. 15–26

ELEN 1989
A. Elen, 'A Codicological Analysis and Reconstruction of Jacopo Bellini's Drawing Books', in Eisler 1989, Appendix A, pp. 454–79

ENGLANDER 1990
D. Englander, *Culture and Belief in Europe 1450–1600: An Anthology of Sources*, Oxford 1990

FACCHINETTI 2005
S. Facchinetti, 'Longhi, Roberto', in *Dizionario biografico degli Italiani*, 65, Rome 2005, pp. 668–76

FAGIOLI 2013
M. Fagioli, 'Un Disegno di Andrea Mantegna', in *Dipinti, Arredi e Disegni Antichi; Dipinti e Sculture del XIX e XX Secolo*, Prato 2013, n.p., lot 234

FAIETTI 2010
M. Faietti, 'Il segno di Andrea Mantegna', in Signorini, Rebonato and Tammaccaro 2010, vol. 1, pp. 15–44

FAIETTI 2014
M. Faietti, 'From Solomon's Temple to Hagia Sophia: A Metaphorical Journey for Andrea Mantegna', in A. Payne (ed.), *Dalmatia and the Mediterranean: Portable Archaeology and the Poetics of Influence*, Leiden 2014, pp. 115–44

FERMOR 1993
S. Fermor, 'Piero and the Depiction of Landscape', in S. Fermor, *Piero di Cosimo: Fiction, Invention and 'Fantasia'*, London 1993, pp. 163–206

FERRARA 2007
M. Natale (ed.), *Cosmè Tura e Francesco del Cossa: l'arte a Ferrara nell'età di Borso d'Este*, exh. cat., Palazzo dei Diamanti and Palazzo Schifanoia, Ferrara 2007

FILTENBORG 2009
T. Filtenborg, 'Mantegna's "Man of Sorrows with Two Angels": Examination and Restoration', in Ravaud and Eveno 2009, pp. 93–8

FIOCCO 1922–3
G. Fiocco, 'Un'anconetta primitiva di Giambellino', *Rassegna marchigiana*, 1 (1922–3), pp. 41–5

FIOCCO 1926a
G. Fiocco, 'Lettere pittoriche. Risposta di G. Fiocco a R. Longhi', *Vita artistica*, I, 12 (1926), pp. 144–7

FIOCCO 1926b
G. Fiocco, 'Felice Feliciano amico degli artisti', *Archivio Veneto Tridentino*, 9 (1926), pp. 188–201

FIOCCO 1927
G. Fiocco, *L'arte di Andrea Mantegna*, Bologna 1927

FIOCCO 1933
G. Fiocco, 'Andrea Mantegna or Giambellino?', *L'Arte*, 36 (1933), pp. 185–99

FIOCCO 1937
G. Fiocco, *Andrea Mantegna*, Milan 1937

FLETCHER 2015
F. Fletcher, 'Mantegna's Fictive Bronze *Judith* and *Dido*: Beyond Exemplarity', in Campbell and Koering 2015, pp. 177–99

FLETCHER 1981–2
J. Fletcher, 'Isabella d'Este: Patron and Collector', in London 1981–2, pp. 51–63

FLETCHER 1990
J. Fletcher, 'Harpies, Venus and Giovanni Bellini's Classical Mirror: Some Fifteenth-Century Venetian Painters' Responses to the Antique', in G. Traversari and I. Favaretto (eds), *Venezia e Archeologia: Un importante capitolo nella storia del gusto dell'antico nella cultura veneziana* (Congresso internazionale, Venezia, 1988) (*Rivista di Archeologia*, Supplementi 7), Rome 1990, pp. 170–6

FLETCHER 1991
J. Fletcher, 'The Painter and the Poet: Giovanni Bellini's Portrait of Raffaele Zovenzoni Rediscovered', *Apollo*, 134 (1991), pp. 153–8

FLETCHER 1993
J. Fletcher, 'Mantegna and Venice', in Ames-Lewis and Bednarek 1993, pp. 17–25

FLETCHER 1998
J. Fletcher, 'I Bellini', in R. Cassanelli (ed.), *La bottega dell'artista tra Medioevo e Rinascimento*, Milan 1998, pp. 131–53

FLETCHER 2004
J. Fletcher, 'Bellini's Social World', in Humfrey 2004, pp. 13–47

FLETCHER 1997
S. Fletcher, 'A Re-evaluation of Two Mantegna Prints', *Print Quarterly*, 14 (1997), pp. 67–77

FOGOLARI 1924
G. Fogolari, 'La chiesa di Santa Maria della Carità di Venezia (ora sede delle Regie Gallerie dell'Accademia). Documenti inediti di Bartolomeo Bon, Antonio Vivarini, di Ercole del Fiore e di altri artisti', *Archivio Veneto-Tridentino*, 5 (1924), pp. 57–118

FOGOLARI 1932
G. Fogolari, 'Disegni per gioco e incunaboli pittorici del Giambellino', *Dedalo*, XII (1932), pp. 360–73

FORLÌ 2016
A. Paolucci et al. (eds), *Piero della Francesca. Indagine su un mito*, exh. cat., Musei San Domenico, Forlì 2016

FORTINI BROWN 1988
P. Fortini Brown, *Venetian Narrative Painting in the Age of Carpaccio*, New Haven and London 1988

FRANCESCHINI 2017
C. Franceschini, *Storia del Limbo*, Milan 2017

FRANKFURT 2006
J. Sander (ed.), *Kult Bild: Das Altar- und Andachtsbild von Duccio bis Perugino*, exh. cat. Städel Museum, Frankfurt 2006

FRANKFURT AND PARIS 2006–7
J. Jacoby (ed.), *Raffael bis Tizian: Italienische Zeichnungen aus dem Städel Museum*, exh. cat., Städel Museum, Frankfurt; Fondation Custodia, Paris 2006–7

FREZZATO 2014
F. Frezzato, 'Aspetti della "téchne" belliniana tra il 1460 e il 1470 rivelati dalle analisi microstratigrafiche sulla "Pietà"', in Milan 2014, pp. 107–10

FRY 1899
R. Fry, *Giovanni Bellini*, London 1899

FURLOTTI AND REBECCHINI 2018
B. Furlotti and G. Rebecchini, '"Rare and Unique in this World": Mantegna's "Triumph" and the Gonzaga Collection', in London 2018, pp. 54–9

GARBOLI AND MONTAGNANI 1993
C. Garboli and C. Montagnani (eds), *Bernard Berenson-Roberto Longhi. Lettere e scartafacci 1912–1957*, Milan 1993

GASPAROTTO 2013
D. Gasparotto, 'Il mito della collezione', in G. Beltramini, D. Gasparotto and A. Tura (eds), *Pietro Bembo e l'invenzione del Rinascimento*, exh. cat., Palazzo del Monte di Pietà, Padua 2013, pp. 48–65

GASPAROTTO 2017–18
D. Gasparotto, 'Giovanni Bellini and Landscape', in Los Angeles 2017–18, pp. 11–24

GASPAROTTO 2018
D. Gasparotto (ed.), *Lives of Giovanni Bellini: Giorgio Vasari, Carlo Ridolfi, Marco Boschini, Isabella d'Este*, Los Angeles 2018

GAYE 1839–40
G. Gaye, *Carteggio inedito d'artisti dei secoli XIV, XV, XVI*, 3 vols, Florence 1839–40

GENTILI 2004
A. Gentili, 'Bellini and Landscape', in Humfrey 2004, pp. 167–81

GHIOTTO AND PIGNATTI 1969
R. Ghiotto and T. Pignatti, *L'opera completa di Giovanni Bellini*, Milan 1969

GIARDINI 2016
C. Giardini, 'Intorno alle vicende storico artistiche di un capolavoro: la *Sacra Conversazione* di Marco Zoppo tra Pesaro, Berlino e Baltimora', in Cleri and Giardini 2016, pp. 69–96

GIARDINI, NEGRO AND PIRONDINI 1993
C. Giardini, E. Negro and M. Pirondini (eds), *Dipinti e Disegni della Pinacoteca di Pesaro*, Modena 1993

GILBERT 1992
C.E. Gilbert, *Italian Art 1400–1500: Sources and Documents*, Evanston 1992

GIOVANNUCCI VIGI 1993
B. Giovannucci Vigi (ed.), *Marco Zoppo. Cento 1433–1478 Venezia*, Bologna 1993

GOFFEN 1975
R. Goffen, 'Icon and Vision: Giovanni Bellini's Half-Length Madonnas', *The Art Bulletin*, 57 (1975), pp. 487–518

GOFFEN 1989
R. Goffen, *Giovanni Bellini*, New Haven and London 1989

GOFFEN 1991
R. Goffen, 'Bellini's Nude with Mirror', *Venezia cinquecento*, 1 (1991), pp. 185–99

GOLDNER 1993
G. Goldner, 'Review: Andrea Mantegna', *Master Drawings*, 31/2 (1993), pp. 172–6

GOLDNER 2004
G. Goldner, 'Bellini's Drawings', in Humfrey 2004, pp. 226–55

GOMBRICH 1963
E.H. Gombrich, 'An Interpretation of Mantegna's "Parnassus"', *Journal of the Warburg and Courtauld Institutes*, 26, no. 1/2 (1963), pp. 196–8

GRAVE 2004
J. Grave, *Landschaften der Meditation. Giovanni Bellinis Assoziationsräume*, Freiburg im Breisgau 2004

GREENSTEIN 1992
J.M. Greenstein, *Mantegna and Painting as Historical Narrative*, Chicago and London 1992

HAMBURG 2008
P. Joannides (ed.), *Raffael und Umkreis: Handzeichnungen aus der Sammlung Wolf Bürgi*, exh. cat., Galerie Hans, Hamburg 2008

HAMBURGER 1997
J. Hamburger, *Nuns as Artists: The Visual Culture of a Medieval Convent*, Berkeley 1997

HARTWIEG 2018
B. Hartwieg, '*La Presentazione di Gesù al tempio* di Andrea Mantegna e Giovanni Bellini: genesi delle opere e paragone tecnologico', in Venice 2018, pp. 75–94

HAUSER 2000
A. Hauser, 'Andrea Mantegnas "Pietà". Ein ikonoklastisches Andachtsbild', in *Zeitschrift für Kunstgeschichte*, 63, no. 4 (2000), pp. 449–93

HEINEMANN 1962–91
F. Heinemann, *Giovanni Bellini e i Belliniani*, 3 vols, Venice / Hildesheim 1962–91

HILLS 2004
P. Hills, 'Bellini's Colour', in Humfrey 2004, pp. 182–94

HIND 1938–48
A.M. Hind, *Early Italian Engraving: A Critical Catalogue with Complete Reproduction of all the Prints Described*, 7 vols, London 1938–48

HIRST 1992
M. Hirst, 'Mantegna: London and New York', *The Burlington Magazine*, 134 (1992), pp. 318–21

HOCHMANN 1992
M. Hochmann, 'Tra Venezia e Roma: il cardinale Francesco Corner', *Saggi e memorie di storia dell'arte*, 18 (1992), pp. 99–109

HOLGATE 2002
I. Holgate, 'Paduan Culture in Venetian Care. The Patronage of Bishop Pietro Donato (1380–1447)', in *Renaissance Studies*, 16 (2002), pp. 1–23

HOPE 1992
C. Hope, 'The Triumphs of Caesar', in London and New York 1992, pp. 350–6

HOWARD 2004
D. Howard, 'Bellini and Architecture', in Humfrey 2004, pp. 143–66

HUMFREY 1990
P. Humfrey, 'Co-ordinated Altarpieces in Renaissance Venice: The Progress of an Ideal', in Humfrey and Kemp 1990, pp. 190–211

HUMFREY 1993a
P. Humfrey, 'Marco Zoppo: la pala di Pesaro', in Giovannucci Vigi 1993, pp. 71–8

HUMFREY 1993b
P. Humfrey, *The Altarpiece in Renaissance Venice*, New Haven and London 1993

HUMFREY 2004
P. Humfrey (ed.), *The Cambridge Companion to Giovanni Bellini*, Cambridge 2004

HUMFREY 2011–12
P. Humfrey, 'The Portrait in Fifteenth-Century Venice', in Berlin and New York 2011–12, pp. 48–63

HUMFREY AND KEMP 1990
P. Humfrey and M. Kemp (eds), *The Altarpiece in the Renaissance*, Cambridge 1990

HUSE 1972
N. Huse, *Studien zu Giovanni Bellini*, Berlin and New York 1972

JANSON 1957
H.W. Janson, *The Sculpture of Donatello*, 2 vols, Princeton 1957

JOOST-GAUGIER 1979
C.L. Joost-Gaugier, 'A Pair of Miniatures by a Panel Painter: The Earliest Works of Giovanni Bellini?', *Paragone*, 30 (1979), pp. 48–71

KASL 2004
R. Kasl (ed.), *Giovanni Bellini and the Art of Devotion*, Indianapolis 2004

KEYDEL 1969
J.H. Keydel, *A Group of Altarpieces by Giovanni Bellini Considered in Relation to the Context for which they were Made*, Cambridge MA 1969

KING 1986
M.L. King, *Venetian Humanism in an Age of Patrician Dominance*, Princeton 1986

KING 2009
M.L. King, *The Death of the Child Valerio Marcello*, Chicago 2009

KNOX 1978
G. Knox, 'The Camerino of Francesco Corner', *Arte veneta*, 32 (1978), pp. 79–84

KOKOLE 1990
S. Kokole, 'Notes on the Sculptural Sources for Giorgio Schiavone's *Madonna* in London', *Venezia Arti*, 4 (1990), pp. 50–6

KORBACHER 2012
D. Korbacher, 'Arcadia in Venice: A Place to be', in L. de Fuccia and C. Brouard (eds), *'Di là dal fiume e tra gli alberi': il paesaggio del Rinascimento a Venezia; nascita e fortuna di un genere artistico (XV–XVII secolo), (atti della giornata di studi: Landscape as genre in the Serenissima from XV to XVIIth; iconography, context and taste, Venice, Fondazione Giorgio Cini, Cenacolo Palladiano, 10 April 2010)*, Ravenna 2012, pp. 19–34

KRISTELLER 1901
P. Kristeller, *Andrea Mantegna*, London 1901

KRISTELLER 1902
P. Kristeller, *Andrea Mantegna*, Berlin and Leipzig 1902

KRÜGER 2001
K. Krüger, *Das Bild als Schleier des Unsichtbaren. Ästhetische Illusion in der Kunst der frühen Neuzeit in Italien*, Munich 2001

KUNZ ET AL. 2018
T. Kunz et al., *Bestandskatalog der nordalpinen Bildwerke 1380–1440 in der Skulpturensammlung der Staatlichen Museen zu Berlin*, Petersberg 2018 (forthcoming)

LABOWSKY 1979
L. Labowsky, *Bessarion's Library and the Biblioteca Marciana: Six Early Inventories*, Rome 1979

LANDAU AND PARSHALL 1994
D. Landau and P. Parshall, *The Renaissance Print 1470–1550*, New Haven and London 1994

LEWKENOR 1599
L. Lewkenor, *The Commonwealth and Gouernment of Venice. Written by the Cardinall Gasper Contareno, and translated out of Italian into English, by Lewes Lewkenor*, London 1599

LIGHTBOWN 1986
R. Lightbown, *Mantegna, with a Complete Catalogue of the Paintings, Drawings and Prints*, Oxford 1986

LILLIE 2007
A. Lillie, 'Fiesole: Locus amoenus or Penitential Landscape?', *I Tatti Studies in the Italian Renaissance*, vol. 11 (2007), pp. 11–55

LIVERPOOL AND LONDON 1998–9
X. Brooke, *Mantegna to Rubens: The Weld-Blundell Drawings Collection*, exh. cat., Walker Art Gallery, Liverpool; British Museum, London 1998–9

LONDON 1981–2
D.S. Chambers and J. Martineau (eds), *Splendours of the Gonzaga*, exh. cat., Victoria and Albert Museum, London 1981–2

LONDON 1998
H. Chapman, *Padua in the 1450s: Marco Zoppo and his Contemporaries*, exh. cat., British Museum, London 1998

LONDON 2001–2
L. Syson and D. Gordon, *Pisanello: Painter to the Renaissance Court*, exh. cat., National Gallery, London 2001–2

LONDON 2003
D. Jaffé (ed.), *Titian*, exh. cat., National Gallery, London 2003

LONDON 2016
A. Robbins, *Painters' Paintings*, exh. cat., National Gallery, London 2016

LONDON 2018
D. Shawe-Taylor and P. Rumberg (eds), *Charles I: King and Collector*, exh. cat., Royal Academy of Arts, London 2018

LONDON AND DÜSSELDORF 2017–18
L. Packer and J. Sliwka, *Monochrome: Painting in Black and White*, exh. cat., National Gallery, London; Museum Kunstpalast, Düsseldorf 2017–18

LONDON AND FLORENCE 2010–11
H. Chapman and M. Faietti, *Fra Angelico to Leonardo: Italian Renaissance Drawings*, exh. cat., British Museum, London; Galleria degli Uffizi, Florence 2010–11

LONDON AND NEW YORK 1992
J. Martineau (ed.), *Andrea Mantegna*, exh. cat., Royal Academy of Arts, London; Metropolitan Museum of Art, New York 1992

LONDON AND NEW YORK 1994–5
J.J.G. Alexander, *The Painted Page: Italian Renaissance Book Illumination 1450–1550*, exh. cat., Royal Academy of Arts, London; Pierpont Morgan Library, New York 1994–5

LONDON AND NEW YORK 2012–13
C.B. Bailey and S. Buck (eds), *Master Drawings from the Courtauld Gallery*, exh. cat., Courtauld Gallery, London; Frick Collection, New York 2012–13

LONGHI 1914 (1961)
R. Longhi, 'Piero dei Franceschi e lo sviluppo della pittura veneziana', *L'Arte*, 17 (1914), pp. 198–221 and 241–56, reprinted in Longhi 1961–2000, I, vol. 1, pp. 61–106

LONGHI 1925–6 (1995)
R. Longhi, 'Escursioni Belliniane' [1925–6], in R. Longhi, *Il Palazzo non finito. Saggi inediti 1910–1925*, F. Frangi and C. Montagnani (eds), Milan 1995, pp. 365–400

LONGHI 1926 (1967)
R. Longhi, 'Lettera pittorica a Giuseppe Fiocco', *Vita artistica*, I (1926), pp. 127–39 and 147–8, reprinted in Longhi 1961–2000, II, vol. I, pp. 77–98

LONGHI 1927 (1963)
R. Longhi, *Piero della Francesca*, Rome 1927, reprinted in Longhi 1961–2000, III

LONGHI 1934 (1968)
R. Longhi, 'Risarcimento di un Mantegna', *Pan*, 2 (1934), pp. 504–12, reprinted in Longhi 1961–2000, IV, pp. 67–73

LONGHI 1946 (1978)
R. Longhi, *Viatico per cinque secoli di pittura veneziana*, Florence 1946, reprinted in Longhi 1961–2000, X, pp. 1–63

LONGHI 1949 (1978)
R. Longhi, 'The Giovanni Bellini Exhibition', *The Burlington Magazine*, 91 (1949), pp. 274–83, reprinted in Longhi 1961–2000, X, pp. 99–109

LONGHI 1961
R. Longhi, 'Avvertenze per il lettore', in Longhi 1961–2000, I, vol. I, pp. VII–XI

LONGHI 1961–2000
R. Longhi, *Edizione delle opere complete*, 14 vols, Florence 1961–2000

LONGHI 1962 (1978)
R. Longhi, 'Crivelli e Mantegna: due mostre interferenti e la cultura artistica nel 1961', *Paragone*, 13 (1962), pp. 7–21, reprinted in Longhi 1961–2000, X, pp. 143–55

LOS ANGELES 2017–18
D. Gasparotto (ed.), *Giovanni Bellini: Landscapes of Faith in Renaissance Venice*, exh. cat., J. Paul Getty Museum, Los Angeles 2017–18

LUCCO 1983
M. Lucco, 'Venezia fra Quattro e Cinquecento', in F. Zeri (ed.), *Storia dell'arte italiana. Parte seconda. Dal Medioevo al Novecento. Volume primo. Dal Medioevo al Quattrocento*, Turin 1983, pp. 447–77

LUCCO 1990a
M. Lucco (ed.), *La pittura nel Veneto. Il Quattrocento*, 2 vols, Milan 1990

LUCCO 1990b
M. Lucco, 'Venezia', in Lucco 1990a, vol. 2, pp. 395–480

LUCCO 2004
M. Lucco, 'Bellini and Flemish Painting', in Humfrey 2004, pp. 75–94

LUCCO 2006
M. Lucco, 'Le occasioni di Antonello', in Rome 2006, pp. 17–25

LUCCO 2008–9
M. Lucco, 'La primavera del Mondo tuto, in ato de Pitura', in Rome 2008–9, pp. 19–37

LUCCO 2013
M. Lucco, *Mantegna*, Milan 2013

LUCHS 1995
A. Luchs, *Tullio Lombardo and Ideal Portrait Sculpture in Renaissance Venice, 1490–1530*, Cambridge 1995

MADRID 2003
M. Falomir (ed.), *Tiziano*, exh. cat., Museo Nacional del Prado, Madrid 2003

MADRID AND PARIS 2004–5
P. Torres Guardiola (ed.), *Masters of Invention. The Edmond de Rothschild Collection from the Musée du Louvre*, exh. cat., Fundación Juan March, Madrid; Musée du Louvre, Paris 2004–5

MANCA 1993
J. Manca (ed.), *Titian 500: Studies in the History of Art*, 45, National Gallery of Art, Washington DC, 1993

MANIERI ELIA 2010
G. Maniera Elia (ed.), *Masterpieces Restored. The Gallerie dell'Accademia and Save Venice Inc.*, Venice 2010

MANTUA 1961
G. Paccagnini (ed.), *Andrea Mantegna*, exh. cat., Palazzo Ducale, Mantua 1961

MANTUA 2006–7
M. Lucco (ed.), *Mantegna a Mantova 1460–1506*, exh. cat., Palazzo Te, Mantua 2006–7

MARCON 1987
S. Marcon, 'Umanesimo veneto e calligrafia monumentale: codici nella Biblioteca di San Marco', *Lettere italiane*, 39 (1987), pp. 252–81

MARIANI CANOVA 1999
G. Mariani Canova, 'La miniatura a Padova dal medioevo al Settecento', in Padua 1999, pp. 13–32

MARIANI CANOVA 2009
G. Mariani Canova, 'La miniatura in Veneto', in A. Putaturo Donati Murano and A. Perricciolі Saggese (eds), *La miniatura in Italia, Vol. II: Dal tardogotico al manierismo*, Naples 2009, pp. 331–71

MARINI 2015
H.F. Marini, 'A New Drawing by Andrea Mantegna', *The Burlington Magazine*, 157 (2015), pp. 155–7

MARTINDALE 1979
A. Martindale, *The Triumphs of Caesar by Andrea Mantegna in the Collection of Her Majesty the Queen at Hampton Court*, London 1979

MASSING 1990
J.M. Massing, *Du texte à l'image: La calomnie d'Apelle et son iconographie*, Strasbourg 1990

MATTHEWS 1998
L.C. Matthews, 'The Painter's Presence: Signatures in Venetian Renaissance Paintings', *The Art Bulletin*, 80 (1998), pp. 616–48

MAZE 2013
D.W. Maze, 'Giovanni Bellini: Birth, Parentage, and Independence', *Renaissance Quarterly*, 66 (2013), pp. 783–823

MAZE 2017–18
D.W. Maze, 'The Life of Giovanni Bellini', in Los Angeles 2017–18, pp. 37–55

MAZZOTTA 2018a
A. Mazzotta, 'In his Father's Workshop: Giovanni Bellini's Paintings for the Scuola di S. Giovanni Evangelista, Venice', *The Burlington Magazine*, 160 (2018), pp. 283–90

MAZZOTTA 2018b
A. Mazzotta, 'Per la Sant'Orsola di Giovanni Bellini', in *Giovanni Bellini '… il migliore nella pittura', atti del convegno di Venezia (27–28 ottobre 2016)*, Venice 2018 (forthcoming)

MEISS 1957
M. Meiss, *Andrea Mantegna as Illuminator: An Episode in Renaissance Art, Humanism and Diplomacy*, New York 1957

MENU AND RAVAUD 2009
M. Menu and E. Ravaud (eds), *La technique picturale d'Andrea Mantegna*, Paris 2009 [*Techné*]

METZ 1801
Catalogue of a Select Collection of Genuine and Capital Drawings … the entire cabinet of C.M. Metz, Esq…, 4–6 May 1801, London 1801

MEYER ZUR CAPELLEN 1985
J. Meyer zur Capellen, *Gentile Bellini*, Stuttgart 1985

MEZZETTI 1958
A. Mezzetti, 'Un "Ercole e Anteo" del Mantegna', *Bollettino d'Arte*, 43/4 (1958), pp. 232–44

MICHIEL 1800
M. Michiel, *Notizia D'Opere di Disegno nella Prima Metà del Secolo XVI, esistenti in Padova Cremona Milano Pavia Bergamo Crema e Venezia*, I. Morelli (ed.), Bassano 1800

MILAN 1991
A. Di Lorenzo (ed.), *Le Muse e il Principe. Arte di corte nel Rinascimento padano*, exh. cat., Museo Poldi Pezzoli, 2 vols, Milan 1991

MILAN 2002–3
A. Di Lorenzo (ed.), *Due collezionisti alla scoperta dell'Italia. Dipinti e sculture dal Museo Jacquemart-André di Parigi*, exh. cat., Museo Poldi Pezzoli, Milan 2002–3

MILAN 2012–13
A. De Marchi, A. Di Lorenzo and L. Galli Michero (eds), *Giovanni Bellini. Dall'icona alla storia*, exh. cat., Museo Poldi Pezzoli, Milan 2012–13

MILAN 2014
E. Daffra (ed.), *Giovanni Bellini. La nascita della pittura devozionale umanistica. Gli studi*, exh. cat., Pinacoteca di Brera, Milan 2014

MORELLI 1893
I. Lermolieff [G. Morelli], *Kunstkritische Studien über die Italienische Malerei. Die Galerie zu Berlin*, Leipzig 1893

MOTTURE 2013
P. Motture, 'Looking Afresh: Reviewing Italian Renaissance Sculpture for the V&A's Medieval and Renaissance Galleries', in P. Motture, E. Jones and D. Zikos (eds), *Carvings, Casts and Collectors. The Art of Renaissance Sculpture*, London 2013, pp. 16–31

NATALE 1982
M. Natale (ed.), *Museo Poldi Pezzoli: Dipinti*, Milan 1982

NEW YORK 2003
Sotheby's, New York, Important Old Master Paintings, 23 January 2003, New York 2003

NEW YORK 2013
K. Christiansen, *Piero della Francesca: Personal Encounters*, exh. cat., Metropolitan Museum of Art, New York 2013

NOVA 2008–9
A. Nova, 'Icona, racconto e *dramatic close-up* nei dipinti devozionali di Giovanni Bellini', in Rome 2008–9, pp. 105–15

OBERTHALER 2009
E. Oberthaler, 'Mantegna's "Saint Sebastian" from Vienna – Condition, Technique and Recent Restoration', in Menu and Ravaud 2009, pp. 99–105

OLIVARI 2006
M. Olivari (ed.), *Andrea Mantegna. La Madonna dei Cherubini*, Milan 2006

PÄCHT 2003
O. Pächt, *Venetian Painting in the Fifteenth Century*, London and Turnhout 2003

PADUA 1999
G. Baldissin Molli, G. Mariani Canova and F. Toniolo (eds), *La miniatura a Padova dal medioevo al Settecento*, exh. cat., Palazzo della Ragione and Palazzo del Monte, Padua 1999

PADUA 2006–7
D. Banzato, A. De Nicolò Salmazo and A.M. Spiazzi (eds), *Mantegna e Padova 1445–1460*, exh. cat., Musei Civici, Padua 2006–7

PANIZON 2007
E. Panizon, 'Una lettura iconografica per "l'Introduzione del Culto di Cibele a Roma" di Andrea Mantegna', *Arte in Friuli, arte a Triste*, XXVI (2007), pp. 57–64

PANOFSKY 1927 (1998)
E. Panofsky, 'Imago Pietatis. Ein Beitrag zur Typengeschichte des "Schmerzensmanns" und der "Maria Mediatrix"' (1927), reprinted in in E. Panofsky, *Deutschsprachige Aufsätze* 2, K. Michels and M. Warnke (eds), Berlin 1998, pp. 186–233

PARIS 1975
S. Béguin (ed.), *Le Studiolo d'Isabella d'Este*, exh. cat., Musée du Louvre, Paris 1975

PARIS 1993
M. Laclotte and G. Nepi Scirè (eds), *Le Siècle de Titien. L'âge d'or de la Peinture à Venise*, exh. cat., Grand Palais, Paris 1993

PARIS 2008–9
G. Agosti and D. Thiébaut (eds), *Andrea Mantegna 1431–1506*, exh. cat., Musée du Louvre, Paris 2008–9 (revised Italian edition: Milan 2008)

PARKER 1928
K.T. Parker, 'An Attribution to Giovanni Bellini', *Old Master Drawings*, 3 (1928), pp. 19–23

PARKER AND BYAM SHAW 1953
K.T. Parker and J. Byam Shaw, in *Old Master Drawings*, exh. cat., Royal Academy of Arts, London 1953, no. 120

PENNY 2008
N. Penny, *National Gallery Catalogues: The Sixteenth Century Italian Paintings, vol. 2, Venice 1540–1600*, London 2008

PERRY 2016
D.M. Perry, 'The Material Culture of Venetian Medieval Identity', in J. Watkins and K.L. Reyerson (eds), *Mediterranean Identities in the Premodern Era*, Abingdon and New York 2016, pp. 15–34

PESCI AND TONIOLO 2008
F. Pesci and L. Toniolo (eds), *Andrea Mantegna. La Pala di San Zeno. La Pala Trivulzio. Conoscenza, conservazione, monitoraggio*, Venice 2008

PINCUS 2004
D. Pincus, 'Bellini and Sculpture', in Humfrey 2004, pp. 122–42

PINCUS 2008
D. Pincus, 'Giovanni Bellini's Humanist Signature. Pietro Bembo, Aldus Manutius and Humanism in Early Sixteenth-Century Venice', *Artibus et Historiae*, 29 (2008), pp. 89–119

PINCUS 2017
D. Pincus, 'Calligraphy, Epigraphy and the Paduan-Venetian Culture of Letters', in Blass-Simmen and Weppelmann 2017, pp. 41–60

PINO 2000
P. Pino, *Dialogo di Pittura* [1548], S. Falabella (ed.), Rome 2000

POLDI AND VILLA 2008
G. Poldi and G.C.F. Villa (eds), *Bellini a Venezia. Sette opere indagate nel loro contesto*, Milan 2008

POLDI AND VILLA 2009
G. Poldi and G.C.F. Villa, *Indagando Bellini*, Milan 2009

POPE-HENNESSY 1964
J. Pope-Hennessy, *Catalogue of Italian Sculpture in the Victoria and Albert Museum*, 3 vols, London 1964

POPE-HENNESSY 1993
J. Pope-Hennessy, *Donatello: Sculptor*, New York 1993

POPHAM AND POUNCEY 1950
A.E. Popham and P. Pouncey, *Italian Drawings in the Department of Prints and Drawings in the British Museum. The Fourteenth and Fifteenth Centuries*, 2 vols, London 1950

POPHAM AND WILDE 1949
A.E. Popham and J. Wilde, *The Italian Drawings of the XV and XVI Centuries in the Collection of His Majesty the King at Windsor Castle*, London 1949

PREVITALI 1980
G. Previtali (ed.), *Storia dell'arte italiana. Parte prima. Materiali e problemi. Volume quarto. Ricerche spaziali e tecnologie*, Turin 1980

PRINZ 1962
W. Prinz, 'Die Darstellung Christi im Tempel und die Bildnisse des Andrea Mantegna', *Berliner Museen*, 12 (1962), pp. 50–4

PROCHNO 2006
R. Prochno, *Konkurrenz und ihre Gesichter in der Kunst. Wettbewerb, Kreativität und ihre Wirkungen*, Berlin 2006

PROUST 1913 (2005)
M. Proust, *Swann's Way* (1913), trans. C.K. Scott Moncrieff and T. Kilmartin, London 2005

PUPPI 1972
L. Puppi, *Il trittico di Andrea Mantegna per la Basilica di S. Zeno Maggiore in Verona*, Verona 1972

RAVAUD ET AL. 2009a
E. Ravaud et al., 'La prédelle du retable de San Zeno / The Predella of San Zeno', in Menu and Ravaud 2009, pp. 74–81

RAVAUD ET AL. 2009b
E. Ravaud et al., 'Matériaux et techniques de quatre toiles d'Andrea Mantegna/Materials and Techniques used in Four Paintings by Andrea Mantegna', in Menu and Ravaud 2009, pp. 27–34

REARICK 2004
W.R. Rearick, 'The Study of Venetian Drawings Today', *Master Drawings*, 42/4 (2004), pp. 299–301

RIGONI 1948–9 (1970)
E. Rigoni, 'Il pittore Niccolò Pizolo', *Arte veneta*, 2 (1948–9), pp. 141–7, reprinted in E. Rigoni, *L'arte rinascimentale in Padova. Studi e documenti*, Padua 1970, pp. 25–46

RIMINI 2012
M. Bona Castellotti and M. Pulini (eds), *Gli angeli della Pietà. Intorno a Giovanni Bellini*, exh. cat., Museo della Città, Rimini 2012

RINGBOM 1965 (1984)
S. Ringbom, *Icon to Narrative. The Rise of the Dramatic Close-Up in Fifteenth-Century Devotional Painting* (1965), Doornspijk 1984

ROBERTSON 1960
G. Robertson, 'The Earlier Work of Giovanni Bellini', *Journal of the Warburg and Courtauld Institutes*, 23 (1960), pp. 45–59

ROBERTSON 1968
G. Robertson, *Giovanni Bellini*, Oxford 1968

ROBERTSON 1981
G. Robertson, *Giovanni Bellini*, New York 1981

ROMANO 1981 (1994)
G. Romano, 'Towards the Modern Manner: From Mantegna to Raphael' [1981], in *History of Italian Art*, trans. C. Dorey, 2 vols, Cambridge 1994, vol. 2, pp. 373–489

ROMANO 1998
G. Romano, *Storie dell'arte. Toesca, Longhi, Wittkower, Previtali*, Rome 1998

ROMANO 2008–9
G. Romano, 'Mantegna dans le Studiolo d'Isabella d'Este Gonzague', in Paris 2008–9, pp. 321–35

ROME 2006
M. Lucco (ed.), *Antonello da Messina. L'opera completa*, exh. cat., Scuderie del Quirinale, Rome 2006

ROME 2008–9
M. Lucco and G.C.F. Villa (eds), *Giovanni Bellini*, exh. cat., Scuderie del Quirinale, Rome 2008–9

ROME 2010–11
G. Valagussa and G.C.F. Villa (eds), *I grandi Veneti. Da Pisanello a Tiziano, da Tintoretto a Tiepolo. Capolavori dell'Accademia Carrara di Bergamo*, exh. cat., Chiostro del Bramante, Rome 2010–11

ROSENAUER 1993
A. Rosenauer, *Donatello*, Milan 1993

ROSSI 2006
F. Rossi (ed.), *Placchette e rilievi di bronzo nell'età del Mantegna*, Milan 2006

ROTHE 1992
A. Rothe, 'Mantegna's Paintings in Distemper', in London and New York 1992, pp. 80–8

ROWLEY 2008
N. Rowley, 'Giovanni Bellini: Rome', *The Burlington Magazine*, 150 (2008), pp. 848–9

ROWLEY 2010
N. Rowley, *'Pittura di luce': la manière claire dans la peinture du Quattrocento*, PhD, Université Paris-Sorbonne 2010, 2 vols

ROWLEY 2016
N. Rowley, 'Portrait of a Soldier (Presumed Portrait of Ludovico III Gonzaga)', *SMB-digital: Online collections database*, http://www.smb-digital.de/eMuseumPlus?service=ExternalInterface&module=collection&objectId=1890962&viewType=detailView

ROWLEY 2018a
N. Rowley, 'Donatello à Berlin: au-delà de la *Madone Pazzi*', in N. Rowley (ed.), *Donatello a Berlino*, Pisa 2018 (forthcoming) [*Predella. Journal of Visual Arts*]

ROWLEY 2018b
N. Rowley, 'Fortune e sfortune della *Presentazione di Gesù al tempio* di Andrea Mantegna ora alla Gemäldegalerie di Berlino', in Venice 2018, pp. 51–61

ROY 2009
A. Roy, 'The Place of the Copenhagen "Man of Sorrows with Two Angels" in Mantegna's Technical Oeuvre', in Ravaud and Eveno 2009, pp. 88–92

RUBIN 2006
P.L. Rubin, 'Signposts of Invention: Artists' Signatures in Renaissance Italian Art', *Art History*, 29, (2006), pp. 563–99

RUTHERGLEN 2015
S. Rutherglen, '"The Footprints of our Lord": Giovanni Bellini and the Franciscan Tradition', in Rutherglen and Hale 2015, pp. 23–57

RUTHERGLEN AND HALE 2015
S. Rutherglen and C. Hale (eds), *In a New Light. Giovanni Bellini's 'St. Francis in the Desert'*, New York 2015

SAFARIK 1974
E.A. Safarik, 'Campagnola, Girolamo', in *Dizionario Biografico degli Italiani*, vol. 17, Rome 1974, pp. 317–18

SANDER 2004
J. Sander, *Italienische Gemälde im Städel 1330–1550. Oberitalien, die Marken und Rom*, Mainz 2004

SCARDEONE 1560
B. Scardeone, *De antiquitate urbis Patavii*, Basel 1560

SCHMIDT ARCANGELI 1990
C. Schmidt Arcangeli, 'La "sacra conversazione" nella pittura veneta', in Lucco 1990a, pp. 703–26

SCHMIDT ARCANGELI 1996
C. Schmidt Arcangeli, 'Un tempio aperto…', *Studi di Storia dell'Arte*, VII (1996), pp. 65–98

SCHMIDT ARCANGELI 2015
C. Schmidt Arcangeli, *Giovanni Bellini e la pittura veneta a Berlino. Le collezioni di James Simon e Edward Solly alla Gemäldegalerie*, Verona 2015

SCHMITTER 2003
M. Schmitter, 'The Dating of Marcantonio Michiel's "Notizia" on works of art in Padua', *The Burlington Magazine*, 145 (2003), pp. 564–71

SCHÖLZEL 2009
C. Schölzel, 'The Restoration and Painting Technique of the "Holy Family" by Mantegna in the Dresden Gallery', in Ravaud and Eveno 2009, pp. 106–13

SCHULZE ALTCAPPENBERG 1995
H.-T. Schulze Altcappenberg, *Die italienischen Zeichnungen des 14. und 15. Jahrhunderts im Berliner Kupferstichkabinett. Kritischer Katalog*, Berlin 1995

SHAPLEY 1979
F.R. Shapley, *Catalogue of the Italian Paintings: National Gallery of Art, Washington*, 2 vols, Washington DC 1979

SHAW WITH BOCCIA-SHAW 1989
K.V. Shaw with T.M. Boccia-Shaw, 'Mantegna's Pre-1448 Years Reexamined: The S. Sofia Inscription', *The Art Bulletin*, 71 (1989), pp. 47–57

SHAW AND BOCCIA-SHAW 1996
K. Shaw and T.M. Boccia-Shaw, 'Further Observations on a Quattrocento "ymago sancti Bernardini" in the Santo', *Il Santo*, 36 (1996), pp. 475–85

SHAW AND BOCCIA 2016
K. Shaw and T.M. Boccia, 'Andrea Mantegna Called Andrea Squarcione', in M. Bourne and A.V. Coonin (eds), *Encountering the Renaissance: Celebrating Gary M. Radke and 50 Years of the Syracuse University Graduate Program in Renaissance Art*, Ramsey 2016, pp. 317–24

SHEPHERD 2014
T. Shepherd, *Echoing Helicon: Music, Art and Identity in the Este Studioli, 1440–1530*, Oxford 2014

SIGNORINI 1985
R. Signorini, *Opus hoc tenue: la camera dipinta di Andrea Mantegna*, Milan 1985

SIGNORINI, REBONATO AND TAMMACCARO 2010
R. Signorini, V. Rebonato and S. Tammaccaro (eds), *Andrea Mantegna. Impronta del genio. Convegno Internazionale di studi (Padova, Verona, Mantova, 8-9-10 novembre 2006)*, 2 vols, Florence 2010

SILVA MAROTO 2013
M.P. Silva Maroto, *La Oración en el Huerto con el donante Luis I de Orleans (hacia 1405–1408), una tabla francesa descubierta*, Madrid 2013

STAATLICHE GRAPHISCHE SAMMLUNG MÜNCHEN 2010
Corpus der italienischen Zeichnungen 1300–1450. Teil III: Verona. Bd. 3, Badile-Album. Studiensammlung einer Veroneser Künstlerwerkstatt, vorliegender Corpus-Bd. 3/3 hg. von Staatlichen Graphischen Sammlung München, Munich 2010

SYSON 2009
L. Syson, 'Reflections on the Mantegna Exhibition in Paris', *The Burlington Magazine*, 151 (2009), pp. 526–35

TEMPESTI 1991
A.F. Tempesti, *The Robert Lehman Collection, vol. 5, Italian Fifteenth- to Seventeenth-Century Drawings*, New York 1991

TEMPESTINI 1992
A. Tempestini, *Giovanni Bellini. Catalogo completo dei dipinti*, Florence 1992

TEMPESTINI 2000
A. Tempestini, *Giovanni Bellini*, Milan 2000

TEMPESTINI 2004
A. Tempestini, 'Bellini and his Collaborators', in Humfrey 2004, pp. 256–71

TEMPESTINI 2008–9
A. Tempestini, 'Temi profane e pittura narrativa in Giovanni Bellini', in Rome 2008–9, pp. 53–65

THIÉBAUT 2008–9
D. Thiébaut, 'Le "premier peintre du monde" au Louvre', in Paris 2008–9, pp. 17–27

TIETZE-CONRAT 1955
E. Tietze-Conrat, *Mantegna: Paintings, Drawings, Engravings*, London 1955

TIETZE AND TIETZE-CONRAT 1944
H. Tietze and E. Tietze-Conrat, *The Drawings of the Venetian Painters in the 15th and 16th Centuries*, New York 1944

TOMASELLA 2002
G. Tomasella, 'Giuseppe Fiocco al crocevia fra Toscana e Veneto. Note a margine di un carteggio', in T. Franco and G. Valenzano (eds), *De lapidibus sententiae. Scritti di storia dell'arte per Giovanni Lorenzoni*, Padua 2002, pp. 383–5

TOURS 2009
P. Le Leyzour, A. De Marchi and A. Gillet (eds), *Mantegna. La Prédelle de San Zeno de Vérone, 1457–1459*, exh. cat., Musée des Beaux-Arts, Tours 2009

TRESIDDER 1992
W. Tresidder, 'A Borrowing from the Antique in Giovanni Bellini's *Continence of Scipio*', *The Burlington Magazine*, 134 (1992), pp. 660–2

VALAGUSSA 2018
G. Valagussa (ed.), *Accademia Carrara Bergamo. Dipinti italiani del Trecento e del Quattrocento. Catalogo completo*, Milan 2018

VASARI 1966–97
G. Vasari, *Le Vite de' più eccellenti pittori, scultori e architettori nelle redazioni del 1550 e 1568*, R. Bettarini and P. Barocchi (eds), 11 vols, Florence 1966–97

VASARI 1568 (1996)
G. Vasari, *Lives of the Painters, Sculptors and Architects*, D. Ekserdjian (ed.), G. du C. de Vere (trans.), 2 vols, New York 1996

VENICE 1949
R. Palucchini (ed.), *Giovanni Bellini. Catalogo illustrato della mostra*, exh. cat., Palazzo Ducale, Venice 1949

VENICE 2000
R. Goffen and G. Nepi Sciré (eds), *Il colore ritrovato. Bellini a Venezia*, exh. cat., Gallerie dell'Accademia, Venice 2000

VENICE 2014–15
A. Robison, *La Poesia della Luce: Disegni Veneziani dalla National Gallery of Art di Washington*, exh. cat., Museo Correr, Venice 2014–15

VENICE 2018
B. Blass-Simmen, N. Rowley and G.C.F. Villa (eds), *Capolavori a confronto. Bellini / Mantegna. Presentazione di Gesù al Tempio*, exh. cat., Fondazione Querini Stampalia, Venice 2018

VENTURA 1995
L. Ventura, *Lorenzo Leonbruno: Un pittore a corte nella Mantova di primo Cinquecento*, Rome 1995

VENTURI 1914
A. Venturi, *Storia dell'arte italiana. VII. La pittura del Quattrocento. Parte III*, Milan 1914

VERONA 2006–7
S. Marinelli and P. Marini (eds), *Mantegna e le Arti a Verona, 1450–1500*, exh. cat., Palazzo della Gran Guardia, Verona 2006–7

VERRI AND AMBERS 2010
G. Verri and J. Ambers, 'Revealing Stratigraphy', in J. Ambers, C. Higgitt and D. Saunders (eds), *Italian Renaissance Drawings: Technical Examination and Analysis*, London 2010, pp. 89–102

VICENZA 2016
G.C.F. Villa (ed.), *Giovanni Bellini. La Trasfigurazione*, exh. cat., Palazzo Leoni Montanari, Vicenza 2016

VICKERS 1976
M. Vickers, 'Mantegna and Constantinople', *The Burlington Magazine*, 118 (1976), pp. 680–7

VILLA 2008
G.C.F. Villa, 'Dall'underdrawing al Disegno. Il caso di Giovanni Bellini', *Mitteilungen Des Kunsthistorischen Institutes in Florenz*, vol. 52, no. 2/3, 2008, pp. 73–87

VILLA 2009
G.C.F. Villa, 'Indagando Bellini. Quattro ancone in un itinerario', in Poldi and Villa 2009, pp. 13–127

VILLA 2017
G.C.F. Villa, 'Andrea Mantegna and Giovanni Bellini. The Hidden Dialogue', in Blass-Simmen and Weppelmann 2017, pp. 79–92

VINCO 2014
M. Vinco, "'L'Istrias" di Raffaele Zovenzoni e Giovanni Bellini ante 1475', in Milan 2014, pp. 97–102

VINCO 2015
M. Vinco, 'Pizzolo, Nicolò', in *Dizionario Biografico degli Italiani*, vol. 84, Rome 2015, pp. 368–72

VINCO 2018
M. Vinco, 'Frammenti innovativi. Le prime pale d'altare di Giovanni Bellini a Venezia', in *Giovanni Bellini '... il migliore nella pittura', atti del convegno di Venezia (27–28 ottobre 2016)*, Venice 2018 (forthcoming)

VON HADELN 1932
D. von Hadeln, 'Giovanni Bellini or Mantegna?', *The Burlington Magazine*, 61 (1932), pp. 228–30

WALKER 1956
J. Walker, *Bellini and Titian at Ferrara: A Study of Styles and Taste*, London 1956

WALTER 1989
I. Walter, 'Andrea Mantegnas "Darbringung Jesu im Tempel". Ein Bild der Befreiung und des Aufbruchs', *Städel-Jahrbuch*, 12 (1989), pp. 59–70

WARNKE 1993
M. Warnke, *The Court Artist: On the Ancestry of the Modern Artist*, Cambridge 1993

WASHINGTON 1973
J.A. Levenson, K. Oberhuber and J.L. Sheehan (eds), *Early Italian Engravings from the National Gallery of Art, Washington*, exh. cat., National Gallery of Art, Washington DC 1973

WASHINGTON 1986
M. Leithe-Jasper (ed.), *Renaissance Master Bronzes from the Collection of the Kunsthistorisches Museum Vienna*, exh. cat., National Gallery of Art, Washington DC 1986

WASHINGTON AND VIENNA 2006–7
D.A. Brown and S. Ferino-Pagden (eds), *Bellini, Giorgione, Titian and the Renaissance of Venetian Painting*, exh. cat., National Gallery of Art, Washington DC; Kunsthistorisches Museum, Vienna 2006–7

WESTON 2009
H. Weston, *Christ's Descent into Limbo at the Bristol City Art Gallery and Museum: A Singular Work of Art*, unpublished MPhil thesis, University of Birmingham, 2009

WHISTLER 2016
C. Whistler, *Venice and Drawing 1500–1800: Theory, Practice and Collecting*, New Haven and London 2016

WILSON 1977
C.C. Wilson, *Bellini's Pesaro Altarpiece: A Study of Context and Meaning*, PhD dissertation, New York University 1977

WILSON 2015
C.C. Wilson (ed.), *Examining Giovanni Bellini: An Art 'More Human and More Divine'*, Turnhout 2015

ZAMPONI 2006–7
S. Zamponi, 'Andrea Mantegna e la maiuscola antiquaria', in Padua 2006–7, pp. 73–9

ZERI 1971
F. Zeri, 'Quattro tempere di Jacopo Bellini', *Diario di lavoro: Quaderni di Emblema*, 1 (1971), pp. 42–9

ZGRAJA 2015
K. Zgraja, 'A Contribution to the Study of Giovanni Bellini's Drawings and Under-drawings', in Wilson 2015, pp. 169–81

ZIMMERMANN 1965
H. Zimmermann, 'Drei Chiaroscuro-Bilder von Andrea Mantegna', *Pantheon*, 23 (1965), pp. 17–21

List of Exhibited Works

Provenance and references compiled by Alexander Röstel

Works are listed chronologically under each artist. Dimensions are given height followed by width. Unless otherwise stated, the works are exhibited in London and Berlin.

Andrea Mantegna
(about 1431–1506)

FIG. 77

ANDREA MANTEGNA
Saint Mark the Evangelist, about 1448
Egg tempera on canvas, 81.1 × 63.6 cm
Städel Museum, Frankfurt am Main (1046)

PROVENANCE
Possibly Duque de Uceda, Madrid; at least since 1859 José de Salamanca y Mayol, 1st Marquess of Salamanca; his sale, Pillet, Paris, 3–6 June 1867, lot 58, from which acquired by the museum.

REFERENCES
Kristeller 1901, p. 457; Fiocco 1937, pp. 28–9, 199; Tietze-Conrat 1955, p. 183; Bellonci and Garavaglia 1967, no. 12, pp. 87–8; Lightbown 1986, p. 475; London and New York 1992, no. 5, pp. 119–21; Padua 2006–7, no. 18, pp. 174–5; Paris 2008–9, no. 6, pp. 70–2.

FIG. 116

ANDREA MANTEGNA
Saint Jerome Penitent in the Desert, 1448–51
Egg tempera on panel, 51 × 40 cm
Museu de Arte de São Paulo Assis Chateaubriand. Gift, Câmera Municipal de São Paulo, 1952 (MASP.00015)

PROVENANCE
C. Raven until November 1936; his sale, 20 November 1936, Christie's, London, lot 97; Elizabeth Batts, London, since November 1936; Prince Paul of Yugoslavia from around 1938–50; Wildenstein, New York, 1951; acquired in 1952.

REFERENCES
Fiocco 1937, pp. 76–7; Tietze-Conrat 1955, p. 197; Lightbown 1986, p. 475; London and New York 1992, no. 3, pp. 115–17; Padua 2006–7, no. 19, pp. 176–7; Paris 2008–9, no. 7, pp. 72–4.

FIG. 221

ANDREA MANTEGNA
The Adoration of the Shepherds, about 1450–2
Egg tempera on canvas, transferred from panel, 40 × 55.6 cm
The Metropolitan Museum of Art, New York. Purchase, Anonymous Gift, 1932 (32.130.2)

PROVENANCE
From 1586 until at least 1598, Margherita Gonzaga, Ferrara; by 1603–21, Cardinal Pietro Aldobrandini, Rome; Cardinal Ippolito Aldobrandini; 1638–81, Olimpia Aldobrandini Borghese Pamphili; 1682–1710, Giovanni Battista Pamphili; 1710–60, Cardinal Girolamo Pamphili; 1760–8, his estate; 1768–92, Paolo Borghese Aldobrandini; 1792–1800, Giovanni Battista Borghese Aldobrandini; 1800–1, Alexander Day, London; by 1808, William Buchanan, London; 1808–24, Richard Payne Knight, Downton Castle, Ludlow, Herefordshire; 1838–1909, Andrew Johnes Rouse-Boughton-Knight, Downton Castle; 1924, A. Ruck, London; 1924–5, Duveen Brothers, New York; 1925–32, Clarence H. Mackay, Roslyn, Long Island, New York; acquired in 1932.

REFERENCES
Kristeller 1901, p. 453; Fiocco 1937, pp. 31, 43–4; Tietze-Conrat 1955, pp. 190–1; Bellonci and Garavaglia 1967, no. 7, p. 87; Lightbown 1986, pp. 59–60; London and New York 1992, no. 8, pp. 126–8; Paris 2008–9, no. 50, pp. 162–3.

FIG. 83

ANDREA MANTEGNA
Saint James led to martyrdom, about 1453
Pen and brown ink on paper, 16.4 × 25.6 cm
The British Museum, London. Accepted by HM Government in lieu of Inheritance Tax and allocated to the British Museum, 1976 (1976,0616.1)

PROVENANCE
Spencer collection; Sir Thomas Lawrence; John Wingfield Malcolm, 1st Baron Malcolm of Poltalloch; A.E. Gathorne-Hardy, Donnington Priory, Newbury, Berkshire; acquired in 1976.

REFERENCES
Kristeller 1901, pp. 101–2; Fiocco 1933, pp. 185–94; Tietze-Conrat 1955, p. 204; Robertson 1968, pp. 22–3; Lightbown 1986, p. 481; London and New York 1992, no. 11, pp. 135–6; London 1998, no. 7, pp. 50–1; Padua 2006–7, no. 29, pp. 200–1; London and Florence 2010–11, no. 20, pp. 136–7.

FIG. 128

ANDREA MANTEGNA
The Presentation of Christ in the Temple, about 1454
Egg tempera on canvas, assembled on wooden construction, 77.5 × 94.4 cm
Gemäldegalerie, Staatliche Museen zu Berlin (29)

PROVENANCE
1520s, Cardinal Pietro Bembo, Padua; by inheritance to the Casa dei Gradenigo, Padua; 1803, sold by the Gradenigo to an unknown person; Edward Solly, Berlin; acquired in 1821.

REFERENCES
Kristeller 1901, pp. 143–5; Fiocco 1937, pp. 48–9; Tietze-Conrat 1955, p. 179; Mantua 1961, no. 17, p. 29; Bellonci and Garavaglia 1967, no. 38, p. 99; Lightbown 1986, pp. 404–5; Schmidt Arcangeli 2015, pp. 316–24; Venice 2018.

FIG. 108

ANDREA MANTEGNA
The Virgin and Child with Saints Jerome and Louis of Toulouse, about 1455
Egg tempera on panel, 69.4 × 44.5 cm
Musée Jacquemart-André, Paris (MJAP-P2184)

PROVENANCE
Private collection in Milan before 1814; Teodoro Lechi, Brescia, from around 1814–66; by descent to Faustino Lechi, Brescia, until his death in 1870; by descent to Alfredo Lechi, Brescia, to around 1887; purchased in 1887 by Michelangelo Guggenheim, Venice, from whom purchased by Édouard André and Nélie Jacquemart; part of the museum since 1913.

REFERENCES
Fiocco 1937, p. 30; Tietze-Conrat 1955, p. 196; Mantua 1961, no. 12, p. 24; Robertson 1968, p. 153; Milan 2002–3, no. 3, pp. 54–9; Paris 2008–9, no. 28, pp. 116–17.

Berlin only

FIG. 125

ANDREA MANTEGNA
The Agony in the Garden, about 1455–6
Egg tempera on panel, 62.9 × 80 cm
The National Gallery, London. Bought, 1894 (NG 1417)

PROVENANCE
Possibly Aldobrandini collection by 1611; Olimpia Aldobrandini by 1626; probably by descent, in the collection of Prince Giovanni Battista Pamphili Aldobrandini, Rome, before 1710; collection of Cardinal Fesch, France, from 1815, Rome, from which sold in February 1845 and purchased by Artaria; owned by Farrer; William Coningham collection in 1845–6, from which sold, 9 June 1849, lot 58; purchased by Chaplin, 12 April 1851, lot 57, in the collection of Thomas Baring by 1853; by bequest to Lord Northbrook, from whom acquired in 1894.

REFERENCES
Kristeller 1901, pp. 163–7; Fiocco 1937, p. 48; Tietze-Conrat 1955, p. 185; Davies 1961, pp. 335–8; Mantua 1961, no. 9, p. 21; Bellonci and Garavaglia 1967, no. 22, pp. 94; Lightbown 1986, p. 404; Paris 2008–9, no. 48, pp. 158–9.

FIG. 188

ANDREA MANTEGNA
The Virgin and Child (Simon Madonna), about 1455–60
Glue size on canvas, 48.4 × 32.2 cm
Gemäldegalerie, Staatliche Museen zu Berlin (S 5)

PROVENANCE
Trissino collection, Vicenza; G. Brauner; Della Porta collection, Piacenza; 1897–1904, James Simon, Berlin; 1904, bequeathed to the museum.

REFERENCES
Kristeller 1901, pp. 124, 438; Fiocco 1937, pp. 26, 49, 58; Tietze-Conrat 1955, pp. 20, 179; Mantua 1961, no. 18, p. 30; Bellonci and Garavaglia 1967, no. 54, p. 108; Lightbown 1986, p. 424; London and New York 1992, no. 41, pp. 205–6; Padua 2006–7, no. 27, pp. 196–7; Schmidt Arcangeli 2015, pp. 325–31.

FIG. 163

ANDREA MANTEGNA
Three studies for the Dead Christ (recto); *Two studies of women* (verso), about 1455–65
Pen and brown ink on paper, 12.2 × 8.8 cm
The British Museum, London (1909,0406.3)

PROVENANCE
Until 1909, John Calthorpe Blofeld, London, from whom acquired by the museum.

REFERENCES
Tietze-Conrat 1955, p. 205; Robertson 1968, pp. 22, 25; London and New York 1992, no. 26, pp. 177–8; London 1998, no. 10, pp. 56–7; Verona 2006–7, no. 9, pp. 209–10; Paris 2008–9, nos 54–5, pp. 146–7, 168–9; Marini 2015.

FIG. 101

ANDREA MANTEGNA
The Crucifixion, 1456–9
Egg tempera on panel, 76 × 96 cm
Musée du Louvre, Paris. Département des Peintures (368)

PROVENANCE
1459–1797, San Zeno, Verona, predella of the High Altarpiece; since 1798, Musée Central des Arts, Paris (now Musée du Louvre).

REFERENCES
Fiocco 1937, pp. 41–2; Tietze-Conrat, 1955, pp. 194, 200; Mantua 1961, no. 6, pp. 18–19; Bellonci and Garavaglia 1967, no. 23E, p. 95; Lightbown 1986, pp. 406–8; Verona 2006–7, no. 2, pp. 195–9; Paris 2008–9, no. 52, pp. 164–7; Tours 2009, no. 2, pp. 50–67.

London only

FIG. 206

ANDREA MANTEGNA
Cardinal Ludovico Trevisan, 1459–60
Egg tempera on poplar, 45.5 × 34.8 cm
Gemäldegalerie, Staatliche Museen zu Berlin (9)

PROVENANCE
Before 1630, Francesco Leone, Padua; Edward Solly, Berlin; acquired in 1830.

REFERENCES
Kristeller 1901, pp. 170–3; Fiocco 1937, p. 47; Tietze-Conrat 1955, p. 196; Mantua 1961, no. 10, p. 22; Bellonci and Garavaglia 1967, no. 26, pp. 95–6; Lightbown 1986, pp. 81–2, 408–10; London and New York 1992, no. 100, pp. 333–5; Berlin and New York 2011–12, no. 142, pp. 324–7; Schmidt Arcangeli 2015, pp. 332–8.

FIG. 193

ANDREA MANTEGNA
Saint Sebastian, about 1459–60
Egg tempera on poplar, 68 × 30 cm
Gemäldegalerie, Kunsthistorisches Museum, Vienna (GG301)

PROVENANCE
From 1659 to at least 1662, Leopold Wilhelm of Habsburg, Brussels and Vienna; 1662–1705, Leopold I of Habsburg, Vienna; Habsburg collections until 1918, exhibited in the Kunsthistorisches Museum since 1891.

REFERENCES
Kristeller 1901, pp. 168–70; Fiocco 1937, pp. 43–4; Tietze-Conrat 1955, p. 200; Mantua 1961, no. 8, p. 20; Bellonci and Garavaglia 1967, no. 43, p. 100; Lightbown 1986, p. 408; Paris 2008–9, no. 71, pp. 202–3.

FIG. 158

ANDREA MANTEGNA
The Deposition of Christ (recto); *Study for a candlestick* (verso), about 1460
Pen and brown ink on paper, 13 × 9.5 cm
BRESCIA – Fondazione Brescia Musei (147)

PROVENANCE
Until 1863, Camillo Brozzoni; 1863–88, Pinacoteca Comunale Tosio, Brescia; since 1888, Pinacoteca Comunale Martinengo (Pinacoteca Tosio Martinengo from 1906).

REFERENCES
Venice 1949, no. 128, p. 215; Tietze-Conrat 1955, p. 203; Robertson 1968, pp. 22, 24; Lightbown 1986, p. 482; London and New York 1992, no. 27, pp. 179–80; Verona 2006–7, no. 10, pp. 211–12; Paris 2008–9, no. 43, pp. 144–5; Marini 2015.

London only

FIG. 159

ANDREA MANTEGNA
Two studies of the Lamentation (recto); *Studies of the Pietà* (verso), early 1460s
Pen and brown ink on paper, 15.1 × 10 cm
Private collection, Milan

PROVENANCE
Sold Farsetti Arte, Prato, 8 November 2013.

REFERENCES
Fagioli 2013; Marini 2015.

FIG. 214

ANDREA MANTEGNA
The Death of the Virgin, about 1460–4
Egg tempera on panel, 54.5 × 42 cm
Museo Nacional del Prado, Madrid (P00248)

PROVENANCE
Until 1576, possibly chapel of the Castello di San Giorgio, Mantua; by 1588–1618, Margherita Gonzaga, Duchess of Ferrara; 1618–26, Ferdinando Gonzaga, 6th Duke of Mantua; 1627, Vincenzo Gonzaga, 7th Duke of Mantua; 1627–49, Charles I of England; sold 1649/50; purchased by John Baptist Gaspars; 1650–65, Philip IV of Spain; Spanish Royal Collections; in the museum since 1829.

REFERENCES
Kristeller 1901, pp. 220–2, 440; Fiocco 1937, pp. 48, 203; Tietze-Conrat 1955, pp. 186–7; Mantua 1961, pp. 31–5; Bellonci and Garavaglia 1967, no. 34E, pp. 97–8; Lightbown 1986, p. 431; London and New York 1992, no. 17, pp. 159–63; Paris 2008–9, no. 60, pp. 184–6.

FIG. 213

ANDREA MANTEGNA
Christ with the Virgin's Soul, about 1460–4
Egg tempera on panel, 27.5 × 17.5 cm
Pinacoteca Nazionale, Ferrara (333)

PROVENANCE
Until 1576, possibly chapel of the Castello di San Giorgio, Mantua; about 1579–97, Chapel of Margherita Gonzaga d'Este, Palazzo Ducale, Ferrara; after 1880 until 1900, Enea Vendeghini, Ferrara; 1900–58, Maria Vendeghini Baldi, Ferrara; 1958–73, Mario Baldi, Ferrara, from whom bequeathed to the museum in 1973.

REFERENCES
Fiocco 1937, pp. 47–8; Tietze-Conrat 1955, pp. 181, 186–7; Mantua 1961, no. 22, p. 34; Bellonci and Garavaglia 1967, no. 34D, p. 97; Lightbown 1986, p. 413; London and New York 1992, no. 16, pp. 159–63; Paris 2008–9, no. 61, pp. 184–6.

Berlin only

FIG. 153

ANDREA MANTEGNA
Pietà, about 1460–5
Pen and brown ink on paper, 12.7 × 9.8 cm
Gallerie dell'Accademia, Venice (115)

PROVENANCE
Until 1810, Francesco Antonio Lapegna, Naples; from 1810–15, Giuseppe Bossi, Milan; 1815–18, Bossi's heirs; until 1822, Luigi Celotti, Venice, from whom acquired by the museum.

REFERENCES
Venice 1949, no. 129, p. 216; Robertson 1968, pp. 24, 36; Goffen 1989, p. 299; London and New York 1992, no. 28, pp. 181–2; Padua 2006–7, no. 30, pp. 202–3; Paris 2008–9, no. 44, pp. 146–7; Milan 2014, no. 18, p. 167.

Berlin only

FIG. 195

ANDREA MANTEGNA
Studies for Christ at the column, 1460–5
Pen and brown ink on paper, 23.7 × 14.5 cm
The Samuel Courtauld Trust.
The Courtauld Gallery, London (D.1978.PG.345)

PROVENANCE
John Skippe; the Martin family; Edward Holland-Martin; Mrs A.C. Rayner-Wood; sale of Edward Holland-Martin, Christie's, London, 20–1 November 1958, lot 36; Count Antoine Seilern, by whom bequeathed in 1978.

REFERENCES
Robertson 1968, p. 22, 24, 36; Washington 1973, p. 202; Lightbown 1986, p. 482; London and New York 1992, no. 35, pp. 193–4; Paris 2008–9, no. 42, pp. 141–3.

FIG. 123

ANDREA MANTEGNA
Reading saint, 1460s
Pen and brown ink on pink prepared paper, 17.4 × 6.9 cm
The British Museum, London (1895,0915.780)

PROVENANCE
Sir Thomas Lawrence; Sir John Charles Robinson; John Wingfield Malcolm, 1st Baron Malcolm of Poltalloch, from whom acquired in 1895.

REFERENCES
Popham and Pouncey 1950, p. 8; Tietze-Conrat 1955, p. 205; Robertson 1968, p. 25; Lightbown 1986, pp. 481–2; London and New York 1992, no. 24, p. 175; Verona 2006–7, no. 5, pp. 203–4.

FIG. 143

ANDREA MANTEGNA
The Descent of Christ into Limbo, about 1468
Pen and brown ink, brown wash on vellum, 37.2 × 28 cm
École Nationale Supérieure des Beaux-Arts, Paris (EBA189)

PROVENANCE
Aimé Charles His de la Salle; donated in 1869.

REFERENCES
Kristeller 1901, p. 103, 459; Hind 1938–48, vol. 5, p. 18; Mantua 1961, no. 130, p. 173; Robertson 1968, p. 25; Washington 1973, no. 80, pp. 208–10; Goffen 1989, pp. 284–6; London and New York 1992, no. 66, pp. 261–3; Paris 2008–9, no. 68, pp. 196–8.

Berlin only

FIG. 198

ANDREA MANTEGNA

A man lying on a stone slab, late 1470s
Pen and brown ink over traces of black chalk on paper, 20.3 × 13.9 cm
The British Museum, London (1860,0616.63)

PROVENANCE

William Young Ottley; Sir Thomas Lawrence; Samuel Woodburn; sold Christie's, London, 6 June 1860, lot 545.

REFERENCES

Kristeller 1901, pp. 405, 445; Tietze-Conrat 1955, p. 205; Lightbown 1986, p. 483; London and New York 1992, no. 43, pp. 209–10; Bätschmann 2008, p. 46; London and Florence 2010–11, no. 21, pp. 138–9.

Berlin only

FIG. 65

ANDREA MANTEGNA

A Roman triumph, 1475–90
Pen and ink on brown paper, 26.6 × 26.6 cm
Private collection

PROVENANCE

Collection of August Grahl; sold Sotheby's, London, 1985, lot 209; Alexander Twietmeyer; from around 1930 private collection in Germany; from whom acquired at local public auction in 2016.

REFERENCES

Unpublished

FIG. 233

ANDREA MANTEGNA

A bird catching a fly, about 1480
Pen and brown ink on paper, 12.8 × 8.8 cm
The British Museum, London. Presented by The Art Fund, 1946 (1946,0713.7)

PROVENANCE

Jonathan Richardson Sr; Sir Thomas Lawrence; Samuel Woodburn; sold Christie's, London, 6 June 1860, lot 552; Sir Thomas Phillipps; by descent to T. Fitzroy Fenwick, from whom acquired in 1946.

REFERENCES

Popham and Pouncey 1950, p. 99; Tietze-Conrat 1955, p. 205; Lightbown 1986, pp. 483–4; London and New York 1992, no. 73, pp. 277–8.

FIG. 235

ANDREA MANTEGNA

The Triumphs of Caesar II: The Standard-Bearers and Siege Equipment, mid-1480s – before 1506
Egg tempera on canvas, 270.3 × 281.1 cm
Lent by Her Majesty The Queen (RCIN 403959)

PROVENANCE

Palace at San Sebastiano, Mantua; by June 1625, nine canvases in the Galleria della Mostra, Palazzo Ducale; 1629, dispatched from Mantua; October 1630, dispatched from Venice; by 1631, in the collection of Charles I, probably at Hampton Court; May 1650, moved to Somerset House; by 1659, returned to Hampton Court.

REFERENCES

Kristeller 1901, pp. 267–97; Tietze-Conrat 1955, pp. 183–4; Bellonci and Garavaglia 1967, no. 63B, p. 111; Martindale 1979, pp. 138–41, 178; Lightbown 1986, pp. 140–53; London and New York 1992, no. 109, pp. 359–60; London 2018, no. 26, pp. 54–9, 72.

FIG. 236

ANDREA MANTEGNA

The Triumphs of Caesar IV: The Vase-Bearers, mid-1480s – before 1506
Egg tempera on canvas, 269.5 × 280 cm
Lent by Her Majesty The Queen (RCIN 403961)

PROVENANCE

As above.

REFERENCES

Kristeller 1901, pp. 267–97; Tietze-Conrat 1955, pp. 183–4; Bellonci and Garavaglia 1967, no. 63D, p. 112; Martindale 1979, pp. 145–7; London and New York 1992, no. 111, pp. 363–4; Paris 2008–9, pp. 362–71, no. 160, pp. 380–2; London 2018, no. 28, pp. 54–9, 74.

FIG. 237

ANDREA MANTEGNA

The Triumphs of Caesar V: The Elephants, mid-1480s – before 1506
Egg tempera on canvas, 270 × 280.7 cm
Lent by Her Majesty The Queen (RCIN 403962)

PROVENANCE

As above.

REFERENCES

Kristeller 1901, pp. 267–97; Tietze-Conrat 1955, pp. 183–4; Bellonci and Garavaglia 1967, no. 63E, p. 112; Martindale 1979, pp. 147–9; London and New York 1992, no. 112, pp. 365–6; London 2018, no. 29, pp. 54–9, 75.

FIG. 107

ANDREA MANTEGNA

The Virgin and Child with an angel, about 1485
Pen and brown ink with brown wash on paper, 19.6 × 13.9 cm
The British Museum, London (1858,0724.3)

PROVENANCE

Count Nils Barck; Walter Benjamin Tiffin, from whom acquired in 1858.

REFERENCES

Kristeller 1901, pp. 404–5; Popham and Pouncey 1950, p. 99; Lightbown 1986, p. 484; London and New York 1992, no. 49, pp. 221–2; London and Florence 2010–11, no. 23, pp. 142–3.

London only

FIG. 150

ANDREA MANTEGNA

The Dead Christ supported by Two Angels, about 1485–1500
Egg tempera on panel, 78 × 48 cm
Statens Museum for Kunst, Copenhagen (KMSsp69)

PROVENANCE

1753, private collection, Florence; 1756, acquired in Bologna by Cardinal Silvio Valenti Gonzaga, Rome; 1756–63, Marchese Carlo and Cardinal Luigi Valenti Gonzaga, Rome; sold Amsterdam, 18 May 1763, no. 68; purchased by Gerhard Morell; 1763–6, King Frederick VII, Copenhagen; Danish Royal Collections.

REFERENCES

Kristeller 1901, pp. 327–30, 442; Fiocco 1937, pp. 70–1, 208; Tietze-Conrat 1955, pp. 180–1; Bellonci and Garavaglia 1967, no. 69, p. 113; Lightbown 1986, pp. 220–2; London and New York 1992, no. 60, pp. 243–5; Mantua 2006–7, no. 13, pp. 94–7; Paris 2008–9, no. 84, pp. 232–5.

FIG. 234

ANDREA MANTEGNA

Orange tree, about 1490
Pen and brown ink on paper, 31.2 × 14.2 cm
Musée du Louvre, Paris. Département des Arts graphiques (776 DR)

PROVENANCE

1887, H.G. Gutekunst Kunst-Auktion, Stuttgart; 1887–1934, Edmond de Rothschild, Paris; acquired from his heirs in 1935.

REFERENCES

London and New York 1992, p. 459; Paris 2008–9, no. 115, pp. 285–6.

Berlin only

FIG. 122

ANDREA MANTEGNA

Three studies for Saint John the Baptist, about 1490
Pen and brown ink on pale pink prepared paper, 17.4 × 18.5 cm
National Museums Liverpool, Walker Art Gallery. Purchased from the Trustees of the Weld Heirlooms Settlement with the assistance of the National Heritage Memorial Fund, The Art Fund, Sir Denis Mahon and British Nuclear Fuels in 1995 (WAG 1995.324)

PROVENANCE

Padre Sebastiano Resta; 1710–16, John Somers, London; before 1729, Nicola Francesco Haym, London; until 1811, George John, 2nd Earl Spencer, Althorp; 1811–16, William Roscoe, Liverpool; Roscoe sale; 1816–37, Charles Robert Blundell, Ince Blundell Hall; 1837–1995, Weld-Blundell family, from whom acquired by the museum.

REFERENCES

Robertson 1968, p. 26; Verona 2006–7, no. 8, pp. 207–9; Paris 2008–9, no. 182, pp. 412–13.

FIG. 231

ANDREA MANTEGNA

Three deities, 1490s
Pen and brown ink with brown, red and blue wash, heightened with white, on paper, 36.3 × 31.6 cm
The British Museum, London (1861,0810.2)

PROVENANCE

From at least 1785 until around 1798, John Strange, Venice and London; from around 1798, Conrad Martin Metz; 6 May 1801, sale Thomas Philipe, lot 91; until 13 June 1814, William Young Ottley, London; 13 June 1814, sale Thomas Philipe, lot 780; until 10 August 1861, John Heywood Hawkins; acquired in 1861.

REFERENCES

Kristeller 1901, pp. 374, 444; Popham and Pouncey 1950, pp. 94–5; Tietze-Conrat 1955, p. 206; London 1981–2, p. 171; Lightbown 1986, p. 486; London and New York 1992, no. 146, pp. 449–50; Paris 2008–9, no. 143, pp. 342–4.

Berlin only

FIG. 229

ANDREA MANTEGNA

Virtus Combusta, 1490s
Pen and brown ink and point of the brush on a brown ground, heightened with white, the black background over red, on paper, 28.6 × 44.1 cm
The British Museum, London. Bequeathed by Richard Payne Knight, 1824 (Pp,1.23)

PROVENANCE

Casa Giovanelli, Venice; purchased by John Strange; sold, 19 March 1800; C.M. Metzl sold, Thomas Philipe, 6 May 1801, lot 92; 1824, Payne Knight bequest.

REFERENCES

Popham and Pouncey 1950, pp. 95–7; Tietze-Conrat 1955, pp. 205–6; London 1981–2, pp. 171–2; London and New York 1992, no. 147, pp. 451–3.

London only

FIG. 190

ANDREA MANTEGNA

The Holy Family, about 1490–1500
Egg tempera with some oil on canvas, 75 × 61.5 cm
Gemäldegalerie Alte Meister, Staatliche Kunstsammlungen, Dresden (51)

PROVENANCE

1648, heirs of Bernardo Giunti, Venice; by 1850, Natale Schiavoni, Venice; from 1854–65, Sir Charles Lock Eastlake, London; 1865–76, Elizabeth Rigby Eastlake, London, from whom acquired by the museum.

REFERENCES

Kristeller 1901, pp. 322–3; Fiocco 1937, p. 70; Tietze-Conrat 1955, p. 181; Mantua 1961, no. 31, p. 48; Bellonci and Garavaglia 1967, no. 84, pp. 115–16; Dresden 2006; Mantua 2006–7, no. 11, pp. 88–9; Paris 2008–9, no. 82, pp. 228–30.

FIG. 173

ANDREA MANTEGNA

The Virgin and Child with the Magdalen and Saint John the Baptist, about 1490–1505
Egg tempera on canvas, 139.1 × 116.8 cm
The National Gallery, London.
Bought, 1855 (NG 274)

PROVENANCE

Probably in the collection of Cardinal Cesari Monti (Archbishop of Milan from 1632); Palazzo Andreani (Adriani), Milan, by 1795; collection of Mario Andreani; collection of Giacomo Mellerio; sold by Mellerio's heir, Conte Cavazzi della Somaglia, to the dealer Giuseppe Baslini in 1855; purchased by Roverselli, from whom acquired in 1855.

REFERENCES

Kristeller 1901, pp. 320–1, 442; Tietze-Conrat 1955, p. 185; Davies 1961, pp. 329–30; Bellonci and Garavaglia 1967, no. 102, p. 120; Lightbown 1986, pp. 436–7.

FIG. 141

ANDREA MANTEGNA

The Descent of Christ into Limbo, probably about 1492
Egg tempera and gold on panel, 38.8 × 42.3 cm
Private collection

PROVENANCE

Probably Ferdinando Carlo Gonzaga, Duke of Mantua, from at least 1700 until 1708, and last mentioned in his posthumous inventory of 1709; probably sold shortly afterwards in Venice and acquired during the second half of the eighteenth century, Marchese Jacopo Durazzo, from about 1775, Genoa; before 1930, Ernesto Bertollo, from whom acquired by Thomas Agnew & Sons Ltd., London, 1930, there purchased, 4 November 1930, by Sir Stephen Courtauld, London and Argyll, 1930–73; sold Sotheby's, London, 11 July 1973, lot 10; P. & D. Colnaghi & Co., London, 1973–4, there purchased by Juan de Beistegui, Paris, from whom acquired in 1988; 1988–2003, Barbara Piasecka Johnson, Princeton (NJ); sold Sotheby's, New York, 15 October 2003, lot 62.

REFERENCES

Fiocco 1937, p. 77; Tietze-Conrat 1955, pp. 197–8; Mantua 1961, pp. 169, 175; Washington 1973, pp. 208–11; Lightbown 1986, pp. 437–8; London and New York 1992, no. 70, pp. 269–70; New York 2003.

FIG. 136

ANDREA MANTEGNA

The Adoration of the Magi, about 1495–1505
Glue size on canvas, 48.6 × 65.6 cm
The J. Paul Getty Museum at the Getty Center, Los Angeles (85/PA.417)

PROVENANCE

By 1871–1903, Louisa, Lady Ashburton; around 1903–15, Spencer Douglas Compton, Castle Ashby, Northants; 1915–78, William Bingham Compton, 6th Marquess of Northampton, Castle Ashby; 1978–85, Spencer Douglas David Compton, 7th Marquess of Northampton, Castle Ashby; sold Christie's, London, 1 April 1985, lot 16.

REFERENCES

Kristeller 1901, pp. 143–5, 438–9; Fiocco 1937, pp. 68, 206; Tietze-Conrat 1955, p. 192; Mantua 1961, p. 76; Bellonci and Garavaglia 1967, no. 106, p. 121; London 1981–2, no. 32, pp. 122–3; Lightbown 1986, pp. 445–6; London and New York 1992, no. 56, pp. 237–8; Carr 1997; Paris 2008–9, no. 181, pp. 411–12.

FIG. 240

ANDREA MANTEGNA

The Vestal Virgin Tuccia with a Sieve, about 1495–1506
Egg tempera on poplar, 72.5 × 23 cm
The National Gallery, London.
Bought, 1882 (NG 1125.1)

PROVENANCE

Possibly in the collection of William Thomas Beckford; in the Duke of Hamilton's collection at Hamilton Palace at least by 1854; purchased at the Hamilton sale, 24 June 1882, lot 398.

REFERENCES

Kristeller 1901, pp. 372, 444; Tietze-Conrat 1955, p. 186; Davies 1961, pp. 340–1; Mantua 1961, p. 74; Bellonci and Garavaglia 1967, no. 97, p. 120; Lightbown 1986, p. 450; London and New York 1992, pp. 393–416.

London only

FIG. 241

ANDREA MANTEGNA

A Woman Drinking, about 1495–1506
Egg tempera on poplar, 71.2 × 19.8 cm
The National Gallery, London.
Bought, 1882 (NG 1125.2)

PROVENANCE

In the Duke of Hamilton's collection at Hamilton Palace at least by 1854; purchased at the Hamilton sale, 24 June 1882, lot 398.

REFERENCES

Kristeller 1901, pp. 372, 444; Tietze-Conrat 1955, p. 186; Davies 1961, pp. 340–1; Bellonci and Garavaglia 1967, no. 98, p. 120; Lightbown 1986, p. 450; London and New York 1992, pp. 393–416; Mantua 2006–7, no. 18, pp. 106–7.

London only

FIG. 189

ANDREA MANTEGNA

The Holy Family with Saint John the Baptist, about 1500
Glue size on canvas, 71.1 × 50.8 cm
The National Gallery, London.
Mond Bequest, 1924 (NG 5641)

PROVENANCE

Recorded in the collection at Verona of Cav. Andrea Monga in 1856; acquired from the Monga collection in 1885 by J.P. Richter, and in his collection at Florence until 1891. Purchased from him by Ludwig Mond; Mond Bequest, 1924; entered the National Gallery in 1946.

REFERENCES

Kristeller 1901, pp. 326–7, 442; Fiocco 1937, p. 70; Tietze-Conrat 1955, p. 185; Davies 1961, pp. 338–9; Mantua 1961, p. 65; Bellonci and Garavaglia 1967, no. 85, p. 116; Lightbown 1986, pp. 448–9.

London only

FIG. 238

ANDREA MANTEGNA

Samson and Delilah, about 1500
Glue size on canvas, 47 × 36.8 cm
The National Gallery, London.
Bought, 1883 (NG 1145)

PROVENANCE

Possibly bought before 1728 from Bartolomeo Buonfiglioli at Bologna by Procurator Zaccaria Sagredo of Venice; Consul Joseph Smith at Venice, from whom purchased in 1763 by Consul John Udny; Duke of Marlborough at Blenheim; purchased at the Sunderland sale, 15 June 1883, lot 82.

REFERENCES

Kristeller 1901, pp. 369–70, 443; Fiocco 1937, p. 68; Tietze-Conrat 1955, pp. 184–5; Davies 1961, pp. 334–5; Mantua 1961, p. 69; Bellonci and Garavaglia 1967, no. 95, p. 119; Lightbown 1986, p. 449; London and New York 1992, pp. 393–416; Paris 2008–9, p. 307.

London only

FIG. 225

ANDREA MANTEGNA

Minerva expelling the Vices from the Garden of Virtue, about 1500–2
Egg tempera on canvas, 159 × 192 cm
Musée du Louvre, Paris. Département des Peintures (371)

PROVENANCE

1502–39, Isabella d'Este, Marchioness of Mantua; 1539–40, Federico Gonzaga, Duke of Mantua; 1540, Margherita Paleologa, Duchess of Mantua; 1540–1627/9, Dukes of Mantua; 1627/9–42, Armand-Jean du Plessis, Cardinal and Duke of Richelieu, Paris and the Château de Richelieu, Poitou; 1642–1715, Armand-Jean de Wignerod du Plessis, Duke of Richelieu, Château de Richelieu; 1715–88, Louis-François-Armand de Wignerod du Plessis, Duke of Richelieu, Château de Richelieu; 1788–1801, Château de Richelieu; 1801, Musée Central des Arts, Paris (now Musée du Louvre).

REFERENCES

Kristeller 1901, pp. 356–8; Fiocco 1937, pp. 135–6; Tietze-Conrat 1955, pp. 195–6; Mantua 1961, no. 46. pp. 66–8; Bellonci and Garavaglia 1967, no. 91B, p. 118; Paris 1975, no. 110, pp. 36–8; Lightbown 1986, pp. 186–208; London and New York 1992, no. 136, pp. 427–30; Mantua 2006–7, no. 15, pp. 100–3; Paris 2008–9, no. 145, pp. 345–7.

FIG. 230

ANDREA MANTEGNA

The Calumny of Apelles, 1505–6
Pen and three shades of brown ink with some white heightening, in part oxidised, on paper, 20.6 × 37.9 cm
The British Museum, London (1860,0616.85)

PROVENANCE

By 1669, Rembrandt Harmensz. van Rijn, Amsterdam; until around 1718, S. van der Schelling, Amsterdam; from around 1718, Salomon Gautier, London; from 1771, John Barnard; sold Greenwood, London, 16 February 1787, lot 88; bought by Benjamin West; Sir Thomas Lawrence, London; since 1835, William Esdaile; sold Christie's, London, 17 June 1840, lot 120; Samuel Woodburn; sold Christie's, London, 7 June 1860, lot 763; acquired in 1860.

REFERENCES
Kristeller 1901, p. 461; Popham and Pouncey 1950, pp. 97–9; Lightbown 1986, pp. 207, 486–7; London and New York 1992, no. 154, pp. 467–8; Paris 2008–9, no. 148, pp. 350–1.

FIG. 245

ANDREA MANTEGNA
The Introduction of the Cult of Cybele at Rome, 1505–6
Glue size on canvas, 76.5 × 273 cm
The National Gallery, London.
Bought, 1873 (NG 902)

PROVENANCE
Ordered by Francesco Cornaro of Venice in 1505; sold to Cardinal Sigismondo Gonzaga in 1506 by Mantegna's son Lodovico; Palazzo Cornaro, later Mocenigo (San Polo, Venice), where recorded in 1815; bought by Antonio Sanquirico; by 1835 in the collection of George Vivian; purchased from Captain Ralph Vivian in 1873.

REFERENCES
Kristeller 1901, pp. 361–9, 443; Fiocco 1937, pp. 67, 205; Tietze-Conrat 1955, pp. 185–6; Bellonci and Garavaglia 1967, no. 96, pp. 119-20; Shapley 1979, pp. 52–4; Lightbown 1986, pp. 214–18, 451–2; London and New York 1992, no. 135, pp. 412–16.

Attributed to Andrea Mantegna

FIG. 98

Attributed to ANDREA MANTEGNA
Child in the manger, 1450
Miniature from Eusebius, *Chronicon*
Tempera, gum or glue on vellum, 27.3 × 18.3 cm
Biblioteca Nazionale Marciana, Venice (Cod. Lat. IX, 1 (3496), fol. 133v)

PROVENANCE
Until 1789, Convent of Santi Giovanni e Paolo, Venice; from where transferred to the library.

REFERENCES
London and New York 1992, no. 7, pp. 123–5; Padua 2006–7, no. 17, pp. 172–3; Paris 2008–9, no. 10, pp. 78–9.

Berlin only

FIG. 139

Attributed to ANDREA MANTEGNA
The Descent of Christ into Limbo, about 1465–70
Pen and brown ink, brown wash on paper, 26.9 × 20 cm
The Metropolitan Museum of Art, New York. Robert Lehman Collection (1975.1.274)

PROVENANCE
Jan Pietersz. van Zomer; John Skippe, Ledbury; his sister, Penelope Skippe; married in 1774 to James Martin, Overbury Court, Worcestershire; James Martin's son, Old Colwall, Malvern, by descent through his mother to Edward Holland; his sister, Mrs A.C. Rayner-Wood; his nephew, Edward Holland-Martin; Skippe sale, Christie's, London, 20 November 1958, lot 37; Colnaghi and Co., London; acquired by Robert Lehman in 1959; bequeathed to the Metropolitan Museum of Art in 1969.

REFERENCES
Kristeller 1901, p. 459; Heinemann 1962–91, vol. 1, p. 54; Washington 1973, pp. 208–10; Tempesti 1991, pp. 31–6; London and New York 1992, no. 65, pp. 259–61.

FIG. 106

Attributed to ANDREA MANTEGNA
Saint Jerome and the lion, 1480s
Black chalk on paper, 17.3 × 13.6 cm
Kupferstichkabinett, Staatliche Museen zu Berlin (KdZ 5114)

PROVENANCE
Until 1902, Adolf von Beckerath, Berlin, from whom acquired in 1902.

REFERENCES
Kristeller 1901, p. 460; Fiocco 1937, pp. 76–7; Tietze-Conrat 1955, p. 203; London and New York 1992, no. 4, pp. 117–18; Schulze Altcappenberg 1995, pp. 60–2; Paris 2008–9, no. 40, pp. 138–9.

FIG. 112

Attributed to ANDREA MANTEGNA
Jupiter and Ganymede, 1490s
Pen and brown ink on laid paper, the two figures incised, 15.2 × 11.9 cm
National Gallery of Art, Washington DC. Ailsa Mellon Bruce Fund 1996 (1996.11.1)

PROVENANCE
Barthold Suermondt, Aachen; Count Grigory Stroganoff, Rome; André de Hevesy, Paris, until at least 1955; Edward Holland-Martin, London; his sale, Christie's, London, 20 May 1966, lot 103; Christie's, 22 November 1966, lot 132; private collection, California; acquired from Olimpia Theodoli and Michael Miller Lucy Vivante Fine Arts, New York, in 1996.

REFERENCES
Tietze and Tietze-Conrat 1944, no. A 320, p. 89 (as Mantegna); Tietze-Conrat 1955, p. 207, fig. 32 (as Mantegna); Heinemann 1962–91, vol. 1, pp. 214, S. 913 (as school of GIOVANNI BELLINI), vol. 3, pp. 75, 79, S. 913, fig. 48 (as school of GIOVANNI BELLINI); Venice 2014–15, no. 6, pp. 40–1.

FIG. 140

Attributed to ANDREA MANTEGNA
The Resurrection of Christ, about 1492
Egg tempera on panel, 48.3 × 37.7 cm
Fondazione Accademia Carrara, Bergamo (81LC00169)

PROVENANCE
Bequest of Guglielmo Lochis, 1866.

REFERENCES
Kristeller 1901, p. 454; Fiocco 1937, p. 227; Heinemann 1962–91, vol. 1, p. 257; Lightbown 1986, p. 474; Agosti 2005, pp. 375, 414; Valagussa 2018.

Circle of Andrea Mantegna

FIG. 157

Circle of ANDREA MANTEGNA
The Entombment, about 1470–80
Bronze, partially gilded silver, 24.4 × 44.9 × 2 cm
Kunstkammer, Kunsthistorisches Museum, Vienna (KK 6059)

PROVENANCE
At least since 1659, collection of Archduke Leopold Wilhelm of Austria, Vienna; before 1735, transferred to Schloss Ambras near Innsbruck; 1821, transferred to the Ambras collection, Vienna; 1891, transferred to the museum.

REFERENCES
Washington 1986, pp. 61–4; Rossi 2006, pp. 40–1; Ferrara 2007, no. 54, pp. 290–1.

FIG. 196

Circle of ANDREA MANTEGNA
The Flagellation, about 1470–80
Engraving, 40.5 × 31.8 cm
The British Museum, London (1845,0825.594)

PROVENANCE
Purchased from W & G Smith in 1845.

REFERENCES
Kristeller 1901, p. 410; Tietze-Conrat 1955, pp. 243–4; Washington 1973, no. 78, pp. 200–5.

London only

(not illustrated)

Circle of ANDREA MANTEGNA
The Flagellation, about 1470–80
Engraving, 44.5 × 34.4 cm
Kupferstichkabinett, Staatliche Museen zu Berlin (208-1901)

PROVENANCE
Amsler & Ruthardt, Berlin; James Reiss sale, London; acquired in 1901.

REFERENCES
Bartsch 1811, XIII, 227.1; Kristeller 1901, p. 410; Tietze-Conrat 1955, pp. 243–4; Washington 1973, no. 78, pp. 200–5; Milan 2014, no. 1.7, p. 188.

Berlin only

FIG. 142

Circle of ANDREA MANTEGNA
The Descent of Christ into Limbo, about 1480–5
Engraving, printed in brown ink, 42.9 × 33.7 cm
Kupferstichkabinett, Staatliche Museen zu Berlin (840-21)

PROVENANCE
Karl Friedrich Ferdinand von Nagler, Berlin; acquired in 1835.

REFERENCES
Bartsch 1811, XIII, 230.5; Washington 1973, no. 80, pp. 208–10.

Berlin only

FIG. 66

Circle of ANDREA MANTEGNA
The Entombment, about 1480–5
Engraving, 30.4 × 44.4 cm
Kupferstichkabinett, Staatliche Museen zu Berlin (95-1893)

PROVENANCE
Acquired before 1878.

REFERENCES
Bartsch 1811, XIII, 229.3; Washington 1973, no. 70, pp. 170–5.

Berlin only

Studio of Andrea Mantegna

FIG. 197

Studio of ANDREA MANTEGNA
Study for a soldier of the Resurrection and other figures (recto); *Study of drapery and figures* (verso), about 1455–65
Pen and light brown ink on orange-brown prepared paper (recto); brush and grey wash with white heightening on orange-brown prepared paper (verso), 25 × 18.8 cm
Lent by Her Majesty The Queen (RCIN 912795)

PROVENANCE
Listed in George III's inventory (1810).

REFERENCES
Popham and Wilde 1949, no. 15, p. 174; London and New York 1992, no. 63, pp. 251–2.

FIG. 183

Studio of ANDREA MANTEGNA
The Virgin and Child, about 1480–5
Engraving, 24.7 × 21 cm
The British Museum, London (1856,0712.1072)

PROVENANCE
Sir Mark Masterman-Sykes; Henry Munn; Sotheby's, London, 14 July 1856, lot 415; Walter Benjamin Tiffin, from whom acquired in 1856.

REFERENCES
Bartsch 1811, XIII, 232.8; Kristeller 1901, pp. 392–3, 445; Hind 1938–48, vol. 5, p. 10; Washington 1973, no. 77, pp. 194–5; London and New York 1992, no. 48, pp. 219–20; Fletcher 1997; London 1998, no. 21, pp. 74–5.

London only

(not illustrated)

Studio of ANDREA MANTEGNA
The Virgin and Child, about 1480–5
Engraving, 18.0 × 13.2 cm
Kupferstichkabinett, Staatliche Museen zu Berlin (95-1893)

PROVENANCE
Amsler & Ruthardt, Berlin, Dietze sale; acquired in 1893.

REFERENCES
Bartsch 1811, XIII, 232.8; Kristeller 1901, pp. 392–3, 445; Hind 1938–48, vol. 5, p. 10; Washington 1973, no. 77, pp. 194–5; London and New York 1992, no. 48, pp. 219–20; Fletcher 1997; London 1998, no. 21, pp. 74–5.

Berlin only

FIG. 144

Studio of ANDREA MANTEGNA
The Descent of Christ into Limbo, about 1490
Brush in dark brown and grey with white heightening on blue prepared paper, 28.3 × 20.1 cm
Kupferstichkabinett, Staatliche Museen zu Berlin (KdZ 622)

PROVENANCE
Padre Anselmo Oliva (?), Van Parijs, Brussels; acquired in 1878.

REFERENCES
Kristeller 1901, p. 103; Fiocco 1937, pp. 77; Mantua 1961, p. 169; Lightbown 1986, p. 488; London and New York 1992, no. 71, pp. 271–2; Schulze Altcappenberg 1995, pp. 64–5.

FIG. 56

Studio of ANDREA MANTEGNA
Dancing muse, about 1497
Pen and black ink, blue-grey wash, white heightening, over black chalk on brown prepared paper, traces of spolvero transfer, 45.6 × 31.2 cm
Kupferstichkabinett, Staatliche Museen zu Berlin (KdZ 5058)

PROVENANCE
Carlo Prayer, Milan; probably H.G. Gutekunst Kunst-Auktion, Stuttgart; until 1902, Adolf von Beckerath, Berlin; acquired in 1902.

REFERENCES
Kristeller 1901, p. 103; Fiocco 1937, p. 77; Mantua 1961, no. 123, p. 166; Lightbown 1986, p. 485; Schulze Altcappenberg 1995, pp. 62–3; Paris 2008–9, no. 138, pp. 334–5.

After Andrea Mantegna

FIG. 113

GIULIO CAMPAGNOLA, after ANDREA MANTEGNA
Jupiter and Ganymede, about 1500–5
Engraving, 16.7 × 12.4 cm
Kupferstichkabinett, Staatliche Museen zu Berlin (52-1886)

PROVENANCE
1886, H.G. Gutekunst Kunst-Auktion, Stuttgart; acquired in 1886.

REFERENCES
Bartsch, 1811, XIII, 372.5; Hind 1938–48, V, p. 196; Tietze-Conrat 1955, p. 207; Heinemann 1962–91, vol. 1, p. 214; Washington 1973, pp. 392–3; Brown 2010, pp. 85–6.

Berlin only

Giovanni Bellini
(about 1435–1516)

FIG. 114

GIOVANNI BELLINI
Saint Jerome in the Wilderness, probably 1453–5
Egg tempera on panel, 44.2 × 30 cm
The Henry Barber Trust, The Barber Institute of Fine Arts, University of Birmingham (49.1)

PROVENANCE
D. Goodyear, Burton House, Gloucester; his sale, Christie's, London, 6 June 1856, lot 537, unsold; Rev. William Davenport Bromley, Wootton Hall, Staffordshire; his sale, Christie's, London, 12 June 1863, lot 59; purchased by James Carnegie, 9th Earl of Southesk; by descent, Southesk collection, Kinnaird Castle, Perthshire; Christie's, London, 23 June 1948, lot 42; Thomas Agnew & Sons Ltd., London, from whom purchased by the Henry Barber Trust, February 1949.

REFERENCES
Venice 1949, no. 24, pp. 48–9; Heinemann 1962–91, vol. 1, p. 219; Robertson 1968, pp. 15–16, 19–20, 29–31, 37; Ghiotto and Pignatti 1969, no. 1, p. 85; Goffen 1989, pp. 4–9, 14, 34, 184, 287, 294, 327; Tempestini 2000, p. 174; Bätschmann 2008, pp. 12–18; Rome 2008–9, no. 2, pp. 136–9; Los Angeles 2017–18, no. 1, pp. 58–63.

FIG. 148

GIOVANNI BELLINI
Pietà, about 1457
Egg tempera on panel, 50.5 × 40.4 cm
Museo Poldi Pezzoli, Milan (1587)

PROVENANCE
Giuseppe Molteni; acquired by Gian Giacomo Poldi Pezzoli between 1853 and 1865.

REFERENCES
Venice 1949, no. 43, pp. 74–5; Robertson 1968, p. 36; Ghiotto and Pignatti 1969, no. 22, p. 87; Natale 1982, pp. 115–16; Goffen 1989, pp. 79, 287, 300; Tempestini 2000, p. 186; Bätschmann 2008, pp. 18, 24–6; Milan 2012–13, no. 4, pp. 56–9.

London only

FIG. 26

GIOVANNI BELLINI
The Lamentation over the Dead Christ, with Saints Mark and Nicholas of Bari, about 1457–9
Oil (?) on canvas, 116 × 319 cm
Ducal Palace, Venice (433)

PROVENANCE
From at least 1648, Palazzo Ducale, Venice.

REFERENCES
Venice 1949, no. 50, pp. 88–9; Heinemann 1962–91, vol. 1, p. 48; Robertson 1968, pp. 14, 46–7; Goffen 1989, pp. 72–8, 83, 96–8, 259, 288, 302, 306; Tempestini 2000, pp. 22, 275; Bätschmann 2008, pp. 95–6; Rome 2008–9, no. 12, pp. 172–5; Milan 2014, no. 23, pp. 170–1.

FIG. 126

GIOVANNI BELLINI
The Agony in the Garden, about 1458–60
Egg tempera on panel, 80.4 × 127 cm
The National Gallery, London. Bought, 1863 (NG 726)

PROVENANCE
Apparently owned by Consul Joseph Smith at Venice; presumably Sir Joshua Reynolds's sale, 13 March 1795, lot 48, bought by Walton; Beckford sale, Fonthill, 16 October 1822, lot 77; the same, 10 October 1823, lot 77, bought by Bentley; Edward Harman sale, 28 May 1847, lot 412, bought by Bromley; Rev. W. Davenport Bromley collection, from which sold, 12 June 1863, lot 62, and bought for the National Gallery.

REFERENCES
Davies 1961, pp. 58–60; Heinemann 1962–91, vol. 1, no. 150, p. 45; Robertson 1968, pp. 16, 19, 32–3, 42, 74, 80, 91, 154; Ghiotto and Pignatti 1969, no. 18, p. 87; Goffen 1989, pp. 16, 74, 106–7, 111, 122, 137, 238, 274, 281–2, 287, 296; Tempestini 2000, pp. 42–5, 175; Bätschmann 2008, pp. 43–7.

FIG. 105

GIOVANNI BELLINI
The Transfiguration of Christ, about 1458–60
Egg tempera and oil on panel, 133 × 90.3 cm
Fondazione Musei Civici di Venezia, Museo Correr, Venice (27)

PROVENANCE
Before 1830, Teodoro Correr; bequeathed to the museum.

REFERENCES
Venice 1949, no. 41, pp. 70–1; Heinemann 1962–91, vol. 1, pp. 55–6; Robertson 1968, pp. 15–16, 30–2, 52, 91; Ghiotto and Pignatti 1969, no. 15, p. 87; Goffen 1989, pp. 14–16, 31, 34, 119, 137–9, 274, 276, 281, 288, 327; Tempestini 2000, pp. 38–41, 175; Padua 2006–7, no. 74, pp. 300–1; Bätschmann 2008, pp. 43, 63, 115, 117–18; Rome 2008–9, no. 6, pp. 148–51.

FIG. 111

GIOVANNI BELLINI
The Virgin and Child (Davis Madonna), about 1460
Egg tempera on panel, 72.4 × 46.4 cm
The Metropolitan Museum of Art, New York. Theodore M. Davis Collection, Bequest of Theodore M. Davis, 1915 (30.95.256)

PROVENANCE
Before 1890, Walther Fol, Rome; by 1893–5, Jean Paul Richter, London and Florence; 1895–1915, Thomas M. Davis, Newport, from whom acquired by the museum.

REFERENCES
Venice 1949, no. 5, pp. 34–5; Heinemann 1962–91, vol. 1, p. 3; Robertson 1968, pp. 36–7, 120; Ghiotto and Pignatti 1969, no. 12, p. 86; Goffen 1989, pp. 28–32, 49, 52, 60, 62–3, 73, 297–8, 308; Tempestini 2000, pp. 34, 174; Padua 2006–7, no. 73, pp. 298–9; Bätschmann 2008, pp. 42–4; Rome 2008–9, no. 5, pp. 146–7.

FIG. 109

GIOVANNI BELLINI
The Virgin and Child, about 1460
Egg tempera on poplar, 66.3 × 48.6 cm
Gemäldegalerie, Staatliche Museen zu Berlin (1177)

PROVENANCE
Edward Solly, Berlin; acquired in 1821.

REFERENCES
Heinemann 1962–91, vol. 1, p. 2; Robertson 1968, pp. 37, 49, 79; Ghiotto and Pignatti 1969, no. 17, p. 87; Goffen 1989, pp. 90, 297; Tempestini 2000, p. 175; Bätschmann 2008, pp. 74, 79; Schmidt Arcangeli 2015, pp. 119–24.

Berlin only

FIG. 119

GIOVANNI BELLINI
Saint Louis of Toulouse holding a staff, early 1460s
Pen and brown ink over stylus on paper, 9.8 × 4.4 cm
National Gallery of Art, Washington DC. William B. O'Neal Fund 1997 (1997.40.1)

PROVENANCE
Charles Gasc, Paris; Charles Molinier, Toulouse; André de Hevesy, Paris, until at least 1955; Edward Holland-Martin; his sale, Christie's, London, 20 May 1966, lot 104; Christie's, London, 22 November 1966, lot 133; P. & D. Colnaghi, London; Denys Sutton, London, and by descent; sale Christie's, New York, 30 January 1997, lot 2; acquired via Colnaghi Drawings, London.

REFERENCES
Tietze and Tietze-Conrat 1944, pp. 82, 93; Venice 2014–15, no. 2, pp. 30–2.

FIG. 118

GIOVANNI BELLINI
Saint Louis of Toulouse holding a book, early 1460s
Pen and brown ink over stylus on paper, 9.8 × 5 cm
National Gallery of Art, Washington DC. William B. O'Neal Fund 1997 (1997.40.2)

PROVENANCE
Charles Gasc, Paris; Charles Molinier, Toulouse; André de Hevesy, Paris, until at least 1955; Edward Holland-Martin; his sale, Christie's, London, 20 May 1966, lot 104; Christie's, London, 22 November 1966, lot 133; P. & D. Colnaghi, London; Denys Sutton, London, and by descent; sale Christie's New York, 30 January 1997, lot 2; acquired via Colnaghi Drawings, London.

REFERENCES
Tietze and Tietze-Conrat 1944, pp. 82, 93; Heinemann 1962–91, vol. 1, no. 343, p. 84; Venice 2014–15, no. 2, pp. 30–2.

FIG. 194

GIOVANNI BELLINI
Saint Sebastian (recto); *Head of a man* (verso), early 1460s
Brush drawing in brown ink, with touches of pen and ink, heightened with white (mostly oxidised), on pink-red prepared paper (recto); Black chalk, on pink-red prepared paper (verso), 18.6 × 5.8 cm
The British Museum, London (1895,0915.800)

PROVENANCE
Acquired from the collection of John Wingfield Malcolm, 1st Baron Malcolm of Poltalloch, in 1895.

REFERENCES
Tietze and Tietze-Conrat 1944, pp. 86–7; Popham and Pouncey 1950, vol. 1, p. 12; Robertson 1968, pp. 42, 49; Goldner 2004, pp. 236, 238.

FIG. 211

GIOVANNI BELLINI
Head of an old man (Saint Anthony Abbot), about 1460–6
Brush and ink with white body colour on paper, 26 × 19 cm
Lent by Her Majesty The Queen (RCIN 912800)

PROVENANCE
First listed in a Royal Collection inventory around 1810.

REFERENCES
Popham and Wilde 1949, no. 2, pp. 171; Robertson 1968, p. 43; Tempestini 2000, p. 185.

FIG. 192

GIOVANNI BELLINI
The Blood of the Redeemer, about 1465
Egg tempera on panel, 47.6 × 35.2 cm
The National Gallery, London. Bought, 1887 (NG 1233)

PROVENANCE
An unidentified seal on the back; Robert Prioleau Roupell sale, 25 June 1887, lot 63; bought by Charles Fairfax Murray, from whom acquired through the Clarke Fund in 1887.

REFERENCES
Davies 1961, pp. 60–1; Heinemann 1962–91, vol. 1, no. 191, pp. 56–7; Robertson 1968, pp. 33–6, 40, 48, 102, 154; Ghiotto and Pignatti 1969, no. 64, p. 92; Goffen 1989, pp. 82, 224–5, 287; Tempestini 2000, pp. 36–7, 175; Bätschmann 2008, pp. 47–9, 131, 136; Rome 2008–9, no. 7, pp. 152–5.

FIG. 102

GIOVANNI BELLINI
The Crucifixion, about 1465
Oil or egg tempera on panel, 71 × 63 cm
Musée du Louvre, Paris. Département des Peintures (RF 1970–39)

PROVENANCE
By about 1807(?), Santa Maria della Carità, Venice; Richard Chester Fisher, Midhurst, Sussex, documented in 1865 and 1887; Agnews, London; Rudolf Kann, Paris, documented in 1900 and 1907; Joseph Duveen, New York, documented in 1907; Elia Volpi, Florence, documented 1907–13; Charles Fairfax-Murray, Florence and London, documented in 1913; Alessandro Contini-Bonacossi, Florence, and his heirs until 1970.

REFERENCES
Venice 1949, no. 42, pp. 72–3; Heinemann 1962–91, vol. 1, p. 218; Robertson 1968, p. 49; Ghiotto and Pignatti 1969, no. 59, p. 92; Tempestini 2000, pp. 21, 57, 176; Rome 2008–9, no. 8, pp. 156–9; Los Angeles 2017–18, no. 3, pp. 70–5.

FIG. 103

GIOVANNI BELLINI
Three Stories of Drusiana and Saint John the Evangelist, about 1465
Oil or egg tempera on panel, 32 × 202 cm
Wittelsbacher Ausgleichsfonds, Munich (B I 34)

PROVENANCE
Santa Maria della Carità, Venice, until 1808; Pinacoteca di Brera, Milan, 1808–32; since 1832 Filippo Benucci; Horace Buttery, London and Berlin; Richard von Kaufmann 1900–8, Berlin, whose heirs kept it until 1917; from whom sold through Cassirer-Helbing, 4 December 1917, lot 41; acquired by Rupprecht of Bavaria; part of the Wittelsbacher Ausgleichsfonds since 1923.

REFERENCES
Robertson 1968, pp. 44, 47; Paris 2008–9, no. 33, pp. 124–7.

Berlin only

FIG. 154

GIOVANNI BELLINI
Pietà, about 1465–70
Pen and brown ink on paper, 13.2 × 9 cm
Musée des Beaux-Arts, Rennes (794.1.2503)

PROVENANCE
Until 1756, Christophe-Paul Gautron, Marquis de Robien, Rennes; 1756–94, Paul-Christophe Gautron, Marquis de Robien, from whom seized; since 1805, property of the municipality, Rennes; since 1855, Musée des Beaux-Arts.

REFERENCES
Venice 1949, no. 133, p. 220; Robertson 1968, p. 25; Paris 2008–9, no. 45, pp. 147–8; Milan 2014, no. 16, p. 166.

Berlin only

FIG. 151

GIOVANNI BELLINI
The Dead Christ supported by Two Angels, about 1465–70
Oil on panel, 95 × 71.7 cm
The National Gallery, London. Mond Bequest, 1924 (NG 3912)

PROVENANCE
Stated to be from the collections of Conte Nuvoloni, Mantua, and the Cav. Cesare Menghini, Mantua; acquired in 1889 by Richter for Ludwig Mond; Mond Bequest in 1924.

REFERENCES
Davies 1961, p. 64; Heinemann 1962–91, vol. 1, no. 164, p. 50; Robertson 1968, p. 64; Ghiotto and Pignatti 1969, no. 69, p. 94; Goffen 1989, pp. 83, 289; Tempestini 2000, pp. 78, 177; Bätschmann 2008, p. 127.

London only

FIG. 162

GIOVANNI BELLINI
Pietà (recto); *Studies of putti* (verso), 1465–70
Pen and brown ink, brown wash on paper, 12.9 × 9.2 cm
The British Museum, London (1895,0915.791)

PROVENANCE
Sir Thomas Lawrence, London; until about 1860, Sir John Charles Robinson, London; by 1869, John Wingfield Malcolm, 1st Baron Malcolm of Poltalloch, London; 1893–5, John Wingfield Malcolm, 1st Baron Malcolm of Poltalloch London; from whom acquired by the museum.

REFERENCES
Popham and Pouncey 1950, p. 8; Robertson 1968, p. 25; London 1998, no. 14, pp. 63–4; Paris 2008–9, no. 46, pp. 149–50.

FIG. 156

GIOVANNI BELLINI
The Dead Christ supported by Four Angels, about 1470
Egg tempera (?) on wood, transferred to fibreglass panel, 80.5 × 120 cm
Museo della Città "Luigi Tonini", Rimini (18 PQ)

PROVENANCE
Mentioned in Rainerio di Lodovico Migliorati's will of 1499 and possibly the Tempio Malatestiano; transferred to the Musei Comunali, Rimini, in 1798.

REFERENCES
Venice 1949, no. 80, pp. 124–5; Heinemann 1962–91, vol. 1, pp. 49–50; Robertson 1968, pp. 62–4, 78, 94 107, 154; Goffen 1989, pp. 82–3, 94, 225, 288, 299, 303; Tempestini 2000, pp. 72–4, 177, 188; Bätschmann 2008, p. 157; Rome 2008–9, no. 14, pp. 178–81; Milan 2012–13, no. 7, pp. 68–71; Rimini 2012, pp. 6–10; Milan 2014, no. 21, pp. 168–9.

FIG. 152

GIOVANNI BELLINI
The Dead Christ supported by Two Angels, about 1470–5
Egg tempera on poplar, 82.9 × 66.9 cm
Gemäldegalerie, Staatliche Museen zu Berlin (28)

PROVENANCE
Edward Solly, Berlin; acquired in 1821.

REFERENCES
Heinemann 1962–91, vol. 1, p. 50; Robertson 1968, pp. 52, 56; Ghiotto and Pignatti 1969, no. 82, p. 85; Goffen 1989, pp. 82–3, 287; Tempestini 2000, pp. 76–7, 177; Bätschmann 2008, pp. 127–8; Schmidt Arcangeli 2015, pp. 125–32.

FIG. 132

GIOVANNI BELLINI
The Presentation of Christ in the Temple, about 1470–5
Oil on panel, 80 × 105 cm
Fondazione Querini Stampalia, Venice (2/29)

PROVENANCE
At least since 1810, Querini Stampalia family.

REFERENCES
Venice 1949, no. 46, pp. 80–1; Heinemann 1962–91, vol. 1, p. 41; Robertson 1968, pp. 75–6, 94, 98; Ghiotto and Pignatti 1969, no. 37, p. 89; Lightbown 1986, pp. 70–3, 429–30; Goffen 1989, pp. 178, 282, 284; Tempestini 2000, pp. 58–60, 176; Bätschmann 2008, pp. 52, 83, 86–7; Rome 2008–9, no. 13, pp. 176–7; Venice 2018.

FIG. 179

GIOVANNI BELLINI
The Virgin and Child, about 1475
Oil on poplar, 76 × 54.2 cm
Gemäldegalerie, Staatliche Museen zu Berlin (10A)

PROVENANCE
Until 1905, collection of Conte Folco, Vicenza; acquired by the museum from the Florentine art market.

REFERENCES
Heinemann 1962–91, vol. 1, p. 6; Robertson 1968, p. 78; Ghiotto and Pignatti 1969, no. 95, p. 96; Goffen 1989, pp. 288, 301; Tempestini 2000, p. 177; Bätschmann 2008, p. 11; Schmidt Arcangeli 2015, pp. 145–50.

FIG. 218

GIOVANNI BELLINI
The Resurrection of Christ, 1475–9
Oil on canvas, transferred from panel, 148 × 128 cm
Gemäldegalerie, Staatliche Museen zu Berlin (1177A)

PROVENANCE
San Michele in Isola; collection of the Counts Roncalli, Bergamo, from whom acquired in 1902.

REFERENCES
Heinemann 1962–91, vol. 1, p. 54; Robertson 1968, pp. 74–6, 85, 87, 111, 115, 126; Ghiotto and Pignatti 1969, no. 65, p. 92; Goffen 1989, pp. 140–4, 284, 287, 310; Tempestini 2000, pp. 79–82, 178; Bätschmann 2008, pp. 119–20, 127; Rome 2008–9, no. 21, pp. 208–11; Schmidt Arcangeli 2015, pp. 133–44.

FIG. 145

GIOVANNI BELLINI
The Descent of Christ into Limbo, about 1475–80
Oil on vellum on panel, 51.8 × 37.3 cm
Bristol Culture: Bristol City Museum & Art Gallery, F.P.M. Schiller Bequest (K.1654)

PROVENANCE
Sold Christie's, London, 7 July 1916, lot 106; acquired by A.H. Buttery; 1917, acquired by F.N. Schiller; 1946, Schiller bequest to Bristol Museums and Art Gallery.

REFERENCES
Robertson 1968, pp. 25–6, 75; Goffen 1989, pp. 284, 287; London and New York 1992, no. 69, pp. 267–8.

FIG. 117

GIOVANNI BELLINI
Saint Jerome reading in a Landscape, about 1480–5
Oil on panel, 46.8 × 33.8 cm
The National Gallery, London. Bought, 1855 (NG 281)

PROVENANCE
Alleged to have been engraved in the collection of Salvatore Rossetti; purchased from Bartolomeo Marcovich, Venice, 1855.

REFERENCES
Davies 1961, pp. 72–3; Heinemann 1962–91, vol. 1, no. 224, p. 66; Robertson 1968, p. 77; Ghiotto and Pignatti 1969, no. 99, p. 97; Tempestini 2000, p. 179; Rome 2008–9, no. 32, pp. 242–5; Los Angeles 2017–18, no. 7, pp. 92–7.

London only

FIG. 155

GIOVANNI BELLINI
The Lamentation over the Dead Christ, about 1490
Pen and brown ink on paper, 12 × 19 cm
Musée du Louvre, Paris. Département des Arts graphiques (RF 436)

PROVENANCE
Giuseppe Vallardi, Milan; until 1878, Aimé Charles His de la Salle, Paris, from whom acquired by the museum.

REFERENCES
Venice 1949, no. 134, p. 221; Robertson 1968, p. 25; Goffen 1989, pp. 82, 127, 301; Paris 2008–9, no. 47, pp. 150–1.

Berlin only

FIG. 161

GIOVANNI BELLINI
The Lamentation over the Dead Christ, about 1490
Ink brush on a lead white imprimatura on panel, 74 × 118 cm
Galleria degli Uffizi, Florence (1890 no. 943)

PROVENANCE
Galleria Aldobrandini, Rome; Alvise Mocenigo, by whom presented to Ferdinand III, Grand Duke of Tuscany, in 1798.

REFERENCES
Venice 1949, no. 105, pp. 168–9; Heinemann 1962–92, vol. 1, p. 52; Robertson 1968, pp. 98, 117–19, 121, 124, 131; Ghiotto and Pignatti 1969, no. 153, p. 103; Goffen 1989, pp. 178, 181, 287, 315; Tempestini 2000, p. 123, 180; Rome 2008–9, no. 27, pp. 228–31.

FIG. 187

GIOVANNI BELLINI
The Virgin and Child with Saints Catherine and Mary Magdalene, about 1490
Oil on panel, 58.8 × 108 cm
Gallerie dell'Accademia, Venice (613)

PROVENANCE
By 1812, Count Bernardino Renier, Venice; by descent to Maria Felicita Bertrand, by whom bequeathed in 1850.

REFERENCES
Venice 1949, no. 96, pp. 160–1; Heinemann 1962–91, vol. 1, p. 29; Robertson 1968, pp. 94–5, 98; Ghiotto and Pignatti 1969, no. 138, p. 101; Goffen 1989, pp. 58–9, 114–15, 288; Tempestini 2000, pp. 120–1, 180; Bätschmann 2008, pp. 87–9; Rome 2008–9, no. 26, pp. 226–7.

FIG. 180

GIOVANNI BELLINI
Madonna of the Meadow, about 1500–5
Oil on synthetic panel, transferred from wood, 66.5 × 85.1 cm
The National Gallery, London (NG 599)

PROVENANCE
Purchased from Achille Farina (Faenza) in 1858.

REFERENCES
Davies 1961, pp. 57–8; Heinemann 1962–91, vol. 2, no. 57, p. 18; Robertson 1968, pp. 114, 119–20, 122–3, 126, 144, 151–2; Ghiotto and Pignatti 1969, no. 148, p. 102; Goffen 1989, pp. 41, 62–3, 163, 287, 299, 315; Tempestini 2000, pp. 142–3, 182; Bätschmann 2008, pp. 9, 199–200.

FIG. 207

GIOVANNI BELLINI
Doge Leonardo Loredan, about 1501–2
Oil on poplar, 61.4 × 44.5 cm
The National Gallery, London. Bought, 1844 (NG 189)

PROVENANCE
Two unidentified seals on the back; acquired from the Grimani Palace, Venice, by the first Lord Cawdor; collection of William Thomas Beckford, from which purchased in 1844.

REFERENCES
Davies 1961, pp. 55–6; Heinemann 1962–91, vol. 1, no. 287, p. 78; Robertson 1968, pp. 19, 107, 109–10, 127; Ghiotto and Pignatti 1969, no. 165, p. 104; Goffen 1989, pp. 84, 161, 191, 197, 205–12, 287, 318–20; Tempestini 2000, pp. 136–7, 181; Bätschmann 2008, pp. 56–7, 130–2.

FIG. 220

GIOVANNI BELLINI
The Assassination of Saint Peter Martyr, about 1505–7
Oil on panel, 99.7 × 165.1 cm
The National Gallery, London. Presented by Lady Eastlake, 1870 (NG 812)

PROVENANCE
Seen by Sir Charles Lock Eastlake in the studio of Natale Schiavone, Venice, in 1854 and purchased from him in that year; presented by Lady Eastlake in 1870.

REFERENCES
Davies 1961, pp. 65–7; Robertson 1968, pp. 125–7, 131, 151; Ghiotto and Pignatti 1969, no. 192, p. 108; Goffen 1989, pp. 246, 249, 315; Tempestini 2000, pp. 152, 183; Bätschmann 2008, p. 210.

London only

FIG. 239

GIOVANNI BELLINI
Two men in antique dress, about 1506–8
Grey wash, lead white, pen and black ink on paper, 41.4 × 26.6 cm
Fondation Custodia, Collection Frits Lugt, Paris (4145)

PROVENANCE
Possibly Francesco Calzolari, Verona; possibly Lodovico Moscardo, Verona; until 1905, Moscardo family, Verona; 1905–29, Luigi Grassi, Florence; 1929–47, Frits Lugt, Maartensdijk and The Hague; since 1947, Fondation Custodia, Paris.

REFERENCES
Paris 2008–9, no. 133, pp. 318–19.

FIG. 246

GIOVANNI BELLINI
The Continence of Publius Cornelius Scipio, about 1506–8
Oil on canvas, 74.8 × 356.2 cm
The National Gallery of Art, Washington DC. Samuel H. Kress Collection (1952.2.7)

PROVENANCE
Commissioned by Francesco Cornaro; Palazzo Corner-Mocenigo (San Polo, Venice); Sir John Charles Robinson, London; sold 1873 to Sir Francis Cook, Richmond, Surrey; by descent to Sir Frederick Lucas Cook; by descent to Sir Herbert Frederick Cook; by descent to Sir Francis Ferdinand Maurice Cook; sold February 1948 to Gualtiero Volterra, London, for Count Alessandro Contini-Bonacossi, Florence; sold March 1949 to the Samuel H. Kress Foundation, New York; gift to the museum in 1952.

REFERENCES
Heinemann 1962–91, vol. 1, p. 259; Robertson 1968, pp. 118, 132–3; Ghiotto and Pignatti 1969, no. 190, pp. 107–8; Goffen 1989, pp. 237–40, 242, 282, 290, 323; Tempestini 2000, p. 183; Rome 2008–9, no. 54, pp. 302–3.

FIG. 226

GIOVANNI BELLINI, with later additions by DOSSO DOSSI and TITIAN
The Feast of the Gods, 1514–29
Oil on canvas, 170.2 × 188 cm
National Gallery of Art, Washington DC. Widener Collection (1942.9.1)

PROVENANCE
Probably commissioned by Alfonso I d'Este, Duke of Ferrara; by descent to his son, Ercole II d'Este, Duke of Ferrara; by descent to his son, Alfonso II d'Este, Duke of Ferrara; by descent to his cousin, Cesare d'Este, Duke of Ferrara; confiscated from the Castello at Ferrara by Cardinal Pietro Aldobrandini in 1598 and recorded in his inventory in 1603; by descent through the Aldobrandini family until the line became extinct in 1760; by descent in 1769 to Paolo Borghese Aldobrandini, Rome; by descent to his nephew, Giovan Battista Borghese Aldobrandini, Rome; purchased in 1796–7 by Pietro Camuccini for the collection of his brother, Vincenzo Camuccini, Rome; by descent through the entire Camuccini collection until sold in 1853, to Algernon Percy, 4th Duke of Northumberland, Alnwick Castle, Northumberland; by descent to subsequent Dukes of Northumberland; sold 16 June 1916 to Thomas Agnew & Sons, London; by descent from the Estate of Peter A.B. Widener by gift through power of appointment of Joseph E. Widener, Elkins Park, Pennsylvania, after purchase in 1921 by funds of the estate; gift to the museum in 1942.

REFERENCES
Robertson 1968, pp. 2, 13, 30, 76, 103, 111, 119, 131–52; Ghiotto and Pignatti 1969, no. 207, p. 109; Goffen 1989, pp. 56, 239, 242–7, 249, 251, 255, 261, 269, 273, 288, 324–5; Tempestini 2000, pp. 164–7, 183; London 2003, no. 15, pp. 108–9; Washington and Vienna 2006–7, no. 32, pp. 172–5; Bätschmann 2008, pp. 197, 200, 207–13.

FIG. 210

GIOVANNI BELLINI
Portrait of Fra Teodoro of Urbino as Saint Dominic, about 1515
Oil on canvas, 62.9 × 50.8 cm
On loan from the Victoria and Albert Museum, London (L 1115)

PROVENANCE
1797, Pietro and Giovanni Pesaro, Pesaro; acquired in 1865 from the collection of Jules Soulages, Paris and Toulouse.

REFERENCES
Davies 1961, pp. 61–4; Heinemann, 1962–91, vol. 1, p. 79; Robertson 1968, p. 153; Goffen 1989, pp. 214–17; Tempestini 2000, p. 184; Bätschmann 2008, p. 212; Berlin and New York 2011–12, no. 167, pp. 371–4.

London only

FIG. 247

GIOVANNI BELLINI
The Drunkenness of Noah, about 1515
Oil on canvas, 103 × 157 cm
Musée des Beaux-Arts et d'Archéologie, Besançon (896.1.13)

PROVENANCE
Jean Gigoux, by bequest to the museum, 1894.

REFERENCES
Venice 1949, no. 126, p. 211; Heinemann 1962–91, vol. 1, pp. 271–2; Robertson 1968, pp. 119, 124, 131; Goffen 1989, pp. 216, 249–52, 273, 287, 325; Paris 1993, no. 3, pp. 270–1; Tempestini 2000, pp. 170, 184; Bätschmann 2008, pp. 212–13; Rome 2008–9, no. 62, pp. 320–3.

London only

Attributed to Giovanni Bellini

FIG. 99

Attributed to GIOVANNI BELLINI
The three crosses, about 1456–7
Pen and brown ink on grey prepared paper, 24 × 21.5 cm
The British Museum, London. Bequeathed by Richard Payne Knight, 1824 (Pp,1.22)

PROVENANCE
Philips Koninck, Amsterdam; until 1824, Richard Payne Knight, Downton Castle, from whom acquired by the museum.

REFERENCES
Kristeller 1901, p. 459; Tietze and Tietze-Conrat 1944, no. 312, pp. 87–8; Popham and Pouncey 1950, p. 15; Los Angeles 2017–18, p. 84.

FIG. 84

Attributed to GIOVANNI BELLINI
Saints Sebastian, John the Baptist and Anthony Abbot (three panels from the *Saint Sebastian Triptych*), 1462–4
Egg tempera on panel; *Saint John the Baptist* 126 × 48.4 cm; *Saint Sebastian* 125.5 × 46.5 cm; *Saint Anthony Abbot* 126 × 46.5 cm
Gallerie dell'Accademia, Venice (621a)

PROVENANCE
Originally in the Saint Sebastian chapel in the Church of Santa Maria della Carità, Venice.

REFERENCES
Venice 1949, nos 10–12, pp. 36–45; Robertson 1968, pp. 14, 36, 39–43, 66, 72, 79, 121; Ghiotto and Pignatti 1969, nos 39–41, p. 90; Eisler 1989, p. 73; Goffen 1989, pp. 276–7; Tempestini 2000, p. 174; Bätschmann 2008, pp. 26–7, 49–50.

FIG. 212

Attributed to GIOVANNI BELLINI
Portrait of a Humanist (Andrea Mantegna?), about 1475–80
Oil on board, 35 × 28 cm
Pinacoteca del Castello Sforzesco, Milan (249)

PROVENANCE
Collection De Cristoforis, Milan.

REFERENCES
Venice 1949, no. 76, pp. 116–17; Robertson 1968, p. 107; Ghiotto and Pignatti 1969, no. 92, p. 96; Goffen 1989, pp. 191–2, 202, 289; Tempestini 2000, p. 188; Rome 2010–11, no. 10, pp. 48–9.

FIG. 216

Attributed to GIOVANNI BELLINI
The Nativity, about 1480
Pen and brush and brown ink on laid paper, 21.1 × 21.1 cm
The Courtauld Gallery, London (D.1978.PG.79)

PROVENANCE
Sir Peter Lely; George Le Hunte, Ireland, by 1842; Misses M.H.L.E. and M.D. Le Hunte, by descent to Archibald George Blomefield Russell, London and Swanage; his sale, Sotheby's, London, 9 June 1955, lot 43; purchased there by Colnaghi, London, on behalf of Count Antoine Seilern; Princes Gate Bequest 1978.

REFERENCES
Robertson 1968, pp. 72–3; London and Florence 2010–11, p. 18; London and New York 2012–13, pp. 52–5; Los Angeles 2017–18, no. 4, pp. 76–81.

Berlin only

FIG. 217

Attributed to GIOVANNI BELLINI
Saint Mark healing Ananias (recto); *Fragment of a spiral ornament* (verso), about 1485
Pen and brown ink on paper (recto); black chalk on paper (verso), 18.4 × 17.2 cm
Kupferstichkabinett, Staatliche Museen zu Berlin (KdZ 1357)

PROVENANCE
Samuel Woodburn, London; Marquis Philippe Chennevières, Paris; Alphonse Wyatt Thibaudeau, London; acquired in 1880.

REFERENCES
Robertson 1968, p. 73; Schulze Altcappenberg 1995, no. 8, pp. 66–8, 189; Tempestini 2000, p. 185; Goldner 2004, pp. 243–4; Bätschmann 2008, pp. 108–9.

Circle of Giovanni Bellini

FIG. 100

Circle of GIOVANNI BELLINI
The Crucifixion, about 1460
Pen and brush and brown ink on vellum, 27.4 × 19.6 cm
Kupferstichkabinett, Staatliche Museen zu Berlin (KdZ 1364)

PROVENANCE
Samuel Woodburn, London; Marquis Philippe Chennevières, Paris; Alphonse Wyatt Thibaudeau, London; acquired in 1880.

REFERENCES
Schulze Altcappenberg 1995, no. 7, pp. 188–9.

Berlin only

Nicolò di Giovanni Baroncelli (died 1453) and Domenico di Paris (active in Ferrara during the second half of the 15th century)

FIG. 202

Attributed to NICOLÒ DI GIOVANNI BARONCELLI and DOMENICO DI PARIS
Portrait of a Soldier, possibly Ludovico III Gonzaga, about 1453
Bronze, 37 × 29 × 28 cm
Skulpturensammlung und Museum für Byzantinische Kunst, Staatliche Museen zu Berlin (52)

PROVENANCE
Frédéric Spitzer, Paris; acquired in 1876.

REFERENCES
London 1981–2, no. 28, pp. 117–18; Rowley 2016.

Berlin only

Jacopo Bellini (about 1400 – about 1470)

FIG. 92

JACOPO BELLINI
The London Drawing Book of Jacopo Bellini, 1440–70
Leadpoint on paper, 41.5 × 33.3 cm
The British Museum, London (1855,0811.97)

PROVENANCE
Possibly the album left by Anna Bellini, widow of the artist, to her son Gentile in 1471, who in turn left in 1507 to his brother, Giovanni; Gabriele Vendramin; Jacopo Soranzano; Marco Cornaro, Bishop of Vicenza; Count Bonomo Algarotti; the Corniani family; acquired from Bonetto Corniani by Giovanni Maria Sasso in 1802; sold by Sasso's executor in 1803 to Girolamo Mantovani, from whom inherited by his nephew Domenico; purchased for the British Museum from Mantovani by Rawdon Brown in 1855.

REFERENCES
Popham and Pouncey 1950, no. 21, p. 14; Eisler 1989; Bätschmann 2008, pp. 13–16, 34–6, 43, 112; London and Florence 2010–11, no. 16, pp. 122–9.

London only

FIG. 89

JACOPO BELLINI
Three dead kings, from *The Paris Drawing Book of Jacopo Bellini*, about 1455–60
Pen and brown ink and metalpoint on vellum, 22 × 41 cm
Musée du Louvre, Paris. Département des Arts graphiques (RF 425)

PROVENANCE
Jacopo Bellini until his death in 1470–1; his wife, Anna Rinversi Bellini, until her death in 1471, both in Venice; Gentile Bellini until 1479, Venice; Sultan Mehmet II from 1479–81, Istanbul; Bibliothèque du Sérail, Istanbul, until 1677; private collection, Smyrna, 1728; Jean-Baptiste Florentin Gabriel de Meryan, Marquess of Lagoy, Paris, until around 1810; Moritz Christian Johann, Reichsgraf von Fries from around 1810, Vienna; Alexandre Lenoir, Paris, until 1838; Aimé Charles His de la Salle, until 1878, Paris; bequeathed in 1878.

REFERENCES
Eisler 1989, pp. 252–3, 261, 525.

London only

FIG. 90

JACOPO BELLINI
Tomb of a prince, from *The Paris Drawing Book of Jacopo Bellini*, about 1455–60
Pen and brown ink on parchment, 12 × 39.7 cm
Musée du Louvre, Paris. Département des Arts graphiques (RF 428)

PROVENANCE
Jacopo Bellini until his death in 1470–1; his wife, Anna Rinversi Bellini, until her death in 1471, both in Venice; Gentile Bellini until 1479, Venice; Sultan Mehmet II from 1479–81 in Istanbul; Bibliothèque du Sérail, Istanbul, until 1677; private collection in Smyrna in 1728; Jean-Baptiste Florentin Gabriel de Meryan, Marquess of Lagoy, Paris, until around 1810; Moritz Christian Johann, Reichsgraf von Fries from around 1810, Vienna; Alexandre Lenoir, Paris, until 1838; Aimé Charles His de la Salle, until 1878, Paris; bequeathed in 1878.

REFERENCES
Eisler 1989, pp. 252–3, 261, 494; Paris 2008–9, no. 5, pp. 69–70.

London only

FIG. 85

JACOPO BELLINI, with possible contributions by GIOVANNI and GENTILE BELLINI
The Adoration of the Magi, about 1459–60
Egg tempera on panel, 29 × 57 cm
Pinacoteca Nazionale, Ferrara (327)

PROVENANCE
After 1880 until 1900, Enea Vendeghini Baldi, Ferrara; 1900–58, Maria Vendeghini Baldi, Ferrara; 1958–73, Mario Baldi, Ferrara, from whom bequeathed to the museum in 1973.

REFERENCES
Eisler 1989, pp. 60, 516–17; Goffen 1989, pp. 8–9, 289; Padua 2006–7, no. 69, pp. 290–1; Bätschmann 2008, pp. 18, 24–6.

Berlin only

FIG. 86

JACOPO BELLINI, with possible contributions by GIOVANNI and GENTILE BELLINI
The Crucifixion, about 1459–60
Egg tempera on panel, 28.6 × 57 cm
Fondazione Musei Civici di Venezia, Museo Correr, Venice (29)

PROVENANCE
By 1830, Teodoro Correr; bequeathed to the museum.

REFERENCES
Venice 1949, no. 1, pp. 27–8; Robertson 1968, pp. 15, 17; Ghiotto and Pignatti 1969, no. 2, p. 85; Goffen 1989, pp. 8–9, 12, 289; Eisler 1989, pp. 60, 516–17; Tempestini 2000, p. 186; Bätschmann 2008, pp. 18, 24–6.

FIG. 87

JACOPO BELLINI, with possible contributions by GIOVANNI and GENTILE BELLINI
The Descent of Christ into Limbo, about 1459–60
Egg tempera on panel, 28.5 × 58 cm
Musei Civici agli Eremitani, Museo d'Arte Medievale e Moderna, Padua (416)

PROVENANCE
Antonio Piazza, Padua; Giovanni Maria Piazza from 1844 to 1856, from whom acquired by the museum.

REFERENCES
Eisler 1989, pp. 60, 516–17; Goffen 1989, pp. 8–9, 289; Tempestini 2000, p. 186; Padua 2006–7, no. 71, pp. 294–5; Bätschmann 2008, pp. 18, 24–6; Paris 2008–9, no. 27, pp. 113–15.

Berlin only

FIG. 95

Attributed to JACOPO BELLINI
Assembly of the Order of the Crescent, 1453
Miniatures from Jacopo Antonio Marcello, *Passio Mauritii et sotiorum eius*
Tempera, gum or glue on vellum, 18.7 × 14 cm (each page)
Bibliothèque de l'Arsenal, Paris (MS 940, fols Cv-1r)

PROVENANCE
Jean Cossa from 1453; Cathedral of Saint-Maurice, Angers, until 1539; Paul Pétau, Orléans, from around 1590 to 1614; Claude Ménard, Anjou; Nicolas-Claude Fabri de Peiresc, Aix-en-Provence; Claude-Nicolas Boucot, Paris, from 1695; Roger de Gaignières, Paris, from 1700; Charles-Adrian Picard, 1763; collection of Antoine-René de Voyer de Paulmy d'Argenson, which formed the nucleus of the Bibliothèque de l'Arsenal, where inventoried since 1797.

REFERENCES
Meiss 1957, pp. 1–29; Robertson 1968, pp. 17–21, 78; Lightbown 1986, pp. 494–5; London and New York 1992, no. 10, pp. 129–34; Padua 2006–7, no. 40, pp. 224–5; Paris 2008–9, no. 30, pp. 129, 131–4.

Berlin only

FIG. 97

Attributed to JACOPO or GIOVANNI BELLINI
Guarino da Verona consigns his translation of Strabo to Jacopo Antonio Marcello; Jacopo Antonio Marcello offers the manuscript to René of Anjou, 1459
Miniatures from Strabo, *De situ orbis geographia*
Tempera, gum or glue on vellum, 37 × 25 cm
Médiathèque d'Albi-Centre Pierre Amalric, Albi (RES.MS 77)

PROVENANCE
René of Anjou, 1459; Louis d'Amboise, Bishop of Albi, 1474–1503, Albi; Palais épiscopal, Albi; Library of the Cathedral Chapter, Albi; from the end of the eighteenth century, Bibliothèque Municipale, Albi.

REFERENCES
Meiss 1957, pp. 20–51; Robertson 1968, p. 50; Lightbown 1986, pp. 494–5; Padua 2006–7, no. 31, pp. 204–7; Paris 2008–9, nos 31–2, pp. 122–3.

Berlin only

FIG. 93

School of JACOPO BELLINI
Two arcades, figures and view, about 1470–80
Pen and brown ink on vellum, 14.2 × 14.1 cm
Kupferstichkabinett, Staatliche Museen zu Berlin (KdZ 418)

PROVENANCE
Acquired before 1878.

REFERENCES
Schulze Altcappenberg 1995, no. 10, pp. 190–1.

Donatello (about 1386–1466)

FIG. 182

DONATELLO
The Virgin and Child with Four Angels, about 1435–40
Terracotta, 99 × 69 × 20 cm
Skulpturensammlung und Museum für Byzantinische Kunst, Staatliche Museen zu Berlin (54)

PROVENANCE
Florence, Santa Maria Maddalena dei Pazzi, until about 1888; Florence, Stefano Bardini; acquired in 1888.

REFERENCES
Pope-Hennessy 1993, pp. 261–2; Rosenauer 1993, no. 74, p. 305; Berlin 2015, pp. 114, 120–1; Rowley 2016.

Berlin only

FIG. 149

Attributed to DONATELLO
The Dead Christ tended by Angels, about 1430–5
Carved marble in low relief, 80.5 × 114.3 cm
Victoria and Albert Museum, London (7577-1861)

PROVENANCE
By 1855, collection of Marquee Ottavio Gigli; 1861, purchased by the South Kensington Museum, London (now Victoria and Albert Museum).

REFERENCES
Pope-Hennessy 1964, vol. 1, pp. 73–5; Pope-Hennessy 1993, pp. 140–2.

Francesco Squarcione (1397–1468)

FIG. 79

FRANCESCO SQUARCIONE
The Virgin and Child, about 1449–52
Egg tempera on poplar, 87 × 69.5 cm
Gemäldegalerie, Staatliche Museen zu Berlin (27A)

PROVENANCE
Since 1798, Giovanni Maria Sasso, Venice; at least since 1817, Giovanni de Lazara, Padua; acquired in 1882.

REFERENCES
Schmidt Arcangeli 2015, pp. 383–9.

Berlin only

Venetian School

FIG. 200

VENETIAN SCHOOL
The Blood of the Redeemer, about 1500
Terracotta, 80 × 45.7 cm
Victoria and Albert Museum, London (1195:1-1903)

PROVENANCE
Until 1863, Webb collection, London; 1863, purchased by the South Kensington Museum, London (now Victoria and Albert Museum).

REFERENCES
Pope-Hennessy 1964, vol. 1, p. 340.

London only

Marco Zoppo (1433–1478)

FIG. 171

MARCO ZOPPO
The Dead Christ supported by angels, about 1455–7
Pen and brown ink, brown wash on vellum, 35 × 28 cm
The British Museum, London. Acquired with contributions from the Heritage Lottery Fund and The Art Fund, 1995 (1995,0506.7)

PROVENANCE
Duke of Anhalt-Dessau; 1937, D. Giese, London; March 1937, P. & D. Colnaghi, London; from whom bought by Lt Col. Norman Colville MC; acquired from the Colville family in 1995.

REFERENCES
Parker and Byam Shaw 1953; Armstrong 1976, no. D.1, pp. 56–72, 392; London 1998, no. 8, pp. 51–4.

FIG. 164

MARCO ZOPPO
The Severed Head of Saint John the Baptist, about 1470
Egg tempera on panel, 28 cm (diameter)
Musei Civici, Pesaro
Il Comune di Pesaro / Servizio Cultura e Patrimonio (4545)

PROVENANCE
By 1777, new Church of San Giovanni Battista, Pesaro; Museo Oliveriano, Pesaro; Museo Civici, Pesaro.

REFERENCES
Venice 1949, no. 37, pp. 62–3; Mantua 1961, no. 63, pp. 90–1; Robertson 1968, p. 53; Armstrong 1976, pp. 381–4; Giardini, Negro and Pirondini 1993, pp. 53–4; Tempestini 2000, p. 187; Rimini 2012, pp. 26–31.

FIG. 169

MARCO ZOPPO
The Dead Christ supported by Two Angels, 1471
Egg tempera on poplar, 102 × 74 cm
Musei Civici, Pesaro
Il Comune di Pesaro / Servizio Cultura e Patrimonio (4546)

PROVENANCE
Originally part of the *Pesaro Altarpiece* in the old Church of San Giovanni Battista, Pesaro; transferred to the new Church of San Giovanni Battista around 1536; Museo Oliveriano, Pesaro; Musei Civici, Pesaro.

REFERENCES
Armstrong 1976, pp. 379–80; Giardini, Negro and Pirondini 1993, pp. 52–3; Rimini 2012, pp. 32–4.

FIG. 167

MARCO ZOPPO
The Virgin and Child between Saints John the Baptist, Francis, Paul and Jerome, also known as the *Pesaro Altarpiece*, 1471
Egg tempera on poplar, 268 × 258 cm
Gemäldegalerie, Staatliche Museen zu Berlin (1170)

PROVENANCE
1471–1536, old Church of San Giovanni Battista, Pesaro; transferred to the new Church of San Giovanni Battista; Edward Solly, Berlin; acquired in 1821.

REFERENCES
Armstrong 1976, pp. 371–3; Schmidt Arcangeli 2015, pp. 394–404

Berlin only

Index

Page numbers in *italic* refer to the illustrations

List of Lenders

ALBI
Médiathèque d'Albi-Centre Pierre Amalric

BERGAMO
Fondazione Accademia Carrara

BERLIN
Staatliche Museen zu Berlin:
- Gemäldegalerie
- Kupferstichkabinett
- Skulpturensammlung und Museum für Byzantinische Kunst

BESANÇON
Musée des Beaux-Arts et d'Archéologie

BIRMINGHAM
The Henry Barber Trust, The Barber Institute of Fine Arts, University of Birmingham

BRESCIA
Fondazione Brescia Musei
Pinacoteca Tosio Martinengo

BRISTOL
Bristol City Museum and Art Gallery

COPENHAGEN
Statens Museum for Kunst

DRESDEN
Gemäldegalerie Alte Meister, Staatliche Kunstsammlungen

FERRARA
Pinacoteca Nazionale

FLORENCE
Galleria degli Uffizi

FRANKFURT
Städel Museum

LIVERPOOL
Walker Art Gallery

LONDON
The British Museum
The Courtauld Gallery
The National Gallery
Victoria and Albert Museum

LOS ANGELES
The J. Paul Getty Museum

MADRID
Museo Nacional del Prado

MILAN
Museo Poldi Pezzoli
Pinacoteca del Castello Sforzesco

MUNICH
Wittelsbacher Ausgleichsfonds

NEW YORK
The Metropolitan Museum of Art

PADUA
Musei Civici agli Eremitani, Museo d'Arte Medievale e Moderna

PARIS
Bibliothèque de l'Arsenal
École Nationale Supérieure des Beaux-Arts
Fondation Custodia, Collection Frits Lugt
Musée Jacquemart-André
Musée du Louvre

PESARO
Il Comune di Pesaro / Servizio Cultura e Patrimonio

RENNES
Musée des Beaux-Arts

RIMINI
Museo della Città

SÃO PAULO
Museu de Arte de São Paulo Assis Chateaubriand

VENICE
Biblioteca Nazionale Marciana
Fondazione Musei Civici di Venezia:
- Museo Correr
- Palazzo Ducale

Fondazione Querini Stampalia
Gallerie dell'Accademia

VIENNA
Kunsthistorisches Museum:
- Gemäldegalerie
- Kunstkammer

WASHINGTON DC
National Gallery of Art

OTHER LENDERS
Private collection, Berlin
Private collection, Milan
Private collection, Switzerland
The Royal Collection Trust / HM Queen Elizabeth II

Photographic Credits

ALBI
Mediathèque Municipale Pierre-Almaric © Réseau des médiathèques de l'Albigeois (médiathèque Pierre-Amalric d'Albi): 97.

BALTIMORE
© The Walters Art Museum, Baltimore: 170.

BERGAMO
Accademia Carrara © Fondazione Accademia Carrara, Bergamo: 140; © Photo Scala, Florence: 133.

BERLIN
Gemäldegalerie © Staatliche Museen zu Berlin, Gemäldegalerie / Photo: Christoph Schmidt: 37, 38, 39, 40, 41, 47, 51, 52, 79, 88, 109, 128, 135, 152, 168, 190, 179; © Staatliche Museen zu Berlin, Gemäldegalerie / Image by Google: 218; © Staatliche Museen zu Berlin, Gemäldegalerie / Photo: Jörg P. Anders: 167, 188, 206; © Staatliche Museen zu Berlin, Gemäldegalerie / Photo: Babette Hartwieg: 42. Kupferstichkabinett © Kupferstichkabinett. Staatliche Museen zu Berlin / Photo: Dietmar Katz: 56, 66, 69, 93, 100, 106, 113, 142, 144, 217. Skulpturensammlung © Staatliche Museen zu Berlin – Preußischer Kulturbesitz / Skulpturensammlung und Museum für Byzantinische Kunst / Photo: Antje, Voigt, Berlin: 78, 130, 165, 182, 202.

BESANCON
Musée des Beaux-Arts et d'Archéologie © C2RMF/Thomas Clot: 247.

BIRMINGHAM
© The Henry Barber Trust, The Barber Institute of Fine Arts, University of Birmingham: 114.

BOSTON
© 2017 Museum of Fine Arts, Boston: 209.

BRESCIA
Pinacoteca Tosio Martinengo © Archivio fotografico dei Musei di Brescia – Fotostudio Rapuzzi: 75, 158.

BRISTOL
© Bristol Museum and Art Gallery, UK / Bridgeman Images: 145.

COPENHAGEN
© Statens Museum for Kunst, Copenhagen: 150.

DRESDEN
Gemäldegalerie Alte Meister © bpk / Staatliche Kunstsammlungen Dresden / Elke Estel / Hans-Peter Klut: 190.

DUBLIN
© The National Gallery of Ireland: 204.

FERRARA
Pinacoteca Nazionale © Su concessione del Ministero dei Beni e delle Attività Culturali e del Turismo, Polo Museale dell'Emilia Romagna: 85, 213.

FLORENCE
Church of San Lorenzo © Photo Scala, Florence: 138. Gabinetto dei Disegni e delle Stampe, Galleria degli Uffizi © Photo Scala, Florence – courtesy of the Ministero Beni e Att. Culturali e del Turismo: 58; © Soprintendenza Speciale per il Polo Museale Fiorentino, Gabinetto Fotografico, Ministero per i Beni e le Attività Culturali: 160. Galleria degli Uffizi © Photo Scala, Florence – courtesy of the Ministero Beni e Att. Culturali e del Turismo: 224; © Soprintendenza Speciale per il Polo Museale Fiorentino: 161.

FRANKFURT AM MAIN
© Städel Museum – U. Edelmann – ARTOTHEK: 77.

GUTENSTETTEN
St Johannis Kirche © 2018 Wolfgang Steeger: 166.

LIVERPOOL
Walker Art Gallery © Courtesy National Museums Liverpool: 122.

LONDON
© The Trustees of The British Museum: 7, 59, 61, 67, 71, 74, 83, 92, 99, 107, 123, 162, 163, 171, 183, 194, 196, 198, 215, 227, 228, 229, 230, 231, 233. © The National Gallery, London: 10, 27, 28, 29, 30, 31, 32, 33, 34, 35, 36, 43, 44, 45, 46, 54, 117, 125, 126, 134, 151, 173, 176, 177, 178, 180, 185, 189, 192, 207, 220, 238, 240, 241, 245. © The Samuel Courtauld Trust, Courtauld Gallery, London: 195, 216. © Victoria and Albert Museum, London: 149, 205, 210. Royal Collection Trust / © Her Majesty Queen Elizabeth II 2018: 197, 211, 235, 236, 237.

LOS ANGELES
The J. Paul Getty Museum, Digital image courtesy of the Getty's Open Content Program: 136.

MADRID
© Photographic Archive Museo Nacional del Prado: 19, 214.

MANTUA
Basilica of Sant'Andrea © Mario Bonotto / Photo Scala, Florence: fig. 243; © Photo Scala, Florence: figs 242, 244; © Photo Scala, Florence / courtesy of Diocesi di Mantova: fig. 256. Ducal Palace © akg-images / De Agostini Picture Lib. / A. Dagli Orti : fig. 3; © akg-images / MPortfolio / Electa: fig. 254; © Photo Scala, Florence – courtesy of the Ministero Beni e Att. Culturali e del Turismo: fig. 203. Museo della Città, Palazzo San Sebastiano © Bridgeman Images: fig. 205. © De Agostini Picture Library / W. Buss / Bridgeman Images: fig. 4.

MILAN
Museo Bagatti-Valsecchi © akg-images / Mondadori Portfolio / Sergio Anelli: 22. © Museo Poldi Pezzoli, Milan: 148, 201. Pinacoteca di Brera © akg / MONDADORI PORTFOLIO / Archivio Magliani / Mauro Magliani & Barbara Piovan: 8; © akg-images / Erich Lessing: 11; © Photo Scala, Florence – courtesy of the Ministero Beni e Att. Culturali e del Turismo: 25, 129, 199; Raccolte d'Arte Antica, Pinacoteca del Castello Sforzesco © Comune di Milano, tutti i diritti riservati: 212.

MUNICH
© Staatliche Graphische Sammlung München: 63. © Wittelsbacher Ausgleichsfonds München (resp. Munich): 18, 103; © Wittelsbacher Ausgleichsfonds München (resp. Munich), photo: Giovanni Villa: 104.

NAPLES
Museo Nazionale di Capodimonte © Photo Scala, Florence – courtesy of the Ministero Beni e Att. Culturali e del Turismo: 172, 222; © Soprintendenza Speciale per il Polo Museale di Napoli © akg-images: 208.

NEW YORK

© The Pierpont Morgan Library, New York: 62. The Frick Collection © Photo Fine Art Images/ Heritage Images / Scala, Florence: 219. The Metropolitan Museum of Art © 2018. Image copyright The Metropolitan Museum of Art / Art Resource / Scala, Florence: 111, 221; © The Metropolitan Museum of Art, New York: 139, 175, 186.

OXFORD

© By permission of the Governing Body of Christ Church, Oxford: 76.

PADUA

Basilica of Sant'Antonio © Photo Scala, Florence: 2, 131, 147. Musei Civici agli Eremitani, Museo d'Arte Medievale e Moderna © Gabinetto Fotografico Musei Civici Padova / Photo: Giuliano Ghiraldini: 87; © Cameraphoto / Scala, Florence – Photo Scala, Florence – courtesy of the Ministero dei Beni e delle Attività Culturali e del Turismo: 80. Ovetari Chapel © Archivio Naya-Bohm, Venezia, image courtesy of Special Collections, Fine Arts Library, Harvard University (172 P138 2E(i)1 Bohm 6480): 250; © akg-images / Mondadori Portfolio / 2004 / Mauro Magliani: 248; © akg-images / Mondadori Portfolio / 2004 / Mauro Magliani: 82; © Alinari / Bridgeman Images: 249, 251; © Alinari Archives, Florence / Bridgeman Images: 81. Piazza del Santo © Photo Scala, Florence: 1. Scrovegni Chapel © A. Dagli Orti / Scala, Florence: 127.

PARIS

© Bibliothèque Nationale de France, Paris: 94, 95. École nationale supérieure des beaux-arts © Beaux-Arts de Paris, Dist. RMN-Grand Palais / image Beaux-arts de Paris: 15, 143. © Fondation Custodia, Collection Frits Lugt, Paris: 239. Musèe Jacquemart-Andrè © Photo Musèe Jacquemart-Andrè / Inst. de France / Scala, Florence: 108. Musée du Louvre, Département d'Arts Graphiques © RMN-Grand Palais (musée du Louvre) / Thierry Le Mage: 137, 234; © RMNGrand Palais (musée du Louvre) / Gérard Blot: 89, 90, 91, 115, 146; © RMN-Grand Palais (musée du Louvre) / Hervé Lewandowski: 155. Musée du Louvre, Département des Peintures, Paris © RMN-Grand Palais (musée du Louvre) / Gérard Blot: 96, 225; © RMN-Grand Palais (musée du Louvre) / Jean-Gilles Berizzi: 110; © RMN-Grand Palais (musée du Louvre) / Michel Urtado: 102; © RMN-Grand Palais (musée du Louvre) / Stéphane Maréchalle: 57; © RMNGrand Palais (musée du Louvre) / Thierry Le Mage: 13, 101.

PESARO

Musei Civici © Photo Scala, Florence – courtesy of Comune di Pesaro / Servizio Musei: 255; © 2018 Pesaro Musei: 164, 169.

PRIVATE COLLECTION

© Courtesy of the owner / Photo: Georg Josef Dietz: 64, 65. © Gabinetto Fotografico Musei Civici Padova / Photo: Giuliano Ghiraldini: 184. © Art Photo Studio di Paolo Manusardi: 73, 159. © 2018. Image copyright The Metropolitan Museum of Art / Art Resource / Scala, Florence: 12. © Courtesy of the owner / Photo: Sotheby's New York: 141.

RENNES

Musée des Beaux-Arts © MBA, Rennes, Dist. RMN-Grand Palais / Adélaïde Beaudoin: 68, 154.

RIMINI

© Museo della Città "L. Tonini", Rimini / Photo: Gilberto Urbinati: 156.

SÃO PAULO

Museu de Arte de São Paulo Assis Chateaubriand © MASP / Photo: João Musa: 116.

TOURS

Musée des Beaux-Arts de Tours © Photo Scala, Florence: 9, 124.

TURIN

Galleria Sabauda © Photo Scala, Florence – courtesy of the Ministero Beni e Att. Culturali e del Turismo: 6.

VATICAN CITY

Vatican Museums © Photo Scala, Florence: 255.

VENICE

Biblioteca Nazionale Marciana © Ministero per i Beni e le Attività Culturali, Biblioteca Nazionale Marciana, Venezia / Photo: Shylock e-Solutions: 98. Church of San Zaccaria © akg-images/Mondadori Portfolio / Mauro Magliani & Barbara Piovan/Archivio Magliani: 257. Church of Santa Maria Gloriosa dei Frari © akg-images / Mondadori Portfolio / Mauro Magliani & Barbara Piovan / Archivio Magliani: 174. Church of Santi Giovanni e Paolo (San Zanipolo) © akg-images / Cameraphoto: 23; © akg-images / Erich Lessing: 253. Gallerie dell'Accademia © akg-images / MPortfolio / Electa: 84 (lunette), 120; © Cameraphoto / Scala, Florence: 21; © Cameraphoto Arte Venezia / Bridgeman Images: 20; © Photo Scala, Florence – courtesy of the Ministero Beni e Att. Culturali e del Turismo: 181, 223; © Su concessione del Ministero dei beni e delle attività culturali e del turismo, Museo Nazionale delle Gallerie dell'Accademia di Venezia: 60, 84, 153, 187. Mascoli Chapel, Basilica of San Marco © Cameraphoto / Scala, Florence: 24. Museo Correr © Cameraphoto / Scala, Florence: 14, 17; 2018 © Photo Archive – Fondazione Musei Civici di Venezia: 16, 86, 105. © Fondazione Querini Stampalia Onlus, Venezia: 48, 49, 50, 53, 132. Ducal Palace 2018 © Photo Archive – Fondazione Musei Civici di Venezia: 26. Scuola Grande di San Marco © Andrea Jemolo / Scala, Florence: 70. © akg-images / Cameraphoto: 5.

VERONA

Basilica of San Zeno © Cameraphoto / Scala, Florence: 252.

VIENNA

Kunsthistorisches Museum © KHM-Museumsverband: 157, 191, 193.

WASHINGTON DC

Image courtesy of the Board of Trustees, National Gallery of Art, Washington, DC: 55, 72, 112, 118, 119, 226, 232, 246.

WHEREABOUTS UNKNOWN

Formerly in the Koenigs collection © RKD Nederlands Instituut voor Kunstgeschiedenis, The Hague: 121.

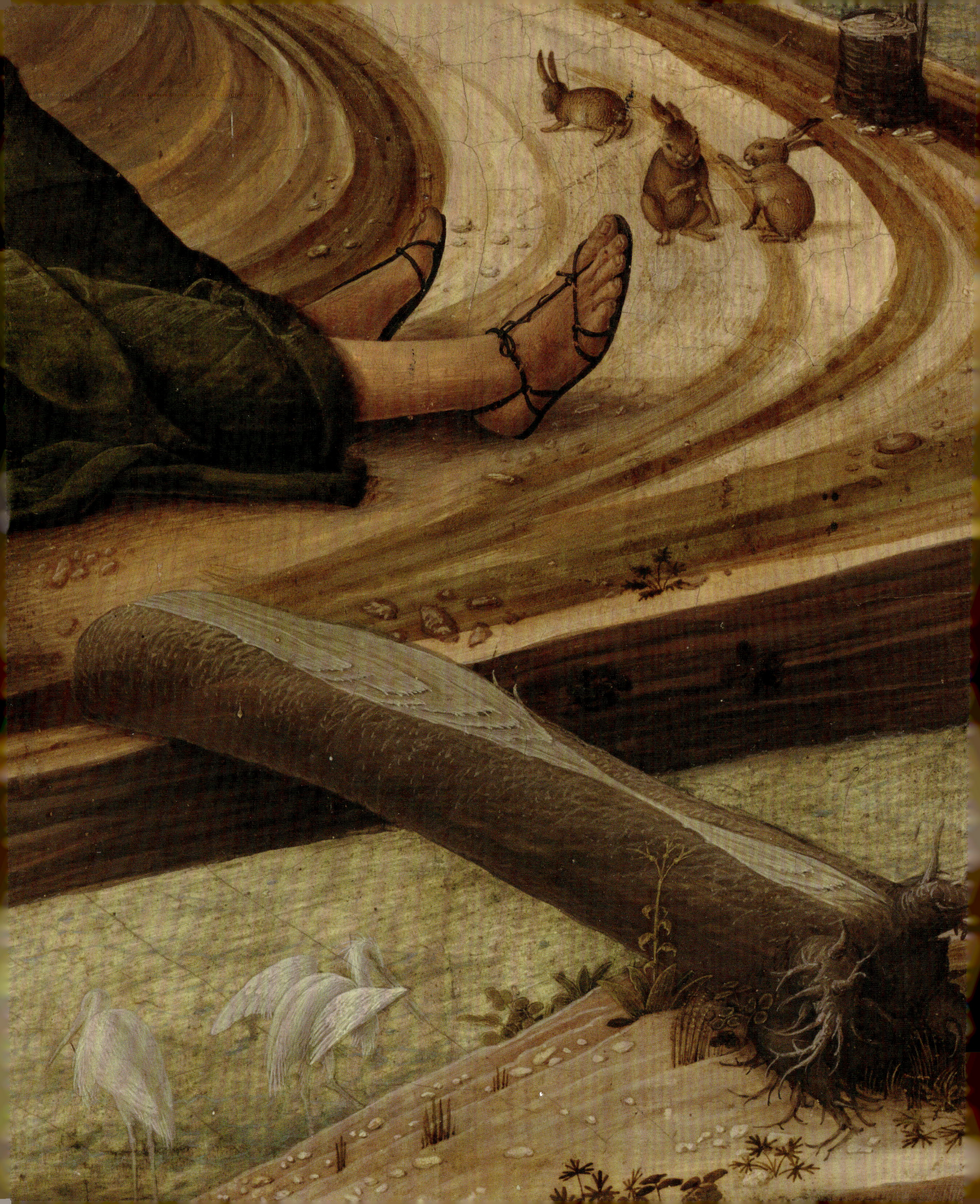